*iText in Action*

# *iText in Action*

## *Creating and Manipulating PDF*

BRUNO LOWAGIE

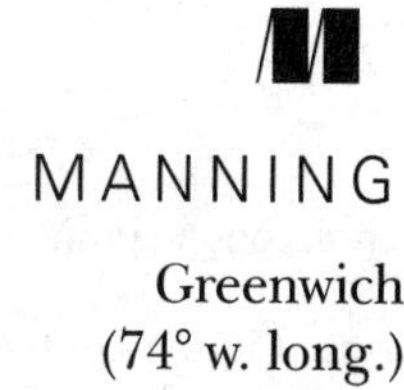

MANNING
Greenwich
(74° w. long.)

For online information and ordering of this and other Manning books, go to www.manning.com. The publisher offers discounts on this book when ordered in quantity. For more information, please contact:

Special Sales Department
Manning Publications Co.
Cherokee Station
PO Box 20386
New York, NY 10021

Fax: (609) 877-8256
email: orders@manning.com



Manning Publications Co.
Cherokee Station
PO Box 20386
New York, NY 10021

Copyeditor: Tiffany Taylor
Typesetter: Denis Dalinnik
Cover designer: Leslie Haimes

ISBN 1932394796

Printed in the United States of America
1 2 3 4 5 6 7 8 9 10 – MAL – 10 09 08 07 06

*To my wife, Ingeborg*

# *brief contents*

# contents

# *preface*

I have lost count of the number of PCs I have worn out since I started my career as a software developer—but I will never forget my first computer.

I was only 12 years old when I started programming in BASIC. I had to learn English at the same time because there simply weren't any books on computer programming in my mother tongue (Dutch). This was in 1982. Windows didn't exist yet; I worked on a TI99/4A home computer from Texas Instruments. When I told my friends at school about it, they looked at me as if I had just been beamed down from the Starship Enterprise.

Two years later, my parents bought me my first personal computer: a Tandy/Radio Shack TRS80/4P. As the *P* indicates, it was supposed to be a portable computer, but in reality it was bigger than my mother's sewing machine. It could be booted from a hard disk, but I didn't have one; nor did I have any software besides the TRSDOS and its BASIC interpreter. By the time I was 16, I had written my own word-processing program, an indexed flat-file database system, and a drawing program—nothing fancy, considering the low resolution of the built-in, monochrome green computer screen.

I don't remember exactly what happened to me at that age—maybe it was my delayed discovery of girls—but it suddenly struck me that I was becoming a first-class nerd. So I made a 180-degree turn, studying Latin and math in high school and taking evening classes at a local art school. I decided that I wanted to become an artist instead of going to college. As a compromise with my parents, I studied civil architectural engineering at Ghent University. In my final year, I bought myself a Compaq portable computer to write my master's thesis. It was like finding a long-lost friend! After I earned my degree as an architect, I decided that it was time to return to the world of computers.

In 1996 I enrolled in a program that would retrain me as a software engineer. I learned and taught a brand-new programming language, Java. During my apprenticeship, I was put in charge of an experimental broadband Internet project. It was my first acquaintance with the Web. This expertise resulted in different assignments for the Flemish government. One of my tasks was to write an R&D report on standard Internet–intranet tools for GIS applications. That's when I wrote my first Java servlets.

I returned to Ghent University as an employee in 1998. When I published my first Free/Open Source Software library, I knew I had finally found my vocation. Now I have had the chance to write a book about it. I tried to give this book the personal touch I often miss when reading technical writings. I hope you will enjoy reading it as much as I have enjoyed writing it.

# *acknowledgments*

Many people have made it possible for me to write this book. First of all, I would like to thank my wife, Ingeborg, and my children, Inigo and Jago, for being patient with me, for giving me the time to write, and for keeping me in touch with the "real world" (reminding me to eat, drink, and sleep).

On behalf of all iText users, I would like to thank Paulo Soares, who started working on iText in the summer of 2000. Thanks to his efforts, a relatively simple Free/Open Source library was changed into a powerful PDF product. Paulo is currently in charge of most of the new developments, including the .NET port *iTextSharp*. I would also like to thank Mark Hall, who is responsible for the capability iText has to produce documents in RTF. Numerous people contributed valuable code, fixed bugs, added new features, and posted useful answers on the mailing list. The list of names is just too long to sum up. Thank you all for making iText the library it is today!

Thanks also to all of my current and former colleagues at Ghent University, especially Bernard Becue, Professor Geert De Soete, Luc Verschraegen, Mario Maccarini, Jurgen Lust, and Evelyne De Cordier. Thanks for supporting iText and for making my job worthwhile.

I would like to thank all the people at Manning Publications for giving me the opportunity to write this book, starting with publisher Marjan Bace, Megan Yockey, Blaise Bace, Jackie Carter, Lianna Wlasiuk, Karen Tegtmeyer, Mary Piergies, Tiffany Taylor, Katie Tenant, Denis Dalinnik, Dottie Marsico, and Olivia DiFeterici. Special thanks go to my development editor, Howard Jones. I am just a craftsman piling up material—Howard is the real artist, the sculptor who shaped it into a book.

Sincere thanks to the people who reviewed this book. Their remarks and suggestions at different stages of the manuscript were valuable to me in making this a better book: Stanley Wang, Paulo Soares, Barry Klawans, Jurgen Lust, Mark Hall, Bernard Becue, Bill Ensley, Leonard Rosenthal, Kris Coolsaet, Pim Van Heuven, Rudi Vansnick, Steve Appling, Mario Maccarini, Justin Lee, Stuart Caborn, Jan Van Campenhout, Alan Dennis, Oliver Ziegermann, Xavier Le Vourch, Doug James, Carl Hume, and Chris Dole. Special thanks to Mark Storer who did a final technical proofread of the book, just before it went to press.

Last, but not least, I would like to thank you, the people who are using iText. You are the ones who have kept me going! Many of you have sent me nice little notes of appreciation. I really like those notes, be they from a student who used iText successfully in a school project or from a developer working for a multinational who integrated iText with the software of a worldwide project. Thanks! I couldn't have written this book without your encouragement.

# about this book

This book will teach you about PDF, Adobe's Portable Document Format, from a Java developer's point of view. You'll learn how to use iText in a Java/J2EE application for the production and/or manipulation of PDF documents. Along the way, you'll become acquainted with lots of interesting PDF features and discover e-document functionalities you may not have known about before.

In addition to the many small code samples, this book includes lots of XML-based, ready-made solutions that can easily be adapted and integrated into your projects.

If you're a .NET developer using the C# or J# port of iText, iTextSharp or iText.NET, you can also benefit from this book, but you'll have to adapt the examples.

## How to use this book

You can read this book chronologically, starting with the introductory part 1. Part 2 describes useful basic building blocks, and part 3 gets into iText's core PDF functionality. You'll finish with part 4, which discusses the interactive features of PDF.

If you haven't convinced your project manager yet that PDF is the way to go, you'll certainly benefit from reading chapters 1 and 3. It sums up some reasonable arguments that will help you help your manager make policy decisions regarding e-documents. Section 1.3 contains a roadmap to the ready-made solutions that are demonstrated throughout the book. The main function of this section is to offer you a menu composed of a series of screenshots, showing all kinds of documents: documents with flowing text, graphics, bookmarks, and so on. If you see something you like, you can use this book as a kind of 'cookbook' and jump to the 'recipe' that was used to create a similar document.

Readers who are new to iText will need to take the "Hello World" crash course in chapter 2. This chapter shows that iText can be used in many different ways. The first three chapters often refer to sections in parts 2, 3, and 4, where you'll find an in-depth explanation of the specific functionality that is being introduced in one of the many "Hello World" examples.

You can also read the book in random order or thematically, starting from the table of contents or the roadmap in chapter 1. Once you're well acquainted with iText, you'll probably use the book as a reference manual, browsing for the many small standalone code samples that can be applied directly to your own code.

## *Roadmap*

Part 1 consists of three chapters which introduce the history of iText and the basics of creating and manipulating PDF documents. These chapters give you a bird's-eye view of PDF in general and iText in particular. You'll get acquainted with different aspects of PDF by first looking at different screenshots and then making a series of small "Hello, World" files demonstrating the concept of PDF creation and manipulation using iText. Chapter 1 also discusses in greater detail how to use and navigate the book.

Part 2 consists of four chapters that explain the building blocks which are used to construct a document, such as phrases, paragraphs, chapters, and sections. A document can also contain images, tables, and columns. Chapters 4 through 7 explain how iText implements these structures, and the examples at the end of each chapter demonstrate how they fit together.

Part 3 goes to the core of iText and PDF. This part is meant to serve as a reference manual for the reader, explaining how to create the actual content of a document and answering many practical questions: How do I choose a font? How do I draw a dashed line? How do I make an image transparent? How do I translate a Swing component to PDF? Chapters 8 through 12 answer these and many other questions, further illustrating them with plenty of examples.

The last six chapters of the book make up part 4, "Interactive PDF," and they deal with meta content. The following questions are answered: How do I add bookmarks to a file? How do I add headers, footers, or a watermark? How do I add comments or a file attachment? How do I create and fill a form? And above all, how do I create a PDF file in a web application? The syntax and design of PDF are discussed.

## *Who should read this book?*

This book is intended for Java developers who want to enhance their projects with dynamic PDF document generation and/or manipulation. It assumes you have some background in Java programming.

For reasons of convenience, most of the examples are constructed as standalone command-line applications. If you want to run these examples in a web application, you should know how to set up an application server, where to put the necessary Java archive files (jars) and resources, and how to deploy a servlet.

The same goes for XML. Although this book could have used database tables, XML was preferred as the technology-independent format to store the data needed for the ready-made solutions. You should be familiar with Simple API for XML (SAX) parsers and how to use them.

Knowledge of the Portable Document Format isn't necessary, because this book will explain a good deal of the PDF functionality and syntax where needed. The PDF Reference (Adobe Systems Inc.) is a good companion for this book, for those who want to know every detail about PDF internals.

## *Code conventions*

First use of technical terms is in *italic*. The same goes for emphasized terms and mathematical variables. Source code in listings or in text is in a `fixed width font`. Java packages, method names, directories, parameters, and XML elements and attributes are also presented using `fixed width font`. Some code lines can be in **`bold fixed width font`** for emphasis. Code that appears in *`italic fixed width font`* is a placeholder, and you should replace it according to your needs.

Code annotations accompany many of the source code listings, highlighting important concepts. In some cases, annotations correspond to explanations that follow the listing.

## *Software requirements and downloads*

iText is a Free/Open Source Software library created by Bruno Lowagie and Paulo Soares, protected by the Mozilla Public License (MPL). You can download it from http://www.sourceforge.net/projects/itext/ or http://www.lowagie.com/iText/.

All jars are compiled with the Java Development Kit (JDK) 1.4. If you need iText to run in another Java Runtime Environment (JRE), it's safest to download the source code and recompile the library with the corresponding JDK.

You can download the source code of the small standalone examples, as well as the ready-made solutions, from itext.ugent.be/itext-in-action/. You can also download the source code for the examples in the book from www.manning.com/lowagie. All examples have been tested with iText 1.4.

## Author Online

Your purchase of *iText in Action* includes free access to a private web forum run by Manning Publications, where you can make comments about the book, ask technical questions, and receive help from the author and from other users. To access the forum and subscribe to it, point your web browser to www.manning.com/lowagie. This page provides information on how to get onto the forum once you are registered, what kind of help is available, and the rules of conduct on the forum. Manning's commitment to our readers is to provide a venue where a meaningful dialogue among individual readers and between readers and the author can take place. It is not a commitment to any specific amount of participation on the part of the author, whose contribution to the AO remains voluntary (and unpaid). We suggest you try asking the author some challenging questions, lest his interest stray!

The Author Online forum and the archives of previous discussions will be accessible from the publisher's website as long as the book is in print.

## About the title

By combining introductions, overviews, and how-to examples, the *In Action* books are designed to help learning *and* remembering. According to research in cognitive science, the things people remember are things they discover during self-motivated exploration.

Although no one at Manning is a cognitive scientist, we are convinced that for learning to become permanent it must pass through stages of exploration, play, and, interestingly, re-telling of what is being learned. People understand and remember new things, which is to say they master them, only after actively exploring them. Humans learn *in action*. An essential part of an *In Action* guide is that it is example-driven. It encourages the reader to try things out, to play with new code, and explore new ideas.

There is another, more mundane, reason for the title of this book: our readers are busy. They use books to do a job or solve a problem. They need books that allow them to jump in and jump out easily and learn just what they want just when they want it. They need books that aid them *in action*. The books in this series are designed for such readers.

## *About the cover illustration*

The figure on the cover of *iText in Action* is a "Dorobautz Valachia" or a Rumanian from Wallachia, a historical region of southeast Romania between the Transylvanian Alps and the Danube River. Founded as a principality in the late thirteenth century, Wallachia was ruled by Turkey from 1387 until it was united with Moldavia to form Romania in 1861. The illustration is taken from a collection of costumes of the Ottoman Empire published on January 1, 1802, by William Miller of Old Bond Street, London. The title page is missing from the collection and we have been unable to track it down to date. The book's table of contents identifies the figures in both English and French, and each illustration bears the names of two artists who worked on it, both of whom would no doubt be surprised to find their art gracing the front cover of a computer programming book...two hundred years later.

The collection was purchased by a Manning editor at an antiquarian flea market in the "Garage" on West 26th Street in Manhattan. The seller was an American based in Ankara, Turkey, and the transaction took place just as he was packing up his stand for the day. The Manning editor did not have on his person the substantial amount of cash that was required for the purchase and a credit card and check were both politely turned down. With the seller flying back to Ankara that evening the situation was getting hopeless. What was the solution? It turned out to be nothing more than an old-fashioned verbal agreement sealed with a handshake. The seller simply proposed that the money be transferred to him by wire and the editor walked out with the bank information on a piece of paper and the portfolio of images under his arm. Needless to say, we transferred the funds the next day, and we remain grateful and impressed by this unknown person's trust in one of us. It recalls something that might have happened a long time ago.

The pictures from the Ottoman collection, like the other illustrations that appear on our covers, bring to life the richness and variety of dress customs of two centuries ago. They recall the sense of isolation and distance of that period—and of every other historic period except our own hyperkinetic present.

Dress codes have changed since then and the diversity by region, so rich at the time, has faded away. It is now often hard to tell the inhabitant of one continent from another. Perhaps, trying to view it optimistically, we have traded a cultural and visual diversity for a more varied personal life. Or a more varied and interesting intellectual and technical life.

We at Manning celebrate the inventiveness, the initiative, and, yes, the fun of the computer business with book covers based on the rich diversity of regional life of two centuries ago, brought back to life by the pictures from this collection.

# Part 1

# Introduction

These three chapters give you a bird's eye view of PDF in general and iText in particular. You'll get acquainted with different aspects of PDF by first looking at different screenshots and then making a series of small "Hello, World" files demonstrating the concept of PDF creation and manipulation using iText.

# 1 iText: when and why

**This chapter covers**

- History and first use of iText
- Overview of iText's PDF functionality
- Introduction to the examples in this book

If you want to enhance applications with dynamic PDF generation and/or manipulation, you've come to the right place. Throughout this book, you'll learn how to build applications that produce professional, high-quality PDF documents. More specifically, you'll learn how to do the following:

- Serve dynamically generated PDF to a web browser
- Generate documents and reports based on data from an XML file or a database
- Create maps and ebooks, exploiting numerous interactive features available in PDF
- Add bookmarks, page numbers, watermarks, and other features to existing PDF documents
- Split and/or concatenate pages from existing PDF files
- Fill out forms, add digital signatures, and much more

You'll create these documents on the fly, meaning you aren't going to use a desktop application such as Adobe Acrobat. Instead, you'll use an API to produce PDF directly from your own applications, which is necessary when a project has one of the following requirements:

- The content needs to be served in a web environment, and PDF is preferred over HTML for better printing quality, for security reasons, or to reduce the file size.
- The PDF files can't be produced manually due to the volume (number of pages/documents) or because the content isn't available in advance (it's calculated and/or based on user input).
- Documents need to be created in unattended mode (for instance, in a batch process).
- The content needs to be customized and/or personalized.

This book is a comprehensive guide to an API that makes all this possible: iText, a free Java-PDF library. For first-time users, this book is indispensable. Although the basic functionality of iText is easy to grasp, this book lowers the learning curve for more advanced functionality.

It's also a must-have for the many developers who are already familiar with iText. With this book, they finally have in one place all the information previously found scattered across the Internet. Even expert developers are likely to discover iText functionality they weren't aware of.

In this chapter, you'll learn how iText was born, and we'll look at some real-world PDF files that were generated using iText.

## 1.1 The history of iText

In the summer of 1998, the university where I worked[1] was starting up a migration project with the intention of redesigning a series of standalone programs used by the student administration. Up until then, entering the grades of students and calculating their final results at the end of the academic year was done using software that worked only on MS-DOS. Documents produced by this software could be printed on only one type of printer. This wasn't an ideal way of working, to say the least. Teachers and their administrative staff were using all kinds of systems: Windows, Mac, Linux, Solaris, and so forth. Yet for one of the most delicate aspects of their job—grading students—they were still forced to use plain old DOS. The university decided it was high time to do something about this situation and hired two developers to create a completely web-based solution. One of them was (and still is) my colleague Mario Maccarini. The other one, as you've probably guessed, was me.

Mario and I immediately started writing some Java servlets using Apache JSERV (it was the stone age of J2EE), and we proudly presented our first online lists with students, courses, and grades in the fall of 1998. It was just some ordinary HTML in a browser, but compared to the MS-DOS box, it was a big leap forward. Everybody was enthusiastic, until somebody asked one of the most crucial questions of the project: *what did we, the developers, plan to do about the "document problem"?*

### 1.1.1 How iText was born

Have you ever tried printing an HTML document in Microsoft Internet Explorer (MSIE), Firefox, or Netscape? If so, you have a good idea of the problem we were facing. Every browser interprets HTML in its own way. A table in MSIE doesn't look completely the same as a table rendered by Firefox. Using Cascading Style Sheets (CSS) can help you fine-tune the end result, but there's another problem: The end-user can disable style sheets, change margins, add page numbers, and so forth. Moreover, just like with Microsoft Word documents, the end user can usually change the content of an HTML document manually, using the application

[1] ICT Department, Ghent University, Belgium.

that renders the document. We wanted to avoid this, so we didn't consider Word and HTML to be options. We needed a technology that allowed us to generate unalterable reports with a reliable layout.

I didn't know much about the Portable Document Format back then. I only knew it was supposed to be a read-only format and that you could make printouts look exactly the way you intended to, regardless of the operating system and/or printer. When the document question arose, my answer was impulsive. Without fully realizing the consequences, I told the university committee, "We'll produce PDF!"

Mind you, it was a good answer, and it was well received. PDF is known as a widespread page-description language (PDL), and it's a de facto industry standard. It's portable. It's reliable. It prints really well. Almost everyone has the free Adobe Reader on their system. I assumed all of these fine qualities automatically meant there would be ample free or open source software available to produce PDF.

Apparently I was wrong. I needed an API, a set of classes, preferably written in Java, and preferably open source, but in the winter of 1998, the only free Java-PDF libraries I found on the Internet weren't able to provide the functionality required in our project. Only then did I become aware that I would have to write a PDF library myself if I wanted to keep my promise. During that period, I spent all my free time reading the PDF Reference.

Within seven months of when we were hired, our new intranet application was brought into production at the university where I worked. Its main users were university professors, their proxies, and the administrative staff of the university.

Registered users could log in to a personalized intranet page and do the following:

- Get an overview of all the courses they were responsible for (as a teacher or a proxy)
- Fetch (empty) grading lists in PDF with all the students enrolled for a specific course
- Get an HTML form to submit grades to the server (this could also have been a PDF AcroForm—a form containing a number of fixed areas—or AcroFields, on one or more pages)
- Get a completed version of the grading lists per course

School administrators were also able to

- Compose a curriculum for each individual student
- Generate application forms for students to sign up for specific examination periods
- Calculate every student's grade at the end of the academic year
- Fetch lists with information on the complete year of study for different purposes: deliberation lists, proclamation lists, feedback for the students, and so forth
- Generate official documents such as report cards and transcripts for the students

Every document that needed to be printed was generated in PDF by a newly created library. I designed this set of classes in such a way that it would be usable in other projects, too. I was encouraged to publish the library as a Free and Open Source Software (FOSS) product even before our project went into production. That's how iText was born.

Almost immediately, many fellow developers started to use the library, contributing source code at the same time. Paulo Soares was one of these early adopters. He joined the project in the summer of the year 2000 and is now one of the main developers of new iText features. He also maintains the .NET port iTextSharp.

### 1.1.2 iText today

Nowadays, iText is used in many online and other services, directly or indirectly. You may have already used iText without being aware of it; a lot of software products ship iText in their distribution. If you've created PDF documents using Macromedia ColdFusion, the file was probably generated by iText. If you're creating reports with one of the most important reporting tools of the moment—JasperReports or Eclipse/BIRT—you'll see that iText is built in as its PDF engine. You could use this book to enhance your own product so that it's capable of producing PDF documents, but the activity on the mailing list tells me it's more likely that you're going to use iText in tailor-made applications similar to the intranet application Mario and I wrote.

In e-commerce applications, you replace students with customers, courses with products, and grades with prices. Energy companies use iText to generate invoices with tables showing customers how much gas, electricity, or water they consumed. The iText library is popular in e-government projects because iText can be used to add a digital signature to a PDF document using an *eID*—a smart card issued by some governments that can be used for proof of identity. The financial sector uses iText to provide clients with reports about investments, or to produce and process loan application forms. Manufacturers can use iText to compose lists of the parts, subassemblies, and raw materials used to make a product (the Bill of Materials) complete with barcodes that allow automating the manufacturing process. I've seen blueprints and city maps that were created with iText. NASA uses iText in a tool that produces PDF documents showing global longitude-latitude images or pole-to-pole latitude-vertical images of the earth. Google Calendar uses iText to produce calendar sheets.

In short, whatever your project, iText can save you a lot of work and time, helping you to create new PDF documents and/or manipulate existing PDF files.

### Ease of use and flexibility

First-time iText users will find lots of examples on the Internet explaining how to create a simple PDF document using iText. On the Java Boutique site is an article by Benoy Jose titled "PDF Generation Made Easy" (http://javaboutique.internet.com/tutorials/iText/). This title reflects the initial idea of iText—that you shouldn't have to be a PDF specialist to be able to generate PDF documents. iText's small set of basic building blocks allows you to create a proof of concept in no time.

Some in the community are occasionally heard to say that working with iText can be demanding, as might be expected of even a well-designed software tool when you're dealing with complicated issues. However, this book is structured so that even iText's complexities are presented painlessly. Don Fluckinger, a freelance writer who has been covering Acrobat and PDF technologies for PDF-Zone since 2000, writes that iText is "a robust little software tool for generating PDFs on the fly that isn't for the technically faint of heart." I must admit that iText code can get complex as soon as you want maximum flexibility when creating a customized PDF document. Don recommends iText "if you feel like rolling up your sleeves, popping open the hood, and getting to work." That's exactly what we're going to do in this book: We're going to go further than the articles you can find on the Internet and in the online tutorial. This book will give you an in-depth overview of what is possible with iText.

A developer who successfully integrated iText into his software writes, "You're able to produce an extremely size-optimized PDF on-the-fly without sacrificing any feature of the desired output." That's the spirit of the true iText user.

#### iText licensing

Although iText is free (you're allowed to use iText in open or closed source software, in standalone or web-based applications, for free or proprietary services, and in commercial or nonprofit projects), this doesn't mean you're free to do anything you want with the library; you have to respect the copyright and the Mozilla Public License (MPL) that protects iText. The first versions of iText were published under the Library (or Lesser) GNU Public License (LGPL), but once iText got interesting for some major players in the Information and Communications Technology (ICT) business, there was increasing pressure to move to another license.

Many company lawyers had issues with some of the quirky details in the LGPL, so we chose the MPL with LGPL as an alternative license, for backward compatibility. Basically, the MPL says that you have to inform your customers that you're using the FOSS library iText (by Bruno Lowagie and Paulo Soares), and you have to tell them where they can find the library's source code. Additionally, if you change the library, you should make your enhancements and bug fixes available to the community. This leads to a win-win situation: You win if you get your fixes in the official release, because you reduce upgrade-related problems. The iText community wins because it can benefit from your enhancements. This is the short explanation. For the long version, see the full text of the MPL that is available on the iText site (http://www.lowagie.com/iText/MPL-1.1.txt) and packaged with the source code.

### 1.1.3 Beyond Java

This book focuses on PDF manipulation with iText seen from a Java developer's point of view, but that doesn't mean you can't use iText in another environment. Companies make choices, and when it comes to building enterprise software, it seems to come down to a choice between two technologies: J2EE or .NET. That's why the .NET ports are religiously synchronized at the release and Concurrent Versioning System (CVS) level.

#### iText.NET and iTextSharp

There are two important .NET ports: *iText.NET* is a J# port by Kazuya Ujihara; and *iTextSharp* is a C# port originally written by Gerald Henson, but which has been taken over by Paulo Soares, the most active developer of iText in the past five years. Paulo has been "converted" from Java to .NET recently and keeps iTextSharp synchronized with the original Java version.

### *iText and pdftk*

The PDF Toolkit (pdftk) by Sid Steward is "a command-line tool for doing everyday things with PDF documents," as defined on the AccessPDF web site (www.accesspdf.com). pdftk is also a good example of how iText can be used in a C++ program by building a native library using the GNU compiler for Java (GCJ). If your program needs some of the PDF-manipulation functionality found in a C++ environment, you should try this toolkit.

### *iText and ColdFusion*

The iText.jar file is shipped with Macromedia's server product ColdFusion. This means it's possible to use iText in your ColdFusion applications for generating PDF documents on the fly. By acquiring Macromedia, Adobe now has an affordable server product that is able to produce PDFs.

### *Using iText in PHP, Python, Ruby*

There aren't any PHP, Python, or Ruby ports, but you can use a PHP/Java bridge for PHP integration, or a Ruby/Java bridge to address iText from a Ruby application. If you search the Internet, you'll find some iText examples written in Jython, the Java implementation of Python.

You won't find any C#, CF, J#, Jython, Python, PHP, Ruby, or VB examples in this book, but it should be fairly easy to adapt the Java examples so that you can use them in your specific development environment. Most of the mechanisms that are explained in this book are independent of the programming language. Let's return to Java and find out how to download and test iText.

## 1.2 *iText: first contact*

Setting up an environment in which to run and test the examples in a book can be cumbersome, especially if you need to install additional services or servers. To reduce the complexity, most examples in this book were conceived as small standalone applications.

All examples were written in Java, so you'll need a Java environment (JDK 1.4 or higher is preferred) and the appropriate Java Archives (jars). Each example writes a short explanation to the `System.out`, telling you what it does. It also lists the necessary resources and the jars needed in the `CLASSPATH` (a variable that tells the Java Compiler and JVM where to find all necessary Java class-files and archives).

iText.jar is an executable jar. If you open it in a Java Runtime Environment (JRE), the iText toolbox opens. This is a GUI application that lets you do some simple PDF experiments without having to write a single line of code.

But first things first: Let's find out how to compile and execute the code samples.

### 1.2.1 Running the examples in the book

You can download a Zip file containing all the examples in this book from http://itext.ugent.be/itext-in-action/. Unzip this file in the directory of your choice, but be sure to name it something you can easily remember. After unzipping the file, you should have a subdirectory called /examples. The examples are organized in packages by chapter.

The code snippets in this book all start with a comment line, for instance: `/* chapter01/HelloWorld.java */`. This line tells you where to find the complete sample code by giving you a subdirectory of <your_dir>/examples/ (in this case <*your_dir*>/examples/chapter01) and the name of the Java source file (HelloWorld. java). If an example needs some extra resources (such as an image or an XML file), you'll find them in a subdirectory: <*your_dir*>/examples/chapter <*chapter_number*>/resources.

Whenever extra fonts are needed (TTF, OTF, or TTC files, for example), they should be in the directory C:/Windows/Fonts. You'll need to adapt this hardcoded path in the example if you're working on a Mac, Linux, or Unix OS, or if the fonts are stored elsewhere on your Windows system.

**NOTE** *Never use hardcoded paths in your production code*. I wanted the examples to be simple, so I didn't use code to load properties files or fetch information from a Java Naming and Directory Interface (JNDI) repository. You should use a more robust solution to refer to fonts or any other resource once you start writing your own code.

You'll also need to download a file containing all the Java archives that are needed to run the examples. The Zip file with the examples comes with a build.xml file that expects these jars to be present in the directory called <*your_dir*>/bin. If you're used to working with ANT—the standard tool used to build and execute Java code—you'll immediately feel comfortable with it.

The `action` target allows you to compile and execute each example like this:

```
$ ant -Dchapter=01 -Dexample=HelloWorld action
```

Although this is the official way to run `ant`, with the target at the end of the command, I find it more practical to switch the order of parameters and target like this:

```
ant action -Dchapter=01 -Dexample=HelloWorld
```

It saves you a few keystrokes to use the Up arrow to repeat and the Backspace key to change a command previously called in your shell (such as DOS or bash). This particular command compiles and executes a "Hello, World" example. The source code can be found in the directory <*your_dir*>/examples/chapter01/HelloWorld.java. This Java source file is compiled to <*your_dir*>/bin/classes/chapter01/HelloWorld.class, and the file HelloWorld.pdf appears in <*your_dir*>/examples/chapter01/results as soon as the compiled code is executed.

After a while, you'll have generated lots of files—compiled Java classes, PDF documents, and so forth. You can remove all these files at once by using the `clean` target for the `ant` command.

Once you succeed in running these examples, integrating iText into your own application should be a piece of cake. Just add the iText.jar to your `CLASSPATH`, and start coding. If you're new to Java development, and you have trouble finding where to put the jar or where to change the `CLASSPATH` in a web application, please consult your application server's manual.

If you're not ready to compile and execute these examples yet, you can turn to the iText toolbox first. This toolbox offers some ready-to-use tools that don't require any knowledge of Java or PDF; you only need a JRE.

### 1.2.2 Experimenting with the iText toolbox

Originally, iText was developed as a developer's library, meaning that it wasn't aimed at an end-user market. Developers could integrate iText into their Java web applications or standalone Java programs, but the library itself didn't have a user interface.

When the first PDF manipulation classes were added to iText, some simple command-line applications for splitting, encrypting, and concatenating PDF files were provided as examples in the iText tutorial. Later, these sample applications were moved to a `com.lowagie.tools` package.

Mailing-list questions made it clear that not many people were using command-line tools, probably because they aren't user-friendly. So, a small GUI called the iText toolbox was developed. The toolbox has now become a means to test part of the iText functionality without having to write any source code.

You can open the toolbox by executing the iText jar file:

```
java -jar iText.jar
```

In figure 1.1, some plug-ins are opened in an internal window of the toolbox.

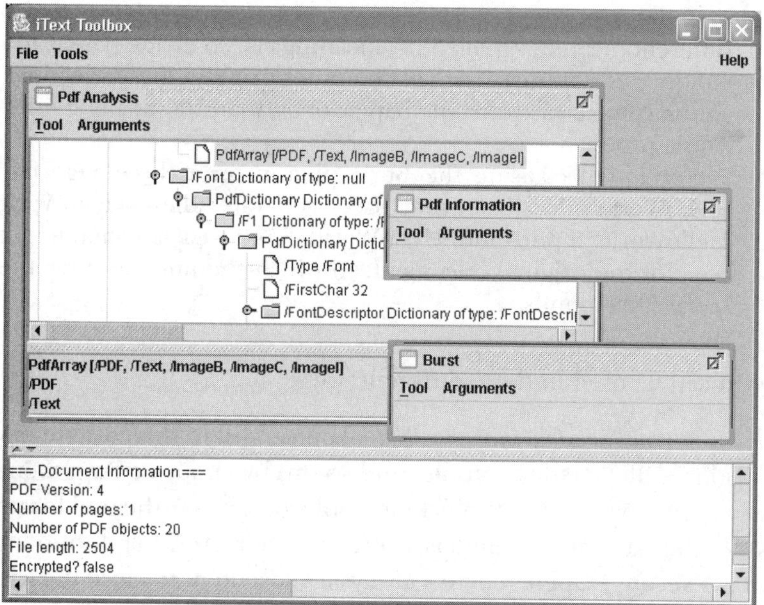


**Figure 1.1 The iText toolbox**

The toolbox contains three menu items:

- *File*—The File > Close command closes the toolbox.
- *Tools*—A selection of plug-ins is loaded from the package `com.lowagie.-tools.plugins` when you open the toolbox. These plug-ins are organized in different categories under the Tools menu.
- *Help*—Choosing Help > About directs you to a web page describing the tools, and Help > Version shows the list of tools that were loaded and their versions.

**NOTE** By going to the URL http://itext.ugent.be/library/itext.jnlp, you can use the Java Network Launching Protocol (JNLP) to download and start the jar as a Java Web Start (JWS) application. The application should start automatically. Notice that you'll get a security warning because I signed the jar with a self-signed certificate.

Most of the plug-ins are self-explanatory. In the chapters that follow, we'll dig into the mechanics of some of these tools. Whenever there's a toolbox tool that illustrates some specific functionality, I'll insert a note about it like this:

**TOOLBOX** `com.lowagie.tools.plugins.Burst` *(Manipulate)* The verb *to burst* has different meanings. One of its meanings is "to divide paper; to separate continuous stationery such as computer printout into individual sheets." In the context of electronic paper, to *burst* a PDF means splitting it into single pages.

For instance, using the Burst plug-in on a three-page file named HelloWorld.pdf generates three separate files—HelloWorld_1.pdf, HelloWorld_2.pdf, and HelloWorld_3.pdf—each containing a single page of the original document, to which the number after the underscore corresponds.

Each plug-in can be used in three different ways:

- *From an internal window in the toolbox*—You can fill in the parameters for the tool (source file, destination file, and so on) by choosing Arguments in the internal window's menu. By clicking Tool, you can ask the tool for its Usage, consult the Arguments, and Execute the tool. Another (optional) menu item is Execute+Open. There's always a Close item to close the window.
- *As a command-line tool*—For instance, if you want to burst a PDF file from the command line, you can call the plug-in like this:

  ```
  java -cp ./iText.jar com.lowagie.tools.plugins.Burst HelloWorld.pdf
  ```

  Calling the plug-in without any arguments will show you the *Usage* information.
- *From another Java application*—Construct a `String` array with the arguments and call the main method of the plug-in:

  ```
  /* chapter01/HelloWorldBurst.java */
  String[] arg = {"HelloWorldRead.pdf"};
  com.lowagie.tools.plugins.Burst.main(arg);
  ```

We'll create some more HelloWorld PDF files in the next chapter to get acquainted with iText. First, let's look at the more interesting examples this book has in store. Let me tell you a story that could have happened to you.

## 1.3 An almost-true story

I graduated as a civil architectural engineer, and I started my professional career in the Geographical Informations Systems (GIS) division of Tractebel Information Systems (TRASYS), in Brussels, which is now owned by the international industrial and services group Suez. While I was looking for an application that could run continuously throughout this book, I started drawing the map of a fictional city called Foobar. On this map, I added a university campus. That way, I combined my GIS background with my current professional situation. I thought of a story that would make an employee of the fictive Technological University of Foobar (TUF) the heroine. Her name is Laura, and she will be your guide throughout the longer examples in this book.

The following subsections tell the beginning of Laura's story, but their main purpose is to give you a preview of the iText features that will be explained in parts 2, 3, and 4. Starting with chapter 2, you'll find lots of small, almost atomic source code examples that explain how to do something; later, some longer real-world examples will show you how it all works together. The screenshots in this section represent the output of these longer examples.

### 1.3.1 Some Foobar fiction

Laura is preparing to attend yet another staff meeting. According to her business card, she's a software architect for the central administration at TUF. When asked for her job title, Laura prefers to call herself a Java developer, plain and simple.

TUF is a small university located in the city of Foobar. Apart from the central administration, it consists of only two departments: the Department of Science and the Department of Engineering. There has been a constant rivalry between the departments, one of the catalysts being the introduction of computer science as a new study discipline. That was over 20 years ago. At that time, the board of the university decided to follow in the footsteps of King Solomon and divided the discipline over both departments. Undergraduates had to enroll in the Department of Science, whereas graduate students enrolled in the Department of Engineering.

It was a great idea in theory, but in practice, it was a burden. Making decisions concerning the educational program of the complete field of study was no longer a sinecure. Hidden agendas and internal differences between the departments often got in the way of good management. Informatics students suffered from this pragmatic division, too—their colleagues from other scientific disciplines didn't consider them to be "real" scientists in the first years of their studies, and during their graduate years, their peers didn't regard them as being "engineer material."

Laura was aware of the feeling, but she was always careful never to be dragged into a discussion about it. For a long time, the university played with the idea of redesigning all the software applications supporting the core business processes of the central administration. Finally, a decision was made, and a committee was formed with authorities from both departments. Laura, of course, was also invited. She feared the worst and decided to keep quiet while the debates between scientists and engineers heated up. At one point, she forgot where she was and began to daydream.

### 1.3.2 A document daydream

Computer sciences, software engineering, Information and Communication Technology (ICT)—all of these disciplines have their differences, but is dividing really the best way to conquer the hearts of students? Laura had given this question a lot of thought. "*Suppose I were given the opportunity to start a new department,*" she said to herself, "*a department that combined all the courses and education in the field of computer science and engineering. What would I need?*

She decided to start with the following:

- Promotional flyers for the new department
- A guide containing study programs (tables)
- A course catalog (columns)

In part 2 of this book, all the elements needed to bring these assignments to completion will be explained step by step throughout four chapters. At the end of each chapter, you'll work with Laura to create the documents she's dreaming of.

#### *Making a flyer*

As Laura's new colleagues, the first thing we'll do is create a flyer with the university's logo, a paragraph welcoming new students, lists of programs offered by the department, and links to the university's web site. See figure 1.2 for an example.

You can consult section 4.3 if you need to generate a flyer with paragraphs, lists, and anchors. If you need images, you'll also need to read section 5.3. These sections explain how to write source code that allows you to create an exact copy of the PDF in figure 1.2.

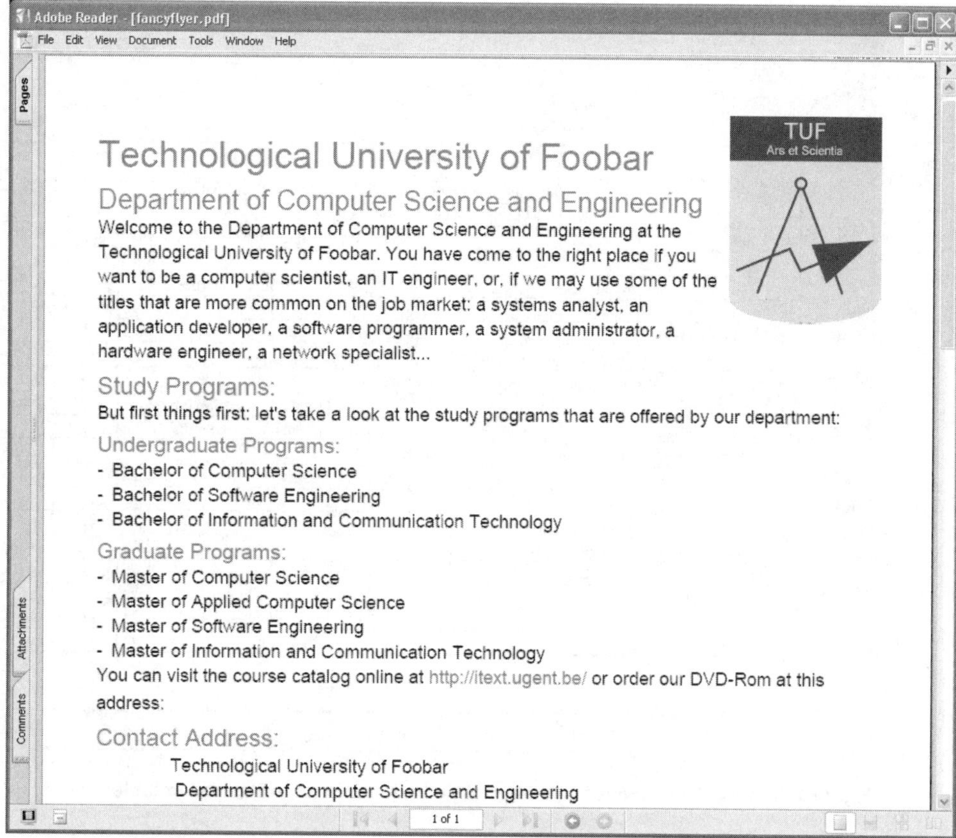


TUF
Ars et Scientia

Technological University of Foobar

Department of Computer Science and Engineering

Welcome to the Department of Computer Science and Engineering at the Technological University of Foobar. You have come to the right place if you want to be a computer scientist, an IT engineer, or, if we may use some of the titles that are more common on the job market: a systems analyst, an application developer, a software programmer, a system administrator, a hardware engineer, a network specialist...

Study Programs:

But first things first: let's take a look at the study programs that are offered by our department:

Undergraduate Programs:

- Bachelor of Computer Science
- Bachelor of Software Engineering
- Bachelor of Information and Communication Technology

Graduate Programs:

- Master of Computer Science
- Master of Applied Computer Science
- Master of Software Engineering
- Master of Information and Communication Technology

You can visit the course catalog online at http://itext.ugent.be/ or order our DVD-Rom at this address:

Contact Address:

Technological University of Foobar
Department of Computer Science and Engineering

**Figure 1.2 A PDF document containing some basic text elements, such as paragraphs, lists, anchors, and images**

### *Composing a study guide*

Once students have seen our flyer, they may be interested in studying at the Department of Computer Science and Engineering. If they contact the university for more information, we should be able to send them a study guide. One part of the study guide should contain tables representing the study programs. Figure 1.3 shows the first page of the program for students who want to earn a graduate degree in complementary studies in applied informatics.

The second part of the study guide should describe the courses that are mentioned in the study program. Figure 1.4 shows how we could organize this information in columns with tables and images.

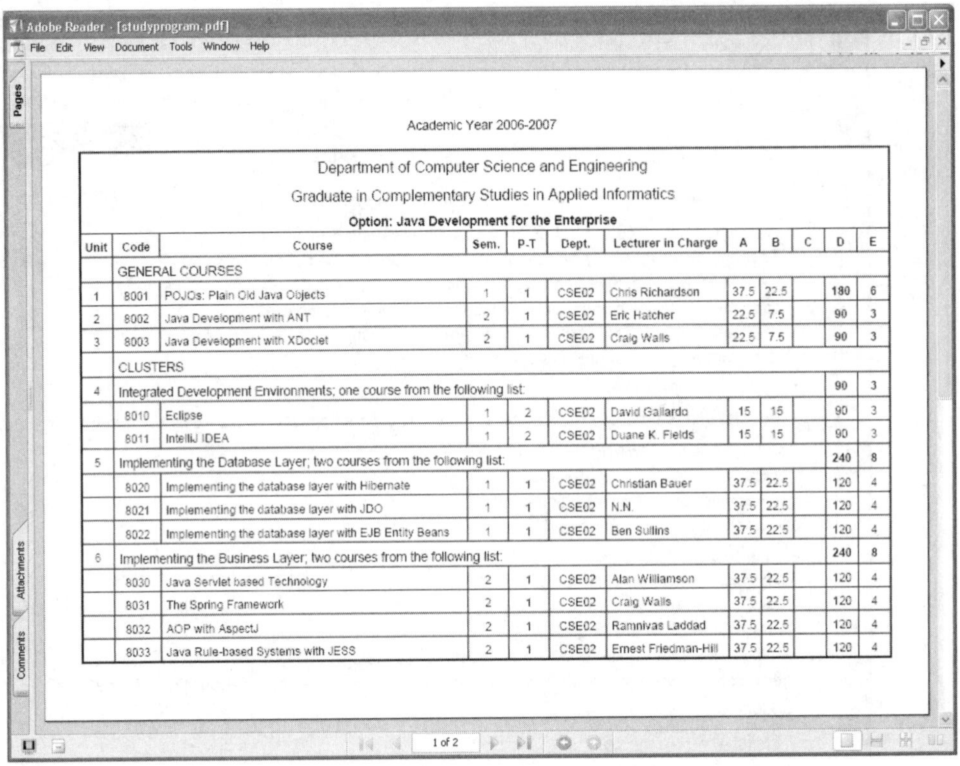

Adobe Reader - [studyprogram.pdf]
File Edit View Document Tools Window Help

Academic Year 2006-2007

Department of Computer Science and Engineering

Graduate in Complementary Studies in Applied Informatics

**Option: Java Development for the Enterprise**

| Unit | Code | Course | Sem. | P-T | Dept. | Lecturer in Charge | A | B | C | D | E |
|---|---|---|---|---|---|---|---|---|---|---|---|
| | GENERAL COURSES | | | | | | | | | | |
| 1 | 8001 | POJOs: Plain Old Java Objects | 1 | 1 | CSE02 | Chris Richardson | 37.5 | 22.5 | | 180 | 6 |
| 2 | 8002 | Java Development with ANT | 2 | 1 | CSE02 | Eric Hatcher | 22.5 | 7.5 | | 90 | 3 |
| 3 | 8003 | Java Development with XDoclet | 2 | 1 | CSE02 | Craig Walls | 22.5 | 7.5 | | 90 | 3 |
| | CLUSTERS | | | | | | | | | | |
| 4 | Integrated Development Environments; one course from the following list: | | | | | | | | | 90 | 3 |
| | 8010 | Eclipse | 1 | 2 | CSE02 | David Gallardo | 15 | 15 | | 90 | 3 |
| | 8011 | IntelliJ IDEA | 1 | 2 | CSE02 | Duane K. Fields | 15 | 15 | | 90 | 3 |
| 5 | Implementing the Database Layer; two courses from the following list: | | | | | | | | | 240 | 8 |
| | 8020 | Implementing the database layer with Hibernate | 1 | 1 | CSE02 | Christian Bauer | 37.5 | 22.5 | | 120 | 4 |
| | 8021 | Implementing the database layer with JDO | 1 | 1 | CSE02 | N.N. | 37.5 | 22.5 | | 120 | 4 |
| | 8022 | Implementing the database layer with EJB Entity Beans | 1 | 1 | CSE02 | Ben Sullins | 37.5 | 22.5 | | 120 | 4 |
| 6 | Implementing the Business Layer; two courses from the following list: | | | | | | | | | 240 | 8 |
| | 8030 | Java Servlet based Technology | 2 | 1 | CSE02 | Alan Williamson | 37.5 | 22.5 | | 120 | 4 |
| | 8031 | The Spring Framework | 2 | 1 | CSE02 | Craig Walls | 37.5 | 22.5 | | 120 | 4 |
| | 8032 | AOP with AspectJ | 2 | 1 | CSE02 | Ramnivas Laddad | 37.5 | 22.5 | | 120 | 4 |
| | 8033 | Java Rule-based Systems with JESS | 2 | 1 | CSE02 | Ernest Friedman-Hill | 37.5 | 22.5 | | 120 | 4 |

1 of 2

**Figure 1.3 A PDF document containing basic text elements, organized in tables**

Chances are, you've been working on projects that deal with similar information. Maybe you've been asked to publish content coming from a database or an XML repository in the form of some neat-looking PDF reports.

If that is the case, you may want to read chapters 6 and 7 and discover how to shape your data into tabular or columnar text elements. The code that was used to create figure 1.3 and figure 1.4 is discussed in sections 6.3 and 7.5.

### 1.3.3 *Welcoming the student*

The university will welcome students from all over the world, so it's important that we provide them with an information package with some information written in different languages. We'll also have to give them a map of the city so that they're able to find their way to the campus. The five chapters of part 3 deal with PDF text and graphics, which we'll need to produce documents using different fonts and writing systems, and a map of the city of Foobar.

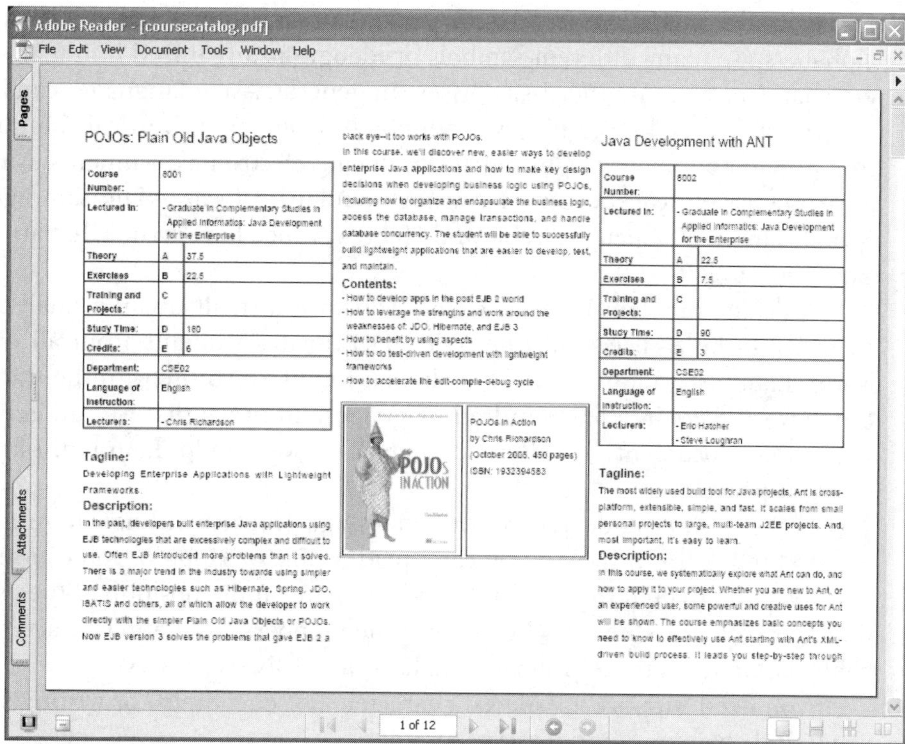

POJOs: Plain Old Java Objects

| Course Number: | 8001 | |
|---|---|---|
| Lectured In: | - Graduate in Complementary Studies in Applied Informatics: Java Development for the Enterprise | |
| Theory | A | 37.5 |
| Exercises | B | 22.5 |
| Training and Projects: | C | |
| Study Time: | D | 180 |
| Credits: | E | 6 |
| Department: | CSE02 | |
| Language of Instruction: | English | |
| Lecturers: | - Chris Richardson | |

**Tagline:**

Developing Enterprise Applications with Lightweight Frameworks.

**Description:**

In the past, developers built enterprise Java applications using EJB technologies that are excessively complex and difficult to use. Often EJB introduced more problems than it solved. There is a major trend in the industry towards using simpler and easier technologies such as Hibernate, Spring, JDO, iBATIS and others, all of which allow the developer to work directly with the simpler Plain Old Java Objects or POJOs. Now EJB version 3 solves the problems that gave EJB 2 a black eye--it too works with POJOs.

In this course, we'll discover new, easier ways to develop enterprise Java applications and how to make key design decisions when developing business logic using POJOs, including how to organize and encapsulate the business logic, access the database, manage transactions, and handle database concurrency. The student will be able to successfully build lightweight applications that are easier to develop, test, and maintain.

**Contents:**

- How to develop apps in the post EJB 2 world
- How to leverage the strengths and work around the weaknesses of: JDO, Hibernate, and EJB 3
- How to benefit by using aspects
- How to do test-driven development with lightweight frameworks
- How to accelerate the edit-compile-debug cycle

POJOs in Action
by Chris Richardson
(October 2005, 450 pages)
ISBN: 1932394583

Java Development with ANT

| Course Number: | 8002 | |
|---|---|---|
| Lectured In: | - Graduate in Complementary Studies in Applied Informatics: Java Development for the Enterprise | |
| Theory | A | 22.5 |
| Exercises | B | 7.5 |
| Training and Projects: | C | |
| Study Time: | D | 90 |
| Credits: | E | 3 |
| Department: | CSE02 | |
| Language of Instruction: | English | |
| Lecturers: | - Eric Hatcher<br>- Steve Loughran | |

**Tagline:**

The most widely used build tool for Java projects, Ant is cross-platform, extensible, simple, and fast. It scales from small personal projects to large, multi-team J2EE projects. And, most important, it's easy to learn.

**Description:**

In this course, we systematically explore what Ant can do, and how to apply it to your project. Whether you are new to Ant, or an experienced user, some powerful and creative uses for Ant will be shown. The course emphasizes basic concepts you need to know to effectively use Ant starting with Ant's XML-driven build process. It leads you step-by-step through

**Figure 1.4 A PDF document containing basic text elements, organized in columns**

Whereas part 2 discusses mainly iText-specific functionality, part 3 goes to the core of iText and focuses on the internal structure of a PDF page.

### *Producing documents in different languages*

In the ICT world, developers have adopted the English language as the de facto standard for human communication. That's why I'm writing this book in English, although my mother tongue is Dutch. At some point, however, you may be asked to create documents with non-English text. You probably won't have a problem displaying text in French, even with all those little accents and cedillas; those characters can be found in the standard *latin-1* encoding. But to display some special characters that are common in languages such as Polish or Turkish, you have to use another encoding. The same goes for Greek and Russian, languages that have completely different alphabets than English.

It gets harder when you need to display text in an Asian alphabet, because such alphabets use many different symbols or ideograms organized into many different character sets. Another issue arises: In general, Asian languages can be written from left to right, but it's also common to write text in vertical columns read from top to bottom and right to left. Producing electronic documents using such a writing system can be complex using standard software. The same goes for Semitic languages, such as Arabic and Hebrew, which have scripts that are written from right to left.

This is the problem Laura is facing. Foobar is a small city in a small country. In order to be a successful university, TUF invites students from all over the world. Laura isn't multilingual, but she has found a web site with the translation of the word *peace* in a few hundred languages. To prove that we can generate a welcoming document in different languages, we'll help Laura display these words of peace.

Figure 1.5 shows a document with a message of peace in English, Arabic, and Hebrew, respectively. Even if you can't read Arabic or Hebrew, you can see these languages are written from right to left by looking at the position of the exclamation point and the comma. The order of the numbers and Latin characters in the abbreviation for Internet Internationalization (I18N) is preserved.

If you need support for special character sets, encodings, or writing systems, you'll find chapters 8 and 9 indispensable.

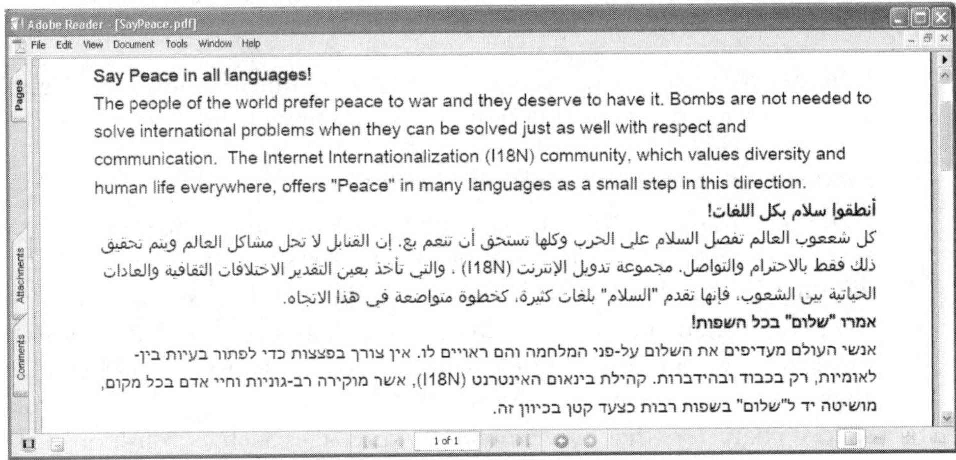


**Say Peace in all languages!**

The people of the world prefer peace to war and they deserve to have it. Bombs are not needed to solve international problems when they can be solved just as well with respect and communication. The Internet Internationalization (I18N) community, which values diversity and human life everywhere, offers "Peace" in many languages as a small step in this direction.

**أنطقوا سلام بكل اللغات!**

كل شعوب العالم تفضل السلام علي الحرب وكلها تستحق أن تنعم بع. إن القنابل لا تحل مشاكل العالم ويتم تحقيق ذلك فقط بالاحترام والتواصل. مجموعة تدويل الإنترنت (I18N) ، والتي تأخذ بعين التقدير الاختلافات الثقافية والعادات الحياتية بين الشعوب، فإنها تقدم "السلام" بلغات كثيرة، كخطوة متواضعة في هذا الاتجاه.

**אמרו "שלום" בכל השפות!**

אנשי העולם מעדיפים את השלום על-פני המלחמה והם ראויים לו. אין צורך בפצצות כדי לפתור בעיות בין-לאומיות, רק בכבוד ובהידברות. קהילת בינאום האינטרנט (I18N), אשר מוקירה רב-גוניות וחיי אדם בכל מקום, מושיטה יד ל"שלום" בשפות רבות כצעד קטן בכיוון זה.

**Figure 1.5 A PDF document demonstrating different writing systems**

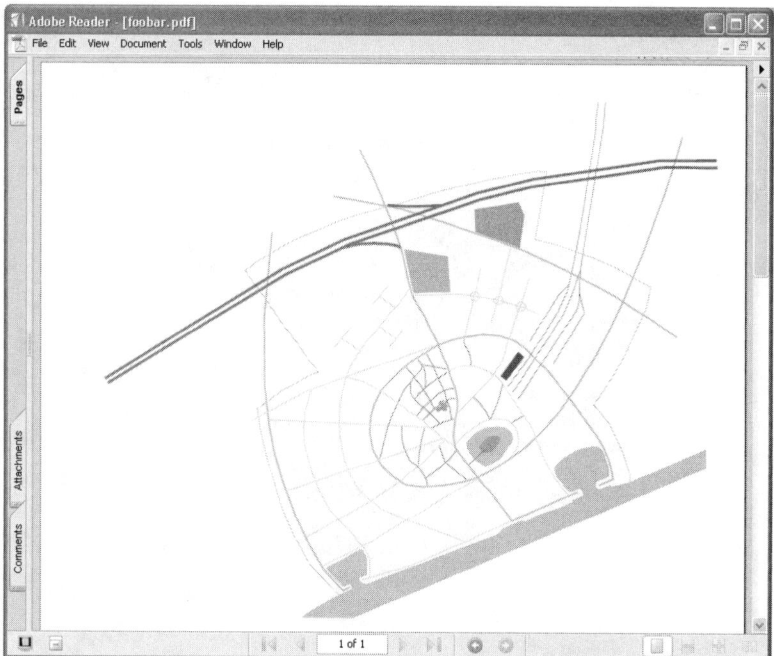


**Figure 1.6 Using iText to draw graphics such as lines and shapes**

### *Drawing a city map*

Laura has made a map of the city of Foobar in the Scalable Vector Graphics (SVG) format, and throughout this book we'll attempt to create a PDF document based on this SVG file. First we'll deal with the streets (paths) and the squares (shapes), as shown in figure 1.6.

In chapter 10, the first chapter on PDF's *graphics state,* you'll learn about path construction and path-painting operators and operands. A first attempt to generate the map of Foobar appears in section 10.5.

### *Adding street names to the map*

We'll continue discussing the graphics state in chapter 11, where you'll learn that PDF's *text state* is a subset of the graphics state. The text state will help us add the street names to the map. Figure 1.7 shows the result of a second attempt to draw the map of Foobar (see section 11.6).

The third attempt at drawing the map will use Apache Batik to parse the SVG.

**Figure 1.7 Using iText to draw text at absolute positions**

### *Adding interactive layers to the map*

Apache Batik is a library that can parse an SVG file and draw the paths, shapes, and text that are described in the form of XML to a `java.awt.Graphics2D` object. Chapters 10 and 11 present custom iText methods that are closely related to the operators and operands listed in the PDF Reference, and chapter 12 explains that you can also use an API you probably know already: the `java.awt` package.

For our first two attempts, we used one SVG file with the graphics and one with the street names in English, but Laura also wants to add the street names in French and Dutch. This task can be achieved using PDF's *optional content* feature, discussed in chapter 12. By adding each set of street names to a different *optional content group*, Laura can give foreign students the option to look at the map in the language of their choice, as shown in figure 1.8.

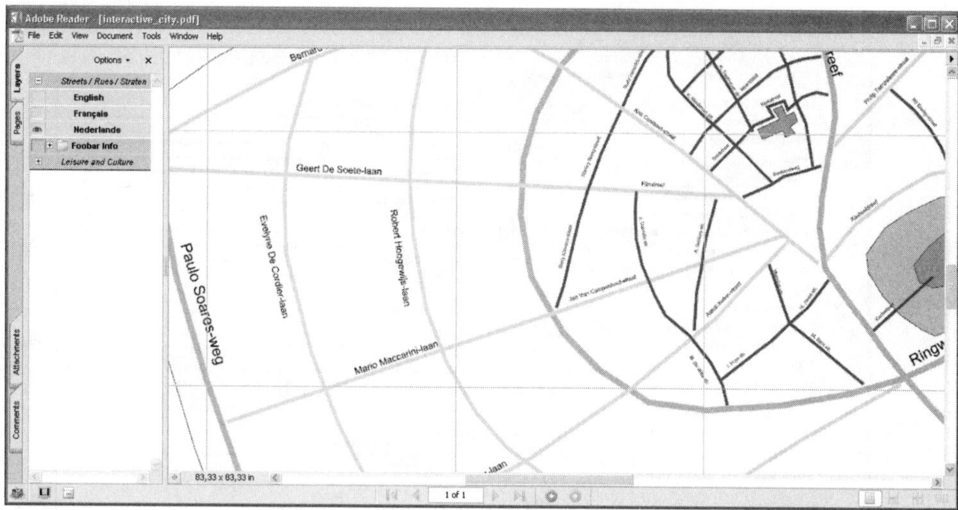


**Figure 1.8 A PDF document demonstrating the use of optional content groups.**

In section 12.4, we'll create a final version of the map of Foobar. Using Apache Batik, we'll parse different SVG files into different layers that can be turned on and off interactively.

This brings us to part 4, "Interactive PDF."

### 1.3.4 *Producing and processing interactive documents*

Laura can be hard on herself sometimes. She isn't quite satisfied with the study guide and course catalog shown in figures 1.3 and 1.4. She wants to add interactivity and extra features such as a watermark and page numbers.

#### *Making documents interactive*

Because a student's curriculum can consist of many different courses, it may be necessary to help students navigate through the course catalog. Let's add some extra links, annotations, and bookmarks to the document.

Chapter 4 discusses some building blocks with interactive features, but if you want the full assortment, you should dig into chapter 13, where you'll learn about setting viewer preferences; page labels and bookmarks; and actions and destinations. In section 13.6, we'll come back to the course catalog example and adapt it, giving it the interactive features shown in figure 1.9.

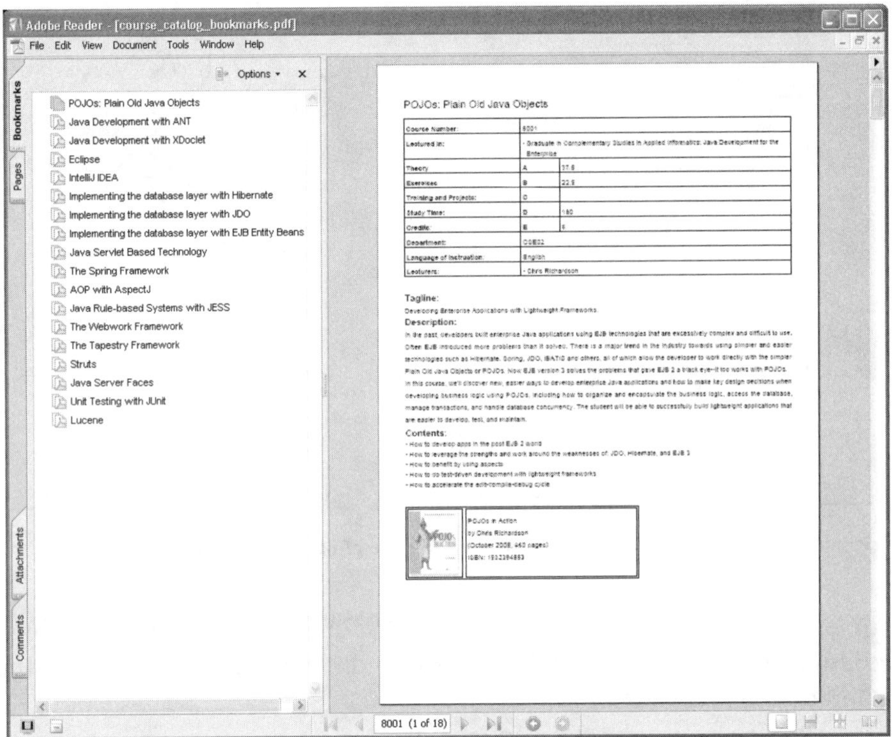


Figure 1.9 A PDF document demonstrating some interactive features.

### Adding watermarks and page numbers

Figure 1.10 shows pages 4 and 5 of the course catalog. The course number has been added as a header, and every file has the university's logo as its watermark.

In chapter 14, "Automating PDF Creation," you'll learn about page events that let you add content (such as watermarks or page numbers) automatically every time a new page is triggered.

### Using iText in a web application

You may have wondered what the letter *i* in iText stands for. You'll find out while reading about *interactive* PDF. You already know that iText was initially designed to generate PDF in a web application and that its original purpose was to serve text interactively based on a user specific query. It's easy to adapt the code of the examples so that they can be integrated in a web application, as long as you know how to avoid some specific browser-related issues.

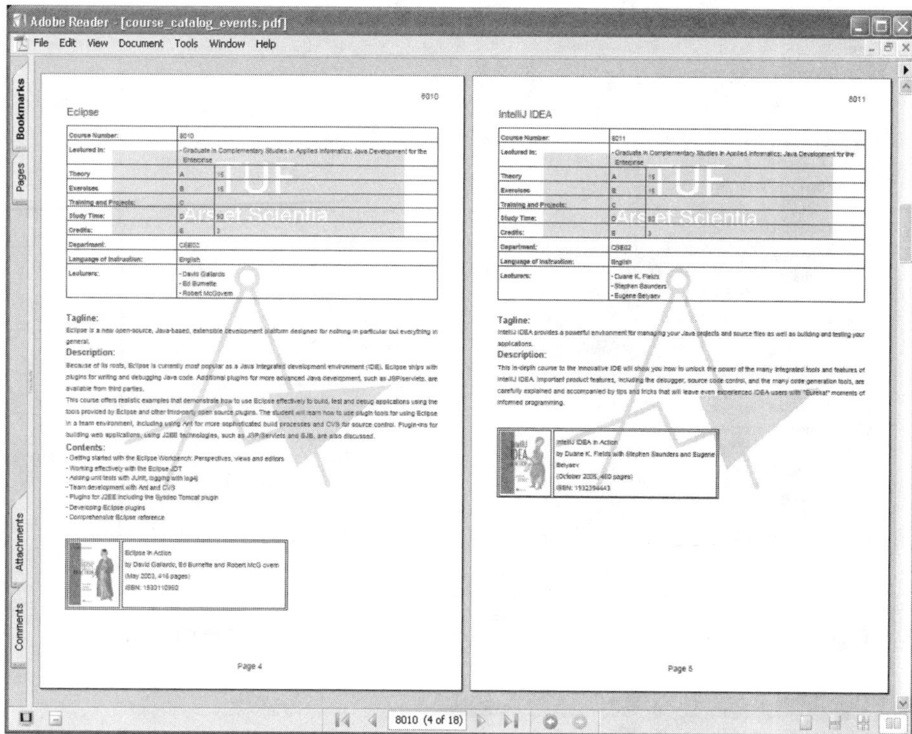


**Figure 1.10 Using page events to add page numbers and watermarks**

You can write a web application that is able to create a personalized course catalog for every student. Figure 1.11 shows a simple HTML form with the different courses that are in the catalog. This form was created dynamically based on the bookmarks inside the course catalog PDF.

Students can select the courses that interest them and create a personalized version of the course catalog. Figure 1.12 shows a PDF file containing information about the three courses that were selected in the HTML form shown in figure 1.11. Note that this screenshot also demonstrates the use of the Pages panel.

Chapter 17 lists the common pitfalls you should avoid when integrating iText in a web application. The source code used to produce the web pages shown in figures 1.11 and 1.12 can be found in section 17.2.

Notice that we've skipped chapters 15 and 16. These two chapters introduce the theory for another example that begins in section 17.2 and is completed in section 18.4.

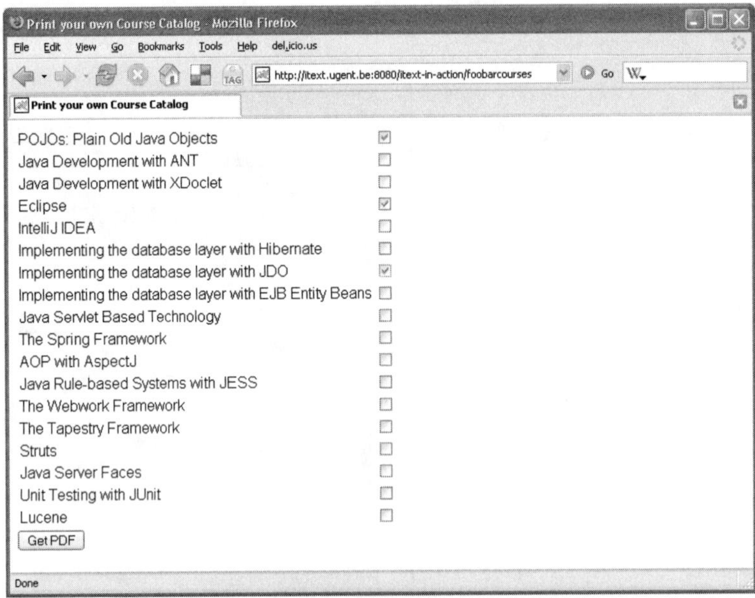


**Figure 1.11 An HTML form listing the different courses in the course catalog**

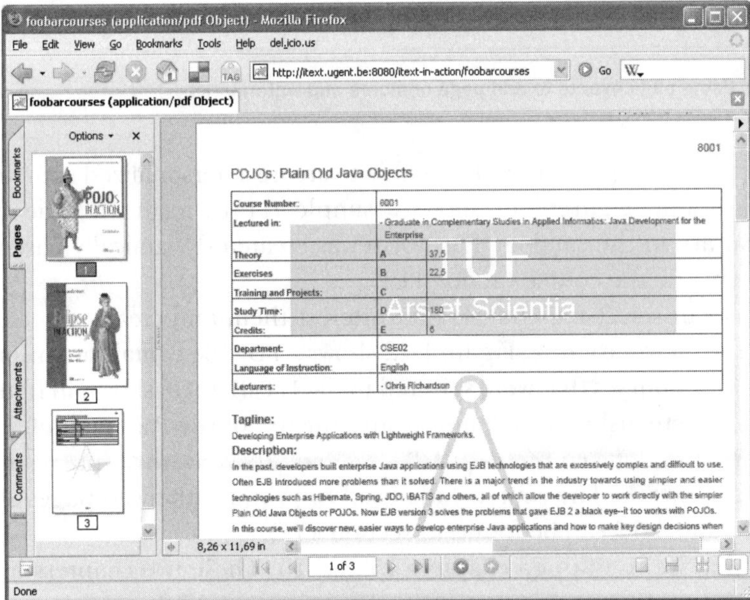


**Figure 1.12 A PDF served by a web application containing a personalized course catalog**

### Creating and filling forms using iText

Exchange students who want to study at the TUF have to fill out a Learning Agreement form, and Laura wants to make this form available online. Students can print this form, fill it out manually, and send it to the university, but it would be nice if they also had the option to submit it online. That way, the courses they've chosen can be preregistered in the database, and when the student arrives on campus, the document can be checked and signed (manually or with a digital signature).

Figure 1.13 shows a PDF document with fillable form fields (the technical term is *AcroFields* in an *AcroForm*); the document is opened in the Adobe Reader browser plug-in. It can be submitted to a server.

Chapter 15 explains how you can create such a form using iText, and chapter 16 explains how you can fill in the form fields programmatically. We'll also *flatten the form* to create a registration card for the students, and you'll learn how to add a digital signature to a PDF file.

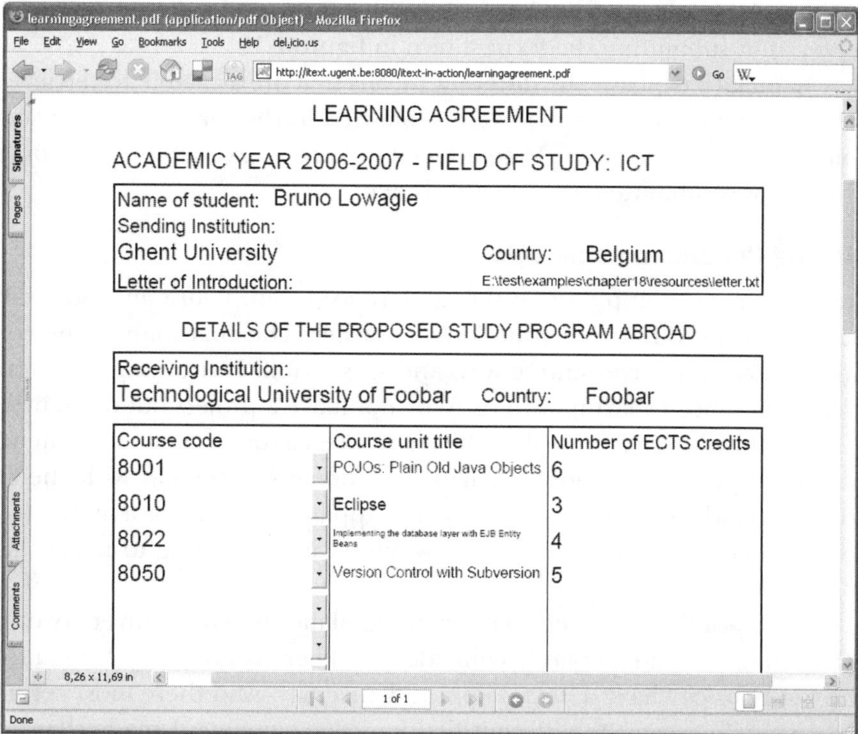



LEARNING AGREEMENT

ACADEMIC YEAR 2006-2007 - FIELD OF STUDY: ICT

Name of student: Bruno Lowagie
Sending Institution:
Ghent University Country: Belgium
Letter of Introduction: E:\test\examples\chapter18\resources\letter.txt

DETAILS OF THE PROPOSED STUDY PROGRAM ABROAD

Receiving Institution:
Technological University of Foobar Country: Foobar

| Course code | Course unit title | Number of ECTS credits |
|---|---|---|
| 8001 | POJOs: Plain Old Java Objects | 6 |
| 8010 | Eclipse | 3 |
| 8022 | Implementing the database layer with EJB Entity Beans | 4 |
| 8050 | Version Control with Subversion | 5 |

**Figure 1.13 A PDF form in a browser**

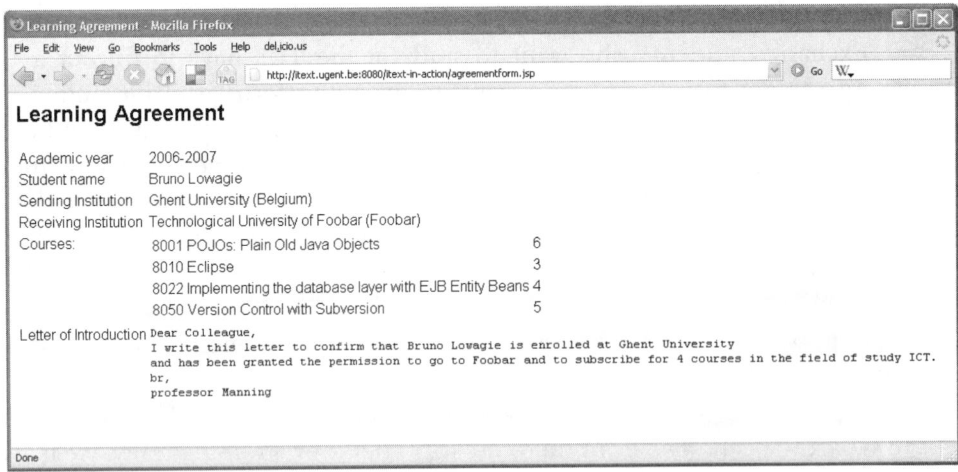


**Figure 1.14 Displaying the data that was submitted using a PDF AcroForm**

In figure 1.14, a Java Server Pages (JSP) page displays the data that was sent to the server after submitting the form shown in figure 1.13.

Chapter 16 explains the different means that are available to retrieve the text values of the parameters that were submitted in the form of an (X)FDF file, but you'll need to read chapter 18 to understand how to extract the letter of introduction that was submitted as a file attachment.

### 1.3.5 *Making the dream come true*

Suddenly there is applause in the conference room. Laura abruptly wakes from her daydream to find everyone looking at her. The chairman of the committee nods at Laura in a consenting way, and says, "Well, Laura, those are some good ideas you've been sharing with us. Why not make a project out of them?"

Only then Laura does realize she hasn't been as quiet as she had intended. She has been speaking out loud, sharing her dreams and ideas with the complete committee, which is now, to her surprise, applauding her. For a moment she panics, but soon she calms down. Why wouldn't it be possible to make this dream come true?

I hope you'll understand that any resemblance to a real university or real persons, living or dead, is purely coincidental. There is no city of Foobar. Nor does this fictitious city have a Technological University. And there most certainly isn't any rivalry between the different fictitious departments; I made that up to add some spice to the story. And yet, if you've read the preface, you know where the inspiration to write this story came from. Stories like this happen to developers all the time; iText was born from a situation that was similar to the one Laura is facing now. This story could happen to you too. If it does, you don't have to worry about document problems anymore—this book can solve most of them for you.

## 1.4 Summary

The iText API was conceived for a specific reason: It allows developers to produce PDF files on the fly. The short history on the origin of the library made it clear that iText can easily be built into a web application to serve PDF documents to a browser dynamically.

We talked about the different ports of iText, but we chose to write all the book samples in Java, using the original iText. We compiled and executed a first example as a simple standalone application, and we also opened the iText toolbox. The toolbox was written to demonstrate some of the iText functionality from a simple GUI; you don't need to write any source code to use it.

The final section of this chapter offered you an à la carte view of what is possible with iText. Every figure in this section corresponds with a milestone in the iText learning process. If you plan on reading this book sequentially, you can use the corresponding sections as exercises to get acquainted with the functionality you've acquired earlier in the chapter.

If you intend to read this book to help you with a specific assignment, and your Chief Technology Officer (CTO) or your customer demands a proof of concept before you're allowed to start coding, just follow the pointers accompanying each screenshot in this section. You'll notice that most of the Foobar examples are XML based. You can feed these ready-made solutions with an XML file adapted to another working environment or another line of business—for instance, replacing students with customers and courses with products. After only a few hours of work, you should be able to convince your CTO or customer that iText may be the answer to their prayers.

I can't guarantee you won't have to do any extra programming to integrate the examples into your final application—but hey, wouldn't we all be out of work if the contrary were true?

# 2 PDF engine jump-start

**This chapter covers**

- Hello World, Hello iText
- Creating a PDF document in five steps
- Manipulating PDF: the basics

If you're new to iText, reading this chapter will be like your first day on a new job. Somebody gives you a quick tour of the building and makes you shake hands with people you don't know, and all the while you're hoping you'll be able to remember all of their names. At the end of the day, you may have the feeling you haven't done anything substantial, but really, you've done something important: You've said "hello" to everyone.

In this chapter, you'll create new PDF documents in five easy steps, and you'll learn several ways to implement one of those steps: adding content. You'll also learn how to read and manipulate existing PDF files using several iText classes.

Whereas the previous chapter gave you an overview of parts 2, 3, and 4 using screenshots of some real-world PDF documents, this chapter presents the most important mechanisms in iText. These mechanisms will return in almost every example.

## 2.1 Generating a PDF document in five steps

Following the principle that you shouldn't try to run before you can walk, we'll start with a simple PDF file. Figure 2.1 shows you a one-page PDF document saying nothing more than "Hello World".

The code that was used to generate this "Hello World" PDF is shown in listing 2.1. Note that the numbers to the side indicate the different steps.

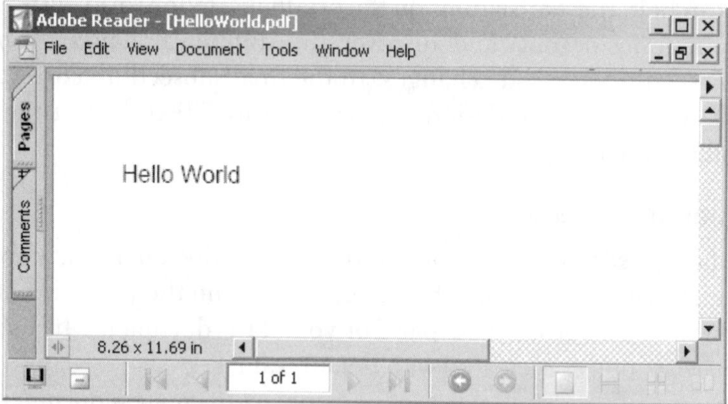


**Figure 2.1 Output of most of the "Hello World "examples in this chapter**

**Listing 2.1 Creating a HelloWorld.pdf in five steps**

```
/* chapter02/HelloWorld.java */
Document document = new Document();    <-❶
try {
  PdfWriter.getInstance(document,
    new FileOutputStream("HelloWorld.pdf"));    ❷
  document.open();    <-❸
  document.add(
    new Paragraph("Hello World"));    ❹
} catch (Exception e) {
  // handle exception
}
document.close();    <-❺
```

We'll devote a separate subsection to each of these five steps:

Step ❶ Create a `Document`.
Step ❷ Get a `DocWriter` instance (in this case, a `PdfWriter` instance)
Step ❸ Open the `Document`.
Step ❹ Add content to the `Document`.
Step ❺ Close the `Document`.

In every subsection, we'll focus on one specific step. You'll apply small changes to step ❶ in the first subsection, to step ❷ in the second, and so forth. This way, you'll create several new documents that are slightly different from the one in figure 2.1. You can hold these variations on the original "Hello World" PDF against a strong light (literally or not) and discover the differences and/or similarities caused by the small source code changes. In the final subsection (corresponding with step ❺), we'll weigh the design pattern used for iText against the Model-View-Controller (MVC) pattern.

## 2.1.1 Creating a new document object

`Document` is the object to which you'll add *content*: the document data and metadata. Upon creating the `Document` object, you can define the page size, the page color, and the margins of the first page of your PDF document. In listing 2.1, step ❶, a `Document` object is created with default values.

You can use a `com.lowagie.text.Rectangle` object to create a document with a custom size. Replace step ❶ in listing 2.1 with this snippet:

```
/* chapter02/HelloWorldNarrow.java */
Rectangle pageSize = new Rectangle(216f, 720f);
Document document = new Document(pageSize);
```

The two `float` values passed to the `Rectangle` constructor are the width and the height of the page. These values represent *user units*. By default, a user unit corresponds with the typographic unit of measurement known as the *point*. There are 72 points in one inch. You've defined a width of 216 pt (3 in) and a height of 720 pt (10 in). If you open the resulting PDF in Adobe Reader and look at the tab File > Document Properties > Description, you can check whether the document indeed measures 3 x 10 in.

### Page size

Theoretically, you could create pages of any size, but the PDF specification[1] imposes limits depending on the PDF version of the document that contains those pages. For PDF 1.3 or earlier, the minimum page size is 72 x 72 units (1 x 1 in); the maximum is 3,240 x 3,240 units (45 x 45 in). Later versions have a minimum size of 3 x 3 units (approximately 0.04 x 0.04 in) and a maximum of 14,400 x 14,400 units (200 x 200 in).

We'll discuss some other, more general version limitations in chapter 3.

**FAQ** *Are there methods in iText to convert points into inches, inches into meters, and so forth?* No. You'll notice that all measurements are done in points and occasionally in thousandths of points (see chapter 9). The conversion from and to the metric system and other systems of measurement has to be handled in your code. Remember that 1 in = 2.54 cm = 72 points.

In most cases, you'll probably prefer using a standard paper size. If you want to write a letter to the world using the standard letter format, you have to change step ❶ like this:

```
/* chapter02/HelloWorldLetter.java */
Document document = new Document(PageSize.LETTER);
```

This creates a PDF document sized at 8.5 x 11 in, whereas the first "Hello World" example was created with the default page size DIN A4 (8.26 x 11.69 in or 210 x 297 mm).

[1] Adobe Systems Inc., *PDF Reference*, fifth edition, Appendix H, section 3, "Implementation notes," http://partners.adobe.com/public/developer/pdf/index_reference.html.

**NOTE** A4 is the most common paper size in Europe, Asia, and Latin America. It's specified by the International Standards Organization (ISO). ISO paper sizes are based on the metric system. The height divided by the width of all these formats is the square root of 2 (1.4142).

`PageSize` is a class written for your convenience. It contains nothing but a list of `static final Rectangle` objects, offering a selection of standard paper sizes: `A0` to `A10`, `B0` to `B5`, `LEGAL`, `LETTER`, `HALFLETTER`, `_11x17`, `LEDGER`, `NOTE`, `ARCH_A` to `ARCH_E`, `FLSA`, and `FLSE`. The orientation of most of these formats is Portrait. You can change this to Landscape by invoking the `rotate` method on the `Rectangle`. Step ❶ now looks like this:

```
/* chapter02/HelloWorldLandscape.java */
Document document = new Document(PageSize.LETTER.rotate());
```

Another way to create a `Document` in Landscape is to create a `Rectangle` object with a width that is greater than the height:

```
/* chapter02/HelloWorldLandscape2.java */
Document document = new Document(new Rectangle(792, 612));
```

The results of both Landscape examples look the same in Adobe Reader. The Reader's Description tab doesn't show any difference in size. Both PDF documents have a page size of 11 x 8.5 in (instead of 8.5 x 11 in), but there are subtle differences internally:

- In the first file, the page size is defined with a size that has a width lower than the height, but with a rotation of 90 degrees.
- The second file has the page size you defined without any rotation (a rotation of 0 degrees).

This difference will matter when you want to manipulate the PDF.

### *Page color*

If you use a `Rectangle` as `pageSize` parameter, you can also change the background color of the page. In the next example, you change the background color to cornflower blue by setting the color of the `Rectangle` with `setBackgroundColor`:

```
/* chapter02/HelloWorldBlue.java */
Rectangle pagesize = new Rectangle(612, 792);
pagesize.setBackgroundColor(new Color(0x64, 0x95, 0xed));
Document document = new Document(pagesize);
```

The `Color` class used in this example is `java.awt.Color`; the colorspace is Red-Green-Blue (RGB) in this case. If you need another colorspace—for instance,

Cyan-Magenta-Yellow-Black (CMYK)—you can use the class `com.lowagie.text.-pdf.ExtendedColor`. You can find a class diagram of the color classes in appendix A, section A.8; you'll read all about colors in chapter 11.

The iText API includes a third constructor of the `Document` class that we didn't discuss yet. This constructor not only takes a `Rectangle` as a parameter, but four float values as well.

### *Page margins*

In step ❹ of the example, you add a `Paragraph` object to the document. This paragraph contains the words "Hello World," but how does iText know where to put those words on the page? The answer is simple: When adding basic building blocks such as `Paragraph`, `Phrase`, `Chunk`, and so forth to a document, iText keeps some space free at the left, right, top, and bottom. These are the margins of your document. All the "Hello World" examples you've created so far have default margins of half an inch (36 units in PDF). Let's change step ❶ one last time:

```
/* chapter02/HelloWorldMargins.java */
Document document = new Document(PageSize.A5, 36, 72, 108, 180);
```

The PDF document now has a left margin of 36 pt (0.5 in), a right margin of 72 pt (1 in), a top margin of 108 pt (1.5 in), and a bottom margin of 180 pt (2.5 in).

You can mirror the margins by adding a line of code after step ❷:

```
/* chapter02/HelloWorldMirroredMargins.java */
document.setMarginMirroring(true);
```

In this example, all the odd pages have a left margin of 36 pt and a right margin of 72 pt. For the even pages, it's the other way around.

## 2.1.2 *Getting a DocWriter instance*

Once you have a document instance, you need to decide if you'll write the document to a file, to memory, or to the output stream of a Java servlet. You also need to decide if you'll produce PDF or another format that is supported by iText.

Step ❷ combines these two actions:

- It tells the `DocWriter` to which `OutputStream` the resulting document should be written.
- It associates a `Document` with an implementation of the abstract `DocWriter` class. In this book, we focus on the class `PdfWriter` because we're interested in generating PDF. It can be useful to know that you can also get a `DocWriter` instance that produces RTF (using `RtfWriter2`) or HTML (using `HtmlWriter`).

These writers translate the content you're adding to the `Document` object into the syntax of some specific document format (PDF, RTF, or HTML).

The class diagram in appendix A, section A.1, shows how the different `DocWriter` classes relate to each other. In the upper-left corner, you'll recognize the `Document` object. One of the member values is an `ArrayList` of listeners. These listeners implement the `DocListener` interface. For instance, if you add an element to the document, the document forwards it to the `add` method of its listeners. The `DocListener` interface is implemented by different subclasses of the abstract class `DocWriter`.

As you can see in the class diagram, the constructors of these classes are protected. You can only create them using the `public static getInstance()` method. This method creates the writer and adds the newly created object as a listener to the document. If necessary, some helper classes are created for internal use by iText only; see, for instance, the `PdfDocument` or `RtfDocument` object.

### *Creating the same document in different formats*

Let's add some extra lines to step ❷ and see what happens:

```
/* chapter02/HelloWorldMultiple.java */
PdfWriter.getInstance(document,
  new FileOutputStream("HelloWorldMultiple.pdf"));
RtfWriter2.getInstance(document,
  new FileOutputStream("HelloWorldMultiple.rtf"));
HtmlWriter.getInstance(document,
  new FileOutputStream("HelloWorldMultiple.htm"));
```

Because you're careful only to use code that is valid for all three presentation formats (PDF, RTF, and HTML), you're able to generate three different files (of different types) using the same code for steps ❶, ❸, ❹, and ❺. Note that this approach won't work with all the building blocks described in this book.

### *Choosing an OutputStream*

While you're adding content to the document, the writer instance gradually writes PDF, RTF, or HTML syntax to the output stream. So far, you've written simple PDF, RTF, and HTML documents to a file using the `java.io.FileOutputStream`. Most examples in this book are written this way so you can try the examples on your own machine without having to install additional software such as a web server or a J2EE container.

In real-world applications, you may want to write a PDF byte stream to a browser (to a `ServletOutputStream`) or to memory (to a `ByteArrayOutputStream`).

All of this is possible with iText; you can write to any `java.io.OutputStream` you want. If you want to write a PDF document to the `System.out` to see what PDF looks like on the inside, you can change step ❷ like this:

```
/* chapter02/HelloWorldSystemOut.java */
PdfWriter.getInstance(document, System.out);
```

If you try this example, you won't recognize the words "Hello World" in the output; but you'll notice different structures: objects marked `obj`, dictionaries between << and >> brackets, and a lot of binary gibberish. In chapter 18, we'll look under the hood of iText and PDF, and you'll learn to distinguish the different parts that make up a PDF file. But this is stuff for people who really want to dig into the Portable Document Format; you're probably more interested in seeing how to serve a PDF file in a web application.

Class `javax.servlet.ServletOutputStream` extends `java.io.OutputStream`, so you could try getting an instance of `PdfWriter` with `response.getOutputStream()` as a second parameter. This works on some—but, unfortunately not all—browsers. Chapter 17 will tell you how to avoid the many pitfalls you're bound to encounter once you start integrating iText (or any other dynamic PDF-producing tool) in a J2EE web application. Notice that those problems are in most cases browser-related, *not* iText-related.

For now, let's look at something simpler: opening the document.

### 2.1.3 Opening the document

Java programmers may not be used to having to open streams before being able to add content. You create a new stream and write `bytes`, `chars`, and `Strings` to it right away.

With iText, it's mandatory to open the document first. When a document object is opened, a lot of initializations take place in iText. If you use the parameterless `Document` constructor and you want to change page size and margins with the corresponding setter methods, it's important to do this *before* opening the document. Otherwise the default page size and margins will be used for the first page, and your page settings will only be taken into account starting from the second page.

The following snippet opens a document in which the first page is letter size, landscape oriented, with a left margin of 0.5 in, a right margin of 1 in, a top margin of 1.5 in, and a bottom margin of 2 in:

```
/* chapter02/HelloWorldOpen.java */
Document document = new Document();
```

```
PdfWriter.getInstance(document, new
  FileOutputStream("HelloWorldOpen.pdf"));
document.setPageSize(PageSize.LETTER.rotate());
document.setMargins(36, 72, 108, 144);
document.open();
```

One of the most common questions iText users ask is why page settings apply to all pages but the first. The answer is almost always the same: You've added the desired behavior *after* opening the `Document` instead of *before*.

Many document types keep version information and metadata in the file header. That's why you should always set the PDF version and add the metadata before opening the document.

### The PDF header

When `document.open()` is invoked, the iText `DocWriter` starts writing its first bytes to the `OutputStream`. In the case of `PdfWriter`, a PDF header is written, and by default it looks like this:

```
%PDF-1.4
%âãÏÓ
```

The first line shows the PDF version of the document; that's obvious. The second line may seem a little odd. It starts with a percent symbol, which means it's a PDF comment line; thus it doesn't seem to have any function. It isn't necessary to add this line, but doing so is recommended to ensure the "proper behavior of file transfer applications that inspect data near the beginning of a file to determine whether to treat the file's content as text or as binary."[2]

PDF documents are binary files. Some systems or applications may not preserve binary characters, and this almost inevitably makes the PDF file corrupt. According to the PDF Reference, this problem can be avoided by including at least four binary characters (codes greater than 127) in a comment near the beginning of the file to encourage "binary treatment."

For the time being, iText generates PDF files with version 1.4 by default. If you look at table 2.1, you'll notice that version 1.4 is rather old.

If you want to use functionality that is available only in a PDF version other than v1.4, you can change the default PDF version with the method `PdfWriter.-`

---

2 See section 3.4.1 of the PDF Reference version 1.6.

**Table 2.1 Overview of the PDF versions**

| PDF version | Year | iText constant |
|---|---|---|
| PDF-1.0 | 1993 | - |
| PDF-1.1 | 1994 | - |
| PDF-1.2 | 1996 | PdfWriter.VERSION_1_2 |
| PDF-1.3 | 1999 | PdfWriter.VERSION_1_3 |
| PDF-1.4 | 2001 | PdfWriter.VERSION_1_4 |
| PDF-1.5 | 2003 | PdfWriter.VERSION_1_5 |
| PDF-1.6 | 2004 | PdfWriter.VERSION_1_6 |

`setPdfVersion()`, using one of the static values displayed in the third column of table 2.1:

```
/* chapter02/HelloWorldVersion_1_6.java */
Document document = new Document();
PdfWriter writer = PdfWriter.getInstance(document,
  new FileOutputStream("HelloWorld_1_6.pdf"));
writer.setPdfVersion(PdfWriter.VERSION_1_6);
document.open();
```

This file is intended to be viewed in Adobe Reader 7.0 or later. If you use an older version of Adobe Reader, you'll get a warning (Acrobat Reader 3.0 and later) or even an error (all versions before Acrobat Reader 3.0). The cause of this error will be explained in the next chapter.

**FAQ** *Why doesn't iText generate PDF in the latest PDF version by default?* The iText developers consider themselves to be early adopters of the newest versions in many ways, but with respect to the end users of their software, they deliberately didn't use the most recent version. An end user may still be using a viewer that only supports older PDF versions.

Changing the version number of the PDF has to be done before opening the document, because you can't change the header once it's written to the `OutputStream`.

The metadata of a PDF document is kept in an *info dictionary*. This dictionary is a PDF object that can be put anywhere in the PDF. In theory, it would be possible to add metadata after opening the document when producing PDF only, but in practice iText doesn't allow this. This was a design decision—an attempt to keep the code to produce HTML, RTF, and PDF as uniform as possible.

### *Adding metadata*

Let's rewrite the HelloWorldMultiple example and change it into HelloWorld-Metadata:

```
/* chapter02/HelloWorldMetadata.java */
document.addTitle("Hello World example");
document.addSubject("This example shows how to add metadata");
document.addKeywords("Metadata, iText, step 3, tutorial");
document.addCreator("My program using iText");
document.addAuthor("Bruno Lowagie");
document.addHeader("Expires", "0");
document.open();
```

In HTML, all this information is stored in the `<head>` section of the resulting file:

```
<head>
  <title>
    Hello World example
  </title>
  <meta name="subject" content="This example shows how to add metadata" />
  <meta name="keywords" content="Metadata, iText, step 3" />
  <!-- Creator: My program using iText -->
  <meta name="author" content="Bruno Lowagie" />
  <meta name="Expires" content="0" />
  <!-- iText 1.4 (by lowagie.com) -->
  <!-- CreationDate: Wed Dec 28 09:44:40 CET 2006 -->
</head>
```

In PDF, the metadata passed to `addHeader` is added as a key-value pair to the PDF info dictionary. This example adds the `Expires` key. This has no meaning in the PDF syntax, so it won't have any effect on the PDF file. Figure 2.2 shows how the metadata added to the info dictionary is visualized in the File > Document Properties > Description dialog box.

Don't change the producer information and the creation date. If you ever need support from the mailing list, the producer information will tell which iText version you're using. In figure 2.2, you can immediately see that an old version of iText is being used (iText 1.3.5 dates from October 2005).

If you experience a problem with an iText-generated PDF file, you can use this version number to check whether the problem is caused by a bug that has been fixed in a more recent version.

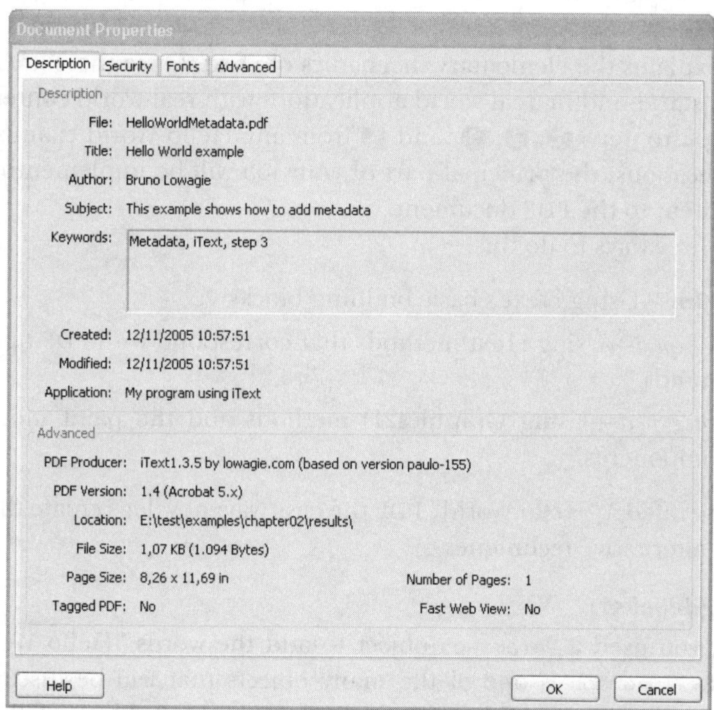


**Figure 2.2 Document properties of HelloWorldMetadata.pdf.**

**FAQ** *How do you retrieve the producer information programmatically?* The iText version, displayed as the producer information in the document properties, can also be retrieved programmatically with the static method `Document.getVersion()`. If you look into the iText source code, you'll see that this method and the corresponding `private static final String ITEXT_VERSION` may only be changed by Paulo Soares and Bruno Lowagie. The underlying philosophy of this restriction is purely a matter of courtesy. You can use iText for free, but in return you implicitly have to give the product some publicity. The iText developers hope you don't mind granting them this small favor. It's better than having a watermark saying "free trial version" spoiling every page of your document. Besides, the average end user never looks at the Advanced section of the Document Properties and thus is never confronted with this hidden persuader.

Now that you've added metadata and opened the document, you can start adding real data.

### 2.1.4 Adding content

This chapter explains the elementary mechanics of iText. Once these are understood, you can start building real-world applications with real-world content. You can copy and paste steps ❶, ❷, ❸, and ❺ from any Hello World example into your own applications; the principal part of your job will be implementing step ❹: adding content to the PDF document.

There are three ways to do this:

- *The easy way*—Using iText's basic building blocks
- *As a PDF expert*—Using iText methods that correspond with PDF operators and operands
- *As a Java expert*—Using Graphics2D methods and the paint method in Swing components

Listing 2.1 generated a "Hello World" PDF the easy way; now let's create the same PDF file using alternative techniques.

#### *Using building blocks*

In listing 2.1, you used a `Paragraph` object to add the words "Hello World" to the document. `Paragraph` is one of the many objects that will be discussed in part 2 of this book, "Basic building blocks." These building blocks will let you programmatically compose a document in a programmer-friendly way without having to worry about layout issues. Each of these building blocks has its own set of methods to parameterize properties such as the leading, indentation, fonts, colors, border widths, and so forth. iText does all the formatting based on these properties.

Note that iText is not a tool to *design* a document. It's not a word processor, nor is it a What You See Is What You Get (WYSIWYG) tool—otherwise I would have called it user-friendly instead of programmer-friendly. It's a library that lets you, the developer, produce PDF documents on the fly—for example, when you want to publish the content of a database in nice-looking reports. In part 2, we'll start with simple text elements and images, but the key chapters will be chapter 6, "Constructing tables," and chapter 7, "Constructing columns." Remember that if you use iText's basic building blocks, you don't need to know anything about PDF.

In some cases, this limited set of building blocks won't be sufficient for your needs, and you'll have to use one of the alternatives.

### *Low-level PDF generation*

The content of every page in a PDF file is defined inside a *content stream*. In chapter 18, "Under the hood," we'll look inside a PDF document. You'll learn that the content stream of a page is a PDF object of type `stream`. Listing 2.2 shows the uncompressed content stream of the "Hello World" page created with listing 2.1.

**Listing 2.2 Content stream of the Hello World page**

```
<</Length 55>>stream
q
BT
36 806 Td
0 -18 Td
/F1 12 Tf
(Hello World)Tj
ET
Q

endstream
```

You immediately recognize the words "Hello World"; after reading part 3, you'll also understand the meaning of the other PDF operators and operands that are between the keywords `stream` and `endstream`. When you use basic building blocks, you add these operators and operands internally using an object called `PdfContentByte`.

iText allows you to grab this object so that you can address it directly—with the method `PdfWriter.getDirectContent()`, for example. Starting from the original listing 2.1, you could replace step ❹ with the following lines:

```
/* chapter02/HelloWorldAbsolute.java */
PdfContentByte cb = writer.getDirectContent();
BaseFont bf = BaseFont.createFont(
    BaseFont.HELVETICA, BaseFont.CP1252, BaseFont.NOT_EMBEDDED);
cb.saveState();               // q
cb.beginText();               // BT
cb.moveText(36, 806);         // 36 806 Td    ❶
cb.moveText(0, -18);          // 0 -18 Td    ❷
cb.setFontAndSize(bf, 12);    // /F1 12 Tf
cb.showText("Hello World");   // (Hello World)Tj    ❸
cb.endText();                 // ET
cb.restoreState();            // Q
```

I have added the corresponding PDF operators and operands in a comment section after each line.

First you move the cursor to the starting position ❶. The default margin to the right was 36 units. Note that the lower-left corner of the page is used as the origin of the coordinate system by default. The height of the page (`PageSize.A4.height()`) is 842 units. You subtract the top margin: 842 – 36 = 806 units. That's the starting position: x = 36; y = 806.

Subsequently, you move down 18 units ❷. This is the line spacing. In the PDF Reference, as well as in iText, the line spacing is called the *leading*. You could reduce these two lines to one: `cb.moveText(36, 788);` that's the position where you add the "Hello World" paragraph using `showText` ❸. The other methods set the state, define a text block, and set the font and font size.

You can print the file that was generated using the first example (HelloWorld.pdf) and the file generated using this code snippet (HelloWorldAbsolute.pdf), hold them both to a strong light, and see that their output is identical. You may ask why one would go through the trouble of learning how to write PDF syntax when adding a simple line of code in current iText versions will do the work for you. But you have to take into account that this isn't really a representative example.

In real-world examples, you'll often write to the direct content using the `PdfContentByte` object—for example, to add page numbers or a page header or footer at an absolute position. This `PdfContentByte` object offers you a maximum of flexibility and PDF power, as long as you take into account the words of Spider-Man's Uncle Ben: "With great power, there comes great responsibility." If you use `PdfContentByte`, it's advised that you know something about PDF syntax.

Don't panic—it won't be necessary to read the complete PDF Reference. Chapters 10 and 11 of this book will explain everything you need to know. You'll learn about PDF's *graphics state* and *text state*, and we'll discuss the PDF coordinate system and most of the operators and operands that are available.

If you want to avoid this low-level PDF functionality, chapter 12 talks about a third way to add content to a page: using the Java Abstract Windowing Toolkit (AWT).

### Using java.awt.Graphics2D

In the original Star Trek series, the character Leonard "Bones" McCoy is often heard to say things like "I'm a doctor, not a bricklayer!" You may now be having a similar reaction—"I'm a Java developer, not a PDF specialist. I want to use iText so that I can avoid learning PDF syntax!"

If that is the case, I have good news for you. The class `PdfContentByte` has a series of `createGraphics()` methods that let you create a subclass of the abstract Java class `java.awt.Graphics2D` called `com.lowagie.text.pdf.PdfGraphics2D`. This subclass overrides all the `Graphics2D` methods, translating them to `PdfContentByte` calls behind the scenes.

Once again, you replace step ❹ in listing 2.1:

```
/* chapter02/HelloWorldGraphics2D.java */
PdfContentByte cb = writer.getDirectContent();
Graphics2D graphics2D =
  cb.createGraphics(PageSize.A4.width(), PageSize.A4.height());
graphics2D.drawString("Hello World", 36, 54);
graphics2D.dispose();
```

You can compare the result of this example to the "Hello World" files you produced using the basic building block or low-level approach. They're identical.

This third way of adding content is especially interesting if you're writing GUI applications using Swing components or objects derived from `java.awt.Component`. These objects can paint themselves to a `Graphics2D` object, and therefore they can also paint themselves to PDF using iText's `PdfGraphics2D` object. Chapter 12 will show you how to write the content displayed on the screen in a GUI application to a PDF file. What you see on the screen is what you'll get on paper. There is no PDF syntax involved; it's just standard Java.

**FAQ** *How do you solve X problems?* On UNIX systems, people working with this `PdfGraphics2D` object—or even with simple methods that use the `java.awt.Color` class—may encounter X11 problems that prompt this error message: *Can't connect to X11 window server using* xyz *as the value of the DISPLAY variable.*

The Sun AWT classes on UNIX and Linux have a dependency on the X Window System: You must have X installed in the machine; otherwise none of the packages from `java.awt` will be installed. When you use the classes, they expect to load X client libraries and to be able to talk to an X display server. This makes sense if your client has a GUI. Unfortunately, it's required even if your client uses AWT but, like iText, doesn't have a GUI.

You can work around this issue by running the AWT in headless mode by starting the Java Virtual Machine (JVM) with the parameter `java.awt.headless=true`.

Another solution is to run an X server. If you don't need to display anything, a virtual X11 server will do.

You've said "Hello" to the world many times, creating PDF documents from scratch in many different ways. You may have an idea by now of which approach suits your needs best. Only one step is left, which you must not forget—or you'll end up with a PDF file that misses its *cross-reference table* and its *trailer*—two important structures that are mandatory in a PDF file.

### 2.1.5 Closing the document

Let's restate the five steps to create a PDF document:

1. Create a `Document`.
2. Create a `PdfWriter` using `Document` and `OutputStream`.
3. Open the `Document`.
4. Add content to the `Document`.
5. Close the `Document`.

Some people may express serious doubts about this choice of design, because the iText approach seems to be in violation of the MVC pattern. You may ask why iText wasn't designed like this:

Model

1. Create a `Document`.
2. Add content to the `Document`.

View

3. Create a `PdfWriter/RtfWriter/...` using `OutputStream`.
4. Write the `Document` using `PdfWriter/RtfWriter/...`.

The advantage of such a design, as advocates of the MVC pattern keep telling me, is that the `Document` would then act as an Object-Oriented (OO) model, encapsulating the document data—the content—so that it can be arbitrarily written to any specific output location and/or format on demand.

#### Design pattern

The iText design was inspired by the *builder pattern*, a pattern that's used to create a variety of complex objects from one source object. With iText, when you're adding content (step ❹), you've already decided how and where this content should be written (step ❷), thus mixing content encapsulation with generation and presentation. Is that so bad? Please look at the other side of the coin before answering this question.

Imagine you have a document consisting of more than 10,000 pages. Are you really going to keep all those pages in memory, risking an `OutOfMemoryError` before writing even the first byte of the document representation? Will you store the content in another format, in an object in memory, or in XML on the file system, before you convert it to PDF or RTF? The answer to these questions could be yes, but you'd only need to do this if you wanted to examine the contents of the document programmatically (which is beyond the scope of iText) or if you didn't find out which output format you wanted until you finished gathering the data. These are typically issues that are difficult, if not impossible, to solve when you're dealing with very large documents. If you compare document generation to XML parsing, the advantages of iText are similar to the advantages of the Simple API for XML (SAX) over the Document Object Model (DOM). Any DOM variant is well known to be suitable only when the data won't be very large, and SAX is provided as an alternative for parsing extremely large XML documents. Behind the scenes, SAX is often used to build the DOM tree. By analogy, you can build an MVC-compliant application that uses iText as the underlying engine to create the View. You can store the Model in a custom service object, create a `Document` instance to which you add a listener, and finally pass it to your service object, so that your object can write its content to the iText `Document`. That isn't a bad design. As a matter of fact, lots of applications use iText for that purpose.

Nevertheless, there are many projects for which this design just doesn't work. Think of business processes that have to be very fast—for instance, the creation of large documents that must be served in a web application, or batch jobs that take a whole night. In such circumstances, you'll be happy iText works the way it does. One of iText's strengths is its high performance. During step ❹, iText writes and flushes all kinds of objects to the `OutputStream`, the most important objects being the page dictionaries and page streams of all the pages as soon as they're completed. All these objects become eligible for garbage collection, keeping the amount of memory used relatively low compared to some other PDF-producing tools. You can't achieve this if you don't specify the `DocWriter` and the `OutputStream` first.

### PDF cross-reference table and trailer

Upon closing the `Document`, the PDF objects that have to be kept in memory (because they must be updated from time to time) are written to the `OutputStream`. These include the following:

- The *PDF cross-reference table*, an important table that contains the byte positions of the PDF objects
- The *PDF trailer*, which contains information that enables an application to quickly find the start of the cross-reference table and certain special objects, such as the info dictionary

Finally, the `String %%EOF` (End of File) is added. After all this is done, the `OutputStream` created in step ❷ is flushed and closed. You've successfully created a PDF file.

The next chapter will list different types of PDF, not all of which are supported in iText. I'll use the phrase *traditional PDF* to refer to the most common type of PDF. Traditional PDF is intended to be a read-only, graphical format; it's designed to be electronic paper. When text is printed on paper, you can't add an extra word in the middle of a sentence and expect the layout of the paragraph to adapt automatically. The same is true for traditional PDF; it's not a format that is suited for editing. This doesn't mean you can't perform a series of other operations: You can stamp a piece of paper, cut it into pieces, copy one or more sheets, and perform other changes as well. Those sorts of changes are exactly what you'll perform on a traditional PDF file with iText classes such as `PdfStamper` and/or `PdfCopy`.

You'll also use `PdfStamper` to fill in the fields of a PDF form programmatically. Such a PDF document has a series of fields at specific coordinates on one or more pages. An end user can fill in these fields, but you, as a developer, can also use a PDF form as a template; iText is able to retrieve the absolute position of each field and add data at these coordinates.

All this functionality will be introduced in the next section, which discusses manipulation classes.

## 2.2 Manipulating existing PDF files

Imagine you're selling audio and video equipment in a branch office of a major electronics dealer. The mother company has sent you a product catalog in PDF with hundreds of pages. It contains sections on computers, digital cameras, televisions, radios, dishwashers, and so forth. Suppose you want to distribute a similar catalog among your clientele.

You can't use the original product catalog from your dealer because you're not even selling half of the products mentioned in it. You know your customers won't be interested in kitchen equipment—they want to read about the new features of the latest-model DVD players. For that reason, you want to compose a reduced catalog that only contains the pages that are relevant for your store. If possible, each page should have a header, footer, or watermark with the name and logo of your store.

Because PDF wasn't conceived to be a word-processing format, creating this new, personalized catalog is complex. It's not sufficient to cut some pages from one PDF file and paste them into another. Searching the Internet, you'll find lots of small tools and applications that offer this specialized functionality—such as Pdftk, jImposition, and SheelApps PDFTools—but if you study these more closely, you'll find that most of them use iText under the hood (even tools that cost several hundred dollars).

Before spending any money or time on a tool that may or may not solve your problem, look at the upcoming subsections. They will show you how these tools work, and you'll be able to tailor your own PDF-manipulation solution using the iText API directly. You'll learn that the `PdfCopy` class is best suited to copy a selection of pages from a series of different, existing PDF files. Adding new content (such as a logo, page numbers, or a watermark) is best done with the `PdfStamper` class.

The relationship between the different manipulation classes is shown in the class diagram in appendix A section A.2. `PdfCopy` is a subclass of `PdfWriter`, whereas `PdfStamper` has an implementation class that is derived from `PdfWriter`. These classes are *writers*, they can't *read* PDF files.

To read an existing PDF file, you need the class `PdfReader`; the actual work is done in the `PdfReaderInstance` class, but you'll never address this instance directly. As shown in the class diagram, `PdfReaderInstance` is for internal use by `PdfWriter` only.

Let's begin by examining the `PdfReader` class and find out what information you can retrieve from a PDF document before you start manipulating one or more PDF files with `PdfStamper`, `PdfCopy`, and the other classes mentioned in the class diagram.

### 2.2.1 Reading an existing PDF file

Before you start manipulating files, let's generate a PDF file with some functionality that is more complex than a "Hello World" document. Figure 2.3 shows the first page of the document HelloWorldToRead.pdf. As you can see, you can open the Bookmarks tab to see the outline tree of the document.

You'll learn how to create bookmarks in chapters 4 and 13. For the moment, we're only interested in `PdfReader` and how to retrieve the information from this

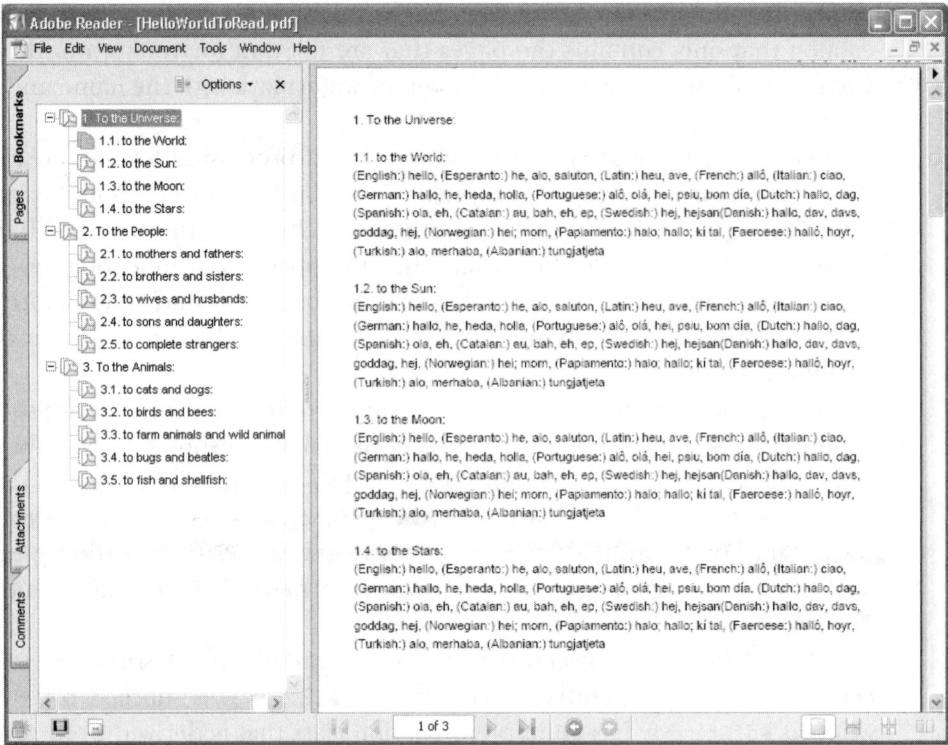


**Figure 2.3 The existing PDF file you'll inspect with PdfReader**

PDF file. You'll retrieve general properties, such as the file size and PDF version, the number of pages, and the page size, and also metadata and the bookmark entries.

### *Document properties*

The following example demonstrates how to perform some of the basic queries: determining the version of the PDF file, the number of pages, the file length, and whether the PDF was encrypted:

```
/* chapter02/HelloWorldReader.java */
PdfReader reader = new PdfReader("HelloWorldToRead.pdf");
System.out.println("PDF Version: " + reader.getPdfVersion());
System.out.println("Number of pages: " +
  reader.getNumberOfPages());
System.out.println("File length: " + reader.getFileLength());
System.out.println("Encrypted? " + reader.isEncrypted());
```

Returns 4

Returns 3

Returns 8439

Returns false

The information returned in this code snippet is related to the complete document, but you can also ask the reader for information on specific pages.

### Page size and rotation

Section 2.1.1 talked about rotating the page size `Rectangle`. In the HelloWorldReader example, you create a PDF document with three pages. The first two are A4 pages in portrait orientation, and the third is rotated with the `rotate()` method.

Now you'll ask those pages for their page size:

```
/* chapter02/HelloWorldReader.java */
System.out.println("Page size p1: " + reader.getPageSize(1));
System.out.println("Rotation p1: " +
  reader.getPageRotation(1));
System.out.println("Page size p3: " +
  reader.getPageSize(3));
System.out.println("Rotation p3: " +
  reader.getPageRotation(3));
System.out.println("Size with rotation p3: " +
  reader.getPageSizeWithRotation(3));
```

**Returns 595.0x842.0 (rot. 0 degrees)**

**Returns 0**

**Returns 595.0x842.0 (rot. 0 degrees)**

**Returns 90**

**Returns 842.0x595.0 (rot. 90 degrees)**

If you ask for the page size with the method `getPageSize()`, you always get a `Rectangle` object without rotation (rot. 0 degrees)—in other words, the paper size without orientation. That's fine if that's what you're expecting; but if you reuse the page, you need to know its orientation. You can ask for it separately with `getPageRotation()`, or you can use `getPageSizeWithRotation()`.

The annotations alongside the code sample show the results of the `toString()` method of class `Rectangle`. The second page size query didn't return what you would expect for page three; the last one gives you the right value and indicates that the page was rotated 90 degrees.

> **TOOLBOX** *`com.lowagie.tools.plugins.InspectPDF` (Properties)* If you want a quick inspection of some of the properties of your PDF file, you can do this with the InspectPDF tool in the iText Toolbox.

Not every PDF tool produces documents that are 100 percent compliant with the PDF Reference. Also, if you have the audacity to change a PDF file manually (something you should attempt only if your PDF Fu is truly mighty), the offsets of the different objects will change. This makes the PDF document corrupt, and there may be a problem if the file is read.

### *Reading damaged PDFs*

When you open a corrupt PDF file in Adobe Reader, you get this message: *The file is damaged and can't be repaired.* PdfReader will probably also throw an exception when you try to read such a file; because it *is* damaged and it *can't* be repaired. There's nothing iText can do about it.

In other cases—for example, if the cross-reference table is slightly changed—Adobe Reader only shows you this warning: *The file is damaged but is being repaired.* PdfReader can also overcome similar small damages to PDF files. Because iText isn't necessarily used in an environment with a GUI, no alert box is shown, but you can check whether a PDF was repaired by using the method isRebuilt():

```
/* chapter02/HelloWorldReader.java */
System.out.println("Rebuilt? " + reader.isRebuilt());
```

When trying to manipulate a large document, another problem can occur: You can run out of memory. Augmenting the amount of memory that can be used by the JVM is one way to solve this problem, but there's an alternative solution.

### *PdfReader and memory use*

When constructing a PdfReader object the way you did in the previous examples, all pages are read during the initialization of the reader object. You can avoid this by using another constructor:

```
/* chapter02/HelloWorldPartialReader.java */
PdfReader reader;
long before;
before = getMemoryUse();
reader = new PdfReader(                              Does full read of
  "HelloWorldToRead.pdf", null);                     PDF file
System.out.println("Memory used by the full read: "          Returns about
  + (getMemoryUse() - before));                              30 KB
before = getMemoryUse();
reader = new PdfReader(                                              Does partial
  new RandomAccessFileOrArray("HelloWorldToRead.pdf"), null);        read of PDF file
System.out.println("Memory used by the partial read: "         Returns about
  + (getMemoryUse() - before));                                3.5 KB
```

The size of HelloWorld.pdf is about 5 KB. If you do a full read, a little less than 30 KB of the memory is used by the (uncompressed) content and the iText objects that contain the object. By using the object com.lowagie.text.pdf.RandomAccesFileOrArray in the PdfReader constructor, barely 3.5 KB of the memory is used initially. More memory will be used as soon as you start working with the object, but PdfReader won't cache unnecessary objects. If you're dealing with large documents, consider using this constructor.

Now that you've tackled some problems with corrupt or large PDFs, you can go on retrieving information.

### *Retrieving bookmarks*

In figure 2.3, the Bookmarks tab is open. The class `com.lowagie.text.pdf.SimpleBookmark` can retrieve these bookmarks if you pass it a `PdfReader` object. You can retrieve the bookmarks in the form of a `List`:

```
/* chapter02/HelloWorldBookmarks.java */
PdfReader reader = new PdfReader("HelloWorldToRead.pdf");
List list = SimpleBookmark.getBookmark(reader);
```

This is an `ArrayList` containing a `Map` with the properties of the bookmark entries. If you run this example, the titles of the outline tree shown in figure 2.3 is written to `System.out`.

With the static method `SimpleBookmark.exportToXML`, this list of bookmarks can also be exported to an XML file:

```
/* chapter02/HelloWorldBookmarks.java */
SimpleBookmark.exportToXML(list,
  new FileOutputStream("bookmarks.xml"), "ISO8859-1", true);
```

You'll learn more about the bookmark properties and about the structure of this XML file in chapter 13.

**TOOLBOX** `com.lowagie.tools.plugins.HtmlBookmarks` *(Properties)* Suppose you have many PDFs on your web site, all having an extensive table of contents in the form of an outline tree. Wouldn't it be great to be able to extract these outlines and serve them to site visitors in the form of an HTML index file with links to every entry in the PDF outline tree? That way, if visitors are looking for a specific chapter, they don't have to download and browse every PDF file. Instead, they can browse through the HTML files first and click a link to go to a specific page within a PDF file. The HtmlBookmarks tool offers such index files—the only thing you have to do is to provide a Cascading Style Sheets (CSS) file that goes with it.

Metadata can also contain information that is useful to display in an HTML file before the visitor of your site downloads the complete document. You can use `PdfReader` to extract the metadata from the PDF files in your repository and store this information somewhere so that the repository can be searched.

### *Reading metadata*

When you created the file HelloWorldToRead.pdf, you added metadata. The PDF-specific metadata of the document is kept in the PDF info dictionary. `PdfReader` can retrieve the contents of this dictionary as a `(Hash)Map` using the method `getInfo()`:

```
/* chapter02/HelloWorldReadMetadata.java */
PdfReader reader = new PdfReader("HelloWorldToRead.pdf");
Map info = reader.getInfo();
String key;
String value;
for (Iterator i = info.keySet().iterator(); i.hasNext(); ) {
  key = (String) i.next();
  value = (String) info.get(key);
  System.out.println(key + ": " + value);
}
```

Now that you've retrieved the metadata, let's try to change the `Map` returned by `getInfo()`. This will introduce the `PdfStamper` class.

## 2.2.2 *Using PdfStamper to change document properties*

`PdfStamper` is the class you'll use if you want to manipulate a single document. This is how you create an instance of `PdfStamper`:

```
/* chapter02/HelloWorldAddMetadata.java */
PdfReader reader = new PdfReader("HelloWorldNoMetadata.pdf");
System.out.println("Tampered? " + reader.isTampered());
PdfStamper stamper = new PdfStamper(reader,
  new FileOutputStream("HelloWorldStampedMetadata.pdf"));
System.out.println("Tampered? " + reader.isTampered());
```

Notice that as soon as you create a `PdfStamper` object, the reader is *tampered*—that is, the `PdfStamper` instance alters the reader behind the scenes so it can't be used with any other `PdfStamper` instance. `PdfStamper` is often used to stamp data from a database on the same document over and over again. For example, suppose you've created a standard letter for your customers using Acrobat. You have all the names of your customers in a database. Now you want to merge the results of a database query with this letter. You can do this by reading the original PDF with `PdfReader` and stamping it with `PdfStamper`.

**FAQ** *Why do I get an exception when I try to create a* `PdfStamper` *instance?* Novice iText users often make the mistake of trying to reuse the reader instance. A `DocumentException` will be thrown, saying: *The original document was reused. Read it again from file.* This is normal: `PdfStamper` needs a unique and exclusive `PdfReader` object. Tampered reader objects can't be reused.

Note that it's impossible to write to the file you're reading. `PdfReader` does random-access file reading on the original file, so it's important to realize that the original and the manipulated file can't have the same name. Few programs read a file and change it at the same time; most of them write to a temporary file and replace the original file afterward. If that's what you want, that's how you should implement it; but you can also read the original file into a byte array, create the `PdfReader` object using this array, and write the output of the stamper to a file with the same name as the original PDF.

That being said, you can write some code to change the metadata of an existing PDF file. You get the information `(Hash)Map` from the reader ❶, add some extra keys and values ❷, and then add it to the stamper object with the method `setMoreInfo()` ❸:

```
/* chapter02/HelloWorldAddMetadata.java */
Map info = reader.getInfo();   <-❶
info.put("Subject", "Hello World");
info.put("Author", "Bruno Lowagie");        ❷
stamper.setMoreInfo(info);   <-❸
stamper.close();   <-❹
```

Don't forget to close the stamper ❹! Otherwise you'll end up with a file of 0 KB.

In the next chapter, you'll learn how to use `PdfStamper` to change other properties of a PDF file, such as the compression, the encryption, and the user permissions of a file. The rest of this chapter will focus on adding content to an existing PDF file.

### 2.2.3 Using PdfStamper to add content

Let's return to our earlier example. You're selling audio and video equipment, and you want to send a standard letter to all of your customers telling them about the personalized catalog they can order. This letter is provided as a PDF document containing a PDF form. In this case, the form's fields (called *AcroFields*) correspond to the fields of individual records in your customer database. You can now use iText to fill in those fields.

#### Filling in a form

It's possible to create a document containing a PDF form (also called an *AcroForm*) with iText, and you'll learn more about that in chapter 15; but using an end-user tool like Acrobat is a better way to make a quality design. Chapter 16 will explain how to fill and process forms. This is a crash course on document manipulation, so let's have a small taste of form functionality.

You start with a simple PDF saying "Hello Who?" The word "Who?" is gray deliberately; you may not notice that it's a form field just by looking at it, but if you hover the cursor over this word, you'll see the cursor changes from a little hand into an I-bar. Click the area, and you can edit the word. One possible use of a PDF form is to have people fill in the form and submit it, but for now you're more interested in using the form as a template and filling it out programmatically:

```
/* chapter02/HelloWorldForm.java */
PdfReader reader = new PdfReader("HelloWorldForm.pdf");
PdfStamper stamper = new PdfStamper(reader,
  new FileOutputStream("HelloWorldFilledInForm.pdf"));
AcroFields form = stamper.getAcroFields();     <-- Gets form from stamper
form.setField("Who", "World");     <-- Sets field in form
stamper.close();
```

Granted, the design of this HelloWorldForm is simple, but that doesn't matter. You can create forms with multiple fields in a complex design; it won't make your code more complex. You just ask the `PdfStamper` object for its `AcroFields` object and change the value of all the fields inside the form.

This example changes the word "Who?" that was in the Who field into the word "World." The result is a new PDF file that still contains a form; but it now says "Hello World" instead of "Hello Who?" If you click the word "World," you can change it into something else. This may not always be what you want; in some cases, you don't want the end user to know you have used a PDF form as a template. The resulting PDF shouldn't be interactive once it's filled in.

That's why you'll *flatten* the form. Flattening means there are no longer any editable field in the new PDF. The field content is added at the position where the field was defined; an end user can't change the text:

```
/* chapter02/HelloWorldForm.java */
stamper.setFormFlattening(true);
```

In chapter 16, you'll discover lots of tips and tricks to optimize the process of filling and flattening a PDF form—for example, how to make sure the text fits the field, or how to use a field as a placeholder for an image.

But what if you need to add content to an existing PDF document *without* a form? Can you still use it as a template and add extra content? The answer is yes, you can—if you know where (on which coordinates) to add the new content.

### Adding content to pages

Think of the personalized catalog you want to compose. The original catalog doesn't contain a form, but you want to take the existing PDF file, add a watermark with your company logo in the middle of each page (under the existing content), and add page numbers to the bottom of the pages. Again, you need the `PdfStamper` class to achieve this.

Do you remember the `PdfContentByte` object, which you used to add text at an absolute position? With `PdfStamper`, you can get two different `PdfContentByte` objects per page. The method `getOverContent(int pagenumber)` gives you a canvas on which to draw text and graphics that are painted on top of the existing content.

The next code snippet uses this method to add page numbers and draws a circle at an absolute position:

```
/* chapter02/HelloWorldStamper.java */
PdfContentByte over = stamper.getOverContent(i);
over.beginText();
over.setFontAndSize(bf, 18);
over.setTextMatrix(30, 30);
over.showText("page " + i);
over.endText();
over.setRGBColorStroke(0xFF, 0x00, 0x00);
over.setLineWidth(5f);
over.ellipse(250, 450, 350, 550);
over.stroke();
```

With the method `getUnderContent(int pagenumber)`, you can get a canvas that appears under the existing content. For example, you can add a watermark to every page, like this:

```
/* chapter02/HelloWorldStamper.java */
PdfReader reader = new PdfReader("HelloWorld.pdf");
PdfStamper stamper = new PdfStamper(reader,
  new FileOutputStream("HelloWorldStamped.pdf"));
Image img = Image.getInstance("watermark.jpg");
img.setAbsolutePosition(200, 400);
PdfContentByte under;
int total = reader.getNumberOfPages() + 1;
for (int i = 1; i < total; i++) {
  under = stamper.getUnderContent(i);
  under.addImage(img);
}
stamper.close();
```

Remember the importance of page orientation. In the HelloWorld.pdf file, the third page has landscape orientation. If you're adding text, graphics, or an image at an absolute coordinate, you have to realize that the coordinate system has been changed, too. You're working on a canvas with dimensions set in `height x width` instead of `width x height`. If this isn't what you want, you can avoid it by setting `setRotateContents` to `false`:

```
/* chapter02/HelloWorldStamper2.java */
stamper.setRotateContents(false);
```

Take a close look at figure 2.4, and compare the third pages of the documents HelloWorldStamped.pdf and HelloWorldStamped2.pdf.

In HelloWorldStamped.pdf, the page rotation has been taken into account, and the text and graphics have been added so that you can read them without having to turn your head 90 degrees. This also means you should have adjusted the position of the watermark—it isn't exactly where you want it to be. In HelloWorldStamped2.pdf, the text and graphics were added as if the page was still in portrait orientation.

Not only can `PdfStamper` be used to change existing pages, but you can also insert new blank pages to which content can be added.

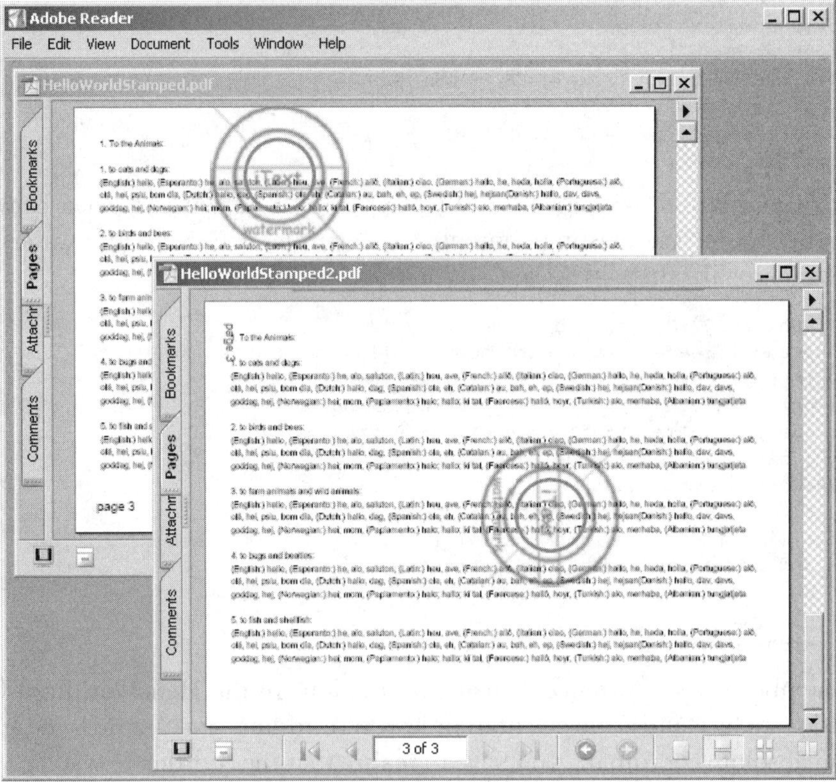


**Figure 2.4 Taking the page rotation into account when stamping a PDF**

### *Inserting new pages*

In the next example, you'll add a title page to an existing PDF document:

```
/* chapter02/HelloWorldStamperAdvanced.java */
stamper.insertPage(1, PageSize.A4);
PdfContentByte cb = stamper.getOverContent(1);
cb.beginText();
cb.setFontAndSize(bf, 18);
cb.setTextMatrix(36, 770);
cb.showText("Inserted Title Page");
cb.endText();
```

I also threw in some more advanced functionality:

```
/* chapter02/HelloWorldStamperAdvanced.java */
stamper.addAnnotation(
  PdfAnnotation.createText(stamper.getWriter(),
    new Rectangle(30f, 750f, 80f, 800f),
    "inserted page", "This page is the title page.",
    true, null), 1);
```

This adds a comment on the first page. When the comment is closed, you see a page icon; the comment title and text are visible only if you move the mouse pointer over the comment. Figure 2.5 shows the text annotation in its opened state. (Annotations are discussed in chapter 15.)

Notice that the page numbers shift when inserting a new page—not the page numbers that are printed on the page, but the indices used to retrieve the page from the `PdfStamper` object. Make sure you keep track of the actual page count if you're inserting and retrieving pages using one stamper object!

Let's return to the idea of a personalized catalog. You already have two useful pieces of the puzzle: You can stamp a logo on each page, and you can add an

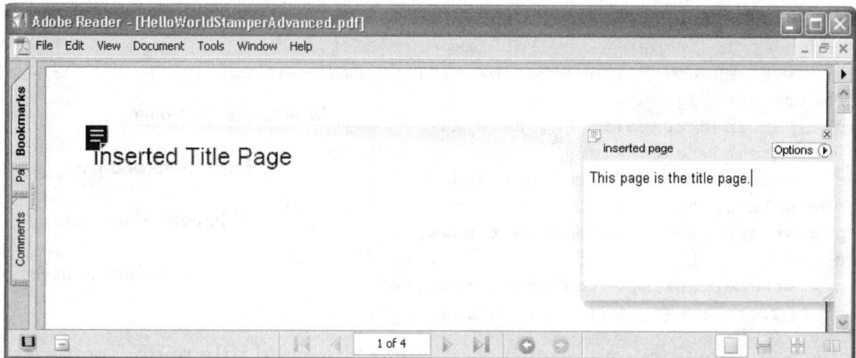


**Figure 2.5 A PDF with an open text annotation**

extra title page. You can't remove the sections presenting the newest types of dishwasher yet, but it would be nice if you could illustrate the title page with thumbnails of existing pages, such as the title page of the section on DVD players. In other words, you want to copy a complete page and paste a smaller version of it on another page. To achieve this, you need *imported pages*.

### 2.2.4 Introducing imported pages

If you browse the API of the `PdfReader` class, you'll discover the method `getPageContent(int pagenumber)`, which returns the content stream of that page. You've already seen the content stream of a simple "Hello World" page in listing 2.2. This stream tells you what's inside a page, but it doesn't necessarily return the complete page.

A content stream normally contains references to external objects, images, and fonts. For example, you can find a reference to a font named /F1 in listing 2.2. This font is stored elsewhere in the PDF file. It's possible to retrieve every object that is needed to copy an existing page, but it takes a fair amount of coding and you need to know the Portable Document Format inside out.

That's why it's never advisable to extract a page from `PdfReader` directly. Instead, you should pass the reader object to the manipulation class (`PdfStamper`, `PdfCopy`, or even `PdfWriter`) and ask the writer (not the reader!) for the imported page. A `PdfImportedPage` object is returned. Behind the scenes, all the necessary resources (such as images and fonts) are retrieved. As you'll see in chapter 18, importing pages this way not only saves you a lot of work, but is also less error-prone.

Here's an example using `PdfStamper`:

```
/* chapter02/HelloWorldStamperImportedPages.java */
PdfReader reader = new PdfReader("HelloWorldRead.pdf");
PdfStamper stamper = new PdfStamper(reader,
  new FileOutputStream("HelloWorldImportedPages.pdf"));
PdfImportedPage p;
stamper.insertPage(1, PageSize.A4);                      <- Inserts new first page
PdfContentByte cb = stamper.getOverContent(1);
p = stamper.getImportedPage(reader, 2);                  <- Imports second page
cb.addTemplate(p, 0.4f, 0f, 0f, 0.4f, 36f, 450);
p = stamper.getImportedPage(reader, 3);                  <- Imports third page
cb.addTemplate(p, 0.4f, 0f, 0f, 0.4f, 300f, 450);
p = stamper.getImportedPage(reader, 4);                  <- Imports fourth page
cb.addTemplate(p, 0.4f, 0f, 0f, 0.4f, 36f, 100);
```

Instead of inserting a page with text saying "inserted title page," you insert a first page that shows downsized versions of the pages that follow. With the method getImportedPage(), you pass the PdfReader object to a PdfStamper, and you tell the stamper which page you want to import.

The object that is returned is of type PdfImportedPage. It contains a description of the contents of the page; the resources that are referred to from this page are passed to PdfStamper behind the scenes. Note that you can't add new content to a PdfImportedPage object; you can only scale, rotate, and/or translate it while adding it to another page. The example uses the addTemplate method to scale and position the thumbnails. The float values that are passed to this method are elements of a *transformation matrix*. (You'll read all about the transformation matrix in chapter 10.)

There's still a lot to say about PdfStamper. We haven't discussed how you can sign an existing document, change viewer preferences, and so forth, but we'll cover all of that in part 4, "Interactive PDF."

Let's elaborate on these imported pages first.

### 2.2.5 Using imported pages with PdfWriter

PdfStamper is able to retrieve and (re)use imported pages, but other classes may be better suited for the job. If you're using PdfStamper, it's assumed that you want to manipulate one and only one existing PDF file. But maybe you want to create a document from scratch and use pages from an existing document as new content. If we're talking about generating a document from scratch, we automatically think of PdfWriter.

What you did in the PdfStamperImportedPages example can also be done in step ❹ of the PDF creation process we'll discuss in chapter 3. If you wrap the PdfImportedPage in an Image object (as will be discussed in section 5.3.4), it's easy to manipulate the imported page. Figure 2.6 shows how the pages of an existing PDF document are used as thumbnails in a new document.

In this example, you wrap the imported page inside an image ❶, scale it to 15 percent of its original size ❷, draw a gray box that is three units thick around it ❸, and add it to the page ❹:

```
/* chapter02/HelloWorldImportedPages.java */
PdfReader reader = new PdfReader("HelloWorldToImport.pdf");
PdfWriter writer = PdfWriter.getInstance(document,
  new FileOutputStream("HelloWorldImportedPages.pdf"));
document.open();
System.out.println("Tampered? " + reader.isTampered());
document.add(new Paragraph("This is page 1:"));
PdfImportedPage page = writer.getImportedPage(reader, 1);
Image image = Image.getInstance(page);    ❶
image.scalePercent(15f);    ❷
```

```
image.setBorder(Rectangle.BOX);
image.setBorderWidth(3f);
image.setBorderColor(new GrayColor(0.5f));     ❸
document.add(image);   ❹
System.out.println("Tampered? " + reader.isTampered());
document.close();
```

This functionality can be handy if you want to invite customers to order the complete product catalog. You can make a flyer with the description of the content of the catalog along with some thumbnails showing the most interesting and attractive pages.

Note the `System.out` lines: I added them to show that importing pages with `PdfWriter` doesn't tamper with the reader object. A reader object used by `PdfWriter` isn't exclusively tied to the writer as was the case with `PdfStamper`. This may sound unimportant, but once you get to know iText well, you'll understand that you can improve your applications drastically by choosing the right object for the right job. Throughout this book, I'll present different ways to achieve the same result. If performance is an issue, you should try different solutions, benchmark them in your specific working environment, and use the best solution in your production software.

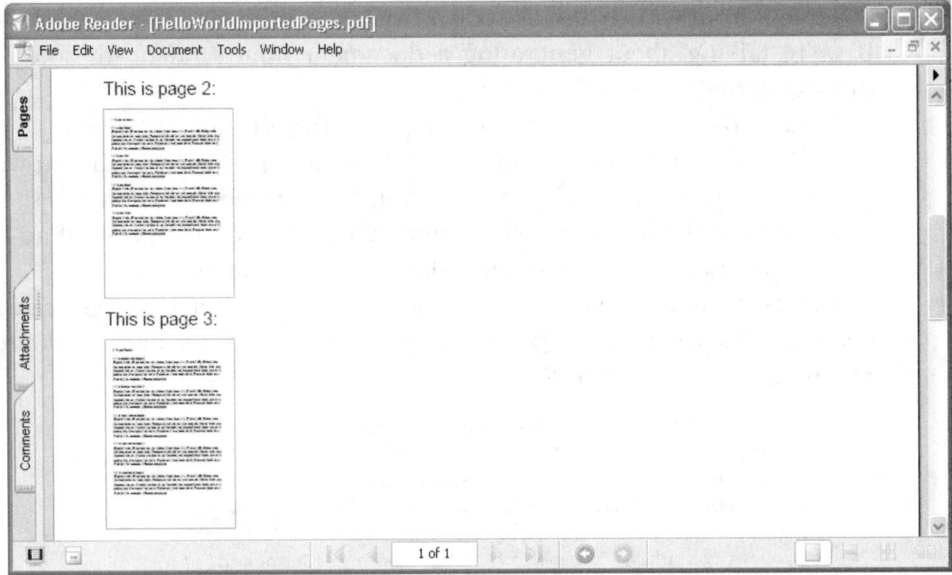


**Figure 2.6 Imported pages as thumbnails**

The next example is a little more complex. It places the four pages of an existing document on one page of a new document, so that the document can be folded into a booklet. If you have a four-page brochure presenting your products, you can use this code to print the four pages on one page in such a way that the page can be folded to fit inside an envelope:

```
/* chapter02/HelloWorldWriter.java */
PdfReader reader = new PdfReader("HelloWorldToImport.pdf");
PdfWriter writer = PdfWriter.getInstance(document,
 new FileOutputStream("HelloWorldFolded.pdf"));
document.open();
PdfContentByte cb = writer.getDirectContent();
PdfImportedPage page;
page = writer.getImportedPage(reader, 1);
cb.addTemplate(page, -0.5f, 0f, 0f, -0.5f,
  PageSize.A4.width() / 2, PageSize.A4.height());        ❶
page = writer.getImportedPage(reader, 2);
cb.addTemplate(page, 0.5f, 0f, 0f, 0.5f, 0f, 0f);        ❷
page = writer.getImportedPage(reader, 3);
cb.addTemplate(page, 0.5f, 0f, 0f, 0.5f,
  PageSize.A4.width() / 2f, 0f);                         ❸
page = writer.getImportedPage(reader, 4);
cb.addTemplate(page, -0.5f, 0f, 0f, -0.5f,
  PageSize.A4.width(), PageSize.A4.height());            ❹
document.close();
```

The height and width of the first imported page ❶ are divided by 2; the page is turned upside down and added at the upper-left side of the new page. The second page ❷ is also scaled; it's added at the lower-left side of the new page. Page three ❸ is scaled and added next to page 2, at the lower-right side of the new page. The fourth page ❹ is scaled, rotated, and added next to page 1 at the upper-right side of the page.

**TOOLBOX** `com.lowagie.tools.plugins.NUp` *(Manipulate)* The N-up tool allows you to create a new PDF document based on an existing one. Each page of the new document contains N pages of the existing document, with N equal to 2, 4, 8, 16, 32, or 64.

There is one major downside when you're adding a page imported using `PdfWriter` (or with `PdfStamper.getImportedPage`) to a document. All interactive features (annotations, bookmarks, fields, and so forth) are lost in the process. If you want to import pages in order to concatenate several PDF files into one, this is a big disadvantage. That's where `PdfCopy` comes into the picture.

### 2.2.6 Manipulating existing PDF files with PdfCopy

You used `PdfStamper` to manipulate one and only one existing PDF file. `PdfCopy` is the class you need if you want to combine a selection of pages from one or multiple existing PDFs. This is the next puzzle piece you can use to create a personalized catalog.

You can distinguish different approaches. If you have different small catalogs per product line, you can concatenate the PDF files that are of importance to your customers into one catalog. If you have one big catalog with all the products, you can make a selection of specific pages and page ranges.

#### Concatenating PDF files

In the next example, you'll concatenate three pages from three different PDF documents into one new document. The first document contains a plain page with a paragraph; the second, a page with a text annotation; and the third, a page with an anchor. All of these features are preserved in the resulting three-page document:

```
/* chapter02/HelloWorldCopy.java */
PdfReader reader = new PdfReader("Hello1.pdf");
Document document = new Document(reader.getPageSizeWithRotation(1));
PdfCopy copy = new PdfCopy(document,
  new FileOutputStream("HelloWorldPdfCopy123.pdf"));
document.open();
System.out.println("Tampered? " + reader.isTampered());
copy.addPage(copy.getImportedPage(reader, 1));
reader = new PdfReader("Hello2.pdf");
copy.addPage(copy.getImportedPage(reader, 1));
reader = new PdfReader("Hello3.pdf");
copy.addPage(copy.getImportedPage(reader, 1));
System.out.println("Tampered? " + reader.isTampered());
document.close();
```

Again, you work with a `getImportedPage()` method, but this time you add the imported page to the manipulation class with the method `addPage()`. You don't scale or position the page; it's added as is. `PdfCopy` is a subclass of `PdfWriter`; the use of both classes is similar, but it's important to realize that `PdfCopy` can't be used to change the content of a PDF file. This time, you can't grab a `PdfContentByte` object; `PdfCopy` doesn't allow new content on a page. If you need to concatenate and stamp different PDF files (as you'll do with the personalized catalog), you must create the resulting PDF in multiple passes (see section 2.3).

When you run the example, you'll see that importing a page with `PdfCopy` doesn't tamper with `PdfReader`. You can reuse the reader object for different instances of PdfCopy—for example, if you need to add the same title page to a series of existing PDF files.

### Selected pages

There are two ways to select pages from an existing PDF file. You can use PdfCopy to import the pages you need and add only those pages to the new document with the method addPage(), but there's a more elegant way to achieve this. You can use the method selectPages() on PdfReader to narrow the selection even before you start reading and copying.

The next code snippet uses this method to select the odd pages from the existing PDF file:

```
/* chapter02/HelloWorldSelectPages.java */
PdfReader reader = new PdfReader("HelloMultiplePages.pdf");
reader.selectPages("o");
int pages = reader.getNumberOfPages();
Document document = new Document();
PdfCopy copy = new PdfCopy(document,
  new FileOutputStream("HelloWorldSelectPagesOdd.pdf"));
document.open();
for (int i = 0; i < pages; ) {
  ++i;
  copy.addPage(copy.getImportedPage(reader, i));
}
document.close();
```

The general syntax for the range that is used in the selectPages() method looks like this: [!][o][odd][e][even]start-end. You can have multiple ranges separated by commas. The ! modifier removes pages from what is already selected. The range changes are incremental—numbers are added or deleted as the range appears. The start or the end can be omitted. If you omit both, you need at least o (odd; selects all odd pages) or e (even; selects all even pages).

**TOOLBOX** *com.lowagie.tools.plugins.SelectedPages (Manipulate)* If you need to quickly create a new document from a selection of pages from an existing PDF file, you don't need to adapt the example that demonstrates the selectPages method. You can go to the iText Toolbox and use the SelectedPages plug-in instead.

Note that if you reuse a reader object from which you've removed pages, the pages remain removed; that's why you have to create a new PdfReader for every new selection in the example. The next code snippet selects pages 1, 2, 3, 7, and 9 (I excluded page 8):

```
/* chapter02/HelloWorldSelectPages.java */
reader = new PdfReader("HelloWorldMultiplePages.pdf");
reader.selectPages("1-3, 7-9, !8");
```

This `PdfReader` functionality can also be used in the context of a `PdfStamper` application.

```
/* chapter02/HelloWorldSelectedPages */
reader = new PdfReader("HelloMultiplePages.pdf");
stamper = new PdfStamper(reader,
  new FileOutputStream("HelloSelectedEven.pdf"));
reader.selectPages("e");
stamper.close();
reader = new PdfReader("HelloMultiplePages.pdf");
stamper = new PdfStamper(reader,
  new FileOutputStream("HelloSelected12379.pdf"));
reader.selectPages("1-3, 7-9, !8");
stamper.close();
```

Again, I'm presenting different ways to solve the same problem. It's up to you to experiment and choose the object that is best suited for your specific needs. For example, if you need to combine a selection of pages from different product catalogs, you'll probably prefer using `PdfCopy` over `PdfStamper`. In some cases, you'll even need another class: `PdfCopyFields`.

### 2.2.7 Concatenating forms with PdfCopyFields

Be careful with the next example: It shows you how *not* to combine PDF files with forms. It doesn't differ much from the example HelloWorldCopy, except that the pages you import now contain *form fields*:

```
/* chapter02/HelloWorldCopyForm.java */
PdfReader reader = new PdfReader("HelloWorldForm1.pdf");
Document document =
  new Document(reader.getPageSizeWithRotation(1));
PdfCopy writer = new PdfCopy(document,
  new FileOutputStream("HelloWorldCopyForm.pdf"));
document.open();
writer.addPage(writer.getImportedPage(reader, 1));
reader = new PdfReader("HelloWorldForm2.pdf");
writer.addPage(writer.getImportedPage(reader, 1));
reader = new PdfReader("HelloWorldForm3.pdf");
writer.addPage(writer.getImportedPage(reader, 1));
document.close();
```

When you open the resulting file HelloWorldCopyForm.pdf, you immediately see that something didn't work out the way you expected. HelloWorldForm1.pdf and

HelloWorldForm2.pdf each have a form containing one text field that has the same name: field1. After concatenating the files with `PdfCopy`, one of these fields got lost in the process.

That's just one of the problems you could potentially experience when copying forms using `PdfCopy`. `PdfCopy` only deals with the form in the first document. The form fields of the other documents are copied but not added to the initial form. The resulting PDF looks good in most cases, but as soon as you start to work with it, it will fail. This is an example of how you *shouldn't* concatenate forms.

To avoid problems when concatenating forms, you should use the class `PdfCopyFields`. This is the safest way to concatenate documents that have forms; but as you probably know, everything comes with a price—unlike `PdfCopy`, `PdfCopyFields` keeps all the documents in memory so the final form can be updated correctly. Make sure you have enough memory available:

```
/* chapter02/HelloWorldCopyFields.java */
PdfCopyFields copy =
  new PdfCopyFields(new FileOutputStream("HelloWorldCopyFields.pdf"));
copy.addDocument(new PdfReader("HelloWorldForm1.pdf"));
copy.addDocument(new PdfReader("HelloWorldForm2.pdf"));
copy.addDocument(new PdfReader("HelloWorldForm3.pdf"));
copy.close();
```

If you look at HelloWorldCopyFields.pdf, you now see that field1 is present on the first and the second page (with `PdfCopy`, it was missing on the second page). If you change one of these fields, the other fields with the same name are changed automatically, which is expected behavior.

I've been stressing the importance of choosing the right manipulation class for the right job. Now that you've worked with the different reader and writer classes for PDF manipulation available in iText, it's a good time for an overview.

### 2.2.8 Summary of the manipulation classes

When dealing with existing PDF documents, you can turn to table 2.2 to determine which manipulation class or classes can be used to perform the different aspects of your assignment.

You'll soon discover that choosing one class that solves all problems isn't possible. You'll have to combine different classes, and the most efficient way to do this is by creating a PDF in multiple passes.

**Table 2.2 An overview of PDF manipulation classes**

| iText class | Usage |
|---|---|
| `PdfReader` | Read PDF files. In most cases, you have to pass an instance of this class to one of the PDF manipulation classes. |
| `PdfStamper` | Manipulate the content of an existing PDF document. For example, you can add page numbers, fill form fields, or sign an existing PDF file. |
| `PdfEncryptor` | Uses `PdfStamper` to encrypt an existing PDF file in a user-friendly way (see chapter 3). |
| `PdfWriter` | Generate PDF documents from scratch; import pages from other PDF documents. The major downside: All interactive features (annotations, bookmarks, fields, and so forth) of the imported page are lost in the process. |
| `PdfCopy` | Concatenate a selection of pages from one or multiple existing PDF forms. Major disadvantages: `PdfCopy` doesn't allow new content, and combining multiple forms into one is problematic. |
| `PdfCopyFields` | Put the fields of the different forms into one new form. Can be used to avoid the problems encountered with form fields when using `PdfCopy`, but remember that memory use can be an issue. |

## 2.3 Creating PDF in multiple passes

You finally have all the pieces of the puzzle when it comes to manipulating existing PDF files, but now you have to start putting the puzzle together. For example, you know how to fill in one standard letter using one user record, but how do you combine all the letters into a single file so you can send it to a printing office?

One solution would be to use `PdfStamper` to fill in the fields of one PDF template form. `PdfStamper` can't add multiple forms that are filled in with different data to the same document. You could keep the stamped PDF in memory temporarily and do the concatenation with `PdfCopy`. As you remember, `PdfCopy` wasn't able to add new data to a document, so you need both classes: `PdfCopy` and `PdfStamper`.

Once you've chosen which manipulation class to use for which aspect of your assignment, you have to determine the best order to perform the manipulation. Will you stamp the existing PDFs first, and then copy? Or is it better to do it the other way around?

### 2.3.1 Stamp first, then copy

Let's say you have a standard letter in PDF (with a form) that says the following:

```
Dear ...
I just wanted to say Hello.
```

In place of the ellipsis, you want a name from your customer database, and you want to create a single document that has all the different versions of this letter, one per addressee. In this case, the first step is to stamp and flatten the original document. You don't need the individual files, so you keep the result in memory (in a `ByteArrayOutputStream`):

```
/* chapter02/HelloWorldStampCopy.java */
RandomAccessFileOrArray letter =
  new RandomAccessFileOrArray("HelloLetter.pdf");
reader = new PdfReader(letter, null);
ByteArrayOutputStream baos = new ByteArrayOutputStream();
stamper = new PdfStamper(reader, baos);
form = stamper.getAcroFields();
form.setField("field", "World,");
stamper.setFormFlattening(true);
stamper.close();
```

Now you read the stamped and flattened file from memory and copy it:

```
/* chapter02/HelloWorldStampCopy.java */
reader = new PdfReader(baos.toByteArray());
Document document =
  new Document(reader.getPageSizeWithRotation(1));
PdfCopy writer = new PdfCopy(document,
  new FileOutputStream("HelloWorldStampCopy.pdf"));
document.open();
writer.addPage(writer.getImportedPage(reader, 1));
```

You can repeat this process as many times as you want:

```
/* chapter02/HelloWorldStampCopy.java */
reader = new PdfReader(letter, null);
baos = new ByteArrayOutputStream();
stamper = new PdfStamper(reader, baos);
form = stamper.getAcroFields();
form.setField("field", "People,");
stamper.setFormFlattening(true);
stamper.close();
reader = new PdfReader(baos.toByteArray());
writer.addPage(writer.getImportedPage(reader, 1));
```

This is just a simple example. You'll probably want to write some loops to handle all the copies with the same code and to copy all pages of the original document (instead of just the first one), but that shouldn't be a problem. Also, if file size and performance are an issue, it may be wiser to work with PdfWriter and page events as discussed in chapter 14.

### 2.3.2 *Copy first, then stamp*

We've dealt with having one form that was filled in multiple times using different data. Now we'll look at the best way to proceed when you want to combine different forms into one and then stamp the result. For example, suppose you have several different loan application forms—one for people who own a house and one for people who don't; one for people who own their own company and one for people who work for someone else. You want to be able to concatenate the forms in a personalized way depending on the applicant's individual situation, so that you have all the necessary data (and nothing more) in one big form.

In this case, it's probably better to start with the concatenation of the different forms:

```
/* chapter02/HelloWorldCopyStamp.java */
ByteArrayOutputStream baos = new ByteArrayOutputStream();
PdfCopyFields copy = new PdfCopyFields(baos);
copy.addDocument(new PdfReader("HelloWorldLetter1.pdf"));
copy.addDocument(new PdfReader("HelloWorldLetter2.pdf"));
copy.close();
```

HelloWorldLetter1.pdf has a form containing field1. HelloWorldLetter2.pdf has a form with field2. The resulting PDF (kept in memory) has one form containing both fields. You can stamp these fields like this:

```
/* chapter02/HelloWorldCopyStamp.java */
reader = new PdfReader(baos.toByteArray());
stamper = new PdfStamper(reader,
  new FileOutputStream("HelloWorldCopyStamp.pdf"));
form = stamper.getAcroFields();
form.setField("field1", "World");
form.setField("field2", "People");
stamper.setFormFlattening(true);
stamper.close();
```

Of course, it could happen that you want to combine different forms having the same field names for entities that are different in reality. For example, suppose you have a form that contains the fields name and income and that allows one person to declare his monthly revenues. When dealing with a couple, you need to know the income of both partners, so you want to combine two versions of the income form: one version with fields named name_husband and income_husband, and another with fields named name_wife and income_wife. In this case, you must rename these fields before you copy them.

### 2.3.3 Stamp, copy, stamp

Let's keep it simple and experiment with the original letter. You'll stamp it and use the method `renameField()` to change the name of the field:

```
/* chapter02/HelloWorldStampCopyStamp.java */
RandomAccessFileOrArray letter =
  new RandomAccessFileOrArray("HelloLetter.pdf");
reader = new PdfReader(letter, null);
ByteArrayOutputStream baos1 = new ByteArrayOutputStream();
stamper = new PdfStamper(reader, baos1);
form = stamper.getAcroFields();
form.renameField("field", "field1");
stamper.close();
reader = new PdfReader("HelloLetter.pdf");
ByteArrayOutputStream baos2 = new ByteArrayOutputStream();
stamper = new PdfStamper(reader, baos2);
form = stamper.getAcroFields();
form.renameField("field", "field2");
stamper.close();
```

Then, repeat what you did in section 2.3.2 (applying some small changes):

```
/* chapter02/HelloWorldStampCopyStamp.java */
ByteArrayOutputStream baos = new ByteArrayOutputStream();
PdfCopyFields copy = new PdfCopyFields(baos);
copy.addDocument(new PdfReader(baos1.toByteArray()));
copy.addDocument(new PdfReader(baos2.toByteArray()));
copy.close();
```

Finally, stamp the fields you've just renamed:

```
/* chapter02/HelloWorldStampCopyStamp.java */
reader = new PdfReader(baos.toByteArray());
stamper = new PdfStamper(reader,
  new FileOutputStream("HelloWorldStampCopyStamp.pdf"));
form = stamper.getAcroFields();
form.setField("field1", "World");
form.setField("field2", "People");
stamper.setFormFlattening(true);
stamper.partialFormFlattening("field2");
stamper.close();
```

Notice this line: `stamper.partialFormFlattening("field2");`.

Although you've set flattening to `true`, the resulting PDF still has a form with editable fields. Only the fields you marked with the method `partialFormFlattening()` are flattened. This is useful if the forms are part of a workflow, being filled in by different instances. For example, suppose some parts of a loan-application form are to be filled in by the couple applying for the loan, whereas other parts are to be filled in by the company granting the loan. The form can go back and forth several times before the loan is approved. Along the way, some fields can be consolidated: for instance, the fields with the applicants' names can be set to read-only.

These are only a few simple examples. In chapters 15 and 16, you'll get an overview of all the possible types, find out more ways to fill forms programmatically, and learn how to process forms that were filled out by end users.

## 2.4 Summary

In this chapter, you've said "Hello" to iText in 35 different Java programs. As in chapter 1, you were introduced to the contents of the rest of this book, but from a different point of view. Instead of looking at screenshots of different PDF documents generated by iText, you've created and manipulated PDF files to get acquainted with different mechanisms that will return throughout the book.

Remember that the creation process always follows five essential steps: ❶ creating a document, ❷ getting a writer instance, ❸ opening the document, ❹ adding content, and ❺ closing the document. Starting with chapter 4, we'll elaborate on the fourth step. In part 2, we'll add content to a document using iText's basic building blocks; in part 3, you'll learn about low-level PDF operators and operands, and you'll discover the benefits of using the Java `Graphics2D` functionality.

We also discussed different ways to manipulate existing PDF documents. Table 2.2 gave you an overview of the different operations available in iText. You can use this table to determine what iText class is best suited for each job. If necessary, you can create a PDF in multiple passes.

In the next chapter, you'll learn more about PDF in general. We'll talk about different types and versions of PDF. You'll find out which types and versions are supported by iText for the moment, and which aren't (yet).

# 3 PDF: why and when

**This chapter covers**

- What is PDF?
- History of the format
- Different types
- Different versions

In chapter 2, you created some simple and some not-so-simple "Hello World" documents. The not-so-simple documents have an initial demonstration of the power of iText as far as document manipulation is concerned. Before we continue with iText at full force, we'll take one step back and look more closely at the Portable Document Format.

In the first section of this chapter, you'll learn why PDF was invented and how it evolved into a de facto standard. In the second section, you'll see that PDF comes in different flavors, some of which are described in an International Standards Organization (ISO) standard. It's important to understand when to choose which specific type of PDF.

Finally, we'll use a table listing the different versions of the PDF specification to focus on specific features such as compression and encryption. We'll conclude with more "Hello World" examples that show how to compress/decompress and encrypt/decrypt PDF files.

## 3.1 A document history

Do you remember when people were talking about the paperless office? It was a utopian concept that surfaced in the 1980s, which didn't make it to the end of the century. The brave new technology that was going to eliminate the paper chase had quite the opposite effect—it generated an avalanche of paper.

Although electronic documents didn't bring about utopia, they do have advantages:

- *They're easy to search*—Even if electronic documents don't have an index, there are tools that can make one for you automatically.
- *They're easy to archive*—Just think of the huge amount of cubic meters needed for paper storage and compare that to the number of electronic documents you can save on a mass-storage device.
- *They're easy to exchange*—You can put electronic documents on a web site or e-mail them if you want to share them with others.

Of course, there are also major downsides. The fact that electronic documents are easy to exchange can be a serious disadvantage when it comes to issues of piracy and illegal copies. When it comes to legal issues, a hard copy still holds more credibility than an electronic one. Even more important, there's the irrefutable fact that a printed document is a lot easier to read than text on a computer screen. As it turns out, paper still rules.

New technologies are emerging that may revive the dream of the paperless office. New devices that provide a better reading experience are finding their way to the market. Technologies that add digital signatures to an electronic document are becoming increasingly accepted by companies and governments. Electronic documents are becoming more reliable and more secure. One of the key protagonists in this process, if not the main player, is Adobe Systems Incorporated. In this section, we'll look at the company and its products, and we'll talk about the intellectual property of the PDF specification.

### 3.1.1 Adobe and documents

Adobe Systems Incorporated was founded in 1982 by John Warnock and Chuck Geschke. Its first products were digital fonts. These days, Adobe Creative Suite (including Photoshop and Illustrator) and Acrobat are the company's flagship products.

It's important to realize that PDF wasn't created out of the blue. The ancestors of PDF still exist and are used in many applications. The best way to understand the difference between PDF and these other specifications is to go back in history and see how it all started.

#### The ancestors of PDF

In 1985, Adobe introduced the PostScript (PS) Page Description Language (PDL). PS is an interpretive programming language. Its primary goal is to describe the appearance of text, graphical shapes, and sampled images. It also provides a framework for controlling printing devices; for example, specifying the number of copies to be printed, activate duplex printing, and so forth.

Also in 1985, Adobe developed an application for the Apple Macintosh called Adobe Illustrator, a vector-based drawing program with its own format, AI, which was derived from PS. Illustrator was ported to Windows in 1989, so it covered an important market in the graphical industry.

Producing high-quality visual materials was the privilege of specialists for a long time, but with the advent of PostScript and Illustrator, anyone with a computer could accomplish high-end document publishing. By introducing these two technologies, Adobe started the desktop publishing revolution. But the founders of Adobe felt there was something missing.

In 1991, John Warnock wrote the "Camelot paper," in which he said the following:

> The specific problem is that most programs print to a wide range of printers, but there is no universal way to communicate and view this printed information electronically. ... What industries badly need is a universal way to communicate documents across a wide variety of machine configurations, operating systems, and communication networks.

As a result of this writing, a new development project was started, and the engineers at Adobe enhanced the PostScript and Illustrator technologies to create a document format and a suite of applications with which to create and visualize documents of this format.

### *The Portable Document Format*

This new document format, originally called Interchange PostScript (IPS), is now known as the Portable Document Format (PDF). Although PostScript (PS) and PDF are related, they're essentially different formats. PDF isn't a programming language like PS; PDF leverages the ability of the PS language to render complex text and graphics and brings this feature to the screen as well as to the printer. As stated in the PDF Reference, "PDF trades reduced flexibility for improved efficiency and predictability."

PDF and PS share the same underlying Adobe imaging model. A PDF document consists of a sequence of pages, with each page including the text, font specifications, margins, layout, graphical elements, and background and text colors. Unlike PS, PDF can contain a lot of document structure, links, and other related information. As opposed to PS, PDF can't tell the printer to use a certain input tray, change the resolution, or use any other hardware-specific feature. One of the key advantages PDF has over PS is page independence. Because PS is a programming language, something in the description of page 1 can affect page 1000, so to view page 1000 you have to interpret all the pages before it. Each page in PDF can be drawn individually.

PDF is called the *Portable* Document Format because a PDF document can be viewed and printed on any platform: UNIX, Macintosh, Windows, Linux, or Palm OS. In theory, a PDF document looks the same on any of these platforms (we'll discuss some exceptions in chapter 8, when we're talking about embedding fonts). In analogy with Java's Write Once, Run Anywhere, you could say PDF is Write Once, Read Anywhere—but in a more reliable way than the catchy Java advertising phrase promises.

*Camelot* was the original code name for what later became Acrobat. It's important not to confuse PDF, the Page Description Language, with Acrobat, the suite of Adobe products that was developed along with the PDF specification.

### 3.1.2 The Acrobat family

The Adobe web site describes the Acrobat family as a suite of products that allow you to "create and exchange documents, collect and compare comments, and tailor the security of a file in order to distribute reliable and polished Adobe PDF documents."

In this book, I assume you and the end users of the PDF files you're producing have Adobe Reader—a free PDF viewer that works with a plethora of operating systems—installed. You can use it as a standalone product or as a plug-in for your browser. It allows you to view, print, and search PDF files. It doesn't let you create or change PDF files. People often confuse Adobe Reader with Acrobat—for example, thinking that the free reader is capable of saving data entered into any PDF form. (That's only possible with reader-enabled PDFs.)

Non-Adobe alternatives for Adobe Reader are available, such as Preview, Ghostview, and Foxit, but these viewers are less feature-rich than Adobe Reader. Note that Mac OS X uses PDF as the basis of its imaging model and ships Preview as the default application for any PDF. Most of the PDF examples generated in this book will be displayed correctly in the other tools, but not all of the functionalities will work. For example, a PDF form is rendered correctly in Apple's Preview, but Preview doesn't know how to submit forms. (I don't know if they plan to add this functionality.)

Even if you're only planning to develop applications using iText, you may need some other Adobe products. For example, a customer may want to design a PDF that can be used as a resource in her software applications. This resource can act as a template that will be manipulated using iText code (see section 2.2). Note that designing a document usually isn't the task of a developer; it's typically a job for a graphic designer using one of the following Acrobat products:

- *Adobe Acrobat Elements* allows you to view, print, and search PDF files, as well as create PDF files from any application that prints. You can manage specialized content from Microsoft Office and protect documents with passwords, granting or revoking permissions. If you're creating PDF files from Microsoft Word, you can use iText to post process and concatenate these files.
- *Adobe Acrobat Standard* has the same functionality as Adobe Elements, but it can also organize comments from multiple reviewers with sorting and filtering tools; combine application files into a single Adobe PDF document; digitally sign and certify documents; and manage specialized content from Microsoft Outlook, MS Internet Explorer, Access, and Publisher.

- *Adobe Acrobat Professional* adds the following features to those of Adobe Standard: enables anyone with free Adobe Reader software to use highlighter, sticky note, pen, and other commenting tools; and builds intelligent forms with Adobe LiveCycle Designer, which is a separate product (that can be executed from Acrobat). For the moment, iText doesn't fully support forms created with Adobe LiveCycle Designer; only static XFA forms. To be sure your forms can be filled with iText, you can create AcroForms (not XFA forms) with Acrobat Professional (not Designer).
- *Adobe LiveCycle Designer* retains layers and object data in technical drawings and manages specialized content from AutoCAD, Microsoft Visio, and Microsoft Project.
- *Adobe Distiller* lets you turn PostScript into PDF.
- *Acrobat Capture* is a powerful Optical Character Recognition (OCR) tool that teams with your scanner to convert volumes of paper documents into searchable PDF files.

These are all commercial products (proprietary software). If you want to use them, you need to purchase them and pay a license fee. Depending on the tool you need, this can be expensive. You may wonder: If Acrobat tools are expensive, how is it possible that everybody can use iText for free? How were the iText developers able to create their PDF-producing software? Did they have to pay a license fee? No, they didn't, and the following explains why not.

### 3.1.3 The intellectual property of the PDF specification

Adobe owns the copyright for the PDF specifications, but to promote the use of the Portable Document Format for information interchange among diverse products and applications—including, but not necessarily limited to, Acrobat products—Adobe gives anyone copyright permission to (I quote section 1.5 of the PDF Reference, version 1.6):

- Prepare files whose content conforms to the Portable Document Format
- Write drivers and applications that produce output represented in the Portable Document Format
- Write software that accepts input in the form of the Portable Document Format and displays, prints or otherwise interprets the contents
- Copy Adobe's copyrighted list of data structures and operators, as well as the example code and PostScript language-function definitions in the

written specification, to the extent necessary to use the Portable Document Format for the purposes above

The conditions of such copyright permissions are:

- Authors of software that accepts input in the form of the Portable Document Format must make reasonable efforts to ensure that the software they create respects the access permissions and permissions controls listed in Table 3.20 of this specification (i.e. the PDF Reference), to the extent that they're used in any particular document. These access permissions express the rights that the document's author has granted to the users of the document. It's the responsibility of Portable Document Format consumer software to respect the author's intent.
- Anyone who uses the copyrighted list of data structures and operators, as stated above, must include an appropriate copyright notice.

Again, these permissions and conditions were copied word-for-word from the PDF Reference. If you need advanced PDF features, I highly recommended this manual as a companion for this book. You can purchase a hardcopy or download it for free from the Adobe web site (www.adobe.com).

The general idea is that developers like you and me are free to build tools that view, generate, change, or manipulate PDF files (as long as you don't crack them). And that's exactly what Paulo Soares and I did—we built a tool that let us create and manipulate PDF.

Of course, we didn't implement the complete specification; some version-specific features aren't implemented (yet), and not all the possible types of PDF are supported in iText.

## 3.2 Types of PDF

PDF is the de facto standard in many different sectors, including the graphic arts industry, prepress companies, and governments. Each of these markets has its own requirements and demands regarding documents, so it's obvious that, although Adobe ensures the integrity of the format through its copyright, many different types of PDF have evolved from the original specifications. Some subsets of the PDF specification were modeled into an ISO standard. Other types of PDF are so new that they aren't supported by (almost) any tools yet.

People who don't know the difference between these types of PDF files risk accepting assignments that might as well be labeled "Mission: Impossible." These are typically the people posting questions on the mailing list with the word "urgent" in the subject, begging for assistance. Unfortunately, we're unable to help them.

It's important to make sure you and your clients are communicating in the same language when talking about PDF. That's why I made a list with different categories, which are discussed in the following sections. People with other backgrounds could organize their lists differently, but I made my list from an iText developer's point of view.

### 3.2.1 Traditional PDF

This isn't an official term, but I use the word *traditional* when I want to refer to the kind of PDF that is intended to be a finished product with unchangeable content and a print-ready layout. The way it looks on the screen is the way it will look when it's printed, in contrast with other formats such as RTF or HTML. The printed output of an RTF or HTML (and even a Microsoft Word) file depends on the application that is used to render it.

Traditional PDF is a read-only paginated document format that can contain all kinds of multimedia, links, bookmarks, and so forth; but it doesn't know anything about text structure. For example, traditional PDF doesn't understand the concept of a table; you can render a table in a PDF file, but you can't retrieve the data that was organized in this tabular structure from the PDF to reuse it in another application. As far as the PDF file is concerned, the table consists of some characters drawn on a canvas, along with some lines. The concept of rows and columns is lost on PDF. You'd need specialized OCR software to retrieve the original content.

In short, creating traditional PDF is a one-way process.

### 3.2.2 Tagged PDF

Sometimes traditional PDF isn't sufficient for your needs. You may want to produce PDF files that can adapt themselves to the device they will be used on, or you may want to repurpose the PDF file if, for example, end users will read the document on the smaller screen of their Palm Pilot. If you need to make the document accessible for the visually impaired, the PDF file should contain the logical reading order (which isn't always the case with traditional PDF). Images should be given alternate descriptions. Also, if you need to be able to recognize document structures such as paragraphs and tables, you'll need *tagged PDF*.

Tagged PDF is a stylized use of PDF; it defines a set of standard structure types and attributes that allow page content to be extracted and reused for other purposes. Page content is represented so that the characters, words, and text order can be determined reliably. There's a basic layout model and a set of standard structure elements and attributes. Limited support for tagged PDF has been added to iText only recently (see appendix F).

### 3.2.3 Linearized PDF

A *linearized PDF* file is organized in a special way to enable efficient incremental access, thus enhancing the viewing performance. Its primary goal is to display the first page as quickly as possible. When data for a page is delivered over a slow channel, the page content is displayed incrementally as it arrives. Linearized PDF isn't supported by iText, but iText can read linearized PDFs just fine—an important distinction.

### 3.2.4 PDFs preserving native editing capabilities

I mentioned briefly that Adobe Illustrator was one of the ancestors of PDF. In Adobe Illustrator, you have the option to save files as a PDF file. If you open such a file in Illustrator, you can continue editing, just like with the native AI format. Note that these PDF files aren't suited for general, online distribution: they're larger than the traditional PDFs because they contain a lot of application-specific data. It's a matter of taste, but I wouldn't recommend using PDF as an editing format. It's not what PDF was designed for. Instead, keep the source of the document in another format and convert to PDF when needed.

### 3.2.5 PDF types that became an ISO standard

There are many ways to create a valid PDF file. This freedom is an advantage, but it can be a disadvantage too. Not all valid PDF files are usable in every context. To tackle this problem, different ISO standards were created.

#### PDF/X

In particular, the prepress sector felt the need to restrict the freedom offered by the Portable Document Format. A consortium of prepress companies got together and released specifications for *PDF/X* (the X stands for *eXchange*). PDF/X is a set of ISO standards (ISO 15930-1, -2, and -3) describing well-defined subsets of the PDF specification that promise predictable and consistent PDF files. The main goal of PDF/X-1a is to support *blind exchange* of PDF documents. Blind exchange means you can deliver PDF documents to a print service provider with hardly any technical discussion. PDF/X-3 is a superset of PDF/X-1a. The primary difference is that a PDF/X-3 file can also contain color managed data. PDF/X-2 is a superset of

PDF/X-3. It was designed for exchanges where there is more discussion between the supplier and receiver of the PDF.

Each standard has its own specific requirements and constraints, but in general, you can say that functionality that will probably break PDF/X conformance includes encryption, the use of fonts that aren't embedded, RGB colors, layers, image masks, transparency, and some blend modes. The two most useful PDF/X standards are supported by iText: PDF/X-1a:2001 and PDF/X-3:2002.

### PDF/A and XMP

*PDF/A* is another ISO specification: ISO 19005-1:2005, "Document management—Electronic document file format for long-term preservation—Part 1: Use of PDF 1.4 (PDF/A-1)." The standard was approved in September 2005. The initiative for PDF/A was started by the Association for Information and Image Management (AIIM) and the Association for Suppliers of Printing, Publishing and Converting Technologies (NPES).

The *A* in PDF/A stands for *archiving*; there are many electronic formats (ASCII, TIFF, PDF, XML) and technologies (databases, repositories) to choose from for archiving. The proprietary nature of many of these formats is one of the biggest disadvantages: They can't be guaranteed to continue for the long term. For example, if you try to open a 10-year-old Microsoft Word file in the most recent version of Word, you can't expect it to look like it looked 10 years ago in the version that was used to create it.

As opposed to most word-processing formats, PDF represents not only the data contained in the document but also the exact form the document takes. The file can be viewed without the originating application. All the revisions of the PDF specification are backward-compatible. For example, if your viewer can read and print a PDF with version 1.6, it can also read a PDF with version 1.2. Moreover, the information about the file format is always in the public domain. Anyone, at any time, using any hardware or software, can create programs to access PDF documents.

This makes PDF an interesting candidate as a format for archiving. PDF/A goes a step further: It's a subset of PDF-1.4 intended to be suitable for long-term preservation of page-oriented documents. Just like PDF/X, PDF/A imposes some constraints: In order to meet level-B conformance, all fonts must be embedded; encryption isn't allowed; audio and video content are forbidden, as are JavaScript and executable file launches; and so forth. Level-A conformance also means the PDF has to be tagged (see the discussion of tagged PDF earlier in this chapter).

Of course, archiving isn't just about storing documents somewhere in some format. You also have to be able to search and find the documents.

Self-documentation of every archived file is important. This is where XML and, more specifically, Adobe's Extensible Metadata Platform (XMP) come into the picture. XMP is a standard format for the creation, processing, and interchange of metadata, not limited to the PDF format. Applications that don't understand PDF, JPG, PNG, or GIF syntax but are able to extract and read XMP can retrieve the metadata from files in either of these formats.

#### PDF/E

Another ISO standard that will emerge soon is PDF/E. You can follow the progress of this standard on the AIIM site (www.aiim.org/), where the PDF/E committee defines their scope as being "responsible for specifying PDF tags for creating, viewing, and printing documents used in engineering workflows."

The PDF/E standard doesn't exist yet, so it's evident that PDF/E isn't supported yet in iText.

### 3.2.6 PDF forms, FDF, and XFDF

A PDF document can contain an interactive form, sometimes referred to as an AcroForm. An *AcroForm* is a collection of fields. These fields can be used to gather information interactively from the user. They can also act as placeholders with fixed coordinates that can be filled with variable content.

In the first situation, the PDF file can be served on a web site, as if it were an HTML page with a single form. If the user clicks the Submit button, the data entered can be submitted to the web server in different formats (depending on how the submit action was defined in the AcroForm):

- *As an HTML query string*—`key1=value1&key2=value2&...` or HTML multipart form data.
- *In the Forms Data Format (FDF)*—An FDF file contains the data of the form and a reference to the PDF file with the AcroForm. When an FDF file is opened in Adobe Reader, the original PDF is fetched, and the fields are filled with the data in the FDF.
- *In XFDF*—This is the XML-based alternative to FDF.
- *As PDF*—In this case, a complete filled-in PDF file is sent to the server (note that this is not possible if you only have Adobe Reader).

In this book, you'll also use PDFs with an AcroForm as a kind of template. You'll fill the fields with data coming from a database, XML, FDF, or XFDF. One special type of form field is the digital signature.

### 3.2.7 *XFA and XDP*

Forms that are made with Acrobat 7.0 (more specifically, with Adobe's LiveCycle Designer, which comes with Acrobat 7.0 Professional but not with the Standard version) are completely different from AcroForms. They're based on the XML Forms Architecture (XFA). The XML Data Package (XDP) provides a mechanism for packaging units of PDF content as XML. XFA resources are described as XDP packages inside the PDF. In this case, you still have a PDF file, but the form is described in XML. Forms like this aren't discussed in this book. You can read more about XFA in the XFA Specification on the Adobe web site (www.adobe.com). There is only basic XFA support.

The XML Data Package is more than just XFA. XDP is intended to be an XML-based companion to PDF. An XDP file is an XML file that encodes a PDF file in XML. An XDP file consists of five parts, many of which are optional:

- *The XML form data*—The user data encoded according to an arbitrary XML schema chosen by the designer of the form.
- *The XML form template*—Contains all the form intelligence. Maps the XML form data to PDF form fields. Holds the business logic to validate fields, calculates results, and so forth.
- *XML configuration information*—A global reference for database and web service connections.
- *Other XML information*—Metadata, schemas, and digital signatures.
- *The PDF file*—Embeds the PDF as base64 encoded.

PDF and XDP are equivalent and interchangeable representations of the same underlying electronic form. PDF offers advantages for large documents, when file size is important, or when forms contain images. XDP is interesting when forms have to fit in an XML workflow and data needs to be manipulated by software that isn't PDF-aware. For the time being, there are no plans to support XDP files in iText.

### 3.2.8 *Rules of thumb*

I'll refer to the different types of PDF files regularly in parts 2, 3, and 4 of this book. It's not essential that you remember all of them, as long as you keep the following points in mind:

- Traditional PDF is a one-way process.
- Don't abuse the phrase *PDF template*. No one will know whether you're referring to a traditional PDF file that can be *stamped*, tagged PDF files that can be *repurposed,* or a PDF form that can be *filled in*.

- If you're talking about a PDF form, always specify whether you're referring to an *AcroForm* or an *XFA* form.
- PDF is a de facto standard; PDF/X, PDF/A, and (soon) PDF/E are ISO standards.

Now that you have an idea of the types of PDF that are supported, let's look at the different PDF versions and discuss some iText-specific issues.

## 3.3 PDF version history

In chapter 2, you learned how to change the PDF version of the documents that are generated with iText. Table 2.1 listed the different versions and the year the specifications of these versions were published; in table 3.1 you'll find a nonrestrictive list of new features that were added in each PDF version.

**Table 3.1 New features in different PDF versions**

| PDF version | Year | Acrobat version | New features |
|---|---|---|---|
| **PDF-1.0** | 1993 | Acrobat 1 | - Ability to render complex text and graphics to the screen as well as to the printer |
| **PDF-1.1** | 1994 | Acrobat 2 | - Ability to create a password-protected PDF<br>- External links<br>- Device-independent color |
| **PDF-1.2** | 1996 | Acrobat 3 | - Flate (zip/gzip) compression<br>- Interactive, fill-in forms<br>- Chinese, Japanese, Korean (CJK) support |
| **PDF-1.3** | 1999 | Acrobat 4 | - File attachments,<br>- Digital signatures,<br>- Logical page numbering |
| **PDF-1.4** | 2001 | Acrobat 5 | - 128-bit encryption<br>- Transparency<br>- Tagged PDF |
| **PDF-1.5** | 2003 | Acrobat 6 | - Additional compression and encryption options<br>- Optional content groups<br>- Enhanced support for embedding and playback of multimedia |
| **PDF-1.6** | 2004 | Acrobat 7 | - Customizable UserUnit value<br>- Support for Advanced Encryption Standard (AES)<br>- Page-scaling option for printing |

For a complete list, see the PDF Reference Manual. Each version of the Reference has a section in its introductory chapter detailing the latest version's new features.

A number of the features listed in table 3.1 were additions to the existing PDF specification (for example, support for 128-bit encryption and support for transparency), whereas other features led to an almost completely different type of PDF (for example, tagged PDF).

When you create a new document using iText, the default version is 1.4. In chapter 2, you used the method `setPdfVersion()` to create a PDF document in another version, but it's important to realize that this method changes only a single character in the PDF header (see section 2.1.3); iText doesn't check the compatibility of every feature you're using in your code.

In this section, we'll look at specific examples that will help you understand the implications of this limitation. You'll learn what happens if you change the user unit, a feature that was introduced in version 1.6; and you'll learn more about the compression and encryption of PDF documents, two important topics that figure in different rows of table 3.1.

### 3.3.1 Changing the user unit

When we discussed the first step of the iText PDF-creation process, we talked about the maximum and minimum size of a page. If you decide to create a PDF document with a version that is different from the default, you have to be careful not to create a PDF that isn't valid.

For example, if you change the PDF version to 1.3, iText won't check the page size. It's your responsibility not to insert pages that are smaller than 72 by 72 units or bigger than 3,240 by 3,240 units.

Since version 1.4, pages can have a minimum size of 3 by 3 units and a maximum of 14,400 by 14,400 units. This corresponds with a minimum page size of approximately 0.04 by 0.04 in and a maximum of 200 by 200 in, because 1 in equals 72 pt. That's true for PDF-1.4 and -1.5; but table 3.1 indicates that you can change the user unit, starting with version 1.6. The minimum value of the user unit is 1 pt (this is the default; 1 unit = 1/72 in); in PDF 1.6 it can be changed to a maximum of 75,000 pt (1 unit = 1042 in).

Let's give it a try and create a "Hello World" document with a page of 15,000,000 by 15,000,000 inches (14,400 ❶ x 75,000 ❷ x 1/72).

```
/* chapter03/HelloWorldMaximum.java */
Document document = new Document(new Rectangle(14400, 14400));    <-❶
PdfWriter writer = PdfWriter.getInstance(document,
```

```
    new FileOutputStream("HelloWorldMaximum.pdf"));
  writer.setPdfVersion(PdfWriter.VERSION_1_6);
  writer.setUserunit(75000f);    <-2
  document.open();
```

Note that this document measures 381 by 381 kilometers! You'll only be able to view it correctly in Adobe Reader 7.0 or later. If you open HelloWorldMaximum.pdf in an earlier version of Acrobat Reader, you'll get a warning similar to the one Adobe Reader 6.0 is giving in figure 3.1.

Adobe Reader 6.0 can't display the page correctly because it doesn't understand the meaning of a user unit of 75,000 pt.

End users get the warning shown in figure 3.1 every time you serve them a PDF that has a higher version than the one supported by their version of Adobe Reader. This happens even if the PDF doesn't contain new functionality that can't be shown in that specific viewer application. For example, Acrobat Reader 3.0 gives a similar warning if you try to open the "Hello World" file you created in chapter 2. Once you click the OK button, the document displays correctly. That's because listing 2.1 doesn't produce any PDF syntax that isn't compatible with PDF version 1.2.

Requiring the end user to click OK can be annoying. Table 3.1 can help you decide when it's necessary to change the PDF version. If you plan to use the optional content group functionality (OCG; see chapter 12), you have to change the version of your PDF file to 1.5 or 1.6 before opening the document. Note that iText can't change the version number automatically. The PDF version number is

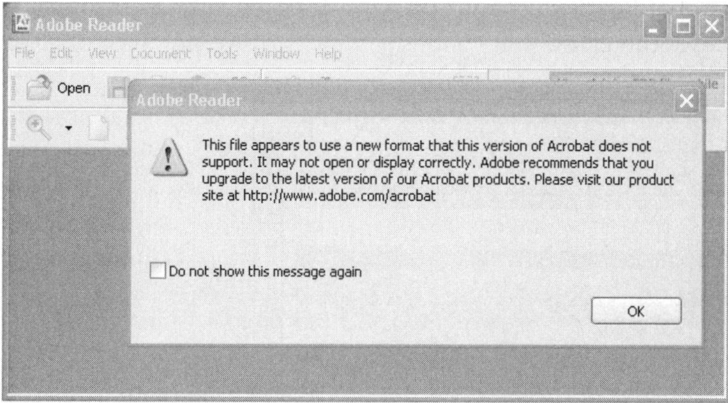


**Figure 3.1 Warning when opening a PDF document with a version higher than the version of the viewer**

written to the output stream in the second step of the PDF creation process; iText notices the use of OCG functionality only in the fourth step.

Changing the user unit, on the other hand, is done *before* the second step. In this case, you could have omitted the line with `setPdfVersion()`. Setting the version is done implicitly in the method `setUserUnit()`. The same happens when you use `setFullCompression()`. A glance at table 3.1 shows that flate/zip compression was introduced in PDF 1.2, but additional full compression functionality wasn't added until version 1.5.

Let's look at some examples that demonstrate the difference between uncompressed, compressed, and fully compressed files.

### 3.3.2 PDF content and compression

Figure 3.1 showed the warning you get when you opened your initial "Hello World" file in Acrobat Reader 3.0. In spite of this warning, Acrobat Reader was able to display the document correctly. This isn't the case if you try to open the file with Acrobat Reader 2.0. Instead of a warning, you get an error message (see figure 3.2).

The document you've generated isn't damaged; you know it opens without any problem in more recent versions of Adobe Reader. After you click OK, Acrobat Reader 2.0 gives you another message box, saying *This file contains information not understood by the viewer. Suppress further errors?*

That's a better error message. Acrobat Reader 2.0 is only supposed to support PDF version 1.1 or earlier. By default, iText compresses the content streams of each page. Acrobat Reader versions prior to 3.0 can't show compressed streams; that's what causes the error.

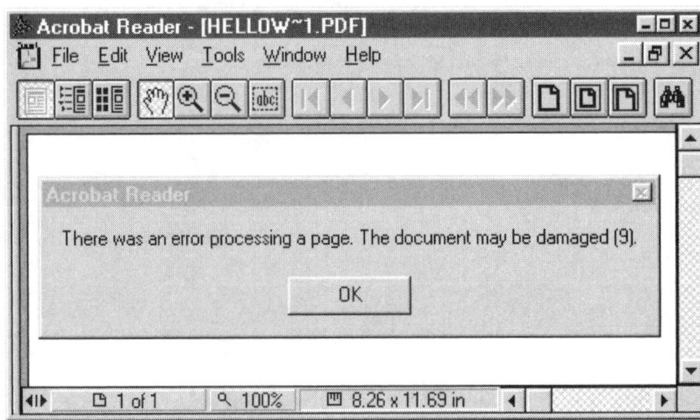


**Figure 3.2 Error message prompted when opening HelloWorld.pdf in Acrobat Reader 2.**

**FAQ** *What is the default compression when creating PDF files with iText?* Since PDF-1.2, flate/deflate compression has been the default compression used by Acrobat. This is an algorithm based on Huffman encoding and LZ77 compression, one of the first versions of Lempel-Ziv-Welch (LZW). It's also the compression iText uses by default.

If you refer again to table 2.1, you'll notice that the iText constant values for PDF-1.0 and -1.1 are missing. This was intentional; it's assumed that you aren't interested in generating a PDF file using a specification that is more than 10 years old.

Nevertheless, you can tweak iText to generate a valid 1.0 or 1.1 PDF file. The PDF header that is written to the output stream upon opening the document is stored in a `HEADER` variable. The `setPdfVersion()` method replaces one character in this `String`. You could tweak iText to generate a PDF-1.1 by calling `setPdfVersion()` and passing the char 1 as a parameter. Additionally, you'd have to turn off the default compression. Note that this example is shown for pedagogic reasons only; I don't recommend that you change the compression variable. It's a static value, so if you set compression to `false`, you do this for the entire JVM (and thus for all the PDFs you're generating in the same process). Doing so may lead to unwanted side effects:

```
/* chapter03/HelloWorldUncompressed.java */
Document.compress = false;
writer.setPdfVersion('1');
```

You can open this particular HelloWorldUncompressed.pdf file in Acrobat Reader 2.0 without getting the error message shown in figure 3.2. Mind my choice of words: You can open this *particular* file in Reader 2.0. I already explained that using `setPdfVersion()` doesn't necessarily result in files that are compliant with that version.

You've just made a PDF that was uncompressed. Why not make one that is fully compressed for a change? *Full compression* means that not only page streams are compressed, but some other objects as well, such as the cross-reference table. This is only possible since PDF-1.5:

```
/* chapter03/HelloWorldFullyCompressed.java */
writer.setFullCompression();
```

You don't set the version in this example; iText changes it to 1.5 automatically.

### *Existing PDF documents and compression*

Suppose you have a large repository of old PDF files that aren't fully compressed. With `PdfStamper`, you can upgrade the version of these PDF files by constructing the `PdfStamper` with a version character as an extra parameter. You can then apply full compression with the method `setFullCompression()`:

```
/* chapter03/HelloWorldFullyCompressed.java */
reader = new PdfReader("HelloWorldCompressed.pdf");
stamper = new PdfStamper(reader,
  new FileOutputStream("HelloWorldFullCompression.pdf"),
  PdfWriter.VERSION_1_5);
stamper.setFullCompression();
stamper.close();
```

Isn't that easy? If you compare the sizes of the files, you'll see that the original file is 4211 bytes, and the one with full compression is only 3179 bytes. Just for fun, you can also decompress the file, which results in a file that is 5561 bytes long:

```
/* chapter03/HelloWorldCompression.java */
reader = new PdfReader("HelloWorldCompressed.pdf");
stamper = new PdfStamper(reader,
  new FileOutputStream("HelloWorldDecompressed.pdf"), '1');
Document.compress = false;
int total = reader.getNumberOfPages() + 1;
for (int i = 1; i < total; i++) {
  reader.setPageContent(i, reader.getPageContent(i));
}
stamper.close();
```

I used a trick to decompress the pages. You can get the uncompressed content stream of a page (see listing 2.2) directly from the reader with `getPageContent()`; this can be interesting if you want to debug a PDF file at the lowest level. You can set the content back with `setPageContent()`. (Note that you should have some experience with PDF before you start experimenting with these methods; you'll read more about them in chapter 18.)

Let's wrap up this chapter by covering one more topic that's mentioned several times in table 3.1: encryption.

## *3.3.3 Encryption*

The FAQs of many tools that produce PDF documents recommend iText as a tool for post-processing PDF files. For example, Apache Formatting Objects Processor (FOP) can be used to convert XML to PDF, but it doesn't encrypt the resulting file; the FOP developers recommend using iText as a post-processor for FOP-generated PDF documents.

In the next example, you'll encrypt an existing PDF document in two different ways, and you'll learn how to decrypt an encrypted PDF file (provided that you have the needed credentials).

### Encrypting existing PDF documents

To encrypt an existing PDF document, you can create a `PdfReader` object, construct a `PdfStamper` object with it, set the encryption parameters, and close the stamper:

```
/* chapter03/HelloWorldEncryptDecrypt.java */
reader = new PdfReader("HelloWorldNotEncrypted.pdf");
stamper = new PdfStamper(reader,
  new FileOutputStream("HelloWorldEncrypted1.pdf"));
stamper.setEncryption(
  "Hello".getBytes(), "World".getBytes(),       <-1
  PdfWriter.AllowPrinting | PdfWriter.AllowCopy,     <-2
  PdfWriter.STRENGTH40BITS);    <-3
stamper.close();
```

This looks simple, but you can do all this in a one-liner using the `PdfEncryptor` class:

```
/* chapter03/HelloWorldEncryptDecrypt.java */
PdfEncryptor.encrypt(new PdfReader("HelloWorldNotEncrypted.pdf"),
  new FileOutputStream("HelloWorldEncrypted2.pdf"),
  "Hello".getBytes(), "World".getBytes(),     <-1
  PdfWriter.AllowDegradedPrinting,    <-2
  PdfWriter.STRENGTH128BITS);    <-3
```

Note that the encrypt methods in `PdfEncryptor` use `PdfStamper` behind the scenes. The end result is exactly the same as if you used the same arguments with `PdfStamper`. In both cases, you need to pass two passwords ❶, an or-ed sequence of permissions ❷, and the strength of the encryption ❸. Let's look more closely at these parameters.

### PDF passwords

The PDF standard security handler allows *access permissions* and up to two passwords to be specified for a document: a *user password* (sometimes referred to as the *open password*) and an *owner password* (sometimes referred to as the *permissions password*). Encryption applies to all strings and streams used in the PDF objects, but not to other types such as integers and boolean values needed to define the document's structure rather than its content.

In the examples, the user must enter the password "Hello" in order to open the files HelloWorldEncrypted1.pdf and HelloWorldEncrypted2.pdf. The PDF file is locked for everyone who doesn't know the password. If you want to read the PDF file in order to change the permissions (and possibly decrypt it), you need the owner password. Remember that the owner password (in this case, "World") will also let you open the PDF file.

The maximum password length is 32 characters: You can enter longer passwords, but only the first 32 characters will be taken into account. One or both of the passwords can be null. If you don't specify a user password, all users will be able to open the document without being prompted for a password, but the permissions and restrictions (if any) will remain in place. This protection is merely psychological. The encryption key is derived from the user password, so omitting this password doesn't provide real security: The content is encrypted as described in the PDF Reference. You could write a program to decrypt such a file, but that would be illegal.

It's even easier to decrypt a file if no owner password was specified; again, you can read the PDF Reference to learn how to change the permissions of the file. If you want decent protection for your document, choose 128-bit key length and always set both passwords, using different strings and all 32 characters for each one. If you choose a password shorter than 32 characters, it will be padded with default padding (as described in the PDF Reference).

Passwords such as "Hello" and "World" are good for simple examples because they make it easy for you to test (reducing the possibility that you can't open the document due to a slip of the keyboard); but in a production environment, you should use passwords that are more complex. Remember that anyone with one of the passwords will be able to remove all the permissions from the file. If users have the owner/permissions password, they can do this legally. If they have the user/open password, they can use rogue software to decrypt the content and create an unprotected copy.

Speaking of protection, let's sum up the permissions that can be applied to a PDF document.

### Overview of the permissions

Encryption is often used to enforce restrictions. The permissions that can be granted or restricted depend on the *strength* of the encryption; there's 40-bit encryption and 128-bit encryption. A quick glance at table 3.1 tells you that 128-bit encryption became possible only in PDF-1.4. In iText, you can use `PdfWriter.STRENGTH40BITS` or `PdfWriter.STRENGTH128BITS` as a parameter to pass to the `setEncryption()` or `encrypt()` method.

Permissions are or-ed like this: `PdfWriter.AllowPrinting | PdfWriter.AllowCopy`.

**TOOLBOX** *`com.lowagie.tools.plugins.Encrypt` (Encrypt)* With this tool, you can encrypt an unencrypted PDF document as you did in the examples. Notice that if you're using this tool from the command line, the permissions argument is a series of 0 and 1 `String` values.

Table 3.2 provides an overview of all the possible values. If you're using 40-bit encryption, every permission that has the remark "128 bit" is granted automatically. If you want to revoke these permissions, you need to use 128-bit encryption. As you can see, 128-bit encryption offers more fine-grained permission levels.

**Table 3.2 Overview of the permission parameters**

| Static final in iText | Description of permission | Remark |
|---|---|---|
| `PdfWriter.AllowPrinting` | Printing the document. | |
| `PdfWriter.AllowDegradedPrinting` | Printing the document, but not with the quality offered by `PdfWriter.AllowPrinting`. | 128 bit |
| `PdfWriter.AllowModifyContents` | Modifying the contents—for example, changing the content of a page, or inserting or removing a page. | |
| `PdfWriter.AllowAssembly` | Inserting, removing, and rotating pages and adding bookmarks is allowed. The content of a page can't be changed (unless the permission `PdfWriter.AllowModifyContents` is granted too). | 128 bit |
| `Pdfwriter.AllowCopy` | Copying or otherwise extracting text and graphics from the document, including assistive technologies such as screen readers or other accessibility devices. | |
| `PdfWriter.AllowScreenReaders` | Extracting text and graphics for use by accessibility devices. | 128 bit |
| `PdfWriter.AllowModifyAnnotations` | Adding or modifying text annotations and interactive form fields. | |
| `PdfWriter.AllowFillIn` | Filling form fields; adding or modifying annotations only if `PdfWriter.AllowModifyAnnotations` is granted too. | 128 bit |

**FAQ** *How do you revoke permission to save or copy a PDF file?* It isn't possible to restrict someone from saving or copying a PDF file. You can't disable the Save (or Save As) option in Adobe Reader. And even if you could, people would always be able to retrieve and copy the file with another tool. This isn't an iText issue—it goes beyond standard PDF security.

If you really need this kind of protection, you must look for a Digital Rights Management (DRM) solution. DRM tools give you fine-grained control over the document. There are different DRM software vendors, but these tools are rather expensive.

If you have an existing file that is encrypted, you can get its permissions with the `getPermissions()` method of `PdfReader`. This method returns a value that is rather cryptic. You can get a verbose overview of the permissions using `getPermissionsVerbose()`, a static method in `PdfEncryptor`:

```
/* chapter03/HelloWorldEncryptDecrypt.java */
System.out.println("Encrypted? " + reader.isEncrypted());
if (reader.isEncrypted()) {
System.out.println("Permissions: " +
  PdfEncryptor.getPermissionsVerbose(reader.getPermissions()));
  System.out.println("128 bit? " + reader.is128Key());
}
```

We have discussed all the parameters needed for encryption. You've used them to encrypt an existing PDF document. In the next example, you'll use these parameters to create a PDF document from scratch.

### *Encrypting a PDF document generated from scratch*

The `PdfWriter` class has a `setEncryption()` method that takes the same parameters as the `PdfStamper` method with the same name. If you go back to the reference example in chapter 2, it's sufficient to add one extra line after the second step:

```
/* chapter03/HelloWorldEncrypted.java */
PdfWriter writer
  = PdfWriter.getInstance(document, new
   FileOutputStream("HelloWorldEncrypted.pdf"));
writer.setEncryption(PdfWriter.STRENGTH128BITS,      <-3
  "Hello", "World",    <-1
  PdfWriter.AllowCopy | PdfWriter.AllowPrinting);     <-2
```

Note that the order of the parameters is slightly different.

You've been encrypting PDF files, both existing and new, but if you want to read an encrypted PDF file with `PdfReader`, you need a constructor that takes a password as parameter.

### Decrypting an existing PDF file

If you try reading an encrypted PDF file with `PdfReader`, an exception will be thrown if you don't provide the owner password. If you *do* know the owner password, decrypting a PDF file with iText is simple. Create the reader object with the constructor that takes the password as parameter ❶, construct the stamper object ❷ and close it immediately afterward ❸:

```
/* chapter03/HelloWorldEncryptDecrypt.java */
reader = new PdfReader("HelloWorldEncrypted1.pdf", "World".getBytes()); ❶
stamper = new PdfStamper(reader,
  new FileOutputStream("HelloWorldDecrypted.pdf"));                     ❷
stamper.close();  <-❸
```

You've just created an unencrypted version of an encrypted PDF file.

**TOOLBOX** *com.lowagie.tools.plugins.Decrypt (Encrypt)* With this tool, you can decrypt an encrypted PDF document as you did in the example.

Note that changing the compression and/or encryption of a PDF file is easy when using iText. It's sufficient to change some settings. If you want to know more about the compression and/or encryption algorithms that are used behind the scenes, please consult the PDF Reference.

We have dealt with three version-specific features that are mentioned in table 3.1. I won't go into detail about the differences between the versions prior to PDF-1.4, but whenever we encounter functionality that was added after version 1.4 (the default version used by iText), I'll mention this in the text. That way, you'll know if and when it's necessary to change the PDF version in your source code.

## 3.4 Summary

This chapter started with a general overview of the Portable Document Format. We talked about the origins and the initial purpose of PDF. PDF has become a de facto standard, but you've seen that along the way different types of PDF and different real ISO standards have emerged. We have discussed how to deal with different PDF versions when using iText. The concepts of user unit, compression, and encryption were introduced in a series of simple examples. This concludes the first part of this book.

In the second part, you'll create traditional PDF documents using iText's basic building blocks. There will be no need to change the PDF version. All the files will be generated in the default version: PDF 1.4. In part 3, we'll encounter some more advanced functionality. You'll still be producing traditional PDF files, but you'll need to change the version once you start working with optional content groups. Part 4 will deal with interactive PDF, including some very recent PDF functionality. You'll also work with other types of PDF: PDF documents with AcroForms and FDF and XFDF files.

If you haven't done so already, now is the time to roll up your sleeves and start doing some real work!

# Part 2

# *Basic building blocks*

Every document is made up of different structures: phrases, paragraphs, chapters, and sections. A document can also contain images, tables, and columns. This part explains how iText implements these structures, and the examples demonstrate how they fit together.

# 4 Composing text elements

**This chapter covers**

- Working with `Chunks`, `Phrases`, and `Paragraphs`
- Working with `Anchors`, `Lists`, and `ListItems`
- Working with `Chapters` and `Sections`
- Advanced `Chunk` functionality

If you wanted to use the first versions of iText back in 1999, you had to be a PDF specialist. Even if you knew what PDF-specific iText methods to use, the Java code to produce a PDF document was obscure. Because I wanted to speed up the development process and make the code maintainable and easier to debug, it wasn't long before I decided to write a layer on top of iText version 0.2x. I had been producing many different types of PDF documents, so I knew which high-level objects would be useful.

This chapter describes a first series of high-level objects that can be used as basic building blocks to generate quality PDF documents without having to bother with PDF syntax. The building blocks that will be discussed in this chapter are presented in class diagram A.3, "Text element classes" (appendix A), which will help you understand the relation between the different text elements available in iText.

A `Chunk` corresponds with a `String` of which all the characters have the same font, font size, font color, and font style. It's the most atomic text element. A `Phrase` is an `ArrayList` of `Chunk` objects. It's the most elementary object you can use to add a complete sentence to a document. You can define the main font of a phrase and the space between the lines. `Anchor` is a special type of `Phrase`. It can be used to define a destination inside a document or to add a clickable link.

Class `Paragraph` is also derived from the `Phrase` object: It's a block of text that can be aligned and indented. Add a list symbol to a `Paragraph`, and you have a `ListItem`. `ListItem` objects are grouped in a `List` object. All of these text elements can be added to a `Chapter` or a `Section`; these two objects can be used to organize the content of your document. They automatically generate a table of contents that is visible as an outline tree in the Bookmarks panel of Adobe Reader.

At the end of this chapter, you'll use most of these text elements to help Laura with her first assignment: making a flyer for the Department of Computer Science and Engineering. Throughout this book, you'll see that the objects discussed in this chapter are the essential ingredients of more complex iText objects such as `Table` (chapter 6) and `ColumnText` (chapter 7).

## 4.1 Wrapping Strings in text elements

Let's go back to the first "Hello World" example from Listing 2.1. The line marked as step ❹ (adding content to the document) looked like this:

```
/* chapter02/HelloWorld.java */
document.add(new Paragraph("Hello World"));
```

The general idea of step ❹ in the PDF-creation process using `document.add()` is that you add objects implementing the interface `Element` to the `Document` object. Behind the scenes, a writer object analyzes these objects and translates them into the appropriate syntax.

Class `PdfWriter` knows how to insert these elements on a PDF page. It also makes sure all the necessary resources, such as fonts and image data, are dealt with and added correctly to the PDF document.

In this chapter, we'll discuss all the objects shown in class diagram A.3 that implement the `Element` interface. These classes have one thing in common: Their main function is to display Java `String` objects. Diagram A.3 shows that all these classes are related to each other, but each one has its own specific characteristics.

Let's find out what makes `Chunks`, `Phrases`, and `Paragraphs` different from each other.

### 4.1.1 The atomic building block: com.lowagie.text.Chunk

A `Chunk` is the smallest significant part of text that can be added to a document. It's the atomic building block of most of the other high-level text objects. A `Chunk` contains a `String` of which all the characters have the same font, font size, font style, font color, rendition, and so forth.

We'll discuss these characteristics in detail in section 4.2. For now, let's look at a short example:

```
/* chapter04/FoxDogChunk1.java */
Font font = new Font(Font.COURIER, 10, Font.BOLD);            ❶
font.setColor(new Color(0xFF, 0xFF, 0xFF));
Chunk fox = new Chunk("quick brown fox", font);
fox.setBackground(new Color(0xa5, 0x2a, 0x2a));
Chunk jumps = new Chunk(" jumps over ", new Font());          ❷
Chunk dog = new Chunk("the lazy dog",
  new Font(Font.TIMES_ROMAN, 14, Font.ITALIC));               ❸
document.add(fox);
document.add(jumps);
document.add(dog);
```

In this example, three chunks of text are constructed. The words *quick brown fox* are in 10-point Courier bold, and the font color is white with a brown background color ❶. The words *jumps over* are in 12-point Helvetica; this is the default font and size when you use `new Font()` ❷. Finally, the words *the lazy dog* are in 14-point Times Roman italic ❸. Note that some lines in this snippet were left out on purpose; we'll discuss the complete sample later.

The end result looks nice because *quick brown fox jumps over the lazy dog* fits on one line; but if you tried to add more text to the document, you'd have a problem.

The `Chunk` object knows how the characters have to advance on a line from left to right. If a line is full, a carriage return is triggered, but a `Chunk` doesn't know about line spacing. If no other object has been added to the document, the default line spacing is 0. So, if you added nothing but `Chunks` to a document, all the text would be printed on the first line, with the different characters overlapping. Let's add some lines to the original `Chunk` example and see what happens:

```
/* chapter04/FoxDogChunk2.java */
Chunk space = new Chunk(' ');
for (int i = 0; i < 10; i++) {
  document.add(fox);
  document.add(jumps);
  document.add(dog);
  document.add(space);
}
```

Look at the overlapping chunks in figure 4.1; what do you think about the result? It's ugly, isn't it? I added this example to demonstrate that, in general, `Chunks` aren't objects you should add to a document directly; instead, they should be used in combination with other objects.

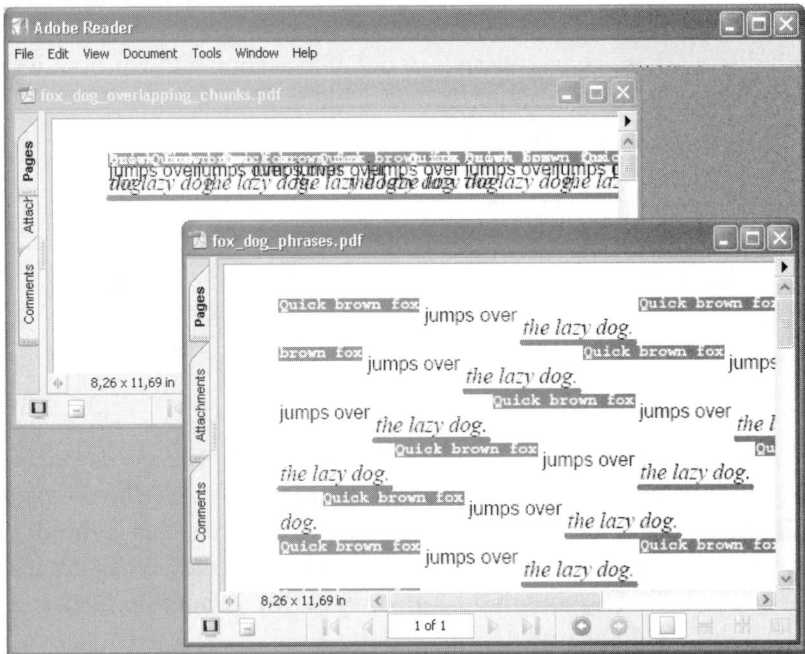


**Figure 4.1 The difference between `Chunks` without leading (background) and `Phrases` with leading (foreground)**

### 4.1.2 An ArrayList of Chunks: com.lowagie.text.Phrase

I chose the word *chunk* for the atomic element because of its first definition in my dictionary: "a solid piece." A *phrase*, on the other hand, is defined as "a string of words." It isn't solid; it's a composed object. I thought it was a good word to use to refer to a concatenation of chunks. Translated to iText and Java, a `Phrase` is an `ArrayList` of `Chunk` objects. Let's adapt the previous example:

```
/* chapter04/FoxDogPhrase.java */
Phrase phrase = new Phrase(30);
phrase.add(fox);
phrase.add(jumps);
phrase.add(dog);
phrase.add(space);
for (int i = 0; i < 10; i++)
document.add(phrase);
```

Now the words *Quick brown fox jumps over the lazy dog* are repeated 10 times, but when the end of the line is reached, a newline is triggered. The space between the baselines of the two lines is 30 user units. You pass this value as a parameter when you construct the `Phrase` object.

If you don't specify a value for the leading, a default is chosen, depending on the font used in the `Phrase`. The default value is 1.5 times the font size. The word *leading* is used as a synonym for line spacing.

**FAQ** *How do I change the space between two lines?* When I wrote the `Phrase` class, I used the word *leading* because that is how the space between two lines is defined in the PDF Reference. Until recently, I thought the word was pronounced "leeding." But while writing this book, I found out it's pronounced "ledding" because the term is derived from the word *lead* (the metal); when type was set by hand for printing presses, strips of lead were placed between lines of type to add space. The word originally referred to the thickness of these strips of lead that were placed between the lines. The PDF Reference redefined the word. In answer to the frequently asked question, you can change the space between the lines of a `Phrase` (and its subclasses) by using the method `setLeading()`.

If you take a closer look at the PDF, you can see that every word that doesn't fit on the line is forwarded to the next line. You can also trigger a newline action by adding the static `Chunk.NEWLINE`:

```
/* chapter04/FoxDogPhrase.java */
document.add(Chunk.NEWLINE);
```

This works because the default leading is no longer 0; it's set to 30 when you add the `Phrase` object. Another way to jump to the next line is by using newline characters (\n):

```
/* chapter04/FoxDogPhrase.java */
phrase.add("\n");
```

I don't know about you, but I don't like all that juggling with newline chunks or characters. I'd rather have an object that adds a newline automatically. That object is a `Paragraph`.

### 4.1.3 A sequence of Phrases: com.lowagie.text.Paragraph

The `Paragraph` class is derived from `Phrase`; this means you can create a `Paragraph` and specify the leading, but you also can do much more. Let's start by composing a `Paragraph` with some `Chunk` and `Phrase` objects:

```
/* chapter04/FoxDogParagraph.java */
Chunk space = new Chunk(' ');
String text = "Quick brown fox jumps over the lazy dog.";
Phrase phrase1 = new Phrase(text);
Phrase phrase2 = new Phrase(new Chunk(text, new Font(Font.TIMES_ROMAN)));
Phrase phrase3 = new Phrase(text, new Font(Font.COURIER));
Paragraph paragraph = new Paragraph();
paragraph.add(phrase1);
paragraph.add(space);
paragraph.add(phrase2);
paragraph.add(space);
paragraph.add(phrase3);
document.add(paragraph);
document.add(paragraph);
```

I used different constructors for the `Phrase` objects to illustrate the different possibilities. You compose a `Paragraph` object with these phrases and add it twice to the document. In the resulting PDF, you see that a newline was added automatically.

But this isn't the most important feature of the `Paragraph` class. In the `Phrase` example, you can see that all the text is added starting from the default right margin, but the left margin is assembled capriciously. With `Paragraphs`, you can specify an alignment:

```
/* chapter04/FoxDogParagraph.java */
paragraph.setAlignment(Element.ALIGN_LEFT);       <- Left alignment is default
document.add(paragraph);
paragraph.setAlignment(Element.ALIGN_CENTER);     <- Center every line of paragraph
document.add(paragraph);
paragraph.setAlignment(Element.ALIGN_RIGHT);      <- Align all lines to right
document.add(paragraph);
```

```
paragraph.setAlignment(Element.ALIGN_JUSTIFIED);    <-- Justify line
document.add(paragraph);
```

You can add some extra spacing before or after a paragraph using the `setSpacingBefore()` and `setSpacingAfter()` methods:

```
/* chapter04/FoxDogParagraph.java */
paragraph.setSpacingBefore(10);
document.add(paragraph);
paragraph.setSpacingBefore(0);
paragraph.setSpacingAfter(10);
document.add(paragraph);
```

The value passed as a parameter is a height in user units that is added to the leading. Whereas leading is responsible for managing the space between *lines*, this value defines the spacing between *paragraphs*..

**TOOLBOX** *`com.lowagie.tools.plugins.Txt2Pdf` (Convert2Pdf)* If you have plain ASCII files that are formatted using space characters, you can convert them to PDF. With this tool, you can choose the page size and orientation. The font used for the PDF file is Courier. Courier is a *monospace* font, meaning that every character has the same width, which is necessary if you want to preserve the original formatting of the plain text file.

With the `Paragraph` object, you can also change the indentation of a paragraph:

```
/* chapter04/FoxDogParagraph.java */
paragraph. setIndentationLeft(20);
document.add(paragraph);
paragraph.setIndentationRight(20);
document.add(paragraph);
```

There are some other methods in class `Paragraph`, but these will be discussed later because they only work in the context of more complex objects. Let's continue with our overview.

## 4.2 Adding extra functionality to text elements

Class `Phrase` is a subclass of `java.util.ArrayList`. You're probably familiar with `java.util.ArrayList`, so this information helps you understand what the `Phrase` object is about. Seen from the point of view of the iText developer, it's probably better to describe a `Phrase` as an implementation of the `com.lowagie.text.TextElementArray` interface, rather than as an `ArrayList` of `Chunk` objects.

This interface has only one method: `public boolean add(Object o)`. The `Phrase` class overrides this method, which is available in its superclass, `ArrayList`. The overridden method makes sure that not every type of object can be added. Each implementation of `TextElementArray` accepts only a limited set of types of `com.lowagie.text.Element` objects.

Except for class `Chunk`, all the objects we'll discuss in this chapter are implementations of the `TextElementArray` interface. Some of these objects do more than just display a `String`; they can act as an anchor or refer to a destination inside or outside of the document (class `Anchor`). They can organize the content in bulleted or numbered lists (classes `List` and `ListItem`). They can even be used to generate a table of contents in the Bookmarks tab of Adobe Reader (classes `Chapter` and `Section`). Let's look at these objects one by one.

### 4.2.1 External and internal links: com.lowagie.text.Anchor

I've been making a lot of examples with the words *Quick brown fox jumps over the lazy dog*, but why did I choose this particular phrase? You can look it up in the free encyclopedia Wikipedia. Or, I can give you a link to the page that explains the origin of this sentence:

```
/* chapter04/FoxDogAnchor1.java */
Anchor anchor =
  new Anchor("Quick brown fox jumps over the lazy dog.");
anchor.setReference("http://en.wikipedia.org/wiki/
  ➥ The_quick_brown_fox_jumps_over_the_lazy_dog");
document.add(anchor);
```

If you hover your mouse over the words in the PDF file, you'll see that the cursor changes into a pointing finger. Click the right mouse button, and your browser opens and a Wikipedia HTML page appears. This is only one of the many ways you can add an *external* link to a PDF file using iText. More complex `Anchor` functionality will follow in section 4.5 and chapter 13.

If you want to add *internal* references with class `Anchor`, you need an `Anchor` that contains the actual reference. In HTML, this is an `<A>` tag with a `HREF` attribute. But you also need an `Anchor` that is referenced. In HTML, this is an `<A>` tag with a `NAME` attribute. If you click the text in the first `Anchor` (the link), you automatically jump to the text of second one (the destination).

Try this example, and see what happens:

```
/* chapter04/FoxDogAnchor2.java */
Paragraph paragraph = new Paragraph("Quick brown ");
Anchor foxReference = new Anchor("fox");          | Reference that can
foxReference.setReference("#fox");                | be clicked
```

```
paragraph.add(foxReference);
paragraph.add(" jumps over the lazy dog.");
document.add(paragraph);
document.newPage();
Anchor foxName = new Anchor("This is the FOX.");
foxName.setName("fox");
document.add(foxName);
```

**Referenced Anchor; destination**

If you click the word *fox*, Adobe Reader changes its view to the second page, to the sentence *This is the FOX*. Notice that when you define the link, you have to add the # sign to the name of the destination. This functionality is important because it can be used to add structural elements that help the end user when browsing the document. We'll elaborate on this functionality in chapter 13.

To help Laura with her first assignment, you'll provide a list with links to the different faculties. You know how to create an `Anchor`, but what about the `List`?

### 4.2.2 Lists and ListItems: com.lowagie.text.List/ListItem

`List` and `ListItem` are both implementations of the `TextElementArray` interface. If you add a `ListItem` to a `List`, the content is indented, and a bullet or a number is added automatically.

Figure 4.2 shows examples of ordered and unordered lists:

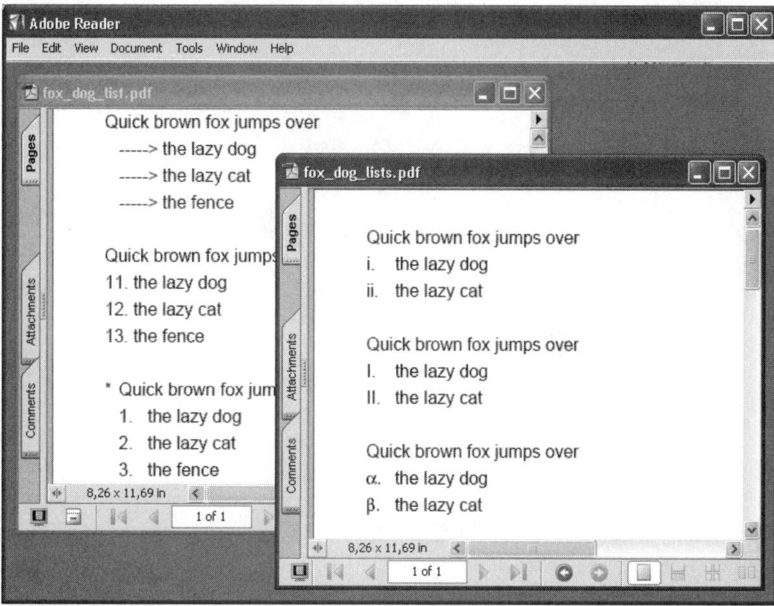


**Figure 4.2 Different types of lists**

`ListItem` is a subclass of `Paragraph`. A `ListItem` has the same functionality as a `Paragraph` (such as leading and indentation), except for two differences:

- You can't add a `ListItem` to a document directly. You have to add `ListItem` objects to a `List`.
- The classes `List` and `ListItem` have a member variable that represents the list symbol.

The default `ListItem` is a number or a letter for ordered lists and a hyphen for unordered lists. With unordered lists, you can change this list symbol for each item individually or set it at the level of the list. The space that is needed for the list symbol isn't calculated automatically. You need to pass the symbol indentation with the constructor of the list:

```
/* chapter04/FoxDogList1.java */
List list1 = new List(List.ORDERED, 20);     <-1
list1.add(new ListItem("the lazy dog"));
document.add(list1);
List list2 = new List(List.UNORDERED, 10);     <-2
list2.add("the lazy cat");     <-3
document.add(list2);
List list3 = new List(List.ORDERED, List.ALPHABETICAL, 20);     <-4
list3.add(new ListItem("the fence"));
document.add(list3);
List list4 = new List(List.UNORDERED, 30);
list4.setListSymbol("----->");     <-5
list4.setIndentationLeft(10);     <-6
list4.add("the lazy dog");
document.add(list4);
List list5 = new List(List.ORDERED, 20);
list5.setFirst(11);                          7
list5.add(new ListItem("the lazy cat"));
document.add(list5);
List list = new List(List.UNORDERED, 10);
list.setListSymbol(new Chunk('*'));
list.add(list1);     <-8
list.add(list3);
list.add(list5);
document.add(list);
```

Here's what happens in the code:

1. Create an ordered list (1, 2, 3, and so on).
2. Create an unordered list (the list symbol is -).
3. Add a `String` instead of a `ListItem`.
4. Create an ordered list (A, B, C, and so on).

❺ Create an unordered list using a custom list symbol.
❻ Change the overall indentation of the list.
❼ Generate an ordered list (11, 12, 13, and so on).
❽ Lists can be nested.

In figure 4.2, you also see some lists that have list symbols that look special:

```
/* chapter04/FoxDogList2.java */
RomanList romanlist = new RomanList(20);            | Create list with Roman
romanlist.setRomanLower(false);                     | numbers (I, II, II, IV...)
romanlist.add(new ListItem("the lazy dog"));
document.add(romanlist);
GreekList greeklist = new GreekList(20);            | Create list with Greek
greeklist.setGreekLower(true);                      | characters (α, β)
greeklist.add(new ListItem("the lazy cat"));
document.add(greeklist);
ZapfDingbatsList zapfdingbatslist = new ZapfDingbatsList(42, 15);
zapfdingbatslist.add(new ListItem("the lazy dog"));    Create list with
document.add(zapfdingbatslist);                        Zapfdingbats symbols
ZapfDingbatsNumberList zapfdingbatsnumberlist
  = new ZapfDingbatsNumberList(0, 15);
zapfdingbatsnumberlist.add(new ListItem("the lazy cat"));
document.add(zapfdingbatsnumberlist);
```

These lists can be handy, but you have to be careful with them. `RomanList` and `GreekList` work well if your list has no more than 26 or 24 items. If you have more list items, other characters appear. The same goes for the `ZapfDingbatsNumberList`. These are lists from ① to ⑩; if you have more than 10 items, the eleventh item is numbered with the next character, for instance ⓿.

The next `TextElementArray` implementations are also elements that structure text on one or more pages, but they add something extra: They automatically generate an outline tree (also known as a bookmark).

### 4.2.3 Automatic bookmarking: com.lowagie.text.Chapter/Section

In the previous chapter, you learned how to retrieve the outline tree of a PDF document. I'll explain bookmarks further in chapter 13, but in the meantime you'll create bookmarks like the ones in figure 4.3 automatically using the `TextElementArray` implementations `Chapter` and `Section`.

The use of chapters and sections isn't limited to novels; you can use these `TextElementArray` objects to offer a structure to the people who consult your document online. For example, if you have a catalog of electronic equipment, you can place all the video equipment in one chapter and the computer-related products in another. In the video equipment section, you can have subsections for cameras,

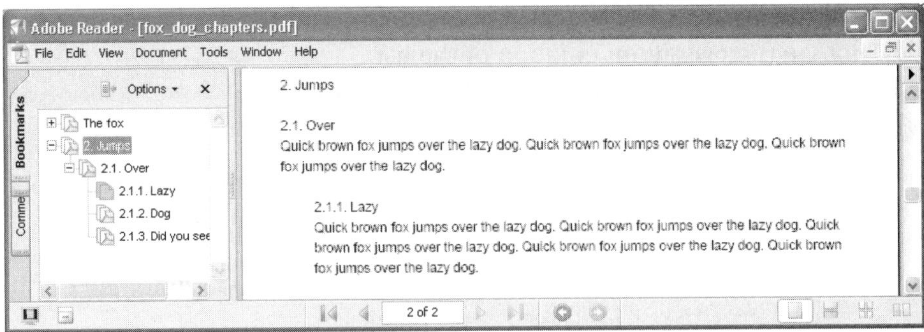


**Figure 4.3 A PDF document with bookmarks**

DVD players, DVD recorders, and so forth. That way, your customers can use the Bookmarks tab to jump directly to the section they're interested in; they don't have to scroll through the complete document.

The top-level bookmarks refer to `Chapter` objects. All sublevels refer to `Section` objects. `Section` objects are created with the method `addSection()`. Let's approach this step by step:

```
/* chapter04/FoxDogChapter1.java */
Chapter chapter1 = new Chapter(
  new Paragraph ("This is a sample sentence:", font), 1);    <-❶
chapter1.add(text);   <-❷
Section section1 = chapter1.addSection("Quick", 0);    <-❸
section1.add(text);   <-❹
document.add(chapter1);   <-❺
```

❶ creates a `Chapter` object with the number 1 (it's the first chapter). Note that a PDF document doesn't necessarily have to start with chapter 1. The title of the chapter (or section) is used as the title for the bookmark. It can be passed as a `String` or a `Paragraph`. You can change this with the method `setBookmarkTitle()` if needed. The outline tree that is visible in the Bookmark tab is open by default. With the method `setBookmarkOpen()`, you can also change this:

```
/* chapter04/FoxDogChapter2.java */
chapter1.setBookmarkTitle("The fox");
chapter1.setBookmarkOpen(false);
```

In steps ❷ and ❹, content is added to the chapter and the section: `Paragraphs`, `Phrases`, `Anchors`, `Lists`, and so forth. You can't construct a `Section` directly; creating a `Section` ❸ only makes sense in the context of a `Chapter` or a parent `Section`. Step ❸ also defines the *number depth*. The `numberDepth` variable tells iText how many parent-level numbers should be shown.

For example, you're now reading section 4.2.3 of part 2 of this book. If the number depth was 1, the title would be "3 Automatic bookmarking: com.lowagie.text.Chapter/Section." With a number depth of 4, the part number (2) would be added to the section number (4.2.3): "2.4.2.3 Automatic bookmarking: com.lowagie.text.Chapter/Section."

In step ❺, the `Chapter` is added to the `Document`. It's important to realize that `Chapters` can consume a lot of memory. This memory can only be released after the `Chapter` is added to the document, after the content is flushed to the `OutputStream`. The `Chapter/Section` functionality isn't memory-friendly.

Let's now return to the atomic text and learn how to change the characteristics of the text that is being added to a `TextElementArray`.

## 4.3 Chunk characteristics

I have already introduced some of the characteristics of `Chunk` objects. In figure 4.1, you saw superscript `Chunks`, subscript `Chunks`, and underlined `Chunks`. Perhaps you've already peeked into the code to see how it was done.

This section will introduce some of the standard `Chunk` functionality, such as retrieving the dimensions of a `Chunk`, adding lines and colors, and changing the way characters inside a `Chunk` are rendered.

### 4.3.1 Measuring and scaling

`Chunks` can be used as elements in the basic building blocks, but they will also be useful for more complex PDF magic later on in this book. On some occasions, you need to know the width of a `Chunk`. For instance, if you write *Quick brown fox jumps over the lazy dog* in 12-point Helvetica, how much space do you need? The `getWidthPoint()` method gives you the width in points. Doing some math will help you find out how many inches or centimeters the `Chunk` takes; see figure 4.4.

The next code snippet shows how the first two lines in figure 4.4 were composed:

```
/* chapter04/FoxDogScale.java */
Chunk c = new Chunk("quick brown fox jumps over the lazy dog");
float w = c.getWidthPoint();
Paragraph p = new Paragraph("The width of the chunk: '");
p.add(c);
p.add("' is ");
p.add(String.valueOf(w));
p.add(" points or ");
p.add(String.valueOf(w / 72f));
p.add(" inches or ");
p.add(String.valueOf(w / 72f * 2.54f));
p.add(" cm.");
```

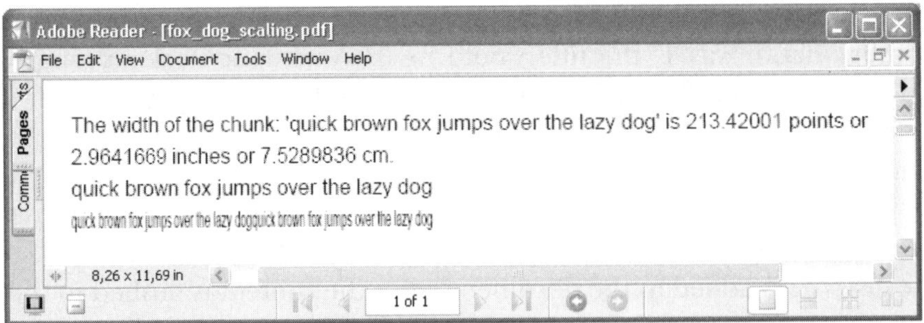


**Figure 4.4 Measuring and scaling a `Chunk`**

Suppose you have to fit a `Chunk` inside a box with a certain width. You can scale the `Chunk` with the method `setHorizontalScaling()`. On line 3 in figure 4.4, the `Chunk` is added as-is once. On line 4, it's added twice, but scaled to 50 percent:

```
/* chapter04/FoxDogScale.java */
document.add(c);
document.add(Chunk.NEWLINE);
c.setHorizontalScaling(0.5f);
document.add(c);
document.add(c);
```

You can see clearly that the two `Chunks` in line 4 take the same space as the one `Chunk` in line 3. Of course, you have to be careful not to exaggerate the scaling. At some point, your text will become almost illegible; you may consider switching to a smaller font size instead of scaling the one you're using. You'll learn more about fonts in chapters 8 and 9.

For now, you'll learn how to add horizontal lines to a `Chunk` so that you can underline or strike through a text string.

### 4.3.2 Lines: underlining and striking through text

In chapter 8, you'll learn about defining the font styles `Font.UNDERLINE` and `Font.STRIKETHRU`. This is nice if you want to underline or strike through some text, but you may wonder if this functionality really belongs in the `Font` class. More important, does the default result correspond with what you expect? Wouldn't you rather have the line striking through the words a few points higher than the default? In some situations, it's better to work at a more atomic level and use one of the variants of the method `Chunk.setUnderline()`. Figure 4.5 shows some of the possibilities.

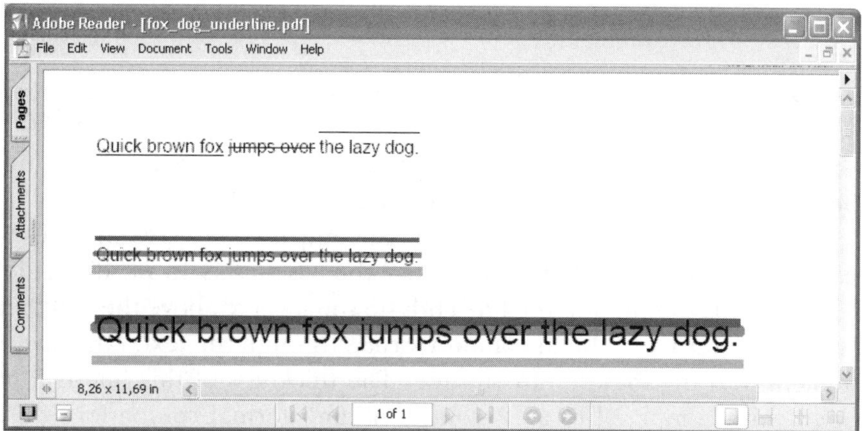


**Figure 4.5 Underlining and striking through text**

The lines drawn under, through, and above the first sentence in figure 4.5 (to underline *Quick brown fox*, strike through *jumps over*, and go above *the lazy dog*) were added at specific distances from the baseline of the text:

```
/* chapter04/FoxDogUnderline.java */
Chunk foxLineUnder = new Chunk("Quick brown fox");
foxLineUnder.setUnderline(0.2f, -2f);
Chunk jumpsStrikeThrough = new Chunk("jumps over");
jumpsStrikeThrough.setUnderline(0.5f, 3f);
Chunk dogLineAbove = new Chunk("the lazy dog.");
dogLineAbove.setUnderline(0.2f, 14f);
```

The first parameter of the `setUnderline()` method defines the thickness of the line; the second specifies the Y position above (Y > 0) or under (Y < 0) the baseline of the `Chunk`. The length of the line depends on the length of the `Chunk`, but if you look at the second and third lines, you can see some variation is possible. Let's look at a method that offers even more flexibility.

Let's define two different `Chunks` with a different font size:

```
/* chapter04/FoxDogUnderline.java */
c = new Chunk("Quick brown fox jumps over the lazy dog.");
c = new Chunk("Quick brown fox jumps over the lazy dog.",
  new Font(Font.HELVETICA, 24));
```

You invoke the same methods with the same parameters on both `Chunks`:

```
/* chapter04/FoxDogUnderline.java */
c.setUnderline(new Color(0x00, 0x00, 0xFF),
  0.0f, 0.2f, 15.0f, 0.0f, PdfContentByte.LINE_CAP_BUTT);
```

**Draw upper (blue) line**

```
c.setUnderline(new Color(0x00, 0xFF, 0x00),
  5.0f, 0.0f, 0.0f, -0.5f,
  PdfContentByte.LINE_CAP_PROJECTING_SQUARE);
c.setUnderline(new Color(0xFF, 0x00, 0x00),
  0.0f, 0.3f, 0.0f, 0.4f, PdfContentByte.LINE_CAP_ROUND);
```

**Draw lower (green) line**

**Draw (red) line that strikes through text**

The most obvious parameter in this method is the first one: It defines the color of the line. But can you see what the other parameters do?

Let's start with the upper line (the blue one, if you're creating the PDF while reading the book). The Y position above the baseline is 15 pt. If you define this height for a 12-point font, the line ends up somewhere above the text; but when a 24-point font is used, the line almost strikes through the text. You have a similar problem with the middle (green) line. The thickness of this line is 5 pt; this is rather thick compared to a 12-point font and normal compared to a 24-point one. The height and thickness of the lower (red) line seem better in proportion with the font size.

Let's look at the javadoc information to see what is happening here:

```
public Chunk setUnderline(Color color,
  float thickness, float thicknessMul,
  float yPosition, float yPositionMul,
  int cap)
```

I've already explained the first parameter:

- `Color`—The color of the line, or `null` to follow the text color

The second and third parameters define the thickness:

- `Thickness`—The absolute thickness of the line
- `ThicknessMul`—The thickness multiplication factor with the font size

The example gives the green line an absolute thickness of 5 pt. This is about half as thick as the 12-point font size of the first line and about a fifth of the 24-point font of the second line. For the blue and red lines, you defined a thickness relative to the size of the font.

The fourth and fifth parameters define the Y position:

- `yPosition`—The absolute Y position relative to the baseline
- `yPositionMul`—The position multiplication factor with the font size

Here, you use an absolute value for the blue line and a relative value for the red and green lines. Finally, there's the `cap` parameter:

- cap—The end line cap. Allowed values are PdfContentByte.LINE_CAP_BUTT, PdfContentByte.LINE_CAP_ROUND, and PdfContentByte.LINE_CAP_PROJECTING_SQUARE

You'll more or less understand the difference between these values by looking closely at the PDF produced by the example. If you need the full explanation, please consult table 10.3 in section 10.3.2.

If you use the Font.UNDERLINE style to underline a text element, you have to accept what you get. With this method, you have almost complete control. By playing with the absolute and relative values, you can fine-tune the position and thickness of the lines.

In the next example, you'll draw a line indicating the baseline and move the text up and down with the method setTextRise().

### 4.3.3 TextRise: sub- and superscript

If you're writing a mathematical function and you need an exponent or an index notation, you want to write a value above (superscript) or below (subscript) the baseline of the chunk. The following example shows how you can use the method setTextRise() to achieve this:

```
/* chapter04/FoxDogSupSubscript.java */
String s = "quick brown fox jumps over the lazy dog";
StringTokenizer st = new StringTokenizer(s, " ");
float textrise = 6.0f;
Chunk c;
while (st.hasMoreTokens()) {
  c = new Chunk(st.nextToken());
  c.setTextRise(textrise);
  c.setUnderline(new Color(0xC0, 0xC0, 0xC0),
  0.2f, 0.0f, 0.0f, 0.0f, PdfContentByte.LINE_CAP_BUTT);
  document.add(c);
  textrise -= 2.0f;
}
```

The result in figure 4.6 is quite jumpy, don't you agree?

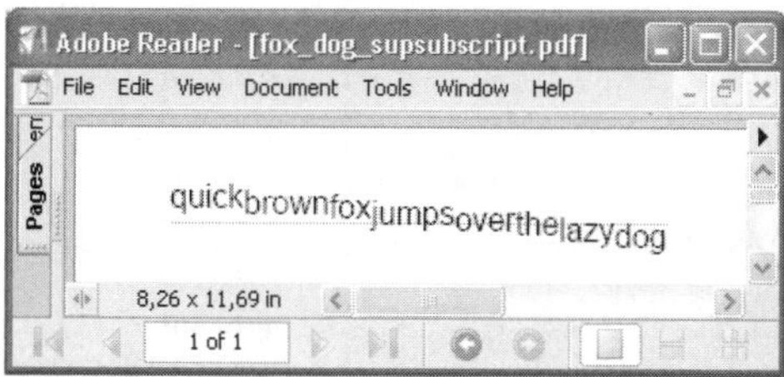


**Figure 4.6**
**Using setTextRise() with Chunks**

Just as you can underline or strike through text using `setUnderline()`, you can now simulate superscript and subscript with `setTextRise()`—that is, if you know how to change the font size. This will be explained in chapter 8.

### 4.3.4 *Simulating italic fonts: skewing text*

In chapter 8, you'll learn how to select fonts with different styles; but in chapter 9, you'll learn that it's not always possible to find the italic or bold version of a font. With some extra `Chunk` magic, you can work around this problem.

The best way to simulate an italic font is by using `chunk.setSkew(0f, 25f)`; figure 4.7 shows the results of using some other parameters:

```
/* chapter04/FoxDogSkew.java */
chunk = new Chunk("Quick brown fox");
chunk.setSkew(15f, -30f);
p.add(chunk);
chunk = new Chunk(" jumps over ");
chunk.setSkew(15f, 15f);
p.add(chunk);
chunk = new Chunk("the lazy dog.");
chunk.setSkew(-30f, 15f);
p.add(chunk);
document.add(p);
```

By changing the value of the first parameter, you change the angle of the baseline. This can lead to strange results. The second parameter defines the angle between the characters and the baseline. If you aren't pleased with the standard

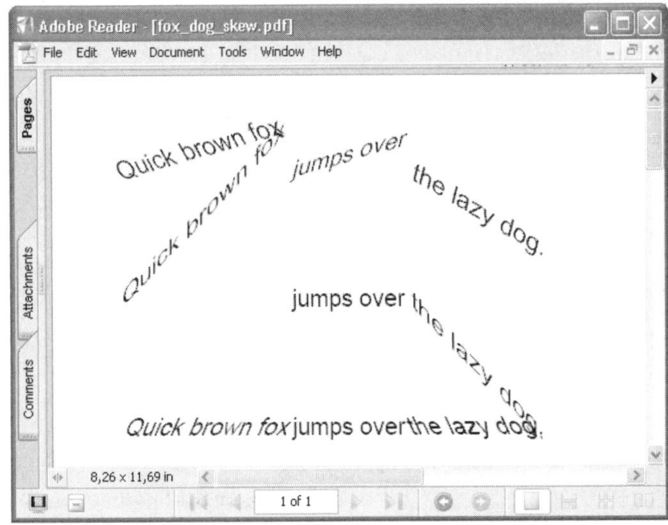


**Figure 4.7 Skewed text**

italic fonts (with the glyphs leaning forward, like a forward slash), you can use this parameter to create your own backward italic font.

The default text color is black. In the next example, you'll learn how to change the text and the background color of the `Chunk`.

### 4.3.5 Changing font and background colors

In figure 4.1, the color of the font and the `Chunk` background of the words *quick brown fox* are different from the other words in the line. Let's look at the code to see how this is done:

```
/* chapter04/FoxDogColor.java */
Font font = new Font(Font.COURIER, 10, Font.BOLD);
font.setColor(new Color(0xFF, 0xFF, 0xFF));          Set font color to white
Chunk fox = new Chunk("quick brown fox", font);
fox.setBackground(new Color(0xa5, 0x2a, 0x2a));      Set background to brown
```

The dimensions of the rectangle are defined automatically, but you can change them if you use another `setBackground()` method:

```
/* chapter04/FoxDogColor.java */
Chunk dog =
  new Chunk("the lazy dog", new Font(Font.TIMES_ROMAN, 14, Font.ITALIC));
dog.setBackground(new Color(0xFF, 0x00, 0x00), 10, -50, 20, -10);
```

The order of the extra parameters that add or subtract space from the original rectangle is as follows: left, bottom, right, top. You can use this function to highlight text.

Let's continue with colors and find out how text is drawn.

### 4.3.6 Simulating bold fonts: stroking vs. filling

In chapter 8, you'll learn that you shouldn't confuse characters with *glyphs*. Glyphs are shapes that can be stroked and/or filled with color. These shapes are defined in a font file. With the method `setTextRenderMode()`, you can change the *rendering* mode that defines whether the glyphs are to be stroked and/or filled, as well as the color and the thickness of the *strokes*.

In figure 4.8, the four rendition modes are demonstrated. In the first line, the shapes are filled in black (the default fill color) ❶. The stroke color of the second line is red; the fill color remains black ❷. The third line is invisible ❸, and the fourth line isn't filled ❹; you can only see the strokes:

```
/* chapter04/FoxDogRender.java */
Chunk chunk = new Chunk("Quick brown fox jumps over the lazy dog.");
chunk.setTextRenderMode(PdfContentByte.TEXT_RENDER_MODE_FILL,
  0f, new Color(0xFF, 0x00, 0x00));                                   ❶
```

```
document.add(new Paragraph(chunk));
chunk.setTextRenderMode(PdfContentByte.TEXT_RENDER_MODE_FILL_STROKE,
  0.3f, new Color(0xFF, 0x00, 0x00));                               ❷
document.add(new Paragraph(chunk));
chunk.setTextRenderMode(PdfContentByte.TEXT_RENDER_MODE_INVISIBLE,
  0f, new Color(0x00, 0xFF, 0x00));                                 ❸
document.add(new Paragraph(chunk));
chunk.setTextRenderMode(PdfContentByte.TEXT_RENDER_MODE_STROKE,
  0.3f, new Color(0x00, 0x00, 0xFF));                               ❹
document.add(new Paragraph(chunk));
```

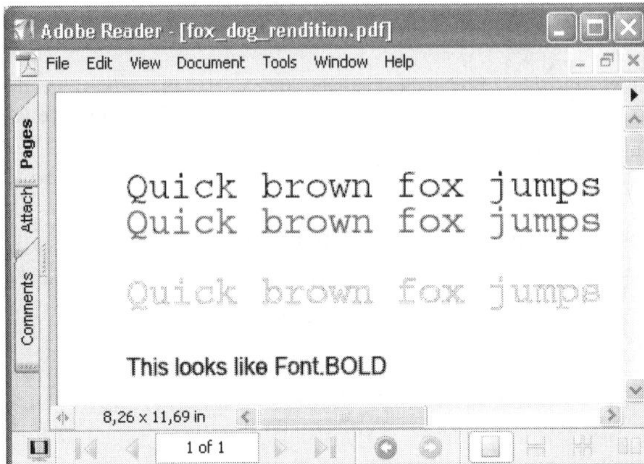


**Figure 4.8**
**Demonstrating text-rendering modes**

The best way to simulate a bold font is by using this code snippet:

```
setTextRenderMode(PdfContentByte.TEXT_RENDER_MODE_FILL_STROKE, 0.5f, null);
```

Observe that `null` is used as the stroke color. In this case, the fill color is used as the stroke color. Note that you should use the `Chunk` functionality to simulate an italic or a bold font only as a last resort. Chapter 8 will explain better ways to change the font style.

The other functionality involving colors and lines we have just discussed will be covered in more detail in part 3, when you'll add text at absolute positions (using PDF text state operators). You'll find that the basic building blocks take away a lot of the complexity of PDF. For example, when using basic building blocks, iText calculates how many characters fit on one line automatically.

## 4.4 Chunks and space distribution

When we discussed the difference between `Chunks`, `Phrases`, and `Paragraphs`, I mentioned that sentences are automatically split at the end of the line. I also mentioned that it's possible to justify paragraphs. In this section, you'll learn how to define split characters and hyphenation rules. You'll also see how you can parameterize the distribution of space (between words and between glyphs).

### 4.4.1 The split character

The default behavior of iText is to try to add as many complete words to a line as possible. iText splits sentences when a space or a hyphen character (-) is encountered. If the `Chunk` is longer than the page width, and it doesn't contain any spaces or hyphens (or any other character that is in one of the Unicode ranges considered to contain split characters), iText splits the `Chunk` just before the first character that doesn't fit the page. This can be annoying in some situations. For example, if you have a long URL, you may want to define the forward slash (/) as a *split character* for chunks that contain a URL. Look at figure 4.9, and think about how you would like to change the default behavior.

To achieve what has been done in the bottom portion of figure 4.9, you need to implement the `SplitCharacter` interface. The method that must be implemented looks a little complicated, but in most cases it's sufficient to copy this method and only change the `return` line:

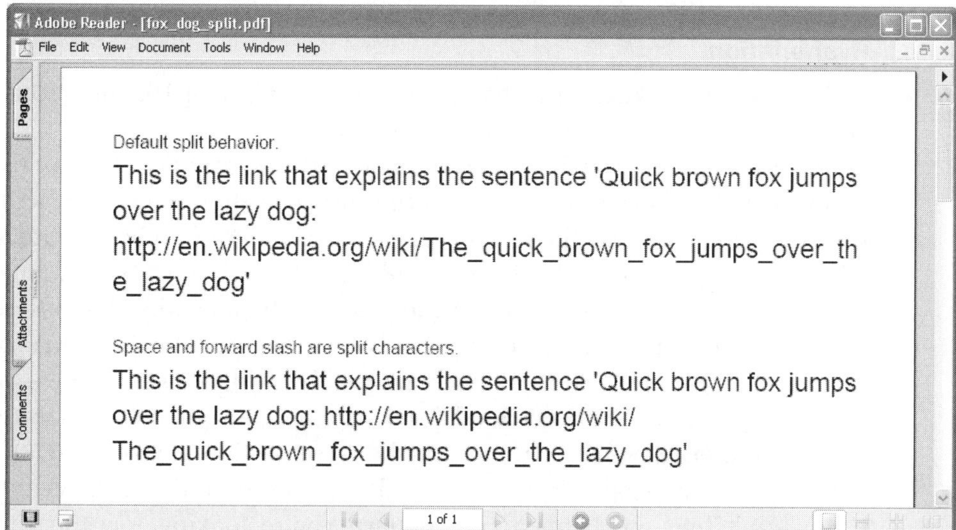


**Figure 4.9 Changing the split character**

```
/* chapter04/FoxDogSplit.java */
public class FoxDogSplit implements SplitCharacter {
public boolean isSplitCharacter(int start, int current, int end,
  char[] cc, PdfChunk[] ck) {
    char c;
    if (ck == null)
      c = cc[current];
    else
      c = ck[Math.min(current, ck.length - 1)]
        .getUnicodeEquivalent(cc[current]);
    return (c == '/');
  }
}
```

Now you tell the URL `Chunk` that it should use your custom `SplitCharacter` implementation instead of the default split functionality:

```
/* chapter04/FoxDogSplit.java */
urlChunk = new Chunk(url, font);
urlChunk.setSplitCharacter(new FoxDogSplit());
```

If the string `url` contains spaces or hyphens, they won't act as split characters. The URL `Chunk` will only be split where there's a forward slash. This is nice, but it isn't as nice as real hyphenation, where words are split according to grammatical rules. We'll discuss this next.

### 4.4.2 Hyphenation

Let's use some real text for a change, as shown in figure 4.10, and quote Charles Dickens, one of the best storytellers who ever lived.

Just like with the split character, you define the magic at the level of the `Chunk`. Before I explain how it's done, I want to draw your attention to the fact that you need to add an extra jar file to your `CLASSPATH` if you want to hyphenate text with iText: itext-hyph-xml.jar. In this jar, you'll find files like en_US.xml, en_GB.xml, nl.xml, and pt.xml. They describe the rules for hyphenation for different languages—in this case, American English, British English, Dutch, and Portuguese.

These XML files weren't created by the iText developers. They were created for Apache FOP, downloaded from Apache, and put in a separate jar for your convenience. Some of them may be General Public License (GPL) or not usable for commercial purposes, so read the licenses and decide what to keep. If you can't find the hyphenation pattern you're looking for, you can create your own as described at the Apache FOP site. Put the XML file in a directory, and call `Hyphenator.setHyphenDir()` or add it as a resource in the package `com.lowagie.text.pdf.hyphenation.hyph`.

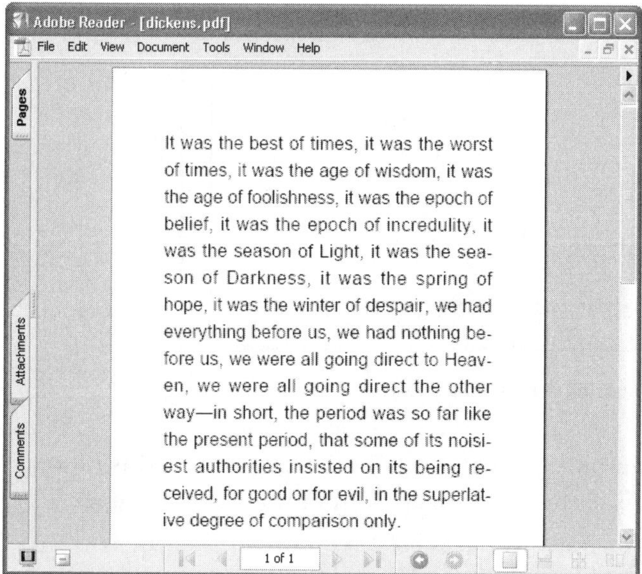


**Figure 4.10**
**A hyphenated excerpt from *A Tale of Two Cities***

Let's see some code that shows how these files are used:

```
/* chapter04/DickensHyphenated.java */
Chunk ck = new Chunk(text);
HyphenationAuto auto = new HyphenationAuto("en", "GB", 2, 2);
ck.setHyphenation(auto);
Paragraph p = new Paragraph(ck);
p.setAlignment(Paragraph.ALIGN_JUSTIFIED);
```

As you can see, the first two parameters of the `HyphenationAuto` constructor correspond with parts of the XML filename, and the third and fourth parameters specify how many characters may be orphaned at the start of a word or the end of a word, respectively. For instance, you wouldn't want to split the word *elephant* like this: *e-lephant*. It doesn't look right if a single letter gets cut off from the rest of the word.

### 4.4.3 Changing the CharSpace ratio

One other issue is important when the end of a line is reached: line justification. Take a close look at figure 4.11. Do you see any difference between the page on the left and the page on the right?

The page on the left shows how characters and words are spaced by default when a paragraph is justified. In order to fit the line exactly, some extra space is added between the words and between the characters. The default ratio between

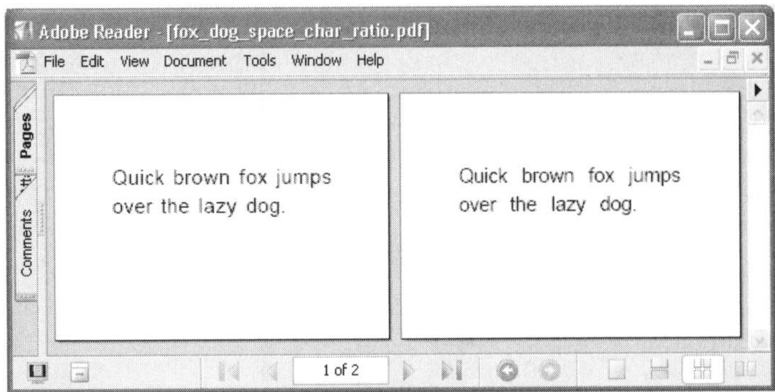


**Figure 4.11 Character spacing versus word spacing**

word spacing and character spacing is 2:5. You can change this ratio at the level of the `PdfWriter` (this is `PdfWriter` magic rather than `Chunk` magic):

```
/* chapter04/FoxDogSpaceCharRatio.java */
Paragraph paragraph = new Paragraph(text);
paragraph.setAlignment(Element.ALIGN_JUSTIFIED);
document.add(paragraph);
document.newPage();
writer.setSpaceCharRatio(PdfWriter.NO_SPACE_CHAR_RATIO);
document.add(paragraph);
```

On the left, there is a lot more space between the words than between the characters. This is because the code tells the writer not to apply character spacing. In reality, `NO_SPACE_CHAR_RATIO` is a big `float`. You can enter any other `float` value if you want to experiment with this feature.

The tricks you've learned until now have concerned visible magic. There's also some magic that won't show up if you print a document, but which you can use to make it easier for a user to read your document online.

## 4.5 Anchors revisited

In section 4.2.1, you added external and internal links using the `Anchor` object. Chapter 13 will tell you more about links and the actions that are invoked when a link is clicked; but in the meantime, let's look at some `Chunk` functionality that lets you add clickable text to jump to another document (HTML, PDF, or another type) or to jump to another place in the current document.

### 4.5.1 Remote Goto

Do you remember the meaning of the *Quick Brown Fox* sentence? In case you've forgotten the Wikipedia link, here's an alternative version of the FoxDog-Anchor1 example:

```
/* chapter04/FoxDogGoto1.java */
Chunk chunk = new Chunk("Quick brown fox jumps over the lazy dog.");
chunk.setAnchor("http://en.wikipedia.org/wiki/
  ➥ The_quick_brown_fox_jumps_over_the_lazy_dog");
document.add(chunk);
```

This code fragment results in the same behavior as `Anchor.setReference()`. If you click the link, the Wikipedia page explaining the Fox/Dog sentence opens. If you need to add an external link, you can choose which object to use, `Anchor` or `Chunk`.

But there is more: With `Chunk`, you can also jump to a specific location on another (remote) PDF document. The document fox.pdf adds a *remote Goto,* like this:

```
/* chapter04/FoxDogGoto2.java */
Paragraph p1 = new Paragraph("The quick brown fox wants to");
Chunk chunk = new Chunk(" jump over ", font);
chunk.setRemoteGoto("dog.pdf", "jump");
p1.add(chunk);
p1.add(" the lazy dog.");
```

**fox.pdf**

You're referring to a destination named *jump* in the file dog.pdf. You could use an `Anchor` with the name `jump`; but for this example I chose to do it this way:

```
/* chapter04/FoxDogGoto2.java */
Paragraph p3 = new Paragraph("The quick brown fox has jumped over ");
p3.add(new Chunk("the lazy dog.").setLocalDestination("jump"));
```

**dog.pdf**

In figure 4.12, both files are open. If you click the words *jump over* in fox.pdf, dog.pdf opens and the focus is set to the line where the destination (named *jump*) was added. The dog.pdf document also has a link to jump to a specific page in another document. Click on it, and page 3 of fox.pdf opens:

```
/* chapter04/FoxDogGoto2.java */
Paragraph p4 = new Paragraph("you can also jump to a ");
p4.add(new Chunk("specific page on another document")
  .setRemoteGoto("fox.pdf", 3));
```

**dog.pdf**

Looking at these code fragments, you'll also notice that these methods return a `Chunk`. What you did in three lines in the first code fragment is reduced to one line in the second and third FoxDogGoto2 sample code fragments.

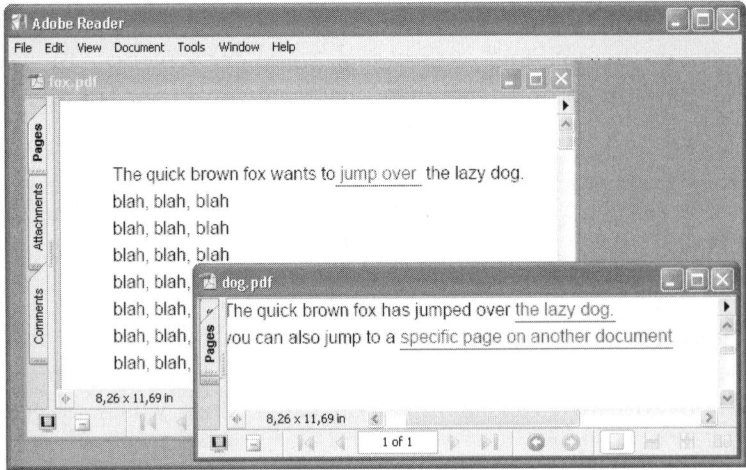


**Figure 4.12 External links from one PDF document to another**

The same functionality exists if you want to navigate *inside* a document not to an external HTML or PDF file.

### 4.5.2 *Local Goto*

With a few changes, you can turn the previous example into one that demonstrates local Goto and local destination functionality:

```
/* chapter04/FoxDogGoto3.java */
Paragraph p1 = new Paragraph("The Quick brown fox wants to");
p1.add(new Chunk(" jump over ").setLocalGoto("jump"));
p1.add("the lazy dog.");
Paragraph p3 = new Paragraph("The fox");
p3.add(new Chunk(" has jumped ").setLocalDestination("jump"));
p3.add("over the lazy dog.");
```

In chapter 13, you'll learn that all of these Goto actions can also be added with a `PdfAction`. Let's write a third variant of the external link example:

```
/* chapter04/FoxDogGoto4.java */
Chunk chunk = new Chunk("Quick brown fox jumps over the lazy dog.");
chunk.setAction(new PdfAction("http://en.wikipedia.org/wiki/
  ➥ The_quick_brown_fox_jumps_over_the_lazy_dog"));
document.add(chunk);
```

The results of FoxDogAnchor1, FoxDogGoto1, and FoxDogGoto4 look identical. Once you start learning about the `PdfAction` class in chapter 13, you'll see that method `setAction()` opens lots of other interesting possibilities.

You've learned (almost) all about the standard `Chunk` functionality. If you're looking to add a circle around a `Chunk` or to strike through a word diagonally, you won't find a specific method in iText to achieve this. This doesn't mean it's impossible; you just need to write custom functionality.

## 4.6 Generic Chunk functionality

Chapters 10 and 11 will explain how to draw a circle or a diagonal line at an absolute position on a page. In chapter 14, you'll learn about page events, which let you retrieve the page coordinates of `Chunks`, `Paragraphs`, `Chapters`, and `Sections`. For instance, by implementing the page event method `onParagraphEnd()`, you can draw a line under every paragraph (if that's one of your requirements).

For now, we'll preview this functionality by looking at the `onGenericTag()` method. First, you'll tag some chunks that need a special background or that need to be marked in some special way. Then, you'll count the occurrence of some tagged chunks. Finally, you'll tag a number of chunks so that you can create an index with references to the page numbers where these chunks occur.

### 4.6.1 Drawing custom backgrounds and lines

You've used specific `Chunk` methods, such as `setUnderline()` and `setBackground()`, to draw lines and rectangles. Suppose you want to draw an ellipse around a word. In that case, you could add an extra ellipse method to the `Chunk` class; but then you'd end up with lots of custom methods, most of which are hardly ever used. You should use generic functionality instead.

This generic functionality is available through page events. For the moment, you're only interested in generic `Chunk` events. Instead of implementing every method of the `PdfPageEvent`, you'll extend the helper class `PdfPageEventhelper` and implement only one method:

```
/* chapter04/FoxDogGeneric1.java */
public class FoxDogGeneric1 extends PdfPageEventHelper {
  public void onGenericTag(PdfWriter writer, Document document,
    Rectangle rect, String text) {
      if ("ellipse".equals(text)) {
        PdfContentByte cb = writer.getDirectContent();
        cb.setRGBColorStroke(0xFF, 0x00, 0x00);
        cb.ellipse(rect.left(), rect.bottom() - 5f,
          rect.right(), rect.top());
        cb.stroke();
        cb.resetRGBColorStroke();
      }
      else if ("box".equals(text)) {
```

```
            PdfContentByte cb = writer.getDirectContentUnder();
            rect.setBackgroundColor(new Color(0xa5, 0x2a, 0x2a));
            cb.rectangle(rect);
        }
    }
}
```

After you create a `PdfWriter` object, you have to declare this event to the writer.

```
/* chapter04/FoxDogGeneric1.java */
PdfWriter writer = PdfWriter.getInstance(document,
  new FileOutputStream("fox_dog_generic1.pdf"));
writer.setPageEvent(new FoxDogGeneric1());
```

Now the method `onGenericTag()` is called by the PDF-generating process every time a tagged `Chunk` is written to the `PdfWriter`. In the example, the word *fox* is put in a box, and an ellipse is drawn around the word *dog*:

```
/* chapter04/FoxDogGeneric1.java */
Paragraph p = new Paragraph();
Chunk fox = new Chunk("Quick brown fox");
fox.setGenericTag("box");
p.add(fox);
p.add(" jumps over ");
Chunk dog = new Chunk("the lazy dog.");
dog.setGenericTag("ellipse");
p.add(dog);
document.add(p);
```

It's important to understand that this event isn't necessarily triggered immediately after the `Chunk` object is added to the document. The only thing you can be sure of is that `onGenericTag()` will be called once the current page is full and a new page is started. This is important because you can use this generic functionality for a number of other interesting applications, as you'll see in the next section.

### 4.6.2 Implementing custom functionality

Suppose you want to write a screenplay about a fox and a dog. For convenience, you can write some helper code that constructs a `Paragraph` displaying the speaker in bold and the text line in a normal font:

```
/* chapter04/FoxDogGeneric2.java */
private static Paragraph getLine(String speaker, String line) {
  Paragraph p = new Paragraph(18);
  Chunk s = new Chunk(speaker + ": ", SPEAKER);
  s.setGenericTag(speaker);
  p.add(s);
  p.add(line);
  return p;
}
```

Now you can write your screenplay like this:

```
/* chapter04/FoxDogGeneric2.java */
document.add(getLine("Fox", "Hello lazy dog."));
document.add(getLine("Dog", "Hello quick brown fox."));
document.add(getLine("Fox", "I want to jump over you."));
document.add(getLine("Dog", "No problem. Go ahead!"));
```

Because you added a generic tag to the speaker `Chunk`, you can count how many lines each actor has:

```
/* chapter04/FoxDogGeneric2.java */
public void onGenericTag(PdfWriter writer, Document document,
  Rectangle rect, String text) {
  Integer count = (Integer) lines.get(text);
  if (count == null) lines.put(text, new Integer(1));
  else lines.put(text, new Integer(count.intValue() + 1));
}
```

Afterward, you can ask the `FoxDogGeneric2` class for the `lines HashMap`, which is defined as a member variable. Remember that the information gathered in the generic tag event is correct only after a `newPage` is invoked on the document. If you try to retrieve the `lines HashMap` earlier, some `Chunks` may not have been written to the `PdfWriter` yet.

If you write implementations of the `PdfPageEvents` interface that can be useful in a broader context, please post them on the mailing list. Maybe they can be bundled in one of the next iText releases, as was the case with the event class in the next section.

### 4.6.3 Building an index

If the previous example inspired you to write a class that builds an index, I have to disappoint you. Another iText developer already had that idea and he contributed the class `IndexEvents`.

In most books, you can find an index at the end. It's a list with the major terms discussed in the book, along with the page numbers on which those discussions can be found. A more detailed index also contains subentries and references to other terms. A good index is an organized map of the contents of the book that helps readers find the information they need. The `IndexEvents` class is able to create an index that is three levels deep. Figure 4.13 gives you an idea: If you look for the word *Yellow*, you see it's a color and that you should also look at the index entry *Color*, where you'll find other colors that might interest you.

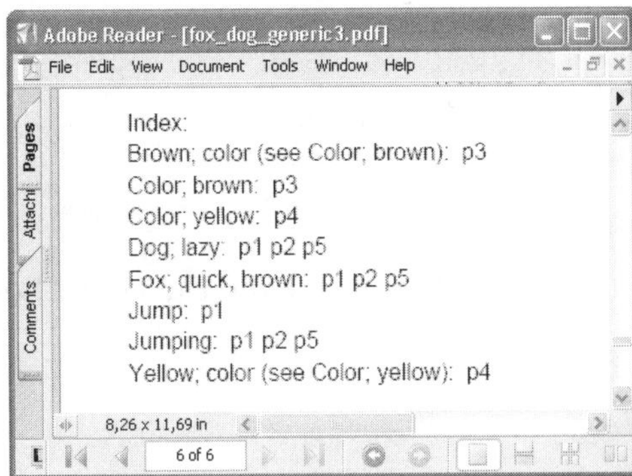


**Figure 4.13**
**An index generated with the `IndexEvents` class**

The following code snippet shows how the content of the index was gathered:

```
/* chapter04/FoxDogGeneric3.java */
PdfWriter writer = PdfWriter.getInstance(document,
  new FileOutputStream("fox_dog_generic3.pdf"));
IndexEvents index = new IndexEvents();                    ❶
writer.setPageEvent(index);
Paragraph p = new Paragraph("Quick brown fox ");
p.add(index.create("jumps", "Jump"));              <-❷
p.add(" over the lazy dog.");
document.add(p);
p = new Paragraph(
  index.create("Quick brown fox", "Fox", "quick, brown"));   <-❸
p.add(new Chunk(" jumps over "));
p.add(index.create("the lazy dog.", "Dog", "lazy"));   <-❹
document.add(p);
Paragraph p = new Paragraph(new Chunk("The fox is "));
p.add(index.create("brown", "Color", "brown"));   <-❺
p.add(index.create(" ", "Brown", "color", "see Color; brown"));   <-❻
```

First you create an instance of `IndexEvents` ❶. The `create` method of this class returns a `Chunk` and keeps a register of keywords. In ❷ the chunk with content *jumps* is created and a single keyword (*Jump*) is registered. This keyword will refer to the page where the word *jumps* was added. Internally, the `onGenericTag()` method was used to achieve this.

You can also create index entries that are two levels deep: For example, the keyword *Fox* with the specification *quick, brown* refers to the `Chunk` containing *Quick brown fox* ❸. Other keywords and specifications such as *Dog; lazy* ❹ and *Color; brown* ❺ are added. The maximum number of levels is three: In ❻, you're creating an empty `Chunk` with a keyword and specification *Brown, color,* but you also add some extra information that can be useful in your index: *see Color;*

*brown*. If people look for the word *Color* in your index, you can refer them to the word *Brown*.

The information in the `IndexEvents` class is sorted by keyword and stored as a `List` of `IndexEvents.Entry` objects. You can write your index like this:

```
/* chapter04/FoxDogGeneric3.java */
document.add(new Paragraph("Index:"));
List list = index.getSortedEntries();
for (int i = 0, n = list.size(); i < n; i++) {
  IndexEvents.Entry entry = (IndexEvents.Entry) list.get(i);
  Paragraph in = new Paragraph();
  in.add(new Chunk(entry.getIn1()));
  if (entry.getIn2().length() > 0) {
    in.add(new Chunk("; " + entry.getIn2()));
  }
  if (entry.getIn3().length() > 0) {
    in.add(new Chunk(" (" + entry.getIn3() + ")"));
  }
  in.add(": ");
  List pages = entry.getPagenumbers();    <-2
  List tags = entry.getTags();    <-3
  for (int p = 0, x = pages.size(); p < x; p++) {
    Chunk pagenr = new Chunk(" p" + pages.get(p));
    pagenr.setLocalGoto((String) tags.get(p));
    in.add(pagenr);
  }
  document.add(in);
}
```

As you can see, you construct strings like *Yellow; color (See Color; Yellow)* by concatenating the different parts of the entry in a paragraph ❶. Then, you retrieve not only the page numbers ❷ but also the tags that were added to the `Chunk` as local destinations ❸ (the `Chunks` are wrapped in an `Anchor`; remember that this is the PDF equivalent of the HTML tag and attribute `<A NAME="tag">`).

By using the local Goto functionality discussed in section 4.5.2, you make the page numbers clickable ❹. By clicking a page number in the index file, you can now jump directly to the place where the referenced word is mentioned.

You can also add custom functionality to paragraphs, chapters, and sections, but we'll cover that in chapter 14. It's high time we help Laura with her first assignment.

## 4.7 Making a flyer (part 1)

In chapter 1, you read that Laura wants to make a flyer introducing the new Department of Computer Science and Engineering. Figure 4.14 shows the HTML

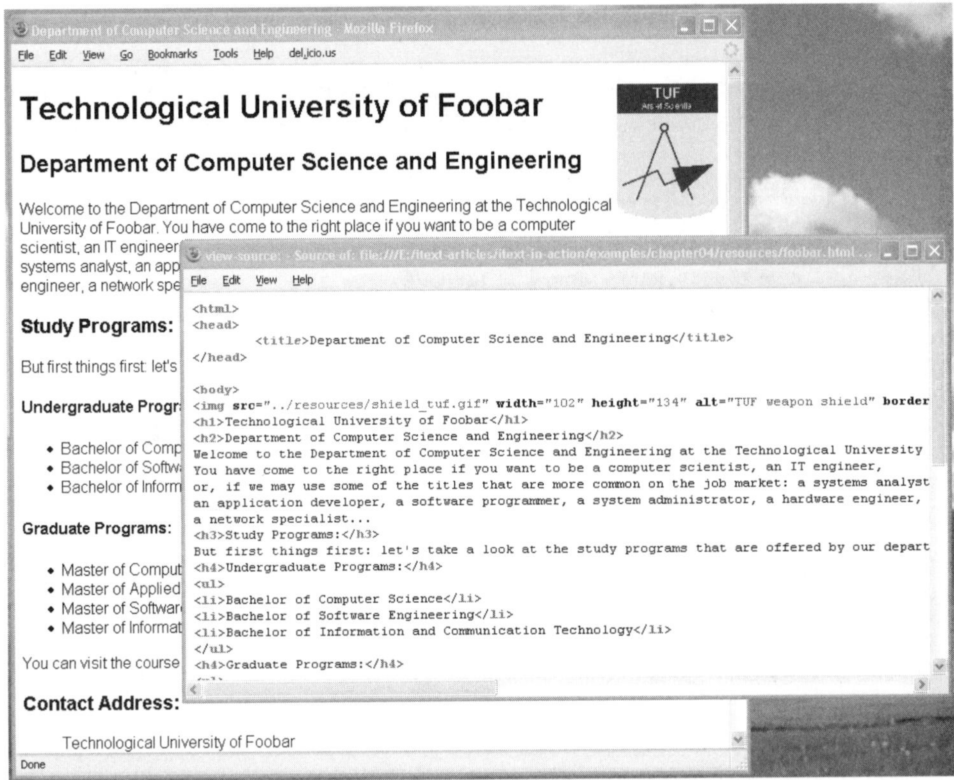


**Figure 4.14 The HTML version of the flyer**

code Laura has written, as well as what this code looks like when rendered in a browser (that's how the PDF page should look). Throughout this chapter, I've covered almost all the elements needed to generate this page in PDF. Only the image functionality is missing. The `H1`, `H2`, and `H3` tags correspond with `Paragraphs`; the `A` tag with an `Anchor`; and the `UL` and `OL` tags with `Lists`. All the text between two tags can be wrapped in `Chunks`.

Maybe you can help Laura to translate the HTML tags she used into iText's basic building blocks. Before you begin, I should tell you that you won't write a full-blown HTML2PDF parser. Chapter 14 will explain that there are better tools if you want to convert HTML to PDF.

For demonstration purposes only, you'll write an extension for the class `org.xml.sax.ContentHandler` and parse the HTML with the Simple API for XML (SAX). Note that you'll need some knowledge of SAX to understand this example. You'll override the `characters()` method of the SAX handler and create a `Chunk` object (`currentChunk`) that contains all the characters between an open and close tag.

You'll also create a `java.util.Stack` object (`stack`), to which you'll add a basic building block every time an open or close tag is encountered. The following code sample shows how to implement the `startElement()` method:

```
/* chapter04/FoobarFlyer.java */
public void startElement(
  String uri, String localName, String qName,
  Attributes attributes) throws SAXException {
  try {
    if (document.isOpen()) {
      updateStack();
      for (int i = 0; i < 6; i++) {
        if (HtmlTags.H[i].equals(qName)) {
          flushStack();
          stack.push(new Paragraph(Float.NaN, "",
            new Font(Font.HELVETICA, FONTSIZES[i], Font.UNDEFINED,       1
            new CMYKColor(0.9f, 0.7f, 0.4f, 0.1f))));
        }
        return;
      }
      if ("blockquote".equals(qName)) {
        flushStack();
        Paragraph p = new Paragraph();
        p.setIndentationLeft(50);                                        2
        p.setIndentationRight(20);
        stack.push(p);
      }
      else if (HtmlTags.ANCHOR.equals(qName)) {
        Anchor anchor = new Anchor("", new Font(
          Font.HELVETICA, Font.UNDEFINED, Font.UNDEFINED,
          new CMYKColor(0.9f, 0.7f, 0.4f, 0.1f)));                       3
        anchor.setReference(attributes.getValue(HtmlTags.REFERENCE));
        stack.push(anchor);
      }
      else if (HtmlTags.ORDEREDLIST.equals(qName)) {
        stack.push(new List(List.ORDERED, 10));                          4
      }
      else if (HtmlTags.UNORDEREDLIST.equals(qName)) {
        stack.push(new List(false, 10));                                 5
      }
      else if (HtmlTags.LISTITEM.equals(qName)) {
        stack.push(new ListItem());                                      6
      }
      else if (HtmlTags.IMAGE.equals(qName)) {
        handleImage(attributes);                                         7
      }
```

```
      }
      else if (HtmlTags.BODY.equals(qName)) {
        document.open();
      }
    } catch (Exception e) {
      e.printStackTrace();
    }
  }
```

Here's what happens in this code snippet:

1. Map h1, h2, h3, h4, h5, and h6 to a Paragraph.
2. Map blockquote to an indented Paragraph.
3. Map the <a> tag to an Anchor.
4. Map ol to an ordered List.
5. Map ul to an unordered List.
6. Map li to a ListItem.
7. The next chapter will deal with img.
8. The <body> tag opens the document.

The method handleImage() isn't implemented yet; it's just some empty braces. We'll deal with it in the next chapter. When looking at this code, you see a lot of common HTML tags and attributes are missing. You didn't implement the name attribute of an <a> tag, add support for different list symbols, and so forth, but I hope you get the general idea: Every time you encounter a starting tag, you add an element—specifically, an implementation of the TextElementArray interface—to the stack.

These objects don't have any content when they're created, but you provide a method updateStack() that regularly adds the currentChunk to the object on top of the stack. The method flushStack() determines whether the elements on top of the stack can be processed.

For example, when the end tag of a list item is encountered, it can be removed from the stack in order to add it to the list that is the next object on the stack. This is what happens in the implementation of the endElement() method:

```
/* chapter04/FoobarFlyer.java */
public void endElement(String uri, String localName, String qName)
  throws SAXException {
  try {
    if (document.isOpen()) {
      updateStack();
      for (int i = 0; i < 6; i++) {
        if (HtmlTags.H[i].equals(qName)) {
          flushStack();
```

```
            return;
          }
        }
        if ("blockquote".equals(qName) ||
          HtmlTags.ORDEREDLIST.equals(qName) ||
          HtmlTags.UNORDEREDLIST.equals(qName)) {
          flushStack();
        }
        else if (HtmlTags.NEWLINE.equals(qName)) {
          currentChunk = Chunk.NEWLINE;
          updateStack();
        }
        else if (HtmlTags.LISTITEM.equals(qName)) {
          ListItem listItem = (ListItem) stack.pop();
          List list = (List) stack.pop();
          list.add(listItem);
          stack.push(list);
        }
        else if (HtmlTags.ANCHOR.equals(qName)) {
          Anchor anchor = (Anchor) stack.pop();
          try {
            TextElementArray previous = (TextElementArray) stack.pop();
            previous.add(anchor);
            stack.push(previous);
          } catch (EmptyStackException es) {
            document.add(anchor);
          }
        }
        else if (HtmlTags.HTML.equals(qName)) {
          flushStack();
          document.close();
        }
      }
      else {
        if (HtmlTags.TITLE.equals(qName)) {
          document.addTitle(currentChunk.content().trim());
        }
        currentChunk = null;
      }
    } catch (Exception e) {
      e.printStackTrace();
    }
  }
```

You can use this custom SAX content handler to parse Laura's HTML file; as a result, you get a PDF file that looks like the screenshot shown in figure 4.15.

Figure 4.15 is already close to the expected result as shown in figure 1.2. The only thing that's missing is the image with the logo of the university.

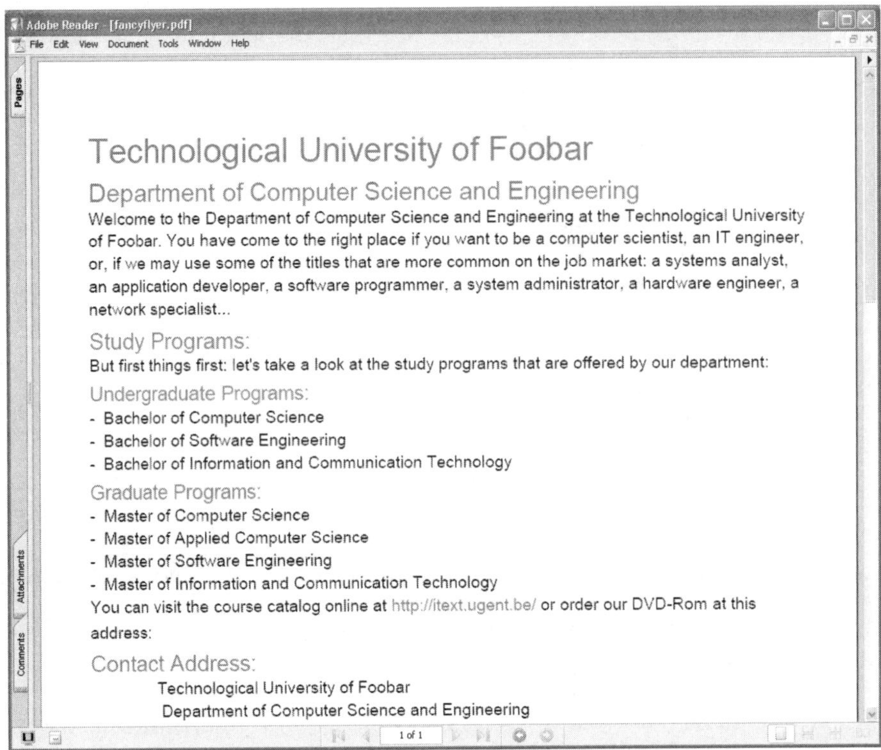


**Figure 4.15 Making a flyer**

## 4.8 Summary

This chapter started with some basic examples. You were introduced to objects such as `Chunk`, `Phrase`, and `Paragraph`. These were designed to make it easy to add straightforward text to a PDF document. In the second section, we added some complexity: We introduced the classes `Anchor`, `List/ListItem`, and `Chapter/Section`.

After this introduction, we questioned some issues that seemed obvious at first—for instance, skipping to the next line—and you saw that there is much more to it than you would think at first sight. You also employed functionality that will be explained when we get to the core of iText: how to navigate through a document using different Goto options, creating generic behavior for `Chunks`, and so forth.

Finally, you helped Laura with her first assignment, but you need to know more about images to complete it. That's what we'll do in the next chapter.

# 5 Inserting images

**This chapter covers**

- Image types supported in iText
- `com.lowagie.text.Image` vs. `java.awt.Image`
- `Image` properties

In the previous chapter, we talked about this quick brown fox jumping over that lazy dog. To take a quote from David Lynch's movie *Wild at Heart*, "Mentally you picture my dog, but I haven't told you the type of dog which I have. Perhaps you even picture Toto, from the 'Wizard of Oz.'" That's definitely not the kind of dog I'm thinking of. Wouldn't it be nice if you could add a picture of a specific fox and a specific dog in the document? If so, what types of images does iText support? Those and other questions will be answered in this chapter.

iText supports a range of standard image types and adds some extra types that are Java or iText specific. You'll work with the `java.awt.Image` class and with raw image data (bytes), and we'll briefly talk about barcodes. Note that you'll find an exhaustive overview of the barcodes supported by iText in appendix B.

Let's start with the standard types: BMP, EPS, GIF, JPEG, PNG, TIFF, and WMF.

## 5.1 Standard image types

Table 5.1 lists the standard image types that are supported by the `Image` class and indicates which format is best to use in which context. For instance, JPG is a better format for photographs than GIF. GIF is better for charts than JPG.

**Table 5.1 Standard image types supported by `com.lowagie.text.Image`**

| Image type | Description |
|---|---|
| BMP | [Windows bitmap] BMP is a common form of bitmap file in Microsoft Windows. It's poorly supported by other operating systems and has limited support for color. |
| EPS | [Encapsulated PostScript] This is a graphics format that describes an image in the PostScript language. It isn't fully supported by iText. It works with only some EPS files; it may or may not work with your EPS files. |
| GIF | [Graphic Interchange Format] GIF is a common format for image files and is especially suitable for images containing large areas of the same color. GIF format files of simple images are often smaller than the same files would be if stored in JPEG format, but GIF format doesn't store photographic images as well as JPEG. |
| JPEG/JPG | [Joint Photographic Experts Group] JPEG or JPG is commonly used to refer to a lossy compression technique, reducing the size of a graphic file by as much as 96%. Usually this is the best file format for photographs on the Web. |
| PNG | [Portable Network Graphics] This graphics format was designed as the successor to GIF. It features compression, transparency, and progressive loading, like GIF. |
| TIFF | [Tagged Image File Format] The TIFF file format is commonly used for digital scanned images. |

*continued on next page*

**Table 5.1 Standard image types supported by `com.lowagie.text.Image` *(continued)***

| Image type | Description |
|---|---|
| WMF | [Windows Metafile Format] WMF is a vector graphics format for Windows-compatible computers, used mostly for word-processing clip art. |

iText has (a) separate class(es) for (almost) each type that is supported (see also section A.4). Fortunately, you don't need to be acquainted with all these different classes; you only need to know about the superclass from which most of them are derived: `com.lowagie.text.Image`.

`Image` is an *abstract* class; you can't construct an instance directly. Instead, you use one of the many static `Image.getInstance()` methods that return an instance of a specific image implementation. This approach is handy if you want to add an image to a PDF document without knowing its type in advance. You don't need to examine an image in order to choose one of the iText classes that deals with some specific type. The `getInstance()` method takes care of this.

Let's start by creating an `Image` object using files of each of the types listed in table 5.1.

### 5.1.1 BMP, EPS, GIF, JPEG, PNG, TIFF, and WMF

I made a picture of a quick brown fox and a lazy dog and converted it to BMP, GIF, JPEG, PNG, TIFF, and WMF. I also added an EPS file of a tiger. Adding images of these types to a document is easy:

```
/* chapter05/FoxDogImageTypes.java */
Image img1 = Image.getInstance("foxdog.jpg");
Document.add(img1);
Image img2 = Image.getInstance("foxdog.gif");
Document.add(img2);
Image img3 = Image.getInstance("foxdog.png");
Document.add(img3);
Image img4 = Image.getInstance("foxdog.tiff");
Document.add(img4);
Image img5 = Image.getInstance("foxdog.wmf");
Document.add(img5);
Image img6 = Image.getInstance("foxdog.bmp");
Document.add(img6);
Image img7 = Image.getInstance("tiger.eps");
Document.add(img7);
```

Figure 5.1 shows what part of the first page generated by the example looks like.

**Figure 5.1 Document with examples of different standard image types**

In the example, I wrote the classname of the seven different images to `System.out`. You'll see that the type of image doesn't always correspond with the iText class you would expect. GIF files, for instance are managed with the class `com.lowagie.text.pdf.codec.GifImage`, but this class isn't derived from `com.lowagie.text.Image`.

The image class returned by `GifImage` is of type `com.lowagie.text.ImgRaw`. This isn't unusual; we'll return to the GIF example and then talk more about `ImgRaw` in the next subsection.

**FAQ** *Why do I get an exception when I try to add an EPS file?* For the moment, iText offers only basic support for EPS. If you have a simple logo in EPS, iText will probably accept it, but iText can't handle all EPS files. You'll have to convert them to another image format before adding them.

One important image type is missing in the standard list of images. You can also use iText to convert a Scalable Vector Graphics (SVG) file to PDF. Chapter 12 will explain how to combine iText and Apache Batik to parse an SVG file (which is an image represented in XML).

Two types mentioned in table 5.1 can contain more than one image. `Image.getInstance()` fetches only the first image. You need other objects and methods to fetch all the pages or frames.

### 5.1.2 TIFF with multiple pages

A TIFF file can contain multiple pages. You can read the TIFF into a `RandomAccessFileOrArray` object ❶, get the number of images (or pages) ❷, and extract the images one by one ❸.

```
/* chapter05/FoxDogMultipageTiff */
RandomAccessFileOrArray ra =
  new RandomAccessFileOrArray("foxdog_multiplepages.tif");   <-❶
int pages = TiffImage.getNumberOfPages(ra);   <-❷
for (int i = 0; i < pages; ) {
  ++i;
  document.add(TiffImage.getTiffImage(ra, i));   <-❸
}
```

TIFF files are common in desktop publishing, faxing, and medical-imaging applications. The iText toolbox provides some useful tools to convert TIFF to PDF.

**TOOLBOX** `com.lowagie.tools.plugins.Tiff2Pdf` *(Convert2Pdf)* This tool allows you to copy a TIFF file into an A4 or Letter PDF file. You can also create a PDF file that keeps the original dimensions of every page in the TIFF.

`com.lowagie.tools.plugins.KnitTiff` *(Convert2Pdf)* TIFF is also a common format for scanned images. When you're scanning, it's often easier to scan the odd pages of a bundle of recto-verso (paper) pages first, followed by the even pages. Unfortunately, you end up with one TIFF that has pages 1, 3, 5… and another TIFF with pages 2, 4…. KnitTiff lets you knit both files together into one PDF document with pages 1, 2, 3, 4….

Multiple GIF images can be packaged into one animated GIF file; but we don't talk of *pages* in this context, because the purpose of these different images is to create an animation.

### 5.1.3 Animated GIFs

In an animated GIF, the animation is created by displaying the different images one after another with a user-defined interval. Animated GIFs aren't supported in

PDF. When an `Image` instance is constructed with an animated GIF, only the first frame of the animation is imported—the animation is lost.

This doesn't mean you can't extract the other images from the combined GIF file. You can create a `GifImage` ❶ and ask it for the number of frames ❷ and extract each specific frame as an `Image` object ❸—more specifically, an `ImgRaw` object.

```
/* chapter05/FoxDogAnimatedGif.java */
GifImage img = new GifImage("animated_fox_dog.gif");;    <-❶
int frames = img.getFrameCount();;    <-❷
for (int i = 0; i < frames; ) {
  ++i;
  document.add(img.getImage(i));;    <-❸
}
```

This is similar to what you've done with TIFF files, but the terminology is different; `getFrameCount()` refers to the fact that you're making a simple movie using a limited set of frames. If you want to add a moving picture, you don't need the `Image` class. Media clips (video and/or sound) are added using annotations (see chapter 15).

In addition to the iText-specific `Image` class, there's also the standard Java class in the AWT package: `java.awt.Image`.

## 5.2 Working with java.awt.Image

You have to pay attention not to confuse the iText object `com.lowagie.text.Image` with the standard Java image class `java.awt.Image`. If you're using both classes in the same source file, you must use the full classname to avoid ambiguity and compile errors.

In figure 5.2, an iText `Image` is constructed using an AWT `Image`.

This is how it's done:

```
/* chapter05/HitchcockAwtImage.java */
java.awt.Image awtImage =
  Toolkit.getDefaultToolkit().createImage("hitchcock.gif");    // Create java.awt.Image from file
com.lowagie.text.Image img1 =
  com.lowagie.text.Image.getInstance(awtImage, null);    // Create iText Image (transparency preserved)
com.lowagie.text.Image img2 =
  com.lowagie.text.Image.getInstance(awtImage, null, true);    // Create iText image (black and white)
com.lowagie.text.Image img3 =
com.lowagie.text.Image.getInstance(awtImage,
  new Color(0xFF, 0xFF, 0x00));    // Create iText image (yellow background)
com.lowagie.text.Image img4 =
com.lowagie.text.Image.getInstance(awtImage,
  new Color(0xFF, 0xFF, 0x00), true);    // Create iText image (black and white)
```

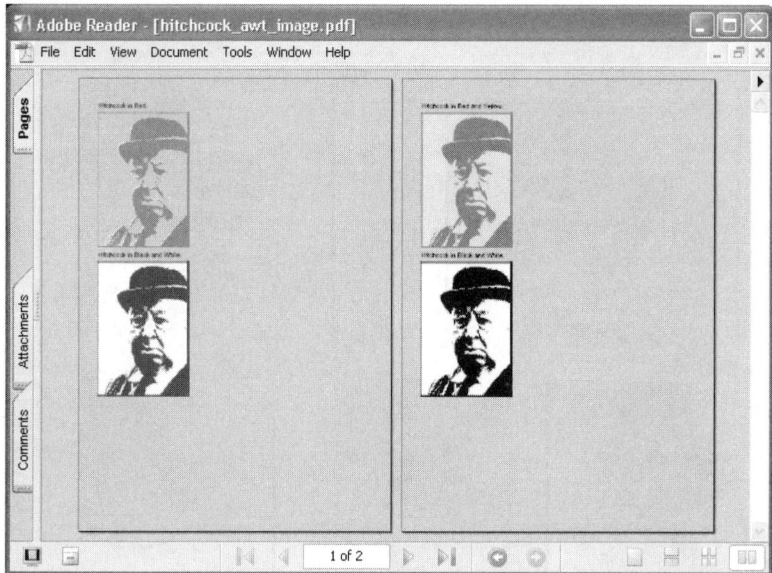


**Figure 5.2 com.lowagie.text.Image and java.awt.Image**

Remember that if you're working on a UNIX/Linux system, you may experience the same problem as mentioned in the FAQ entry about solving X problems in section 2.2.4. You're creating an image with the `java.awt.Toolkit`, so you need an X Server. Note that the other `getInstance()` methods of class `com.lowagie.text.Image` didn't need real X functionality.

One of the big disadvantages of constructing a `com.lowagie.text.Image` using a `java.awt.Image` is the fact that the image is added pixel per pixel. Figure 5.3 show five different PDF files to which this image was added.

The image added to the PDF files shown in figure 5.3 is a 16 KB PNG. When the image is added with the `getInstance()` method used in the previous section, the size of the resulting PDF is 17 KB; this is the upper-left PDF in the screenshot. When the image is added with the method discussed in this section using `java.awt.Image`, the file size is almost 19 KB; this is the upper-right PDF. Although both PDF files look identical, there is a little overhead because the image was added pixel per pixel.

You can convert the `java.awt.Image` to a JPG file by using a different method that also lets you define the quality of the conversion. The three lower PDFs are created like this:

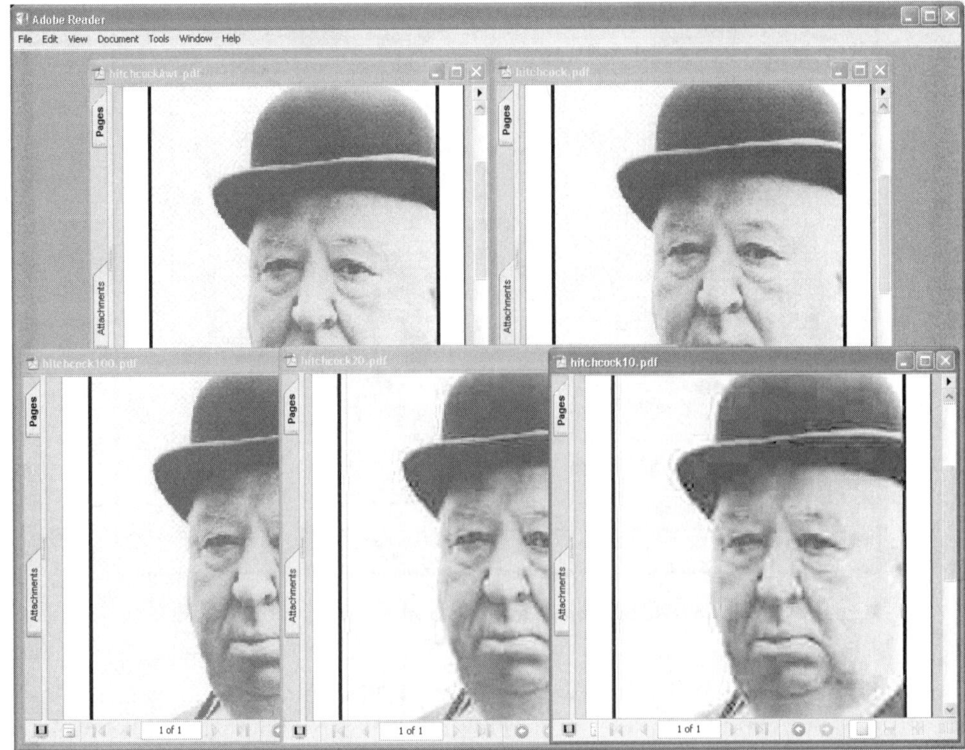


**Figure 5.3 Different ways to add a java.awt.Image**

```
/* chapter05/HitchcockAwt.java */
Document document = new Document(new Rectangle(200, 280));
try {
  PdfWriter writer = PdfWriter.getInstance(document,
    new FileOutputStream("hitchcock20.pdf"));
  document.open();
  img = Image.getInstance(writer, awtImage, 0.2f);
  img.setAbsolutePosition(15, 15);
  document.add(img);
} catch (Exception e) {
  System.err.println(e.getMessage());
}
document.close();
```

This leads to some surprising results. By using this special image constructor, you add the image to the document compressed as a JPG. The quality of the conversion is expressed as a value between 0 (0 percent) and 1 (100 percent). In the screenshot, the quality of the images seen from left to right is 100 percent (file size 35 KB), 20 percent (6 KB), and 10 percent (4 KB).

Observe that the size of the PDF has increased due to the conversion of the image from PNG to a JPG with a quality of 100 percent. Reducing the quality (for instance to 10 percent) may lead to unacceptable results, but for this example there's not that much difference if you compare the image added with a quality of 20 percent and the one with a quality of 100 percent. This can be an interesting way to reduce the final file size if you're creating a document with lots of high-resolution photographs.

We've been constructing images read from files; and we've been constructing images wrapped in the `java.awt.Image` object. Another common way is to construct an image using a byte array retrieved from a database.

## 5.3 Byte arrays with image data

An image can be stored as a Binary Large Object (BLOB) in your database. You could retrieve the image from the database, store it somewhere on the file system, and call it using its path, but that isn't efficient. Performance-wise, it's better to create a `com.lowagie.text.Image` object from memory using the `byte` array with the image data retrieved from the database directly.

Figure 5.4 shows a PDF with two images. The first image was read from a file into a byte array, and the `Image` object was constructed by passing this array to the `Image.getInstance()` method:

```
/* chapter05/FoxDogRawImage.java */
RandomAccessFile rf = new RandomAccessFile("foxdog.jpg", "r");
int size = (int)rf.length();
byte imagedata[] = new byte[size];
rf.readFully(imagedata);
rf.close();
Image img1 = Image.getInstance(imagedata);
```

The `Image` class reads the raw data and, in this case, detects the JPG header. It knows it should return an instance of class `com.lowagie.text.Jpeg`.

The second image in figure 5.4 wasn't read from a file, nor was it stored in a database. The image data was constructed on the fly using an algorithm that generates raw image bytes. The `getInstance()` method returns an image of type `com.lowagie.text.ImgRaw`.

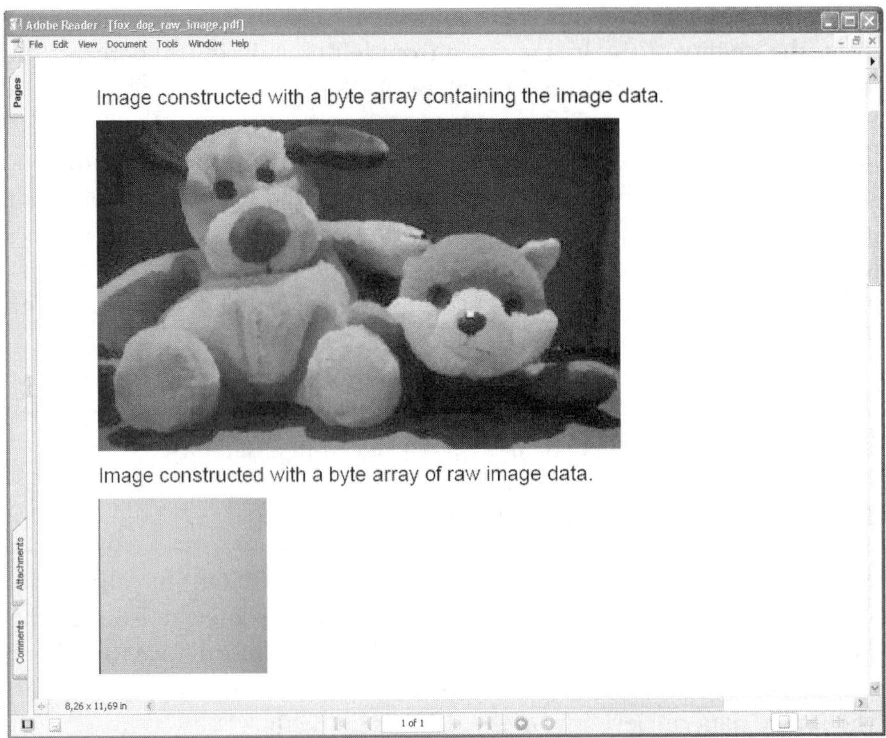


**Figure 5.4 A PDF with images constructed using the raw image data**

### 5.3.1 Raw image data

Sometimes, you need to create an image on the fly. In section 5.4.3, for instance, you'll construct a black-and-white image (an image with one component) that acts as a mask to cover part of another image.

Suppose you want to create an image with three components that measures 100 x 100 pixels. You can define the color of every pixel with three bytes: one for the red value, one for the green value, and one for the blue value. The size of the byte array with the image data will be 30,000: 100 pixels x 100 pixels x 3 components.

To get the effect demonstrated in the lower image in figure 5.2, you use a mathematical algorithm as follows:

```
/* chapter05/FoxDogRawImage.java */
byte data[] = new byte[100*100*3];
for (int k = 0; k < 100; ++k) {
  for (int j = 0; j < 300; j += 3) {
```

```
        data[k * 300 + j] =
          (byte)(255 * Math.sin(j * .5 * Math.PI / 300));
        data[k * 300 + j + 1] =
          (byte)(256 - j * 256 / 300);
        data[k * 300 + j + 2] =
          (byte)(255 * Math.cos(k * .5 * Math.PI / 100));
      }
    }
    Image img2 = Image.getInstance(100, 100, 3, 8, data);
```

As you can see, this example doesn't use the `ImgRaw` constructor. It composes the image manually without any standard image header. The `Image` object can't recognize its type, as well as some other properties such as the image size. You only pass an array of red, green, and blue values. You need to pass more information to the `Image` class with the `getInstance()` method—the width and the height (100 x 100), the number of components (the three colors), and the number of bits per component (you use a byte, and 1 byte is 8 bits). You can also add an `int` array to define a transparency value: The length of this array needs to be two times the number of components.

Another suite of images type you may be generating using an algorithm is defined in the CCITT standard.

## 5.3.2 *CCITT compressed images*

CCITT stands for Comité Consultatif International Téléphonique et Télégraphique, a standards organization that is now part of the International Telecommunication Union (ITU). This organization is responsible for defining many of the standards for data communications. PDF supports Group 3 and Group 4 compression, which are facsimile (fax) standards (until now, you've only worked with flate compression; see section 2.2.3). With iText, you can insert CCITT-encoded images using this method:

```
Image.getInstance(int width, int height,
  boolean reverseBits, int typeCCITT, int parameters, byte[] data)
```

The `reverseBits` parameter indicates whether the bits need to be swapped (bit 7 swapped with bit 0, and so on). The type can be `Element.CCITTG31D`, `Element.CCITTG32D`, or `Element.CCITT4`.

The parameters associated with the stream can be (a combination of) the following values:

- `Element.CCITT_BLACKIS1`—A flag indicating whether 1 bits are to be interpreted as black pixels and 0 bits as white pixels

- `Element.CCITT_ENCODEDBYTEALIGN`—A flag indicating whether the filter expects extra 0 bits before each encoded line so that the line begins on a byte boundary
- `Element.CCITT_ENDOFLINE`—A flag indicating whether end-of-line bit patterns are required to be present in the encoding
- `Element.CCITT_ENDOFBLOCK`—A flag indicating whether the filter expects the encoded data to be terminated by an end-of-block pattern

The CCITT protocols described in this section are used to send a document as an image from one fax to another. You could use iText to import a stream received from your fax server into a PDF file.

In iText CCITT is also used to construct images that need to be read by a machine, such as a two-dimensional barcode.

### 5.3.3 *Creating barcodes*

You may not look at barcodes as images, but in iText it's common to add a barcode to a document as an instance of the `Image` object. The purpose of a barcode is to encode a string of characters as a sequence of spaces and bars so that it's machine-readable. Barcodes are used wherever physical objects need to be tagged with information that is to be processed by computers. An operator can use a barcode reader to enter the information instead of typing the strings of data into a terminal. Fully automated processes can use barcodes—for instance, to ship packages by postal services.

The different barcode classes are presented in section A.5. The following code snippet shows how to add an `Image` object with a Barcode 3 of 9 representing the text "ITEXT IN ACTION":

```
/* chapter05/Barcodes.java */
document.add(new Paragraph("Barcode 3 of 9"));
Barcode39 code39 = new Barcode39();
code39.setCode("ITEXT IN ACTION");
document.add(code39.createImageWithBarcode(cb, null, null));
```

If you want to know when and where to use the different types of barcodes and how to create them using iText, you'll find all the information you need in appendix B. You'll also see how to get the barcode as a `java.awt.Image` or a `PdfTemplate` object.

Any `PdfTemplate` object can be wrapped in an `Image` class, as you'll see next.

### 5.3.4 Working with com.lowagie.text.pdf.PdfTemplate

When you took the crash course on PDF manipulation, I did a little trick with the `Image` class and an imported page to create a thumbnail of an existing page:

```
/* chapter02/HelloWorldImportedPages.java */
PdfImportedPage page = writer.getImportedPage(reader, 1);
Image image = Image.getInstance(page);
```

I told you `PdfImportedPage` is a subclass of `PdfTemplate`. `PdfTemplate` is like a canvas. In chapter 10, you'll learn about the transformation matrix, and the parameters needed to position a `PdfTemplate`. If you want to avoid doing math, it can be useful to wrap such a template in an `Image` so that you can more easily change its properties, such as its width, its height, and its absolute position.

## 5.4 Setting image properties

In the previous sections, you've been adding images to the document at the current pointer in the page, in its original size, with the default (left) alignment. In this section, you'll change these defaults, and you'll also deal with image positioning, rotation, and scaling.

### 5.4.1 Adding images to the document

With some minor changes, you can have the image aligned to the right or in the middle (horizontally):

```
/* chapter05/FoxDogImageAlignment.java */
Image img1 = Image.getInstance("foxdog.jpg");
img1.setAlignment(Image.ALIGN_LEFT);
Image img2 = Image.getInstance("foxdog.gif");
img2.setAlignment(Image.ALIGN_MIDDLE);
Image img3 = Image.getInstance("foxdog.png");
img3.setAlignment(Image.ALIGN_RIGHT);
```

This example also adds some text to see what happens when an image is added. The image aligned to the left starts on a new line. The images added in the middle and right start on the same line as the text, because there is sufficient space to begin with the image. Text that comes after the image is added on a new line.

#### Alignment and wrapping

You can change this behavior by adding extra alignment properties, such as `Image.TEXTWRAP` and `Image.UNDERLYING`.

Using the first constant indicates that you want iText to try to wrap the text around the image. The second constant tells iText not to bother about wrapping; the image will be added under the text:

```
/* chapter05/FoxDogImageWrapping.java */
Phrase p = new Phrase(
  "Quick brown fox jumps over the lazy dog. ");
Image img1 = Image.getInstance("../resources/foxdog.jpg");
img1.setAlignment(Image.RIGHT | Image.TEXTWRAP);
document.add(img1);
for (int i = 0; i < 20; i++) document.add(p);
Image img2 = Image.getInstance("../resources/foxdog.gif");
img2.setAlignment(Image.MIDDLE | Image.UNDERLYING);
document.add(img2);
for (int i = 0; i < 30; i++) document.add(p);
```

Figure 5.5 shows what happens. Text is wrapped around the first image (which is aligned to the right). Text is written on top of the second image (which is aligned in the middle).

Note that `Image.MIDDLE` and `Image.TEXTWRAP` can't be combined. This is one of the limitations of using basic building blocks. In the screenshot, notice that the spacing of the images and wrapped text doesn't always look nice. In chapter 7, we'll deal with this problem using the `ColumnText` object.

You can also wrap an `Image` inside a `Chunk` object, so that you can use the image as if it were a chunk of text.

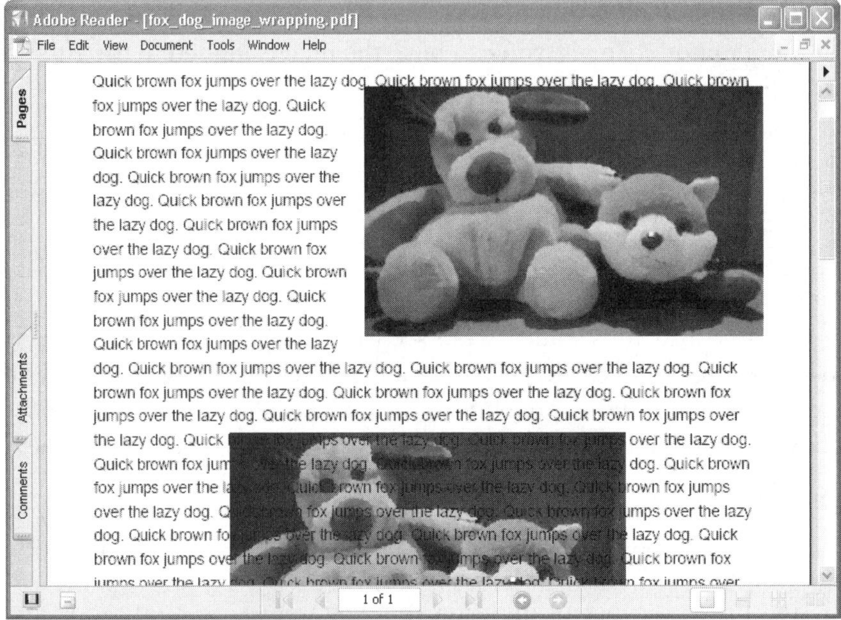


**Figure 5.5 Images and text**

**Figure 5.6 Images wrapped inside a `Chunk`**

### *Images and Chunks*

Even before they could read, I bought books for my children and encouraged them to read. Because they didn't understand words and letters, I bought books that had lots of images and sentences like the ones in figure 5.6.

As you can see, some of the words are replaced by images. You probably won't use this functionality to produce books for children, but it may be handy if you need to integrate a company logo into your text. You can do this by wrapping an `Image` object into a `Chunk` object:

```
/* chapter05/FoxDogImageChunk.java */
Chunk fox = new Chunk(Image.getInstance("fox.gif"), 0, -15);
Chunk dog = new Chunk(Image.getInstance("dog.gif"), 0, -15);
Paragraph p = new Paragraph("Quick brown ");
p.add(fox);
p.add(" jumps over the lazy ");
p.add(dog);
p.add(".");
```

This code sample uses small GIFs representing a fox and a dog. You create a `Chunk` object with the `Image` instance that contains these GIFs, and you define an offset. In this case, x = 0 and y = –15. This means the images are drawn 15 pt under the base line of the `Chunk`. Once the images are wrapped in the `Chunk`, you can use the chunks as if they contained text.

If you want to make these images more presentable, you can add borders.

### *Image borders*

Class `Image` extends class `Rectangle`. You already used this class to define the size of your page, but `Rectangle` is also the superclass of several other rectangular objects. This means you can use some of the methods of this superclass to add a border around the image:

```
/* chapter05/FoxDogImageRectangle.java */
Image jpg = Image.getInstance("foxdog.jpg");
jpg.setBorder(Image.BOX);
jpg.setBorderColor(new Color(0xFF, 0x00, 0x00));
jpg.setBorderWidth(5);
```

More on the `Rectangle` object will follow in the next chapter, when we'll discuss tables and cells.

### *Image sequence*

When you add an image to a document without specifying a coordinate, iText tries to add the image at the current position—that is, where the previous element ended. If the image doesn't fit on the current page, adding the image is postponed. This was a design decision; iText doesn't cut images in two, but it adds other content first.

In the two PDF documents displayed in figure 5.7, a large image is added, followed by a smaller image. This is repeated a number of times. In the PDF on the left, eventually the large image doesn't fit on the page. The smaller image is added first, and the large image is forwarded to the next page. You can change this default behavior by forcing the `PdfWriter` to respect the image sequence, like this:

```
/* chapter05/FoxDogImageSequence.java */
PdfWriter writer = PdfWriter.getInstance(document,
  new FileOutputStream("fox_dog_imageInSequence.pdf"));
writer.setStrictImageSequence(true);
```

This code snippet is responsible for the PDF document on the right in figure 5.7. Just like in the PDF on the left, the fifth image didn't fit the first page, but instead of adding the sixth image, a new page is triggered.

**FAQ** *Can I reuse an* `Image` *more than once?* If you try this example, look at the size of the generated PDF files. The JPEG is about 12 KB; the GIF is about 4 KB. We added both images three times to the document, and the resulting PDF is 17 KB. If you do some math, you see the image data is added to the PDF file only once, no matter how many times the same image shows up in the document.

The sequence problem doesn't apply if you add an image at an absolute position, at specific coordinates on the page.

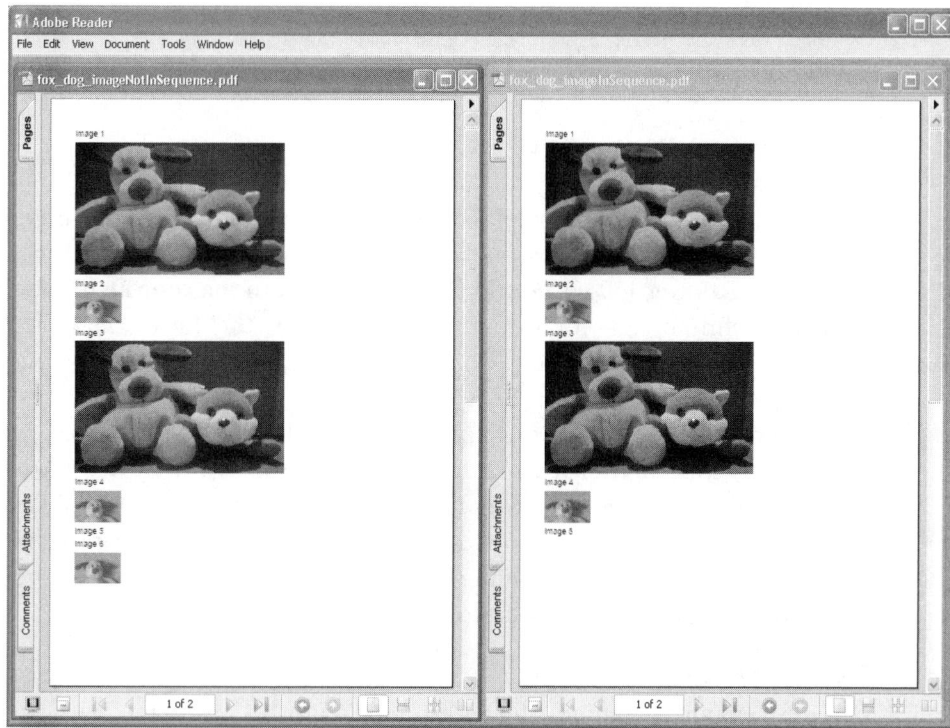


**Figure 5.7 One PDF document demonstrating the image sequence**

## 5.4.2 Translating, scaling, and rotating images

Chapter 10 will offer a short course in analytical geometry. Using some algebra and matrices, you'll learn how to translate, scale and rotate objects in the two-dimensional PDF coordinate system. That's the advanced stuff; in this chapter, we'll start by explaining how to translate, scale, and rotate images.

### Adding an image at an absolute position

When you move an object to another place without scaling or rotating it, you perform a *translation*. This is what happens when you set the absolute positions of an `Image` object. With the method `setAbsolutePosition()`, you pass the coordinate of lower-left corner of the `Image`:

```
/* chapter05/FoxDogImageTranslation.java */
Image img = Image.getInstance("foxdog.jpg");
img.setAbsolutePosition(50, 600);
document.add(img);
```

```
Phrase p =
  new Phrase("Quick brown fox jumps over the lazy dog. ");
for (int i = 0; i < 80; i++) {
  document.add(p);
}
img.setAbsolutePosition(50, 300);
document.add(img);
```

The coordinates of the lower-left corner of the images on the page are (50, 600) and (50, 300). In chapter 10, you'll learn that the origin of the coordinate system (0, 0) is in the lower-left corner. This is different from the coordinate system used in other technologies—for instance, in SVG or in the Java `Graphics2D` object, where the origin is in the upper-left corner. Remember that the y-axis in PDF points up; in SVG or `Graphics2D`, it points down.

I added some text in this example. In the resulting PDF, the images are added *under* the text; no matter if you add the image before or after `document.add(p)`. Images are always added to a layer under the text. In chapter 10, you'll learn how to add the image on top of the text. Note that iText isn't able to wrap text around images that are added at absolute positions. In chapter 7, we'll use a `ColumnText` object with irregular columns to work around this issue.

### Scaling images

The next example changes the width and height of an image; with or without respect to the X/Y ratio. We are *scaling* the image. Figure 5.8 shows an example of an image that is scaled to 50 percent and another in which the scaling in the X direction is different than the scaling in the Y direction.

You can scale an image with `scalePercent()`, but you can also scale it to absolute dimensions with `scaleAbsolute()`.

```
/* chapter05/FoxDogImageScaling1.java */
Image jpg = Image.getInstance("foxdog.jpg");
jpg.scaleAbsolute(154, 94)    <-❶
document.add(jpg);
jpg.scalePercent(50);    <-❷
document.add(new Paragraph("scalePercent(50)"));
document.add(jpg);
jpg.scaleAbsolute(308, 94);    <-❸
document.add(new Paragraph("scaleAbsolute(320, 120)"));
document.add(jpg);
jpg.scalePercent(100, 50);    <-❹
document.add(new Paragraph("scalePercent(100, 50)"));
document.add(jpg);
```

The original image is 308 by 188 pixels. In ❶, you scale the image to half its size by specifying a new width and a new height. You can do the same with the

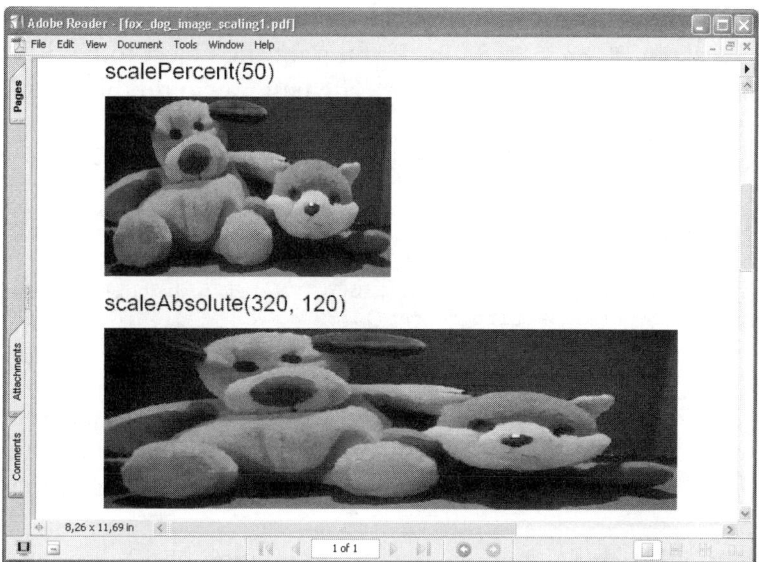


**Figure 5.8 Scaled images**

method `scalePercent()` ❷. With the method `scaleAbsolute()` ❸, you can also change the X/Y ratio of the image. If you want to define a different scale for the X and Y direction, you can define different percentages for `scalePercent()` ❹. The result of line ❹ is identical to the result of line ❸. Note that you can also set the width and height separately with the methods `scaleAbsoluteWidth()` and `scaleAbsoluteHeight()`.

> **NOTE** It's important to understand that iText doesn't change the image's size in bytes. Scaling only changes the resolution that is used to render the image.

There are a lot of misunderstandings about the resolution used by iText when images are added to a document. The next example should shed some light on this matter.

### *Image resolution*

For images, iText always uses a resolution of 72 dots per inch (dpi), regardless of the resolution specified inside the image. Suppose you have a paper image that measures 5 x 5 in. You scan this image at 300 dpi. The resulting image is 1500 x 1500 pixels. If you get an iText `Image` instance, the width and height will be 1500 user units. Taking into account that 1 in equals 72 user units, the image will be about 20.83 x 20.83 in. If you want the object to be displayed as an image of 5 x 5 in, you need to scale it. The best way to do this is with `scalePercent(100 * 72 / 300)`.

Let's look at a concrete example, to see what happens:

```
/* chapter05/FoxDogImageScaling2.java */
Image tiff = Image.getInstance("foxdog.tiff");
document.add(tiff);
document.add(new Paragraph("Original width: " + tiff.width()
+ "; original height: " + tiff.height()));
document.add(new Paragraph("DPI X: " + tiff.getDpiX()
  + "; DPI Y: " + tiff.getDpiY()));
```

**Returns 619x381**

**Returns 360**

The image foxdog.tiff is 619 x 381 pixels. These are the values that are returned by `tiff.width()` and `tiff.height()`. But as you can see, the value returned by `tiff.getDpiX()` and `tiff.getDpiY()` is 360. This means the image has a resolution of 360 dpi.

By default, iText shows the image with a resolution of 72 dpi, but you can change this by scaling it:

```
/* chapter05/FoxDogImageScaling2.java */
tiff.scalePercent(72f / tiff.getDpiX() * 100);
document.add(new Paragraph("Show the image with 360 Dpi (scaled "
  + (7200f / tiff.getDpiX()) + "%):"));
document.add(tiff);
document.add(new Paragraph("Scaled width: " + tiff.scaledWidth()
+ "; scaled height: " + tiff.scaledHeight()));
```

The scaled width and height of the image are 123.8 by 76.2 user units. The image is now rendered with a resolution of 360 dpi instead of 72 dpi.

### *Scale to fit a rectangle*

It's likely that you'll have to fit an image inside a predefined rectangle on your PDF page, keeping the X/Y ratio of the original image. Suppose you have an application form with a rectangular area that can be used for a photo. Not every applicant hands in a photograph that has the correct dimensions; so you'll have to scale the photo if you want to fit it into the rectangle. You don't want to stretch the face on the photograph by using `scaleAbsolute()`, as is done in the lower image in figure 5.8. You could do the math to calculate new dimensions, preserving the aspect ratio, but it's much easier to use the method `scaleToFit()`:

```
/* chapter05/FoxDogImageScaling2.java */
tiff.scaleToFit(200, 200);
document.add(tiff);
```

```
document.add(new Paragraph("Scaled width: " + tiff.scaledWidth()
  + "; scaled height: " + tiff.scaledHeight()));
document.add(new Paragraph("DPI X: "
  + (72f * tiff.width() / tiff.scaledWidth())
  + "; DPI Y: " + (72f * tiff.height() / tiff.scaledHeight())));
```

You know the image is 619 x 381 user units, but you need to make it fit in a square of 200 x 200 user units. If you use the `scaleToFit()` method, the image is resized to 200 x 123.1 user units.

The resolution of the resulting image can be found by doing some extra math: `72f * tiff.width() / tiff.scaledWidth()` equals 222.84 dpi.

We'll finish this subsection on transformations by discussing the *rotation* of an image.

### Image rotation

Figure 5.9 shows an image in which the angle of the base line was changed to 30 degrees.

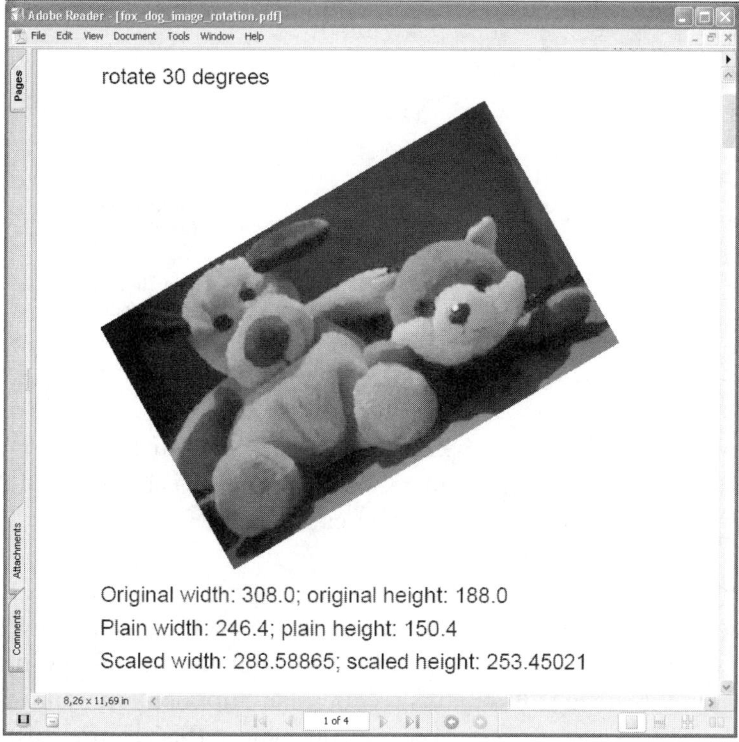


**Figure 5.9 A rotated image**

This rotation can be achieved with the method `setRotation()` or `setRotationDegrees()`:

```
/* chapter05/FoxDogImageRotation.java */
Image jpg2 = Image.getInstance("foxdog.jpg");
jpg2.setRotationDegrees(45);                      // Rotates image 45 degrees
jpg2.setRotation((float)Math.PI / 2);             // Rotates image 90 degrees
jpg2.setRotationDegrees(135);                     // Rotates image 135 degrees
jpg2.setRotation((float)Math.PI);                 // Rotates image 180 degrees
jpg2.setRotation((float)
  (2.0 * Math.PI));                               // Rotates image 360 degrees
```

If you don't rotate the image, plain width/height and scaled width/height return the same values. A rotated image often needs more space. In this case, the methods to return the plain width/height still give you the dimensions of the image itself, but the scaled width/height methods return the dimensions of the rectangle that is needed to display the image—the image plus extra space around it.

The text under each image in the PDF will help you understand the difference between the methods that get the width and height of the image:

```
/* chapter05/FoxDogImageRotation.java */
Image jpg1 = Image.getInstance("foxdog.jpg");
jpg1.scalePercent(80);
jpg1.setRotation((float)Math.PI / 6);
document.add(new Paragraph("rotate 30 degrees"));
document.add(jpg1);
document.add(new Paragraph("Original width: " +
  jpg1.width() + "; original height: " +
  jpg1.height()));                                // Returns 308 x 188 (original dimensions)
document.add(new Paragraph("Plain width: " +
  jpg1.plainWidth() + "; plain height: " +
  jpg1.plainHeight()));                           // Returns 264.4 x 150.4 (scaled dimensions)
document.add(new Paragraph("Scaled width: " +
  jpg1.scaledWidth() + "; scaled height: " +
  jpg1.scaledHeight()));                          // Returns 288.59 x 253.45 (actual dimensions)
```

In the example, 288.59 is the horizontal distance between the upper-left and lower-right corners of the rotated image, whereas 253.45 is the vertical distance between the upper-right and lower-left corner.

### 5.4.3 Image masks

Whatever type of image you create, JPEG, GIF, PNG, TIFF, or something else, it's going to be rectangular or square. You can rotate an image, as you saw in the previous section, but its form still remains rectangular. Suppose you want to add an image that has the form of a circle; how can you achieve this? Figure 5.10 shows a

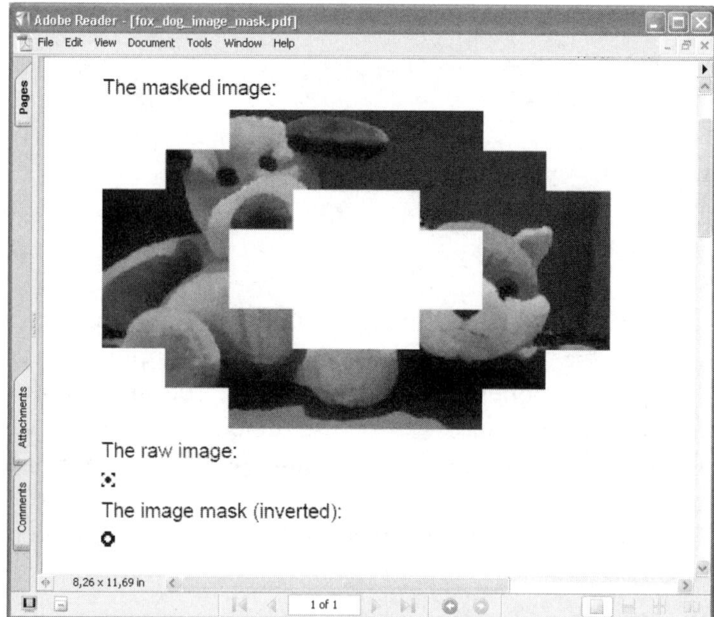


**Figure 5.10 Masking an image**

rudimentary example of how I put a mask that looks somewhat like a donut over the foxdog.jpg image.

In real life, you'll want something that looks much better than figure 5.10, but this example serves mainly to introduce the theory of *hard* and *soft* masks in images. A hard mask has only one bit per component; 1 covers the image and 0 is transparent. A soft mask contains a gradient from 0 to 1. We'll deal with this concept in more depth later on in chapter 11; this is just a simple example that serves as an introduction. In chapter 11, you'll learn how to create masks that are more spectacular.

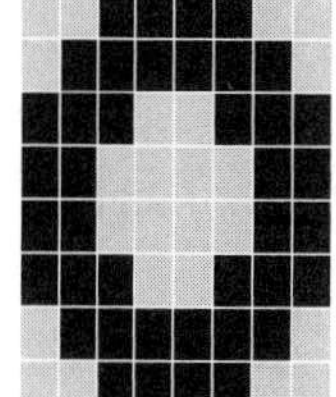

**Figure 5.11 The image mask is an image of 8 x 8 pixels.**

In section 5.3.1, you generated an image with three components and eight bits per component. Now, you need an image with one 1-bit component: black/white. Figure 5.11 represents an image of 8 x 8 pixels. Each line can be described as 1 byte (8 bits, 1 bit per pixel). The first line is 00111100 or 0x3C; the second line 01111110 or 0x7e; and so on.

The hexadecimal `byte` stream of this mask looks like this: 3C7EE7C3C3E77E3C. If you want rounded corners instead of this donut shape, the stream looks like this: 3C7EFFFFFFFF7E3C.

This is how to create the image shown in figure 5.11:

```
/* chapter05/FoxDogImageMask.java */
byte circledata[] =
{(byte)0x3c, (byte)0x7e, (byte)0xe7, (byte)0xc3,
   (byte)0xc3, (byte)0xe7, (byte)0x7e, (byte)0x3c};     1
Image mask = Image.getInstance(8, 8, 1, 1, circledata);  <- 2
mask.makeMask();  <- 3
mask.setInvertMask(true);  <- 4
img.setImageMask(mask);  <- 5
document.add(img);
```

First, you create a `byte` array with the image data ❶. You use this `byte` array to create an `Image` with a size of 8 x 8 pixels. It has one component (it's monochrome) and 1 bit per component (black or white) ❷. You indicate that you're planning to use this image as a mask ❸. You use the donut shape as a stencil for another image ❺ (see figure 5.5); if you omit line ❹, the inverse will happen: The donut shape will cover the other image.

This is a theoretical example. Let's return to the real world and see if we can finish Laura's first assignment.

## 5.5 Making a flyer (part 2)

In the previous chapter, Laura made an HTML file, and you wrote a simple parser that parsed this HTML into a PDF file. You dealt with all the tags that concerned text. You didn't write any code that handled the `<img>` tag because you didn't know anything about images in iText yet. When such a tag was encountered, you called the method `handleImage()`, but you left the body of this method empty.

Now that you know how to get an instance of the `Image` class and set its properties, you can implement this method.

### 5.5.1 Getting the Image instance

Let's start by getting the values of the `url` and `alt` attributes passed with the `<img>` tag. You'll try to create an image with the `url`; if you don't succeed, you'll add a paragraph with the contents of the `alt` attribute:

```
/* chapter05/FoobarFlyer.java */
private void handleImage(Attributes attributes)
  throws MalformedURLException, IOException, DocumentException {
  String url = attributes.getValue(HtmlTags.URL);     Get the src
  String alt = attributes.getValue(HtmlTags.ALT);     attributes
  if (url == null) return;
  Image img = null;
```

```
try {
  img = Image.getInstance(url);       <-- Try to get image instance
  if (alt != null) {
    img.setAlt(alt);      <-- Set alternative string
  }
}
catch(Exception e) {
  if (alt == null) {
    document.add(new Paragraph(e.getMessage()));
  }
  else {
    document.add(new Paragraph(alt));
  }
    return;
  }
}
```

This code snippet uses the method that hasn't been discussed yet: `setAlt()`. This method is useless when generating PDF, but in chapter 2 you saw that you can also use iText to generate HTML. With the method `setAlt()`, you can set the alternative string of an HTML `<img>` tag.

If something goes wrong while trying to get the image instance, the text of the error message or the alternative string is added to the document instead of the image. You can, of course, choose to throw an error. It's up to you; this is just an example, not a full-blown HTML parser.

The `<img>` tag can also have attributes defining the border, the alignment, and the dimensions of the image. Let's complete the `handleImage()` method so that these `Image` properties are set.

### 5.5.2 Setting the border, the alignment, and the dimensions

This example gets the values of the border and the alignment and sets the properties discussed in section 5.4. Note that no border width was defined for the image in Laura's HTML document, so the first part of the code snippet will be skipped when the example is executed. I add it for the sake of completeness:

```
/* chapter05/FoobarFlyer.java */
String property;
property = attributes.getValue(HtmlTags.BORDERWIDTH);
if (property != null) {
  int border = Integer.parseInt(property);
  if (border == 0) {
    img.setBorder(Image.NO_BORDER);
  }
```

```
      else {
        img.setBorder(Image.BOX);
        img.setBorderWidth(border);
      }
    }
    property = attributes.getValue(HtmlTags.ALIGN);
    if (property != null) {
      int align = Image.DEFAULT;
      if (ElementTags.ALIGN_LEFT.equalsIgnoreCase(property))
        align = Image.LEFT;
      else if (ElementTags.ALIGN_RIGHT.equalsIgnoreCase(property))
        align = Image.RIGHT;
      else if (ElementTags.ALIGN_MIDDLE.equalsIgnoreCase(property))
        align = Image.MIDDLE;
      img.setAlignment(align | Image.TEXTWRAP);
    }
```

Finally, you deal with the attributes `width` and `height`. The logo is 411 x 537 pixels, which is much too large for the flyer. Laura has set the dimensions to 102 x 134, so the image will be scaled (see section 5.2.2):

```
/* chapter05/FoobarFlyer.java */
int w = 0;
property = attributes.getValue(HtmlTags.PLAINWIDTH);
if (property != null) {
  w = Integer.parseInt(property);
  int h = 0;
  property = attributes.getValue(HtmlTags.PLAINHEIGHT);
  if (property != null) {
    h = Integer.parseInt(property);
    img.scaleAbsolute(w, h);
  }
}
document.add(img);
```

The only thing that remains is to run the code and take a look at the result.

### 5.5.3 The resulting PDF

Laura has now finished a flyer that she can distribute to promote her new department (see figure 5.12).

I must admit that this example isn't really real-world. If you want to create a flyer like this, you're better of with a word processor or professional software like Acrobat. Keep in mind that this example is only the first step. In the next chapter, you'll help Laura create more documents, with complex elements such as tables and columns.

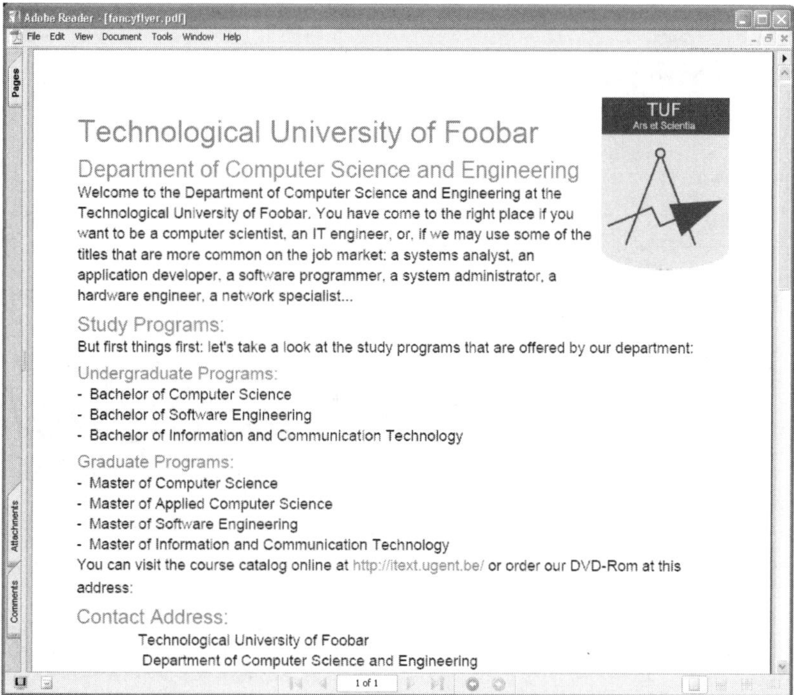


**Figure 5.12 A fancy flyer**

## 5.6 Summary

In this chapter, you've learned what types of images are supported in iText. It's important to remember how to get an instance of an image, because you're going to use the `Image` object in different contexts later. An issue that turns up on the iText mailing list regularly concerns resolution: Remember that iText looks at the size in pixels of the image, regardless of the resolution.

You made a single example with lots of barcodes because barcodes are treated as images in iText; if you need to know more about the different types of barcodes supported in iText, see appendix B. In part 3, we'll return to images; you'll learn how to add an image to a `PdfContentByte` object, how to clip images, and how to make them transparent.

In most cases, you'll use images in combination with other objects and structures. You've seen how to wrap an `Image` inside a `Chunk`. In the chapters that follow, you'll see how to add images to the cells of a table (chapter 6) and how to combine them with columns of text (chapter 7).

# 6 *Constructing tables*

***This chapter covers***

- Working with `PdfPTable`
- Working with `PdfPCell`
- What about class `Table`?

If asked what iText's primary goal is, different people provide different answers depending on the way they use iText. I use iText mostly to produce reports. If you ask me for the most important components when generating such a report, I don't have to think twice. My answer is: tables, tables, and tables. I repeat the word three times and not without reason; the table class comes in three different flavors: `PdfPTable`, `Table`, and `SimpleTable`.

In this book, we'll focus mainly on the most flexible and most important table class: `PdfPTable`. We'll spend two examples on class `Table`, but only to list some of its advantages. We'll use `SimpleTable` for the Foobar example.

## 6.1 Tables in PDF: PdfPTable

If you're generating PDF only—you aren't using `HtmlWriter` or `RtfWriter2`—and if you want full control over the way the table will be rendered, you shouldn't doubt what table class to use. You should go for `PdfPTable` without hesitation.

We'll start with some simple examples, demonstrating how to change the alignment and how to set the width of the table and its columns. Then we'll do the same for cells. Additionally, you'll learn to tune the height of a cell and to change the color of its background and borders. Finally, you'll learn what to do if a table doesn't fit on one page, or if you want to add the table at a specific absolute position.

### 6.1.1 Your first PdfPTable

Suppose you need to create a simple table that looks like figure 6.1.

The code to generate this kind of table is pretty easy, as shown in listing 6.1.

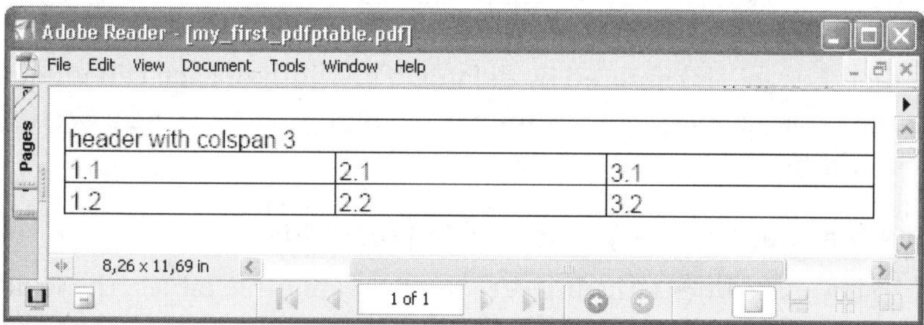


**Figure 6.1 Your first PdfPTable**

**Listing 6.1 Creating a PdfPTable**

```
/* chapter06/MyFirstPdfPTable.java */
PdfPTable table = new PdfPTable(3);        <-- Create PdfPTable with 3 columns
PdfPCell cell =
  new PdfPCell(new Paragraph("header with colspan 3"));   <-- Create PdfPCell with a paragraph
cell.setColspan(3);      <-- Change colspan of PdfPCell
table.addCell(cell);      <-- Add custom PdfPCell to PdfPTable
table.addCell("1.1");
table.addCell("2.1");
table.addCell("3.1");     <-- Add String objects to PdfPTable
table.addCell("1.2");
table.addCell("2.2");
table.addCell("3.2");
document.add(table);
```

When you create a PdfPTable, you always need to pass the number of columns to the constructor (creating a table with zero columns results in a RuntimeException). You can add different objects to a PdfPTable object using the method addCell().

There is an object PdfPRow in the com.lowagie.text.pdf package, but you aren't supposed to address it directly; iText uses this class internally to store the cells that belong to the same row. In this example, the table has three columns. After adding the first cell with column span three, the first row is full. The next cell is added to a second row that is created automatically by iText. In other words, you don't have to worry about rows—you just have to make sure you're adding the correct number of cells.

The default width of a table is 80 percent of the available width. Let's do the math for the table in figure 6.1: The width page is 595 pt minus the margins, which are 36 pt. In short, the width of the table is (595 – (2 * 36)) * 80 percent, or 418.4 pt.

Note that the table is centered by default. The width of each cell is equal to the width of the table divided by the number of columns. In the next section, you'll tune these widths.

## 6.1.2 Changing the width and alignment of a PdfPTable

Let's add a few extra lines to listing 6.1. You'll create three tables; the width of the first one is 100 percent of the available width on the page. The other two have a width of only 50 percent. You'll align one of these tables to the right and the other to the left:

```
/* chapter06/PdfPTableAligned.java */
table.setWidthPercentage(100);
```

```
document.add(table);
table.setWidthPercentage(50);
table.setHorizontalAlignment(Element.ALIGN_RIGHT);
document.add(table);
table.setHorizontalAlignment(Element.ALIGN_LEFT);
document.add(table);
```

You set the horizontal alignment of the complete table object using `setHorizontalAlignment()`. Note that this doesn't have any impact on the alignment of the content inside the cells!

### *Relative versus absolute width of the PdfPTable*

Working with width percentage is easy because it saves you from calculating the width yourself. If you want to set the absolute width, you should use the methods `setTotalWidth()` and `setLockedWidth()`:

```
/* chapter06/PdfPTableAbsoluteWidth.java */
PdfPTable table = new PdfPTable(3);
table.setTotalWidth(216f);
table.setLockedWidth(true);
```

Note that iText stores two width parameters: a percentage of the available width and an absolute width. By setting locked width to true, you indicate that the value of the absolute width should be used.

The example sets the total width to 216 user units and has three columns, so every column in the table is 1 in wide (216 user units / 3 = 72 user units = 1 in).

### *Column widths*

To change the way the available space is distributed over the columns, you can use a table constructor that takes an array of floats as parameter:

```
/* chapter06/PdfPTableColumnWidths.java */
float[] widths1 = { 1f, 1f, 2f };
PdfPTable table = new PdfPTable(widths1);
```

Except for these two lines, this example is identical to the one in listing 6.1; but as you can see in figure 6.2, the distribution of the columns is different from the table shown in figure 6.1.

An array with three values was used to construct the table object, defining a table with three columns. The floats in the array define *relative* widths; `PdfPTable` will calculate the absolute widths internally. The first two columns take a quarter of the horizontal space each (1 / (1 + 1 + 2)). The third column takes half of the available horizontal space. After constructing the `PdfPTable`, you can also change the relative width with the `setWidths()` method:

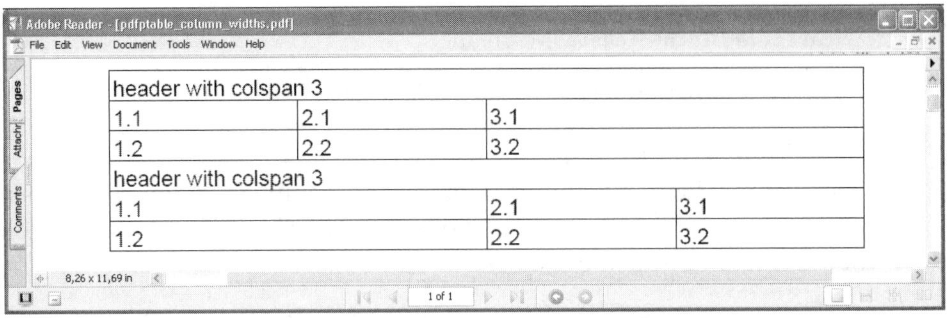
Adobe Reader - [pdfptable_column_widths.pdf]
File Edit View Document Tools Window Help
header with colspan 3
1.1
2.1
3.1
1.2
2.2
3.2
header with colspan 3
1.1
2.1
3.1
1.2
2.2
3.2
8,26 x 11,69 in
1 of 1

**Figure 6.2 Changing the width of the columns**

```
/* chapter06/PdfPTableColumnWidths.java */
float[] widths2 = { 2f, 1f, 1f };
table.setWidths(widths2);
```

**FAQ** *Is it possible to have the column width change dynamically based on the content of the cells?* PDF isn't HTML, and a PdfPTable is completely different from an HTML table rendered in a browser; iText can't calculate column widths based on the content of the columns. The result would depend on too many design decisions and wouldn't always correspond with what a developer expects. It's better to have the developer define the widths.

I repeat that the widths entered with the `widths` array are *relative* values. If you enter an array with absolute widths, every column width is recalculated depending on the available width on the page, which is a percentage of the available page width. You can avoid this result by letting the width percentage of the table depend on the absolute column widths and the page size:

```
/* chapter06/PdfPTableAbsoluteWidths.java */
float[] widths = { 72f, 72f, 144f };
Rectangle r =
  new Rectangle(PageSize.A4.right(72), PageSize.A4.top(72));
table.setWidthPercentage(widths, r);
```

The table generated in the PdfPTableColumnWidths example has two columns with a width of 1 in and a third column with a width of 2 in. There's more than one way to make such a table. You can set the total width to 4 in (288pt) and the relative column widths to `{1, 1, 2}`; or you can do it like this:

```
/* chapter06/PdfPTableAbsoluteColumns.java */
float[] widths = { 72f, 72f, 144f };
```

```
table.setTotalWidth(widths);
table.setLockedWidth(true);
```

Don't forget to set the locked width to true, otherwise, the floats in the `widths` array will be considered as relative widths.

### Spacing before and after a PdfPTable

If you look at the resulting PDF documents generated with the previous examples, you'll notice that consecutive tables are glued to each other: There is no vertical space between the tables. This is handy if you want the different tables to look like one big table.

If the tables are completely different, or if you need extra spacing between a table and other high-level objects (such as a previous or a following `Paragraph`), you should use the methods `setSpacingBefore()` and `setSpacingAfter()`:

```
/* chapter06/PdfPTableSpacing.java */
table.setSpacingBefore(15f);
table.setSpacingAfter(10f);
```

We have dealt with some general table defaults and showed you how to change them. Now, let's look at the way a cell is constructed.

## 6.1.3 Adding PdfPCells to a PdfPTable

Adding a `String`, a `Phrase`, or a `Paragraph` to a table with the method `addCell()` is equivalent to these two lines of code:

```
PdfPCell cell = new PdfPCell(new Phrase("some text"));
table.addCell(cell);
```

If you create a `PdfPCell` with a `Paragraph` as a parameter, then all paragraph specific properties are lost. The leading, alignment, and indentation of the `PdfPCell` are used instead.

When you use `addCell(String text)`, you can define default properties for the cells. For instance, the next code snippet changes the border values of the default table cell to `NO_BORDER`:

```
/* chapter06/PdfPTableWithoutBorders.java */
PdfPTable table = new PdfPTable(3);
table.getDefaultCell().setBorder(PdfPCell.NO_BORDER);
PdfPCell cell =
  new PdfPCell(new Paragraph("header with colspan 3"));
cell.setColspan(3);
table.addCell(cell);
table.addCell("1.1");
table.addCell("2.1");
table.addCell("3.1");
```

The cell containing "header with column span 3" will have borders because `PdfPCell.BOX` is the default value of every newly created `PdfPCell`. The cells that contain "1.1," "2.1," and so on are added without any border, because the border property of the default cell was changed to `PdfPCell.NO_BORDER`.

Note that there is a huge difference between the following line:

```
PdfPCell cell = new PdfPCell(new Paragraph("some text"));   <- ❶
```

and this code snippet:

```
PdfPCell cell = new PdfPCell();
cell.addElement(new Paragraph("some text"));   ❷
```

In the next chapter, you'll see that a `PdfPCell` is rendered as a `ColumnText` object, and you'll learn about the difference between *text mode* (option ❶; see section 7.3.1) and *composite mode* (option ❷; see section 7.3.2):

- Text mode means the properties of the paragraph are ignored.
- Composite mode means the properties of the elements that are added to the cell are respected.

Don't mix these two modes. If you've created a `PdfPCell` in text mode, you shouldn't use `addElement()`. If you do, the original (text mode) content will be lost.

### Alignment of the cell content

In text mode, cell content is aligned horizontally to the left and vertically to the top of the cell by default. Changing the horizontal alignment is done with `setHorizontalAlignment()`:

```
/* chapter06/PdfPTableCellAlignment.java */
PdfPCell cell;
Paragraph p = new Paragraph(
  "Quick brown fox jumps over the lazy dog.
  ➥ Quick brown fox jumps over the lazy dog.");
table.addCell("centered alignment");
cell = new PdfPCell(p);
cell.setHorizontalAlignment(Element.ALIGN_CENTER);
table.addCell(cell);
```

The first four rows in figure 6.3 demonstrate four different ways to align a content cell. When the alignment is set to `Element.ALIGN_JUSTIFIED`, you can change the ratio of word spacing to character spacing with the method `PdfPCell.setSpaceCharRatio()`. Turn to figure 4.11 to see the effect of changing this value.

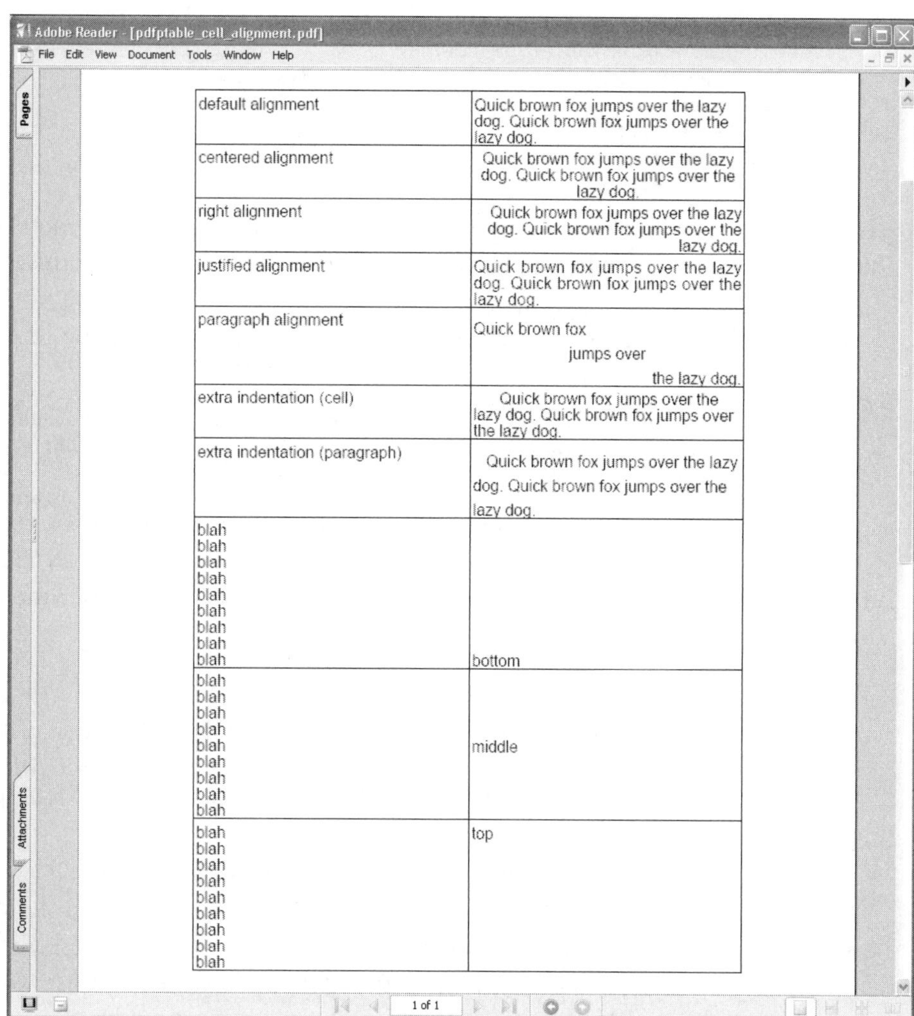


| | |
|---|---|
| default alignment | Quick brown fox jumps over the lazy dog. Quick brown fox jumps over the lazy dog. |
| centered alignment | Quick brown fox jumps over the lazy dog. Quick brown fox jumps over the lazy dog. |
| right alignment | Quick brown fox jumps over the lazy dog. Quick brown fox jumps over the lazy dog. |
| justified alignment | Quick brown fox jumps over the lazy dog. Quick brown fox jumps over the lazy dog. |
| paragraph alignment | Quick brown fox<br>jumps over<br>the lazy dog. |
| extra indentation (cell) | Quick brown fox jumps over the lazy dog. Quick brown fox jumps over the lazy dog. |
| extra indentation (paragraph) | Quick brown fox jumps over the lazy dog. Quick brown fox jumps over the lazy dog. |
| blah<br>blah<br>blah<br>blah<br>blah<br>blah<br>blah<br>blah<br>blah | bottom |
| blah<br>blah<br>blah<br>blah<br>blah<br>blah<br>blah<br>blah<br>blah | middle |
| blah<br>blah<br>blah<br>blah<br>blah<br>blah<br>blah<br>blah<br>blah | top |

**Figure 6.3 Changing the alignment and indentation of a `PdfPCell`**

The previous code snippet sets the alignment for the complete cell. In composite mode, you can use a different alignment per paragraph (row five in figure 6.3):

```
/* chapter06/PdfPTableCellAlignment.java */
table.addCell("paragraph alignment");
Paragraph p1 = new Paragraph("Quick brown fox");
Paragraph p2 = new Paragraph("jumps over");
p2.setAlignment(Element.ALIGN_CENTER);
```

```
Paragraph p3 = new Paragraph("the lazy dog.");
p3.setAlignment(Element.ALIGN_RIGHT);
cell = new PdfPCell();
cell.addElement(p1);
cell.addElement(p2);
cell.addElement(p3);
table.addCell(cell);
```

In both modes, the vertical alignment can be changed with the method `setVerticalAlignment()`. The final 3 rows in figure 6.3 are created like this:

```
/* chapter06/PdfPTableCellAlignment.java */
table.addCell("blah\nblah\nblah\nblah\nblah\nblah\nblah\nblah\nblah\n");
table.getDefaultCell().setVerticalAlignment(Element.ALIGN_BOTTOM);
table.addCell("bottom");
table.addCell("blah\nblah\nblah\nblah\nblah\nblah\nblah\nblah\nblah\n");
table.getDefaultCell().setVerticalAlignment(Element.ALIGN_MIDDLE);
table.addCell("middle");
table.addCell("blah\nblah\nblah\nblah\nblah\nblah\nblah\nblah\nblah\n");
table.getDefaultCell().setVerticalAlignment(Element.ALIGN_TOP);
table.addCell("top");
```

The second column of the PDF file shown in figure 6.3 also experiments with the indentation.

### Indentation and leading of the cell content

You can set the left indentation of the first paragraph in a cell with `setIndent()`; the indentation of the following paragraphs are set with `PdfPCell.setFollowingIndent()`. The indentation to the right can be changed with `PdfPCell.setRightIndent()`.

In chapter 4, you saw some methods to change the indentation of a `Paragraph`. The same rules we discussed for the alignment of a cell/paragraph apply. Rows six and seven shown in figure 6.3 demonstrate the method `Paragraph.setFirstLineIndent()` was used. This is an example of a method that doesn't work with paragraphs added with `document.add()`; it only works if you add a `Paragraph` to a `PdfPTable` or a `ColumnText` object:

```
/* chapter06/PdfPTableCellAlignment.java */
table.addCell("extra indentation (cell)");
cell = new PdfPCell(p);
cell.setIndent(20);
table.addCell(cell);
table.addCell("extra indentation (paragraph)");
p.setFirstLineIndent(10);
cell = new PdfPCell();
cell.addElement(p);
```

In composite mode, the leading of the elements added to the cell is used. In text mode, you can define an absolute value for the leading and/or a value relative to the size of the font:

```
/* chapter06/PdfPTableCellSpacing.java */
PdfPCell cell = new PdfPCell(
  new Paragraph("Quick brown fox jumps over the lazy dog.
  ➥ Quick brown fox jumps over the lazy dog."));
table.addCell("default leading / spacing");
table.addCell(cell);
table.addCell("absolute leading: 20");
cell.setLeading(20f, 0f);                 Absolute leading of 20 pt
table.addCell(cell);
table.addCell("absolute leading: 3; relative leading: 1.2");
cell.setLeading(3f, 1.2f);                Leading of 3 pt + 1.2 times font size
table.addCell(cell);
table.addCell("absolute leading: 0; relative leading: 1.2");
cell.setLeading(0f, 1.2f);                Leading of 1.2 times font size
table.addCell(cell);
table.addCell("no leading at all");
cell.setLeading(0f, 0f);                  Leading of 0
table.addCell(cell);
```

Regardless of whether you're working in text or in composite mode, you can also define the *padding* of the cell content.

### *Padding of the cell content*

The *padding* is the space between the content of a cell and its borders. You can define different padding for the left and right side of the cell, as well as for the top and bottom:

```
/* chapter06/PdfPTableCellSpacing.java */
cell = new PdfPCell(
  new Paragraph("Quick brown fox jumps over the lazy dog."));
table.addCell("padding 10");
cell.setPadding(10);
table.addCell(cell);
table.addCell("padding 0");
cell.setPadding(0);
table.addCell(cell);
table.addCell("different padding for left, right, top and bottom");
cell.setPaddingLeft(20);
cell.setPaddingRight(50);
cell.setPaddingTop(0);
cell.setPaddingBottom(5);
table.addCell(cell);
```

You can adjust the top padding depending on the *ascender* of the first line in the cell. The bottom padding can be adapted to the *descender* of the last line.

When a character is drawn, the ascender is the space needed above its baseline; the *descender* is the space needed below the baseline to draw the character. Here an example:

```
/* chapter06/PdfPTableCellSpacing.java */
Phrase p =
  new Phrase("Quick brown fox jumps over the lazy dog");
table.getDefaultCell().setPadding(2);
table.getDefaultCell().setUseAscender(true);
table.getDefaultCell().setUseDescender(true);
table.addCell("padding 2; ascender and descender");
cell.setPadding(2);
```

Setting the padding is important to increase the readability of your tables. Otherwise, the content of the cell sticks to the borders—and that's not pretty. If the padding is relatively small, you should also consider using the ascender and descender to make sure all the characters fit nicely inside the cell borders.

Changing the leading and/or padding and using the ascender/descender have an impact on the height of a cell and, by extension, on the height of a row. In the previous examples, the height of each row was calculated automatically. Now you'll learn how to change the row height.

### Changing the row height

In figure 6.4, the second column of rows one and two contain the same paragraph. The first row shows the default behavior. When the content of a cell doesn't fit on one line, the text is wrapped and the height of the cell is adapted.

In row two the text isn't wrapped. It's a common misunderstanding that iText truncates the content when you use `setNoWrap(true)`. If you want your table to have a fixed size, you shouldn't turn on the cell wrapping. Instead, you should fix the height to a certain size. This is done in rows three and four.

The height of row three is fixed at 1 in (72 pt) with `setFixedHeight()`; that's more than sufficient to show three lines of "blah blah blah." Row four has a fixed height of 0.5 in (36 pt), which isn't sufficient; so the third line is lost.

If it's your intention to create a table with fixed dimensions, this is a good way to add as many full words as possible to the cell. Words that don't fit the cell are omitted. This is a feature, not a bug.

The method `setMinimumHeight()` is less strict. If the previous example used it instead of `setFixedHeight()`, row four would show all the content, but the cell height would be more than half an inch. The `setMinimumHeight()` method is demonstrated in row five. It has only one line of content, but the cell is half an inch high; that's the minimum height defined in the code. Here's the code for these examples:

```
/* chapter06/PdfPTableCellHeights.java */
cell = new PdfPCell(new Paragraph("blah blah … blah"));
table.addCell("wrap");
cell.setNoWrap(false);                                    Row 1
table.addCell(cell);
table.addCell("no wrap");
cell.setNoWrap(true);                                     Row 2
table.addCell(cell);
cell = new PdfPCell(
  new Paragraph("1. blah blah\n2. blah blah blah\n3. blah blah"));
table.addCell("fixed height (more than sufficient)");
cell.setFixedHeight(72f);                                 Row 3
table.addCell(cell);
table.addCell("fixed height (not sufficient)");
cell.setFixedHeight(36f);                                 Row 4
table.addCell(cell);
table.addCell("minimum height");
cell = new PdfPCell(new Paragraph("blah blah"));          Row 5
cell.setMinimumHeight(36f);
table.addCell(cell);
```

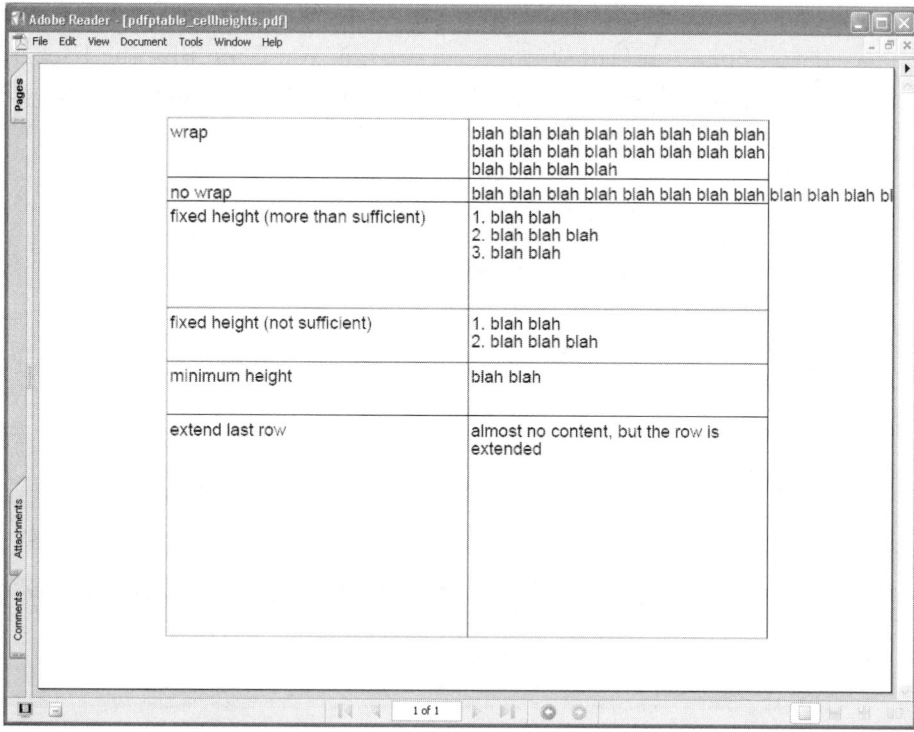


| wrap | blah blah blah blah blah blah blah blah blah blah blah blah blah blah blah blah blah blah blah blah |
|---|---|
| no wrap | blah blah blah blah blah blah blah blah blah blah blah bl |
| fixed height (more than sufficient) | 1. blah blah<br>2. blah blah blah<br>3. blah blah |
| fixed height (not sufficient) | 1. blah blah<br>2. blah blah blah |
| minimum height | blah blah |
| extend last row | almost no content, but the row is extended |

**Figure 6.4 Different row heights**

Note that the height of the final row is extended to the bottom margin of the page. This isn't a cell property; it's something that has to be defined at the table level:

```
/* chapter06/PdfPTableCellHeights.java */
table.setExtendLastRow(true);
table.addCell("extend last row");
cell = new PdfPCell(
  new Paragraph("almost no content, but the row is extended"));
table.addCell(cell);
document.add(table);
```

**Row 6**

Only one method left affects the height of a cell: `setUseBorderPadding()`. But in order to know what this method is about, you need to learn more about setting the width and the color of cell borders.

### *Changing cell borders and colors*

If you want to make your table more colorful, or if you wish to stress the header row by using a thicker line for the borders, you can benefit from the fact that the `PdfPCell` class extends `Rectangle`. You can use all kinds of methods to change rectangle borders and colors.

If you open the PDF shown in figure 6.5, you'll see that the background of the second cell of row one is red. The cells in row two have shades of gray as background color. These colors are set with the methods `setBackgroundColor()` and `setGrayFill()`:

```
/* chapter06/PdfPTableColors.java */
cell = new PdfPCell(new Paragraph("red / no borders"));
cell.setBorder(Rectangle.NO_BORDER);
cell.setBackgroundColor(Color.red);
table.addCell(cell);
cell = new PdfPCell(new Paragraph("0.5"));
cell.setBorder(Rectangle.NO_BORDER);
cell.setGrayFill(0.5f);
table.addCell(cell);
```

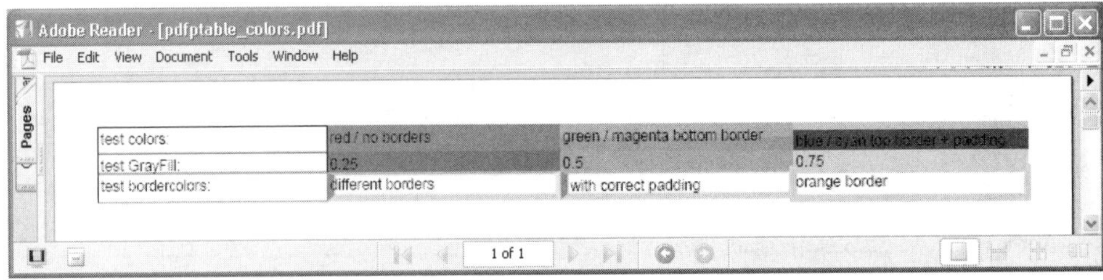


**Figure 6.5 Changing the colors of a cell and its borders**

The following code fragment was used to change the border width and color of the lower-right cell:

```
/* chapter06/PdfPTableColors.java */
cell = new PdfPCell(new Paragraph("orange border"));
cell.setBorderWidth(6f);
cell.setBorderColor(Color.orange);
table.addCell(cell);
```

Do you see the difference from the other cells in row three? The previous snippet sets the width and color of the border box. The next example defines different widths and colors for the right, left, top, and bottom border. This automatically sets the "use variable borders" attribute to true. If you don't want the border to overlap with other cells, as does the orange border cell in figure 6.5, you must add the line `cell.setUseVariableBorders(true);` to the previous code fragment.

The following lines are responsible for creating the cell in the second column of the row three:

```
/* chapter06/PdfPTableColors.java */
cell = new PdfPCell(new Paragraph("different borders"));
cell.setBorderWidthLeft(6f);
cell.setBorderWidthBottom(5f);
cell.setBorderWidthRight(4f);
cell.setBorderWidthTop(2f);
cell.setBorderColorLeft(Color.red);
cell.setBorderColorBottom(Color.orange);
cell.setBorderColorRight(Color.yellow);
cell.setBorderColorTop(Color.green);
table.addCell(cell);
```

If you look at the cells with thick borders, you see that the border and the content of the cell can overlap. This can be avoided by calculating the border into the padding as is done with the cell in the third column of row three:

```
/* chapter06/PdfPTableColors.java */
cell = new PdfPCell(new Paragraph("with correct padding"));
cell.setUseBorderPadding(true);
```

Until now, you've been creating cells with content that is rendered in horizontal lines. Sometimes it's useful to be able to add text that is written vertically. The first column could, for instance, contain a short title, and the second might contain a description.

### *Changing the rotation of a PdfPCell*

Figure 6.6 shows an example of cells that are rotated 90 degrees.

There are different ways to create a table with cells like these. The easiest technique is to change the rotation of the cell with the `setRotation()` method:

```
/* chapter06/PdfPTableVerticalCells.java */
PdfPCell cell = new PdfPCell(new Paragraph("fox"));
cell.setBackgroundColor(Color.YELLOW);
cell.setHorizontalAlignment(Element.ALIGN_CENTER);
cell.setRotation(90);
table.addCell(cell);
```

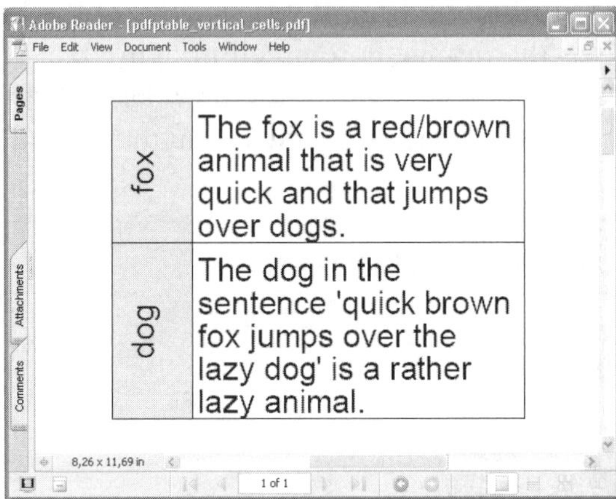


**Figure 6.6**
**Cells with vertical text**

There is no method `setRowspan()` in `PdfPTable/PdfPCell`. If you want to have a title "fox and dog" that spans the two rows, you need to use a workaround: nested tables. Tables can be nested using one of the `PdfPCell` constructors we'll discuss in the next section.

## *6.1.4 Special PdfPCell constructors*

In the previous subsections, you've been constructing cells containing objects from chapter 4—text-only objects. Tables aren't limited to text only; there are also `PdfPCell` constructors that take a `PdfPTable` or an `Image` object as parameter.

### *Nested tables*

To work around the row-span problem, you create a `PdfPCell` with a `PdfPTable` as a parameter. In figure 6.7, cell 1 is really a table with one row and two columns containing the values 1.1 and 1.2. The space between the inner table and the outer cell is the default padding.

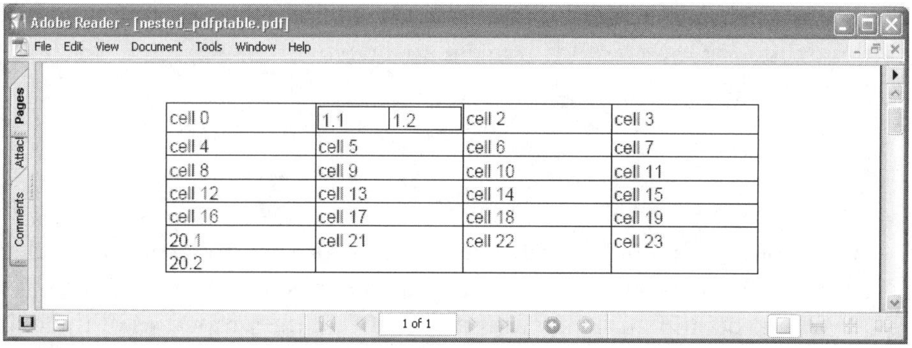

| cell 0 | 1.1 / 1.2 | cell 2 | cell 3 |
|---|---|---|---|
| cell 4 | cell 5 | cell 6 | cell 7 |
| cell 8 | cell 9 | cell 10 | cell 11 |
| cell 12 | cell 13 | cell 14 | cell 15 |
| cell 16 | cell 17 | cell 18 | cell 19 |
| 20.1 / 20.2 | cell 21 | cell 22 | cell 23 |

**Figure 6.7 Cells 1 and 20 contain a nested table**

Cell 20 contains a one-column table with two rows. This nested table is wrapped in a `PdfPCell` so the padding is zero; this way, it looks as if cells 21, 22, and 23 have a row span equal to 2. The following code snippet shows how it's done:

```
/* chapter06/PdfPTableNested.java */
PdfPTable table = new PdfPTable(4);
PdfPTable nested1 = new PdfPTable(2);
nested1.addCell("1.1");
nested1.addCell("1.2");
PdfPTable nested2 = new PdfPTable(1);
nested2.addCell("20.1");
nested2.addCell("20.2");
for (int k = 0; k < 24; ++k) {
  if (k == 1) {
    table.addCell(nested1);
  }
  else if (k == 20) {
    table.addCell(new PdfPCell(nested2));
  }
  else {
    table.addCell("cell " + k);
  }
}
document.add(table);
```

Table to be used for cell I

Table to be used for cell 20

Add tables as cell

Another interesting `PdfPCell` constructor can be used to add images.

### *Tables and images*

Suppose you want to make a table containing the specifications of all the products that are sold by your company. One of the columns should contain an image displaying the product. These images have various heights and widths, so you want iText to scale each image so that it fits into the table.

That's easy to achieve, but make sure you use the right method. There are three different ways to add an image to a table:

```
/* chapter06/PdfPTableImages.java */
PdfPTable table = new PdfPTable(1);
table.addCell(img);   <-❶
table.addCell(new PdfPCell(img, true));   <-❷
table.addCell(new PdfPCell(img, false));   <-❸
```

When you add an image directly to the table ❶, the properties of the default cell are used (for instance, `padding` = 2); the image is scaled to fit the cell by default.

When you add an image wrapped in a cell, the properties of the default cell aren't taken into account. If you set the parameter `fit` to true ❷, the image is scaled so that it fits the cell. If it's set to false ❸, iText tries to adapt the cell dimension to the image.

Having all these small examples to demonstrate different table features is nice, but in real life, you'll probably have to deal with much larger tables than the ones we've shown. Let's look at what happens if a table doesn't fit on one page.

## 6.1.5 Working with large tables

When a cell doesn't fit on a page, what do you expect iText to do? Do you want to trigger a new page and start the cell on a new page? Do you want to split the cell in two parts? Or do you want to drop the cell if it's too large to fit the page? When in doubt, try the next example.

### Tables spanning multiple pages

This example adds the same table to three different documents, demonstrating three different options. You create three `Document` and `PdfWriter` instances:

```
/* chapter06/PdfPTableSplit.java */
PdfWriter.getInstance(document1,
  new FileOutputStream("SplitRowsBetween.pdf"));
PdfWriter.getInstance(document2,
  new FileOutputStream("SplitRowsWithin.pdf"));
PdfWriter.getInstance(document3,
  new FileOutputStream("OmitRows.pdf"));
```

The table is created only once and added to three different documents:

```
/* chapter06/PdfPTableSplit.java */
String text = ". Quick brown fox jumps over the lazy dog.";
PdfPTable table = new PdfPTable(2);
PdfPCell largeCell = new PdfPCell();
for (int i = 1; i < 13; i++) {
  largeCell.addElement(new Paragraph(String.valueOf(i) + text));
}
```

```
for (int i = 1; i < 11; i++) {
  table.addCell(String.valueOf(i));
  table.addCell(largeCell);
  if (i == 8) {
  for (int j = 13; j < 31; j++) {
      largeCell.addElement(new Paragraph(String.valueOf(j) + text));
    }
  }
}
document1.add(table);          <-1
table.setSplitLate(false);     2
document2.add(table);
table.setSplitRows(false);     3
document3.add(table);
```

First, you add the table to `document1` as is ❶. Once this is done, you tell the table that cells shouldn't be kept together and add the table to `document2` ❷. Finally, you indicate that the rows don't need to be split and add the table to `document3` ❸.

What is happening here? The default behavior is that iText tries to add complete cells that aren't split in two. You can change this default by setting "split late" to false. The example adds eight rows with a 12-line cell to a table.

The first four pages of SplitRowsBetween.pdf contain two complete rows each. With `setSplitLate(false)`, the first page contains two complete rows and four lines of the third row. Lines 5 to 12 of row three are forwarded to the next page, and so on. Starting from row eight, you augment the number of lines in the large cell to 30. A cell with 30 lines is too large to fit on one page. This isn't a problem in the file SplitRowsWithin.pdf; these large rows are split over several pages anyway.

If "split late" is true, a choice has to be made. The default is to start the large row on a new page and split it anyway. The alternative is to drop the row. You can do this by setting "split rows" to false, as demonstrated in OmitRows.pdf. If you open this PDF file, you'll see the last two rows are missing.

This table splitting is done automatically, so you don't have to count rows and row positions yourself. But what if you want to repeat the table header on every new page? Again, you don't have to worry about this—`PdfPTable` knows how to take care of it. The previous examples were rather theoretical; the next example is more realistic.

### Repeating the table header and footer

Suppose you have to generate large administrative reports with lots of users, some information about the users, company and department information, and a list of privileges. This example is based on some production code that was sent to me, but instead of filling in data based on a database query, I added some nonsense data.

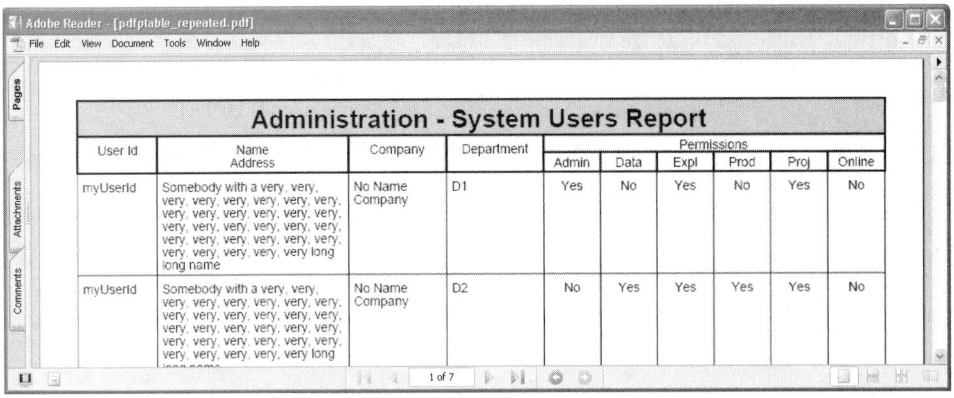

**Figure 6.8 A PdfPTable with some header rows**

Figure 6.8 shows a table with some header rows. The screenshot shows only part of page 1 of 7; the actual report spans multiple pages. If you want to repeat the header (the part with the thick borders) on the pages that contain the rest of the table, you have to use the method `setHeaderRows()` and define the number of rows that are part of the header:

```
/* chapter06/PdfPTableRepeatHeader.java */
datatable.setHeaderRows(2);
```

You can also define a footer for the table. The final row with the permissions in the System Users Report shown in figure 6.9 is repeated on every page, just like the header.

If you want to have the last row repeated, you should add it after the two header rows and before adding any other data. Then you do a little trick:

```
/* chapter06/PdfPTableRepeatHeaderFooter.java */
datatable.setHeaderRows(3);
datatable.setFooterRows(1);
```

You still have two header rows, but the first line of the code snippet says that three rows should be repeated. The second line of the sample says that one of these lines is a footer. When building a table, you add the rows in the following order: header row, header row, footer row, data row 1, data row 2, …, data row *n*.

Once you start experimenting with this functionality, you'll find that this is an easy way to distribute large tables over different pages. There's only one serious caveat: Creating a large table object demands a lot of memory. The memory needed to store table data can exceed the memory available to your JVM. This

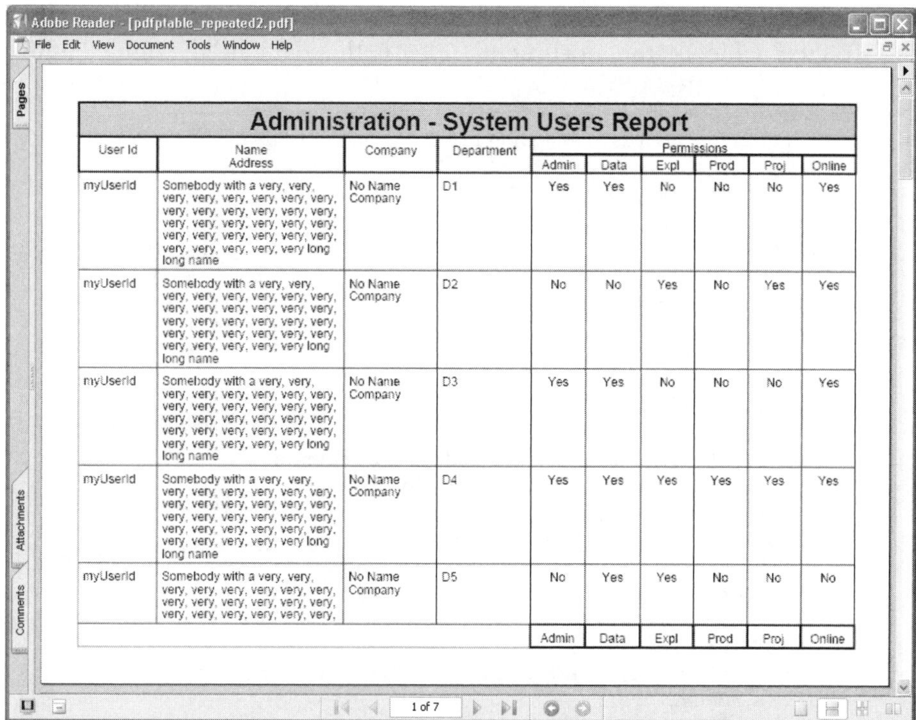


| Administration - System Users Report | | | | | | | | | |
|---|---|---|---|---|---|---|---|---|---|
| User Id | Name<br>Address | Company | Department | Permissions | | | | | |
| | | | | Admin | Data | Expl | Prod | Proj | Online |
| myUserId | Somebody with a very, very, very, very, very, very, very, very, very, very, very, very, very, very, very, very, very, very, very, very, very, very, very, very, very, very, very, very, very, very, very long long name | No Name Company | D1 | Yes | Yes | No | No | No | Yes |
| myUserId | Somebody with a very, very, very, very, very, very, very, very, very, very, very, very, very, very, very, very, very, very, very, very, very, very, very, very, very, very, very, very, very, very, very long long name | No Name Company | D2 | No | No | Yes | No | Yes | Yes |
| myUserId | Somebody with a very, very, very, very, very, very, very, very, very, very, very, very, very, very, very, very, very, very, very, very, very, very, very, very, very, very, very, very, very, very, very long long name | No Name Company | D3 | Yes | Yes | No | No | No | Yes |
| myUserId | Somebody with a very, very, very, very, very, very, very, very, very, very, very, very, very, very, very, very, very, very, very, very, very, very, very, very, very, very, very, very, very, very, very long long name | No Name Company | D4 | Yes | Yes | Yes | Yes | Yes | Yes |
| myUserId | Somebody with a very, very, very, very, very, very, very, very, very, very, very, very, very, very, very, very, very, very, very, very, | No Name Company | D5 | No | Yes | Yes | No | No | No |
| | | | | Admin | Data | Expl | Prod | Proj | Online |

**Figure 6.9 A PdfPTable with a footer row**

memory can be released only once the table is added to the document and the table object goes out of scope or is set to null. If you construct a large `PdfPTable` and keep adding new cells, you risk the dreaded `OutOfMemoryError`.

This can be problematic when dealing with really large tables, but there are several workarounds.

### *Memory management for large tables*

When you add objects to a document, these objects are written to the `OutputStream` as soon as possible (in most cases, when a page is full). The objects that have been added to the document should be made eligible for destruction.

One solution is to fragment a large table into different small tables. In section 6.1.2, you saw how consecutive tables are glued together unless you set the spacing before or after the table. You can use this feature to fake one large table while in reality you're adding multiple small tables that are destroyed once they're added to the document.

But there is another, more elegant way. You can add a partially constructed table to the document, release the data in the table, and continue adding new cells:

```
/* chapter06/PdfPTableMemoryFriendly.java */
PdfPTable table = new PdfPTable(2);
table.setWidthPercentage(100);
table.setHeaderRows(1);
PdfPCell h1 = new PdfPCell(new Paragraph("Header 1"));
h1.setGrayFill(0.7f);
table.addCell(h1);
PdfPCell h2 = new PdfPCell(new Paragraph("Header 2"));
h2.setGrayFill(0.7f);
table.addCell(h2);
PdfPCell cell;
for (int row = 1; row <= 2000; row++) {       <-- Table will have 2000 rows
  if (row % 50 == 0) {                         Add table to document
    document.add(table);                       every 50 rows
    table.deleteBodyRows();                    <-- Delete 50 rows from table
    table.setSkipFirstHeader(true);            <-- Header added only on new page
  }
  cell = new PdfPCell(new Paragraph(String.valueOf(row)));
  table.addCell(cell);                                                       Add new
  cell = new PdfPCell(                                                       cells
    new Paragraph("Quick brown fox jumps over the lazy dog."))
  table.addCell(cell);
}
document.add(table);     <-- Add final rows (fewer than 50)
```

Did you notice that the code is gradually getting more complex? The next subsection goes a step further and tells you how to add tables at absolute positions and split them vertically.

### 6.1.6 Adding a PdfPTable at an absolute position

In section 2.2.4, you saw different ways to add content to a page. Until now, you've been adding content using high-level objects with `document.add()`. In the next examples, you'll use an object that is discussed in part 3: `PdfContentByte`. It can be used to write objects at absolute positions. For instance, if you want to use a table as a header or footer, you have to be able to add this table at exact coordinates above or below the actual content.

#### Comparing document.add() with writeSelectedRows()

Let's add the same table twice in two different ways: once with `document.add()` and once using one of the `writeSelectedRows()` methods:

```
/* chapter06/PdfPTableCompare.java */
PdfPTable table = new PdfPTable(3);
table.addCell("the quick brown fox");          Create regular
table.addCell("jumps over");                   PdfPTable
table.addCell("the lazy dog");
document.add(new Paragraph(
  "The table below is added with document.add():"));
document.add(table);          <- Add table with document.add()
document.add(new Paragraph(
  "The table below is added with writeSelectedRows() at
  ➥ position (x = 50; y ="
  ➥ + PageSize.A4.height() * 0.75f + "):"));    Start and
table.writeSelectedRows(0, -1,                  <- end row
  50, PageSize.A4.height() * 0.75f,    <- Coordinates
  writer.getDirectContent());     <- PdfContentByte object
```

In this case, all the rows of the table are added to the direct content, because you use 0 as the starting row and –1 as end row (which means "show all the remaining rows").

The next example uses the method `writeSelectedRows()` to distribute a table over different pages. Observe that there's a big difference from what you did in section 6.1.5:

```
/* chapter06/PdfPTableAbsolutePositions.java */
PdfContentByte cb = writer.getDirectContent();
PdfPTable table = new PdfPTable(2);
float[] rows = { 50f, 250f };
table.setTotalWidth(rows);
for (int k = 0; k < 200; ++k) {
  table.addCell("row " + k);
  table.addCell("blah blah blah " + k);
}
document.add(new Paragraph("row 0 - 49"));
table.writeSelectedRows(0, 50, 150, 820, cb);     <- 1
document.newPage();
document.add(new Paragraph("row 50 - 99"));
table.writeSelectedRows(50, 100, 150, 820, cb);     <- 2
document.newPage();
document.add(new Paragraph(
  "row 100 - 149 DOESN'T FIT ON THE PAGE!!!"));
table.writeSelectedRows(100, 150, 150, 200, cb);     <- 3
document.newPage();
document.add(new Paragraph("row 150 - 199"));     <- 4
table.writeSelectedRows(150, -1, 150, 820, cb);
```

Here's what happens:

1. Rows 0 to 49 are added at coordinate x = 150; y = 820.

❷ Rows 50 to 99 are added at coordinate x = 150; y = 820. Notice that you have to trigger a `newPage()` manually; this isn't done automatically by iText.

❸ Rows 100 to 149 are added at coordinate x = 150; y = 200. This means the starting point of the table is much lower than it should be. Part of the table doesn't fit the page and will be invisible. It's your responsibility to make sure the table fits.

❹ Rows 150 to 199 are added at coordinate x = 150; y = 820.

Note that the method `writeSelectedRows()` returns the current Y position after the table was added. This information is important if you choose not to use `document.add()` but decide to add all the content at absolute positions.

In the previous example, you were in luck that the first page was big enough to fit rows 0 to 49. In a real-life application, you can calculate the total height of the first 50 rows before selecting and positioning the rows.

**FAQ** *Why is the returned height 0 when I use `table.getRowHeight(0)`?* This result is normal. You've forgotten to set an important property. Before iText can calculate the height of each row, the available horizontal width must be known. Otherwise, it's impossible to determine how much space will be needed vertically to display the content of all the cells in a row. The available width is known to iText when the table is added to the document, but at that moment, any information about the row height comes too late. If you want to know the height before adding the table to a page, you have to set the total width of the table.

The following code snippets demonstrate two different ways to get the height of a selection of rows. In the first example, you loop over the first 50 rows, assuming that the total width of the table is set:

```
/* chapter06/PdfPTableAbsolutePositions.java */
System.out.println("Total table height: " + table.getTotalHeight());
float rowheight = 0;
for (int i = 0; i < 50; i++) {
  rowheight += table.getRowHeight(i);
}
System.out.println("Height of the first 50 rows: " + rowheight);
```

In the second code snippet, you get the height of each row in the `ArrayList` of `PdfPRow` objects:

```
/* chapter06/PdfPTableAbsolutePositions.java */
System.out.print("Heights of the individual rows:");
PdfPRow row;
for (Iterator i = table.getRows().iterator(); i.hasNext(); ) {
  row = (PdfPRow)i.next();
```

```
    System.out.print(" ");
    System.out.print(row.getMaxHeights());
  }
```

A more elegant way to find out if a table that is added at an absolute position fits the current page is to add it to a `ColumnText` object. You can then ask iText to do all the calculations that are performed when a column is added to a page. These calculations can also return a Y position. Depending on this Y value, you can decide if it's necessary to add the table at another position. The `ColumnText` object will be discussed in the next chapter.

Until now, you've split tables horizontally, row per row. For tables that have a lot of columns, it can be interesting to split the table vertically. To do this, you'll use a second variety of the method `writeSelectedRows()`.

### Splitting a PdfPTable vertically

Figure 6.10 shows a table with ten columns. If you tried to fit all these columns on one page, the column width would be insufficient for the cell content.

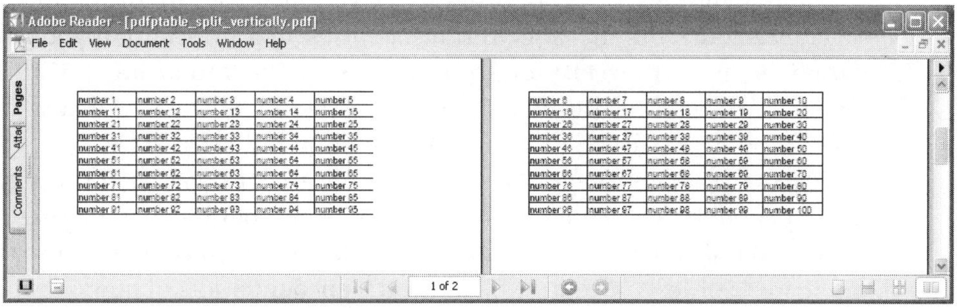

**Figure 6.10 A table that has been split vertically**

With the method `writeSelectedRows()`, you can select the columns that have to be rendered:

```
/* chapter06/PdfPTableSplitVertically.java */
PdfPTable table = new PdfPTable(10);
for (int k = 1; k <= 100; ++k) {
  table.addCell("number " + k);
}
table.setTotalWidth(800);
table.writeSelectedRows(0, 5,                         // Write first 5 columns
  0, -1, 50, 650, writer.getDirectContent());        // Write all rows at coordinate x = 50; y = 650
document.newPage();
table.writeSelectedRows(5, -1,                        // Write remaining columns
  0, -1, 50, 650, writer.getDirectContent());        // Write all rows at coordinate x = 50; y = 650
```

Again, you need to do some extra calculations to see if the table fits on the page. For example, you can call the method `PdfPTable.getAbsoluteWidths()` to retrieve the absolute width of each column.

There's a lot more to say about `PdfPTable`. In chapter 10, you'll learn how to customize cells using table events and cell events. Chapter 10 deals with PDF's graphics state; you'll also learn how to draw cell borders with rounded corners, how to strike a line through a cell, and so on. But for now, let's talk about some alternatives to PdfPTable.

## 6.2 Alternatives to PdfPTable

This chapter focuses on tables created with `PdfPTable`. If you look at the iText API, you'll also find some other table classes. `com.lowagie.text.Table` is the original table class; it dates from the early iText days. It uses class `com.lowagie.text.pdf.PdfTable` internally to render a table to PDF (don't confuse this class with `PdfPTable`).

There's also the newer `SimpleTable` class, which tries to form a link between `PdfPTable` and `Table`. It's able to translate itself to a `PdfPTable` if you add it to a document that writes PDF or to a `Table` if you're producing HTML or RTF. Because this book focuses mainly on PDF generation, I won't discuss the other table classes in detail; I'll just sum up some pros and cons.

The major disadvantage of the `Table` class is that it's no longer supported. Different people have fixed most of the known issues, but today not a single person understands if and how all the `Table`-methods work. If you decide to use this class, you're more or less on your own, and you'll encounter lots of quirky layout issues based on historical design decisions. However, this doesn't mean you can't make good use of the `Table` class. Let's look at some of the advantages.

### Advantages of the Table class

The following code sample illustrates three advantages of using the `Table` class:

```
/* chapter06/MyFirstTable.java */
Document document = new Document();
PdfWriter.getInstance(document,
  new FileOutputStream("my_first_table.pdf"));
RtfWriter2.getInstance(document,
  new FileOutputStream("my_first_table.rtf"));      ❶
HtmlWriter.getInstance(document,
  new FileOutputStream("my_first_table.htm"));
document.open();
Table table = new Table(3);
```

```
table.setBorderWidth(1);
table.setBorderColor(new Color(0, 0, 255));
table.setPadding(5);
table.setSpacing(5);                              ❷
Cell cell = new Cell("header");
cell.setHeader(true);
cell.setColspan(3);
table.addCell(cell);
cell = new Cell("example cell with colspan 1 and rowspan 2");
cell.setRowspan(2);      <-❸
cell.setBorderColor(new Color(255, 0, 0));
table.addCell(cell);
table.addCell("1.1");
table.addCell("2.1");
table.addCell("1.2");
table.addCell("2.2");
table.addCell("cell test1");
cell = new Cell("big cell");
cell.setRowspan(2);
cell.setColspan(2);
cell.setBackgroundColor(new Color(0xC0, 0xC0, 0xC0));
table.addCell(cell);
table.addCell("cell test2");
document.add(table);
document.close();
```

❶ You can generate a table in PDF, HTML, or RTF using the same code.

❷ You can set padding and spacing the way it's done in HTML.

❸ You can use the row span without having to resort to nested table.

With the `Table` class, you can generate a table structure that can be rendered in PDF, RTF, and HTML. If you compare the results, you'll see there are small differences in the way the table is rendered. This is normal; not every table feature is supported in every document format.

The next example demonstrates more advantages of the `Table` class:

```
/* chapter06/SpecificCells.java */
Table table = new Table(2,2);
table.setAlignment(Element.ALIGN_LEFT);
table.setAutoFillEmptyCells(true);
table.addCell("0.0");
table.addCell("0.1");
table.addCell("1.0");
table.addCell("1.1");
table.addColumns(2);      <-❹
float[] f = {2f, 1f, 1f, 1f};
table.setWidths(f);
table.addCell("2.2", new Point(2,2));      <-❺
table.addCell("3.3", new Point(3,3));
```

```
table.addCell("2.1", new Point(2,1));
table.addCell("1.3", new Point(1,3));
table.addCell("5.3", new Point(5,3));
table.addCell("5.0", new Point(5,0));
table.deleteColumn(2);    <-6
document.add(table);
document.add(new Paragraph("converted to PdfPTable:"));
table.setConvert2pdfptable(true);    <-7
document.add(table);
document.add(new Paragraph("positioned PdfPTable:"));
PdfPTable pTable = table.createPdfPTable();    <-8
pTable.setTotalWidth(400);
PdfContentByte cb = writer.getDirectContent();
pTable.writeSelectedRows(0, -1, 36, 550, cb);
```

❹ You can change the number of columns even after you've added cells.

❺ You can add cells at specific positions (the number of rows is augmented dynamically).

❻ You can delete a column before adding the table to the document.

❼ You can let iText add the `Table` as if it was a `PdfPTable`.

❽ You get a `PdfPTable` object based on the `Table` object.

As opposed to `PdfPTable`, you can add cells to a `Table` in a random order, and add or delete columns if needed. You can even translate a `Table` to a `PdfPTable` if you didn't use `setRowspan()`.

There's also the `SimpleTable`, class, which is a simplified version of `(PdfP)-Table`. When adding a `SimpleTable` to a PDF document, iText first attempts to add the table as a `PdfPTable`; if this fails, it's added as a `Table`. When adding a `SimpleTable` to an RTF or HTML document, it's added as a `Table`. `SimpleTable` differs from the `Table` and `PdfPTable` in the sense that it reintroduces the concept of rows. This can be handy if you're parsing an XML file that has a table-row-cell structure. If the tag corresponding with the rows has attributes, you don't have to define this property for each cell in the row separately; you can set the property for the entire row at once.

This being said, we can use this `SimpleTable` class to help Laura with her second assignment. We'll ask her to make an XML file with all the information that needs to be displayed in a study program at Foobar University, and we'll parse this XML into a PDF and an HTML file.

## 6.3 Composing a study guide (part 1)

Do you remember Laura's second assignment? She had to make a nice brochure with information about the available study programs and the different courses that are taught in the new department. Let's start with the study programs and create some sheets with all the necessary data.

### 6.3.1 The data source

For my job, I need to create similar PDF documents with data coming from a database. In other words, I use iText as a database publishing tool. I write a database query, I create a table with as many columns as there are fields returned by my result set, and I start populating a `PdfPTable` class, adding it in small portions as described in section 6.1.4.

At Foobar, Laura wants to create code that is database independent. She uses XML as an intermediary format to store the database results. (Personally, I think this is overkill for most applications, but it's handy to use an example that you can run without having to install a database.) Laura composed an appealing study program. She took some of the most interesting Manning books on Java development and turned them into courses, appointing the writers as teachers. Listing 6.2 shows an excerpt of the XML with the data:

**Listing 6.2 Excerpt of the study program data source**

```
<studyprogram>
  <faculty>Department of Computer Science and Engineering</faculty>
  <programme code="CSE_GCAI0101">Graduate in Complementary
  Studies in Applied Informatics</programme>
  <option>Java Development for the Enterprise</option>
  <group>
    <title>GENERAL COURSES</title>
    <unit>
      <course>
        <coursenumber>8001</coursenumber>
        <title>POJOs: Plain Old Java Objects</title>
        <semester>1</semester>
        <pt>1</pt>
        <department>CSE02</department>
        <teacher>Chris Richardson</teacher>
        <a>37.5</a>
        <b>22.5</b>
        <c />
        <d count="true">180</d>
        <e count="true">6</e>
      </course>
```

```
</unit>
    ...
</group>
   ...
</studyprogram>
```

The data structure is pretty realistic. That's not a coincidence: The data fields are based on the way study programs are composed at Ghent University.

### 6.3.2 Generating the PDF

The data in the XML contains information that fits perfectly into a table structure. That's why a class `FoobarStudyProgram` was created that can parse the XML file (see listing 6.2) into a `SimpleTable` object:

```
/* chapter06/FoobarStudyProgram.java */
public FoobarStudyProgram(String html) throws Exception {
  table = new SimpleTable();
  table.setWidthpercentage(100f);
  currentRow = new SimpleCell(SimpleCell.ROW);
  SAXParser parser = SAXParserFactory.newInstance().newSAXParser();
  parser.parse(new InputSource(new FileInputStream(html)), this);
}
```

Now you have to implement the methods of the SAX `DefaultHandler` interface, just as you did when you created the flyer in the previous chapters. You map every tag with specific cell properties. `SimpleCell` objects are constructed in this manner:

```
/* chapter06/FoobarStudyProgram.java */
private SimpleCell getCell(String s, int style, float width) {
  SimpleCell cell = new SimpleCell(SimpleCell.CELL);
  Paragraph p;
  switch(style) {
    case EMPTY:
      cell.setBorder(SimpleCell.BOX);
      break;
    case TITLE:
      p = new Paragraph(s,
        FontFactory.getFont(BaseFont.HELVETICA, BaseFont.WINANSI,
        BaseFont.NOT_EMBEDDED, 14));
      p.setAlignment(Element.ALIGN_CENTER);
      cell.add(p);
      cell.setColspan(NUMCOLUMNS);
      cell.setBorder(SimpleCell.NO_BORDER);
      break;
    ...
  }
  cell.setBorderWidth(0.3f);
```

```
    cell.setPadding_bottom(5);
    return cell;
}
```

If you have lots of tables to generate, you can write an abstract class with a `getCell()` method that returns all kinds of standard cell layouts. For every type of table, you can then write a subclass that implements the structure of your XML schema or your database query. Once you get some experience with this functionality, you'll see it's not that difficult to create tables like the one in figure 6.11.

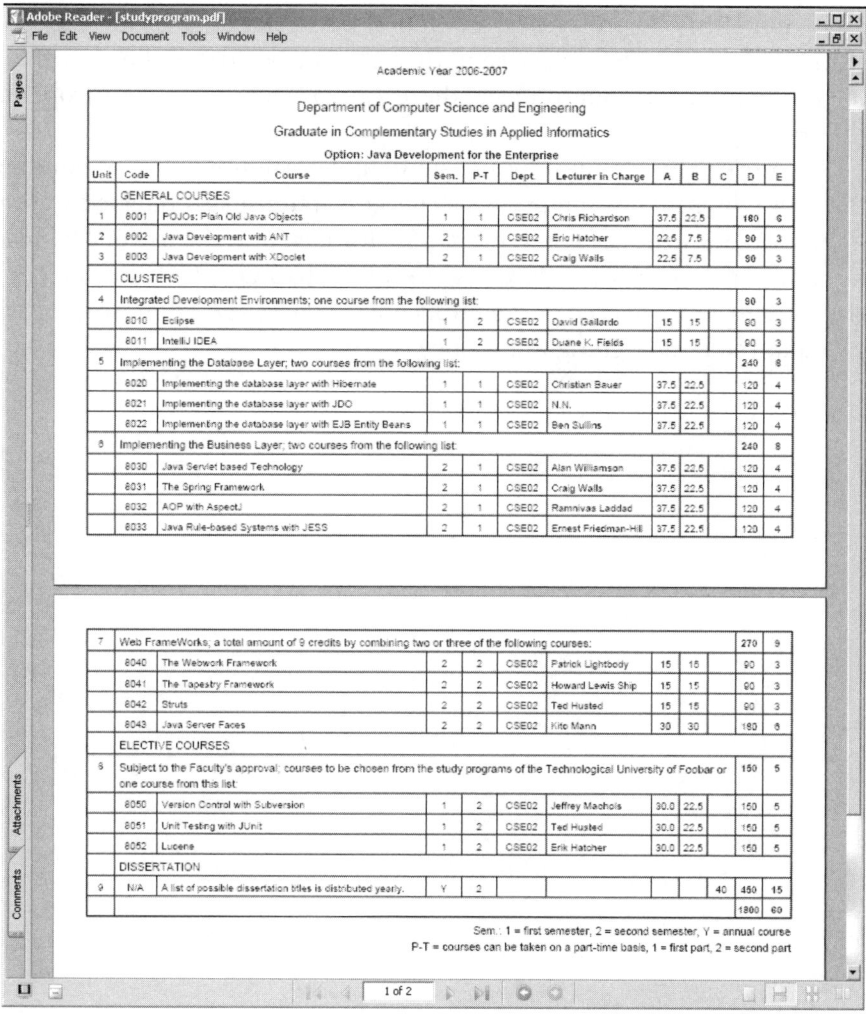

Academic Year 2006-2007

Department of Computer Science and Engineering

Graduate in Complementary Studies in Applied Informatics

**Option: Java Development for the Enterprise**

| Unit | Code | Course | Sem. | P-T | Dept. | Lecturer in Charge | A | B | C | D | E |
|---|---|---|---|---|---|---|---|---|---|---|---|
| | GENERAL COURSES | | | | | | | | | | |
| 1 | 8001 | POJOs: Plain Old Java Objects | 1 | 1 | CSE02 | Chris Richardson | 37.5 | 22.5 | | 180 | 6 |
| 2 | 8002 | Java Development with ANT | 2 | 1 | CSE02 | Eric Hatcher | 22.5 | 7.5 | | 90 | 3 |
| 3 | 8003 | Java Development with XDoclet | 2 | 1 | CSE02 | Craig Walls | 22.5 | 7.5 | | 90 | 3 |
| | CLUSTERS | | | | | | | | | | |
| 4 | Integrated Development Environments; one course from the following list: | | | | | | | | | 90 | 3 |
| | 8010 | Eclipse | 1 | 2 | CSE02 | David Gallardo | 15 | 15 | | 90 | 3 |
| | 8011 | IntelliJ IDEA | 1 | 2 | CSE02 | Duane K. Fields | 15 | 15 | | 90 | 3 |
| 5 | Implementing the Database Layer; two courses from the following list: | | | | | | | | | 240 | 8 |
| | 8020 | Implementing the database layer with Hibernate | 1 | 1 | CSE02 | Christian Bauer | 37.5 | 22.5 | | 120 | 4 |
| | 8021 | Implementing the database layer with JDO | 1 | 1 | CSE02 | N.N. | 37.5 | 22.5 | | 120 | 4 |
| | 8022 | Implementing the database layer with EJB Entity Beans | 1 | 1 | CSE02 | Ben Sullins | 37.5 | 22.5 | | 120 | 4 |
| 6 | Implementing the Business Layer; two courses from the following list: | | | | | | | | | 240 | 8 |
| | 8030 | Java Servlet based Technology | 2 | 1 | CSE02 | Alan Williamson | 37.5 | 22.5 | | 120 | 4 |
| | 8031 | The Spring Framework | 2 | 1 | CSE02 | Craig Walls | 37.5 | 22.5 | | 120 | 4 |
| | 8032 | AOP with AspectJ | 2 | 1 | CSE02 | Ramnivas Laddad | 37.5 | 22.5 | | 120 | 4 |
| | 8033 | Java Rule-based Systems with JESS | 2 | 1 | CSE02 | Ernest Friedman-Hill | 37.5 | 22.5 | | 120 | 4 |
| 7 | Web FrameWorks; a total amount of 9 credits by combining two or three of the following courses: | | | | | | | | | 270 | 9 |
| | 8040 | The Webwork Framework | 2 | 2 | CSE02 | Patrick Lightbody | 15 | 15 | | 90 | 3 |
| | 8041 | The Tapestry Framework | 2 | 2 | CSE02 | Howard Lewis Ship | 15 | 15 | | 90 | 3 |
| | 8042 | Struts | 2 | 2 | CSE02 | Ted Husted | 15 | 15 | | 90 | 3 |
| | 8043 | Java Server Faces | 2 | 2 | CSE02 | Kito Mann | 30 | 30 | | 180 | 6 |
| | ELECTIVE COURSES | | | | | | | | | | |
| 8 | Subject to the Faculty's approval; courses to be chosen from the study programs of the Technological University of Foobar or one course from this list: | | | | | | | | | 150 | 5 |
| | 8050 | Version Control with Subversion | 1 | 2 | CSE02 | Jeffrey Machols | 30.0 | 22.5 | | 150 | 5 |
| | 8051 | Unit Testing with JUnit | 1 | 2 | CSE02 | Ted Husted | 30.0 | 22.5 | | 150 | 5 |
| | 8052 | Lucene | 1 | 2 | CSE02 | Erik Hatcher | 30.0 | 22.5 | | 150 | 5 |
| | DISSERTATION | | | | | | | | | | |
| 9 | N/A | A list of possible dissertation titles is distributed yearly. | Y | 2 | | | | | 40 | 450 | 15 |
| | | | | | | | | | | 1800 | 60 |

Sem.: 1 = first semester, 2 = second semester, Y = annual course

P-T = courses can be taken on a part-time basis, 1 = first part, 2 = second part

**Figure 6.11 A table with a study program**

This is only the first part of a study guide. It lists the courses offered in a certain study program; it doesn't explain what these courses are about. In the next chapter, we'll return to this study program and generate a brochure with some information on every course.

## 6.4 Summary

This was the key chapter of this book if you need to produce reports filled with data retrieved with a database query. You've produced all kinds of tables, and I hope this chapter gave you a good understanding of the different possibilities. `PdfPTable` should be your first choice; but depending on the requirements defined for your project, there can be good reasons to opt for `Table` or `SimpleTable`.

Of course, this chapter doesn't stand alone. We used a lot of building blocks that were discussed in the previous chapters, but we also referred to some functionality that will be discussed in part 3—for instance, the use of `PdfContentByte`.

You'll also need this object in the next chapter, which introduces another structure that can be used to organize content on a page. After working with tabular data, you're now going to produce columns.

# 7 Constructing columns

***This chapter covers***

- Advanced page layout with `ColumnText`
- Text mode vs. composite mode
- Automated columns with `MultiColumnText`

In the examples so far, you've created a `Document` object defining a certain page size and well-defined margins. The layout of the building blocks you added to this document was adapted to fit inside this rectangle (`PageSize` minus margins). With class `ColumnText`, you have an object at your disposal that is similar. You can create a column object, add different types of building blocks, and then decide how the content has to be laid out: You can define a Y position; you can define the left and right borders of the column as straight or irregular lines; and you can also control the flow of the content.

Working with this class isn't always simple, but if you don't mind trading some flexibility for ease of use, you can use a `MultiColumnText` object. This class uses `ColumnText` internally, but it comes with some extra functionality that would otherwise be repeated frequently in your code.

But let's start with a typical problem that can be solved by introducing `ColumnText`. Suppose you want to add a paragraph to a document. How can you know if this paragraph will fit on the current page? If it doesn't fit, how many lines will be added on the current page, and how many lines will be forwarded to the next page?

## 7.1 Retrieving the current vertical position

If a paragraph is cut in two and there's only one line of the paragraph on the current page, we call this line an *orphan*. If there's only one line of the paragraph on the next page, it's called a *widow*. Word processors avoid orphans and widows automatically, but iText isn't a word processor; you have to take care of this issue programmatically.

Figure 7.1 illustrates a similar layout problem.

For this example, we took an excerpt from a famous work by Julius Caesar: "De Bello Gallica." You read the first lines of his report on the Gallic War from the plain ASCII file caesar.txt, wrap every line inside a `Paragraph` object, and add these paragraphs one by one:

```
/* chapter07/ParagraphText.java */
BufferedReader reader = new BufferedReader(
  new FileReader("../resources/caesar.txt"));
String line;
Paragraph p;
float pos;
while ((line = reader.readLine()) != null) {
  p = new Paragraph(line);
  p.setAlignment(Element.ALIGN_JUSTIFIED);
  document.add(p);
}
```

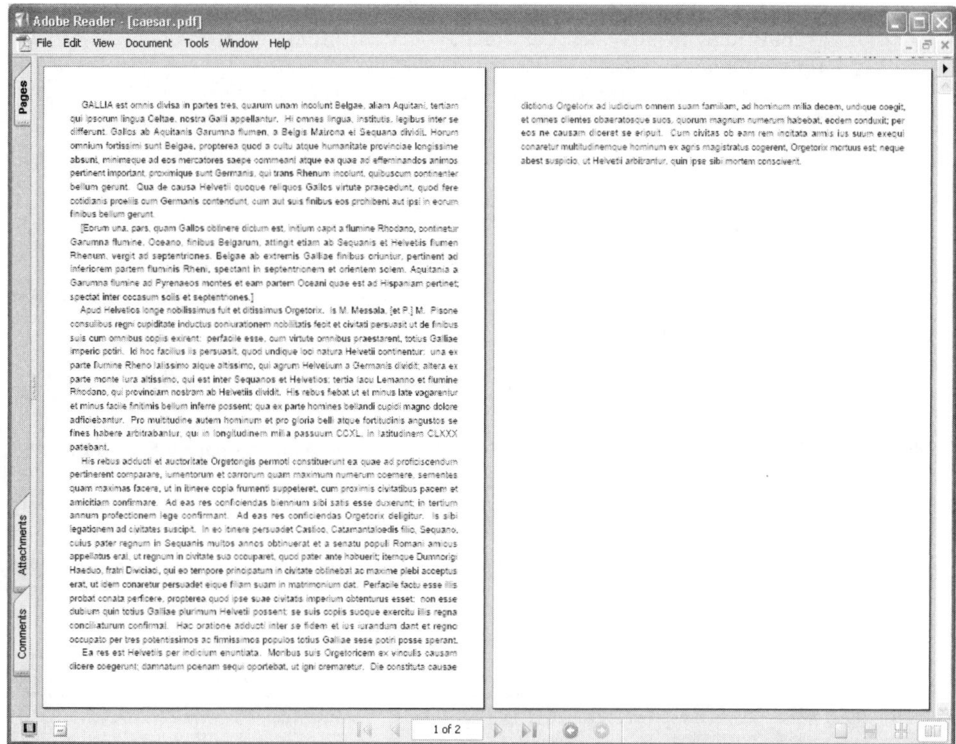


**Figure 7.1 Text composed using `Paragraph` objects and illustrating a layout that could be improved**

The result looks good at first sight, but there is room for improvement. If you give the text a closer look, you'll see the last two lines of the first page belong to a separate paragraph. Suppose you want to keep this last paragraph together on one page.

One possibility is to ask the `PdfWriter` for its vertical Y position after adding a high-level object and evaluate how close you are to the bottom border of the page. This way, you can trigger a new page if you think the next paragraph will cause an orphaned line—for instance, if the space available is less than the bottom margin plus the paragraph leading times two or three. Avoiding widows is more difficult. You don't know how many lines the next paragraph will take, so you have to do quite a bit of math to see if there's enough space available on the current page.

In the second example of this chapter, you'll go to a new page if a paragraph ends less than 1¼ in (90 user units) from the bottom border:

```
/* chapter07/ParagraphPositions.java */
PdfContentByte cb = writer.getDirectContent();
BufferedReader reader =
  new BufferedReader(new FileReader("caesar.txt"));
String line;
Paragraph p;
float pos;
while ((line = reader.readLine()) != null) {
  p = new Paragraph(line);
  p.setAlignment(Element.ALIGN_JUSTIFIED);
  document.add(p);
  pos = writer.getVerticalPosition(false);      <- Get current Y coordinate
  System.out.println(pos);
  cb.moveTo(0, pos);
  cb.lineTo(PageSize.A4.width(), pos);          <- Draw line at this exact Y-position
  cb.stroke();
  if (pos < 90) document.newPage();             <- Open new page if Y < 90 pt
}
```

The resulting PDF is shown in figure 7.2.

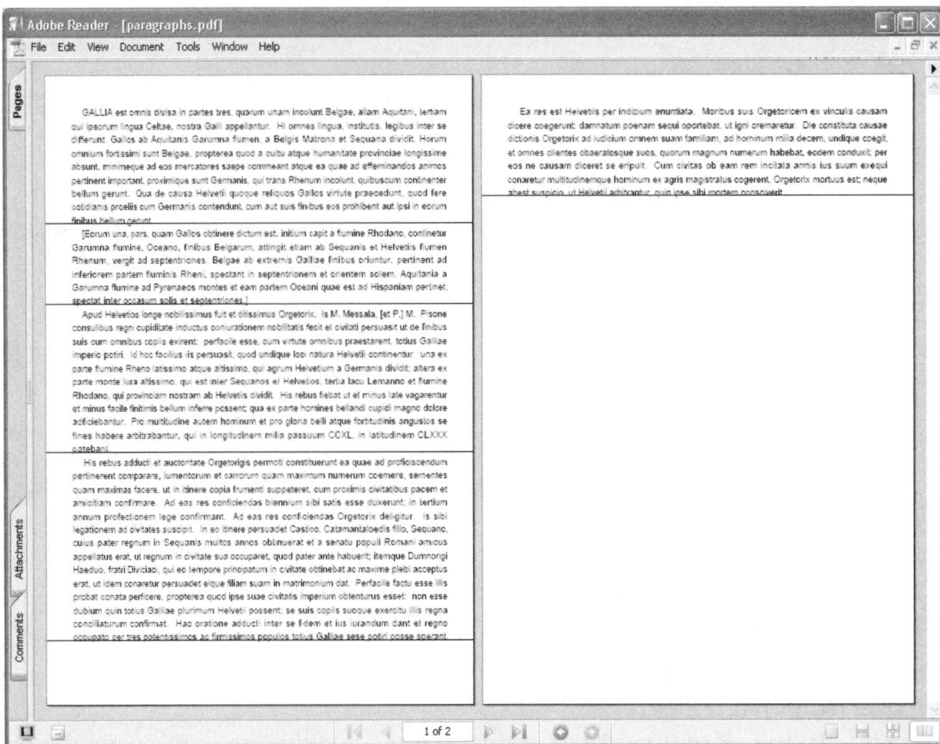


**Figure 7.2 Retrieving the Y position after adding a high-level object**

Look at the horizontal lines that were added with the moveTo()/lineTo() methods (these methods will be explained in part 3). These lines indicate the Y position of the baseline of every last paragraph line. This value is returned by getVerticalPosition(). As you can see, the lines that were orphaned in figure 7.1 are now forwarded to the next page.

In the next section, you'll try to achieve the same result using the ColumnText class.

## 7.2 Adding text to ColumnText

Let's start with Phrases and Chunks. Remember that a Chunk is the atomic building block, containing a String in one specific font, font size, font style, and font color. A Phrase is an ArrayList of chunks for which you've defined a leading. Please don't think about more complex building blocks (such Paragraphs, Images, and Tables) until you've reached the next section.

First, you'll produce a PDF that looks exactly the same as the PDF shown in figure 7.1. You'll use an approach that differs from all the previous examples: Instead of performing a series of document.add() invocations, you'll create a ColumnText object and position it on the page.

### 7.2.1 Different ways to add text to a column

This is a complex matter, so I'll throw in a good deal of code to help you get acquainted with the interesting ColumnText object. The PDF shown in figure 7.1 could have been generated in three different ways.

#### ColumnText.addText(Phrase p)

When you create a ColumnText object, you always need a PdfContentByte object. By now, you probably understand that objects that are added at absolute positions generally can't do without PdfContentByte.

You add different portions of text to this ColumnText object. Furthermore, you use the method setSimpleColumn() to define a rectangle (the lower-left and upper-right corner of the column), a leading, and an alignment:

```
/* chapter07/ColumnWithAddText.java */
PdfContentByte cb = writer.getDirectContent();
ColumnText ct = new ColumnText(cb);          <- Create ColumnText object
BufferedReader reader =
  new BufferedReader(new FileReader("caesar.txt"));
String line;
```

```
while ((line = reader.readLine()) != null) {
  ct.addText(new Phrase(line + "\n"));        <- Add Phrase
}
reader.close();
ct.setSimpleColumn(36, 36,                    <- Define lower-left coordinate
  PageSize.A4.width() - 36, PageSize.A4.height() - 36     <- Define upper-right coordinate
  18, Element.ALIGN_JUSTIFIED);               <- Define leading and alignment
int status = ColumnText.START_COLUMN;
while (ColumnText.hasMoreText(status)) {
  status = ct.go();
  ct.setYLine(PageSize.A4.height() - 36);
  document.newPage();
}
```

The `go()` method renders as much text as possible on the current page. As long as more text is left in the column, you create a new page and reset the Y position of the column so that you can continue rendering text until there's none left.

**NOTE** *Don't write a* `ColumnText` *object to different writers simultaneously.* Invoking `go()` removes content from the column object, so it can only be used once—that is, with one `PdfWriter` at a time.

If the text doesn't fit the column (you've reached the end of the column and there is still content left in the `ColumnText` object), the `go()` method returns `ColumnText.NO_MORE_COLUMN`. If you're out of text, but you still have space available in the column, `ColumnText.NO_MORE_TEXT` is returned. It's also possible that the text fits the column exactly; in this case, an or-ed combination of both values is returned: `ColumnText.NO_MORE_COLUMN | ColumnText.NO_MORE_TEXT`.

**NOTE** You should never check the status like this: `status == ColumnText.NO_MORE_TEXT`. Instead, you can use the condition `(status & ColumnText.NO_MORE_TEXT) == 0` or the convenience method `ColumnText.hasMoreText(status)`.

Another way to get a document similar to the one in figure 7.1 using the `ColumnText` object is to read the text completely into a `String` (including all the newline characters) and add this `String` to a column in a single statement.

### *ColumnText.setSimpleColumn(Phrase p, ... )*

You can read the entire text into a `StringBuffer` and pass the `toString()` of this buffer object to the `setSimpleColumn()` method:

```
/* chapter07/ColumnWithSetSimpleColumn.java */
StringBuffer sb = new StringBuffer(1024);
BufferedReader reader =
  new BufferedReader(new FileReader("caesar.txt"));
int c;
while( (c = reader.read()) > -1){
  sb.append((char)c);
}
reader.close();
PdfContentByte cb = writer.getDirectContent();
ColumnText ct = new ColumnText(cb);
ct.setSimpleColumn(new Phrase(sb.toString()), 36, 36,
  PageSize.A4.width() - 36, PageSize.A4.height() - 36,
  18, Element.ALIGN_JUSTIFIED);
```

When you add content with the `setSimpleColumn()` method, it's appended to the content that was previously added with `addText()`. After setting the simple column, you have to invoke the `go()` method in a loop, as was done in the previous example.

Finally, there's a third way to set the text; it doesn't differ much from the previous example.

#### *ColumnText.setText(Phrase p)*

You can also read the complete text into the `StringBuffer sb`, define the column, and set the text:

```
/* chapter07/ColumnWithSetText.java */
ColumnText ct = new ColumnText(cb);
ct.setSimpleColumn(36, 36,
  PageSize.A4.width() - 36, PageSize.A4.height() - 36,
  18, Element.ALIGN_JUSTIFIED);
ct.setText(new Phrase(sb.toString()));
```

Again, you need to loop until all text has been added. The difference from the previous examples is that using `setText()` discards all the content that was already added to the column. Soon you'll see why this is important.

You've now created three PDF files that look like the one in figure 7.1, but what you really need is a PDF that keeps paragraphs together as shown in figure 7.2.

### 7.2.2 *Keeping paragraphs together*

With class `ColumnText`, it's possible to simulate the `go()` method before you add the content of the column to the document. If you use a `boolean` parameter like `ct.go(true)`, iText will pretend to add the column, but in reality nothing will show up on the page. This is interesting because the result of this simulation provides a lot of information.

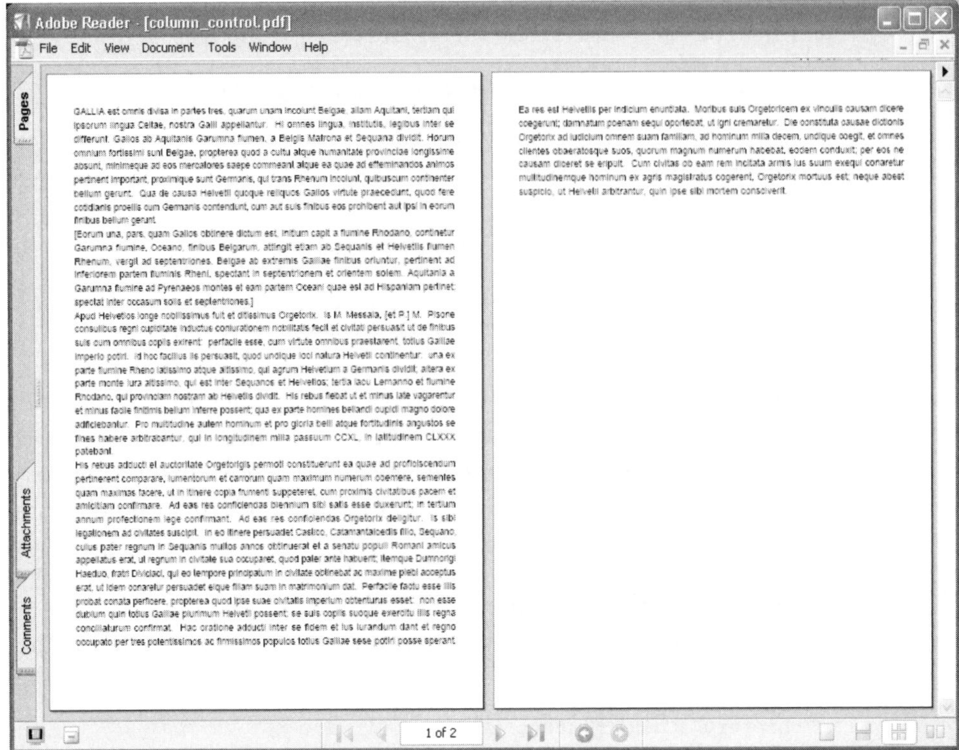


**Figure 7.3 Columns that keep paragraphs together on one page**

It tells you the number of lines that will be rendered, as well as the Y position that will be reached after the content is added. These values can help you to decide whether a block of text will be widowed or orphaned. Compare figure 7.3 with figures 7.2 and 7.1. In figure 7.3, the last paragraph of the text is forwarded to the next page instead of being split.

You use the method `ColumnText.hasMoreText()` to decide if you're going to add the column to this page or forward it to the next page:

```
/* chapter07/ColumnControl.java */
PdfContentByte cb = writer.getDirectContent();
BufferedReader reader =
  new BufferedReader(new FileReader("caesar.txt"));
ColumnText ct = new ColumnText(cb);
float pos;
String line;
Phrase p;
int status = ColumnText.START_COLUMN;
```

```
ct.setSimpleColumn(36, 36,
PageSize.A4.width() - 36, PageSize.A4.height() - 36,
  18, Element.ALIGN_JUSTIFIED);
while ((line = reader.readLine()) != null) {
  p = new Phrase(line);
  ct.addText(p);
  pos = ct.getYLine();
  status = ct.go(true);          <-- Simulate go() method
System.err.println("Lines written:" + ct.getLinesWritten()
    + " Y-positions: " + pos + " - " + ct.getYLine());
  if (!ColumnText.hasMoreText(status)) {
    ct.addText(p);
    ct.setYLine(pos);
    ct.go(false);
  }
  else {
    document.newPage();
    ct.setText(p);
    ct.setYLine(PageSize.A4.height() - 36);
    ct.go();
  }
}
reader.close();
```

Add as much text as possible to page

There are things going on in this code that need some extra explanation. The most important issue is that `go(true)` does everything `go()` or `go(false)` does, except add the content to the page. Observe that `go(true)` also removes the content from the `ColumnText` object as if it was added.

If the text fits, you can use `addText()` or `setText()` to reintroduce the phrase before invoking `go()` for real. In the other case, you have to use `setText()` to discard the content that is still present in the `ColumnText` because it didn't fit. If you used `addText()`, part of the content would be duplicated. This answers the question you probably wanted (but were afraid?) to ask in the previous subsection: Why do you need all these different methods?

Being able to simulate the `go()` method to gain control over what happens when adding data to a page is one interesting feature of class `ColumnText`, but it isn't the most important, as you'll see in the next section.

### 7.2.3 Adding more than one column to a page

You've been using `ColumnText` as an alternative for `document.add()` using a single column, but nothing stops you from adding more than one column to the same page. Figure 7.4 shows you the same text in two columns, as if it was a news article reporting on the Gallic War in the Gazetta di Roma.

**Figure 7.4 Adding more than one column to a page**

You don't need any new functionality to achieve this format. We've already discussed all the necessary methods; but let's look at the source code to produce these regular columns.

### *Regular columns*

If you want to add two columns of text per page, then you only need to make some changes in the `go()` loop:

```
/* chapter07/ColumnsRegular.java */
ColumnText ct = new ColumnText(cb);
ct.setAlignment(Element.ALIGN_JUSTIFIED);
ct.setText(new Phrase(sb.toString()));
float[] left = { 36, (PageSize.A4.width() / 2) + 18 };
float[] right = { (PageSize.A4.width() / 2) - 18,
  PageSize.A4.width() - 36 };
int status = ColumnText.NO_MORE_COLUMN;
int column = 0;
```

**Define left borders**

**Define right borders**

```
while (ColumnText.hasMoreText(status)) {
  ct.setSimpleColumn(left[column], 36,
    right[column], PageSize.A4.height() - 36);
  status = ct.go();
  column++;
  if (column > 1) {
    column = 0;
    document.newPage();
  }
}
```

**Set dimensions of column**

This example doesn't teach you anything new, but it's an ideal way to move on to the next topic.

### *Irregular columns*

Figure 7.5 looks nicer than figure 7.4, which only has regular columns; don't you agree?

This example illuminates the document with an image of Caesar and an extra geometric ornament that is repeated on every page. You don't want the text to overlap the illustrations, so you need to find a way to define irregular borders for the `ColumnText` object.

You can't use the method `setSimpleColumn()` any more; instead, you must define the right and left borders of the column and pass them to the `ColumnText` with the method `setColumns()`:

```
/* chapter07/ColumnsIrregular.java */
PdfContentByte cb = writer.getDirectContent();
Image caesar = Image.getInstance("caesar.jpg");
cb.addImage(caesar, 100, 0, 0, 100, 260, 595);
PdfTemplate t = cb.createTemplate(600, 800);
t.setGrayFill(0.75f);
t.moveTo(310, 112); t.lineTo(280, 60);
t.lineTo(340, 60);  t.closePath();
t.moveTo(310, 790); t.lineTo(310, 710);
t.moveTo(310, 580); t.lineTo(310, 122);
t.fillStroke();
cb.addTemplate(t, 0, 0);
ColumnText ct = new ColumnText(cb);
ct.setText(new Phrase(sb.toString()));
ct.setAlignment(Element.ALIGN_JUSTIFIED);
float[][] left  = {
  {70,790, 70,60} ,
  {320,790, 320,700, 380,700, 380,590,
  320,590, 320,106, 350,60} };
float[][] right = {
  {300,790, 300,700, 240,700, 240,590,
  300,590, 300,106, 270,60} ,
  {550,790, 550,60} };
```

**Define left border, first column**

**Define left border, second column**

**Define right border, first column**

**Define right border, second column**

```
int status = ColumnText.NO_MORE_COLUMN;
int column = 0;
while ((status & ColumnText.NO_MORE_TEXT) == 0) {
  if (column > 1) {
    column = 0;
    document.newPage();
    cb.addTemplate(t, 0, 0);
    cb.addImage(caesar, 100, 0, 0, 100, 260, 595);
  }
  ct.setColumns(left[column], right[column]);
  ct.setYLine(790);
  status = ct.go();
  column++;
}
```

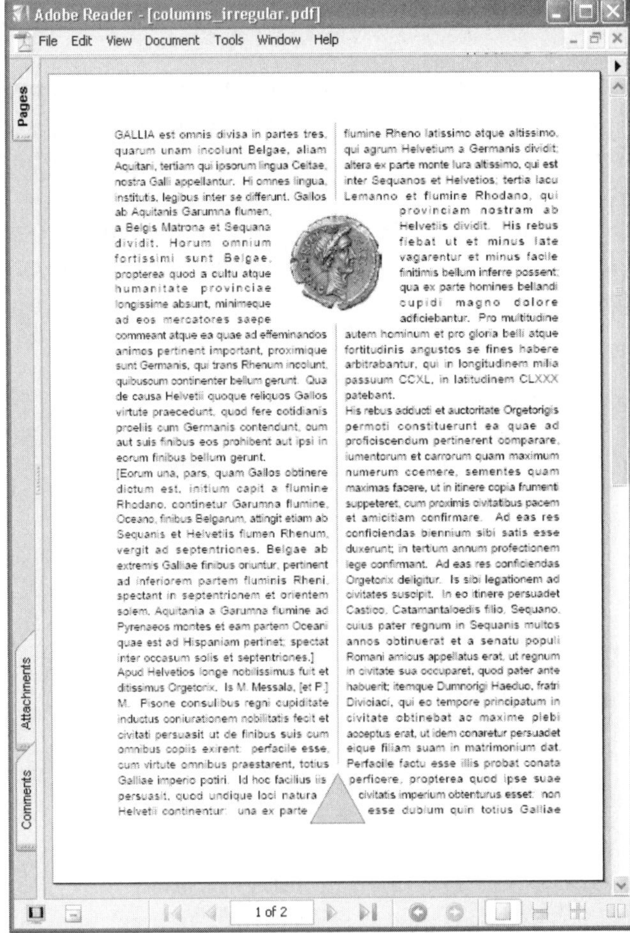


**Figure 7.5 Columns with irregular borders**

Note that the irregular-columns functionality works only when you work with text (the addText() and setText() methods). Once you start working with other high-level objects in the next section, this functionality is no longer available; you'll get a RuntimeException saying: *Irregular columns are not supported in composite mode.*

### Text mode versus composite mode

In the previous chapter, I talked about PdfPTable and the difference between the properties of a PdfPCell and the properties of basic building blocks added with PdfPCell.addElement(). In my explanation, I didn't go into the details. Let's do that now.

The content of a PdfPCell is internally stored as a ColumnText object. If a cell is created by passing a Phrase object to the constructor, the internal ColumnText object of the cell is in *text mode*. When in text mode, you define the properties at the level of the cell/column. Figure 7.6 demonstrates the effect when the default properties of a ColumnText object are changed.

```
/* chapter07/ColumnProperties.java */
ColumnText ct = new ColumnText(cb);
ct.setAlignment(Element.ALIGN_JUSTIFIED);
ct.setExtraParagraphSpace(12);
ct.setFollowingIndent(18);
ct.setLeading(0, 1.2f);
ct.setSpaceCharRatio(PdfWriter.NO_SPACE_CHAR_RATIO);
ct.setUseAscender(true);
```

You recognize the methods we have already used in the previous chapter, "Constructing tables," when we discussed the PdfPCell object:

- setAlignment() defines the alignment of the content.
- setExtraParagraphSpace() adds extra space between paragraphs.
- setFollowingIndent() sets the indentation of the lines following the first line.
- setLeading() defines the leading (an absolute value and a value that is relative to the font size).
- setSpaceCharRatio() defines the SpaceChar ratio.
- setUseAscender() makes sure the ascender is taken into account (or not, if set to false).

PdfPCell uses a ColumnText object behind the scenes. When working with PdfPCell, you saw that changing the properties at the cell level doesn't have any effect as soon as you add other building blocks (not just Phrases and Chunks, but also Paragraphs, Images, and so on). This is because the ColumnText object that

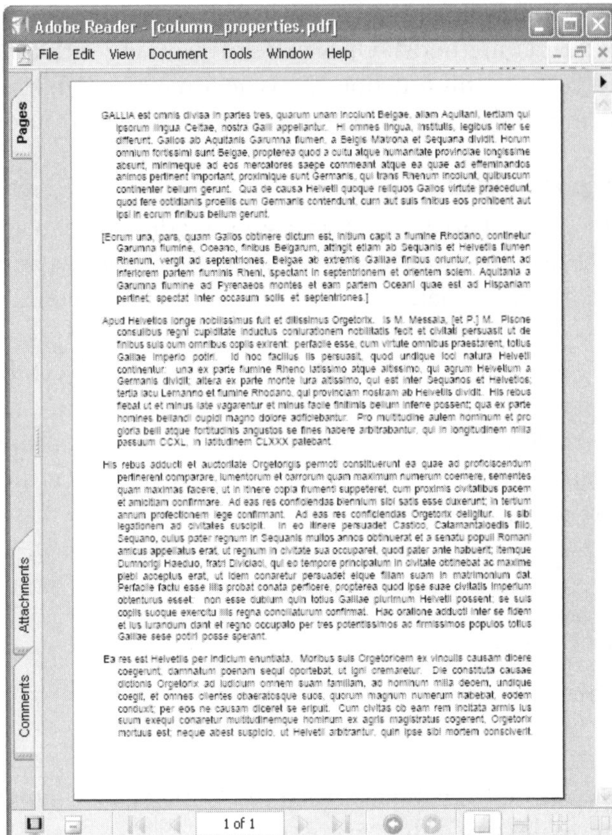


**Figure 7.6 Changing the properties of `ColumnText`**

stores the content of the cell switches to *composite mode* as soon as a `Paragraph`, `Image`, or `PdfPTable` is added. Properties such as leading should then be defined at the level of the content (the objects) instead of the container (the cell). The next section deals with the differences between text mode and composite mode.

## 7.3 Composing ColumnText with other building blocks

If you don't need irregular columns, you can use the method `addElement()` instead of `addText()` and `setText()`. Using `addElement()` causes the `ColumnText` object to switch to *composite mode*. This means you aren't limited to chunks and phrases anymore. Text mode is text-only. In composite mode, you're allowed to add an `Image` object, `PdfPTables`, `Paragraphs`, and so on.

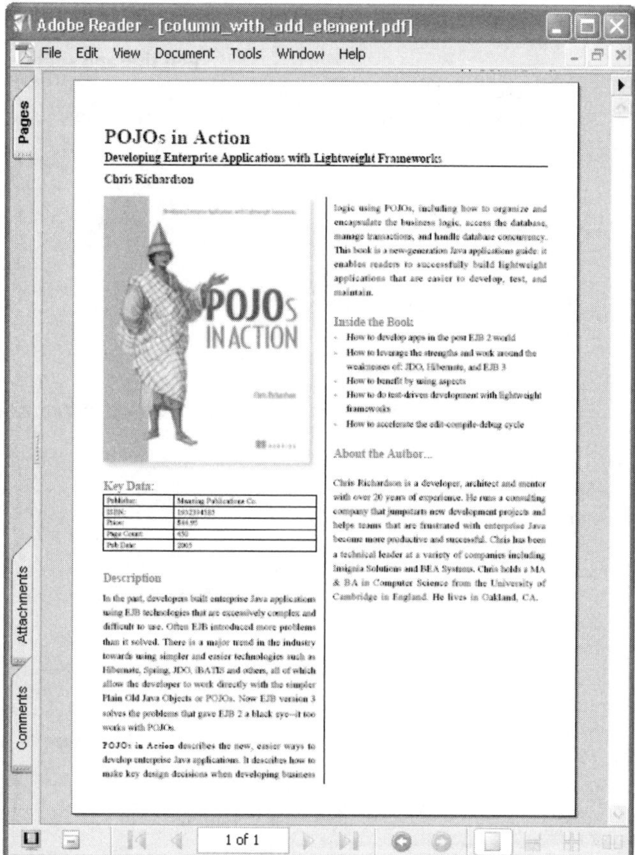


**Figure 7.7 Mixing text and other high-level objects**

The best way to explain the advantages and disadvantages of text mode versus composite mode is by trying to make a document that looks like figure 7.7 in two different ways.

## 7.3.1 Combining text mode with images and tables

If for one reason or another, you want to stick to text mode, the code to produce a document that looks like the screenshot in figure 7.7 gets rather complex:

```
/* chapter07/ColumnElements.java */
PdfContentByte cb = writer.getDirectContent();
ColumnText ct = new ColumnText(cb);
ct.setAlignment(Element.ALIGN_JUSTIFIED);
ct.setLeading(0, 1.5f);
ct.setSimpleColumn(document.left(), 0,
  document.right(), document.top());         Define column width
```

```
Phrase fullTitle = new Phrase("POJOs in Action", FONT24B);
ct.addText(fullTitle);
ct.go();                                          Add title and subtitle
Phrase subTitle = new Phrase(
"Developing Enterprise Applications with Lightweight Frameworks",
  FONT14B);
ct.addText(subTitle);
ct.go();
float currentY = ct.getYLine();
currentY -= 4;
cb.setLineWidth(1);
cb.moveTo(document.left(), currentY);             Get Y position
cb.lineTo(document.right(), currentY);
cb.stroke();
ct.setYLine(currentY);
ct.addText(new Chunk("Chris Richardson", FONT14B));   Add author name
ct.go();
currentY = ct.getYLine();
currentY -= 15;
float topColumn = currentY;
for (int k = 1; k < numColumns; ++k) {
  float x = allColumns[k] - gutter / 2;
  cb.moveTo(x, topColumn);                        Draw column lines
  cb.lineTo(x, document.bottom());
}
cb.stroke();
Image img = Image.getInstance("resources/8001.jpg");
cb.addImage(img, img.scaledWidth(), 0,
0, img.scaledHeight(),                            Add image
  document.left(), currentY - img.scaledHeight());
currentY -= img.scaledHeight() + 10;              Adjust Y pointer
ct.setYLine(currentY);
ct.setSimpleColumn(allColumns[0], document.bottom(),
  allColumns[0] + columnWidth, currentY);         Define rectangle
ct.addText(new Chunk("Key Data:", FONT14BC));
ct.go();
currentY = ct.getYLine();
currentY -= 4;
PdfPTable ptable = new PdfPTable(2);
float[] widths = {1, 2};
ptable.setWidths(widths);
ptable.getDefaultCell().setPaddingLeft(4);
ptable.getDefaultCell().setPaddingTop(0);         Create PdfPTable
ptable.getDefaultCell().setPaddingBottom(4);
ptable.addCell(new Phrase("Publisher:", FONT9));
ptable.addCell(new Phrase("Manning Publications Co.", FONT9));
(...)
ptable.setTotalWidth(columnWidth);    <-- Set table width
currentY = ptable.writeSelectedRows(0, -1,
  document.left(), currentY, cb) - 20;            Write table rows
```

```
ct.addText(new Phrase("Description\n", FONT14BC));
ct.addText(new Phrase("In the past, developers (…).\n\n", FONT11));
Phrase p = new Phrase();
Chunk anchor = new Chunk("POJOs in Action", FONT11B);
anchor.setAnchor("http://www.manning.com/books/crichardson");
p.add(anchor);
p.add(new Phrase(" describes (…).\n\n", FONT11));          Add content
ct.addText(p);
ct.addText(new Phrase("Inside the Book\n", FONT14BC));
ct.addText(new Phrase("* How to develop apps (…)\n\n", FONT11));
ct.addText(new Phrase("About the Author...\n", FONT14BC));
ct.addText(new Phrase("Chris Richardson is a developer, (…).", FONT11));
int currentColumn = 0;     <-- Track column numbers
while (true) {
  int status = ct.go();    <-- Render column
  if ((status & ColumnText.NO_MORE_TEXT) != 0)
    break;
  ++currentColumn;
  if (currentColumn >= allColumns.length)          Define next
    break;                                         column borders
ct.setSimpleColumn(allColumns[currentColumn], document.bottom(),
    allColumns[currentColumn] + columnWidth, topColumn);
}
```

I hate it when a code sample spans more than one page, but in this case it was unavoidable. It also makes my point that you should only mix the `ColumnText` text mode with other objects if there is no alternative. However, you can learn a few new things by examining this large code fragment.

Looking at figure 7.7, you might assume that different `ColumnText` objects are involved. In reality, all the text is added to the same column, but you change the columns borders and the Y position according to your needs while you add text.

Also note that when you add the table with `writeSelectedRows()`, you receive the bottom Y coordinate as a return value.

Working this way offers a lot of flexibility, but it also makes your code less readable and more error prone. If you want to get the result shown in figure 7.7, you're better off using composite mode.

### 7.3.2 ColumnText in composite mode

The first part of the next example is identical to the first part of the previous example. You add the title, subtitle, and author in text mode. There's nothing wrong with that, but as soon as you get to the snippet that adds the image, you'd better switch to composite mode.

Switching to composite mode is done implicitly by using the method `addElement()`. All the text that was added in text mode previously and that hasn't been rendered yet will be cleared as soon as you use `addElement()`. You may already have noticed this when using `PdfPCell`. If you create a cell with a paragraph as a parameter for the constructor and subsequently use `PdfPCell.addElement()`, the first paragraph is lost. This isn't a bug; it's a feature. (Honest!)

But let's return to the `ColumnText` example:

```
/* chapter07/ColumnWithAddElement.java */
int currentColumn = 0;
ct.setSimpleColumn(allColumns[currentColumn], document.bottom(),
  allColumns[currentColumn] + columnWidth, currentY);
Image img = Image.getInstance("resources/8001.jpg");        | Create Image
ct.addElement(img);                                         |
ct.addElement(newParagraph("Key Data:",    | Add paragraph with
  FONT14BC, 5));                           | addElement()
PdfPTable ptable = new PdfPTable(2);
float[] widths = {1, 2};
ptable.setWidths(widths);
ptable.getDefaultCell().setPaddingLeft(4);
ptable.getDefaultCell().setPaddingTop(0);              Add PdfPTable
ptable.getDefaultCell().setPaddingBottom(4);
ptable.addCell(new Phrase("Publisher:", FONT9));
ptable.addCell(new Phrase("Manning Publications Co.", FONT9));
(...)
ptable.setSpacingBefore(5);
ptable.setWidthPercentage(100);
ct.addElement(ptable);
ct.addElement(newParagraph("Description", FONT14BC, 15));    | Add paragraphs
ct.addElement(newParagraph("In the past (...)", FONT11, 5)); |
Paragraph p = new Paragraph();
p.setSpacingBefore(5);
p.setAlignment(Element.ALIGN_JUSTIFIED);                      Add
Chunk anchor = new Chunk("POJOs in Action", FONT11B);         paragraph
anchor.setAnchor("http://www.manning.com/books/crichardson"); with
p.add(anchor);                                                Anchor
p.add(new Phrase(" describes (...)", FONT11));
ct.addElement(p);
ct.addElement(newParagraph("Inside the Book",     | Add paragraph
  FONT14BC, 15));                                 |
List list = new List(List.UNORDERED, 15);
ListItem li;
li = new ListItem("How to develop (...)", FONT11);   Add list
list.add(li);
(...)                                                       Add paragraphs
ct.addElement(list);
ct.addElement(newParagraph("About the Author...", FONT14BC, 15));
ct.addElement(newParagraph("Chris Richardson is (...)", FONT11, 15));
```

I didn't repeat the `go()` loop because it's identical to the loop in the previous example. I know, I cheated a little by using a private static `newParagraph()`

method to make this code look shorter and more attractive, but I hope you agree that this example is much more elegant than the previous one.

Observe that in composite mode, you can add objects of type `Paragraph`, `List`, `SimpleTable`, `PdfPTable`, and `Image`. If you add a `Phrase` or a `Chunk`, it's wrapped in a `Paragraph`. Adding `Anchor` objects directly isn't possible; you can wrap them in a `Paragraph` or use `Chunk.setAnchor()`. This example uses a `Chunk` with an `Anchor`, wrapped in a `Paragraph`.

> **NOTE** Be careful when you mix `addElement()` and `addText()`. Always invoke `go()` before you switch from text mode to composite mode (or vice versa); otherwise, you risk losing part of your data.

Looking at the source code of the previous examples, you realize that gaining more control over what happens on a page also means you have to deal with more complexity. Some code snippets are repeated in almost every `ColumnText` example. Can't we automate some of the processes ? For instance, do we really have to copy/paste the `go()` loop for every new example ? Let's find out in the next section.

## 7.4 Automatic columns with MultiColumnText

If you use the `ColumnText` class extensively, you'll notice that you need to write a lot of code that is repeated over and over. To avoid this code repetition, Steve Appling wrote the `MultiColumnText` class. This is a convenience class written around class `ColumnText` that can save you a lot of work if you only need standard column functionality; for more complex functionality, you'll still need `ColumnText`. With class `MultiColumnText`, the same rules about text and composite mode apply, but much of the complexity is hidden.

You'll make some regular and irregular columns to get acquainted with this new class.

### 7.4.1 Regular columns with MultiColumnText

Steve Appling has provided an example that generates poetry at random, as shown in figure 7.8.

The code to generate these columns is much more user-friendly than the code you had to write when you used class `ColumnText`:

```
/* chapter07/MultiColumnPoem.java */
MultiColumnText mct = new MultiColumnText();      <-- Create MultiColumnText object
mct.addRegularColumns(document.left(),            | Define dimensions
  document.right(), 10f, 3);                      | of column
```

```
for (int i = 0; i < 30; i++) {
  mct.addElement(new Paragraph(String.valueOf(i + 1)));
mct.addElement(newParagraph(
    randomWord(noun), Element.ALIGN_CENTER, Font.BOLDITALIC));
  for (int j = 0; j < 4; j++) {
mct.addElement(newParagraph(
      poemLine(), Element.ALIGN_LEFT, Font.NORMAL));
  }
mct.addElement(newParagraph(
    randomWord(adverb), Element.ALIGN_LEFT, Font.NORMAL));
mct.addElement(newParagraph(
    "\n\n", Element.ALIGN_LEFT, Font.NORMAL));
}
document.add(mct);
```

**Generate 30 random poems**

**Add MultiColumnText to document**

When reading the code sample, the first thing that pops into your mind is probably *what happened to the Y pointer*? The method `addRegularColumns()` defines the

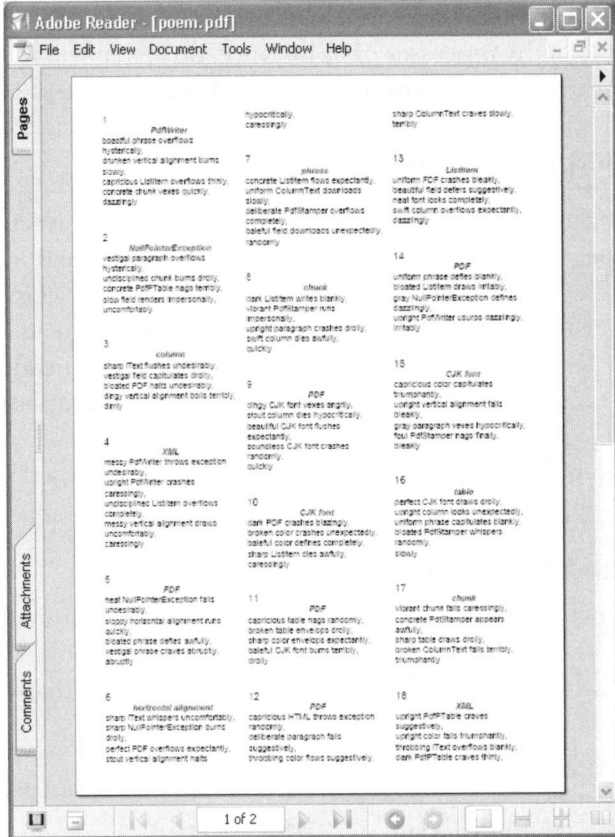


**Figure 7.8**
**Adding `MultiColumnText` columns with `document.add()`**

left and right border, a gutter, and the number of columns, but you don't indicate the Y position where the column should start. What will happen?

The answer is simple: If you don't specify a height for the columns, `MultiColumnText` asks the document for the current vertical position and the bottom margin of the page; this is the available height. Furthermore, iText distributes the available width over the columns, taking into account some space between the columns (specified by the `gutter` parameter).

By default, the columns are added from left to right. If you want to reverse this order, add one extra line to the previous example:

```
/* chapter07/MultiColumnPoemReverse.java */
MultiColumnText mct = new MultiColumnText();
mct.setColumnsRightToLeft(true);
```

You can also define the columns one by one:

```
/* chapter07/MultiColumnPoemCustom.java */
MultiColumnText mct = new MultiColumnText();
mct.addSimpleColumn(100, 280);
mct.addSimpleColumn(300, 480);
```

`MultiColumnText` doesn't have an `addText()` method, only an `addElement()` method; but behind the scenes, it uses `addText()` for `Phrase`s and `Chunk`s as long as you're in text mode. As soon as you use `Image`s, `PdfPTable`s, and so on, it switches to composite mode. The `MultiColumnText` class uses `ColumnText` in the background. When using `MultiColumnText`, you give up some of the `ColumnText` functionality, but in return, you get extra ease of use.

There is a method in `MultiColumnText` to set the alignment of the internal `ColumnText` object; but for the other properties, you need to construct a `ColumnText` object, set its properties, and pass this `ColumnText` object as a parameter with the `useColumnParams()` method.

If you stay in text mode, you can also automate the rendition of irregular columns.

### 7.4.2 Irregular columns with MultiColumnText

Let's return once more to Caesar's report on the Gallic War to demonstrate how you can define irregular columns with `MultiColumnText` (see figure 7.9).

To produce this kind of output, you add a little complexity. You define the height of the columns when constructing the `MultiColumnText` object. However, doing so disables the automatic column repetition over different pages. Only the columns that fit on the current page will be added, so you have to write a loop—

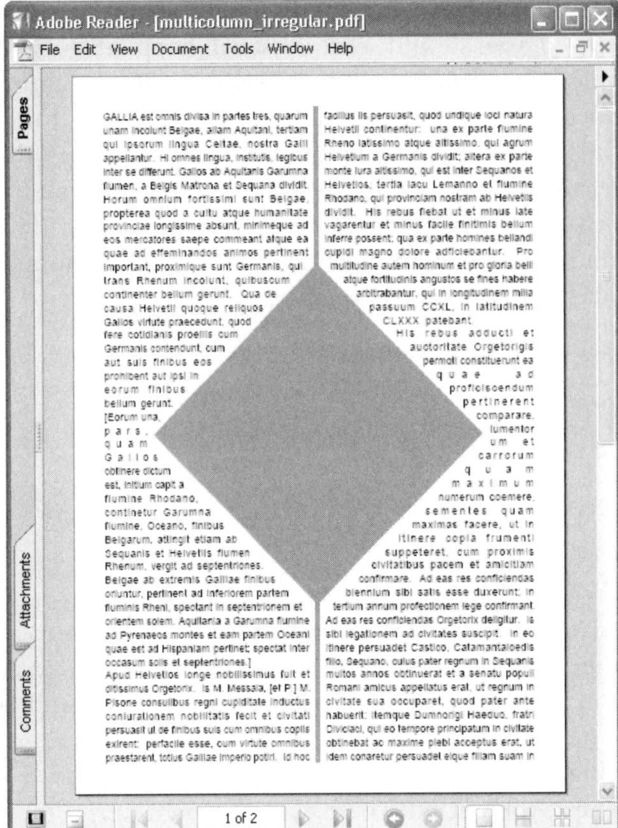


**Figure 7.9**
**Adding irregular columns with `document.add()`**

not to keep track of the column count, but to tell iText that it can continue on the next page. The example clarifies why this can be useful:

```
/* chapter07/MultiColumnIrregular.java */
float[] left = {document.left(), document.top(),          ❶
  document.left(), document.bottom()};
float[] right = {document.left() + colMaxWidth, document.top(),
  document.left() + colMaxWidth, diamondTop,
  document.left() + diamondInset, diamondTop - diamondHeight / 2,   ❷
  document.left() + colMaxWidth, diamondTop - diamondHeight,
  document.left() + colMaxWidth, document.bottom() };
mct.addColumn(left, right);   ❸
left = new float[] { document.right() - colMaxWidth, document.top(),
  document.right() - colMaxWidth, diamondTop,
  document.right() - diamondInset, diamondTop - diamondHeight / 2,   ❹
  document.right() - colMaxWidth, diamondTop - diamondHeight,
  document.right() - colMaxWidth, document.bottom() };
```

```
right = new float[] { document.right(), document.top(),
  document.right(), document.bottom() };                     ⑤
mct.addColumn(left, right);    ⑥
String line;
while ((line = reader.readLine()) != null) {
  mct.addElement(new Phrase(line + "\n"));    ⑦
}
reader.close();
PdfContentByte cb = writer.getDirectContent();
do {
  cb.saveState();
  cb.setLineWidth(5);
  cb.setColorStroke(Color.GRAY);
  cb.moveTo(centerX , document.top());
  cb.lineTo(centerX, document.bottom());
  cb.stroke();
  cb.moveTo(centerX, diamondTop);
cb.lineTo(centerX - (diamondWidth/2),                        ⑧
    diamondTop - (diamondHeight / 2));
  cb.lineTo(centerX, diamondTop - diamondHeight);
cb.lineTo(centerX + (diamondWidth/2),
    diamondTop - (diamondHeight / 2));
  cb.lineTo(centerX, diamondTop);
  cb.setColorFill(Color.GRAY);
  cb.fill();
  cb.restoreState();
  document.add(mct);    ⑨
  mct.nextColumn();    ⑩
} while (mct.isOverflow());    ⑪
```

This example works as follows:

1. Define the left border of the first column.
2. Define the right border of the first column.
3. Add these borders to the `MultiColumnText`.
4. Define the left border of the second column.
5. Define the right border of the second column.
6. Add these borders to the `MultiColumnText`.
7. Add the content; you stay in text mode!
8. Add some lines and the diamond shape.
9. Add two columns of content on the current page.
10. Skip to the next column.
11. Keep on looping as long as there is text.

Do you see why it can be useful to prevent iText from going to the next page automatically? This way, you can add extra content to every new page inside the loop (in this case, the lines and the diamond shape).

You can make the example even more complex by replacing `document.add(mct)` with the method `write(cb, document, documentY)`. This method is similar to the `writeSelectedRows()` method you saw in the previous chapter. It returns the Y position that was reached after the column was added.

## 7.5 Composing a study guide (part 2)

You're almost able to finish Laura's second assignment. Laura needs to create a course catalog with study program tables (section 6.3) and course descriptions (see figure 7.10). If you look at the screenshot of the PDF you want to generate, you see that the best solution is to use a `MultiColumnText` object in composite mode: `MultiColumnText` because you only need standard columns (three per page

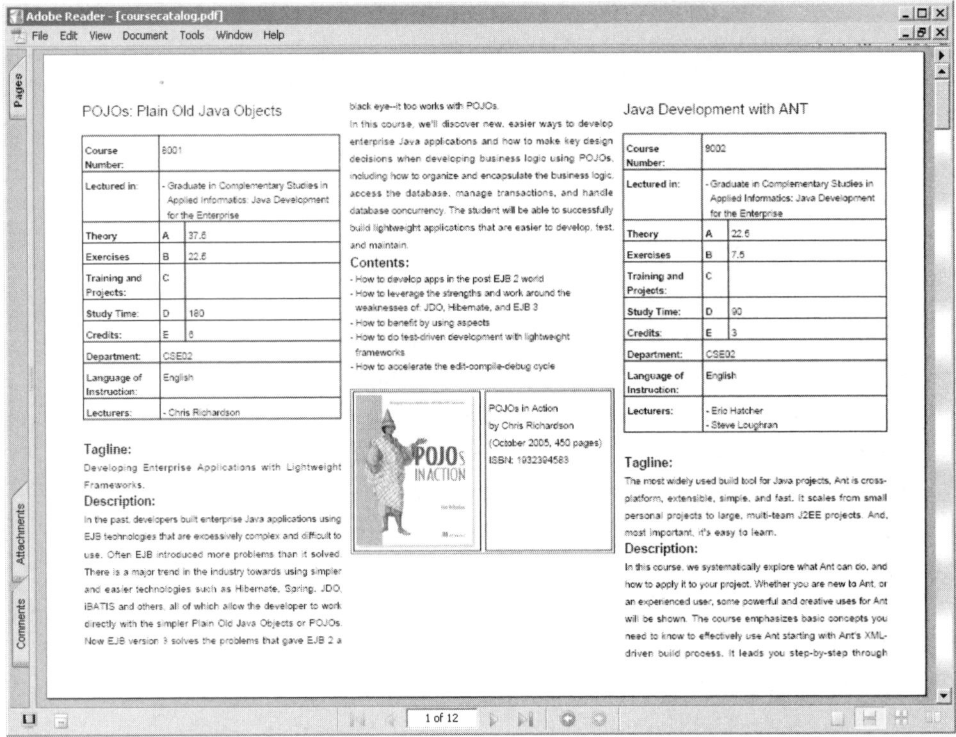


POJOs: Plain Old Java Objects

| Course Number: | 8001 | |
|---|---|---|
| Lectured in: | - Graduate in Complementary Studies in Applied Informatics: Java Development for the Enterprise | |
| Theory | A | 37.5 |
| Exercises | B | 22.5 |
| Training and Projects: | C | |
| Study Time: | D | 180 |
| Credits: | E | 6 |
| Department: | CSE02 | |
| Language of Instruction: | English | |
| Lecturers: | - Chris Richardson | |

**Tagline:**
Developing Enterprise Applications with Lightweight Frameworks.

**Description:**
In the past, developers built enterprise Java applications using EJB technologies that are excessively complex and difficult to use. Often EJB introduced more problems than it solved. There is a major trend in the industry towards using simpler and easier technologies such as Hibernate, Spring, JDO, iBATIS and others, all of which allow the developer to work directly with the simpler Plain Old Java Objects or POJOs. Now EJB version 3 solves the problems that gave EJB 2 a black eye--it too works with POJOs.

In this course, we'll discover new, easier ways to develop enterprise Java applications and how to make key design decisions when developing business logic using POJOs, including how to organize and encapsulate the business logic, access the database, manage transactions, and handle database concurrency. The student will be able to successfully build lightweight applications that are easier to develop, test, and maintain.

**Contents:**
- How to develop apps in the post EJB 2 world
- How to leverage the strengths and work around the weaknesses of: JDO, Hibernate, and EJB 3
- How to benefit by using aspects
- How to do test-driven development with lightweight frameworks
- How to accelerate the edit-compile-debug cycle

POJOs in Action
by Chris Richardson
(October 2005, 450 pages)
ISBN: 1932394583

Java Development with ANT

| Course Number: | 8002 | |
|---|---|---|
| Lectured in: | - Graduate in Complementary Studies in Applied Informatics: Java Development for the Enterprise | |
| Theory | A | 22.5 |
| Exercises | B | 7.5 |
| Training and Projects: | C | |
| Study Time: | D | 90 |
| Credits: | E | 3 |
| Department: | CSE02 | |
| Language of Instruction: | English | |
| Lecturers: | - Eric Hatcher<br>- Steve Loughran | |

**Tagline:**
The most widely used build tool for Java projects, Ant is cross-platform, extensible, simple, and fast. It scales from small personal projects to large, multi-team J2EE projects. And, most important, it's easy to learn.

**Description:**
In this course, we systematically explore what Ant can do, and how to apply it to your project. Whether you are new to Ant, or an experienced user, some powerful and creative uses for Ant will be shown. The course emphasizes basic concepts you need to know to effectively use Ant starting with Ant's XML-driven build process. It leads you step-by-step through

**Figure 7.10 A page from the course catalog**

with a small gutter); composite mode because you need more than just text—you also need tables, lists, and images.

Again, you'll start from an XML file, or rather a series of XML files. The course descriptions are stored in separate XML files. For some courses, you have a JPG showing the cover of the course manual. Each XML file looks like listing 7.1.

**Listing 7.1 XML file describing the course on POJOs: 8001.xml**

```
<course>
<title>POJOs: Plain Old Java Objects</title>
<specs>
  <coursenumber>8001</coursenumber>
  <programs><program>Graduate in Complementary Studies
  in Applied Informatics: Java Development for the
  Enterprise</program></programs>
  <a>37.5</a>
  <b>22.5</b>
  <c />
  <d>180</d>
  <e>6</e>
  <department>CSE02</department>
  <language>English</language>
  <lecturers>
    <lecturer inCharge="true">Chris Richardson</lecturer>
  </lecturers>
</specs>
<tagline>Developing Enterprise Applications
  with Lightweight Frameworks.</tagline>
<description>In the past,
  developers built enterprise Java applications…</description>
<contents>
  <topic>How to develop apps in the post EJB 2 world</topic>
  <topic>...</topic>
</contents>
<book>
  <img src="8001.jpg" border="0" alt="POJOs in Action" align="Left" />
  POJOs in Action<newline />by Chris Richardson<newline />
  (October 2005, 450 pages)<newline />
  ISBN: 1932394583
</book>
</course>
```

As with part 1 of Laura's study guide assignment, this is similar to the real-life situation at Ghent University. In the XML, you immediately recognize objects that will be rendered as a `Paragraph` (`tagline`, `description`), as a `List` (`lecturers`, `contents`), or as an `Image` (`img`). This time, you don't add these objects to a

`Document` or to a `SimpleTable` as in the previous Foobar examples. Instead, you store them in an `objectsStack`:

```
/* chapter07/FoobarCourseCatalog.java */
protected Stack objectStack;
```

Once you have this stack of iText objects representing the content of one course (one XML file), you need a method to flush this stack to a `MultiColumnText` object:

```
/* chapter07/FoobarCourseCatalog.java */
public void flushToColumn(MultiColumnText mct)
  throws DocumentException {
  for (Iterator i = objectStack.iterator(); i.hasNext(); ) {
    Element e = (Element) i.next();
    if (e instanceof SimpleTable) {
      mct.addElement(((SimpleTable)e).createPdfPTable());
    }
    else {
      mct.addElement(e);
    }
  }
}
```

In the main method, you make sure you loop over all the XML files:

```
/* chapter07/FoobarCourseCatalog.java */
MultiColumnText mct = new MultiColumnText();                               (1)
mct.addRegularColumns(document.left(), document.right(), 10f, 3);
String[] courses = {"8001", "8002", "8003", "8010", "8011",
"8020", "8021", "8022", "8030", "8031", "8032", "8033",
  "8040", "8041", "8042", "8043", "8051", "8052"};                       (2)
for (int i = 0; i < courses.length; i++) {
  new FoobarCourseCatalogue(courses[i]).flushToColumn(mct);         <-(3)
  document.add(mct);    <-(4)
  mct.nextColumn();    <-(5)
}
```

This code snippet works as follows:

1. Create one `MultiColumnText` object.
2. List the courses that have to be added.
3. Parse the XML file of one course.
4. Render all the content of one course.
5. Skip to the next column for the next course.

This example differs from the previous ones in this chapter in the sense that it's much closer to what you'll do in a real-life situation. Previously, you filled the column with content; once it was full, you rendered this content to the page. This isn't a good idea if you expect your column to contain a lot of data. You risk the same problems concerning memory use that we discussed when dealing with large tables. Remember that with ColumnText and MultiColumnText, you should render the content from time to time in order to release memory.

In the course catalog example, you add the column object to the document after every course. If you didn't call nextColumn(), the next course would be added directly after the previous one. MultiColumnText keeps track of the current column and Y position. The nextColumn() method tells iText that it should skip to the next column even if there's space left in the current one. It resets the Y pointer to the top of the column. If no columns are left on this page, the newPage() method is triggered.

If you combine the output from this example with the output of the Foobar example in the previous example, you have a study guide you can print for your students. Later, we'll return to these PDFs and add some interactive features.

## 7.6 Summary

Whereas the sample code in the previous chapters looked theoretical, chapters 6 and 7 brought you some examples that are useful in a real-life situation. I mention both chapters in the same breath, because you have seen that ColumnText and PdfPCell are closely related.

MultiColumnText is the most user-friendly solution if you need to organize text and other data in a columnar structure. Class ColumnText is more complex, but it offers you almost as much flexibility as if you were writing to the PdfContentByte directly. This object will be discussed in chapters 10–12 in the next part of the book.

# Part 3

# PDF text and graphics

This part goes to the core of iText and PDF. It also serves as a reference manual for you: How do you choose a font? draw a dashed line? make an image transparent? translate a Swing component to PDF? These and many other questions are answered in five chapters that are illustrated with plenty of examples.

# 8 Choosing the right font

***This chapter covers***

- What is a font?
- What is a font program?
- What font do you need?

The previous part of this book was iText specific. You created some interesting building blocks that were translated to PDF by iText. In this part, we'll focus mainly on PDF-related issues. In chapters 10–12, you'll learn a lot about the syntax used in PDF. In chapters 8 and 9, we'll focus on fonts.

Previous examples have used the font Helvetica. You may have wondered why I didn't use Arial. In this chapter, you'll learn that Helvetica offers some advantages because it's a so-called *built-in* font. It also has some downsides, so it's important to learn how to select another font. In a series of small examples, you'll learn how to produce text written in other languages—for instance, using Eastern European characters and Asian ideographs. But let's start with the most essential question: What is a font?

## 8.1 Defining a font

Some dictionaries say a font is "a complete assortment of *type* of one style and size"[1] or "a set of letters and symbols in a particular design and size."[2] That's true, but other dictionaries tell you that *font* is "a synonym for *typeface*, a coordinated set of designs for *characters*, or a computer *file* that stores these designs."[3] We'll use the word in both senses, depending on the iText object we're using.

Like *font*, *type* is another word that has many different definitions. In this chapter, you'll encounter a lot of words that find their origin in book printing and *typography*. In chapter 4, I explained the origin of the word *leading*. Now you need to add the words *type* and *typeface* to the typography vocabulary.

*Type* can be a synonym for printed characters or *printing blocks*: "the set of small metal blocks used in printing, especially formerly, each of which has a raised figure that is the mirror image of a number or letter on one of its sides." *Typeface* is "the side of a printing block that has the shape of the printed character on it."[4] By the way, the word *font* originally comes from the French word *fondre*, which means "to melt"; all the metal blocks of a font were cast at the same time.

In this section, you'll encounter 14 sets of virtual metal blocks that are supposed to be known by every PDF product (including iText), and you'll learn how to change some font characteristics. That's after we present an overview of more terminology and the different types of font programs.

1 Random House Unabridged Dictionary
2 Cambridge Advanced Learner's Dictionary
3 Wikipedia
4 Encarta World English Dictionary (both definitions)

### 8.1.1 Using the right terminology

Depending on the definition you choose for *font*, you may refer to different meanings of the word. You could be talking about 12 pt Arial Bold Italic, while I'm thinking of the file arial.tff and not specifying any size. Some people talk about the font Arial, but in reality they have the complete *font family* in mind. The fonts Arial, Arial Bold, Arial Italic, and so on all belong to the same family, but they're *different* fonts.

Many tools, iText included, make an ambiguous use of this small word, mixing different definitions. I realize this can get quite confusing, but this chapter should help you understand what fonts are all about as far as using them in iText is concerned.

It's also important to understand the difference between a *character* and a *glyph*. The PDF Reference says, "A character is an abstract symbol, whereas a glyph is a specific rendering of a character. For example, the glyphs A, **A** and *A* are renderings of the abstract A character." You can also use the word *grapheme* in this context. A grapheme is a unit of a writing system: a letter, a number, a punctuation mark, a Chinese ideograph, or any other symbol. Different glyphs can represent the same grapheme.

The PDF Reference manual continues: "Glyphs are organized into fonts. A font defines glyphs for a particular character set." We're especially interested in computer fonts. In the sections that follow, we'll deal with many different font formats that can be used in a PDF. Each of these formats has its own conventions for organizing and representing the information within it.

Table 5.1 of the PostScript Language Reference provides a complete overview of all the font types. Not all of them apply to PDF. I have listed the types that are relevant to you in table 8.1.

**Table 8.1 PostScript font types**

| Type | Description |
|---|---|
| Type 0 | A *composite font* composed of other fonts called *base fonts*. |
| Type 1 | A *base font* that defines character shapes by using specially encoded procedures. Details on this format are provided in the book *Adobe Type 1 Font Format* (Adobe Systems Inc.). |
| Type 2 | A *Compact Font Format* (CFF) font. |
| Type 3 | A *user-defined* font that defines character shapes as ordinary PostScript language procedures. |

All the fonts used in a PDF file are defined in a *font dictionary*. This is a PDF dictionary in which the value of the `Type` entry is set to `Font`.

Another interesting item in this dictionary is the `SubType` entry. Table 8.2 roughly corresponds with table 5.7 in the PDF Reference and lists some possible values for the `SubType` entry. They're listed more or less in the order we'll discuss them.

**Table 8.2 PDF Font dictionary subtype values**

| Subtype value | Description |
|---|---|
| Type1 | A font that defines glyph shapes using PostScript Type 1 font technology. |
| Type3 | A font that defines glyphs with streams of PDF graphics operators. |
| TrueType | A font based on the TrueType font format.<br>Note that the PostScript Type 42 font format (also based on TrueType) doesn't apply to PDF. |
| Type0 | A composite font—a font composed of glyphs from a descendant CIDFont. |
| CIDFontType0 | A CIDFont whose glyph descriptions are based on Type 1 font technology. |
| CIDFontType2 | A CIDFont whose glyph descriptions are based on TrueType font technology. |

I'm introducing a lot of new terminology here: base fonts, user defined fonts, composite fonts, and more. Soon we'll disentangle all these types and font formats in a series of examples.

Let's begin gently with an easy example, introducing the standard Type 1 fonts, a set of 14 fonts that are required to be available in all PDF consumer applications.

### 8.1.2 Standard Type 1 fonts

I was tempted to name this section "Simple fonts"; but that would have been a bad idea because the term *simple font* officially refers to a font in which the glyphs are selected by *single-byte* character and each glyph has a single set of metrics.

An alternative title could have been "The simplest way to construct a font"; but that would have been misleading too, because this subsection will only tell you how to create an iText `Font` object for the 14 Type 1 fonts listed in table 8.3.

**Table 8.3 Standard Type 1 fonts**

| PostScript name | Font family | Font style | AFM file |
|---|---|---|---|
| Courier | Font.COURIER | Font.NORMAL | Courier.afm |
| Courier-Bold | Font.COURIER | Font.BOLD | Courier-Bold.afm |
| Courier-Oblique | Font.COURIER | Font.ITALIC | Courier-Oblique.afm |
| Courier-BoldOblique | Font.COURIER | Font.BOLDITALIC | Courier-BoldOblique.afm |
| Helvetica | Font.HELVETICA | Font.NORMAL | Helvetica.afm |
| Helvetica-Bold | Font.HELVETICA | Font.BOLD | Helvetica-Bold.afm |
| Helvetica-Oblique | Font.HELVETICA | Font.ITALIC | Helvetica-Oblique.afm |
| Helvetica-BoldOblique | Font.HELVETICA | Font.BOLDITALIC | Helvetica-BoldOblique.afm |
| Times-Roman | Font.TIMES_ROMAN | Font.NORMAL | Times-Roman.afm |
| Times-Bold | Font.TIMES_ROMAN | Font.BOLD | Times-Bold.afm |
| Times-Italic | Font.TIMES_ROMAN | Font.ITALIC | Times-Italic.afm |
| Times-BoldItalic | Font.TIMES_ROMAN | Font.BOLDITALIC | Times-BoldItalic.afm |
| Symbol | Font.SYMBOL | - | Symbol.afm |
| ZapfDingbats | Font.ZAPFDINGBATS | - | ZapfDingbats.afm |

In the past, these 14 fonts were often referred to as the *Base 14 fonts*. In more recent reference manuals, this terminology has been replaced; you should now call them *standard fonts*.

### The iText Font class

The iText `Font` class allows you to construct a `Font` object as defined in the first set of dictionaries I mentioned: It's a "set of type of a particular face and size."[5] When you create an iText `Font` object, imagine a box with a number of metal blocks that can be used to form words and sentences. Each line of the PDF shown in figure 8.1 was composed using a different `Font` object—a different "box."

[5] Compact Oxford English Dictionary

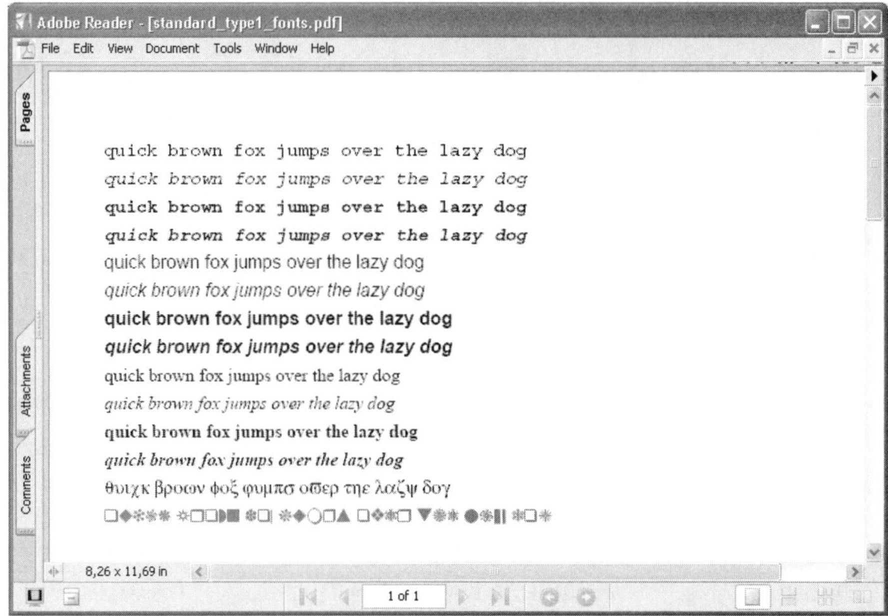

**Figure 8.1 The standard Type 1 fonts**

The code sample demonstrates the original constructors of the `Font` class dating from the time iText supported only the standard fonts. They only work for standard Type 1 fonts:

```
/* chapter08/StandardType1Fonts.java */
Font[] fonts = new Font[14];
fonts[0] = new Font(Font.COURIER, Font.DEFAULTSIZE, Font.NORMAL);
fonts[1] = new Font(Font.COURIER, Font.DEFAULTSIZE, Font.ITALIC);
fonts[2] = new Font(Font.COURIER, Font.DEFAULTSIZE, Font.BOLD);
fonts[3] = new Font(Font.COURIER, Font.DEFAULTSIZE,
  Font.BOLD | Font.ITALIC);
(...)
fonts[11] = new Font(Font.TIMES_ROMAN, Font.DEFAULTSIZE,
  Font.BOLDITALIC);
fonts[12] = new Font(Font.SYMBOL, Font.DEFAULTSIZE);
fonts[13] = new Font(Font.ZAPFDINGBATS, Font.DEFAULTSIZE,
  Font.UNDEFINED, new Color(0xFF, 0x00, 0x00));
for (int i = 0; i < 14; i++) {
  document.add(new Paragraph(
    "quick brown fox jumps over the lazy dog", fonts[i]));
}
```

The first parameter is one of the values from the Font family column in table 8.3.

**FAQ** *Can you change the default font family used by iText from HELVETICA to another font?* If you create a font with the constructor `new Font()`, a font with family `Font.HELVETICA`, size 12, and style `Font.NORMAL` is created. The default values are static. If you changed them, you'd change the default for the complete JVM, which might lead to unexpected (unwanted) side effects. This isn't the way to go. If you need another font, don't depend on the default font; create a `Font` object with the desired font, instead.

The second parameter is the size of the font. The other parameters define the style and color.

### Defining the font style and color

The style can be defined with a single style constant, as listed in the third column of table 8.3. It can also be defined by an or-ed combination of styles; for instance, `Font.BOLD | Font.ITALIC` is equivalent to `Font.BOLDITALIC`. Other possible styles are `Font.UNDERLINE` and `Font.STRIKETHRU`, but in chapter 4 you saw better ways to underline or strike through a `Chunk`; these styles were the predecessors of this functionality.

There is also a parameter that defines the color. Here the meaning of the class name diverges a little from our agreed-on meaning for the word *font*; *color* is a quality of the ink, not a property of the type(face).

### Defining the font size

The size isn't the height of any specific glyph; it's an indication of the vertical space used by a line of text. As you saw in chapter 4, we usually define the leading as a factor of this size (for instance, 1.5 times the font size).

In chapter 2, we talked about metrics, and I wrote that all measurements are done in points. With fonts, you work with points too, but also with glyph metrics. In *glyph space*, 1000 units correspond with 1 unit in *text space*. For instance, for a 12 pt font, 1000 units correspond with 12 pt (see figure 8.2).

This example measures the strings *0123456789* and *abcdefghijklmnopqrstuvwxyz*. The width of the string with the numbers in glyph space is 5560. The width in points is 5560 / 1000 x 12, or 66.72 pt.

The *ascent* is the space needed above the baseline, and the *descent* is the space below the baseline. If you subtract the descent from the ascent, you can calculate the height of the string. In the font Helvetica with size 12, the height required by numbers is 8.664 pt; the height required by the lowercase letters is 11.376 pt.

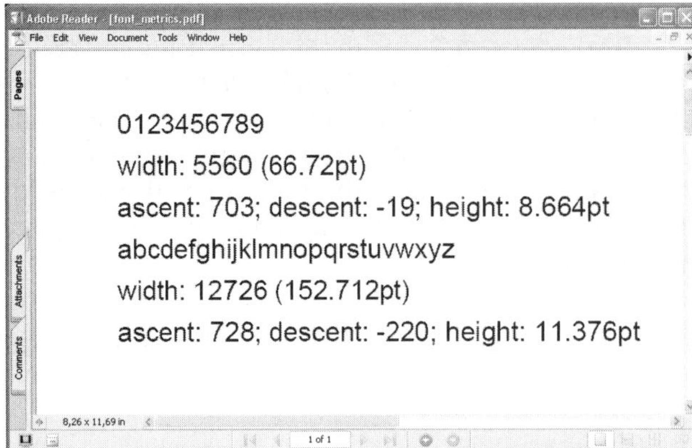


**Figure 8.2 Font metrics**

These values were retrieved from the `BaseFont` object corresponding with the `Font`. This object will be the main topic of the next two sections. First, let's look at the source code that was used to produce figure 8.2:

```
/* chapter08/FontMetrics.java */
Font font = new Font(Font.HELVETICA, 12);
BaseFont bf = font.getCalculatedBaseFont(false);
String numbers = "0123456789";
document.add(new Paragraph(numbers, font));
document.add(new Paragraph("width: " + bf.getWidth(numbers)
  + " (" + bf.getWidthPoint(numbers, 12) + "pt)", font));
document.add(new Paragraph("ascent: " + bf.getAscent(numbers)
  + "; descent: " + bf.getDescent(numbers)
  + "; height: " + (bf.getAscentPoint(numbers, 12)
    - bf.getDescentPoint(numbers, 12) + "pt"), font));
```

The standard fonts are special in the sense that the PDF specification requires that PDF viewers should be able to render every glyph available in the font; iText can give you the width and height values because the metrics of the standard fonts are built into the library. A viewer application needs a font program to draw the shapes corresponding with the characters in your PDF document.

If you're writing a web application, and you don't need any special characters, it's interesting to use one (or more) of the standard fonts. You can be sure the end-user's PDF viewer will be able to render the font, and using a standard font is the best way to keep the file size of your PDF documents within limits.

If you use another font, there is no guarantee that the font will be installed on the client side. The only way to make sure the end user will be able to read your file is to *embed* a font program.

### *Embedded versus nonembedded fonts*

If a font can't be found on the client side, the viewer tries to use another font instead. In a document with the nonembedded font Avenir, its look-alike Century Gothic may be used; Palatino can be replaced by Book Antiqua; and so on.

Adobe Reader does a good job of approximating the most common fonts, but there's always a risk that the text in your document will look different on different machines or even be illegible. Do you remember that in chapter 3 I said a PDF document always looks the same on every system? This is the most important exception to this rule. The only way to make sure the correct font is used and to ensure the document looks exactly the way you intended on every viewer and on every printout is to embed the font program into the PDF document, in a PDF stream object.

Note that embedding the font is mandatory to comply with the PDF/X and PDF/A ISO standards (for eXchanging and Archiving documents). If you send a document to a printing office, you don't want to receive it printed in a different font. If you consult an archive, you need all the used resources to be available.

**FAQ** *Why does iText say my font can't be embedded due to licensing restrictions?* Font programs are subject to copyright, and not all fonts can be used for free. Some fonts have the restriction that you aren't allowed to embed them. When restrictions recorded in the font program are encountered, iText throws a `DocumentException`. This is a licensing problem, not an iText problem.

Of course, by embedding a font, you increase the file size. If file size is an issue, you can opt for a standard font or, if you need characters that aren't available in a standard font, choose to embed only a subset of the font. This way, the PDF document will only contain the glyph descriptions corresponding with the characters that were used. That's the theory; but how is it done in iText?

## *8.2 Introducing base fonts*

In the PostScript Language Reference, fonts of Types 1, 2, 3, 14, and 42 are called *base fonts*, as opposed to Type 0 and character identifier (CID) fonts (PostScript Types 9, 10, 11, and 32). In a base font, every character corresponds with a glyph. The mapping between characters and glyphs isn't a part of the glyph descriptions; this information is stored in a separate *encoding vector*.

This section will demonstrate how to use different types of base fonts: You'll load a Type 1 font in different ways and create your own Type 3 font. We'll also talk about TrueType fonts and what's so different about OpenType fonts.

### 8.2.1 Working with an encoding

The descriptions of individual glyphs can be keyed by character names (Type 1, Type 3) or by means of an internal structure called a *cmap*. The association between characters and glyphs is called the *encoding*. Every base font must have an encoding.

In a font dictionary of a Type 1 and Type 3 font, the descriptions of the individual glyphs are keyed by character *names*, not by character *codes*. The PS Language Reference says, "Character names are ordinary PostScript name objects. Descriptions of Latin alphabetic characters are normally associated with names consisting of single letters, such as A or a. Other characters are associated with names composed of words, such as three, ampersand, or parenleft."

A Type 1 font can have a special built-in encoding; as is the case for Symbol and Zapfdingbats. With other fonts, multiple encodings may be available. Appendix D of the PDF Reference lists the character sets and encodings of the Latin-text standard fonts. If you look up the glyph known as *dagger* (†), you see that it corresponds with `(char) 134` in the encoding known as WinAnsi, aka Western European Latin (code page 1252), a superset of Latin-1 (ISO-8859-1). The same dagger glyph corresponds with different character values in the Adobe Standard encoding (178), Mac Roman encoding (160), and PDF Doc Encoding (129).

You need this information to be able to create an iText `BaseFont` object.

#### Creating a BaseFont object

If you look at the class diagram in appendix A, section A.7, you'll see a lot of implementations of the abstract class `BaseFont`. Notice that the class names correspond vaguely with the types listed in table 8.2. You don't have to worry about what class to use for what type; you get a specific implementation automatically by using the abstract method `BaseFont.createFont()`.

The parameters of this method are as follows:

- A `String` that refers to the font name or file
- The character encoding
- A `boolean` value that indicates if the font needs to be embedded

The name of the BaseFont class is somewhat misleading, because the class is also used to create composite fonts. You won't always pass a real encoding with the encoding parameter; and even if you pass the value true for the embedded parameter, the font won't always be embedded (or vice versa). But let's pretend you don't know that, and start by creating a BaseFont object for a Type 1 font with the createFont() method.

### 8.2.2 Class BaseFont and Type 1 fonts

For every name in the first column of table 8.3, there's a corresponding public static String in the BaseFont object. Let's try to construct a BaseFont object for an embedded font like this:

```
/* chapter08/StandardType1FontFromAFM.java */
BaseFont bf = BaseFont.createFont(
  BaseFont.TIMES_ROMAN,
  BaseFont.CP1252,
  BaseFont.EMBEDDED);                         <-- Ignore BaseFont.EMBEDDED!
System.err.println(bf.getClass().getName());  <-- Return com.lowagie.text.pdf.Type1Font
Font font = new Font(bf, 12);
document.add(new Paragraph("0123456789", font));
```

As opposed to the Font constructor, you don't specify a size when creating a BaseFont object. Here, you're using the definition that says a font is a set of designs. You pass the BaseFont object to a Font object, along with the size.

Figure 8.3 is somewhat surprising. Adobe Reader replaced the Type 1 font Times-Roman with the TrueType font Times New Roman PS MT. The font wasn't embedded!

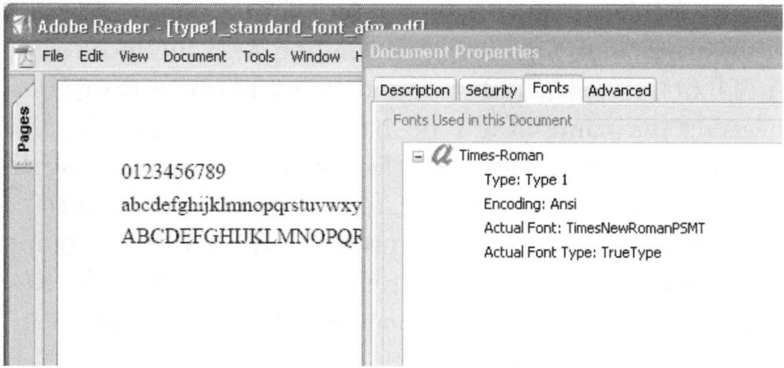


**Figure 8.3 Adobe Reader replaced a font that wasn't embedded.**

This is normal behavior; `BaseFont` is designed to ignore the value of the `embedded` parameter if you use `createFont()` with the name of a standard font. To understand why, you need to know the difference between AFM files and PFB files.

### *Adobe Font Metrics files*

Look inside iText.jar, and you'll find a com/lowagie/text/pdf/fonts directory containing 14 files with the extension AFM. You'll recognize these files from the fourth column in table 8.3. AFM files are plain-text files with *Adobe Font Metrics*: They store information about widths, kerning pairs, and bounding boxes of glyphs. iText uses them to calculate how many glyphs fit on one line and to retrieve the ascender value, descender value, and so on.

Even if you tell iText to embed a standard font, the font won't be embedded *unless you provide a font program*. AFM files don't contain any information about the font shape. If you only have an AFM file, you can only create a `BaseFont` object that isn't embedded.

**FAQ** *Why do I get an* `IOException` *when I use the default or a standard font?* The complete message of the exception is, for instance, *Helvetica is not found as a resource. (The *.afm files must exist as resources in the package com. lowagie.text.pdf.fonts)*. This message explains exactly what went wrong. The AFM files can't be loaded as a resource into your JVM. This is often the result of building iText.jar from source code, forgetting the AFM files. Add them to the jar, and/or check their access permissions.

To create a `BaseFont` object using another Type 1 font, you can pass the name of the font, and iText will look for the corresponding AFM file in directory /com/-lowagie/text/pdf/fonts. If no such file is found, an exception is thrown.

Instead of using the name of a Type 1 font, you can also refer to the AFM file directly by passing the path to the file instead of the name of the font. I downloaded the AFM files of the fonts Utopia Regular (copyright © 1989 by Adobe Systems Incorporated) and Computer Modern Regular (copyright © 1997 American Mathematical Society, a font designed by Donald Knuth) and used them to create the PDF file shown in figure 8.4. These fonts can be used for free as long as you respect the copyright.

Figure 8.4 shows how Adobe Reader tries to visualize these fonts that weren't embedded.

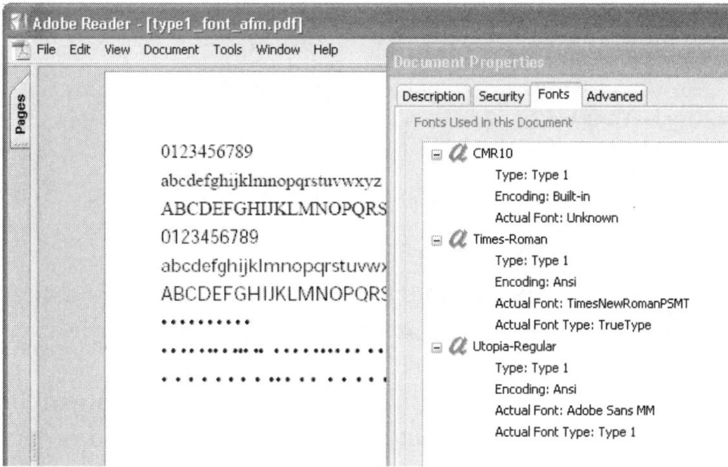


**Figure 8.4 Type 1 fonts that weren't embedded**

You immediately see some problems if you use this approach. Times-Roman is again replaced by Times New Roman PS MT. (You already knew that.) Utopia-Regular is replaced by the Type 1 font Adobe Sans MM. The text is readable, but I was expecting a *serif* font instead of a *sans* font.

**FAQ** *What is the difference between serif and sans(-serif)?* *Serifs* are the small features at the end of the strokes within letters. A font without serifs is called sans-serif (*sans* is the French word for *without*). Compare the first three lines in figure 8.4 (Times New Roman PS MT: serif) with the following three lines (Adobe Sans MM: sans-serif) to understand the difference. Serif is assumed to be easier to read on paper. Sans-serif is better suited to read on a screen. In print, sans-serif is used for headers and smaller sections of text. There's no such thing as a general rule; this is just a rule of thumb.

The biggest problem is that you can't read the text written in the nonembedded font Computer Modern. When you open the file, a warning is shown: *Cannot find or create the font 'CMR10'*. Some characters may not display or print correctly. In figure 8.4, you only see dots, and the spacing between the dots is irregular. What happened? The code looks OK:

```
/* chapter08/Type1FontFromAFM.java */
BaseFont bf1 = BaseFont.createFont(
  "/com/lowagie/text/pdf/fonts/Times-Roman.afm",
  "", BaseFont.NOT_EMBEDDED);
```

```
Font font1 = new Font(bf1, 12);
document.add(new Paragraph("0123456789 ", font1));
BaseFont bf2 = BaseFont.createFont(
  "../resources/putr8a.afm", "", BaseFont.NOT_EMBEDDED);
Font font2 = new Font(bf2, 12);
document.add(new Paragraph("0123456789 ", font2));
BaseFont bf3 = BaseFont.createFont(
  "../resources/cmr10.afm", "", BaseFont.NOT_EMBEDDED);
Font font3 = new Font(bf3, 12);
document.add(new Paragraph("0123456789\ ", font3));
```

Note that the code doesn't specify an encoding. For the Times-Roman and Utopia font, the default encoding (ANSI) was used. Computer Modern has a built-in encoding that is used, but this isn't what's causing the problem.

The issue is that Adobe Reader didn't understand the acronym/font name CMR10. This results in an unknown actual font. The code should provide a font program instead of just the metrics in the AFM file. This example prevents iText from looking up a font program by setting the `embedded` parameter to false. Would setting this value to true without further changes to the code solve the problem?

### *PostScript Font Binary files*

For Utopia and Computer Modern, I have put the files putr8a.pfb and cmr10.pfb in the same directory as the cmr10.afm file. Now, you can set the `embedded` parameter to true for these fonts. You'll still encounter problems with Times-Roman, because I didn't provide a Times-Roman.pfb file. An exception will be thrown, saying *Times-'/com/lowagie/text/pdf/fonts/Times-Roman.pfb' is not found as file or resource.*

PostScript Font Binary (PFB) is a format for storing Type 1 fonts. If you copy the font program from the PFB file to the PDF, you get the PDF shown in figure 8.5.

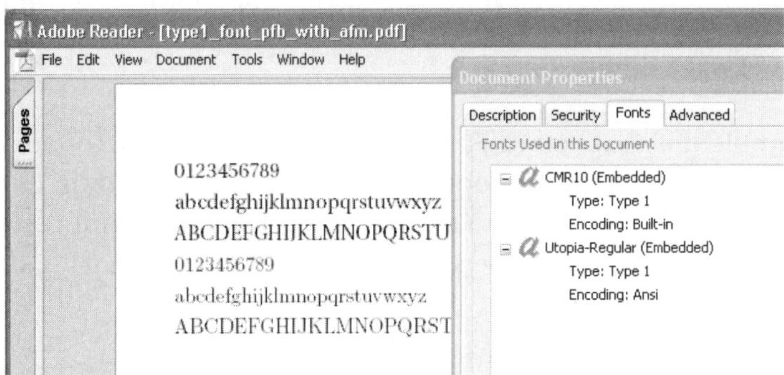


**Figure 8.5 Embedded Type 1 font**

You can finally read the text in Computer Modern. If you compare the text in Utopia-Regular with the Adobe Sans font in figure 8.4, you see why I expected a serif font. In figure 8.5, the letters have these little extra strokes. In the Fonts tab both fonts are marked Embedded.

The only difference in the code is the value of the `embedded` parameter:

```
/* chapter08/Type1FontFromPFBwithAFM.java */
BaseFont bf = BaseFont.createFont(
  "../resources/putr8a.afm", "", BaseFont.EMBEDDED);
Font font = new Font(bf, 12);
document.add(new Paragraph("0123456789 ", font));
bf = BaseFont.createFont(
  "../resources/cmr10.afm", "", BaseFont.EMBEDDED);
font = new Font(bf, 12);
document.add(new Paragraph("0123456789", font));
```

You don't have to pass the path of the PFB files in the `BaseFont` constructor; iText looks for the PFBs in the same directory as the AFM file (by replacing the extension AFM with PFB).

If you look at the resources directory with the AFM and PFB files for these fonts, you'll also find a cmr10.pfm file. This is a Printer Font Metric (PFM) file.

### *Printer Font Metric files*

PFM files are the Microsoft version of AFM; iText is able to convert PFM files to AFM, so you can replace the reference to an AFM file in all the previous examples with a reference to a PFM file (provided you have a PFM version of the AFM):

```
/* chapter08/Type1FontFromPFBwithPFM.java */
BaseFont bf = BaseFont.createFont(
  "../resources/cmr10.pfm", "", BaseFont.EMBEDDED);
Font font = new Font(bf, 12);
document.add(new Paragraph("0123456789", font));
```

The resulting PDF file of this example is about 26 KB. If you set the `embedded` parameter to `BaseFont.NOT_EMBEDDED`, the file is only 2 KB. A larger file size is the price you have to pay for embedding the Type 1 font program.

Some fonts always have to be embedded. For instance, it's evident that a user-defined font always needs to be embedded. Tables 8.1 and 8.2 tell you that such a font is also known as a Type 3 font.

### 8.2.3 *Embedding Type 3 fonts*

In chapter 10, you'll learn about PDF operators and operands. This is PDF syntax, and you can use it to create your own fonts (see figure 8.6).

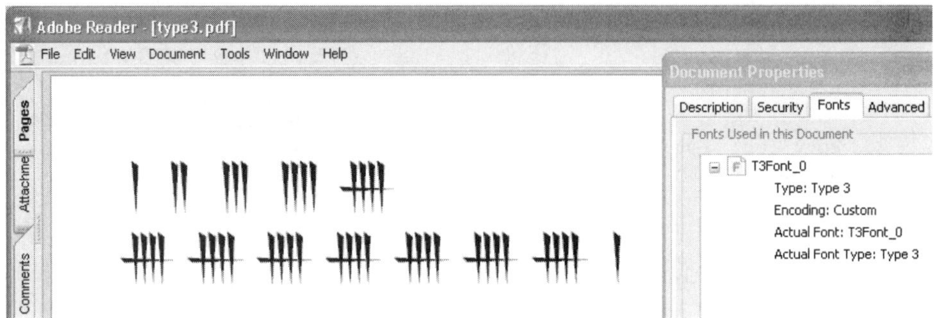


**Figure 8.6 PDF file with a user-defined font**

I created glyphs corresponding with the characters " ", "1", "2", "3", "4", and "5" so that I could mark in fives my age in the year this book was first published. The first line shows the `String` "1 2 3 4 5"; my age in the year 2006 (36) corresponds with the String "5 5 5 5 5 5 5 1."

This is how it's done:

```
/* chapter08/Type3Characters.java */
Type3Font t3 = new Type3Font(writer,                         <-- Type3Font constructor
  new char[]{' ', '1', '2', '3', '4', '5'}, false);          <-- Characters to redefine
PdfContentByte g;                                            <-- One PdfContentByte
g = t3.defineGlyph(' ', 300, 0, 0, 600, 1200);                   object per character
g = t3.defineGlyph('1', 600, 0, 0, 600, 1200);
g.moveTo(250, 1200);                                         Define glyph for
g.lineTo(350, 100);                                          character "1"
g.lineTo(400, 1100);
g.closePathFillStroke();
...
Font font = new Font(t3, 24);
document.add(new Paragraph("1 2 3 4 5", font));
```

You can create a font with class `Type3Font` (extending the abstract class `BaseFont`) and define all the characters with the method `defineGlyph()`. This example passes the value false for the `colorized` parameter in the constructor, so you're limited to characters in one color. Change this parameter to true if you need more color. The metrics parameters passed with the `defineGlyph()` method are the *advance* of the character and the definition of the bounding box of the glyph:

the lower left X-coordinate, the lower-left Y coordinate, the upper-right X coordinate, and the upper-right Y coordinate. All values are measured in glyph space.

There are some rules to take into account if you define your own glyphs. For instance, if you stroke lines instead of filling shapes, you should explicitly set the line width, line join, line cap, and dash pattern. The meaning of these terms is explained in detail in chapter 10.

Although Type 1 and Type 3 fonts are interesting, you may be more familiar with TrueType fonts, or OpenType fonts with TrueType outlines. Those are the fonts you know from Word, Windows, or Mac.

### 8.2.4 Working with TrueType fonts

The TrueType specification was originally developed by Apple Computer, Inc. to compete with Adobe's Type 1 fonts. Apple licensed the TrueType technology to Microsoft, and it was adopted as a standard font format for the Microsoft Windows operating system. This may seem odd, but it was part of a strategy by Apple to distance itself from Adobe. I won't go into the details of corporate politics; what matters is how to use a TrueType font, and whether you can embed it.

If you look at the Fonts tab in figure 8.7, you see that Arial-BlackItalic is mentioned twice: once not embedded, and once with only a subset embedded. On my PC, the name of the actual font corresponds with the PostScript font name retrieved from the TTF file. If you look at this PDF on another machine, another font may be used, instead.

You have to be careful with nonembedded TrueType fonts. Not only do you risk that end users don't have this font on their computers, but TrueType fonts

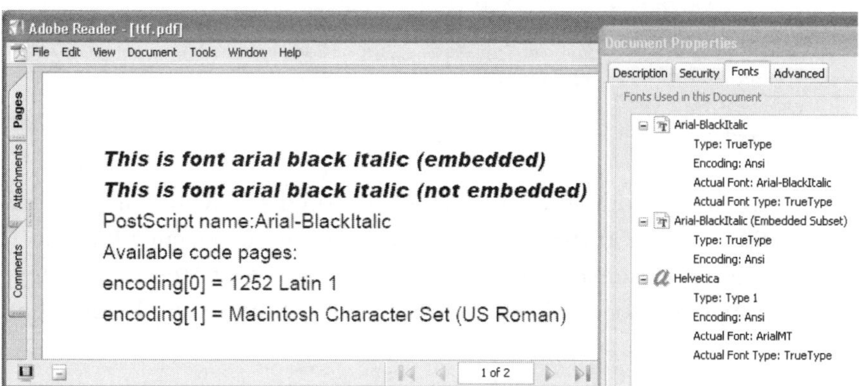


**Figure 8.7 Nonembedded TrueType fonts**

are also platform dependent. You should always embed TrueType fonts. As you can see in the Fonts tab in figure 8.7, iText doesn't embed the complete font, as was the case with Type 1 fonts; only a subset is embedded. You didn't have to set a parameter; iText does this automatically:

```
/* chapter08/TrueTypeFontExample.java */
bf = BaseFont.createFont("c:/windows/fonts/ARBLI___.ttf",
  BaseFont.CP1252,
  BaseFont.EMBEDDED);
font = new Font(bf, 12);
System.err.println(bf.getClass().getName());      <-- Return com.lowagie.text.pdf.TrueTypeFont
document.add(new Paragraph(
  "This is font arial black italic (embedded)", font));
bf = BaseFont.createFont("c:/windows/fonts/ARBLI___.ttf",
  BaseFont.CP1252,
  BaseFont.NOT_EMBEDDED);
font = new Font(bf, 12);
document.add(new Paragraph(
  "This is font arial black italic (not embedded)", font));
document.add(new Paragraph("PostScript name:"
                           + bf.getPostscriptFontName()));   Return PS name Arial-BlackItalic
```

As opposed to Type 1 and Type 3 fonts, glyphs aren't referenced by name (not by names like "a," "parenleft," and "three"). Instead, an internal data structure is used: a cmap table (not to be confused with CMap, another term you'll encounter later). A cmap can contain one or more subtables that represent multiple encodings.

If you want to know the encodings available in a TTF file, you can use the method `getCodePagesSupported()`:

```
/* chapter08/TrueTypeFontExample.java */
document.add(new Paragraph("Available code pages:"));
String[] encoding = bf.getCodePagesSupported();
for (int i = 0; i < encoding.length; i++) {
  document.add(
    new Paragraph("encoding[" + i + "] = " + encoding[i]));
}
```

In the iText source code, the term *code page* is used as a synonym for *encoding*. *Code page* is "the traditional IBM term for a specific character encoding table: a mapping in which a sequence of bits, usually a single octet representing integer values from 0 to 255, is associated with a character."[6] In this example, only Latin 1 and

[6] Wikipedia

the Macintosh Character Set are available, but soon, you'll use font formats that provide many more possible encodings.

This example retrieves the PostScript font name with method `getPostscriptFontName()`, but you can also retrieve the font family and the full font names. As you can see in figure 8.8, you get the same name in different languages. If you replace `getFullFontNames()` with `getFamilyFontName()` in the source code sample, you get the names of the font family:

```
/* chapter08/TrueTypeFontExample.java */
document.add(new Paragraph("Full font names:"));
String[][] name = bf.getFullFontName();    <-❶
for (int i = 0; i < name.length; i++) {
  document.add(new Paragraph(
    name[i][3]    <-❷
    + " (" + name[i][0] + "; "    <-❸
    + name[i][1] + "; "    <-❹
    + name[i][2] + ")"));    <-❺
}
```

In this example, ❶ gets the full font names (2D array). Element 3 is the actual name ❷, element 0 is the platform ID ❸, element 1 is the platform encoding ID ❹, and element 2 is the language code ❺.

I added some numbers between parentheses after the font name. Each subtable inside a cmap is identified by two numbers: a platform ID and a platform-specific encoding ID. Table 8.4 (taken from Microsoft's OpenType specification) lists the platform IDs. Figure 8.8 shows the platform IDs for Mac (1) and Microsoft (3).

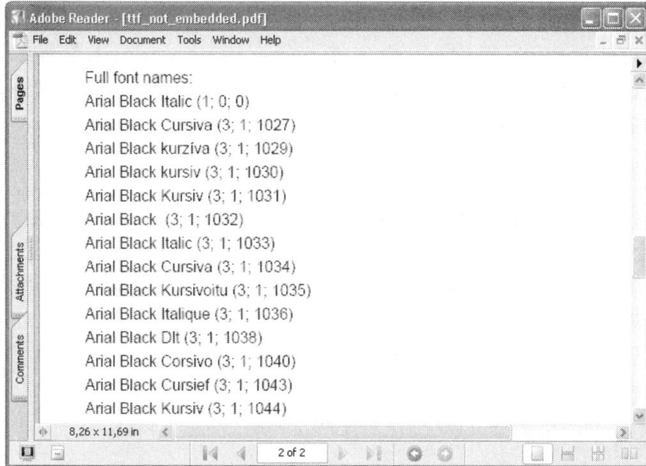


**Figure 8.8 Different names of the font Arial Black Italic**

**Table 8.4 Platform IDs in a TrueType or OpenType font**

| Id | Platform | Platform-specific encoding IDs | Language IDs |
|---|---|---|---|
| 0 | Unicode | Various | None |
| 1 | Macintosh | Script manager code | Various |
| 2 | ISO (deprecated) | ISO encoding (deprecated) | None |
| 3 | Microsoft | Microsoft encoding | Various |
| 4 | Custom | Custom | None |

The second number is the platform encoding ID. The encoding number for Microsoft (1) means "Unicode BMP only" (consult the OpenType specification for more information on the other numbers).

The third number in figure 8.8 is the language identifier. The figure shows the name of the font in Catalan (1027), Czech (1029), Danish (1030), and so on. The language identifier for English is 1033. Notice that these values are returned only for TrueType and OpenType fonts, not for the other fonts that are handled by the `BaseFont` object.

I've dropped the name *OpenType* three times in the last few paragraphs. To explain how OpenType fonts relate to the TrueType font, I should insert a little history lesson. TrueType is a *font standard*; that is, both Apple and Microsoft started with the same standard. But as you have seen happen with a lot of standards, the standard according to Apple and the standard according to Microsoft diverged. Both companies added their own proprietary extensions, and soon they had their own versions and interpretations of (what once was) the standard. When looking for a commercial font, you had to be careful and buy a font that could be used on your system. A TrueType font for Windows didn't necessarily work on a Mac.

**FAQ** *How can I convert my fonts on OS X to fonts that can be used in iText?* Some fonts on your Macintosh will be recognized by iText, and you'll be able to use them in a PDF document. But if you wish to use a Mac font that isn't supported by iText, you should download and install the tool fondu (http://fondu.sourceforge.net/). You can, for instance, switch to your personal Fonts directory (/Users/*username*/Library/Fonts) and issue `fondu *`. Fondu will replace all the Mac-specific files with font files supported in iText.

To resolve the platform dependency of TrueType fonts (and because Apple refused to license its advanced typography technology GX Typography), Microsoft started developing a new font format. Microsoft was joined by Adobe, and support for Adobe's Type 1 fonts was added. A new font format was born: OpenType fonts.

There are some interesting stories to be told about the rivalry between Apple, Microsoft, and Adobe, in the past as well as in the present. But I'll restrain myself and stick to the technical stuff, telling you more about this new font type.

## 8.2.5 Working with OpenType fonts

Adobe's Q&A on OpenType Fonts says, "The OpenType format is a superset of the existing TrueType and Adobe PostScript Type 1 font formats. It provides improved cross-platform document portability, rich linguistic support, powerful typographic capabilities, and simplified font management requirements." Let's analyze this sentence bit by bit.

### OpenType font with PostScript outlines

OpenType fonts can have PostScript Type 1 outlines or TrueType outlines. If an OpenType font has PS outlines, the font file always has the extension OTF. The font is stored in the Compact Font Format (Type 2). Most of these fonts aren't free, but I found some freeware OTF files that were developed by Ethan Lamoreaux. They contain the Shavian alphabet. This alphabet is named after George Bernard Shaw (winner of the Nobel Prize for Literature in 1925). In his will, Shaw stipulated that there should be a contest to create a simple, phonetic orthography (because he didn't think the Latin alphabet was suited to write in English). The competition took place in 1958, and the £500 prize was won by Kingsley Read.

Figure 8.9 shows the first article of the Universal Declaration of Human Rights in English (Latin alphabet) and in … English (Shavian alphabet). Looking at the screenshot, you see that the complete font is embedded as a Type 1 font (not a subset). The corresponding source code has a few peculiarities:

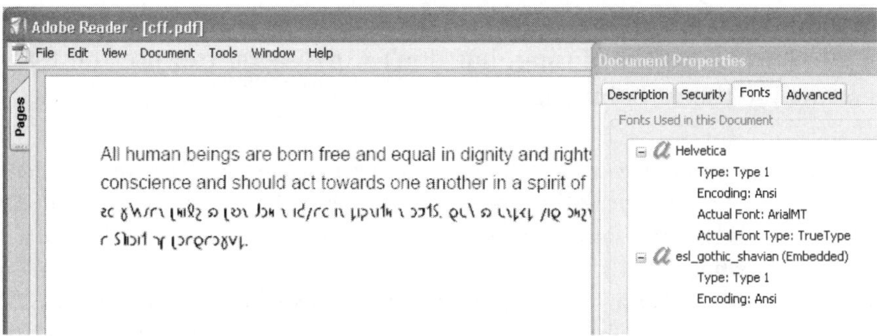


**Figure 8.9 Using an OpenType font (Compact Font Format)**

```
/* chapter08/CompactFontFormatExample.java */
BaseFont bf = BaseFont.createFont(
  "../resources/esl_gothic_shavian.otf", "Cp1252", BaseFont.EMBEDDED);
System.err.println(bf.getClass().getName());    <-- Return com.lowagie.text.
Font font = new Font(bf, 12);                        pdf.TrueTypeFont

document.add(new Paragraph("All human beings are born free and equal      (1)
➥ in dignity and rights. They are endowed with reason and conscience
➥ and should act towards one another in a spirit of brotherhood."));
document.add(new Paragraph("Yl hVman bIiNz R bPn frI n ikwal in          (2)
➥ dignitI n rFts. Hej R endQd wiH rIzn n konSans n Sud Akt tawPds
➥ wan anaHr in a spirit ov braHarhUd.", font));
```

The `String` passed to the paragraph with the Shavian font ❷ looks odd when compared to the `String` in plain English ❶. In this specific OTF, the ranges that are normally reserved for the Latin alphabet are used to store the Shavian alphabet. That way, if you're using a word processor, you can type Shavian directly with regular strokes on your keyboard.

But the real reason the same characters are often used to refer to different graphemes is the limitation that is inherent in the encoding system: A font can contain more than 256 glyphs (OpenType fonts can have up to 65,536 glyphs), but in each code page you can use only 256 characters to refer to them. It happens regularly that a character referring to a certain grapheme in one encoding refers to another grapheme in another encoding.

Furthermore, you probably think the annotation with `bf.getClass().getName()` is a copy/paste error. You expect either an instance of `CFFFont` (because that's the format of the OTF) or `Type1Font` (the type shown in figure 8.9). But no, it isn't an error.

The class `TrueTypeFont` deals with all font files that have the extension OTF or TTF. But in this case the `CFFFont` class does the work, because the font is stored in the Compact Font Format. In Adobe Reader, the font is seen as a Type 1 font, because the glyphs are defined and stored in the PDF as PostScript outlines.

This may sound confusing, but don't worry—you can use the font without knowing the theory behind it.

**FAQ** *Can I use these fonts on operating systems other than Mac and Windows?* One of the biggest differences between OpenType and Type 1/TrueType fonts is that the same font file works on a Windows PC as well as on a Mac. But what about Linux and Solaris? Can you create an iText `BaseFont` object that takes a TTF or OTF file on a UNIX system? The answer is, Yes. With iText, it doesn't matter on which operating system you're working as long as a valid font file is provided.

We started this section by saying that a file with the extension OTF can also be an OpenType font using TrueType technology. Let's look at such a font.

### *OpenType font with TrueType outlines*

In most cases, OpenType font files using TrueType technology have the extension TTF, but OTF is also a valid extension. When we discussed plain old TrueType fonts, we used Arial Black Italic. We didn't have a lot of choice for the encoding. Adobe's Q&A answer says that OpenType provides "rich linguistic support." Let's see if we have more choice if we use the OpenType font ArialBoldMT (arialbd.ttf) instead of Arial Black Italic (ARBLI___.ttf). Compare figure 8.10 with figure 8.7; there's now a list with 26 available codepages.

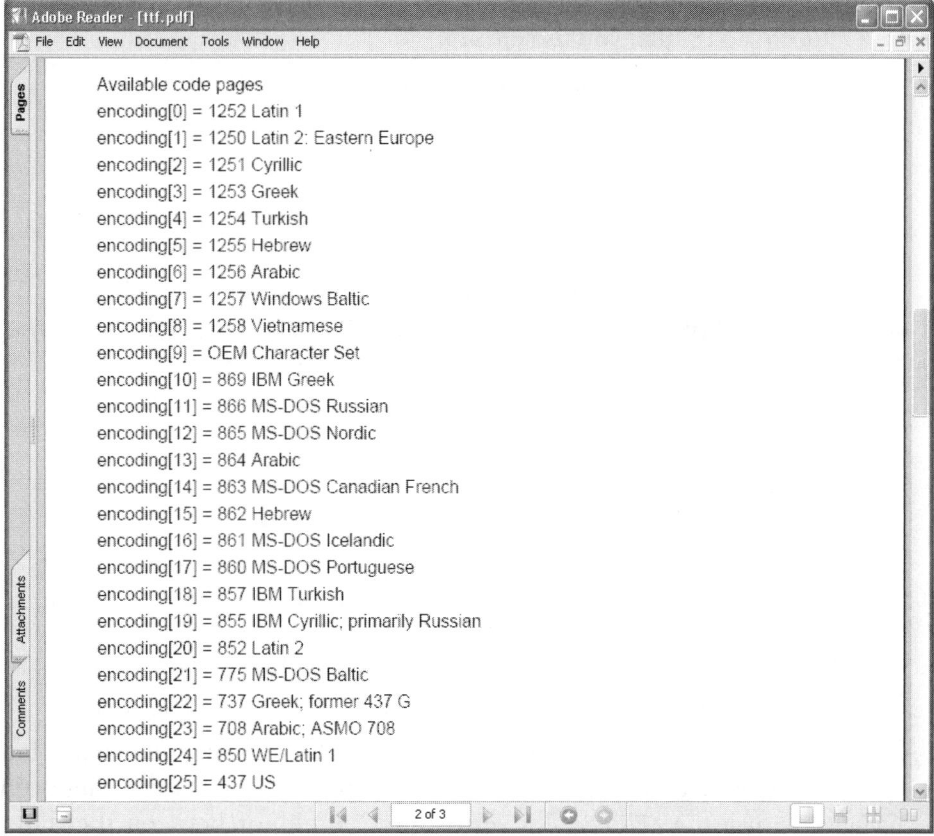

Adobe Reader - [ttf.pdf]
File Edit View Document Tools Window Help
Pages
Attachments
Comments
Available code pages
encoding[0] = 1252 Latin 1
encoding[1] = 1250 Latin 2: Eastern Europe
encoding[2] = 1251 Cyrillic
encoding[3] = 1253 Greek
encoding[4] = 1254 Turkish
encoding[5] = 1255 Hebrew
encoding[6] = 1256 Arabic
encoding[7] = 1257 Windows Baltic
encoding[8] = 1258 Vietnamese
encoding[9] = OEM Character Set
encoding[10] = 869 IBM Greek
encoding[11] = 866 MS-DOS Russian
encoding[12] = 865 MS-DOS Nordic
encoding[13] = 864 Arabic
encoding[14] = 863 MS-DOS Canadian French
encoding[15] = 862 Hebrew
encoding[16] = 861 MS-DOS Icelandic
encoding[17] = 860 MS-DOS Portuguese
encoding[18] = 857 IBM Turkish
encoding[19] = 855 IBM Cyrillic; primarily Russian
encoding[20] = 852 Latin 2
encoding[21] = 775 MS-DOS Baltic
encoding[22] = 737 Greek; former 437 G
encoding[23] = 708 Arabic; ASMO 708
encoding[24] = 850 WE/Latin 1
encoding[25] = 437 US
2 of 3


**Figure 8.10 Code pages in the font ArialBoldMT**

This answers one of the initial questions: Can you create a basic building block that contains Eastern European characters (or Greek, or Turkish, or…)?

Some Western European languages (for instance, French) have letters that get a cedilla (¸) or a circumflex (^). Those letters are in Code Page 1252. For a change, you pass the encoding as a `String`:

```
/* chapter08/TrueTypeFontEncoding.java */
bf = BaseFont.createFont("c:/windows/fonts/arialbd.ttf",
  "Cp1252", BaseFont.EMBEDDED);
System.err.println(bf.getClass().getName());   <-- Return instance of com.lowagie.text.pdf.TrueTypeFont
font = new Font(bf, 12);
document.add(new Paragraph("Un long dimanche de fiançailles", font));
```

Eastern Europe uses letters that get, for instance, a hacek (ˇ, aka a caron). These characters are in Code Page 1250 (also known as Latin 2). If you want to add such a letter to a PDF file, you use `cp1250`:

```
/* chapter08/TrueTypeFontEncoding.java */
bf = BaseFont.createFont("c:/windows/fonts/arialbd.ttf",
  "Cp1250", BaseFont.EMBEDDED);
font = new Font(bf, 12);
byte[] noMansLand = { 'N', 'i', 'k', 'o', 'g', 'a', 'r',
  (byte) 0x9A, 'n', 'j', 'a', ' ', 'z', 'e', 'm', 'l', 'j', 'a' };
document.add(new Paragraph(new String(noMansLand), font));
```

The resulting PDF in figure 8.11 lists some interesting movie titles.

You aren't limited to Latin text; figure 8.11 also shows original movie titles in Cyrillic (Code Page 1251) and Greek (Code Page 1253):

```
/* chapter08/TrueTypeFontEncoding.java */
bf = BaseFont.createFont("c:/windows/fonts/arialbd.ttf",
  "Cp1251", BaseFont.EMBEDDED);
font = new Font(bf, 12);
char[] youILove = { 1071, ' ', 1083, 1102, 1073, 1083, 1102,
  ' ', 1090, 1077, 1073, 1103 };
document.add(new Paragraph(new String(youILove), font));
bf = BaseFont.createFont("c:/windows/fonts/arialbd.ttf",
  "Cp1253", BaseFont.EMBEDDED);
font = new Font(bf, 12);
byte[] brides = { -51, -3, -10, -27, -14 };
document.add(new Paragraph(new String(brides, "Cp1253"), font));
```

I've been showing the Fonts tab so that you can compare which font is (or isn't) embedded into the PDF. The screenshots don't show much difference between using AMF/PFB files versus an OTF file, or between the different flavors of TTF files.

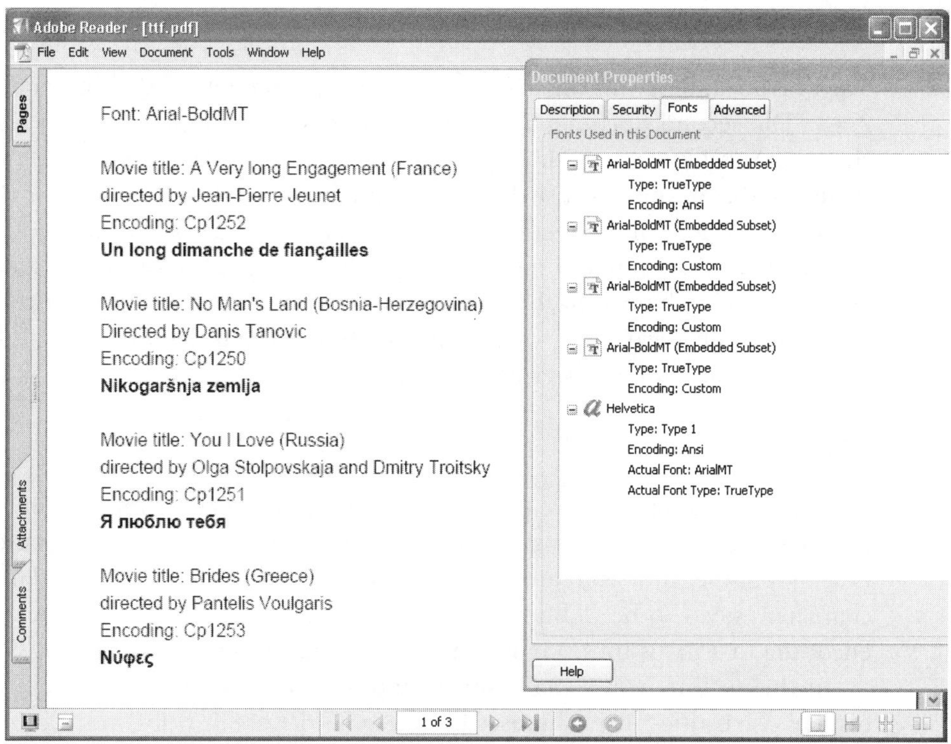


**Figure 8.11 OpenType TrueType font with different encodings**

**FAQ** *When I try the examples in the book, why is the text garbled?* In most cases, this isn't a PDF problem or even an iText problem; it's a simple Java issue. If you have hard-coded `String` values in your source, make sure you compile your code using the correct encoding. The same goes for values that are retrieved from a database: Check the encoding that is used by your database. Java uses a default encoding to translate bytes into `Strings`. If you use the wrong encoding, you can get garbled text.

Notice that in the last example, only a subset of the font is embedded (just like in the other TrueType example). The next example gives you an idea of the impact of embedding a font into your documents:

```
/* chapter08/FileSizeComparison.java */
document1.add(new Paragraph(
  "quick brown fox jumps over the lazy dog", font_not_embedded));
document2.add(new Paragraph(
  "quick brown fox jumps over the lazy dog", font_embedded));
```

```
document3.add(new Paragraph(
  "ooooo ooooo ooo ooooo oooo ooo oooo ooo", font_embedded));
```

The first document with the fox/dog sentence doesn't embed the font and is about 2 KB. The second document embeds 26 letters of the alphabet (plus the space character) and is about 13 KB. In the third document, you add a `String` with the same length, but you only use the letter *o* and the space character. You use the same embedded font as in the second document. The resulting file is only 7 KB.

I've already explained some of the aspects in the Q&A quote at the start of this section on OpenType fonts, but I'll have to postpone the part on advanced typography till after we've dealt with composite fonts. You'll need composite fonts to create basic building blocks with Asian text.

## 8.3 Composite fonts

The previous examples have used single-byte characters to compose text `Strings`. Now we'll look at some languages with huge character sets—for instance, Chinese, Japanese, and Korean. You need a composite font for these languages; characters need to be defined using two or more bytes, and you use a special encoding that maps these characters to the corresponding glyphs.

In this section, you'll make some more movie examples, but this time you'll display Asian titles. For Chinese, Japanese, and Korean titles, you can choose a CJK font. Such a font can't be embedded into the PDF; Adobe Reader will ask you to download and install the font as you open a file that uses one of these fonts. If you want to avoid this, you can embed a CID font using an OpenType font or a TrueType collection that has the required glyph descriptions.

In any case, you need to know about Unicode, so let's start with a definition.

### 8.3.1 What is Unicode?

The opening sentence of the "What is Unicode?" page at the site of the Unicode Consortium[7] is clear and simple:

> Unicode provides a unique number for every character,
>
> - no matter what the platform
> - no matter what the program
> - no matter what the language

[7] http://www.unicode.org/standard/WhatIsUnicode.html

In the Shavian example, two different code pages use the same character number for two different graphemes. It's also possible for two different character numbers to be used for the same grapheme. This is dangerous when you're passing files from one system to another. If they use a different encoding, the data risks getting corrupted. By providing a unique number for every grapheme, Unicode avoids this kind of problem.

Unicode characters vary between U+000000 and U+10FFFF; this means there are 1,114,112 *code points*, of which more than 96,000 are assigned. The most common graphemes can be represented by two-byte characters. The area U+0000–U+FFFF is called the *basic multilingual plane* (BMP). Notice that this is the platform-specific encoding ID you already met in the example with the arial. ttf font.

All the graphemes are listed in the Unicode Standard and in the International Standard ISO/IEC 10646. The characters are organized in blocks (for reasons of convenience). The first 256 code points correspond with ISO-8859-1 (Latin-1). The Braille symbols, for instance, are in the range U+2800–U+28FF. You can look for the character you need in the Unicode Standard 4.1 or on the "Where is my character?" page at Unicode.org.

### *Using Unicode in CID fonts*

1,114,112 code points—that's a large number of possible addresses for a glyph. Even if you know that fewer than 10 percent of the code points have been assigned, you realize that working with code pages that can map only 256 characters won't be efficient; certainly not when dealing with languages with huge character sets such as Chinese, Japanese, and Korean. That's why the CID-keyed font architecture was developed. CID-keyed fonts don't have an encoding built into the font, and the glyphs don't have names. Instead, a character identifier (CID) is used to refer to glyphs in the character collections.

These glyphs are stored in a CIDFont. CIDFonts are font-like objects: A Type 0 CIDFont contains glyph descriptions based on the Type 1 font format; a Type 2 CIDFont contains glyph descriptions based on the TrueType format. Notice that the numbers of the types have different meanings in different contexts. In PDF, a composite font is also called a Type 0 font, but Type 0 has a different meaning when used in the context of a CIDFont. But again, you don't have to worry about the theory.

A CID can be a number between 0 and 65,535. The association between the Unicode code point and its CID is specified in a CMap. A *CMap* is like a very large code page, but it's different from the encodings you've seen up till now. In PDF, a CMap may be specified in two ways:

- As a name object identifying a predefined CMap, whose definition is known to the consumer application
- As a stream object whose contents are a CMap file

Table 5.15 in the PDF Reference lists the names of the predefined CMaps. Table 8.5 lists the CMaps that are provided in the extra iTextAsian.jar file (to be downloaded separately), along with some property files.

**Table 8.5 CJK fonts supported in the iTextAsian.jar file**

| Language | Fonts | CMap names |
|---|---|---|
| Chinese (Simplified) | STSong-Light<br>STSongStd-Light | UniGB-UCS2-H<br>UniGB-UCS2-V |
| Chinese (Traditional) | MHei-Medium<br>MSung-Light<br>MSungStd-Light | UniCNS-UCS2-H<br>UniCNS-UCS2-V |
| Japanese | HeiseiMin-W3<br>HeiseiKakuGo-W5<br>KozMinPro-Regular | UniJIS-UCS2-H<br>UniJIS-UCS2-V<br>UniJIS-UCS2-HW-H<br>UniJIS-UCS2-HW-V |
| Korean | HYGoThic-Medium<br>HYSMyeongJo-Medium<br>HYSMyeongJoStd | UniKS-UCS2-H<br>UniKS-UCS2-V |

The *UCS-2* in the CMap names stands for Universal Character Set. There's also the Unicode Transformation Format (UTF). Both standards map Unicode code points to a unique byte sequence:

- UTF-8 is a variable length encoding using 1 to 4 bytes (sequences of 8 bit).
- UCS-2 is almost identical to UTF-16 and uses 16-bit words.
- UCS-4 corresponds with UTF-32, using the fixed amount of exactly 32 bits.

The *H* in the CMap names refers to horizontal writing mode and the *V* to vertical writing mode. Many Asian languages can be written from left to right; but often you can also use a writing system that writes glyphs from top to bottom in columns from right to left. You'll see an example using this vertical writing system in the next chapter.

I have looked at my personal movie database and I found some titles of Asian movies I really liked. I have put them in a PDF document using some of the fonts mentioned in table 8.5.

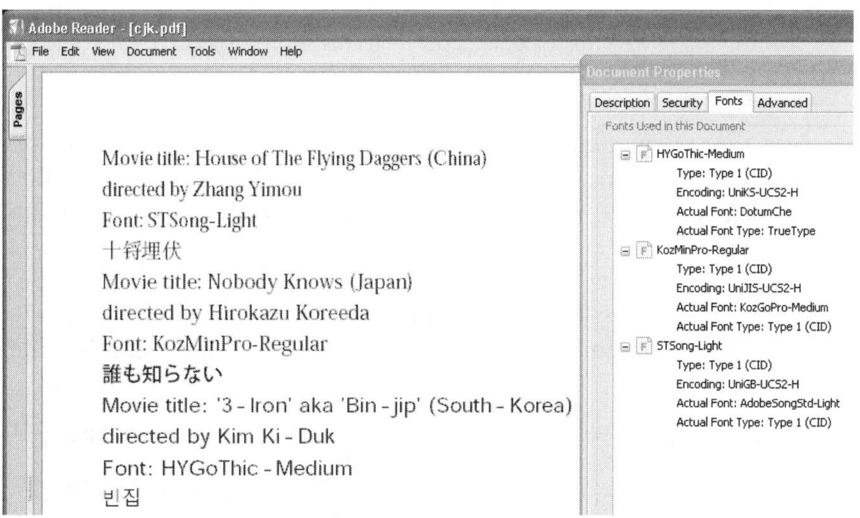


**Figure 8.12 CJK fonts in a PDF**

## 8.3.2 *Introducing Chinese, Japanese, Korean (CJK) fonts*

Figure 8.12 demonstrates the use of some of the CJK fonts listed in table 8.5.

The fonts aren't embedded (even if you set the embedded parameter to true), but if you open Adobe Reader and the fonts aren't available, a dialog box opens and asks if you want to update the reader. If you agree, the necessary font packs are downloaded and installed. You'll find the font files in the directory where Adobe Reader was installed, such as C:/Program Files/Adobe/Acrobat 7.0/Resource/.

Creating a `BaseFont` object for one of the fonts listed in table 8.5 is as easy as creating any other `BaseFont` object: You just combine a value from the second column with a value from the third column in the same row:

```
/* chapter08/ChineseKoreanJapaneseFonts.java */
bf = BaseFont.createFont(
  "STSong-Light", "UniGB-UCS2-H", BaseFont.NOT_EMBEDDED);
font = new Font(bf, 12);
System.err.println(bf.getClass().getName());        <-- Return com.lowagie.text.pdf.CJKFont
document.add(new Paragraph("\u5341\u950a\u57cb\u4f0f", font));
bf = BaseFont.createFont(
  "KozMinPro-Regular", "UniJIS-UCS2-H", BaseFont.EMBEDDED);
font = new Font(bf, 12);
document.add(
  new Paragraph("\u8ab0\u3082\u77e5\u3089\u306a\u3044", font));
```

```
bf = BaseFont.createFont(
  "HYGoThic-Medium", "UniKS-UCS2-H", BaseFont.NOT_EMBEDDED);
font = new Font(bf, 12);
document.add(new Paragraph("\ube48\uc9d1", font));
```

You pass the original movie titles as Java Unicode characters. In most cases, you're not going to write a `String` this way; that would be quite a bit of work. Instead, you get the `String` from a database—for instance, in UCS-2/UTF-16.

### *Using other CMaps*

If you want to use this functionality for an encoding that isn't supported by the CMaps in iTextAsian.jar, you can download the iTextAsianCmaps.jar file and use it like this:

```
PdfEncodings.loadCmap("GBK2K-H", PdfEncodings.CRLF_CID_NEWLINE);    <-❶
byte text[] = my_GB_encoded_text;   <-❷
String cid = PdfEncodings.convertCmap("GBK2K-H", text);   <-❸
BaseFont bf = BaseFont.createFont("STSong-Light",
  BaseFont.IDENTITY_H, BaseFont.NOT_EMBEDDED);
Paragraph p = new Paragraph(cid, new Font(bf, 14));
document.add(p);
```

I insert this sample for the sake of completeness. In the past three years, only a handful of people have posted questions about it on the iText mailing list. I won't go much deeper into the code in this book; I only want to point to these special encodings. `BaseFont.IDENTITY_H` and `BaseFont.IDENTITY_V` are the horizontal and vertical identity mapping for 2-byte CIDs. The `PdfConvertEncodings` class can convert a `String` in a specific encoding to a `String` with 2-byte CIDs ❸. In this case, the original `String` ❷ was encoded in the GB 18030-2000 character set ❶; GB is the abbreviation of the People's Republic of China's National Standards.

In iText, you use Identity-H and Identity-V to embed a CIDFont.

## 8.3.3 *Embedding CIDFonts*

The Identity-H and Identity-V CMaps map 2-byte character codes to the same 2-byte CID value; they can be used to refer to glyphs directly by their CIDs. If you were allowed to use the fonts from the Adobe font packs, you could generate a PDF file like the one in figure 8.13.

Unfortunately, if you download the font packs for free, the font software is licensed to you solely for use with Adobe Reader and is subject to the terms and conditions of the End-User License Agreement accompanying Acrobat Reader. It's hard to find an OTF font that can be distributed freely, so I'll only insert an example using a Type 2 CIDFont.

**Figure 8.13 A document with a Type 0 CIDFont (glyph descriptions based on the Type 1 font format)**

When you use Identity-H and Identity-V with an OpenType font with TrueType outlines, the two-byte characters values in your strings correspond with the indices for the glyph descriptions in the font program. The PDF Reference explains that you can get this to work only if the TrueType font program is embedded. That's why iText always embeds fonts created with Identity-H or Identity-V, no matter what value you're passing with the `embedded` parameter.

One of the previous examples combined different fonts to write a text in the Latin alphabet and the same text in the Shavian alphabet. It used the same characters for different graphemes. I downloaded another font file from Ethan Lamoreaux's site: esl_gothic_unicode.ttf. In this font, the Shavian glyphs are added in the range U+E700–U+E72F, in the private use area.

**FAQ** *Can font designers use unassigned code points as they wish?* The Unicode.org FAQ is clear: "Absolutely not!" Just because there are a lot of unused characters in the Unicode standard doesn't mean you can use unassigned characters for new graphemes at will. Only the values in the private-use area (U+E000–U+F8FF, U+F0000–U+FFFFD, and U+100000–U+10FFFD) are legal for private use.

Figure 8.14 shows the result of adapting the `String` representing the first article of the Universal Declaration of Human Rights.

In the Fonts tab, you see that only one font is used for both the Latin and the Shavian alphabet. The `BaseFont` object is created exactly the same way it's always been up to this point:

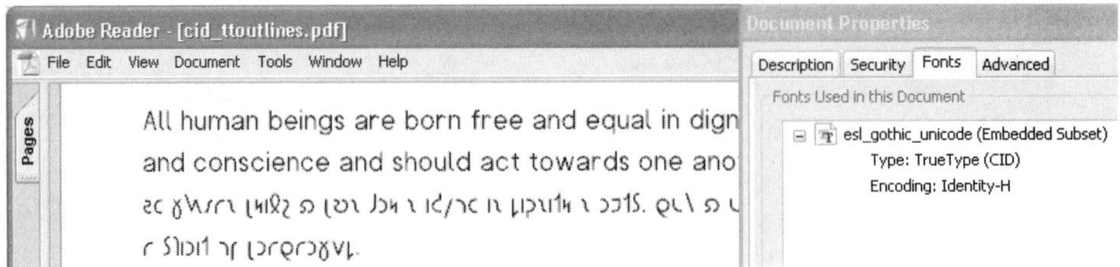


**Figure 8.14 A document with a Type 2 CIDFont (glyph descriptions based on the TrueType font format)**

```
/* chapter08/CIDTrueTypeOutlines.java */
BaseFont bf =
  BaseFont.createFont("../resources/esl_gothic_unicode.ttf",
    BaseFont.IDENTITY_H, BaseFont.NOT_EMBEDDED);
Font font = new Font(bf, 12);
System.err.println(bf.getClass().getName());
document.add(new Paragraph("All human beings ...", font));
document.add(new Paragraph(
  "\ue727\ue714 \ue713\ue72f\ue715\ue719\ue71f ...", font));
```

**Return com.lowagie.text.pdf.TrueTypeFontUnicode** (annotation on the `System.err.println` line)

If you go to Ethan Lamoreaux's site, you'll also find an OTF version of the Shavian Unicode font. Unfortunately, replacing the TTF with the OTF in the source code of the previous example won't work. You can only use the Identity-H or Identity-V encoding on OTF fonts that contain CIDFonts.

We're almost done with the overview of the font types and font files supported in iText. Let's finish this section with Type 2 CIDFonts bundled in a TrueType collection.

### 8.3.4 Using TrueType collections

A *TrueType collection* (TTC) is—as the name indicates—a collection of TrueType fonts bundled in one TTC file. With the static method `BaseFont.enumerateTTCNames()`, you can ask a file which fonts it contains:

```
/* chapter08/TrueTypeCollections.java */
String[] names =
  BaseFont.enumerateTTCNames("c:/windows/fonts/msgothic.ttc");
for (int i = 0; i < names.length; i++) {
  document.add(new Paragraph("font " + i + ": " + names[i], font));
}
```

I used a font that can be found on the CD that comes with the Windows OS (it isn't installed automatically). In figure 8.15, you see that this TTC file contains three fonts: MS-Gothic, MS-PGothic, and MS-UIGothic.

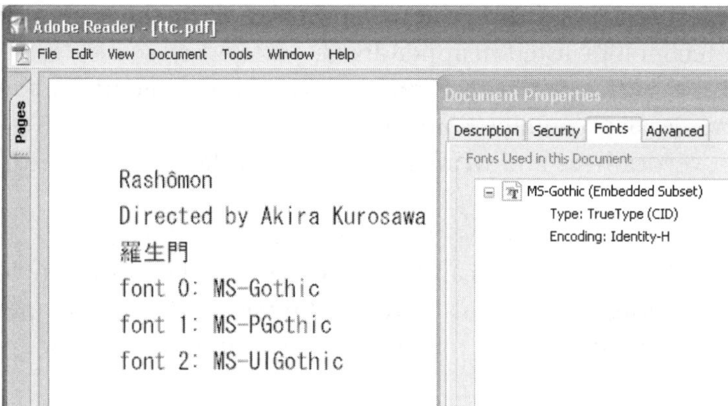


**Figure 8.15 A PDF with a Type 2 CIDFont that comes from a TrueType collection**

You need the index of these fonts in the `createFont()` method. When you use TrueType collections, it isn't sufficient to pass the path to the file; you need to add the index of the font you want to use. In the case of msgothic.ttc, you can pass `"c:/windows/fonts/msgothic.ttc,0"`, `"c:/windows/fonts/msgothic.ttc,1"`, or `"c:/windows/fonts/msgothic.ttc,2"`:

```
/* chapter08/TrueTypeCollections.java */
bf = BaseFont.createFont(
  "c:/windows/fonts/msgothic.ttc,0",        <-- Use first font in ttc: MS-Gothic
  BaseFont.IDENTITY_H, BaseFont.EMBEDDED);
font = new Font(bf, 12);                                   Return com.lowagie.text.pdf.
System.err.println(bf.getClass().getName());          <-- TrueTypeFontUnicode
document.add(new Paragraph("Rashômon", font));
document.add(new Paragraph("Directed by Akira Kurosawa", font));
document.add(new Paragraph("\u7f85\u751f\u9580", font));
```

We're finished with the font-type overview. You know how to create `Font` and `BaseFont` objects using paths to font files, but there's still a lot to learn about fonts.

If you want to create a movie database for the world, you can't add movies from Israel or from Arabic countries, because you don't know how to add text that is written from right to left. We'll discuss this and much more in the next chapter.

## 8.4 Summary

This wasn't an easy chapter. It juggles font types and all sorts of font files. It must have been hard to follow from time to time because of the terminology, which is sometimes confusing. If you really want to know more about the types, consult the books on font technology listed in appendix G.

You now have sufficient information to start using different fonts in iText. The next chapter also contains some interesting functionality; as promised, we'll deal with vertical text and writing from right to left, but also with diacritics and ligatures.

Furthermore, we'll introduce two convenience classes, `FontFactory` and `FontSelector`. These classes can significantly reduce the complexity of your code.

We also haven't forgotten Laura's next assignment. In the next chapter, you'll use the fonts that were introduced to help her send a message of peace.

# 9 Using fonts

**_This chapter covers_**

- How to write from top to bottom
- How to write from right to left
- How to deal with diacritics and ligatures
- How to automate font selection

In the previous chapter, you learned how to *get* a font object of type `Font` or `BaseFont`. You've worked with these objects in the most common situations: using paragraphs of text written from left to right in horizontal lines. In this chapter, we'll look at some other writing directions. I'll have to find extra Asian movie titles to demonstrate how you can write a text in vertical columns; and I need Hebrew and Arabic titles to explain how to change the run direction so that text is written from right to left. This will allow you to implement the first part of Laura's "message of peace" assignment.

Furthermore, we'll discuss some advance typography issues, such as diacritics and ligatures. You'll also learn how to manage fonts in a `FontFactory` and how to automate the font-selection process with class `FontSelector`. This functionality will be useful once you complete Laura's assignment, writing the word *peace* in hundreds of languages. You'll let the `FontSelector` select the appropriate font for each language. But before we start with the examples, I have to make a confession.

## 9.1 Other writing directions

I plead guilty: I'm a movie addict. I like to watch movies from all over the world, and when I'm watching a film from the Middle or Far East, I'm always intrigued by the way the opening titles appear on the screen. I'm interested to see how protagonists in the film use a computer—for instance, working with a Hebrew version of Windows or chatting with a Japanese chat program.

You, on the other hand, may have been waiting for examples on how to create a PDF document with text that is written in vertical right-to-left columns—that is, if you live in Asia. If you need to write text in Hebrew or Arabic, you're probably more interested to know how to write text horizontally from right to left. That's what you're going to do in this section.

### 9.1.1 Vertical writing

I ended the previous chapter with an example that printed the movie title Rashômon in Japanese. I'll continue with the Japanese director Akira Kurosawa, and add a quote from his movie *The Seven Samurai* (1954) vertically (see figure 9.1).

The text starts at the right, with the movie title in Japanese. In the next column, you see the first words of the quote, and you can read the lines from right to left (starting with "You embarrass me. You're overestimating me."). This text was added with the class `VerticalText`.

`VerticalText` is similar to the `ColumnText` object. The method `go()` also returns `VerticalText.NO_MORE_TEXT` or `VerticalText.NO_MORE_COLUMN`. You can use these values in a loop. This example invokes `go()` and assumes that the text fits the page:

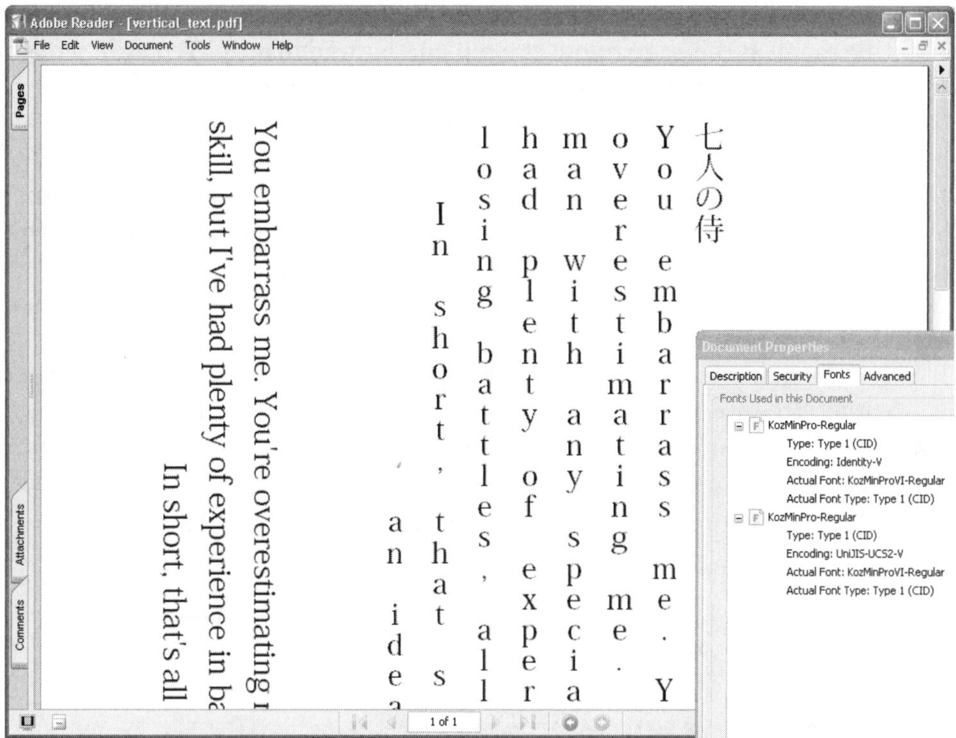


**Figure 9.1 The vertical writing system**

```
/* chapter09/VerticalTextExample.java */
PdfContentByte cb = writer.getDirectContent();
BaseFont bf = BaseFont.createFont(
  "KozMinPro-Regular", "UniJIS-UCS2-V", BaseFont.NOT_EMBEDDED);
Font font = new Font(bf, 20);
vt = new VerticalText(cb);                                        ❶
vt.setVerticalLayout(PageSize.A4.width() * 0.75f,
  PageSize.A4.height() - 36, PageSize.A4.height() - 72, 8, 30);  ❷
vt.addText(new Chunk(movie, font));                               ❸
vt.go();
vt.addText(new Phrase(quote_p1, font));                           ❹
vt.go();
vt.setAlignment(Element.ALIGN_RIGHT);
vt.addText(new Phrase(quote_p2, font));                           ❺
vt.go();
```

Note that you create the `VerticalText` object the same way you created a `ColumnText` object, using a `PdfContentByte` object ❶. You define an area and a number of lines ❷: The upper-right corner of the rectangle is positioned at three-quarters of the page width and at the top of the page minus the margin. The columns can be as tall as the page minus the top and bottom margin. You want a maximum of eight lines, and the space between the columns (the leading) is 30.

First, you add the Japanese text to the `VerticalText` object and call `go()` to write it to the `PdfContentByte` ❸. Then, you add the English text ❹. The default alignment is `Element.ALIGN_LEFT`. In a `VerticalText` object, left corresponds with the top of the columns. Finally, you add the English text again, but you change the alignment to `Element.ALIGN_RIGHT` ❺. In a `VerticalText` object, right corresponds with the bottom of the columns. Note that there is something special about the last string you added.

In figure 9.1, you can see that Latin text isn't well suited to be printed vertically. To solve this problem, the original quote is converted to a `String` that contains the character identifiers (CIDs) of glyphs that represent graphemes of the Latin alphabet, but of which every letter is rotated 90 degrees clockwise. The method `convertCIDs()` calculates the CIDs of the rotated glyphs:

```
/* chapter09/VerticalTextExample.java */
bf = BaseFont.createFont(
  "KozMinPro-Regular", "Identity-V", BaseFont.NOT_EMBEDDED);
font = new Font(bf, 20);
vt = new VerticalText(cb);
vt.setVerticalLayout(PageSize.A4.width() * 0.25f,
  PageSize.A4.height() - 36, PageSize.A4.height() - 72, 8, 30);
vt.addText(new Phrase(convertCIDs(quote_p1), font));
vt.go();
```

Note that the example uses Identity-V for the encoding parameter (V for Vertical).

With class `VerticalText`, you write from right to left; but when you look at the result, you see that it's different from what you need to write Semitic languages. To write movie titles in Hebrew or Arabic, you must be able to write horizontal lines from right to left.

### 9.1.2 Writing from right to left

Some interesting films were made in Israel over the past years: *James' Journey to Jerusalem*, *The Syrian Bride*, and so on; but let's look at the winner of 11 Israeli Oscars in 2003. At first sight, you won't see anything different from the previous examples in figure 9.2, except for the fact that Hebrew glyphs are used.

If you don't know Hebrew, you'll probably try to read the Hebrew glyphs from left to right. You see four glyphs, a space, two glyphs, a space, and the rest of the title. Let's compare this with the original `String` in the source code:

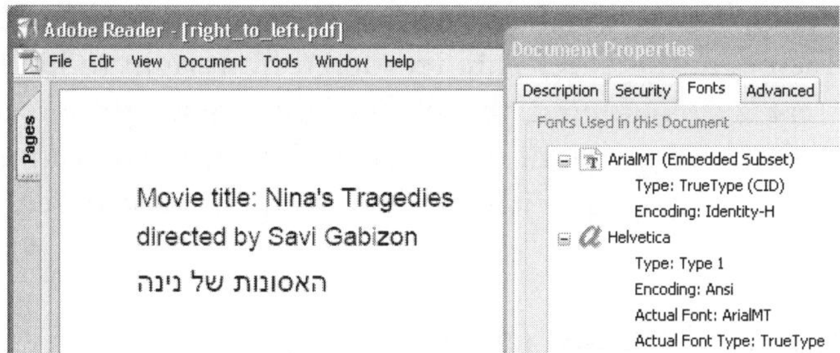


**Figure 9.2**
**Right-to-left writing in iText**

```
/* chapter09/RightToLeftExample.java */
BaseFont bf = BaseFont.createFont(
  "c:/windows/fonts/arial.ttf", BaseFont.IDENTITY_H, true);
Font font = new Font(bf, 14);
MultiColumnText mct = new MultiColumnText();
mct.addSimpleColumn(36, PageSize.A4.width() - 36);
mct.setRunDirection(PdfWriter.RUN_DIRECTION_RTL);
mct.addElement(new Paragraph(
  "\u05d4\u05d0\u05e1\u05d5\u05e0\u05d5\u05ea \u05e9\u05dc "
  + "\u05e0\u05d9\u05e0\u05d4", font));
document.add(mct);
```

The `String` that's passed to the `ColumnText` object includes seven two-byte characters, space, two characters, space, and four characters. In reality, the first glyph on the title line in figure 9.2 is \u05d4, followed by \u05e0, and so on. In other words, the characters are added in reverse order.

Notice that the text is wrapped in a `MultiColumnText` object. Unless you add the `String` at an absolute position (see part 3), you can only add text written from right to left if you wrap it in a `PdfPCell`, `ColumnText` or `MultiColumnText` object.

These objects have a `setRunDirection()` method that takes one of the following parameters:

- `PdfWriter.RUN_DIRECTION_DEFAULT`—Use the default run direction.
- `PdfWriter.RUN_DIRECTION_LTR`—Use bidirectional reordering with a left-to-right preferential run direction.
- `PdfWriter.RUN_DIRECTION_NO_BIDI`—Don't use bidirectional reordering.
- `PdfWriter.RUN_DIRECTION_RTL`—Use bidirectional reordering with a right-to-left preferential run direction.

To explain what *bidirectional* means, let's look at Laura's next assignment: She needs to write a message in different languages. In her text, the term *I18N* (Internationalization) is used. If you choose RTL as the run direction, you don't want this term to be reordered as *N81I*; you want to preserve the order of the

Latin text. That's what bidirectional reordering is about. `RUN_DIRECTION_RTL` means that the characters in the `String` are reordered from right to left by preference, but if Latin text is encountered, the left-to-right order is preserved.

Arabic text is also written from right to left. Does this mean you can now also write a movie title in Arabic? Let's give it a try and write some code to send a message of peace.

## 9.2 Sending a message of peace (part 1)

Frank Da Cruz, Marco Cimarosti, and others have made a web page translating the word *peace* in (almost) all languages. This page starts with a message in English, Arabic, and Hebrew. I wrote to Frank and Marco and received permission to copy the page and make some XML files for Laura; I made an XML file with the *Say Peace* message.

The encoding of this XML file is UTF-8; as explained in the previous chapter, this means a sequence of one or more bytes is used per character. If you open it in WordPad (see figure 9.3), you can see that the English text is readable. One byte is used for the Latin characters. In the Arabic and Hebrew text, you only recognize

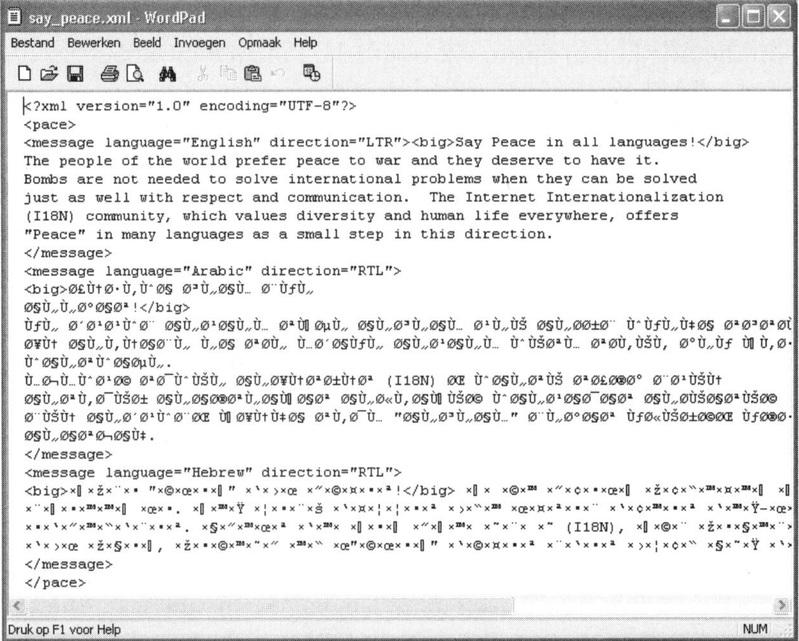


**Figure 9.3 UTF-8 encoded XML file**

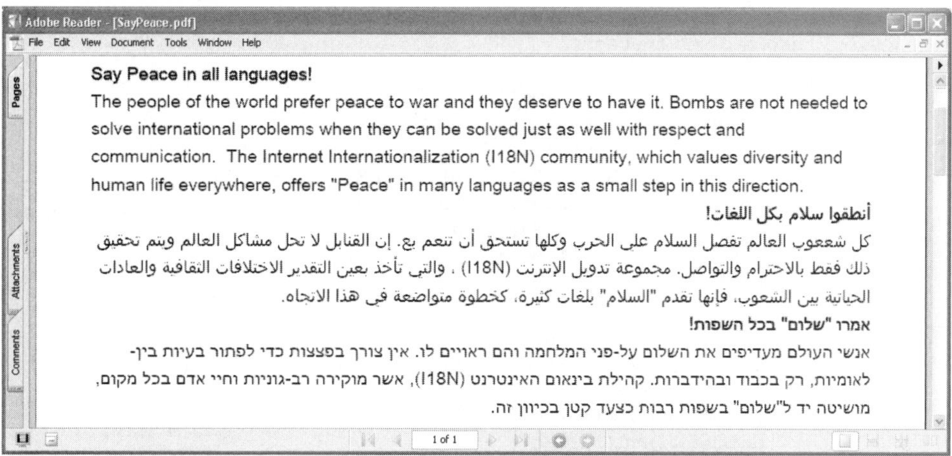


**Figure 9.4 PDF file with a message of peace in English, Arabic, and Hebrew**

the exclamation mark and the abbreviation of Internationalization (I18N). All the other glyphs are represented by two-byte characters.

The text in the XML is written in logical order, starting with the glyphs that should be read first at the left. In figure 9.4, if you read the text from left to right, it starts with the exclamation point. The order has been reversed, except for the string "(I18N)."

The example SayPeace.java is similar to the previous Foobar examples. It parses the XML file shown in figure 9.3 and converts it to a PDF document as demonstrated in figure 9.4.

Only one font file was used to produce this text: Arial Unicode MS (arialuni.ttf). The sentence in bold was rendered differently by using `setTextRenderMode()` (discussed in chapter 4). Here is the code:

```
/* chapter09/SayPeace.java */
public void startElement(
  String uri, String localName, String qName, Attributes attributes)
  throws SAXException {
  if ("message".equals(qName)) {
    buf = new StringBuffer();
    column = new MultiColumnText();
    column.addSimpleColumn(36, PageSize.A4.width() - 36);
    if ("RTL".equals(attributes.getValue("direction"))) {
      column.setRunDirection(PdfWriter.RUN_DIRECTION_RTL);
    }
  }
}
```

**Map <message> to MultiColumn Text**

**Change run direction if necessary**

```
public void endElement(String uri, String localName, String qName)
  throws SAXException {
  try {
    if ("big".equals(qName)) {
      Chunk bold = new Chunk(strip(buf), f);
      bold.setTextRenderMode(
        PdfContentByte.TEXT_RENDER_MODE_FILL_STROKE,
        0.5f, new Color(0x00, 0x00, 0x00));
      Paragraph p = new Paragraph(bold);
      p.setAlignment(Element.ALIGN_LEFT);
      column.addElement(p);
    }
    if ("message".equals(qName)) {
      Paragraph p = new Paragraph(strip(buf), f);
      p.setAlignment(Element.ALIGN_LEFT);
      column.addElement(p);
      document.add(column);
      column = null;
    }
  } catch (DocumentException e) {
    e.printStackTrace();
  }
  buf = new StringBuffer();
}
```

**Map </big> to chunk with style bold**

The Arabic text looks all right, but it's important to understand that iText has done a lot of work behind the scenes. Not every character in the XML file is rendered as a separate glyph. Some characters/glyphs are combined and replaced.

To understand what happens, we need to talk about diacritics and ligatures.

## 9.3 *Advanced typography*

I once saw a Thai cowboy movie with a poor hero who fell in love with a girl from the upper classes. It was a very good and entertaining movie. Figure 9.5 shows the poster and the title of this film.

The first version of the title in Thai was written with the font AngsanaNew (angsa.ttf), a font that comes with Windows XP if you install the OS with extended (international) font support. The second version was written using Arial Unicode MS (arialuni.ttf):

```
/* chapter09/Diacritics1.java */
String movieTitle = "\u0e1f\u0e49\u0e32\u0e17" +
  "\u0e30\u0e25\u0e32\u0e22\u0e42\u0e08\u0e23";
...
bf = BaseFont.createFont("c:/windows/fonts/angsa.ttf",
  BaseFont.IDENTITY_H, BaseFont.EMBEDDED);
font = new Font(bf, 20);
```

```
document.add(new Paragraph("Font: " + bf.getPostscriptFontName()));
document.add(new Paragraph(movieTitle, font));
bf = BaseFont.createFont("c:/windows/fonts/arialuni.ttf",
  BaseFont.IDENTITY_H, BaseFont.EMBEDDED);
font = new Font(bf, 12);
document.add(new Paragraph("Font: " + bf.getPostscriptFontName()));
document.add(new Paragraph(movieTitle, font));
```

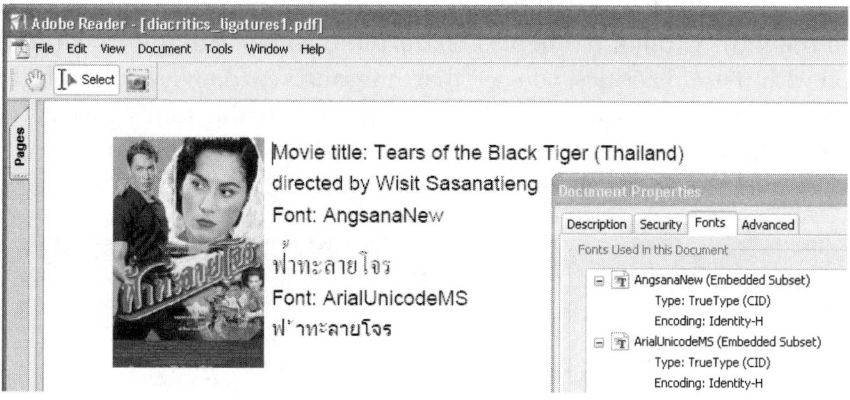


**Figure 9.5 Problems with diacritics**

The `Strings` in the code sample are identical, but the titles in the screenshot aren't quite the same. The second character in the `String` is a curl that looks like a separate character when you write it in Arial Unicode MS. In AngsanaNew, it's positioned almost on top of the first character. In reality, it should be above the first character, as you can see on the movie poster (if you look closely).

This is a *diacritical mark*. We talked about diacritical marks earlier, before you knew what they're called; when we discussed different encodings, we talked about the cedilla, the hacek, and so on. You used different character codes for combinations of a letter and diacritical marks; but in some languages, diacritical marks are stored in a separate character, using two characters instead of one.

## 9.3.1 *Handling diacritics*

For the moment, I'm typing on an AZERTY keyboard (instead of QWERTY). This keyboard has a key with an umlaut and a circumflex. If I type the keys ^ and e, I get the character *ê* (as in the French word *être*).

If you want to save the word *être* in a file, you may expect it to be four characters long; but in some languages, it's common to store both characters separately—for instance, *^etre* or *e^tre* instead of *être*. That is what happened in the previous example; iText just shows the glyphs corresponding with the characters. In most cases, no mechanism replaces the letter and its diacritical mark with another combined character.

### *Changing the character advance*

Some fonts deal with this issue by adapting the character advance. The *advance* of a character is the horizontal distance between the starting point of the character and the starting point of the next character. If you look at the way different fonts deal with these diacritics, you see that AngsanaNew does a better job than Arial Unicode MS. The character advance is stored in the font's metrics. You can change this value in the iText `BaseFont` object. This can be useful to deal with diacritics, as shown in the PDF document in figure 9.6.

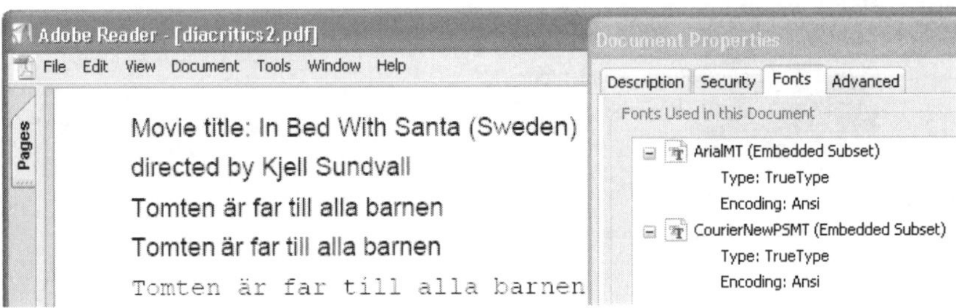


**Figure 9.6 Dealing with diacritics**

Here's the code:

```
/* chapter09/Diacritics2.java */
bf = BaseFont.createFont("c:/windows/fonts/arial.ttf",
  BaseFont.CP1252, BaseFont.EMBEDDED);
font = new Font(bf, 12);
document.add(new Paragraph("Tomten är far till alla barnen", font));  <-❶
System.err.println("Width in arial.ttf: " + bf.getWidth('¨'));
bf.setCharAdvance('¨', -100);  <-❷
document.add(new Paragraph("Tomten ¨ar far till alla barnen", font));  <-┐
bf = BaseFont.createFont("c:/windows/fonts/cour.ttf",                    |
  BaseFont.CP1252, BaseFont.EMBEDDED);                                   ❸
System.err.println("Width in cour.ttf: " + bf.getWidth('¨'));          <-┘
bf.setCharAdvance('¨', 0);
font = new Font(bf, 12);
document.add(new Paragraph("Tomten ¨ar far till alla barnen", font)); <-❹
```

The first time the example adds the Swedish title, it uses the `String` "Tomten är far till alla barnen" ("Santa Claus is the father of all children") ❶. The second ❸ and third time ❹, it uses *¨ar* instead of *är*.

The width of the umlaut/dieresis glyph is 333 units in Arial (glyph space). To get the umlaut or dieresis above the letter *a*, you change the width of the ¨ character to a negative value ❷.

In CourierNew, you can set the advance to 0 without any problem ❸. Courier is a *monospace* or *fixed-width* font: Every character has the same width (in this case, 600 units). If you set the width of the character to 0 in Arial, the diacritic doesn't exactly match with the letter *a*. The width of this font is *proportional*, which means glyphs of varying widths are used. The example uses a negative value (in glyph space), and it looks all right, but in reality it isn't OK. The space before the ä isn't as wide as it should because of the negative character advance of the umlaut/dieresis. If the ä was in the middle of a word, you'd have overlapping glyphs. This is only a good idea for fixed-width fonts.

### Changing a proportional font into a monospace font

Now that you know how to change the width of the glyphs, you can turn a proportional font into a monospace font, as is done with the last line in figure 9.7.

The first title line is written in a proportional font, the second in a real fixed-width font, and the third in a proportional font whose glyph widths have been changed so they're all 600 units wide (in glyph space). This doesn't look nice for Latin text, but it can be a useful feature if, for instance, you're writing Chinese text. Here's the code:

```
/* chapter09/Monospace.java */
bf3 = BaseFont.createFont("c:/windows/fonts/arialbd.ttf",
  BaseFont.CP1252, BaseFont.EMBEDDED);
font3 = new Font(bf3, 12);
int widths[] = bf3.getWidths();
for (int k = 0; k < widths.length; ++k) {
  if (widths[k] != 0)
    widths[k] = 600;
}
bf3.setForceWidthsOutput(true);
```

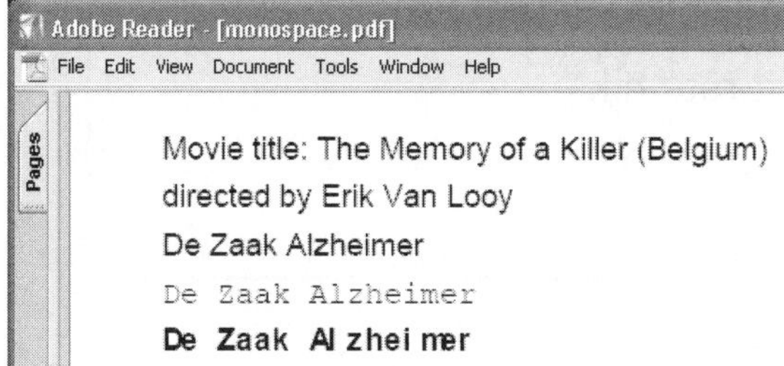


**Figure 9.7 Proportional font versus monospace font**

Changing the character advance is a possible solution to deal with diacritics, but you also have to tackle problems that arise when you use languages that have ligatures. Maybe we can think of a global solution that deals with both problems at the same time.

## 9.3.2 Dealing with ligatures

A *ligature* occurs when a combination of two or more characters is considered to be one and only one glyph. A letter with a diacritic isn't usually called a ligature, but the same principle applies. One of the ligatures we all know (but we may have forgotten it's a ligature) is the ampersand sign (&).

### Ligatures in the Latin alphabet

The ampersand sign was originally a ligature for the Latin word *et* (meaning *and*). As is the case with diacritics, you usually aren't confronted with a problem in languages using Latin text.

Figure 9.8 shows a movie title containing a ligature.

The first title line uses the character æ in the `String`. This is a ligature of the letters *a* and *e*. In the second title line, both characters are written separately:

```
/* chapter09/Ligatures1.java */
bf = BaseFont.createFont("c:/windows/fonts/arial.ttf",
  BaseFont.CP1252, BaseFont.EMBEDDED);
font = new Font(bf, 12);
document.add(new Paragraph("Kærlighed ved første hik", font));
document.add(new Paragraph(ligaturize("Kaerlighed ved f/orste hik"),
   font));
```

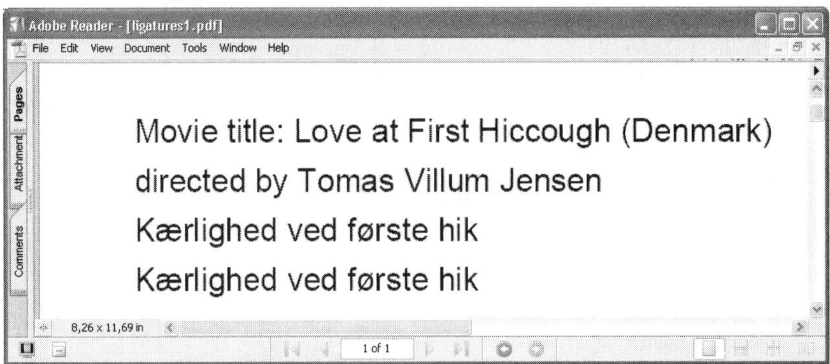


**Figure 9.8 Writing your own ligaturizer**

If you write *Kaerlighed* instead of *Kærlighed*, iText doesn't make the ligature automatically. You need to write a method that makes the ligatures. In the example, I wrote a simple method that deals with the æ ligature and the ø diacritic:

```
/* chapter09/Ligatures1.java */
private static String ligaturize(String s) {
  int pos;
  while ((pos = s.indexOf("ae")) > -1) {
    s = s.substring(0, pos) + 'æ' + s.substring(pos + 2);
  }
  while ((pos = s.indexOf("/o")) > -1) {
    s = s.substring(0, pos) + 'ø' + s.substring(pos + 2);
  }
  return s;
}
```

In Laura's assignment, you'll have to write the word *peace* in many different languages. You'll see that some translations aren't rendered correctly. The Indic rendering of the word *śānti* will be completely wrong because iText can't handle the ligatures. For the moment, only Arabic ligatures are supported.

### Arabic ligatures

I have seen several Arabic and Persian films (*Zinat*, *The Girl in the Sneakers*, *The Riverside*, and so on), but it's difficult to find those titles in their original language on the Web because I don't understand Arabic or Persian. I do know a pretty good English film about Arabia (see figure 9.9).

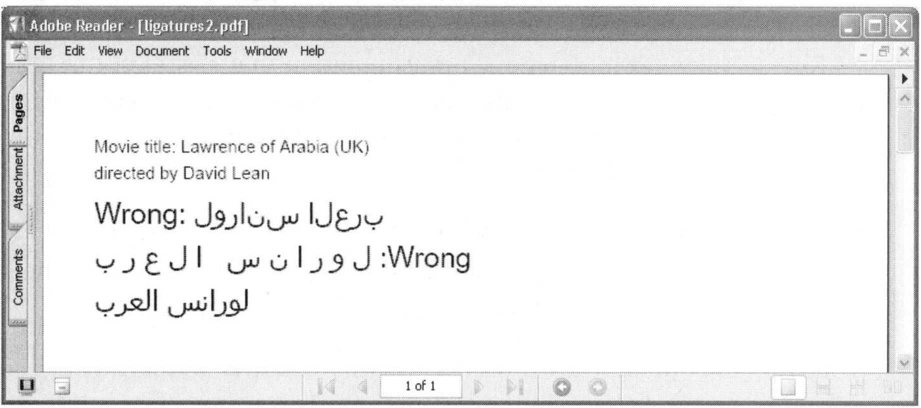


**Figure 9.9 Automatic ligatures in Arabic**

The first version of the Arabic title is wrong, because the different glyphs are added from left to right. For the second version, I added all the Arabic characters individually, separated by the space character. This is also wrong because the ligatures weren't made. Compare the second line with the third line: The same characters are used in the Java `String`, but iText applies the ligatures automatically. Do you see the differences?

```
/* chapter09/Ligatures2.java */
String movieTitle = "\u0644\u0648\u0631\u0627\u0646\u0633 " +
  "\u0627\u0644\u0639\u0631\u0628";
String movieTitleWithExtraSpaces = "\u0644 \u0648 \u0631 \u0627 " +
  "\u0646 \u0633   \u0627 \u0644 \u0639 \u0631 \u0628";
...
document.add(new Paragraph("Wrong: " + movieTitle, font));
MultiColumnText mct = new MultiColumnText();
mct.addSimpleColumn(36, PageSize.A4.width() - 36);
mct.setRunDirection(PdfWriter.RUN_DIRECTION_RTL);
mct.addElement(new Paragraph(
  "Wrong: " + movieTitleWithExtraSpaces, font));
document.add(mct);
mct = new MultiColumnText();
mct.addSimpleColumn(36, PageSize.A4.width() - 36);
mct.setRunDirection(PdfWriter.RUN_DIRECTION_RTL);
mct.addElement(new Paragraph(movieTitle, font));
document.add(mct);
```

If you study the source code, you can see that you don't have to do anything special to invoke the methods of class `ArabicLigaturizer`. If the run direction is RTL and Unicode characters in the Arabic character set are used, this is done automatically.

For the sake of completeness, I must mention that classes `PdfPTable`, `ColumnText`, and `MultiColumnText` also have a method `setArabicOptions()`. That's because there are different ways to deal with vowels in Arabic. These are possible values for the Arabic Options:

- `ColumnText.AR_NOVOWEL`—Eliminates Arabic vowels
- `ColumnText.AR_COMPOSEDTASHKEEL`—Composes the tashkeel in the ligatures
- `ColumnText.AR_LIG`—Does some extra double ligatures

None of these options have any effect on this example, but it can be useful information if you need advanced Arabic support. This is specialized stuff; it's time to return to everyday use of iText and look at some classes that make working with fonts easier.

## 9.4 Automating font creation and selection

In the previous section, you created instances of the `Font` class with a `BaseFont` object as a parameter. In most cases, you needed to pass the path to a filename. That's not very elegant. For instance, I'm used to developing on Windows, but my projects are in most cases deployed on a Sun server with Solaris as the operating system. It's evident that all references to the C:/windows/fonts directory won't work in my production environment. A possible workaround would be to jar the font and ship this jar with my web application (in my war or my ear file). If iText doesn't find a font on the file system, it will try to load the file as a resource from the jars. Remember that you already did this once: In the previous chapter, you loaded an AFM file from iText.jar.

Font files can be large, and if they're already present somewhere on the file system, it can be overkill to ship them with every application. Using a properties file with the location of each font on the file system is one option to solve this problem, but there's a better way. If you use class `FontFactory`, you can avoid some of the most common problems that occur when you want to get a font the way you did in the previous chapter.

### 9.4.1 Getting a Font object from the FontFactory

The `FontFactory` class has a series of static `getFont()` methods that allow you to replace the two lines used in the previous chapter with one line. For instance:

```
BaseFont bf = BaseFont.createFont("c:/windows/fonts/arial.ttf",
  BaseFont.CP1252, BaseFont.EMBEDDED);
Font font = new Font(bf, 14);
```

can be replaced by the following single line:

```
Font font = FontFactory.getFont("c:/windows/fonts/arial.ttf",
  BaseFont.CP1252, BaseFont.EMBEDDED, 14);
```

At first sight, there's nothing special about this single line. The real strength of `FontFactory` is that you can register font files and font directories when your application starts up. Once registered, all applications using the same JVM can ask the `FontFactory` for the font by its name, or even by an alias.

If you're writing web applications, you no longer need to work with the path to the font file; you can load these files in the start-up script of your application server.

### *Registering separate fonts*

Figure 9.10 shows a PDF with our fox/dog sentence displayed using different fonts.

There's a big difference between the way the font was retrieved for the first five lines and the way the fonts of the last lines were created. For the first five lines, the code uses the name of a standard Type 1 font or the path to a TTF file:

```
/* chapter09/FontFactoryExample1.java */
fonts[0] = FontFactory.getFont("Times-Roman");
fonts[1] = FontFactory.getFont("Courier", 10);
fonts[2] = FontFactory.getFont("Courier", 10, Font.BOLD);
fonts[3] = FontFactory.getFont(
  FontFactory.TIMES, 10, Font.BOLD, new CMYKColor(255, 0, 0, 64));
fonts[4] = FontFactory.getFont(
  "c:/windows/fonts/arial.ttf", BaseFont.CP1252, BaseFont.EMBEDDED);
```

You immediately recognize the parameters; there's little difference from what you did to get a font in the previous chapter. Then there's the sixth line, in Computer Modern:

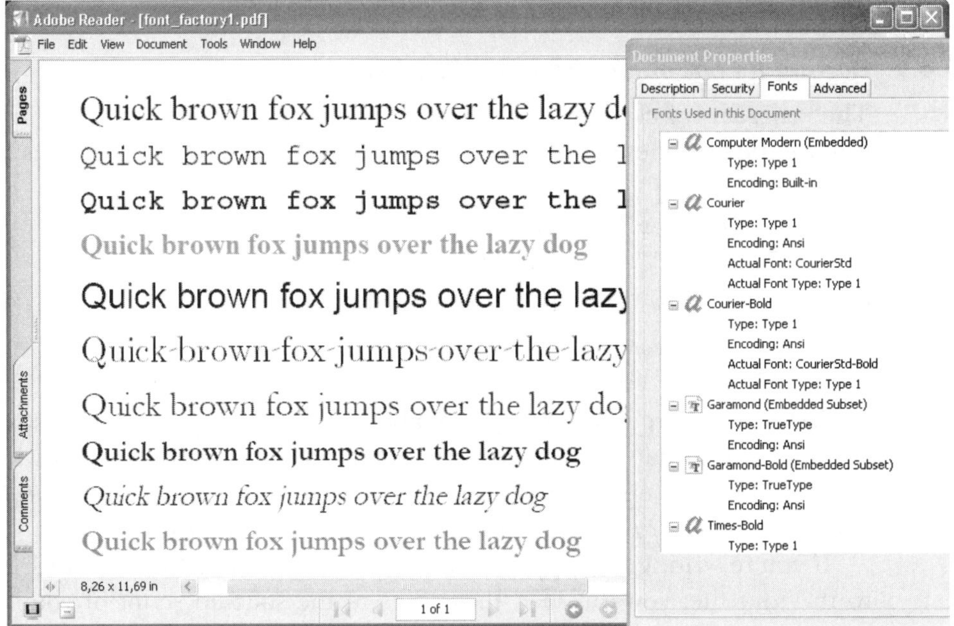


**Figure 9.10 Different ways to get a font from `FontFactory`**

```
/* chapter09/FontFactoryExample1.java */
FontFactory.register("../../chapter08/resources/cmr10.afm");
fonts[5] = FontFactory.getFont(
  "CMR10", BaseFont.CP1252, BaseFont.EMBEDDED);
fonts[5].getBaseFont().setPostscriptFontName("Computer Modern");
```

First you register the AFM file to the `FontFactory`. Remember from the previous chapter that the name of this font is CMR10. From now on, this name will be known to the `FontFactory` for the complete JVM. This means you can get the font with its name: `"CMR10"`.

I did an extra trick in the last line of the code snippet. In the previous chapter, the font is listed in the Fonts tab as *CMR10* (see figure 8.5). Instead of this acronym, I want a readable name to show up, so I changed it to *Computer Modern*. The font appears in the Fonts tab with this name (see figure 9.10). This is only a cosmetic operation; it doesn't mean you can call `getFont()` using the name Computer Modern from now on. If you want to use the font by referring to the name Computer Modern, you should pass this name as an alias when you register the font file.

The font family that is used in Manning books is Garamond. Let's register some fonts in the Garamond family with the alias *Manning*.

```
/* chapter09/FontFactoryExample1.java */
FontFactory.register("c:/windows/fonts/gara.ttf", "Manning");
FontFactory.register(
  "c:/windows/fonts/garabd.ttf", "Manning-bold");
FontFactory.register(
  "c:/windows/fonts/garait.ttf", "Manning-italic");
fonts[6] = FontFactory.getFont(
  "Manning", BaseFont.CP1252, BaseFont.EMBEDDED);
fonts[7] = FontFactory.getFont(
  "Manning-bold", BaseFont.CP1252, BaseFont.EMBEDDED, 10);
fonts[8] = FontFactory.getFont(
  "Manning", BaseFont.CP1252, BaseFont.EMBEDDED, 10, Font.ITALIC);
```

You register different styles of the Garamond font family, each with a different alias. In the `Font` instances `font[6]` and `font[7]`, you get the font based on this alias. If you check figure 9.10, you see that lines 7 and 8 are printed in Garamond regular and Garamond bold.

But look at what happens with line 9. When you ask the `FontFactory` for `font[8]`, you pass the name *Manning* and the style *Italic*. Because you registered different fonts of the same family, you're now able to switch from one font to the other, not by changing the name, but by passing a style parameter!

Finally, you can also get the registered Garamond font by passing one of its original names; it doesn't matter in what language. For instance, I can get the font Garamond bold by passing its name in Dutch:

```
/* chapter09/FontFactoryExample1.java */
fonts[9] = FontFactory.getFont("garamond vet",
  BaseFont.CP1252, BaseFont.EMBEDDED, 10,
  Font.UNDEFINED, new CMYKColor(0, 255, 0, 64));
```

This won't work with all fonts. Not every font file has all the names of the font in every language. An interesting static method allows you to retrieve all the valid names of the fonts and font families supported in the `FontFactory`:

```
/* chapter09/FontFactoryExample1.java */
System.out.println("Registered fonts");
for (Iterator i = FontFactory.getRegisteredFonts().iterator();
  i.hasNext(); ) {
  System.out.println((String) i.next());
}
System.out.println("Registered font families");
for (Iterator i = FontFactory.getRegisteredFamilies().iterator();
  i.hasNext(); ) {
  System.out.println((String) i.next());
}
```

The names that are printed to `System.out` resemble the output shown in figure 8.8, with one difference: All font names are changed to lowercase. Note that the process of getting a `Font` with the `FontFactory` is case insensitive.

You've already seen some interesting features of the `FontFactory`, but you still have to pass a path to the individual font files. If you register Garamond regular and bold, but you forget to register Garamond italic, you can't benefit from the functionality that switches from font to font based on the style parameter. It would be handy to register a complete font directory in one statement.

### *Registering font directories*

The output of the next examples resembles figure 9.10, but some different fonts were used to produce the PDF shown in figure 9.11.

The first five lines used fonts that you encountered in the previous chapter. You register the resources directory from chapter 8:

```
/* chapter09/FontFactoryExample2.java */
FontFactory.registerDirectory("../../chapter08/resources");
System.out.println("Registered fonts");
for (Iterator i = FontFactory.getRegisteredFonts().iterator();
  i.hasNext(); ) {
  System.out.println((String) i.next());
}
fonts[0] = FontFactory.getFont("utopia-regular");
fonts[1] = FontFactory.getFont("cmr10", 10);
fonts[2] = FontFactory.getFont("utopia-regular", 10, Font.BOLD);
fonts[3] = FontFactory.getFont("esl gothic unicode", 10,
```

```
    Font.UNDEFINED, new CMYKColor(255, 0, 0, 64));
  fonts[4] = FontFactory.getFont("utopia-regular",
    BaseFont.CP1252, BaseFont.EMBEDDED);
```

List the font names with `getRegisteredFonts()`, and use some of those names to create a `Font` object. Notice the difference between line 1 and line 5 in figure 9.11: Line 1 is supposed to be in the font Utopia, but the nonembedded font was replaced. Line 5 uses the embedded Utopia font.

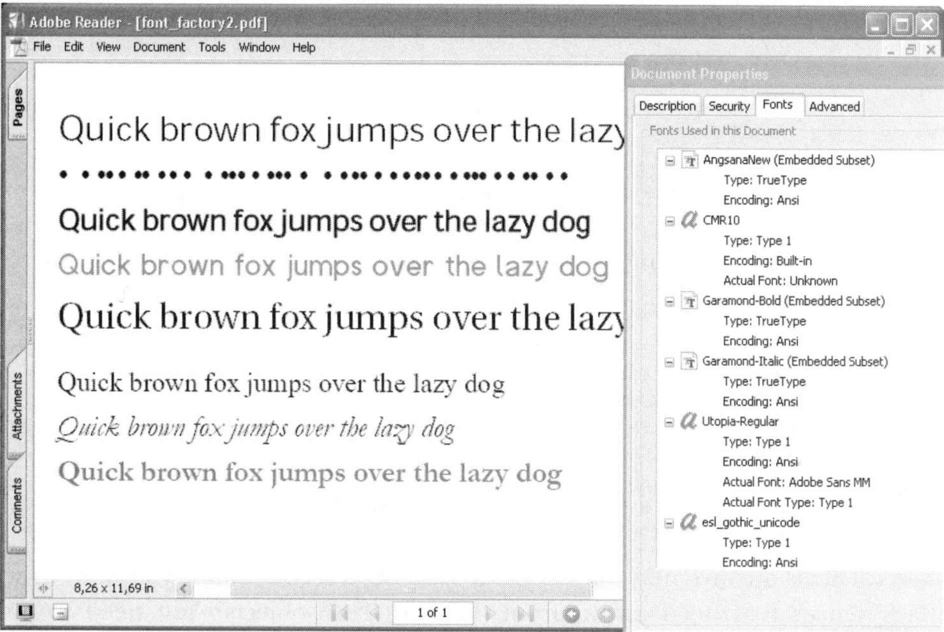


**Figure 9.11 Registering font dictionaries to get a font from a `FontFactory`**

The method `registerDirectory()` registers all the files with extensions AFM, OTF, TTF, and TTC (see chapter 8) in the directory that is passed as a parameter.

There's also a method `registerDirectories()` that doesn't need a parameter. It tries to register all the directories that are normally used by Windows, Linux, or Solaris to store fonts. In the current iText version, the following directories are registered:

- c:/windows/fonts
- c:/winnt/fonts
- d:/windows/fonts

- d:/winnt/fonts
- /usr/X/lib/X11/fonts/TrueType
- /usr/openwin/lib/X11/fonts/TrueType
- /usr/share/fonts/default/TrueType
- /usr/X11R6/lib/X11/fonts/ttf

You can get a list of the font families available on your machine by running this code sample:

```
/* chapter09/FontFactoryExample2.java */
FontFactory.registerDirectories();
System.out.println("Registered font families");
for (Iterator i = FontFactory.getRegisteredFamilies().iterator();
   i.hasNext(); ) {
  System.out.println((String) i.next());
}
```

If the families AngsanaNew and Garamond are present, you can get them by name:

```
/* chapter09/FontFactoryExample2.java */
fonts[5] = FontFactory.getFont("angsana new", BaseFont.CP1252,
  BaseFont.EMBEDDED, 14);
fonts[6] = FontFactory.getFont("garamond", BaseFont.CP1252,
  BaseFont.EMBEDDED, 10, Font.ITALIC);
fonts[7] = FontFactory.getFont(
  "garamond bold", BaseFont.CP1252, BaseFont.EMBEDDED, 10,
  Font.UNDEFINED, new CMYKColor(0, 255, 0, 64));
```

This is a convenient way to get a `Font` object, but what if you want to write sentences that need glyphs from different `Font` objects? You need to get all the different font objects, use them to create `Chunk` and `Phrase` objects, and concatenate everything into a `Paragraph`. That's quite a bit of work. Can't iText do this for us?

## 9.4.2 Automatic font selection

When I started to work at Ghent University, I had to produce lots of documents with the names of dissertation subjects chosen by the students. The thesis titles from students in the Department of Sciences, in particular, contained many Greek symbols that are used in mathematical formulas.

### Automatic selection of Greek symbols

Figure 9.12 shows a title of a fictional dissertation: What is the α-coefficient of the β-factor in the γ-equation?

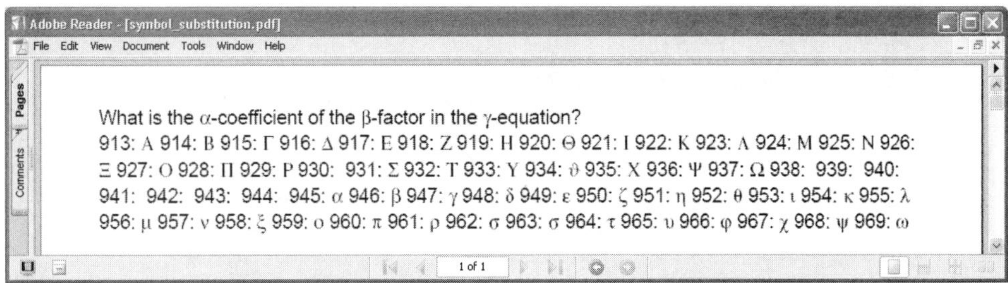


**Figure 9.12 Automatic symbol substitution**

One way to produce this title would be to create `Chunk` objects with "What is the", "-coefficient of the", "-factor in the", and "-equation" in the font Helvetica; and `Chunks` with the Symbol glyphs α, β, and γ. Then you would have to concatenate everything in the right order to get the final `Phrase`. But I was kind of lazy. I wanted iText to recognize a range of symbols, so I wrote the class `SpecialSymbol`. This class knows how to change characters with values 913 to 969 into the corresponding Greek symbols. Maybe you've already used these numbers when writing an HTML page. If you want to add an α symbol in a web page, you can do so by inserting the entity `α`.

This class `SpecialSymbol` is used in a special static method of `Phrase`. You can use it to produce the title shown in figure 9.12 in a more user-friendly way:

```
/* chapter09/SymbolSubstitution.java */
String text = "What is the " + (char) 945 + "-coefficient of the "
  + (char) 946 + "-factor in the " + (char) 947 + "-equation?";
document.add(Phrase.getInstance(text));
```

In figure 9.12, you can look up the symbols and their corresponding numbers. This feature isn't useful in a broader context, but maybe it inspired Paulo Soares to write the class `FontSelector`.

### *Automatic selection of glyphs*

Imagine that you need to write some text in Times-Roman, but the text contains lots of Chinese glyphs. You'll have the same problem I had with the Greek symbols in the mathematical formulas.

Figure 9.13 lists the names of the protagonists in the movie *Hero* by Zhang Yimou. Again, it would be possible to construct the complete sentence using separate `Chunks` or `Phrases`, with the English text in Times-Roman and the Chinese names in a traditional Chinese font. But there's an easier way; you can use the `FontSelector` class to do this work for you:

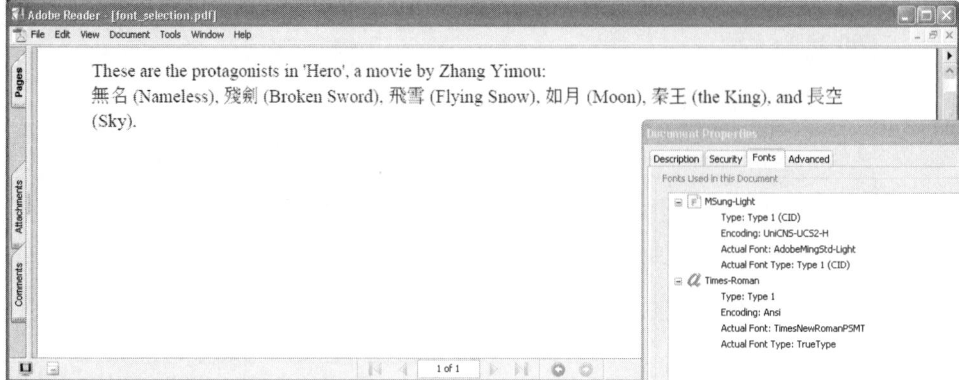


**Figure 9.13 Automatic font selection**

```
/* chapter09/FontSelectionExample.java */
String text = "These are the protagonists in 'Hero', "
  + "a movie by Zhang Yimou:\n"
  + "\u7121\u540d (Nameless), \u6b98\u528d (Broken Sword), "
  + "\u98db\u96ea (Flying Snow), \u5982\u6708 (Moon), "
  + "\u79e6\u738b (the King), and \u9577\u7a7a (Sky).";
FontSelector selector = new FontSelector();        <- Create FontSelector object
selector.addFont(
  FontFactory.getFont(FontFactory.TIMES_ROMAN, 12));
selector.addFont(
  FontFactory.getFont("MSung-Light", "UniCNS-UCS2-H",
  BaseFont.NOT_EMBEDDED));                          <- Add fonts to FontSelector
Phrase ph = selector.process(text);   <- Process String
document.add(new Paragraph(ph));
```

What happens in this code sample? You have a `String` containing characters referring to glyphs from the Latin alphabet as well as to Chinese glyphs. You pass this `String` to a `FontSelector` object, and iText looks at the `String` character per character. If the glyph corresponding with the character is available in the standard Type 1 font Times-Roman (the first font added to the selector object), it's added as a `Chunk` with the font Times-Roman. It the character isn't available, the selector object looks it up in the next font that was registered (in this case, MSung-Light), and so on.

The only thing you have to be careful about is the order you use to add the fonts. If you switch the order of both fonts, there will be a clear difference (compare figures 9.13 and 9.14). Because the Latin characters are also available in the Chinese font, Times-Roman wasn't used.

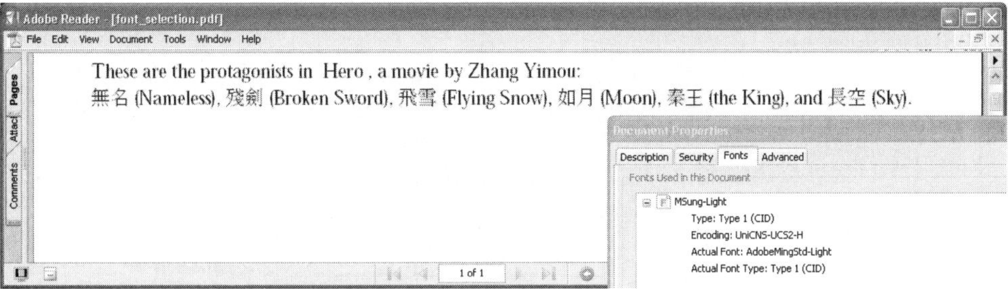


**Figure 9.14 Automatic font selection**

Now that she knows about `FontFactory` and `FontSelector`, Laura can write some code to produce a `PdfPTable` showing the translation of the word *peace* in hundreds of languages.

## 9.5 Sending a message of peace (part 2)

You know that an OpenType font can contain 65,536 characters, but no font can contain all the glyphs that are in the Unicode standard. You'll need more than one font file to finish Laura's assignment: writing the word *peace* in different languages.

As a primary font, you'll use arialuni.ttf. Next, you'll add the free font Aboriginal Serif (© Chris Harvey) that is distributed on the Language Geek site.[1] It contains, among others, the glyphs for the Inuktitut language. Finally, you'll add the public-domain font Damase and the free font Fixedsys Excelsior. But this won't be enough to render each character in the data source. Also remember that the word *peace* in Thai (pronounced "santipap") won't be rendered correctly due to the diacritics. Nor will the word *śānti* in Hindi, because of the ligatures.

Just as with the "Say Peace" message, I parsed the web page made by Frank Da Cruz and put all the translations in an XML file (see figure 9.15). I put the translations inside a `pace` tag (*pace* is Latin for *peace*). The name of each language and the countries where the language is spoken are added as attributes of the tag. Languages that are written from right to left get the attribute `direction="RTL"`.

There are some languages for which the composers of the list don't know the translation yet. In that case, a question mark was added (for instance,

---

1 www.languagegeek.com

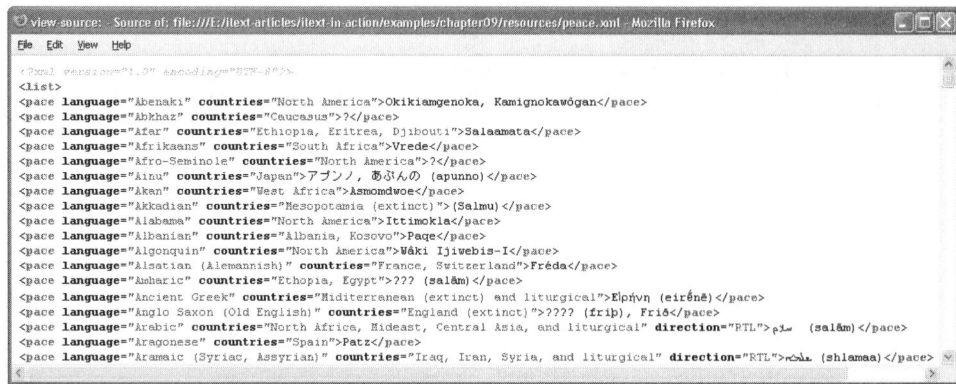

```
<?xml version="1.0" encoding="UTF-8"?>
<list>
<pace language="Abenaki" countries="North America">Okikiamgenoka, Kamignokawôgan</pace>
<pace language="Abkhaz" countries="Caucasus">?</pace>
<pace language="Afar" countries="Ethiopia, Eritrea, Djibouti">Salaamata</pace>
<pace language="Afrikaans" countries="South Africa">Vrede</pace>
<pace language="Afro-Seminole" countries="North America">?</pace>
<pace language="Ainu" countries="Japan">アプンノ, あぷんの (apunno)</pace>
<pace language="Akan" countries="West Africa">Asmomdwoe</pace>
<pace language="Akkadian" countries="Mesopotamia (extinct)">(Salmu)</pace>
<pace language="Alabama" countries="North America">Ittimokla</pace>
<pace language="Albanian" countries="Albania, Kosovo">Paqe</pace>
<pace language="Algonquin" countries="North America">Wâki Ijiwebis-I</pace>
<pace language="Alsatian (Alemannish)" countries="France, Switzerland">Fréda</pace>
<pace language="Amharic" countries="Ethopia, Egypt">??? (salãm)</pace>
<pace language="Ancient Greek" countries="Miditerranean (extinct) and liturgical">Εἰρήνη (eirḗnē)</pace>
<pace language="Anglo Saxon (Old English)" countries="England (extinct)">???? (friþ), Frið</pace>
<pace language="Arabic" countries="North Africa, Mideast, Central Asia, and liturgical" direction="RTL">سلام (salãm)</pace>
<pace language="Aragonese" countries="Spain">Patz</pace>
<pace language="Aramaic (Syriac, Assyrian)" countries="Iraq, Iran, Syria, and liturgical" direction="RTL">ܫܠܡܐ (shlamaa)</pace>
```

**Figure 9.15 The XML source of the translations of the word *peace***

for the Caucasian language Abkhaz). The fonts I listed don't contain every glyph you need; that's why you'll see a gap in the PDF here and there. Figure 9.16 gives you a good idea of the resulting PDF.

The XML file in figure 9.15 doesn't exactly look like a tabular structure, but that doesn't mean you can't parse the XML into a `PdfPTable` object. Notice that you need a `PdfPTable` because `PdfPCell` allows RTL text; the other table objects don't.

When creating the `Peace` object, you add the fonts you want to use to the `FontSelector` and construct a `PdfPTable` object with three columns:

| Cimbrian (Tzimbro, Tàuc') | Bride, Vride | Trentino, Ven |
|---|---|---|
| Comanche | Tsumukikiatu | North Americ |
| Coptic | ϩιρηνη (hirīnī) | Egypt (extinct |
| Cornish | Cres | Cornwall (exti |
| Corsican | Pace | Corsica (Fran |
| Cree | Wetaskiwin, Papayatik | North Americ |
| Croatian | Mir | Croatia |
| Czech | Mír | Czech Repub |
| Danish | Fred | Denmark, Gre |
| Dari | (sulh) صلح | Afghanistan, I |
| Darja | (esslama) عسلامة | Algeria |
| Divehi (Maldivian) | (sulha) | Maldives |
| Dschang (Yemba) | Mbwɛ´né | Cameroon |

**Figure 9.16 The word *peace* in different languages**

```
/* chapter09/Peace.java */
public Peace() {
  fs = new FontSelector();
  fs.addFont(FontFactory.getFont("c:/windows/fonts/arialuni.ttf",
    BaseFont.IDENTITY_H, BaseFont.EMBEDDED));
  fs.addFont(FontFactory.getFont("../resources/abserif4_5.ttf",
    BaseFont.IDENTITY_H, BaseFont.EMBEDDED));
  fs.addFont(FontFactory.getFont("../resources/damase.ttf",
    BaseFont.IDENTITY_H, BaseFont.EMBEDDED));
  fs.addFont(FontFactory.getFont("../resources/fsex2p00_public.ttf",
    BaseFont.IDENTITY_H, BaseFont.EMBEDDED));
  table = new PdfPTable(3);
  table.getDefaultCell().setPadding(3);
  table.getDefaultCell().setUseAscender(true);
  table.getDefaultCell().setUseDescender(true);
}
```

While parsing the XML, you keep track of the properties of each tag in the `startElement()` method:

```
/* chapter09/Peace.java */
public void startElement(
  String uri, String localName, String qName, Attributes attributes)
  throws SAXException {
  if ("pace".equals(qName)) {      ❶
    buf = new StringBuffer();
    language = attributes.getValue("language");      ❷
    countries = attributes.getValue("countries");      ❸
    if ("RTL".equals(attributes.getValue("direction"))) {
      rtl = true;
    }                                                          ❹
    else {
      rtl = false;
    }
  }
}
```

Every time you encounter a starting tag ❶, you store the name of the language ❷, the countries where it's spoken ❸, and whether the word *peace* should be written from right to left ❹.

When you encounter an ending tag, you add three cells to the table. Note that you read the word *peace* into a `StringBuffer` object `buf` in the `characters()` method of the SAX handler:

```
/* chapter09/Peace.java */
public void endElement(String uri, String localName, String qName)
  throws SAXException {
  if ("pace".equals(qName)) {
    PdfPCell cell = new PdfPCell();
    cell.addElement(fs.process(buf.toString()));
```

```
      cell.setPadding(3);
      cell.setUseAscender(true);
      cell.setUseDescender(true);
      if (rtl) {
        cell.setRunDirection(PdfWriter.RUN_DIRECTION_RTL);
      }
      table.addCell(language);
      table.addCell(cell);
      table.addCell(countries);
    }
  }
```

Laura is happy with the result. Perhaps this example will also be useful for you if you need to prove that iText is capable of rendering text in different languages. It also demonstrates the limits of the library: For instance, Indic languages aren't rendered the way they should be because there is no Indic ligaturizer as there is for Arabic languages.

## 9.6 Summary

In the previous chapter, the emphasis was on the different font types. This chapter showed "fonts in action" (wouldn't that be a great title for a book?) in an international context.

You can use a plethora of fonts and font types in combination with the basic building blocks discussed in part 2. In chapter 11, you'll see how to use class `BaseFont` to write text to the direct content. In chapter 12, you'll even learn a way to work around the Indic ligatures problem.

The next chapter will focus on graphics. You'll learn all about the methods you've already experimented with when creating a Type 3 font.

# 10 Constructing and painting paths

**This chapter covers**

- PDF's graphics state
- iText's direct content
- PDF's Coordinate System

This chapter will discuss the *graphics state* of a PDF page. This is a data structure that describes the appearance of a page using PDF operators and operands. This is the short explanation; the PDF Reference spends almost 300 pages on graphics and text, so you'll understand this definition is incomplete.

I have selected the most important issues, and I'll explain them from the point of view of the iText developer in the next three chapters. You'll learn how to draw lines and shapes, and you'll use this newly acquired knowledge in combination with class `PdfPTable` (see chapter 6) to draw custom cell borders and backgrounds. We'll talk about graphics state operators, for instance, to change the line style. One of the most important sections in this chapter will deal with the coordinate system in PDF.

After reading this chapter, you'll be able to help Laura draw a map of the city of Foobar. The first thing you need to know is how to draw lines and shapes; in PDF terminology this is called *constructing and painting paths*.

## 10.1 Path construction and painting operators

In chapter 7, you used the `PdfContentByte` class to draw a horizontal line at specific Y positions. You created an instance of this object by asking the writer object for its *direct content* (as opposed to content that was added using high-level objects). You drew lines without knowing much about the background of the iText methods you were using or the corresponding PDF operators. You've been passing coordinates as parameters (iText) or operands (PDF), but you don't know much about the coordinate system yet.

Remember from chapter 2 that the width of an A4 page is 595 units; the height is 842 units. On a side note, I already mentioned that the origin of the coordinate system (x = 0, y = 0) is the lower-left corner of the page. This means that the coordinate of the upper-right corner is (x = 595, y = 842). You'll learn how to change the origin, the orientation of the x- and the y-axis, and the length of the units along each axis in section 10.4.

For now, you'll work in the default coordinate system, and you'll construct some paths.

### 10.1.1 Seven path construction operators

In PDF, there are seven path construction operators. Table 10.1 lists the operators, their operands, and their corresponding method in iText (see also Table 4.9 in the PDF Reference).

**Table 10.1 PDF path construction operators and operands**

| Operator | iText method | Operands / parameters | Description |
|---|---|---|---|
| `m` | `moveTo` | `(x, y)` | Moves the current point to coordinates (x, y), omitting any connecting line segment. This begins a new (sub)path. |
| `l` | `lineTo` | `(x, y)` | Moves the current point to coordinates (x, y), appending a line segment from the previous to the new current point. |
| `c` | `curveTo` | `(x1, y1, x2, y2, x3, y3)` | Moves the current point to coordinates (x3, y3), appending a cubic Bézier curve from the previous to the new current point, using (x1, y1) and (x2, y2) as Bézier control points. |
| `v` | `curveTo` | `(x2, y2, x3, y3)` | Moves the current point to coordinates (x3, y3), appending a cubic Bézier curve from the previous to the new current point, using the previous current point and (x2, y2) as Bézier control points. |
| `y` | `curveFromTo` | `(x1, y1, x3, y3)` | Moves the current point to coordinates (x3, y3), appending a cubic Bézier curve using (x1, y1) and (x3, y3) as control points. |
| `h` | `closePath` | `()` | Closes the current subpath by appending a straight line segment from the current point to the starting point of the subpath. |
| `re` | `Rectangle` | `(x, y, width, height)` | Appends a rectangle to the current path as a complete subpath. (x, y) is the lower-left corner; `width` and `height` define the dimensions of the rectangle. |

The following code snippet constructs the path of a rectangle twice:

- Once using a sequence of `moveTo` and `lineTo` operators
- Once using a single rectangle operator

```
/* chapter10/InvisibleRectangles.java */
PdfContentByte cb = writer.getDirectContent();
cb.moveTo(30, 700);
cb.lineTo(490, 700);
cb.lineTo(490, 800);
cb.lineTo(30, 800);
cb.closePath();
cb.rectangle(30, 700, 460, 100);
```

If you open the resulting PDF file in a text editor, you immediately see that something went wrong. The complete example code adds a paragraph of text in a `document.add()` statement. This paragraph is rendered on the page. Unfortunately, you don't see a rectangle anywhere on the page.

For debugging purposes, you set the `Document` member variable `public static compress` to false. When you read chapter 18, "Under the hood," you'll learn about the content stream of a page in a PDF file. In most PDF files, this stream is compressed; but if you tell iText not to compress these streams, you can inspect the PDF syntax in a text editor. In this case, you'll see that the iText path-construction methods were invoked correctly, and you'll find this snippet of PDF syntax in the content stream (this example has only one content stream, so it's easy to find):

```
30 700 m
490 700 l
490 800 l
30 800 l
h
30 700 460 100 re
```

**moveTo, lineTo, and closePath**

**Single rectangle operator**

You've made an error that almost every iText newbie has made before: You've constructed paths, and these constructions are added to the content stream of the page, but you've forgotten to paint the path. Before you try the other path-construction operators, let's look at the path-painting operators.

### 10.1.2 Path-painting operators

There are 10 path-painting operators; they don't have any operands. Table 10.2 is based on table 4.10 in the PDF Reference. Again I added a column with the corresponding iText method.

**Table 10.2 PDF path-painting operators**

| Operator | iText method | Description |
|---|---|---|
| `S` | `stroke()` | Stroke the path (lines only; the shape isn't filled). |
| `s` | `closePathStroke()` | Close and stroke the path. This is the same as doing `closePath()` followed by `stroke()`. |
| `f` | `fill()` | Fill the path (using the nonzero winding number rule). Open subpaths are closed implicitly. |

*continued on next page*

**Table 10.2 PDF path-painting operators** *(continued)*

| Operator | iText method | Description |
|---|---|---|
| `F` | - | Deprecated! Equivalent to `f`; included only for compatibility. The PDF Reference says that PDF producer applications should use `f`; so there's no method to add `F` in iText. |
| `f*` | `eoFill()` | Fill the path (using the even-odd rule). |
| `B` | `fillStroke()` | Fill the path using the nonzero winding number rule, and then stroke the path (equivalent to the operator f followed by the operator `S`). |
| `B*` | `eoFillStroke()` | Fill the path using the even-odd rule, and then stroke the path (equivalent to the operator `f*` followed by the operator `S`). |
| `b` | `closePathFillStroke()` | Close, fill, and stroke the path, as is done with the operator `h` followed by `B`. |
| `b*` | `closePathEoFillStroke()` | Close, fill, and stroke the path, as is done with the operator `h` followed by `B*`. |
| `n` | `newPath()` | End the path object without filling or stroking it. |

I have introduced a lot of new information in table 10.1 and 10.2; paths that are shaped as Bézier curves and/or filled using the nonzero winding number or the even-odd rule—this all needs further explaining, but let me jump ahead and introduce two graphics state operators that will make the examples much easier to understand: `setColorStroke()` and `setColorFill()`.

### *Stroking versus filling*

When you've constructed a path using the methods described in table 10.1, you can stroke those paths. *Stroking* a path means you're going to draw the line segments of the subpaths. The color used by default is black. You can change this color with a number of methods, `setColorStroke()` being one of them. In PDF, we talk about *graphics state operators*.

You can also fill the subpaths. Again, the default color is black. In the next example, you'll change this default with the method `setColorFill()`. We'll discuss the different color classes in the next chapter, but for the moment you'll use the `GrayColor` class. Figure 10.1 shows different squares of which the borders were (or weren't) stroked in dark gray (value 0.2) and the shape was (or wasn't) filled with light gray (value 0.9). You can clearly see the difference of the effect using five different path-painting operators.

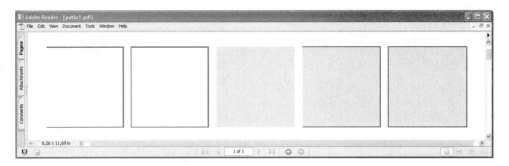

**Figure 10.1 Painting and filling paths**

Let's look at the source code:

```
/* chapter10/ConstructingPaths1.java */
PdfContentByte cb = writer.getDirectContent();
cb.setColorStroke(new GrayColor(0.2f));
cb.setColorFill(new GrayColor(0.9f));
cb.moveTo(30, 700);
cb.lineTo(130, 700);
cb.lineTo(130, 800);          Draw first (incomplete) square
cb.lineTo(30, 800);
cb.stroke();
cb.moveTo(140, 700);
cb.lineTo(240, 700);
cb.lineTo(240, 800);          Draw second square (not filled)
cb.lineTo(140, 800);
cb.closePathStroke();
cb.moveTo(250, 700);
cb.lineTo(350, 700);
cb.lineTo(350, 800);          Draw third square (filled, no border)
cb.lineTo(250, 800);
cb.fill();
cb.moveTo(360, 700);
cb.lineTo(460, 700);
cb.lineTo(460, 800);          Draw fourth square (incomplete border)
cb.lineTo(360, 800);
cb.fillStroke();
cb.moveTo(470, 700);
cb.lineTo(570, 700);
cb.lineTo(570, 800);          Draw fifth square (body and border)
cb.lineTo(470, 800);
cb.closePathFillStroke();
```

You construct five paths using one `moveTo()` and three `lineTo()` statements; you render these paths in five different ways (see figure 10.1). By default, shapes are filled using the nonzero winding number rule. To understand the difference from the even-odd rule, you need to construct more complex shapes.

### *Nonzero winding number vs. even-odd rule*

Look at figure 10.2. First, I constructed five stars, but you only see four of them because I invoked `newPath()` after the third star. (This star isn't painted.) Then, I drew a series of concentric circles that are constructed and/or rendered in different ways.

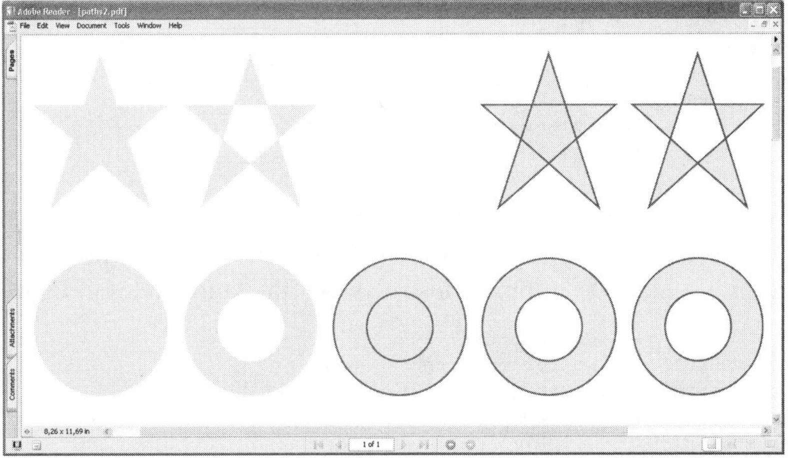

**Figure 10.2 Illustrating the nonzero winding number rule versus the even-odd rule**

To know what happened, you need to look at the source code. The example contains two convenience methods: one that draws a star, and one that draws a circle. The code to draw the star is straightforward.

```
/* chapter10/ConstructingPaths2.java */
public static void
  constructStar(PdfContentByte cb, float x, float y) {
  cb.moveTo(x + 10, y);
  cb.lineTo(x + 80, y + 60);
  cb.lineTo(x, y + 60);
  cb.lineTo(x + 70, y);
  cb.lineTo(x + 40, y + 90);
  cb.closePath();
}
```

The code to draw a circle uses the `curveTo()` method to draw four segments of a circle. You have the option to draw the circle clockwise or counterclockwise:

```
/* chapter10/ConstructingPaths2.java */
public static void constructCircle(PdfContentByte cb,
  float x, float y, float r, boolean clockwise) {
  float b = 0.5523f;
  if (clockwise) {
    cb.moveTo(x + r, y);
    cb.curveTo(x + r, y - r * b, x + r * b, y - r, x, y - r);
    cb.curveTo(x - r * b, y - r, x - r, y - r * b, x - r, y);
    cb.curveTo(x - r, y + r * b, x - r * b, y + r, x, y + r);
    cb.curveTo(x + r * b, y + r, x + r, y + r * b, x + r, y);
  }
  else {
    cb.moveTo(x + r, y);
    cb.curveTo(x + r, y + r * b, x + r * b, y + r, x, y + r);
    cb.curveTo(x - r * b, y + r, x - r, y + r * b, x - r, y);
    cb.curveTo(x - r, y - r * b, x - r * b, y - r, x, y - r);
    cb.curveTo(x + r * b, y - r, x + r, y - r * b, x + r, y);
  }
}
```

We'll go into the details of the `curveTo()` methods and Bézier curves soon, but first let's focus on the difference between the nonzero winding number and the even-odd rule. This code snippet constructs the stars and circles in figure 10.2:

```
/* chapter10/ConstructingPaths2.java */
PdfContentByte cb = writer.getDirectContent();
cb.setColorStroke(new GrayColor(0.2f));
cb.setColorFill(new GrayColor(0.9f));
constructStar(cb, 30, 720);
constructCircle(cb, 70, 650, 40, true);
constructCircle(cb, 70, 650, 20, true);
cb.fill();                                      <-❶
constructStar(cb, 120, 720);
constructCircle(cb, 160, 650, 40, true);
constructCircle(cb, 160, 650, 20, true);
cb.eoFill();                                    <-❷
constructStar(cb, 250, 650);
cb.newPath();                                   <-❸
constructCircle(cb, 250, 650, 40, true);
constructCircle(cb, 250, 650, 20, true);
constructStar(cb, 300, 720);
constructCircle(cb, 340, 650, 40, true);
constructCircle(cb, 340, 650, 20, false);
cb.fillStroke();                                <-❹
constructStar(cb, 390, 720);
constructCircle(cb, 430, 650, 40, true);
constructCircle(cb, 430, 650, 20, true);
cb.eoFillStroke();                              <-❺
```

These paths are filled in five different ways. The star and circles are filled using the nonzero winding number rule ❶. The inner circle overlaps the outer circle, but it has the same color; you can't distinguish the inner circle from the outer one.

The star and circle are filled using the even-odd rule ❷. The middle part of the star isn't filled; nor is the inner circle.

Now, you start a new path after drawing the star; the star isn't rendered ❸. You stroke the star and circles and fill them using the nonzero winding number rule ❹. Note the difference between the third and fourth concentric circles. In the third column, the subpaths of the concentric circles are constructed clockwise. In the fourth column, the subpath of the outer circle is constructed clockwise and the subpath of the inner circle counterclockwise. Then, you stroke the star and circles ❺ and fill them using the even-odd rule. You'll find the definitions of the nonzero winding number rule and the even-odd rule in the PDF reference,[1] but I hope figure 10.2 gives you a good idea.

Bézier curves[2] are used to draw the circles.

### Bézier curves

*Bézier curves* are parametric curves developed in 1959 by Paul de Casteljau (using de Casteljau's algorithm). They were widely publicized in 1962 by Paul Bézier, who used them to design automobile bodies. Nowadays they're important in computer graphics.

*Cubic Bézier curves* are defined by four points: the two *endpoints*—the current point and point (x3, y3)—and two *control points*, (x1, y1) and (x2, y2). The curve starts at the first endpoint going toward the first control point, and it arrives at the second endpoint coming from the second control point. In general, the curve doesn't pass through the control points; they're only there to provide directional information. The distance between an endpoint and its corresponding control point determines how long the curve moves toward the control point before turning toward the other endpoint.

But why write these difficult definitions if I can generate examples that illustrate what all this means? In figure 10.3, the three curve methods listed in table 10.1 are demonstrated.

The extra lines in figure 10.3 connect the endpoints with the corresponding control points. Here's the code that generates the curves in the figure:

---

1 PDF Reference 1.6 (5th ed) section 4.4.2 and figure 4.10 (pages 202–203)

2 PDF Reference 1.6 (5th ed) section 4.4.1 and figure 4.8 and 4.9 (pages 197–199)

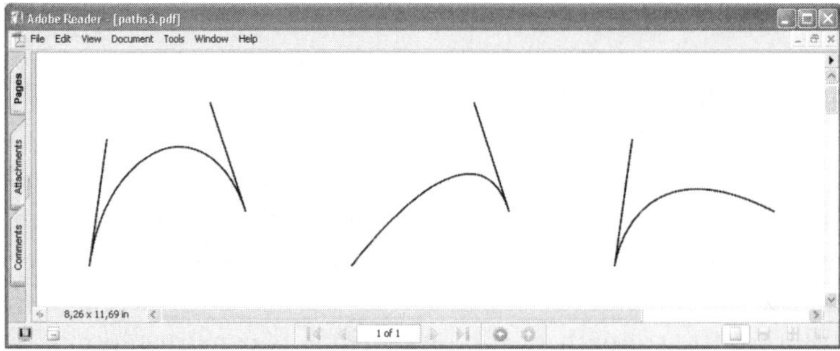

**Figure 10.3 Bézier curves**

```
/* chapter10/ConstructingPaths3.java */
PdfContentByte cb = writer.getDirectContent();
float x0, y0, x1, y1, x2, y2, x3, y3;
x0 = 30; y0 = 720;
x1 = 40; y1 = 790;
x2 = 100; y2 = 810;
x3 = 120; y3 = 750;
cb.moveTo(x0, y0);
cb.lineTo(x1, y1);
cb.moveTo(x2, y2);
cb.lineTo(x3, y3);
cb.moveTo(x0, y0);
cb.curveTo(x1, y1, x2, y2, x3, y3);     <-❶
x0 = 180; y0 = 720;
x2 = 250; y2 = 810;
x3 = 270; y3 = 750;
cb.moveTo(x2, y2);
cb.lineTo(x3, y3);
cb.moveTo(x0, y0);
cb.curveTo(x2, y2, x3, y3);     <-❷
x0 = 330; y0 = 720;
x1 = 340; y1 = 790;
x3 = 420; y3 = 750;
cb.moveTo(x0, y0);
cb.lineTo(x1, y1);
cb.moveTo(x0, y0);
cb.curveTo(x1, y1, x3, y3);     <-❸
cb.stroke();
```

In the second example, the endpoint to the left coincides with the first control point ❷; the same goes for the endpoint to the right in the third example ❸. You could draw these curves using one `curveTo()` method with six parameters ❶, the coordinates of the control points and the coordinates of one endpoint; the current point would then act as the other endpoint. But in accordance with the operators included in the PDF Reference, two extra methods are provided.

The code to draw a circle in the previous example looked complex, but you don't need to worry about that: iText comes with convenience methods that make it easy to draw custom shapes. Behind the scenes, Bézier curves are used.

### *Convenience methods to draw shapes*

`PdfContentByte` has different methods that make it easier for you to draw circles, ellipses, arcs, rectangles, and combinations of these shapes. Figure 10.4 shows these methods in action.

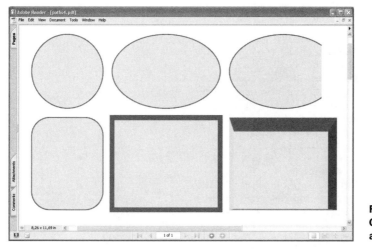

**Figure 10.4 Circles, ellipses, arcs, and rectangles**

The shapes in the first row and the first shape in the second row were constructed using only one line of code:

```
/* chapter10/ConstructingPaths4.java */
PdfContentByte cb = writer.getDirectContent();
cb.setColorStroke(new GrayColor(0.2f));
cb.setColorFill(new GrayColor(0.9f));
cb.circle(70, 770, 40);    ❶
cb.ellipse(120, 730, 240, 810);    ❷
cb.arc(250, 730, 370, 810, 45, 270);    ❸
cb.roundRectangle(30, 620, 80, 100, 20);    ❹
cb.fillStroke();
```

The centre of the first circle is (70, 770); its radius is 40 user units ❶. The ellipse next to the circle fits into the rectangle with lower-left corner (120, 730) and upper-right corner (240, 810) ❷. Note that if you define a square instead of a rectangle, the ellipse will be a circle. The ellipse on the right fits inside the rectangle (250, 730) and (370, 810); but only 270 degrees of the ellipse are drawn, starting at 45 degrees ❸. In the next row, you see a rectangle with rounded corners. The lower-left corner is (30, 620); the width is 80, the height is 100 user units; the radius of the circle segments in the corners is 20 user units ❹. These four shapes are constructed using `moveTo()`, `lineTo()`, and/or `curveTo()` methods internally. The convenience methods don't stroke or fill the path.

The two rectangles with the thick borders are constructed with the `Rectangle` object and added with a method that not only constructs the path, but also strokes and fills it:

```
/* chapter10/ConstructingPaths4.java */
Rectangle rect;
rect = new Rectangle(120, 620, 240, 720);
rect.setBorder(Rectangle.BOX);
rect.setBorderWidth(5);
rect.setBorderColor(new GrayColor(0.2f));
rect.setBackgroundColor(new GrayColor(0.9f));
cb.rectangle(rect);
rect = new Rectangle(250, 620, 370, 720);
rect.setBorder(Rectangle.BOX);
rect.setBorderWidthTop(15);
rect.setBorderWidthBottom(1);
rect.setBorderWidthLeft(5);
rect.setBorderWidthRight(10);
rect.setBorderColorTop(new GrayColor(0.2f));
rect.setBorderColorBottom(new Color(0xFF, 0x00, 0x00));
rect.setBorderColorLeft(new Color(0xFF, 0xFF, 0x00));
rect.setBorderColorRight(new Color(0x00, 0x00, 0xFF));
rect.setBackgroundColor(new GrayColor(0.9f));
cb.rectangle(rect);
cb.variableRectangle(rect);
```

Before we move on to the graphics state operators, let's look at some practical examples.

## 10.2 Working with iText's direct content

Originally, the methods of `PdfContentByte` were designed for internal use by iText only—for instance, to draw the borders of a `PdfPTable`. Later, the class and most of its methods were made public because they can be used to customize iText's functionality—for instance, to create `PdfPCell` objects with rounded borders. When we discussed the `(Multi)ColumnText` object, we used some of the methods to draw extra shapes in the examples with irregular columns. Let's add more examples.

First we'll look at content layers in general; then, you'll discover interesting table functionality that allows you to draw custom cell and table borders and backgrounds.

### 10.2.1 Direct content layers

When you add basic building blocks to a document (also referred to as adding *high-level content*), two `PdfContentByte` objects are created: one with text (the content of chunks, phrases, paragraphs, and so on) and another one with graphics (the background of a chunk, the borders of a cell, images, and so forth). When a page is full, iText draws these layers on top of each other: first the graphics layer, and then the text layer (otherwise, the background of a chunk or cell would cover the text). You can't manipulate these two `PdfGraphics` objects directly; they're managed by iText internally.

There are two extra layers that you can use directly: one that goes on top of the high-level text and graphics layers, and one that goes under them. In iText terminology, this is called *direct content*; figure 10.5 shows how it works. The `Paragraph` *quick brown fox jumps over the lazy dog* was added in the text layer. The gray background of the *jumps* `Chunk` was added in the graphics layer. But extra shapes were added above and below these two layers.

In the source code, the first two shapes are inserted before adding the paragraphs; the next two shapes are added after the paragraphs and chunks:

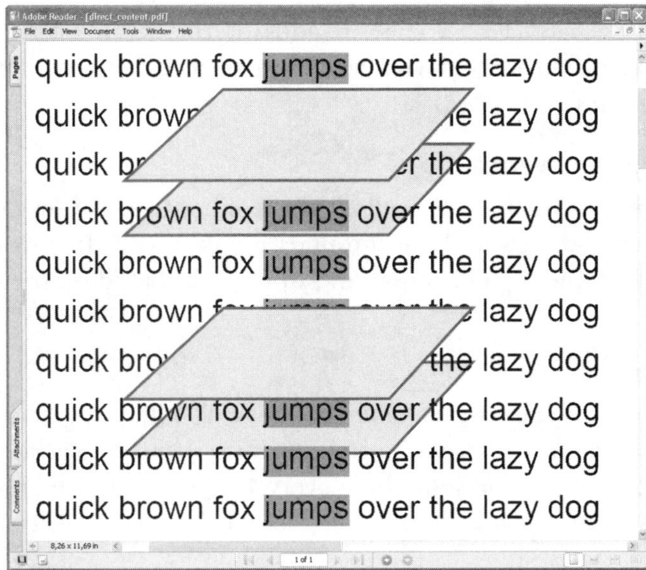


**Figure 10.5 Direct content under and above the high-level layers**

```
/* chapter10/DirectContent.java */
PdfContentByte over = writer.getDirectContent();          ❶
PdfContentByte under = writer.getDirectContentUnder();          ❷
drawLayer(over, 70, 750, 150, 100);    ❸
drawLayer(under, 70, 730, 150, 100);    ❹
Paragraph p = new Paragraph("quick brown fox ");
Chunk c = new Chunk("jumps");
c.setBackground(new GrayColor(0.5f));
p.add(c);
p.add(" over the lazy dog");
for (int i = 0; i < 10; i++) {
  document.add(p);
}
drawLayer(over, 70, 670, 150, 100);    ❸
drawLayer(under, 70, 650, 150, 100);    ❹
```

If you compare the code with figure 10.5, you see that the shapes written to the `PdfContentByte` object obtained with the method `getDirectContent()` ❶ cover the other content ❸, even the shape you draw before adding anything else. When you use the method `getDirectContentUnder()` ❷, you can add shapes that go under the rest of the content ❹.

**NOTE** You saw similar functionality before when we talked about `PdfStamper` in chapter 2. With `PdfStamper`, you use the methods `getOverContent()` and `getUnderContent()` to write on top of or under existing content. The existing content is seen as one layer.

In chapter 14, you'll use `getUnderContent()` to add watermarks. You can use `getOverContent()` to cover parts of the document. In the next section, you'll use four layers to customize tables.

## 10.2.2 PdfPTable and PdfPCell events

In chapter 6, you drew tables and cells with all kinds of borders. But suppose you want to define custom borders and backgrounds for each cell. In this case, it would be handy to grab the direct content and draw paths based on the coordinates of the cell.

### Implementing PdfPCellEvent

Figure 10.6 shows a simple sheet with a table that has cells with rounded borders. This could be an insert for a pharmaceutical product. It shows a period of 30 days: You need to remember to do something every 4 days (the days marked with a red ellipse), and you must avoid something every 3 days (these cells stricken through in blue).

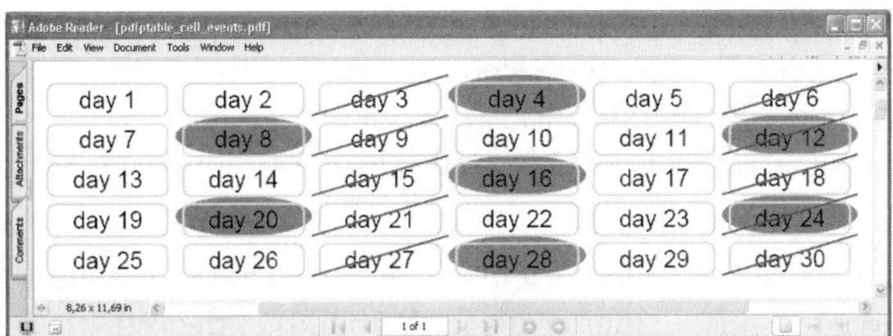


**Figure 10.6 Custom `PdfPCell` behavior**

The text in this table (day 1, day 2, and so on) is added using methods already discussed in chapter 6, but the lines and shapes are drawn in a cell event. The example uses three inner classes implementing the `PdfPCellEvent` interface:

```
/* chapter10/PdfPTableCellEvents.java */
class RoundRectangle implements PdfPCellEvent {
  public void cellLayout(PdfPCell cell, Rectangle rect,
    PdfContentByte[] canvas) {
    PdfContentByte cb = canvas[PdfPTable.LINECANVAS];
    cb.setColorStroke(new GrayColor(0.8f));
    cb.roundRectangle(rect.left() + 4, rect.bottom(),
      rect.width() - 8, rect.height() - 4, 4);
    cb.stroke();
  }
}
class Ellipse implements PdfPCellEvent {
  public void cellLayout(PdfPCell cell, Rectangle rect,
    PdfContentByte[] canvas) {
    PdfContentByte cb = canvas[PdfPTable.BACKGROUNDCANVAS];
    cb.setRGBColorFill(0xFF, 0x00, 0x00);
    cb.ellipse(rect.left(), rect.bottom(),
      rect.right(), rect.top());
    cb.fill();
    cb.resetRGBColorFill();
  }
}
class Strike implements PdfPCellEvent {
  public void cellLayout(PdfPCell cell, Rectangle rect,
    PdfContentByte[] canvas) {
    PdfContentByte cb = canvas[PdfPTable.TEXTCANVAS];
    cb.setRGBColorStroke(0x00, 0x00, 0xFF);
    cb.moveTo(rect.left(), rect.bottom());
    cb.lineTo(rect.right(), rect.top());
    cb.stroke();
    cb.resetRGBColorStroke();
  }
}
```

**Draw borders with rounded corners**

**Draw red ellipse**

**Draw blue diagonal**

The rectangle that is passed to the event holds the coordinates of the cell. As you can see in the examples, you use these coordinates to construct your paths—for instance, to draw an ellipse that fits inside the cell.

The `canvas` array needs more explanation. This array holds four `PdfContentByte` objects:

- `PdfPTable.BASECANVAS`—The original `PdfContentByte`. Anything placed here is under the surface (under the background) of the cell.
- `PdfPTable.BACKGROUNDCANVAS`—The layer where the background goes (for instance, if you define a background color at the cell level).
- `PdfPTable.LINECANVAS`—The layer where the (border) lines go. Content added to this layer is under the text.
- `PdfPTable.TEXTCANVAS`—The layer where the text goes. Anything placed here covers the cell content.

As you can see in figure 10.6, the ellipse is drawn under all the other content (`BACKGROUNDCANVAS`); the borders cover the ellipse (`LINECANVAS`). The blue line that strikes through the cell covers the text (`TEXTCANVAS`).

**NOTE** The `PdfPCell` object passed to the `cellLayout()` method should be considered `ReadOnly`. At the moment the method `cellLayout()` is triggered, the cell has already been rendered, so don't perform actions on it such as `setBackgroundColor()`. They won't have any effect. The cell is passed to the event to allow the retrieval of properties such as padding, dimensions, and so on.

Now that you've defined the events, you can add them to a `PdfPCell`:

```
/* chapter10/PdfPTableCellEvents.java */
PdfPTableCellEvents example = new PdfPTableCellEvents();
RoundRectangle border = example.new RoundRectangle();
Ellipse ellipse = example.new Ellipse();
Strike strike = example.new Strike();
PdfPTable table = new PdfPTable(6);
PdfPCell cell;
for (int i = 1; i <= 30; i++) {
  cell = new PdfPCell(new Phrase("day " + i));
  cell.setHorizontalAlignment(Element.ALIGN_CENTER);
  cell.setBorder(Rectangle.NO_BORDER);
  cell.setPadding(4);
  cell.setCellEvent(border);
  if (i % 3 == 0) cell.setCellEvent(strike);
  if (i % 4 == 0) cell.setCellEvent(ellipse);
```

```
    table.addCell(cell);
  }
  document.add(table);
```

You set the border of the `PdfPCell` to `NO_BORDER`. Otherwise, each cell would have two borders: one drawn by the high-level object, and the other drawn in your custom cell event.

Cell events are practical, but you can work with only one cell at a time. If you want to construct paths that affect all cells, you can implement the `PdfPTableEvent` class.

### *Implementing PdfPTableEvent*

The `PdfPTableEvent` interface has a `tableLayout()` method. It allows you to construct paths based on the coordinates of multiple cells. For instance, you can draw a rectangle around all the header cells, as is done in figure 10.7.

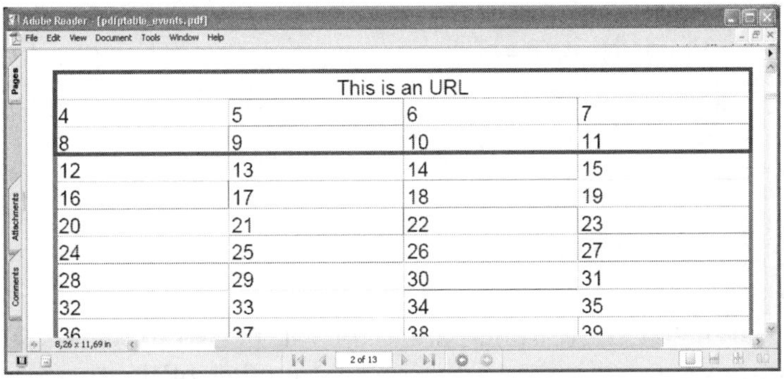

**Figure 10.7 Implementing `PdfPTableEvent`**

This `tableLayout()` method is more complex than the `cellLayout()` method. Let's split the body of the implementation that was used to produce the PDF shown in figure 10.7 into different parts.

```
/* chapter06/PdfPTableEvents.java */
public void tableLayout(PdfPTable table, float[][] width,
  float[] height, int headerRows, int rowStart,
  PdfContentByte[] canvas) {
  float widths[] = width[0];                          <- Get widths array of first row
  PdfContentByte cb = canvas[PdfPTable.TEXTCANVAS];
  cb.saveState();
  cb.setLineWidth(2);
  cb.setRGBColorStroke(255, 0, 0);
  cb.rectangle(widths[0],                             <- Left X coordinate
    height[height.length - 1],                        <- Bottom Y coordinate
```

```
    widths[widths.length - 1] - widths[0],      <— Table width
    height[0] - height[height.length - 1]);     <— Table height
  cb.stroke();
```

The table that is passed is the `PdfPTable` to which the event was added (use it as if it was read-only). The `canvas` parameter contains the four `PdfContentByte` objects as described when we discussed cell events. The parameter `width` is a two-dimensional array, containing the positions of all the borders of every row in the table. In the code fragment, you get the widths of the first row and use this array to get the left and right X coordinate of the table. The parameter `height` contains the heights of all the rows. You use this array to get the top and bottom Y coordinate of the table. With these coordinates, you draw a rectangle around the complete table.

The example continues by adding an extra border around the header rows. The code is similar, but now the bottom of the rectangle is the height of the last header row:

```
/* chapter06/PdfPTableEvents.java */
if (headerRows > 0) {
  cb.setRGBColorStroke(0, 0, 255);
  cb.rectangle(widths[0], height[headerRows],
    widths[widths.length - 1] - widths[0],
    height[0] - height[headerRows]);
  cb.stroke();
}
cb.restoreState();
```

The `rowStart` parameter is the same parameter you passed to the `writeSelectRows()` method in section 6.1.5. It gives you the number of the first row that is written after the header. It doesn't have a meaning when you add the table with `document.add()`. The example also draws borders with random colors around each cell and even adds an action (see chapter 13) to one specific cell:

```
/* chapter06/PdfPTableEvents.java */
cb = canvas[PdfPTable.BASECANVAS];
cb.saveState();
cb.setLineWidth(.5f);
for (int line = 0; line < height.length - 1; ++line) {     <— Loop over rows
  widths = width[line];
  for (int col = 0; col < widths.length - 1; ++col) {      <— Loop over columns
    if (line == 0 && col == 0)
      cb.setAction(new PdfAction(
        "http://www.lowagie.com/iText/"),                  Add action to cell
        widths[col], height[line + 1],
        widths[col + 1], height[line]);
```

```
        cb.setRGBColorStrokeF((float)Math.random(),
          (float)Math.random(), (float)Math.random());
        cb.moveTo(widths[col], height[line]);
        cb.lineTo(widths[col + 1], height[line]);      Draw horizontal border
        cb.stroke();
        cb.setRGBColorStrokeF((float)Math.random(),
          (float)Math.random(), (float)Math.random());
        cb.moveTo(widths[col], height[line]);
        cb.lineTo(widths[col], height[line + 1]);      Draw vertical border
        cb.stroke();
    }
  }
  cb.restoreState();
```

Cell and table events work for tables that are added with `document.add()` as well as with `writeSelectedRows()`:

```
/* chapter06/PdfPTableEvents.java */
PdfPTable table = new PdfPTable(4);
table.getDefaultCell().setBorder(Rectangle.NO_BORDER);
for (int k = 0; k < 24; ++k) {
  if (k != 0)
    table.addCell(String.valueOf(k));
  else
    table.addCell("This is an URL");
}
PdfPTableEvents event = new PdfPTableEvents();
table.setTableEvent(event);
document.add(table);
table.setTotalWidth(300);
table.writeSelectedRows(0, -1, 100, 600,
    writer.getDirectContent());
```

Table events can also deal with tables added with `document.add()` that are split over several pages:

```
/* chapter06/PdfPTableEvents.java */
table = new PdfPTable(4);
table.getDefaultCell().setBorder(Rectangle.NO_BORDER);
for (int k = 0; k < 500 * 4; ++k) {
  if (k == 0) {
    table.getDefaultCell().setColspan(4);
    table.getDefaultCell()
      .setHorizontalAlignment(Element.ALIGN_CENTER);
    table.addCell(new Phrase("This is an URL"));
    table.getDefaultCell().setColspan(1);
    table.getDefaultCell()
      .setHorizontalAlignment(Element.ALIGN_LEFT);
    k += 3;
  }
  else
```

```
        table.addCell(new Phrase(String.valueOf(k)));
    }
    table.setTableEvent(event);
    table.setHeaderRows(3);
    document.add(table);
```

As you can see, you set the colspan of the first cell to 4. This way, the array `width[0]` contains only two values: the left and the right border of the table. You also define the header rows to demonstrate that the event that adds an extra border around the header really works.

Notice that instead of putting all these events in one event class, you could use separate `PdfPTable` implementation classes as you did in the `PdfPCellEvent` example.

### *Combining table and cell events*

In a final example, you'll combine table and cell events to put a border around the table and simulate the HTML table attribute `cellspacing` (complementary to `cellpadding`), which defines the space between the cells. I won't repeat the code to add the table border, only the `cellLayout()` implementation to draw the cell border:

```
/* chapter06/PdfPTableFloatingBoxes.java */
public void cellLayout(
  PdfPCell cell, Rectangle position, PdfContentByte[] canvas) {
  float x1 = position.left() + 2;
  float x2 = position.right() - 2;
  float y1 = position.top() - 2;
  float y2 = position.bottom() + 2;
  PdfContentByte cb = canvas[PdfPTable.LINECANVAS];
  cb.setRGBColorStroke(0xFF, 0x00, 0x00);
  cb.rectangle(x1, y1, x2 - x1, y2 - y1);
  cb.stroke();
  cb.resetRGBColorStroke();
}
```

Because you want every cell to have such a border, you add the cell event to the default cell:

```
/* chapter06/PdfPTableFloatingBoxes.java */
PdfPTable table = new PdfPTable(2);
PdfPTableFloatingBoxes event = new PdfPTableFloatingBoxes();
table.setTableEvent(event);
table.getDefaultCell().setBorder(Rectangle.NO_BORDER);
table.getDefaultCell().setCellEvent(event);
table.getDefaultCell().setPadding(5f);
table.addCell("value");
table.addCell("name");
```

```
table.addCell(new Paragraph("fox"));
table.addCell(new Paragraph("dog"));
document.add(table);
```

We have illustrated the theory about path construction and painting operators with interesting `PdfPTable` functionality, but we still have a lot of graphics state theory to deal with. In the last two examples, you used methods to set the color and the line width. These are graphics state operators.

## 10.3 Graphics state operators

The graphics state is initialized at the beginning of each page. Inside the page, the graphics state can be changed and stacked. All parameters, such as current color (one for filling and one for stroking), current line width, and so on, have default values. When using iText, you can change most of these defaults with `PdfContentByte` methods. Some parameters can only be changed with the `PdfGState` object, as you'll see in the next chapter when we discuss colors and transparency.

In this section, we'll discuss how to change colors and line characteristics.

### 10.3.1 The graphics state stack

The PDF Reference says the following:

> [A] well-structured PDF document typically contains many graphical elements that are essentially independent of each other and sometimes nested to multiple levels. The Graphics State stack allows these elements to make local changes to the graphics state without disturbing the graphics state of the surrounding environment. The stack is a LIFO (last in, first out) data structure in which the contents of the graphics state can be saved and later restored.

What does this mean? Let's look at the cell event you wrote earlier that draws a red ellipse:

```
/* chapter10/PdfPTableCellEvents.java */
class Ellipse implements PdfPCellEvent {
  public void cellLayout(PdfPCell cell, Rectangle rect,
    PdfContentByte[] canvas) {
    PdfContentByte cb = canvas[PdfPTable.BACKGROUNDCANVAS];
    cb.setRGBColorFill(0xFF, 0x00, 0x00);   <-- Change current fill color
    cb.ellipse(rect.left(), rect.bottom(),     | Construct path
      rect.right(), rect.top());               |
    cb.fill();   <-- Paint path
    cb.resetRGBColorFill();   <-- Reset color
  }
}
```

There are different reasons why this code isn't elegant. When you reset the RGB color, you set the color to black. This may not be what you want. Maybe the current fill color was yellow before you set it to red. If you reset the color, you want it to be yellow, not black.

If you're changing not only the fill color but also the stroke color, the line width, and so on, you have to reset all these values. You can save a lot of work (and write less error-prone code) if you do it this way:

```
PdfContentByte cb = canvas[PdfPTable.BACKGROUNDCANVAS];
cb.saveState();
cb.setRGBColorFill(0xFF, 0x00, 0x00);
cb.ellipse(rect.left(), rect.bottom(), rect.right(), rect.top());
cb.fill();
cb.restoreState();
```

The method `saveState()` (corresponding with the PDF operator `q`) saves the current graphics state (for instance, a state with yellow as the fill color). You change the current fill color to red, do other stuff, and then call `restoreState()` (corresponding with the PDF operator `Q`). All the changes you've made to the graphics state after `saveState()` are then reset to the state before `saveState()`.

An example should clarify what this means in practice. In figure 10.8, you see five concentric circles in different colors depending on the color in the current graphics state.

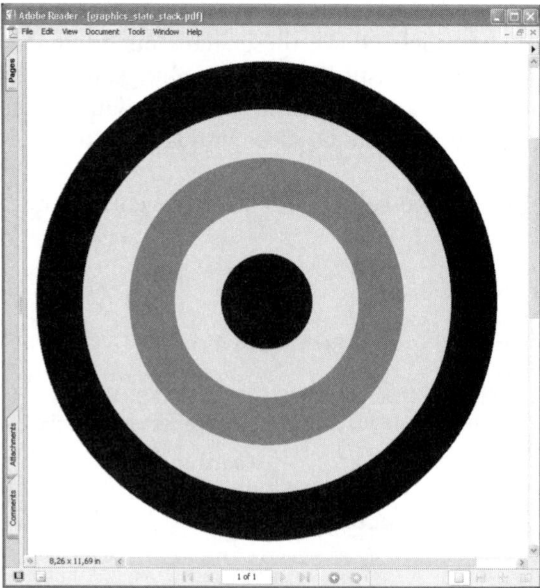

**Figure 10.8**
**Illustrating the graphics state stack**

The source code makes clear how the graphics state stack works:

```
/* chapter10/GraphicsStateStack.java */
PdfContentByte cb = writer.getDirectContent();
cb.circle(260.0f, 500.0f, 250.0f);
cb.fill();   <-❶
cb.saveState();   <-❷
cb.setColorFill(Color.yellow);   <-❸
cb.circle(260.0f, 500.0f, 200.0f);
cb.fill();   <-❹
cb.saveState();   <-❺
cb.setColorFill(Color.red);   <-❻
cb.circle(260.0f, 500.0f, 150.0f);
cb.fill();   <-❼
cb.restoreState();   <-❽
cb.circle(260.0f, 500.0f, 100.0f);
cb.fill();   <-❾
cb.restoreState();   <-❿
cb.circle(260.0f, 500.0f, 50.0f);
cb.fill();   <-⓫
```

First you draw a circle in the default fill color (black) ❶. Before you save the state, the fill color is black ❷, but you change it to yellow ❸. Therefore, the next circle that is drawn is yellow ❹. You save the state a second time (this adds another graphics state to the graphics stack) ❺, and you change the fill color to red ❻. The circle that is drawn in this graphics state is red ❼. But then you restore the state ❽ and remove one graphics state from the stack. You return to the graphics state with fill color yellow. This is why the fourth circle is yellow ❾. Finally, you go back to the initial graphics state ❿ and draw another black circle ⓫.

This is a simple example because you only change one characteristic of the graphics state: the fill color. In the next sections, you'll change line characteristics and the coordinate system. These changes can be complex, and saving and restoring the state can help keep your code maintainable. Remember that the `saveState()` and `restoreState()` methods must be balanced. If you try to restore the state without having saved the state, an exception will be thrown.

Let's start with some of the simplest graphics state operators and gradually increase the complexity.

### 10.3.2 Changing the characteristics of a line

If you stroke a path in the default graphics state, the subpaths are drawn using solid lines that are 1 point thick. Figure 10.9 shows a series of lines painted with different line widths.

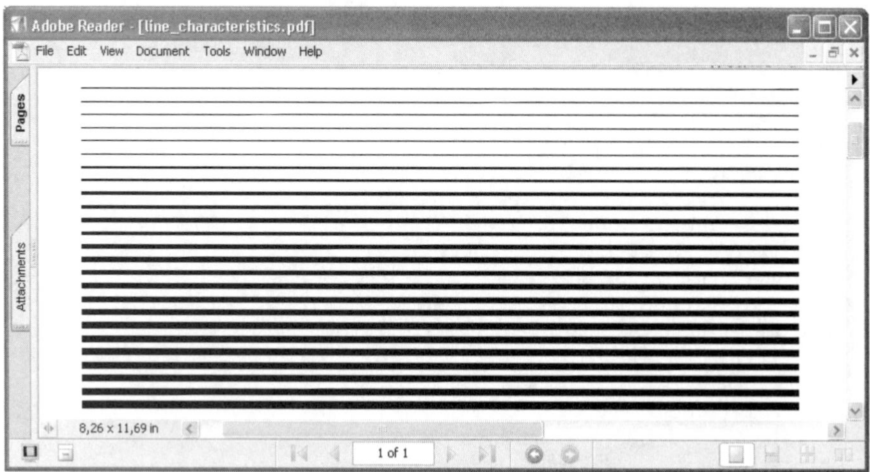


**Figure 10.9 Different line widths**

A `float` value in a range from 0.1 to 2.5 is used as the line width for the lines in figure 10.9:

```
/* chapter10/LineCharacteristics.java */
for (int i = 25; i > 0; i--) {
  cb.setLineWidth((float)i / 10);
  cb.moveTo(40, 806 - (5 * i));
  cb.lineTo(320, 806 - (5 * i));
  cb.stroke();
}
```

It's important to understand that not all devices are able to render lines with the width you specify in your PDF. The actual line width can differ from the requested width by as much as 2 device pixels, depending on the positions of the lines with respect to the pixel grid.

**NOTE** With the method `PdfContentByte.setFlatness()`, you can set the precision with which curves are rendered on the output device. The parameter gives the maximum error tolerance, measured in output device pixels. Smaller numbers give smoother curves at the expense of more computation and memory use.

The PDF Reference advises against it, but you can also define a 0 width. When setting the line width to 0, you indicate you want the thinnest line that can be rendered at device resolution: 1 device pixel wide. The PDF Reference warns that "some devices cannot reproduce 1-pixel lines, and on high-resolution devices, they are nearly invisible."

When you draw lines from one point to another, other parameters can be set.

### *Line cap and line join styles*

Figure 10.10 demonstrates the different *line cap* and *line join* possibilities.

**Figure 10.10 Line cap and line join styles**

The three parallel lines at the left in figure 10.10 theoretically have the same length (1 in). They're drawn between x=72 and x=144 (see the two vertical lines), but the style used at the ends of the horizontal lines is different:

- *Butt cap*—The stroke is squared off at the end point of the path.
- *Round cap*—A semicircular arc with diameter equal to the line width is drawn around the end point.
- *Projecting square cap*—The stroke continues beyond the endpoint of the path for a distance equal to half the line width.

For each of these styles, there's a static final member variable in class `PdfContentByte`:

```
/* chapter10/LineCharacteristics.java */
cb.setLineWidth(8);
cb.setLineCap(PdfContentByte.LINE_CAP_BUTT);
cb.moveTo(72, 640);  cb.lineTo(144, 640);  cb.stroke();
cb.setLineCap(PdfContentByte.LINE_CAP_ROUND);
cb.moveTo(72, 625); cb.lineTo(144, 625); cb.stroke();
cb.setLineCap(PdfContentByte.LINE_CAP_PROJECTING_SQUARE);
cb.moveTo(72, 610);  cb.lineTo(144, 610);  cb.stroke();
```

The three hook shapes to the right in figure 10.10 demonstrate different line join styles. If a subpath consists of different line segments, they can be joined in three ways:

- *Miter join*—The outer edges of the strokes for two segments are extended until they meet at an angle.
- *Rounded join*—An arc of a circle with diameter equal to the line width is drawn around the point where the two line segments meet.
- *Bevel join*—The two segments are finished with butt caps.

There are also static final member variables in `PdfContentByte` for the line join styles:

```
/* chapter10/LineCharacteristics.java */
cb.setLineWidth(8);
cb.setLineJoin(PdfContentByte.LINE_JOIN_MITER);
cb.moveTo(200, 610);  cb.lineTo(215, 640);
cb.lineTo(230, 610);  cb.stroke();
cb.setLineJoin(PdfContentByte.LINE_JOIN_ROUND);
cb.moveTo(240, 610);  cb.lineTo(255, 640);
cb.lineTo(270, 610);  cb.stroke();
cb.setLineJoin(PdfContentByte.LINE_JOIN_BEVEL);
cb.moveTo(280, 610);  cb.lineTo(295, 640);
cb.lineTo(310, 610);  cb.stroke();
```

When you define mitered joins (the default), and two line segments meet at a sharp angle, it's possible for the miter to extend far beyond the thickness of the line stroke. If φ is the angle between both line segments, the miter limit equals the line width divided by sin(φ/2).

You can define a maximum value for the ratio of the miter length to the line width. This maximum is called the *miter limit*. When this limit is exceeded, the join is converted from a miter to a bevel. Figure 10.11 shows two rows of hooks that were drawn using the same line widths and almost the same paths. The angle of the hooks decreases from left to right. In the first row, the miter limit is set to 2; in the second row, the miter limit is 2.1.

**Figure 10.11 Miter limit of 2 (top row) and 2.1 (bottom row)**

The miter limit for the hooks in the first row is exceeded in the fourth hook of the first row. In the second row, it's exceeded just after the fourth hook. Let's compare the code for the fourth hook for both rows:

```
/* chapter10/LineCharacteristics.java */
cb.setLineWidth(8);
cb.setLineJoin(PdfContentByte.LINE_JOIN_MITER);
cb.setMiterLimit(2);
cb.moveTo(198, 560);
cb.lineTo(215, 590);
cb.lineTo(232, 560);
cb.stroke();
cb.setMiterLimit(2.1f);
cb.moveTo(198, 500);
cb.lineTo(215, 530);
cb.lineTo(232, 500);
cb.stroke();
```

Until now, you've been drawing solid lines; you can also paint dashed lines.

### *Line dash pattern*

Before a path is stroked, the *dash array* is cycled through, adding the lengths of dashes and gaps. When the accumulated length equals the *phase*, stroking of the path begins. (The phase defines where the pattern starts.) The default dash array is empty, and the phase is 0; when you stroke a line, you get a solid line just like the first line in figure 10.12. This screenshot also shows lines drawn using different dash arrays and phases.

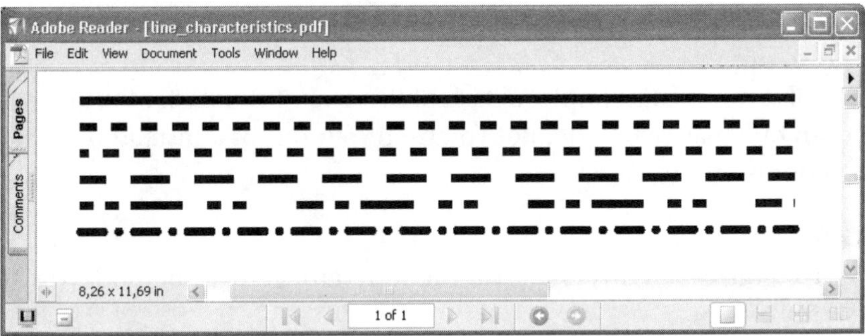


**Figure 10.12 Dash patterns**

Let's examine the source code to understand the meaning of the dash array and the phase:

```
/* chapter10/LineCharacteristics.java */
cb.setLineWidth(3);
cb.moveTo(40, 480);  cb.lineTo(320, 480);  cb.stroke();     ❶
cb.setLineDash(6, 0);
cb.moveTo(40, 470);  cb.lineTo(320, 470);  cb.stroke();     ❷
cb.setLineDash(6, 3);
cb.moveTo(40, 460);  cb.lineTo(320, 460);  cb.stroke();     ❸
cb.setLineDash(15, 10, 5);
cb.moveTo(40, 450);  cb.lineTo(320, 450);  cb.stroke();     ❹
float[] dash1 = { 10, 5, 5, 5, 20};
cb.setLineDash(dash1, 5);
cb.moveTo(40, 440);  cb.lineTo(320, 440);  cb.stroke();     ❺
float[] dash2 = { 9, 6, 0, 6 };
cb.setLineCap(PdfContentByte.LINE_CAP_ROUND);
cb.setLineDash(dash2, 0);
cb.moveTo(40, 430);  cb.lineTo(320, 430);  cb.stroke();     ❻
```

The first line drawn in figure 10.12 is solid ❶; this is the default graphics state. You set the line dash to a pattern of 6 units with phase 0 ❷: This means you start the line with a dash 6 units long, leave a gap of 6 units, paint a dash of 6 units, and so on. The same goes for the third line, but you use a different phase ❸.

In line 4, you paint a dash of 15 units, then leave a gap of 10 units, and so on. The phase is 5, so the first dash you see is only 10 units long (15 – 5) ❹. Line 5 uses a more complex pattern ❺: You start with a dash of 5 (10 – 5) long, then you have a gap of 5, a dash of 5, a gap of 5 and a dash of 20. The next sequence is as follows: a gap of 10, a dash of 5, a gap of 5, a dash of 5, a gap of 20, and so on.

❻ is also a special example: a dash of 9, a gap of 6, a dash of 0, and a gap of 6. The dash of 0 may seem odd, but you used round caps—instead of a zero-length dash, a dot is drawn.

### Overview

Table 10.3 gives an overview of the operators/iText methods discussed in this section.

You almost have sufficient information to help Laura with her first graphical assignment: You can stroke and fill paths that represent streets and squares on the

**Table 10.3 Graphics state operators relating to lines**

| Operator | iText method | Operands / parameters | Description |
|---|---|---|---|
| w | setLineWidth | (width) | The parameter represents the thickness of the line in user units (default = 1). |
| J | setLineCap | (style) | Defines the line cap style, which can be one of the following values:<br>LINE_CAP_BUTT (default)<br>LINE_CAP_ROUND<br>LINE_CAP_PROJECTING_SQUARE |
| j | setLineJoin | (style) | Defines the line join style, which can be one of the following values:<br>LINE_JOIN_MITER (default)<br>LINE_JOIN_ROUND<br>LINE_JOIN_BEVEL |
| M | setMiterLimit | (miterLimit) | The parameter is a limit for joining lines. When it's exceeded, the join is converted from a miter to a bevel. |
| d | setLineDash | (unitsOn, phase)<br><br>(unitsOn, unitsOff, phase)<br><br>(array, phase) | The default line dash is a solid line, but by using the different iText methods that change the dash pattern, you can create all sorts of dashed lines. |

map of Foobar. But before you reward yourself with a visit to Laura, let's see how to transform the coordinate system.

To demonstrate how the different transformations work, I need an irregular shape—for instance, the eye that is used for the iText logo. I'll teach you a trick that allows you to write your own PDF syntax.

### *Literal PDF syntax*

For the examples in this chapter, I set compression to false. If you open the PDF files in a text editor, you can see what the different PDF operators look like. If you need a PDF operator that isn't supported in iText, you can construct your own strings of operators and operands and use the `setLiteral()` method in `PdfContentByte`.

Do you recognize the following sequence of operators and operands?

```
12 w
22.47 64.67 m
37.99 67.76 52.24 75.38 63.43 86.57 c
120 110 m
98.78 110 78.43 101.57 63.43 86.57 c
S
1 J
120 110 m
97.91 110 80 92.09 80 70 c
80 47.91 97.91 30 120 30 c
125 70 m
125 72.76 122.76 75 120 75 c
117.24 75 115 72.76 115 70 c
115 67.24 117.24 65 120 65 c
122.76 65 125 67.24 125 70 c
S
```

If you study tables 10.1, 10.2, and 10.3 (or if your knowledge of the PDF syntax is fluent), you may recognize the eye of the iText logo. You can put this syntax inside a `String` and add it directly to the `PdfContentByte`:

```
/* chapter10/EyeLogo.java */
PdfContentByte cb = writer.getDirectContent();
String eye = "12 w\n22.47 64.67 m\n"
  + "37.99 67.76 52.24 75.38 63.43 86.57 c\n"
  + "120 110 m\n98.78 110 78.43 101.57 63.43 86.57 c\n"
  + "S\n1 J\n120 110 m\n97.91 110 80 92.09 80 70 c\n"
  + "80 47.91 97.91 30 120 30 c\n125 70 m\n"
  + "125 72.76 122.76 75 120 75 c\n"
  + "117.24 75 115 72.76 115 70 c\n"
  + "115 67.24 117.24 65 120 65 c\n"
  + "122.76 65 125 67.24 125 70 c\nS\n";
cb.setLiteral(eye);
```

The resulting PDF shows the iText eye at the bottom of the page (see figure 10.13).

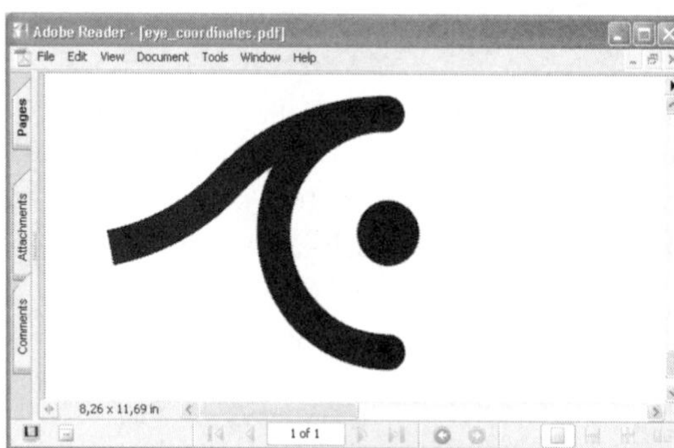


**Figure 10.13**
**Drawing the iText eye**

There's little chance you'll ever need this functionality, but we'll use this eye string to demonstrate the effect of changing the coordinate system.

## 10.4 Changing the coordinate system

The coordinates you use to draw the iText eye in figure 10.13 assume that the origin of the coordinate system is in the lower-left corner and that the x-axis points to the left and the y-axis points to the top of the page. Let's start by turning the coordinate system upside down so that the eye looks like figure 10.14.

**Figure 10.14 Drawing the iText eye upside down**

The eye variable is identical to the String used to draw the eye in figure 10.13:

```
/* chapter10/EyeCoordinates.java */
PdfContentByte cb = writer.getDirectContent();
String eye = "12 w\n22.47 64.67 m ...";
cb.saveState();
cb.concatCTM(1f, 0f, 0f, -1f, 0f, PageSize.A4.height());
cb.setLiteral(eye);
cb.restoreState();
```

With the method concatCTM(), you use the PDF operator that changes the current transformation matrix (CTM). In figure 10.13, the eye is in the lower-left corner; in figure 10.14, the eye is mirrored in the upper-left corner.

### 10.4.1 The CTM

Section 5.4.2 discussed translating, scaling, and rotating images. I referred to analytical geometry, and I told you it's possible to translate, scale, and rotate images using algebra and matrices. Let's take a closer look at these matrices.

### *Doing the math*

The six values in the `concatCTM()` method are elements of a matrix that has three rows and three columns. This is what the CTM looks like:

$$\begin{bmatrix} a & b & 0 \\ c & d & 0 \\ e & f & 1 \end{bmatrix}$$

I was about 17 years old when I first learned this elementary algebra. In case it's been a long time for you, too, let's refresh your memory. Coordinate transformations in a two-dimensional system can be expressed as matrix multiplications:

$$[\ x'\ y'\ 1\ ] = [\ x\ y\ 1\ ] \times \begin{bmatrix} a & b & 0 \\ c & d & 0 \\ e & f & 1 \end{bmatrix}$$

Or like this, if you carry out the multiplication:

```
x' = a * x + c * y + e;
y' = b * x + d * y + f;
```

The third column in the CTM is fixed: You're working in two dimensions, and you don't need to calculate a new Z coordinate.

Suppose you want to transform the iText eye. You could recalculate all the coordinates you used in the literal string, but that's not elegant. It's better to change the CTM. To do this, you need to define values for `a`, `b`, `c`, `d`, `e`, and `f`. Let's disentangle the transformations we already discussed when dealing with images:

Translating a shape is done like this:

```
x' = 1 * x + 0 * y + dX;
y' = 0 * y + 1 * y + dY;
```

These formulas scale a shape:

```
x' = sX * x + 0 * y + 0;
y' = 0 * x + sY * y + 0;
```

There formulas rotate the shape with an angle φ:

```
x' = cos(φ) * x - sin(φ) * y + 0;
y' = sin(φ) * x + cos(φ) * y + 0;
```

Finally, you can also skew the shape, where α is the new angle of the x-axis and β is the new angle of the y-axis:

```
x' = x + tan(β) * y + 0;
y' = tan(α) * x + y + 0;
```

If you want to combine the most common transformations in one operation—translation (dX, dY), scaling (sX, sY), and rotation φ—you can calculate your `a`, `b`, `c`, `d`, `e`, and `f` values like this:

```
a = sX * cos(φ);
b = sY * sin(φ);
c = sX * -sin(φ);
d = sY * cos(φ);
e = dX;
f = dY;
```

You now understand the code that was used to turn the eye in figure 10.13 into the eye on figure 10.14: φ is 0 degrees, but `sY` is -1, so the y-axis points down instead of up. You also perform a translation `dY = PageSize.A4.height();` otherwise, your shape would be drawn outside the page.

**NOTE** The order is important when performing transformations one after the other. For example, a translation (using a matrix $M_T$) followed by a rotation ($M_R$) doesn't necessarily have the same result as the same rotation (using $M_R$) followed by the same translation ($M_T$).

In mathematics, these transformations are called *affine*. If you don't like doing the math that is necessary to get the parameter values for method `concatCTM()`, you can use the standard Java class `java.awt.geom.AffineTransform`.

### Affine transformations

The standard Java class `AffineTransform` has constructors that help you define transformations in a more intuitive way. Apart from the constructors, there are the static methods `getTranslateInstance()` and `getScaleInstance()` and two different `getRotateInstance()` methods that return an `AffineTransform` instance.

Figure 10.15 shows a complete page made in the example EyeCoordinates. You've already seen how the eyes in the left corners were added; the following code snippet demonstrates how you can use the `AffineTransform` class to add the eyes in the middle of the page:

```
/* chapter10/EyeCoordinates.java */
PdfContentByte cb = writer.getDirectContent();
String eye = "12 w\n22.47 64.67 m ...";
cb.transform(AffineTransform.getTranslateInstance(100, 400));
cb.setLiteral(eye);
cb.transform(AffineTransform.getRotateInstance(-Math.PI / 2));
cb.transform(AffineTransform.getScaleInstance(2, 2));
cb.setLiteral(eye);
```

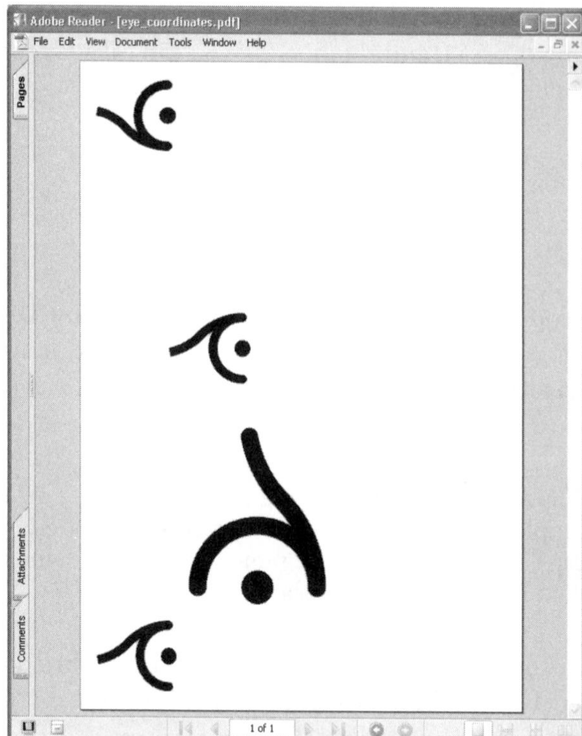


**Figure 10.15**
**Affine transformations**

You didn't save and restore the state as you did before. Be careful when you work like this: Invoking `concatCTM()` or `transform()` doesn't *replace* the current transformation matrix. These methods add a transformation on top of the existing transformation. If you look closely, you also see that the edge of the eye that was scaled is rounded instead of butt-capped. The line cap style was changed to round cap while drawing the iris of the previous eye.

You may prefer working with method `transform()` because it looks easier than working with `concatCTM()` (it's a matter of taste), but that doesn't mean you'll never have to use the formulas to calculate the `a`, `b`, `c`, `d`, `e`, and `f` values of the transformation matrix. You'll still need these values when you want to add an XObject to the direct content.

## 10.4.2 Positioning external objects

I want to stress that what you did in the previous example isn't how you'll work in practice. I used the string with the PDF syntax only to show how you can add the same path definition in different positions by changing the current transformation matrix.

If you open the PDF file in a text editor, you'll see that the same string (`"12 w\n22.47 64.67 m..."`) is repeated four times (because you're drawing the iText eye four times). If you'd like to add the iText eye as a watermark on every page in a document with hundreds of pages, you'll have a lot of syntax that is repeated over and over. There is a better solution: Add the syntax to draw the iText eye as an *external object* (XObject). There are three types of external objects: image XObjects, PostScript XObjects, and form XObjects. You've already encountered one XObject type in chapter 5: images.

### *Image XObjects*

In chapter 5, you added images to a document with `document.add()`. It's also possible to add an image directly to the content with `PdfContentByte.addImage()`. Figure 10.16 shows a PDF file to which iTextLogo.gif was added twice.

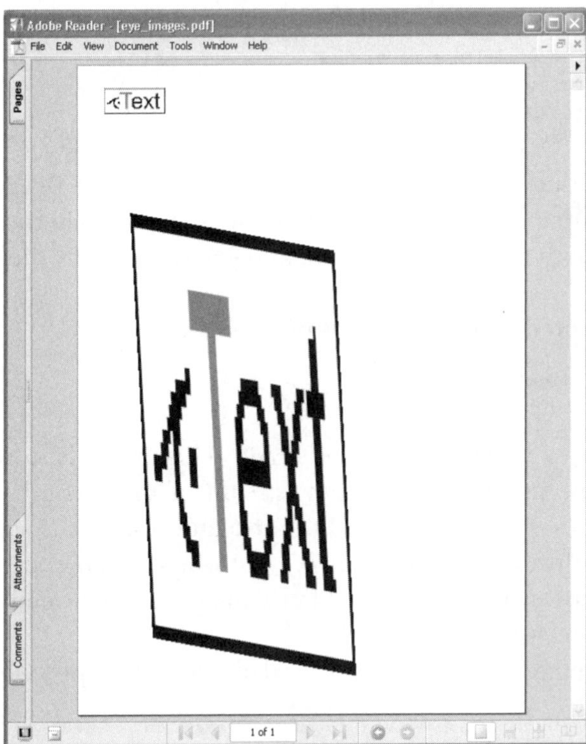


**Figure 10.16**
**Adding `Image` objects to the direct content**

If you only need a translation (like the logo in the upper-left corner), you can use the method you used in chapter 5 (`Image.setAbsolutePositions()`) and `PdfContentByte.addImage(Image img)`. If you want to perform other transformations as well, you need the `addImage()` method with the parameters `a`, `b`, `c`, `d`, `e`, and `f` that define the transformation matrix.

In figure 10.16, the image is skewed, scaled, and translated:

```
/* chapter10/EyeImages.java */
PdfContentByte cb = writer.getDirectContent();
Image eye = Image.getInstance("../resources/iTextLogo.gif");
eye.setAbsolutePosition(36, 780);
cb.addImage(eye);
cb.addImage(eye, 271, -50, -30, 550, 100, 100);
```

Note that images can also be added inline. In this case, the image is added directly within the content stream. The source code is almost identical to images added as XObjects:

```
/* chapter10/EyeInlineImage.java */
PdfContentByte cb = writer.getDirectContent();
Image eye = Image.getInstance("../resources/iTextLogo.gif");
eye.setAbsolutePosition(36, 780);
cb.addImage(eye, true);
cb.addImage(eye, 271, -50, -30, 550, 100, 100, true);
```

If you compare the resulting PDF files of both examples in Adobe Reader, they look identical. If you compare the file size, the first file is about 3 KB; the second file is about 4 KB. Open both files in a text editor, and you can see why the file size is different.

In the first file, the content stream contains only two lines:

```
q 80 0 0 32 36 780 cm /img0 Do Q
q 271 -50 -30 550 100 100 cm /img0 Do Q
```

There is only a reference to an XObject named `/img0`. This image is stored only once, outside the content stream. The content stream of the second PDF file includes the same graphics state operators `q`/`Q` (to save and restore the state) and `cm` (to change the current transformation matrix); but where you'd expect `/img0 Do'`, find a sequence of PDF syntax including binary image data between a begin image (`BI`) and end image (`EI`) statement.

For the sake of completeness, I'll also say a word about PostScript XObjects.

### *PostScript XObjects*

A PostScript XObject contains a fragment of code expressed in PostScript. There is basic support for PostScript XObjects in iText with the class `PdfPSXObject`. It has all the methods that are in `PdfContentByte`, and you can add PS code using the method `setLiteral()`. I won't discuss this functionality because it's no longer recommended that you use PostScript XObjects in PDF. These PS fragments are used only when printing to a PostScript output device. They should be used with extreme caution, because they can cause PDF files to print incorrectly. See section 4.7.1 in the PDF Reference manual: "This feature is likely to be removed from PDF in a future version."

There is one XObject type left; it's called a *form XObject*, but the word *form* is confusing. We aren't talking about forms that can be filled in. To avoid confusion with AcroForms, I prefer talking about `PdfTemplate` objects in iText instead of using the PDF term *form XObjects*.

### *PdfTemplates*

A `PdfTemplate` is a PDF content stream that is a self-contained description of any sequence of graphics objects. `PdfTemplate` extends `PdfContentByte` and inherits all its methods. A `PdfTemplate` object is a kind of extra layer with custom dimensions that can be used for different purposes:

- To create a graphical object using the methods discussed in this chapter (and in the next one) and add this object to your PDF file in a user friendly way. This is what you'll do when you draw the map of Foobar. You'll create a `PdfTemplate`, wrap it in an `Image` object, and add it to your document with `document.add()`.
- To repeat a certain sequence of PDF syntax (for instance, the code that generated the iText eye), but reuse the byte stream to save disk space, processing time, and/or band width. You'll see how this is done in the next example.
- To add content to a page when you don't know in advance what that content will be. For instance, you want to add a footer saying *this is page x of y*, but at the moment the page is constructed and sent to the output stream, you don't know the value of *y* (you don't know how many pages will be in your document). In this case, you can add a template for *y* but wait to add content to this template until you know the exact number of pages. This will be demonstrated in chapter 14.

Let's rewrite the example repeating the iText eye at different positions and produce a PDF that looks (almost) exactly like the one in figure 10.15, but reducing the file size by reusing the eye syntax-string:

```
/* chapter10/EyeTemplate.java */
PdfContentByte cb = writer.getDirectContent();
PdfTemplate template = cb.createTemplate(150, 150);     <-1
template.setLineWidth(12f);
template.arc(
  40f - (float) Math.sqrt(12800), 110f + (float) Math.sqrt(12800),
  200f - (float) Math.sqrt(12800), -50f + (float) Math.sqrt(12800),
  281.25f, 33.75f);
template.arc(40f, 110f, 200f, -50f, 90f, 45f);
template.stroke();                                          2
template.setLineCap(PdfContentByte.LINE_JOIN_ROUND);
template.arc(80f, 30f, 160f, 110f, 90f, 180f);
template.arc(115f, 65f, 125f, 75f, 0f, 360f);
template.stroke();
cb.addTemplate(template, 0f, 0f);
cb.addTemplate(template, 1f, 0f, 0f, -1f, 0f, PageSize.A4.height());
cb.addTemplate(template, 100, 400);
cb.addTemplate(template, 0, -2, 2, 0, 100, 400);          3
```

1. Create a `PdfTemplate` object with the method `createTemplate()`, defining the dimensions of the XObject. Everything drawn outside these dimensions will be invisible.
2. Compose the iText eye. This code creates the same syntax you used before.
3. Add the iText eye four times to the direct content. The actual PDF stream describing the eye is added to the PDF file only once.

Again, the PDF file created with XObjects is smaller in size than the PDF file that repeated the syntax over and over (1388 bytes versus 2023 bytes). The eye string is now in a separate object. If you inspect the PDF file, you see that there's a reference to this object in the content stream:

```
q 1 0 0 1 0 0 cm /Xf1 Do Q
q 1 0 0 -1 0 842 cm /Xf1 Do Q
q 1 0 0 1 100 400 cm /Xf1 Do Q
q 0 -2 2 0 100 400 cm /Xf1 Do Q
```

Comparing the iText source code with the resulting PDF syntax, you immediately understand the meaning of the two `addTemplate()` methods in the class `PdfContentByte`. The method that adds the template along with two `float` parameters can be used to translate the XObject. The `a`, `b`, `c`, and `d` values of the transformation matrix are 1, 0, 0, and 1. The second `addTemplate()` method allows you to define the complete matrix needed for a two-dimensional transformation. iText gives a name to the XObject: `/Xf1`.

With the class `PdfTemplate`, you have the final puzzle piece that is needed to draw a map of Foobar.

## 10.5 Drawing a map of a city (part 1)

Readers familiar with PS will say that there's nothing new about this chapter; all these path-construction and painting operators are identical to what you know from PostScript. Other readers who know something about Scalable Vector Graphics (SVG) will say this looks much like SVG. Both are right. As I mentioned in the chapter 3, PDF has evolved from PostScript, and the imaging system is similar. PDF and PS have many graphic operators and operands in common. But people who define graphics in XML format—more specifically, in SVG—also have a point.

SVG is an XML markup language for describing 2D vector graphics. It was developed by the World Wide Web Consortium (W3C) after Macromedia and Microsoft introduced Vector Markup Language (VML) and Adobe and Sun developed a competing format Precision Graphics Markup Language (PGML). If you read the SVG specification,[3] you'll find path construction and painting operators and operands that are similar to the ones described in this chapter.

Laura has an SVG file that contains the streets and squares of Foobar, and she want to convert this file to a PDF document.

### 10.5.1 The XML/SVG source file

If you look at the file foobar.svg, you'll immediately recognize the terminology (see figure 10.17).

There are `path` tags with move-to (`M`) and line-to (`L`) commands in the path data (`d`) attribute; there are also `fill` and `stroke` attributes defining the fill and stroke color. The attribute `points` in the `polyline` tags defines all the coordinates of the points in the polyline.

Different browsers and tools let you view this file, but you want to render the SVG file on a page in a PDF file as shown in figure 10.18.

Laura suggests that you should write your own SVG parser. Given the number of pages in the SVG Specification, you immediately realize that this will be a lot of work; but against your better judgment, you start writing some code.

---

[3] http://www.w3.org/Graphics/SVG/ contains links to the specifications of the different SVG versions.

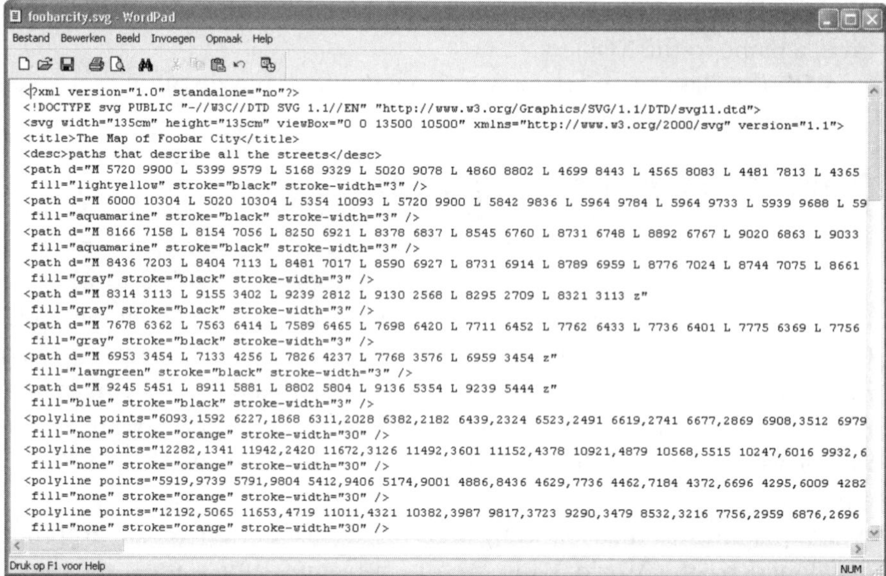

foobarcity.svg - WordPad
Bestand Bewerken Beeld Invoegen Opmaak Help
<?xml version="1.0" standalone="no"?>
<!DOCTYPE svg PUBLIC "-//W3C//DTD SVG 1.1//EN" "http://www.w3.org/Graphics/SVG/1.1/DTD/svg11.dtd">
<svg width="135cm" height="135cm" viewBox="0 0 13500 10500" xmlns="http://www.w3.org/2000/svg" version="1.1">
<title>The Map of Foobar City</title>
<desc>paths that describe all the streets</desc>
<path d="M 5720 9900 L 5399 9579 L 5168 9329 L 5020 9078 L 4860 8802 L 4699 8443 L 4565 8083 L 4481 7813 L 4365
fill="lightyellow" stroke="black" stroke-width="3" />
<path d="M 6000 10304 L 5020 10304 L 5354 10093 L 5720 9900 L 5842 9836 L 5964 9784 L 5964 9733 L 5939 9688 L 59
fill="aquamarine" stroke="black" stroke-width="3" />
<path d="M 8166 7158 L 8154 7056 L 8250 6921 L 8378 6837 L 8545 6760 L 8731 6748 L 8892 6767 L 9020 6863 L 9033
fill="aquamarine" stroke="black" stroke-width="3" />
<path d="M 8436 7203 L 8404 7113 L 8481 7017 L 8590 6927 L 8731 6914 L 8789 6959 L 8776 7024 L 8744 7075 L 8661
fill="gray" stroke="black" stroke-width="3" />
<path d="M 8314 3113 L 9155 3402 L 9239 2812 L 9130 2568 L 8295 2709 L 8321 3113 z"
fill="gray" stroke="black" stroke-width="3" />
<path d="M 7678 6362 L 7563 6414 L 7589 6465 L 7698 6420 L 7711 6452 L 7762 6433 L 7736 6401 L 7775 6369 L 7756
fill="gray" stroke="black" stroke-width="3" />
<path d="M 6953 3454 L 7133 4256 L 7826 4237 L 7768 3576 L 6959 3454 z"
fill="lawngreen" stroke="black" stroke-width="3" />
<path d="M 9245 5451 L 8911 5881 L 8802 5804 L 9136 5354 L 9239 5444 z"
fill="blue" stroke="black" stroke-width="3" />
<polyline points="6093,1592 6227,1868 6311,2028 6382,2182 6439,2324 6523,2491 6619,2741 6677,2869 6908,3512 6979
fill="none" stroke="orange" stroke-width="30" />
<polyline points="12282,1341 11942,2420 11672,3126 11492,3601 11152,4378 10921,4879 10568,5515 10247,6016 9932,6
fill="none" stroke="orange" stroke-width="30" />
<polyline points="5919,9739 5791,9804 5412,9406 5174,9001 4886,8436 4629,7736 4462,7184 4372,6696 4295,6009 4282
fill="none" stroke="orange" stroke-width="30" />
<polyline points="12192,5065 11653,4719 11011,4321 10382,3987 9817,3723 9290,3479 8532,3216 7756,2959 6876,2696
fill="none" stroke="orange" stroke-width="30" />
Druk op F1 voor Help
NUM


**Figure 10.17 An SVG file with the map of Foobar**

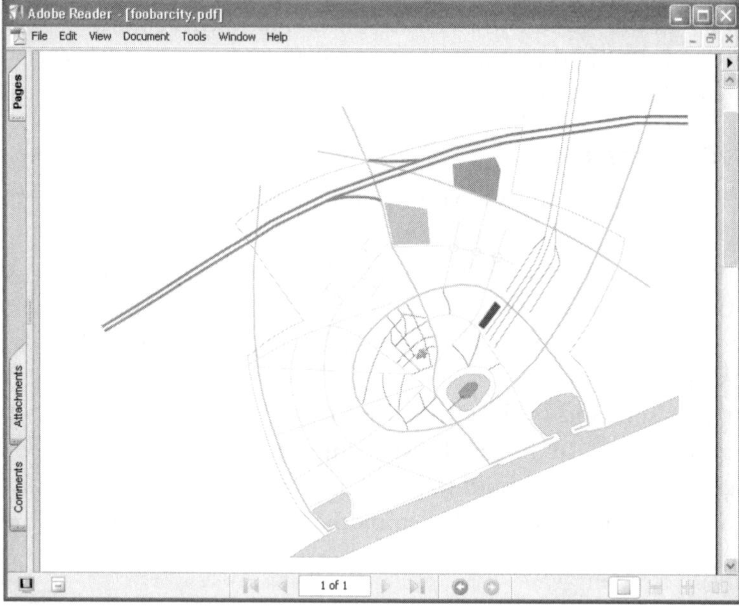


**Figure 10.18 The SVG file rendered on a PDF page**

### 10.5.2 *Parsing the SVG file*

The code of the main class `FoobarCity` is simple. You create a `FoobarSvgHandler` instance and ask this custom SVG handler to return an image:

```
/* chapter10/FoobarCity.java */
FoobarSvgHandler handler = new FoobarSvgHandler(writer,
  new InputSource(
    new FileInputStream("../resources/foobarcity.svg")));
Image image = handler.getImage();
image.scaleToFit(PageSize.A4.width(), PageSize.A4.height());
image.setAbsolutePosition(0,
  PageSize.A4.height() - image.scaledHeight());
document.add(image);
```

The image you retrieve from the handler is constructed using a `PdfTemplate`:

```
/* chapter10/FoobarSvgHandler */
public Image getImage() throws BadElementException {
  return Image.getInstance(template);
}
```

The content of this `PdfTemplate` is added by parsing the SVG file. The custom SVG handler, written especially for this example, takes the following tags into account: `svg` (the root tag), `polyline`, and `path`:

```
/* chapter10/FoobarSvgHandler */
public void startElement(String uri, String localName,
  String qName, Attributes attributes) throws SAXException {
  if ("polyline".equals(qName)) {
    drawPolyline(attributes);
  }
  else if ("path".equals(qName)) {
    drawPath(attributes);
  }
  else if ("svg".equals(qName)) {
    calcSize(attributes);
  }
}
```

The `PdfTemplate` member variable is created in the `calcSize()` method, based on coordinates that are retrieved from the `viewbox` attribute or the `width` and `height` attributes in the `svg` root tag (see the SVG specification for more information on this subject):

```
/* chapter10/FoobarSvgHandler */
template = content.createTemplate(coordinates[4], coordinates[5]);
```

Paths and polylines are drawn in the methods `drawPolyline()` and `drawPath()`:

```
/* chapter10/FoobarSvgHandler */
private void drawPolyline(Attributes attributes) {
```

```
    template.saveState();
    setFill(attributes);
    setStroke(attributes);
    computePoints(attributes);
    template.stroke();
    template.restoreState();
  }
  private void drawPath(Attributes attributes) {
    template.saveState();
    setFill(attributes);
    setStroke(attributes);
    computeData(attributes);
    template.stroke();
    template.restoreState();
  }
```

The methods `setFill()` and `setStroke()` invoke the `PdfTemplate` methods `setColorFill()`, `setColorStroke()`, and `setLineWidth()` based on the values of the attributes; `computePoints()` and `computeData()` invoke the `moveTo()`, `lineTo()`, and `closePathFillStroke()` methods.

This example is interesting because it demonstrates how graphics operators work in PDF as well as in SVG, but I must stress that this isn't a good way to convert SVG to PDF. In chapter 12, you'll write an example converting the file foobar.svg in a way that is much more robust.

For now, Laura is happy with the result. In the next chapter, we'll extend the example and add some street names—that is, after we have discussed a subset of the graphics state: text state.

## 10.6 Summary

This was the first of a set of three chapters discussing how the basic building blocks discussed in part 2 are translated to PDF syntax by iText. We've worked through a lot of theory, but we've also dealt with practical issues.

You've learned how to construct and paint paths, and you've used this functionality to add custom borders, lines, and shapes to a `PdfPTable`. You can now create your own Type 3 font—maybe one that contains a character that corresponds with the iText eye. You've also learned about the coordinate system and `PdfTemplate`, and you created an `Image` object based on a file containing vector graphics.

In the next chapter, we'll continue discussing the graphics state. We'll talk about color and colorspaces. We'll also deal with text state so that we can add street names to the map of Foobar.

# 11 Adding color and text

**This chapter covers**

- PDF and Color spaces
- Transparency and clipping
- PDF's text state

We already dealt with a great deal of the theory described in chapter 4 of the PDF Reference ("Graphics"). We'll continue by discussing colors and colorspaces. Each object in PDF can be in 11 different colorspaces, but you don't have to worry about that; iText provides color classes that hide the complex theory.

While we're talking about color, we'll also discuss rendering (chapter 6 of the PDF Reference) and transparency (chapter 7). You'll also learn how to apply masks to an image.

We'll complete this chapter by explaining how text state is implemented in iText. This will let you add street names to the map of Foobar.

## 11.1 Adding color to PDF files

You've worked with colors in previous examples, mostly using the class `java.awt.Color`. If you look at the class diagram in appendix A, section A.8, you see that iText extends this class. There's an abstract class `ExtendedColor` and lots of subclasses. You can pass any of these subclasses as a color property of iText's basic building blocks. To change the color of the direct content, you can use one of the `setColorFill()` and `setColorStroke()` methods.

The Java class `Color` defines an RGB color. When we talked about PDF/X, we said RGB colors aren't allowed; you should use the class `CMYKColor` instead. In the previous chapter, you used the `GrayColor` class to define a fill or a stroke color. These three classes correspond with the colorspace families that are referred to as the *DeviceRGB*, *DeviceCMYK*, and *DeviceGray* colorspaces.

### 11.1.1 Device colorspaces

A *colorspace* is an abstract mathematical model describing the way colors can be represented a sequence of numbers. Gray color is expressed as the intensity of achromatic light, on a scale from black to white:

```
/* chapter11/DeviceColor.java */
PdfContentByte cb = writer.getDirectContent();
cb.setColorFill(new GrayColor(0.5f));     <-❶
cb.rectangle(252, 770, 36, 36);
cb.fillStroke();
cb.setColorFill(new GrayColor(255));    <-❷
cb.rectangle(470, 770, 36, 36);
cb.fillStroke();
cb.setGrayFill(0.75f);    <-❸
cb.rectangle(360, 716, 36, 36);
cb.fillStroke();
```

The intensity can be expressed as a `float` between 0 and 1 ❶ or as an `int` between 0 and 255 ❷. These values can be used as parameters to construct an instance of the `GrayColor` class. The parameter of the methods `setGrayFill()` ❸ and `setGrayStroke()` has to be a `float`.

For RGB, values for red, green, and blue are defined. RGB is an *additive* color model: Red, green, and blue light is used to produce the other colors (for instance, the colors on your TV are composed of red, green, and blue dots). RGB is typically used for graphics that need to be rendered on a screen. Here's an example:

```
/* chapter11/DeviceColor.java */
cb.setColorFill(new Color(0x00, 0xFF, 0x00));       <-❶
cb.rectangle(144, 662, 36, 36);
cb.fillStroke();
cb.setColorFill(new Color(1f, 1f, 0));      <-❷
cb.rectangle(360, 662, 36, 36);
cb.fillStroke();
cb.setRGBColorFill(0x00, 0xFF, 0xFF);      <-❸
cb.rectangle(198, 608, 36, 36);
cb.fillStroke();
cb.setRGBColorFillF(1f, 0f, 1f);     <-❹
cb.rectangle(306, 608, 36, 36);
cb.fillStroke();
```

The `java.awt.Color` class can be constructed using `int` (0–255) ❶ or `float` (0–1) ❷ values for the red, green, and blue values. In `PdfContentByte`, you can also use `setRGBColorFill()` (`setRGBColorStroke()`) if you define the color as a series of `int` values ❸, or `setRGBColorFillF()` (`setRGBColorStrokeF()`) if you use `float` values ❹.

You may recognize cyan, magenta, and yellow, the CMY in CMYK, as the colors in the cartridge of an ink-jet printer. The K (key) corresponds with black. CMYK is a *subtractive* color model. If you look at a yellow object using white light, the object appears yellow because it reflects and absorbs some of the wavelengths that make up the white light. A yellow object absorbs blue and reflects red and green. In comparison with RGB, you have white (#FFFFFF) minus blue (#0000FF) equals yellow (#FFFF00). CMYK is typically used for graphics that need to be printed. Here's an example:

```
/* chapter11/DeviceColor.java */
cb.setColorFill(new CMYKColor(0x00, 0x00, 0xFF, 0x00));     <-❶
cb.rectangle(90, 554, 36, 36);
cb.fillStroke();
cb.setColorFill(new CMYKColor(1f, 0f, 0f, 0.5f));     <-❷
cb.rectangle(360, 554, 36, 36);
cb.fillStroke();
cb.setCMYKColorFill(0x00, 0xFF, 0xFF, 0x0F);     <-❸
```

```
cb.rectangle(144, 500, 36, 36);
cb.fillStroke();
cb.setCMYKColorFillF(0f, 0f, 0f, 1f);     <-4
cb.rectangle(416, 500, 36, 36);
cb.fillStroke();
```

The `CMYKColor` class extends iText's `ExtendedColor` class and can be constructed using `int` (0–255) ❶ or `float` (0–1) ❷ values for cyan, magenta, yellow, and black. Just as with RGB, there's also `setCMYKColorFill()` (`setCMYKColorStroke()`) ❸ or `setCMYKColorFillF()` (`setCMYKColorStrokeF()`) ❹.

This was the simple part. Now, let's look at the other classes that extend `ExtendedColor`.

### 11.1.2 Separation colorspaces

I referred to ink in the printer on your desk when I talked about CMYK colors, but not all printing devices use (only) these colors. Some device can apply special colors, often called *spot colors*, to produce effects that can't be achieved with CMYK—for instance, metallic colors, fluorescent colors, and special textures.

A spot color is any color generated by an ink (pure or mixed) that is printed in a single run. The PDF Reference says the following:

> When printing a page, most devices produce a single *composite* page on which all process colorants (and spot colors, if any) are combined. However, some devices such as imagesetters, produce a separate, monochromatic rendition of the page, called a *separation*, for each colorant. When the separations are later combined—on a printing press, for example—and the proper inks or other colorants are applied to them, the result is a full-color page.

Using the separation colorspace allows you to specify the use of additional colors or to isolate the control of individual color components. The current color is a single-component value, called a *tint* (defined in iText by a `float` in the range from 0 to 1). There are two spot color classes in iText: `PdfSpotColor` is the actual class, and `SpotColor` is a wrapper class, a subclass of `java.awt.Color`. Use the first class if you need to define a spot color for the direct content and the latter if you need a spot color in a high-level object.

The dominant spot-color printing system in the United States is Pantone. Pantone Inc. is a New Jersey company, and the company's list of color numbers and values is its intellectual property. Free use of the list isn't allowed; but if you buy a house style and the colors include Pantones, you can replace the name `iTextSpotColorX` in the following example with the name of your Pantone color, as well as the corresponding color value:

```
/* chapter11/SeparationColor.java */
PdfSpotColor psc_g = new PdfSpotColor(
  "iTextSpotColorGray", 0.5f, new GrayColor(0.9f));
PdfSpotColor psc_rgb = new PdfSpotColor(
  "iTextSpotColorRGB", 0.9f, new Color(0x64, 0x95, 0xed));
PdfSpotColor psc_cmyk = new PdfSpotColor(
  "iTextSpotColorCMYK", 0.25f, new CMYKColor(0.3f, .9f, .3f, .1f));
SpotColor sc_g = new SpotColor(psc_g);
SpotColor sc_rgb1 = new SpotColor(psc_rgb, 0.1f);
SpotColor sc_cmyk = new SpotColor(psc_cmyk);
cb.setColorFill(sc_g);
cb.rectangle(36, 770, 36, 36);
cb.fillStroke();
cb.setColorFill(psc_g, psc_g.getTint());
cb.rectangle(90, 770, 36, 36);
cb.fillStroke();
cb.setColorFill(sc_rgb1);
cb.rectangle(36, 716, 36, 36);
cb.fillStroke();
cb.setColorFill(psc_rgb, 0.1f);
cb.rectangle(36, 662, 36, 36);
cb.fillStroke();
cb.setColorFill(psc_cmyk, psc_cmyk.getTint());
cb.rectangle(90, 608, 36, 36);
cb.fillStroke();
```

The next type of color isn't really a color in the strict sense of the word. In the PDF Reference, it's listed with the special colorspaces.

### 11.1.3 Painting patterns

When stroking or filling a path, you always used a single color, but it's also possible to apply paint that consists of repeating graphical figures or a smoothly varying color gradient. In this case, we're talking about a *pattern*. There are two kinds of patterns: *tiled* (a repeating figure) and *shading* (a smooth gradient).

#### Tiling patterns

To use a pattern as fill or stroke color, you must create a *pattern cell*. This cell is repeated at fixed horizontal and vertical intervals when you fill a path (the area is tiled). See figure 11.1 for some examples of tiled patterns.

We distinguish two kinds of tiling patterns: *colored tiling patterns* and *uncolored tiling patterns*. A colored tiling pattern's color is self-contained. A `PdfPatternPainter` object is created with the `PdfContentByte` method `createPattern()`. You define the width and the height of the pattern cell. Optionally, you can also define an X and Y step: the desired horizontal and vertical spacing between pattern cells.

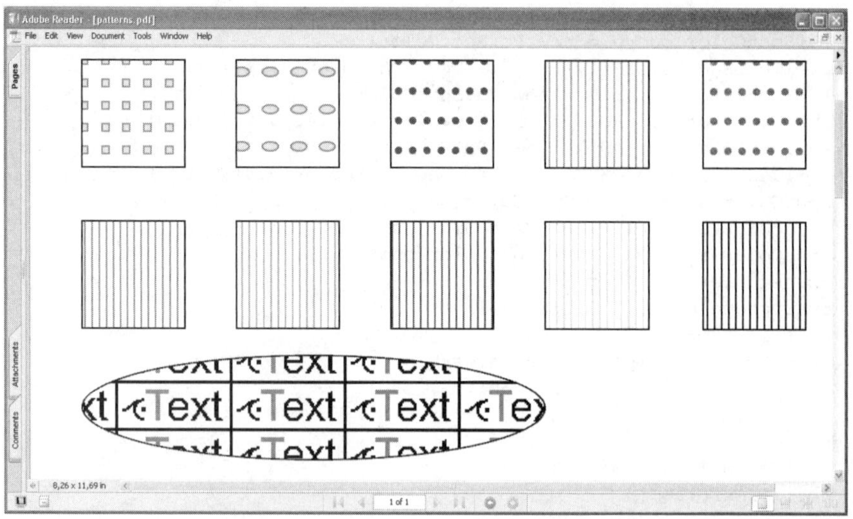

**Figure 11.1 Tiled patterns**

In the course of painting the pattern cell, the pattern's content stream explicitly sets the color of each graphical element it paints. A pattern cell can contain elements that are painted in different colors.

```
/* chapter11/Patterns.java */
PdfPatternPainter square = cb.createPattern(15, 15);
square.setColorFill(new Color(0xFF, 0xFF, 0x00));
square.setColorStroke(new Color(0xFF, 0x00, 0x00));
square.rectangle(5, 5, 5, 5);
square.fillStroke();
PdfPatternPainter ellipse = cb.createPattern(15, 10, 20, 25);
ellipse.setColorFill(new Color(0xFF, 0xFF, 0x00));
ellipse.setColorStroke(new Color(0xFF, 0x00, 0x00));
ellipse.ellipse(2f, 2f, 13f, 8f);
ellipse.fillStroke();
```

An uncolored tiling pattern is a pattern that has no inherent color: The color must be specified separately whenever the pattern is used. The content stream describes a *stencil* through which the color is poured.

You can create a `PdfPatternPainter` for an uncolored tiling pattern with the same methods you used to create a colored pattern, but with an extra parameter: the color that has to be applied to the stencil. You can pass `null` as color value; in that case, you'll have to define the color each time you use the pattern.

```
/* chapter11/Patterns.java */
PdfPatternPainter circle =
  cb.createPattern(15, 15, 10, 20, Color.blue);
circle.circle(7.5f, 7.5f, 2.5f);
circle.fill();
PdfPatternPainter line = cb.createPattern(5, 10, null);
line.setLineWidth(1);
line.moveTo(3, -1);
line.lineTo(3, 11);
line.stroke();
```

With these `PdfPatternPainter` objects, you can create `PatternColor` objects that can be used in iText's building blocks or as parameter for the methods `setColor-Fill()` and `setColorStroke()`:

```
/* chapter11/Patterns.java */
PatternColor squares = new PatternColor(square);
PatternColor ellipses = new PatternColor(ellipse);
PatternColor circles = new PatternColor(circle);
PatternColor lines = new PatternColor(line);
```

You defined the fill color of the squares and the ellipse in figure 11.1 in different ways:

```
/* chapter11/Patterns.java */
cb.setColorFill(squares);                  <-┐
cb.rectangle(36, 716, 72, 72);               │
cb.fillStroke();                             │
cb.setColorFill(ellipses);                 <-┤
cb.rectangle(144, 716, 72, 72);              │ As fill color
cb.fillStroke();                             │
cb.setColorFill(circles);                  <-┤
cb.rectangle(252, 716, 72, 72);              │
cb.fillStroke();                             │
cb.setColorFill(lines);                    <-┘
cb.rectangle(360, 716, 72, 72);
cb.fillStroke();
cb.setPatternFill(circle, Color.red);      <-┐
cb.rectangle(470, 716, 72, 72);              │
cb.fillStroke();                             │
cb.setPatternFill(line, Color.blue);       <-┤ Using setPatternFill()
cb.rectangle(252, 608, 72, 72);              │
cb.fillStroke();                             │
cb.setPatternFill(img_pattern);            <-┘
cb.ellipse(36, 520, 360, 590);
cb.fillStroke();
```

Notice that we forgot to specify a color for the uncolored tiling pattern `line`: We passed a `null` value to the `createPattern()` method. The square with the lines in the first row looks OK, but you can't count on that. You should always define a color for uncolored tiling patterns as is done for the squares in the second row of figure 11.1. For colored tiling patterns, adding a color will throw an exception.

Observe that the `img_pattern` looks kind of special because you use a GIF file in the pattern cell. In reality, there's nothing special about it. As you can see in the class diagram in appendix A, section A.8, the class `PdfPatternPainter` extends `PdfTemplate`, and you've been using standard operators and operands of the graphics state.

The other pattern type is more complex. I won't go into much detail about it; we'll just look at some examples that will help you get the idea. For more information, please consult the PDF Reference.

### *Shading patterns*

First you need to know something about shading. Shading patterns provide a smooth transition between colors across an area to be painted. The PDF Reference lists seven types of shading. iText provides convenience methods for two types: *axial shadings* and *radial shadings*. These two shadings are demonstrated in figure 11.2. (Try the example if you want to see the PDF in full color.)

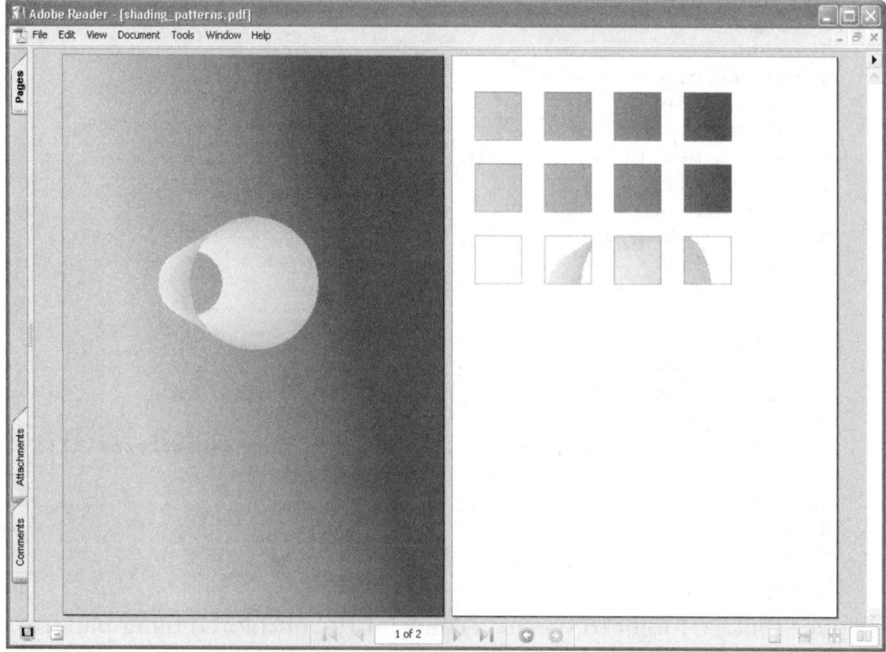


**Figure 11.2 Axial and radial shading**

The background color of the first page in figure 11.2 changes from orange (lower-left corner) to blue (upper-right corner). This is an axial shading; axial shadings (type 2 in the PDF Reference) define a color blend that varies along a linear axis between two endpoints and extends indefinitely perpendicular to that axis. In the iText object `PdfShading`, a static method `simpleAxial()` allows you to pass the start and end coordinates of the axis, as well as a start and end color:

```
/* chapter11/ShadingPatterns.java */
PdfShading axial = PdfShading.simpleAxial(writer,
  36, 716, 396, 788, Color.orange, Color.blue);
cb.paintShading(axial);
```

This code snippet defines that the color at coordinate (36, 716) should be orange; the color at coordinate (396, 788) should be blue. The color of the lines perpendicular to the axis connecting these two points varies between these two colors. With the method `paintShading()`, you fill the page (or, as you'll see later, the current *clipping path*) with this shading; see the background of figure 11.3.

Radial shadings (type 3 in the PDF Reference) define a color blend that varies between two circles; see the shape in the middle of the first page in figure 11.2. You define these circles in the static method `PdfShading.simpleRadial()`:

```
/* chapter11/ShadingPatterns.java */
PdfShading radial = PdfShading.simpleRadial(writer,
  200, 500, 50, 300, 500, 100,
  new Color(255, 247, 148), new Color(247, 138, 107),
  false, false);
cb.paintShading(axial);
```

If you pass two extra `boolean` values with these methods, you can define whether the shading has to be extended at the start and/or the ending. You could define axial shading like this:

```
PdfShading axial = PdfShading.simpleAxial(writer,
  36, 716, 396, 788, Color.orange, Color.blue, false, false);
```

In this case, only the strip with the varying color would be painted. In figure 11.12, the complete page is painted—the part beyond the starting point in orange, the part beyond the ending in blue.

**NOTE** As I already mentioned, the PDF Reference includes five more types of shadings. If you want to use the other types, you need to combine one or more of the static `type` functions of class `PdfFunction`. Please consult the PDF Reference to learn which type of function you need, and inspect the iText source code for inspiration (look at how the methods `simpleAxial()` and `simpleRadial()` work).

Now that you have a `PdfShading` object, you can create a `PdfShadingPattern` object and (if you need it as a color for a basic building block) a `ShadingColor`. This code snippet generates the rectangles on the second page in figure 11.2:

```
/* chapter11/ShadingPatterns.java */
PdfShadingPattern axialPattern = new PdfShadingPattern(axial);
cb.setShadingFill(axialPattern);
cb.rectangle(36, 716, 72, 72);
cb.fillStroke();
ShadingColor axialColor = new ShadingColor(axialPattern);
cb.setColorFill(axialColor);
cb.rectangle(144, 608, 72, 72);
cb.fillStroke();
PdfShadingPattern radialPattern = new PdfShadingPattern(radial);
ShadingColor radialColor = new ShadingColor(radialPattern);
cb.setColorFill(radialColor);
cb.rectangle(252, 500, 72, 72);
cb.fillStroke();
```

To conclude the overview of colors supported in iText, let's use these colors in an example with colored paragraphs.

### 11.1.4 Using color with basic building blocks

Using `Color`, `CMYKColor` or `GrayColor` is easy; you can define these colors with only one class. With `SpotColor`, `PatternColor`, and `ShadingColor`, more classes are needed. You created `PdfSpotColor`, `PdfPatternPainter`, and `PdfShadingPattern` objects when you added direct content, but you need subclasses of `ExtendedColor` if you want to use color in basic building blocks.

Figure 11.3 shows paragraphs created using these special colors. The first paragraph is painted in a spot color. If you look closely, you'll recognize the fox

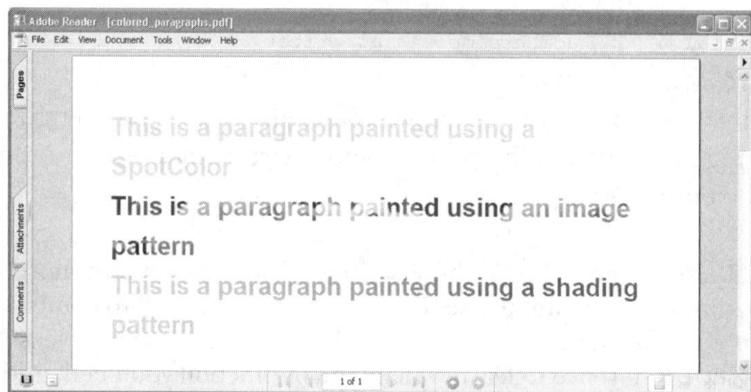


**Figure 11.3 Paragraphs painted with a spot color, a pattern color, and a shading color**

and the dog image in the second paragraph. In the third paragraph, the color varies from orange to blue using the axial shading displayed in figure 11.2.

Compose the color as you did in the previous sections, and construct a `font` object with this color:

```
/* chapter11/ColoredParagraphs.java */
PdfShading axial = PdfShading.simpleAxial(writer, 36, 716, 396, 788,
  Color.orange, Color.blue);
PdfShadingPattern axialPattern = new PdfShadingPattern(axial);
ShadingColor axialColor = new ShadingColor(axialPattern);
document.add(new Paragraph(
  "This is a paragraph painted using a shading pattern",
  new Font(Font.HELVETICA, 24, Font.BOLD, axialColor)));
```

I'm sure you can think of many other examples where it's useful to combine one of these special colors with basic building blocks. You can, for instance, use an image pattern to paint a cell; that way, you have a cell with a tiled image as a background.

Before we move on, look again at figure 11.2. You filled the first page with axial shading and then added radial shading. The radial shading overlaps the axial shading, covering part of it. At first sight, this seems normal; but if you look at table 3.1, you see that PDF-1.4 introduced a new concept into the PDF specification: transparency.

With the introduction of the *transparent imaging model*, overlapping content doesn't necessarily cover the content below it ("cover" in the sense of making it disappear). In the next section, you'll add one shape over the other and learn how to blend the colors of the different shapes so that all the layers contribute to what is shown on a page.

## 11.2 The transparent imaging model

If you think of the graphical objects on a page like a stack similar to the canvases we talked about in the previous chapter (but more fine-grained), the color at each point on the page is that of the topmost object by default. You can change this such that the color at each point is composed using a combination of the color of the object with the colors below the topmost object (the *backdrop*), following the compositing rules defined by the transparency model.

These rules involve variables such as the *blend mode*, *shape*, and *opacity*. The blend mode determines how the colors interact; both shape and opacity vary from 0 (no contribution) to 1 (maximum contribution). Shape and opacity can usually be combined into a single value, called *alpha*, which controls both the color compositing computation and the fading between an object and its backdrop.

Again, I won't go deeper into the theory, but I'll explain some concepts using examples. You'll learn about transparent groups, isolation and knockout, and soft masks for images.

### 11.2.1 Transparency groups

One or more consecutive objects in a stack can be collected into a *transparency group*. The group as a whole can have properties that modify the compositing behavior of objects within the group and their interactions with its backdrop.

Figure 11.4 shows four identical paths. The background (referred to as the *backdrop*) is a square that is half gray, half white. Inside the square, three circles are painted. The first one is red, the second is blue, and the third is yellow. Each version of the paths shown in figure 11.4 is filled using a different transparency model.

Figure 11.4 is a reconstruction of plate 16 in the PDF Reference. The figure is explained like this (PDF Reference, section 7.1):

> In the upper two figures, three colored circles are painted as independent objects with no grouping. At the upper left, the three objects are painted opaquely (opacity = 1.0); each object completely replaces its backdrop (including previously painted objects) with its own color. At the upper right, the same three independent objects are painted with an opacity of 0.5 causing them to composite with each other and with the gray and white backdrop.

The upper-left square and circles show the default behavior; the examples include two methods, one that draws the backdrop and another that draws the circles:

```
/* chapter11/Transparency1.java */
pictureBackdrop(gap, 500, cb);
pictureCircles(gap, 500, cb);
```

You repeat these two lines four times, but in between you change the graphics state. This is one of the examples for which you need the `PdfGState` object. Before painting the circles of the upper-right square, set the opacity to 0.5 like this:

```
/* chapter11/Transparency1.java */
PdfGState gs1 = new PdfGState();
gs1.setFillOpacity(0.5f);
cb.setGState(gs1);
```

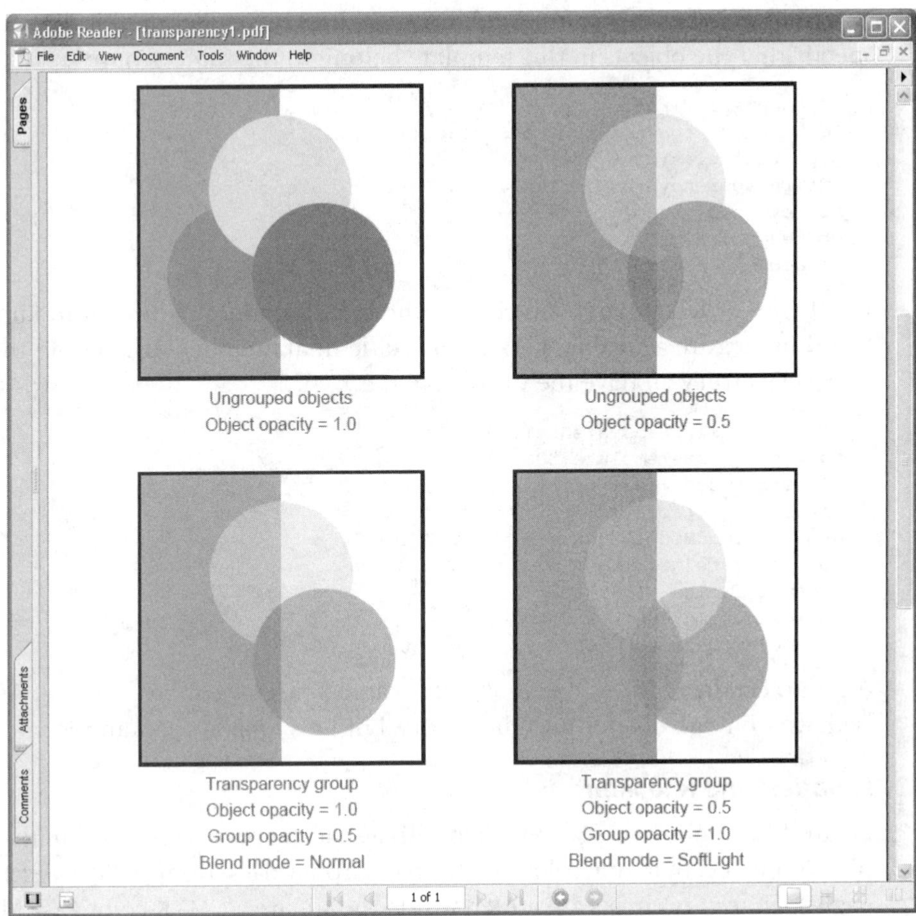


**Figure 11.4 Transparency groups**

The PDF Reference continues:

> In the two lower figures, the three objects are combined as a transparency group. At the lower left, the individual objects have an opacity of 1.0 within the group, but the group as a whole is painted in the *Normal* blend mode with an opacity of 0.5. The objects thus completely overwrite each other within the group, but the resulting group then composites transparently with the gray and white backdrop. At the lower right, the objects have an opacity of 0.5 within the group and thus composite with each other. The group as a whole is painted against the backdrop with an opacity of 1.0 but in a different blend mode (*HardLight*), producing a different visual effect.

To group objects, you create a `PdfTemplate`, draw the circles on this template, and specify that the objects in this template belong to the same group:

```
/* chapter11/Transparency1.java */
PdfTemplate tp = cb.createTemplate(200, 200);
pictureCircles(0, 0, tp);
PdfTransparencyGroup group = new PdfTransparencyGroup();
tp.setGroup(group);
cb.setGState(gs1);
cb.addTemplate(tp, gap, 500 - 200 - gap);
```

For the lower-left square, you change the blend mode. If you want to know what blend modes are available, look at the static final member variables in the `PdfGState` class (they all have the prefix `BM`):

```
/* chapter11/Transparency1.java */
tp = cb.createTemplate(200, 200);
PdfGState gs2 = new PdfGState();
gs2.setFillOpacity(0.5f);
gs2.setBlendMode(PdfGState.BM_SOFTLIGHT);
tp.setGState(gs2);
pictureCircles(0, 0, tp);
tp.setGroup(group);
cb.addTemplate(tp, 200 + 2 * gap, 500 - 200 - gap);
```

A group can be *isolated* or *nonisolated*; it can be *knockout* or *nonknockout*. As promised, we won't go deeper into the theory, but let's look at an example.

### 11.2.2 Isolation and knockout

Figure 11.5 shows four squares filled with a shading pattern. If you run this example, you'll see that the color of the backdrop varies from yellow (left) to red (right). Four gray circles are added inside the squares (CMYK color C = M = Y = 0 and K = 0.15; opacity = 1.0; blend mode Multiply).

The code to draw the four squares and their circles is almost identical (similar to what you did in the previous example); the only difference is the isolation and knockout mode:

```
/* chapter11/Transparency2.java */
tp = cb.createTemplate(200, 200);
pictureCircles(0, 0, tp);
group = new PdfTransparencyGroup();
group.setIsolated(true);
group.setKnockout(true);
tp.setGroup(group);
```

For the two upper squares, the group with the circles is *isolated* (it doesn't interact with the backdrop); for the two lower squares, the group is nonisolated (the

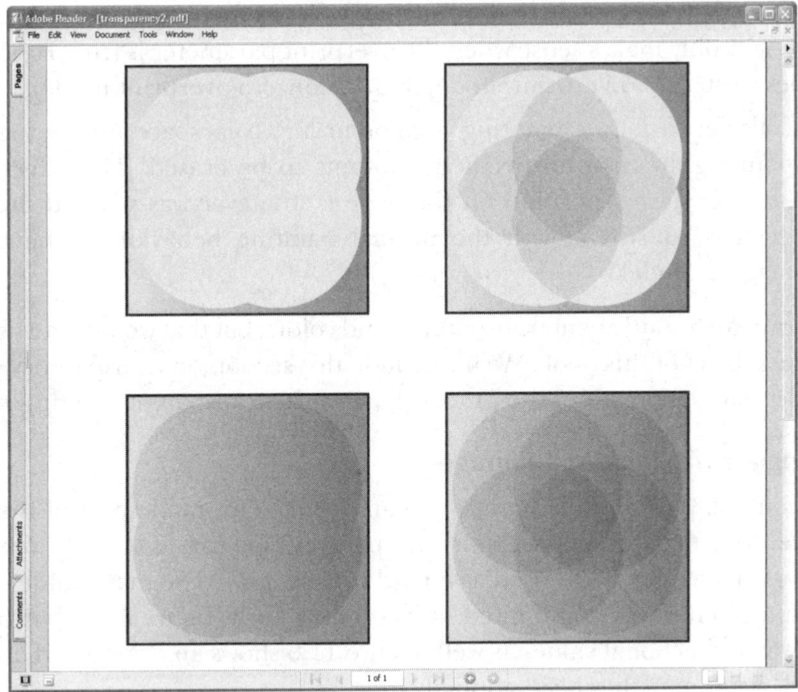


**Figure 11.5 Examples of isolation and knockout**

group composites with the backdrop). For the two squares to the left, *knockout* is set to `true` (they don't composite with each other); for the two to the right, it's set to `false` (they composite with each other).

The `PdfGState` object includes other methods to set the *overprint parameter* and *overprint mode*, such as `setOverPrintStroking()` (for stroking operations), `setOverPrintNonStroking()` (for other painting operations) and `setOverprintMode()`. Note that not all devices support overprinting. Let me summarize some of the definitions listed in section 4.5.6 of the PDF Reference:

The overprint parameter is "a boolean flag that determines how painting operations affect colorants other than those explicitly or implicitly specified by the current colorspace":

- If it's set to true and the output device supports overprinting, "anything previously painted in other colorants is left undisturbed. Consequently, the color at a given position may be a combined result of several painting operations in different colorants." In a deviceCMK colorspace, this combined result depends on the overprint mode. Note that method `setOverprint-Mode()` only makes sense when the overprint parameter is true. Possible values are 0 (zero overprint mode) and 1 (nonzero overprint mode).

- If it's set to false, "painting a color in any colorspace causes the corresponding areas of unspecified colorants to be erased. The effect is that the color at any position on the page is whatever was painted there last, which is consistent with the normal painting behavior of the Opaque Imaging Model."

A lot more can be said about transparency and colors, but that would lead us too far from the subject of this book. We'll conclude this section on transparency with an example that demonstrates the practical use of the transparent imaging model.

### 11.2.3 Applying a soft mask to an image

In section 5.2.3, you applied a mask to an image. This made part of the image invisible. Now that you know about transparency, you can also apply a *soft mask*. The mask in chapter 5 was used as a hard *clipping path*. The mask value of a soft mask at a given point isn't limited to just 0 or 1 (as in figure 5.11) but can take intermediate fractional values as well. Figure 11.6 shows an example of an image to which a soft mask has been applied.

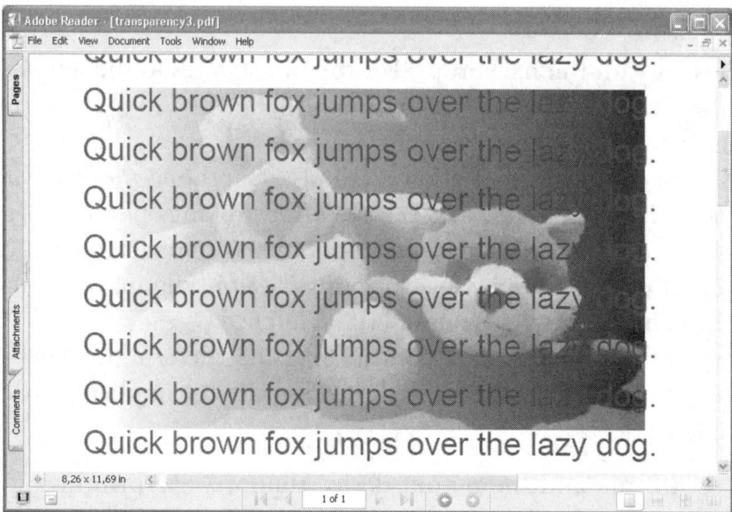


**Figure 11.6 Images and transparency: using a soft mask**

The source code of this example is similar to the source code from chapter 5:

```
/* chapter11/Transparency3.java */
Image img =
  Image.getInstance("../../chapter05/resources/foxdog.jpg");
img.setAbsolutePosition(50, 550);
byte gradient[] = new byte[256];
for (int k = 0; k < 256; ++k)
  gradient[k] = (byte)k;
Image smask = Image.getInstance(256, 1, 1, 8, gradient);
smask.makeMask();
img.setImageMask(smask);
writer.getDirectContent().addImage(img);
```

You use `getDirectContent().addImage()` instead of `document.add()`, to make sure the image is added on top of the text instead of to the graphics layer below the text layer.

Another difference from the earlier example is the way you define the mask. I referred to the example with the mask shown in figure 5.11 as an example of using a hard clipping path. You defined this clipping path using an image, but it would be interesting if you could use a clipping path defined using path construction operators and operands. Let's try an example with a PDF that is similar to the one in figure 5.10, but that looks a lot better.

## 11.3 Clipping content

A question that pops up on the iText mailing list now and then concerns how to cut an image in pieces—for instance, to spread it over different pages. You can do this several ways. One way is to add the `Image` to different `PdfTemplate` objects with a smaller size. Figure 11.7 shows the result of doing this to cut the foxdog.jpg from chapter 5 into four pieces.

You should already know how this is done; to refresh your memory, here's a short code snippet:

```
/* chapter11/TemplateClip.java */
Image img =
  Image.getInstance("../../chapter05/resources/foxdog.jpg");
float w = img.scaledWidth();
float h = img.scaledHeight();
PdfContentByte cb = writer.getDirectContent();
PdfTemplate t1 = cb.createTemplate(w / 2, h / 2);
t1.addImage(img, w, 0, 0, h, 0, - h / 2);
cb.addTemplate(t1, 36, PageSize.A4.height() - 36 - h / 2);
```

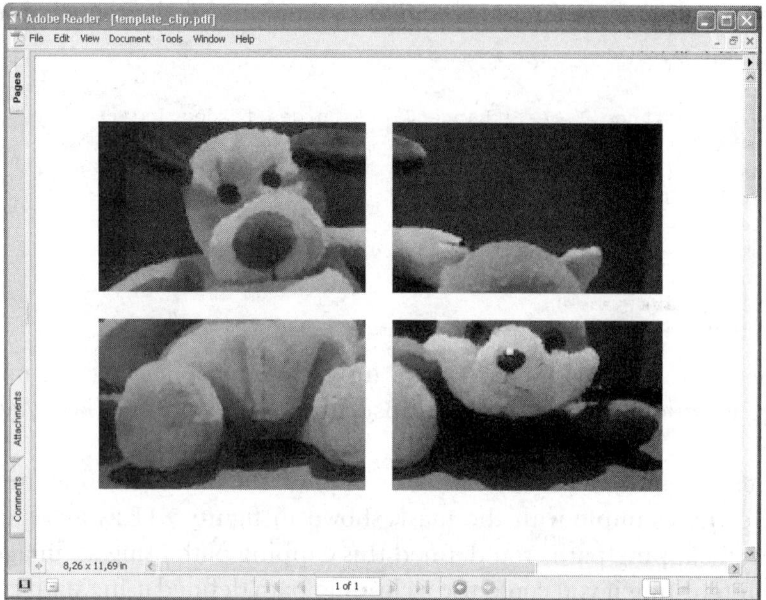


**Figure 11.7 Clipped image using `PdfTemplate`**

What happens with the image in the template is valid for all the objects you add to the direct content. If you add objects that are outside the boundaries of a `PdfTemplate` or a page, these objects are in the PDF, but you won't necessarily see them in Adobe Reader.

This is one way to clip an image (or any other type of content), but a `PdfTemplate` is always rectangular. Suppose you want to define a hard clipping path that has the form of a circle, a rectangle with rounded borders, or even a star, as in figure 11.8.

You achieve this result by constructing a path as you did in the previous chapter and define it as a clipping path. You don't want to fill or stroke this path, so don't forget to call `newPath()` after `clip()`:

```
/* chapter11/ClippingPath.java */
cb.saveState();
cb.circle(260, 700, 70);
cb.clip();
cb.newPath();
cb.addImage(img, w, 0, 0, h, 36, 620);
cb.restoreState();
```

**Figure 11.8 Hard clipping paths in different shapes**

In other words, you change the graphics state so that the canvas is limited to a circle with a radius of 70 user units. If you add an image to the direct content afterward, only the part that is inside the clipping path (the head of the fox in figure 11.8) is visible. The math to make the clipping path and the corresponding content gets easier if you use `PdfTemplate`:

```
/* chapter11/ClippingPath.java */
PdfTemplate tp1 = cb.createTemplate(w, h);
img.setAbsolutePosition(0, 0);
tp1.roundRectangle(0, 0, w, h, 10);
tp1.clip();
tp1.newPath();
tp1.addImage(img);
cb.addTemplate(tp1, 36, 420);
```

In addition to the method `clip()`, there's also a method `eoClip()`. In figure 11.8, you recognize the stars from the previous chapter. The clipping path for the full star is defined using the nonzero winding number rule (`clip()`); the star with the missing body is defined using the even-odd rule (`eoClip()`).

Any graphical shape can be used as a clipping path, including text. You'll see how to do so in the next section, which deals with text state.

## 11.4 PDF's text state

The *text state* is a subset of the graphics state. A glyph is a graphical shape and is subject to all graphical manipulations, such as coordinate transformations, but PDF also includes some text-specific objects and operators. You encountered some of them in chapter 2 (see listing 2.2):

```
BT
36 806 Td
0 -18 Td
/F1 12 Tf
(Hello World)Tj
ET
```

The part between `BT` (begin text) and `ET` (end text) is responsible for putting the words *Hello World* on the page. A sequence of operators and operands inside the `BT` and `ET` operator is called a *text object*.

First we'll give you an overview of these text objects. Afterward, you'll learn about convenience methods that let you add text to the direct content in a more programmer-friendly way.

### 11.4.1 Text objects

*Text space* is the coordinate system in which text is shown. By default, the *text matrix* is the identity matrix (`a` = `c` = 1; `b` = `d` = `e` = `f` = 0), meaning text space and user space coincide. There are three types of text-specific operators:

- Text-positioning operators
- Text-showing operators
- Text-state operators

Text-showing operators update the text matrix (changing the value of `e` and `f`). Additionally, a text object keeps track of a *text-line matrix*, which captures the value of the text matrix at the beginning of a line of text. The text-positioning and text-showing operators read and set the text-line matrix. The *text-rendering matrix* is an intermediate result that combines the effects of text-state parameters, the text matrix, and the current transformation matrix.

### Text-positioning and text-showing operators

Table 11.1 is based on table 5.5 in the PDF Reference and shows which iText methods correspond with the different text-positioning operators in PDF.

**Table 11.1 PDF text-positioning operators and the corresponding iText methods**

| Operator | iText Method | Operands / parameters | Description |
|---|---|---|---|
| `Td` | `moveText` | `(tx, ty)` | Moves to the start of the next line, offset from the start of the current line by (`tx`, `ty`). |
| `TD` | `moveTextWithLeading` | `(tx, ty)` | The same as `Td`, but sets the leading to `-ty`. |
| `Tm` | `setTextMatrix` | `(e, f)`<br>`(a, b, c, d, e, f)` | Sets the text matrix and the text-line matrix. The parameters `a`, `b`, `c`, `d`, `e`, and `f` have the same meaning as described in section 10.4.1. |
| `T*` | `newlineText` | - | Moves to the start of the next line (depending on the leading). |

Notice that the concept of leading is also used when working with the direct content. The text state is aware of the start of a line and of the space between the lines.

Table 11.2 is based on table 5.6 in the PDF Reference.

**Table 11.2 PDF text-showing operators and the corresponding iText methods**

| Operator | iText Method | Operands / parameters | Description |
|---|---|---|---|
| `Tj` | `showText` | `(string)` | Shows a text string. |
| `'` | `newlineShowText` | `(string)` | Moves to the next line, and shows a text string. |
| `"` | `newlineShowText` | `(aw, ac, string)` | Moves to the next line, and shows a text string using `aw` as word spacing and `ac` as character spacing. |
| `TJ` | `showText` | `(array)` | Shows one or more text strings, allowing individual glyph positioning. |

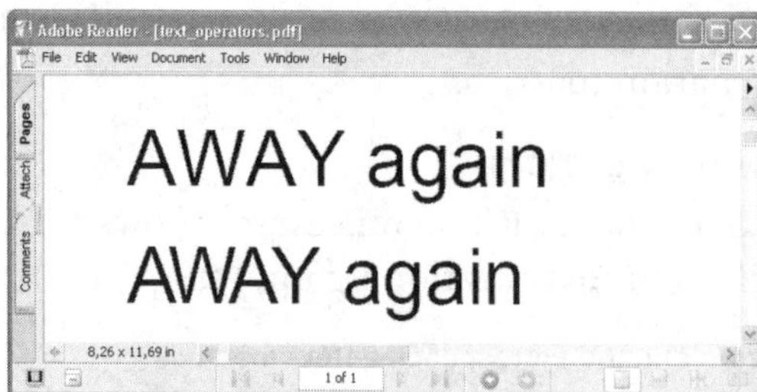

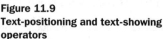

**Figure 11.9**
**Text-positioning and text-showing operators**

Let's use these operators in an example. The words *AWAY again* in figure 11.9 look much like what is shown in figure 5.11 of the PDF Reference.

Let's look at the source code that writes these words:

```
/* chapter11/TextOperators.java */
cb.beginText();
cb.moveText(36, 806);                    <-1
cb.setFontAndSize(bf, 24);
cb.moveTextWithLeading(0, -36);          <-2
cb.showText(text);                       <-3
cb.newlineText();                        <-4
PdfTextArray array = new PdfTextArray("A");  |
array.add(120);                              |
array.add("W");                              |
array.add(120);                              | 5
array.add("A");                              |
array.add(95);                               |
array.add("Y again");                        |
cb.showText(array);                      <-6
cb.endText();
```

In this example, you do the following:

1. Move to the top of the page.
2. Move down 36 points (setting the leading).
3. Show the text.
4. Move down 36 units.
5. Create a PDF text array.
6. Show the text array.

You add the words *AWAY again* twice: once using the character advance as described in the font program (see chapter 9), and a second time specifying some extra glyph-positioning information (in thousandths of a unit). The amount is subtracted from the current horizontal or vertical coordinate, depending on the writing mode.

In the code snippet, you see one method that changes the text state: `setFontAndSize()`; in the next code sample, you'll see the other text-state operators in action.

### *Text-state operators*

Table 5.2 of the PDF Reference lists the text-state operators; table 11.3 lists the corresponding iText methods.

**Table 11.3 PDF text-state operators and the corresponding iText methods**

| Operator | iText Method | Operands / parameters | Description |
|---|---|---|---|
| `Tc` | `setCharacterSpacing` | `(charSpace)` | Sets the character spacing (initially 0). |
| `Tw` | `setWordSpacing` | `(wordSpace)` | Sets the word spacing (initially 0). |
| `Tz` | `setHorizontalScaling` | `(scale)` | Sets the horizontal scaling (initially 100). |
| `TL` | `setLeading` | `(leading)` | Sets the leading (initially 0). |
| `Tf` | `setFontAndSize` | `(font, size)` | Sets the text font (a `BaseFont` object) and size. |
| `Tr` | `setTextRenderingMode` | `(render)` | Specifies a rendering mode (a combination of stroking and/or filling). By default, glyphs are filled. |
| `Ts` | `setTextRise` | `(rise)` | Sets the text rise (initially 0). |
| `TK` | `PdfGState.setTextKnockout` | `(true \| false)` | Determines whether text elements are considered elementary objects for purposes of color compositing in the transparent imaging model. |

Let's look at what some of these operators do in a PDF file (see figure 11.10).

You've already added chunks using this functionality to a document in chapter 4, when we did some `Chunk` magic, but now you can see how iText does it internally:

```
/* chapter11/TextOperators.java */
cb.setWordSpacing(50);    <-❶
cb.newlineShowText(text);
```

```
cb.setCharacterSpacing(20);    ❷
cb.newlineShowText(text);
cb.setWordSpacing(0);
cb.setCharacterSpacing(0);
cb.setLeading(56);    ❸
cb.newlineShowText("Changing the leading: " + text);
cb.setLeading(36);
cb.setHorizontalScaling(50);    ❹
cb.newlineShowText(text);
cb.setHorizontalScaling(100);
cb.newlineShowText(text);
cb.setTextRise(15);             ❺
cb.setFontAndSize(bf, 12);
cb.setColorFill(Color.red);
cb.showText("2");
```

First, you change the word spacing ❶. As you can see, there is more space between the words *AWAY* and *again* than before. Then, you change the character spacing ❷; there's a lot more space between the letters. Do you remember the character/space ratio you set for table cells with justified content? The two methods we discussed are used by iText internally to justify a line of text. For the next line, you increase the leading: There's more space between the lines ❸. Next, you change the scaling to 50 percent ❹. In the last line, you add a red 2 after changing the fill color, the font size, and the text rise ❺.

In chapter 4, you learned how to change the way text is rendered. Figure 11.11 shows the rendering modes you already knew and adds examples of rendering modes that can be used for clipping.

The stroke color of the strings in figure 11.11 is black, and the fill color is red. In the left column, some extra lines are added, but they're clipped by the characters. Table 11.4 shows the rendering modes used. Every row in the table corresponds with a row in figure 11.11.

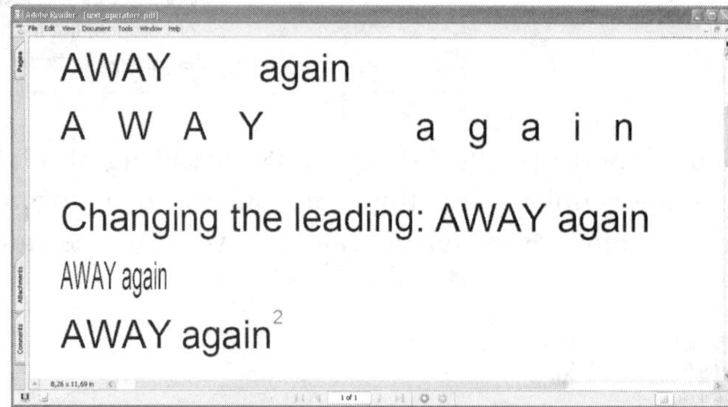


**Figure 11.10 Text-state operators**

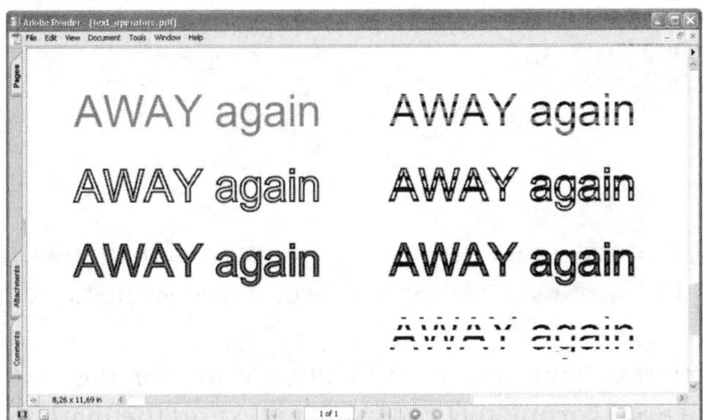


**Figure 11.11**
**Examples of rendering modes**

**Table 11.4 Rendering modes used in figure 11.11**

| | |
|---|---|
| PdfContentByte.<br>TEXT_RENDER_MODE_FILL | PdfContentByte.<br>TEXT_RENDER_MODE_FILL_CLIP |
| PdfContentByte.<br>TEXT_RENDER_MODE_STROKE | PdfContentByte.<br>TEXT_RENDER_MODE_STROKE_CLIP |
| PdfContentByte.<br>TEXT_RENDER_MODE_FILL_STROKE | PdfContentByte.<br>TEXT_RENDER_MODE_FILL_STROKE_CLIP |
| PdfContentByte.<br>TEXT_RENDER_MODE_INVISIBLE | PdfContentByte.<br>TEXT_RENDER_CLIP |

The code used to write the words in the first column looks like this:

```
/* chapter11/TextOperators.java */
PdfTemplate tp1 = cb.createTemplate(160, 36);
tp1.beginText();
tp1.setTextRenderingMode(PdfContentByte.TEXT_RENDER_MODE_FILL);
tp1.setFontAndSize(bf, 24);
tp1.moveText(6, -6);
tp1.showText(text);
tp1.endText();
cb.addTemplate(tp1, 36, 240);
```

The code for the words and lines in the second column looks like this:

```
/* chapter11/TextOperators.java */
PdfTemplate tp5 = cb.createTemplate(200, 36);
tp5.beginText();
tp5.setTextRenderingMode(PdfContentByte.TEXT_RENDER_MODE_FILL_CLIP);
tp5.setFontAndSize(bf, 24);
tp5.moveText(6, -6);
tp5.showText(text);
tp5.endText();
```

```
tp5.setLineWidth(2);
for (int i = 0; i < 6; i ++) {
  tp5.moveTo(0, i * 6 + 3);
  tp5.lineTo(200, i * 6 + 3);
}
tp5.stroke();
cb.addTemplate(tp5, 210, 240);
```

All the text-state operators (and the corresponding iText methods) in tables 11.1, 11.2, and 11.3 are useful—for instance, if you want to add text at an absolute position.

If you want to rotate text, you have to calculate a value for the text matrix, defining the transformation. Fortunately you can let iText do the math using one of its convenience methods.

### 11.4.2 Convenience methods to position and show text

To add text at an absolute position, you can set the text matrix like this:

```
/* chapter11/TextMethods.java */
cb.setTextMatrix(50, 700);
cb.showText(text);
```

The text—you're still working with the `String` "AWAY again"—is added starting from position (X = 50, Y = 700). Suppose you don't want to start the text at that coordinate, but you want to center the text at this position. In that case, you must calculate the *effective* width of the glyphs "AWAY again" and subtract half of it from the translation in the X direction. The effective width isn't necessarily the width you can retrieve with the `BaseFont` object (as you did in chapter 8). You may have to take into account the current text state (scaling, word spacing, and character spacing). You can get this effective width with the method `getEffectiveStringWidth()`. This method needs a `String` object, and you also have to say whether you plan to add the text with `showText()` (the method you encountered in table 11.2) or `showTextKerned()`.

You did some manual kerning when you wrote the word *AWAY* the second time as shown in figure 11.10. To kern characters, you reduce (or augment) the character spacing depending on the sequence of the glyphs. This can be done automatically if the font program contains kerning information (this is a value in thousandths of a user unit per character pair).

If you use `showTextKerned()` and the font allows kerning, iText transforms the `String` into a `PdfTextArray` before adding it. Figure 11.12 shows an unkerned version of the text *AWAY again Left* and a kerned version (see the lower-right corner of the screenshot).

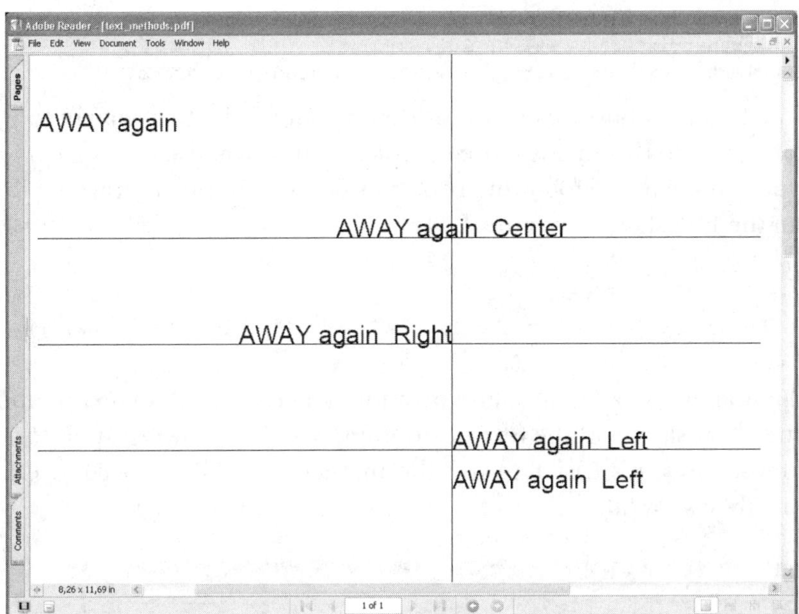


**Figure 11.12 Aligning text**

The text you added after changing the text matrix is in the upper-left corner. You also see some lines and text that is aligned relative to the intersections of these lines. Because you want to avoid doing the math and measuring the length of the `Strings`, you use the convenience method `showTextAligned()` (or `showTextAlignedKerned()`):

```
/* chapter11/TextMethods.java */
cb.showTextAligned(PdfContentByte.ALIGN_CENTER,
  text + " Center", 250, 650, 0);
cb.showTextAligned(PdfContentByte.ALIGN_RIGHT,
  text + " Right", 250, 600, 0);
cb.showTextAligned(PdfContentByte.ALIGN_LEFT,
  text + " Left", 250, 550, 0);
cb.showTextAlignedKerned(PdfContentByte.ALIGN_LEFT,
  text + " Left", 250, 532, 0);
```

First you define the alignment (`ALIGN_CENTER`, `ALIGN_RIGHT`, or `ALIGN_LEFT`), and then you pass the `String` you want to add, followed by the coordinate (the translation values `e` and `f`). With the final parameter, you define the angle.

To rotate text, you can change the text matrix like this:

```
/* chapter11/TextMethods.java */
cb.setTextMatrix(0, 1, -1, 0, 100, 200);
cb.showText("Text at position 100,200, rotated 90 degrees.");
```

Figure 11.13 shows how this text is added. Defining the text matrix to write the text that is next to this line is more complex, unless you use `showTextAligned()`.

As you can see in the following code snippet, it's simple to draw the flowerlike words in the PDF shown in figure 11.13:

```
/* chapter11/TextMethods.java */
for (int i = 0; i < 360; i += 30) {
  cb.showTextAligned(PdfContentByte.ALIGN_LEFT, text, 200, 300, i);
}
```

To add a line of text at an absolute position, you can use the iText methods that are a direct translation of the text-positioning and text-showing operators to PDF; but in most cases, it's easier to use the method `showTextAligned()`. Of course, there are always caveats.

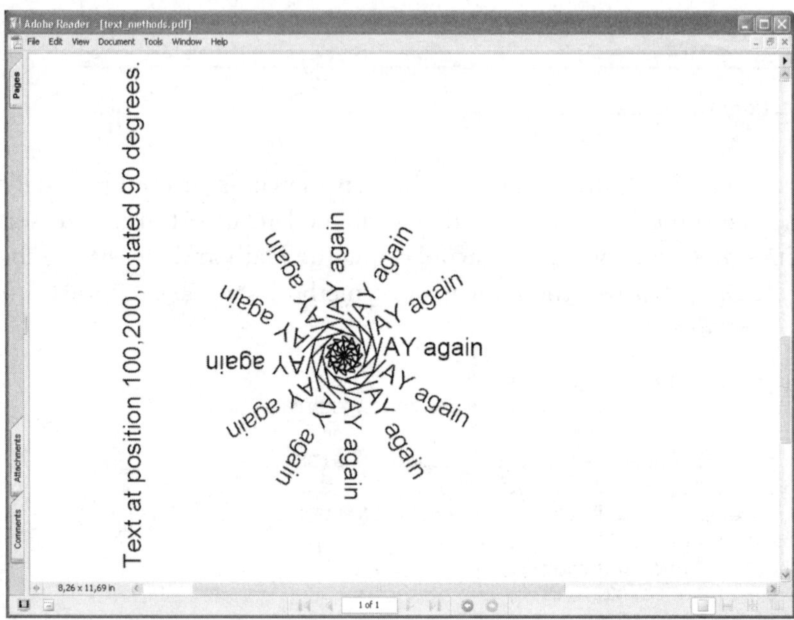


**Figure 11.13 Rotating text**

### *Caveats*

One of the most common newbie problems leads to specific error messages given by Adobe Reader: for instance, *Illegal Operation 'Td' outside text object* or *Illegal operation 're' inside text object*. These errors are caused by using a text operation outside a block that begins with `BT` (begin text) and ends with `ET` (end text), or by using a path construction operator inside such a text block.

When you use iText's basic building blocks, you won't encounter problems like this; iText takes care of everything. But when you write to the direct content, you're responsible for constructing the correct syntax. If you don't, no exception will be thrown at compile time (and not even at runtime), but the resulting PDF will be corrupt. If you forget to begin and/or end the text, iText can't throw an exception. In short, if you want to produce PDF with iText's low-level methods, you're responsible for writing code that makes sense.

You'll see some practical examples where you need to add text at absolute positions as soon as we discuss page events. For now, we've kept Laura waiting long; let's enhance the SVG parsing capabilities so that you can add street names to the map of Foobar.

## 11.5 The map of Foobar (part 2)

In the previous chapter, you drew a map (see figure 10.18) based on an SVG file (see figure 10.17); but at that point, you only knew how to construct and paint lines and shapes. Now that you've learned how to add text, you can insert the street names.

Laura has made you an additional SVG file with path definitions and text tags referring to these paths. For instance:

```
<defs>
  <path id="s08" d="M 4487 7033 L 4720 7788" />
</defs>
<text font-size="80">
  <textPath xlink:href="#s08">Paulo Soares Way</textPath>
</text>
```

In the `text` tag, you recognize the name of a street. There's also a `textPath` tag that refers to a path with coordinates. The text is drawn along this path, as you can see in figure 11.14.

You reuse the `FoobarSvgHandler` class from chapter 10 to draw the map to a `PdfTemplate`, but you write an extra `FoobarSvgTextHandler` to construct a `Map` with all the necessary parameters to write the text to the direct content at the correct positions:

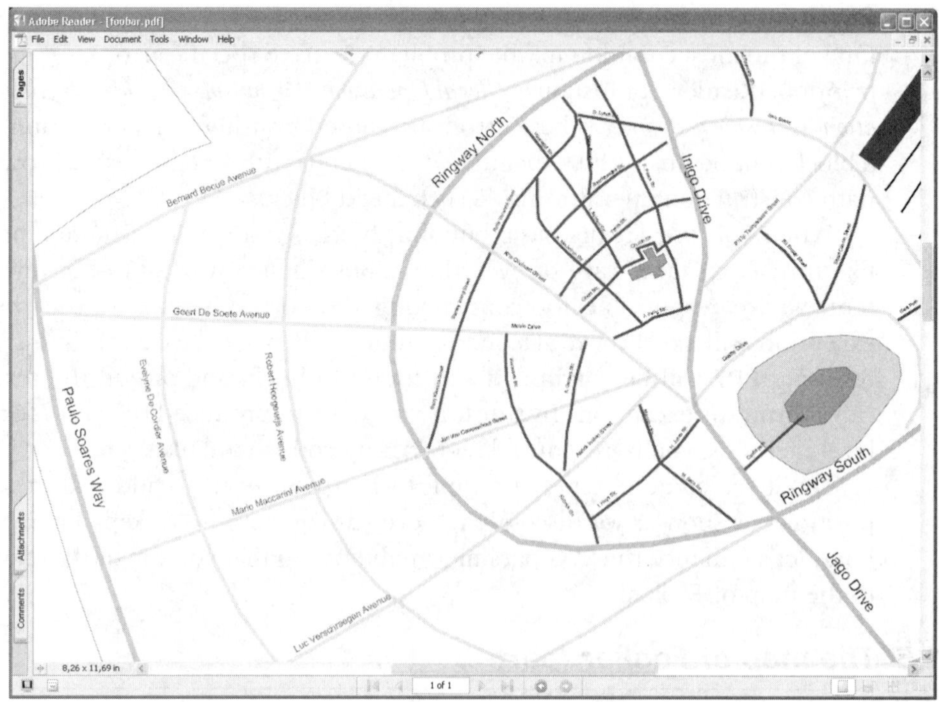


**Figure 11.14 The map of Foobar with street names**

```
/* chapter11/FoobarCityStreets.java */
FoobarSvgHandler handler =
  new FoobarSvgHandler(writer,
  new InputSource(new FileInputStream(
    "../../chapter10/resources/foobarcity.svg")));
PdfTemplate template = handler.getTemplate();
FoobarSvgTextHandler text =
  new FoobarSvgTextHandler(new InputSource(
    new FileInputStream("../resources/streets.svg")));
Map streets = text.getStreets();
FoobarSvgTextHandler.Street street;
BaseFont bf = BaseFont.createFont(
  BaseFont.HELVETICA, BaseFont.WINANSI, BaseFont.NOT_EMBEDDED);
template.beginText();
for (Iterator i = streets.keySet().iterator(); i.hasNext(); ) {
  street = (FoobarSvgTextHandler.Street) streets.get(i.next());
  template.setFontAndSize(bf, street.fontsize);
  template.showTextAligned(PdfTemplate.ALIGN_LEFT,
    street.name, street.x, street.y, street.alpha);
}
template.endText();
```

You can look at the `FoobarSvgTextHandler` code if you want to, but you'll immediately notice that a lot of SVG functionality is missing. You started writing an SVG parser against your better judgment, and that wasn't smart. It would have been better to first look for an existing library that can parse SVG. Apache Batik is such a library: It can write the content to a `Graphics2D` object. The only thing you have to find out is how to fit this library into iText, so that it writes SVG content to a PDF file. That's what we'll do in the next chapter.

## 11.6 Summary

In this chapter, we continued exploring PDF's graphics state. The previous chapter mainly discussed constructing and painting paths, but you didn't use a lot of paint. This changed drastically in the first sections of this chapter. You learned how to construct and apply colors; and with your newly acquired knowledge, you refined some of the functionality you encountered in the chapter about images.

The second part of this chapter dealt with a subset of the graphics state: text state. You learned about the iText mechanics that render basic building blocks and how you can use this functionality directly—for instance, to add a street name on a map.

This wasn't an easy chapter in the sense that I skipped some of the technical details. For example, if you want to apply a specific type of shading, you'll have to look at the PDF Reference.

In the next chapter, you'll rewrite the code that generates the map of Foobar; this time, you'll let the cobbler stick to his last. More specifically, you'll use Apache Batik to parse the SVG and iText to produce the PDF.

12

# *Drawing to Java Graphics2D*

**This chapter covers**

- iText and Java's `Graphics2D`
- `java.awt.font` vs. `com.lowagie.text.Font`
- Swing components and PDF
- PDF and Optional Content

In the two previous chapters, we've been discussing methods to draw graphics and text using iText's direct content object `PdfContentByte`. You may have recognized some of the examples from other books on SVG, PostScript, or Java graphics. For instance, all the graphical shapes you drew in chapter 10 also exist in the standard Java Developer Kit (JDK): The package `java.awt.geom` has objects such as `Rectangle2D`, `Ellipse2D`, `CubicCurve2D`, and so on.

Maybe you're already familiar with these objects. If that is the case, you can use iText as a PDF engine for all your `Graphics2D` requirements. We'll start adapting a simple example from Sun's tutorial on AWT so that it produces PDF. You'll learn how you can integrate iText in Swing applications, and you'll use external libraries to draw charts and a better version of the map of Foobar.

Before you can draw this map, you'll learn about an aspect of the graphics state that was omitted in the previous chapters: *optional content*. But first things first: Let's start by getting a `Graphics2D` instance that can be used to generate PDF.

## 12.1 Obtaining a Java.awt.Graphics2D instance

The Java API says that `java.awt.Graphics` is "the abstract base class for all graphics contexts that allow an application to draw onto components that are realized on various devices, as well as onto off-screen images."

In the JSDK, the abstract class `java.awt.Graphics2D` extends `java.awt.Graphics`. Sun's description of the `Graphics2D` object matches exactly what you did using PDF syntax in the previous two chapters; its purpose is "to provide more sophisticated control over geometry, coordinate transformations, color management, and text layout. This is the fundamental class for rendering two-dimensional shapes, text and images on the Java platform."

In the previous chapters, you grabbed a `PdfContentByte` object to add graphical content and text, to perform transformations, and so on. Wouldn't it be nice if you could also grab a special implementation of the abstract `Graphics2D` class? I'm thinking of a `Graphics2D` object that doesn't draw graphics onto Java components or to off-screen images, but that produces PDF instead. This is possible with only a handful of extra lines in your code.

### 12.1.1 A simple example from Sun's tutorial

In iText's `com.lowagie.text.pdf` package, you'll find the object `PdfGraphics2D` and its subclass `PdfPrinterGraphics2D`. `PdfGraphics2D` extends `java.awt.Graphics2D`. `PdfPrinterGraphics2D` implements the `java.awt.print.PrinterGraphics` interface.

In these objects, most of the standard `Graphics2D` methods are implemented so that they produce PDF. For instance, the implementation of the abstract Java method `drawstring()` uses some of the methods discussed in the previous chapter: `beginText()`, `showText()`, and `endText()`.

In other words, all the Java methods are translated to a sequence of iText methods. Having the "fundamental class for rendering 2-dimensional shapes, text and images on the Java platform" produce PDF makes it easy for you to integrate iText into your existing applications.

**NOTE** *What's the most important feature in iText?* In chapter 6, I told you there can be different answers to the question about the primary goal of iText, depending on the way you intend to use iText. The table functionality is the most important functionality in my projects, but other people say that `PdfGraphics2D` is the most important class in iText. It will soon become clear why.

Let's look at Sun's tutorial on 2D graphics first:

#### The 2D Graphics tutorial trail

At java.sun.com, a Tutorials link appears in the Resources category. Choose the Java Tutorial, and you'll find a link to 2D Graphics under Specialized Trails and Lessons. Browse the pages of this tutorial; many words should sound familiar after reading the previous chapters—stroking, filling, transforming, clipping, and so on.

The second chapter of this trail ("Displaying Graphics with Graphics2D") includes a section titled "Constructing Complex Shapes from Geometry Primitives." This section has an interesting example called Pear.java; you can use it to construct a pear shape from several ellipses, as shown in figure 12.1.

Now comes the amazing part: You can render this shape to PDF by pasting the code from this tutorial example into your iText examples. The original example extends `JApplet`. You copy the `init()` and `paint()` methods and make slight changes:

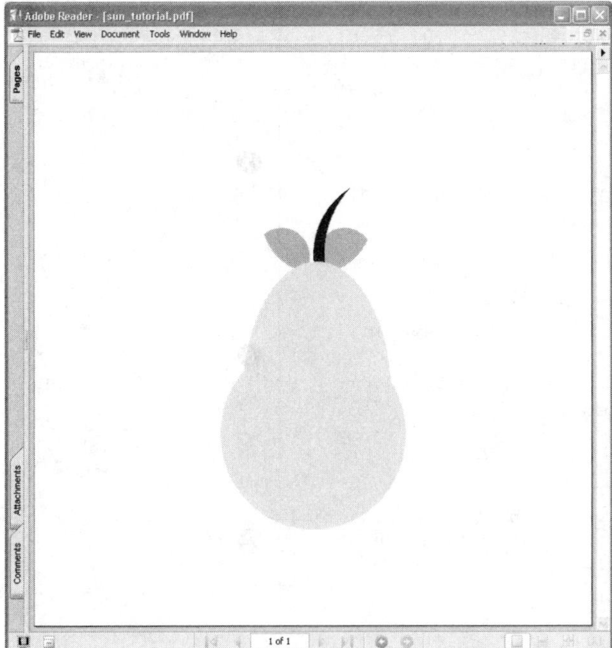


**Figure 12.1 Sun's 2D Graphics example rendered in PDF**

```
/* chapter12/SunTutorialExample.java */
Ellipse2D.Double circle, oval, leaf, stem;
Area circ, ov, leaf1, leaf2, st1, st2;            (1)
public void init() {
  circle = new Ellipse2D.Double();
  oval = new Ellipse2D.Double();
  leaf = new Ellipse2D.Double();
  stem = new Ellipse2D.Double();
  circ = new Area(circle);                         (2)
  ov = new Area(oval);
  leaf1 = new Area(leaf);
  leaf2 = new Area(leaf);
  st1 = new Area(stem);
  st2 = new Area(stem);
  // setBackground(Color.white);                   (3)
}
public void paint(Graphics g) {
  Graphics2D g2 = (Graphics2D) g;
  // Dimension d = getSize();                      (4)
  // int w = d.width;
  // int h = d.height;
  double ew = w/2;
  double eh = h/2;
```

```
    g2.setColor(Color.green);
    leaf.setFrame(ew-16, eh-29, 15.0, 15.0);
    leaf1 = new Area(leaf);
    leaf.setFrame(ew-14, eh-47, 30.0, 30.0);
    leaf2 = new Area(leaf);
    leaf1.intersect(leaf2);
    g2.fill(leaf1);                                  ❺
    leaf.setFrame(ew+1, eh-29, 15.0, 15.0);
    leaf1 = new Area(leaf);
    leaf2.intersect(leaf1);
    g2.fill(leaf2);
    g2.setColor(Color.black);
    stem.setFrame(ew, eh-42, 40.0, 40.0);
    st1 = new Area(stem);                            ❻
    stem.setFrame(ew+3, eh-47, 50.0, 50.0);
    st2 = new Area(stem);
    st1.subtract(st2);
    g2.fill(st1);
    g2.setColor(Color.yellow);
    circle.setFrame(ew-25, eh, 50.0, 50.0);
    oval.setFrame(ew-19, eh-20, 40.0, 70.0);         ❼
    circ = new Area(circle);
    ov = new Area(oval);
    circ.add(ov);
    g2.fill(circ);
  }
```

You first specify the shapes needed to draw a pear ❶ and initialize the `Ellipse2D` and `Area` objects ❷. The only difference between the `init()` method and the original example is that you don't set the background color ❸. In the original `paint()` method, you remove the lines that define the width and height ❹; instead, you declare the `w` and `h` as member variables so you can use them to define the page size of the PDF document. Just like in the original example, you draw the green leaves ❺, the black stem ❻, and the yellow pear body ❼.

Compare the previous code snippet with the original code in Sun's tutorial; the differences are minimal. You haven't yet used any iText-specific code.

### *Integrating iText into this example*

When you create the `SunTutorialExample` object, you initialize the values of the member variables `w` and `h`. You also call the `init()` method you inherited from the original applet example:

```
/* chapter12/SunTutorialExample.java */
public SunTutorialExample() {
  w = 150;
```

```
    h = 150;
    init();
  }
```

After creating an instance of this object, you invoke your custom method `createPdf()`. This is the only iText-specific code in this example:

```
/* chapter12/SunTutorialExample.java */
public void createPdf() {
  Document document = new Document(new Rectangle(w, h));
  try {
    PdfWriter writer = PdfWriter.getInstance(document,
      new FileOutputStream("sun_tutorial.pdf"));
    document.open();
    PdfContentByte cb = writer.getDirectContent();
    Graphics2D g2 = cb.createGraphics(w, h);          <-- Create Graphics2D instance
    paint(g2);          <-- Call original paint method
    g2.dispose();          <-- DO NOT FORGET THIS LINE!
  } catch (Exception e) {
    System.err.println(e.getMessage());
  }
  document.close();
}
```

If you have an existing application that draws shapes to a `Graphics2D` object (for instance, to a component used in your GUI), you can use this code snippet to add these shapes to a PDF file. The object returned by the `createGraphics()` method is an instance of `PdfGraphics2D`, but this shouldn't matter. Your applications will see it as an instance of the standard Java classes `Graphics` or `Graphics2D`.

You must admit that this is really simple. It would be surprising if there weren't any caveats:

- Don't forget to call the `dispose()` method once you finish drawing to the `Graphics2D` object; otherwise, nothing will be added to the direct content.
- The coordinate system in Java's `Graphics2D` is different from the default coordinate system in PDF's graphics state. The tutorial trail on 2D Graphics says, "the origin of user space is the upper-left corner of the component's drawing area. The *x* coordinate increases to the right and the *y* coordinate increases downward."
- Java works in standard Red-Green-Blue (sRGB) as the default color space internally, so colors need to be translated. Anything with four colors is assumed to be ARGB when it's probably CMYK. (ARGB includes the RGB components plus an alpha transparency factor that specifies what happens when one color is drawn over another.)

- Watch out when using fonts. There is a big difference between the font classes `java.awt.Font` and `com.lowagie.text.Font`.

The next section elaborates on the use of fonts. We'll add some text with the `Graphics2D` `drawString()` method as shown in figure 12.2.

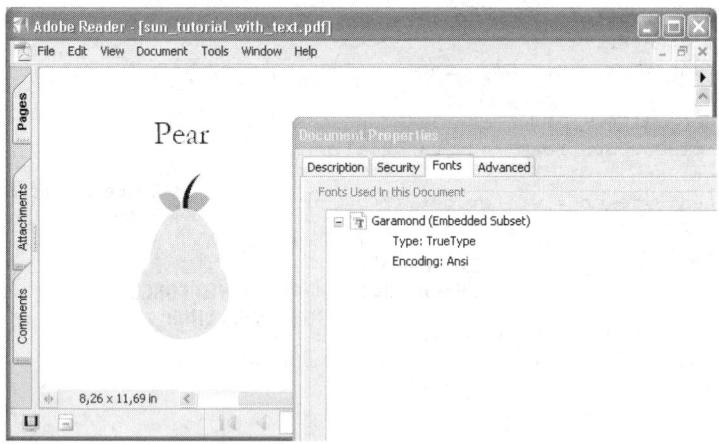


**Figure 12.2 Sun's tutorial example with extra text**

### *12.1.2 Mapping AWT fonts to PDF fonts*

One way to deal with the difference between the way fonts are handled in AWT and fonts in PDF is to create the `PdfGraphics2D` object using an instance of the `FontMapper` interface. This font mapper interface has only two methods:

```
public com.lowagie.text.pdf.BaseFont awtToPdf(java.awt.Font font);
public java.awt.Font pdfToAwt(
  com.lowagie.text.pdf.BaseFont font, int size);
```

I use the fully quantified class names here so that nobody confuses the AWT class `Font` with iText's `Font` class. There isn't an exact correlation between fonts in Java and fonts in PDF, so each application can define the appropriate mapping.

There is a default font mapper class called `DefaultFontMapper`. By default, it maps some font names to the standard Type 1 fonts:

- DialogInput, Monospaced, and Courier are mapped to a font from the Courier family.
- Serif and TimesRoman are mapped to a font from the Times-Roman family.
- Dialog and SansSerif are mapped to a font from the Helvetica family (this is also the default).

If you need more fonts, you can add font directories to the mapper with the method insertDirectory(). Let's extend the previous example and override the createPdf() method so that text is added using the font Garamond.

This example creates the Graphics2D instance from a PdfTemplate object instead of creating it from the direct content. This allows you to add the graphics canvas at a specific position on the page:

```
/* chapter12/SunTutorialExampleWithText.java */
PdfContentByte cb = writer.getDirectContent();            ❶
PdfTemplate tp = cb.createTemplate(w, h);
DefaultFontMapper mapper = new DefaultFontMapper();            ❷
mapper.insertDirectory("c:/windows/fonts");
String name;
Map map = mapper.getMapper();
for (Iterator i = map.keySet().iterator(); i.hasNext(); ) {            ❸
  name = (String)i.next();
  System.out.println(name + ": "
    + ((DefaultFontMapper.BaseFontParameters)map.get(name)).fontName);
}
Graphics2D g2 = tp.createGraphics(w, h, mapper);   ❹
paint(g2);
g2.setColor(Color.black);
java.awt.Font thisFont =            ❺
  new java.awt.Font("Garamond", java.awt.Font.PLAIN, 18);
g2.setFont(thisFont);
String pear = "Pear";
FontMetrics metrics = g2.getFontMetrics();            ❻
int width = metrics.stringWidth(pear);
g2.drawString(pear, (w - width) / 2, 20);   ❼
g2.dispose();
```

You first create a PdfTemplate with dimensions w x h ❶. Next, you create a font mapper instance ❷ and print the list of mapped fonts ❸. Then, create a Graphics2D object ❹ and a Java Font object ❺. ❻ shows the Java metrics, and ❼ draws the string.

In this code sample, the list of font names that are registered in the mapper is written to the output of the console. In addition to getMapper(), there's a method getAliases() that returns all the names that can be used to create the Java AWT Font object. This includes the name of the font in different languages, provided the translations are present in the font file. You can also add your own aliases with the method putAlias().

In this example, you get the java.awt.FontMetrics so that you can calculate the width of the text when rendered to the Graphics2D. This is the width according to Java. In most cases, you won't notice any difference; but when you need special fonts, you'll find that the metrics in Java don't always correspond with the metrics according to PDF. In the next section, you'll learn to deal with this problem by obtaining a `Graphics2D` instance using `createGraphicsShapes()`.

`DefaultFontMapper` works for the most common examples; it uses CP1252 as default encoding. If you need another encoding, you have to write your own implementation of the `FontMapper` interface. The class `AsianFontMapper` in iText extends the `DefaultFontMapper` and lets you define a default font and encoding. For instance, the PDF in figure 12.3 was created using Java's `Graphics2D` and a CJK font.

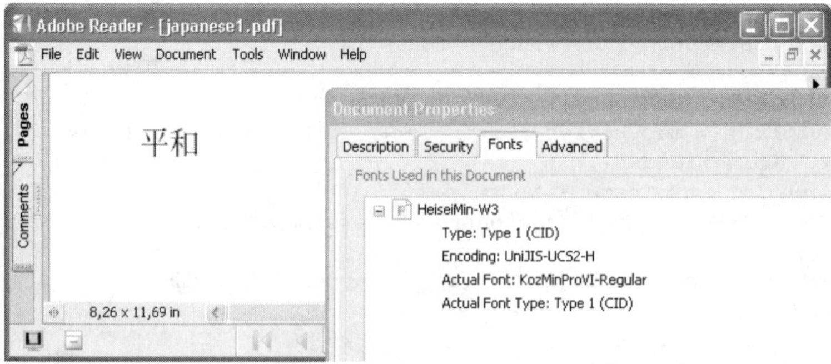


**Figure 12.3 A `String` drawn with a `Graphics2D` method using a CJK font**

There's something strange about the code used to create this example:

```
/* chapter12/JapaneseExample1.java */
String text = "\u5e73\u548C";
PdfContentByte cb = writer.getDirectContent();
PdfTemplate tp = cb.createTemplate(100, 50);
AsianFontMapper mapper =
  new AsianFontMapper(
    AsianFontMapper.JapaneseFont_Min,
    AsianFontMapper.JapaneseEncoding_H);
Graphics2D g2 = tp.createGraphics(100, 50, mapper);
java.awt.Font font =
  new java.awt.Font("Arial Unicode MS", java.awt.Font.PLAIN, 12);
g2.setFont(font);
g2.drawString(text, 0, 40);
g2.dispose();
cb.addTemplate(tp, 36, 780);
```

The code creates an AWT font using the name Arial Unicode MS. But if you look at figure 12.3, you see that a different font was used. This is normal behavior. The font mapper can't find a reference to the font file arialuni.ttf that contains the glyphs of Arial Unicode, so the mapper uses its default font and encoding. You define these defaults in the AsianFontMapper constructor: JapaneseFont_Min (corresponding with HeiseiMin-W3) and JapaneseEncoding_H (UniJIS-UCS2-H).

**NOTE** This AsianFontMapper class contains static String values corresponding with CJK fonts. Its name refers to Asian fonts, but you can pass any font name (or any path to a font file) and any encoding with the constructor. As soon as a font is used that isn't found in the font map or in the aliases, the method awtToPdf() returns a BaseFont object that is created with the first String used to construct this special FontMapper instance as font name, and with the second String as an encoding value.

One of the most obvious problems when using this approach lies with the font metrics. As far as the Java part is concerned, the font Arial Unicode MS is used in this example, and all the metrics are based on this assumption. In reality, a CJK font is used. If the Java font metrics differ from the PDF font metrics, you'll run into problems.

Let's consider another approach: You can drop the PDF font part, and let the Java code draw the shapes of the glyphs onto the Graphics2D canvas instead of using fonts.

### 12.1.3 Drawing glyph shapes instead of using a PDF font

If you create a PdfGraphics2D object using the method createGraphicsShapes() instead of createGraphics(), you don't need to map any fonts. The JSDK includes the object java.awt.font.TextLayout, which uses a font program to draw the glyphs to the Graphics2D object. This is what happened in figure 12.4.

There's a significant difference between this approach and using FontMapper. When you look at figure 12.4, you see that although the same Java font was used for both examples, there was definitely another font used in the PDF. In the

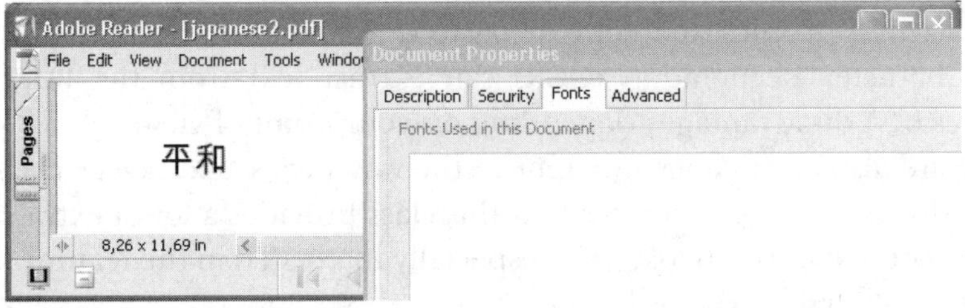


**Figure 12.4 Drawing the shapes of the glyphs to a Graphics2D object**

screenshot, the Fonts tab in the Document Properties window of Adobe Reader is empty. What happened?

Compare the following code snippet with the previous sample:

```
/* chapter12/JapaneseExample2.java */
String text = "\u5e73\u548C";
PdfContentByte cb = writer.getDirectContent();
PdfTemplate tp = cb.createTemplate(100, 50);
Graphics2D g2 = tp.createGraphicsShapes(100, 50);
java.awt.Font font =
  new java.awt.Font("Arial Unicode MS", java.awt.Font.PLAIN, 12);
g2.setFont(font);
g2.drawString(text, 0, 40);
g2.dispose();
cb.addTemplate(tp, 36, 780);
```

Because this example uses the method `createGraphicsShapes()` instead of `createGraphics()`, the glyphs are painted on the canvas using PDF operators and operands as discussed in chapter 10, not using text state operators as discussed in chapter 11. As far as the PDF document is concerned, there is no text in this PDF—just shapes!

**NOTE** Adobe Reader's Basic toolbar includes a Select button that you can use to select characters in a PDF document—for instance, if you want to copy and paste words or sentences. You can copy and paste the Japanese word for *peace* in the first example, but it's impossible to select the same word in the second example: It isn't recognized as text, it's just some paths that have been filled.

The fact that paths are drawn with pure graphics state operators instead of showing characters using text state operators has advantages and disadvantages. If you plan to add a lot of text this way, file size may be an issue because the glyph descriptions aren't reused as is the case if you use a font. The same goes for performance.

The fact that people can't copy or paste words, and that only tools that use Optical Character Recognition (OCR) can extract text from the PDF, can be advantages or a disadvantages depending on your point of view.

There are also advantages inherent in the way Java's `TextLayout` class works. Sun's API documentation indicates that this class provides a lot of extra capabilities. In the context of this book, we're especially interested in the feature "implicit bidirectional analysis and reordering."

You probably remember that we dealt with diacritics, ligatures, and bidirectional writing in chapter 9. You saw that iText can write Hebrew and Arabic from

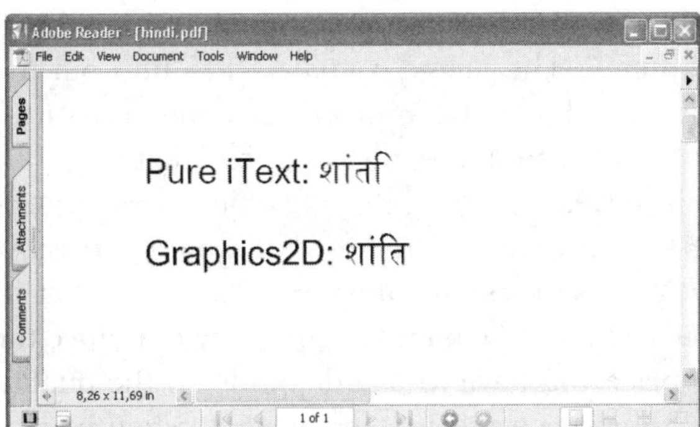


**Figure 12.5**
**Comparing the way ligatures are (or aren't) made in iText and `Graphics2D`**

right to left, and an example mixed content that was written in two directions. But there were languages with problems you couldn't tackle: for instance, the diacritics in the Thai example and the ligatures in Hindi. For the moment, iText supports the generation of PDFs using Indic fonts, but iText isn't able to deal with diacritics and ligatures.

You can work around this problem by letting Java's `TextLayout` class do the work. Figure 12.5 clearly shows how iText fails to write the word *Peace* in Hindi but succeeds in rendering it correctly when using `Graphics2D`.

The same `String` is used for both lines shown in the screenshot. I don't understand Hindi, but I'm told that the glyph order is wrong in the first line and correct in the second line. The difference is that iText shows the glyphs using the characters order in the `String`, whereas Java's `TextLayout()` method reorders the characters and makes ligatures before painting the glyphs on the canvas. Here's the example code:

```
/* chapter12/HindiExample.java */
String text = "\u0936\u093e\u0902\u0924\u093f";
BaseFont bf = BaseFont.createFont("c:/windows/fonts/arialuni.ttf",
  BaseFont.IDENTITY_H, BaseFont.EMBEDDED);
document.add(new Paragraph(
  "Pure iText: " + text, new com.lowagie.text.Font(bf, 12)));
PdfContentByte cb = writer.getDirectContent();
PdfTemplate tp = cb.createTemplate(100, 50);
Graphics2D g2 = tp.createGraphicsShapes(100, 50);
java.awt.Font font = new java.awt.Font(
  "Arial Unicode MS", java.awt.Font.PLAIN, 12);
g2.setFont(font);
g2.drawString("Graphics2D: " + text, 0, 40);
g2.dispose();
cb.addTemplate(tp, 36, 750);
```

If you add an image to a `Graphics2D` object, the Java code does something similar to what is described in chapter 5: The image is analyzed to find out the image type, and the image data is parsed with the appropriate image class in the JDK. Note that these classes are different from the ones used by iText.

The two types of methods to create a `PdfGraphics2D` object—`createGraphics()` and `createGraphicsShapes()`—also exist with two extra parameters: `convertImagesToJPEG` and `quality`. You use these parameters to tell Java that it should convert the images to a JPEG. This can be an interesting way to reduce the size of your PDF documents. The price you have to pay depends on the quality of this conversion. This is similar to what you saw in section 5.2, when you created a `com.lowagie.text.Image` object using a `java.awt.Image` object.

Now that you know the meaning of all the parameters and the methods to obtain a `Graphics2D` object from iText, let's look at real-world situations where you can take advantage of the power of iText and Java two-dimensional graphics.

## 12.2 Two-dimensional graphics in the real world

The fact that you can use iText to translate `Graphics2D` methods to graphics state operations has many interesting implications. If you're writing Swing applications, you can benefit from iText's `Graphics2D` functionality. I could rewrite the previous chapters from the point of view of the Java Swing developer. Do you remember chapter 6, about tables? To construct a table, you chose one of the table objects available in iText; but why not use a `JTable`? The same goes for the text objects in chapter 4. Why not use standard Java text objects?

Using the `PdfGraphics2D` object, you can export any Swing component to PDF.

### 12.2.1 Exporting Swing components to PDF

Suppose you've written an application with a GUI using Swing components such as `JTable` or `JTextPane`. All these components are derived from the abstract class `javax.swing.JComponent`. `JComponent` has methods that are of interest in the context of this chapter. One of them is `print(Graphics g)`: You can use this method to let the Swing component print itself to your `PdfGraphics2D` object.

Figure 12.6 shows a simple Java application with a `JFrame`. It contains a `JTable` found in Sun's Java tutorial on Swing components. If you click the first button, the contents of the table are added to a PDF using `createGraphicsShapes()` (the upper PDF in the screenshot). If you click the second button, the table is added using `createGraphics()` (the lower PDF, using the standard Type 1 font Helvetica). Notice the subtle differences between the fonts used for both variants.

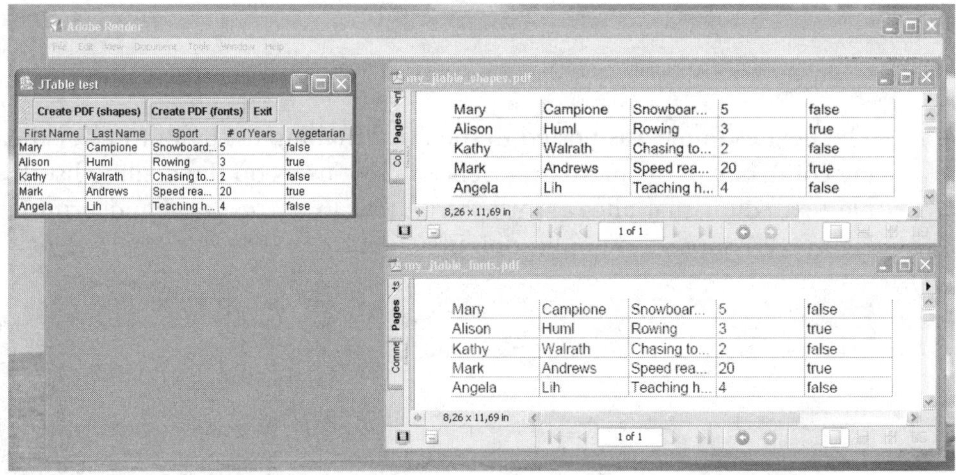


**Figure 12.6 A Swing application with a `JTable` that is printed to PDF two different ways**

If you run this example, try changing the content of the `JTable`; the changes are reflected in the PDF. If you select a row, the background of the row is shown in a different color in the Java applications as well as in the PDF.

The code to achieve this is amazingly simple:

```
/* chapter12/MyJTable.java */
public void createPdf(boolean shapes) {
  Document document = new Document();
  try {
    PdfWriter writer;
    if (shapes)
      writer = PdfWriter.getInstance(document,
        new FileOutputStream("my_jtable_shapes.pdf"));
    else
      writer = PdfWriter.getInstance(document,
        new FileOutputStream("my_jtable_fonts.pdf"));
    document.open();
    PdfContentByte cb = writer.getDirectContent();
    PdfTemplate tp = cb.createTemplate(500, 500);
    Graphics2D g2;
    if (shapes)
      g2 = tp.createGraphicsShapes(500, 500);
    else
      g2 = tp.createGraphics(500, 500);
    table.print(g2);
    g2.dispose();
    cb.addTemplate(tp, 30, 300);
  } catch (Exception e) {
```

```
        System.err.println(e.getMessage());
    }
    document.close();
}
```

The next example was posted to the iText mailing list by Bill Ensley (bearprinting.com), one of the more experienced iText users on the mailing list. It's a simple text editor that allows you to write text in a `JTextPane` and print it to PDF. Figure 12.7 shows this application in action.

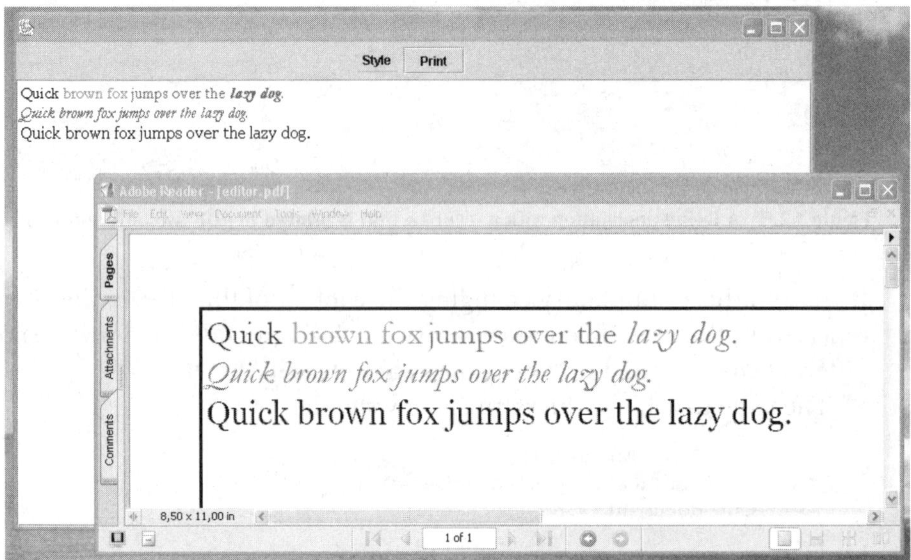


**Figure 12.7 A simple editor with a JTextPane that is drawn onto a PDF file**

The code is a bit more complex than the `JTable` example. This example performs an affine transformation before the content of the `JTextPane` is painted. You already learned about these transformations in section 10.4.1:

```
/* chapter12/JTextPaneToPdf.java */
Graphics2D g2 = cb.createGraphics(612, 792, mapper, true, .95f);
AffineTransform at = new AffineTransform();
at.translate(convertToPixels(20), convertToPixels(20));
at.scale(pixelToPoint, pixelToPoint);
g2.transform(at);
g2.setColor(Color.WHITE);
g2.fill(ta.getBounds());
Rectangle alloc = getVisibleEditorRect(ta);
ta.getUI().getRootView(ta).paint(g2, alloc);
```

**Define transformations**

**Fill white rectangle**

**Paint JTextPane to PDF**

```
g2.setColor(Color.BLACK);
g2.draw(ta.getBounds());
g2.dispose();
```

**Draw black border**

Numerous applications use iText this way. Let me pick two examples; one Free/ Open Source Software (FOSS) product and one proprietary product:

- JasperReports, a free Java reporting tool from JasperSoft (jaspersoft.com), allows you to deliver content onto the screen; to the printer; or into PDF, HTML, XLS, CSV, and XML files. If you choose to generate PDF, iText's `PdfGraphics2D` object is used behind the scenes.
- ICEbrowser is a product from ICEsoft (icesoft.com). ICEbrowser parses and lays out advanced web content (XML/HTML/CSS/JS); PDF is generated by rendering the parsed documents to the `PdfGraphics2D` object.

It's not my intention to make a complete list of products that use iText. The main purpose of these two examples is to answer the following question.

**FAQ** *Can I build iText into my commercial product?* Lots of people think open source is the opposite of commercial, but that's a misunderstanding. It's not because iText is FOSS that it can only be used in other free products. It's not because iText is free that it isn't a "commercial" product. As long as you respect the license, you can use iText in your closed-source or proprietary software.

Another useful aspect of iText's `Graphics2D` functionality is that it opens the door to using iText in combination with other libraries with graphical output—for instance, Apache Batik, a library that is able to parse SVG; or JFreeChart, a library that will be introduced in the next section.

### 12.2.2 Drawing charts with JFreeChart

This isn't one of Laura's assignments, but as a bonus you'll help her make charts showing demographic information. You'll take the student population of the Technological University of Foobar and graph the number of students per continent.

To make these charts, you'll combine iText with JFreeChart, an interesting library developed by David Gilbert and Thomas Morgner. The web site jfree.org explains that JFreeChart is "a free Java class library for generating charts, including pie charts (2D and 3D), bar charts (regular and stacked, with an optional 3D effect), line and area charts, scatter plots and bubble charts, time series, high/low/

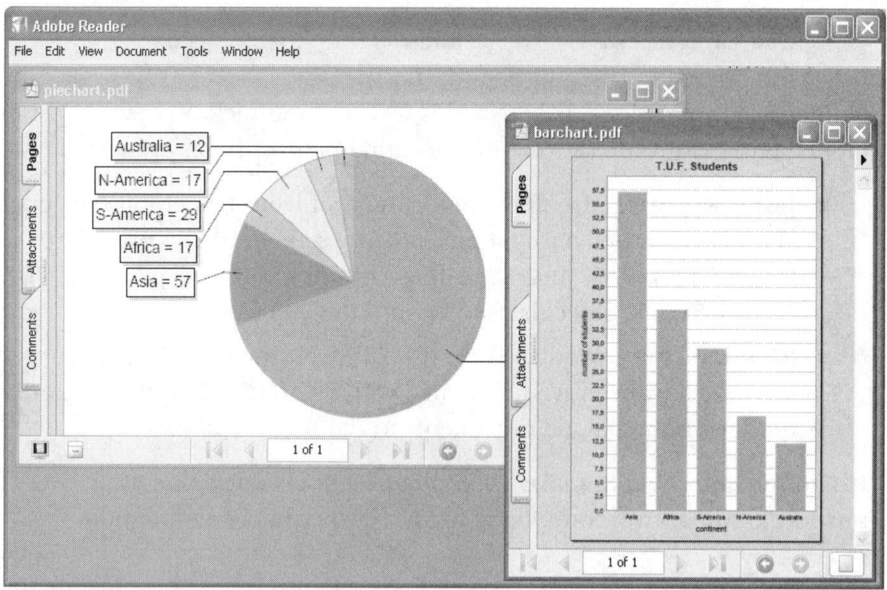


**Figure 12.8 Foobar statistics represented in a pie chart and a bar chart**

open/close charts and candle stick charts, combination charts, Pareto charts, Gantt charts, wind plots, meter charts and symbol charts, and wafer map charts." (I won't go into the details of the JFreeChart library. David Gilbert's "The JFree-Chart Developer Guide" can be purchased on the jfree.org web site.)

These charts can be rendered on an AWT or Swing component, they can be exported to JPEG or PNG, and you can combine JFreeChart with Apache Batik to produce SVG or with iText to produce PDF.

Figure 12.8 shows PDFs with a pie chart and a bar chart created using JFree-Chart and iText.

In JFreeChart, you construct a `JFreeChart` object using the `ChartFactory`. One of the parameters passed to one of the methods to create the chart is a dataset object. The code to create the charts shown in figure 12.8 is simple:

```
/* chapter12/FoobarCharts.java */
public static JFreeChart getBarChart() {
  DefaultCategoryDataset dataset = new DefaultCategoryDataset();
  dataset.setValue(57, "students", "Asia");
  dataset.setValue(36, "students", "Africa");
  dataset.setValue(29, "students", "S-America");
  dataset.setValue(17, "students", "N-America");
  dataset.setValue(12, "students", "Australia");
```

```
    return ChartFactory.createBarChart("T.U.F. Students",
      "continent", "number of students", dataset,
      PlotOrientation.VERTICAL, false, true, false);
  }
  public static JFreeChart getPieChart() {
    DefaultPieDataset dataset = new DefaultPieDataset();
    dataset.setValue("Europe", 302);
    dataset.setValue("Asia", 57);
    dataset.setValue("Africa", 17);
    dataset.setValue("S-America", 29);
    dataset.setValue("N-America", 17);
    dataset.setValue("Australia", 12);
    return ChartFactory.createPieChart("Students per continent",
      dataset, true, true, false);
  }
```

The previous code snippet creates two `JFreeChart` objects. The following code snippet shows how to create a PDF file per chart:

```
/* chapter12/FoobarCharts.java */
public static void convertToPdf(JFreeChart chart,
  int width, int height, String filename) {
  Document document = new Document(new Rectangle(width, height));
  try {
    PdfWriter writer;
    writer = PdfWriter.getInstance(document,
      new FileOutputStream(filename));
    document.open();
    PdfContentByte cb = writer.getDirectContent();
    PdfTemplate tp = cb.createTemplate(width, height);
    Graphics2D g2d = tp.createGraphics(width, height,
      new DefaultFontMapper());
    Rectangle2D r2d = new Rectangle2D.Double(0, 0, width, height);
    chart.draw(g2d, r2d);
    g2d.dispose();
    cb.addTemplate(tp, 0, 0);
  }
  catch(Exception e) {
    e.printStackTrace();
  }
  document.close();
}
```

The chart is drawn on a `PdfTemplate`. This object can easily be wrapped in an iText `Image` object if you want to add it to the PDF with `document.add()`.

This was a nice Foobar interlude. Before you can continue and create a new version of the map of Foobar, you need to learn about optional content.

## 12.3 PDF's optional content

All the content you've added to documents until now was either visible or invisible—for instance, because it was clipped or because the rendering was set to invisible. Beginning with PDF-1.5, you can also add *optional* content to a document; it can be selectively viewed or hidden by document authors or consumers.

In this section, you'll learn more about these optional content layers. You'll organize them in different structures and define different properties for each layer. You'll learn how to define actions to change the state of a layer and discover some convenient methods to add a `PdfTemplate` or `Image` object to a layer. The simplest way to turn a layer on or off is using the Layers panel in Adobe Reader.

### 12.3.1 Making content visible or invisible

Graphics that can be made visible/invisible dynamically are grouped in *optional content groups*. Content that belongs to a certain group is visible when the group is *on* and invisible when the group is *off*. In iText, such groups are called *layers*. You can create a `PdfLayer` object; when adding content to a `PdfContentByte` object, you can specify in which layer (or content group) the content should be shown (or hidden).

Figure 12.9 shows a simple example of a PDF with optional content.

In the example, the Layers tab in Adobe Reader shows one layer or optional content group with the title "Do you see me?" If you see an eye in the check box preceding the title of the content group, the status of the layer is *on*; everything in the content group is visible. You can change the status to *off* by clicking the eye. Figure 12.10 shows what happens if you change the status in this example.

**Figure 12.9 PDF document with optional content (visible)**

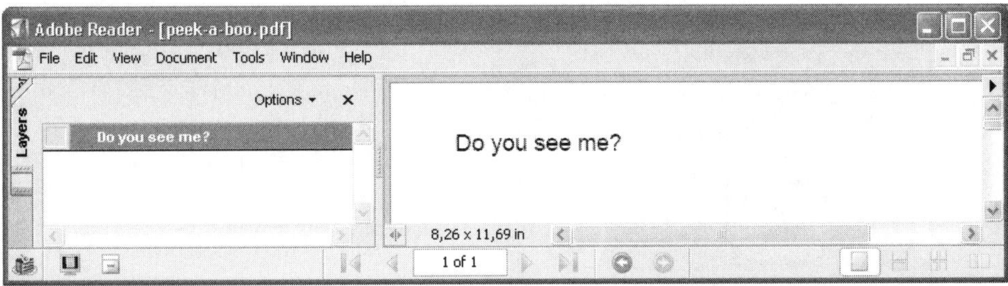


**Figure 12.10 PDF document with optional content (invisible)**

The text *Peek-a-Boo!!!* has disappeared, because this word was added as optional content. Here's how it's done:

```
/* chapter11/PeekABoo.java */
PdfLayer layer = new PdfLayer("Do you see me?", writer);      <-- Define optional content group
BaseFont bf = BaseFont.createFont(
  BaseFont.HELVETICA, BaseFont.WINANSI, BaseFont.NOT_EMBEDDED);
PdfContentByte cb = writer.getDirectContent();
cb.beginText();
cb.setTextMatrix(50, 790);
cb.setLeading(24);
cb.setFontAndSize(bf, 18);
cb.showText("Do you see me?");
cb.beginLayer(layer);           <-- Start sequence of optional content
cb.newlineShowText("Peek-a-Boo!!!");     <-- Add content
cb.endLayer();      <-- End of optional content
cb.endText();
```

Note that you set the version of the PDF to `PdfWriter.VERSION_1_5`. This functionality wasn't available yet in PDF 1.4 (the default version of PDF files generated with iText).

The optional content of a group can reside anywhere in the document. It doesn't have to be consecutive in drawing order or belong to the same content stream (or page). The previous example was simple, with one layer and one sequence of optional content. Let's see how you can work with different layers that are organized in different structures.

### 12.3.2 Adding structure to layers

Figure 12.11 demonstrates different features of the `PdfLayer` class. Let's start with the structure that is visible in the Layers tab. It shows a tree with three branches: Nested Layers, Grouped Layers, and Radio Group. Let's find out the differences between these groups.

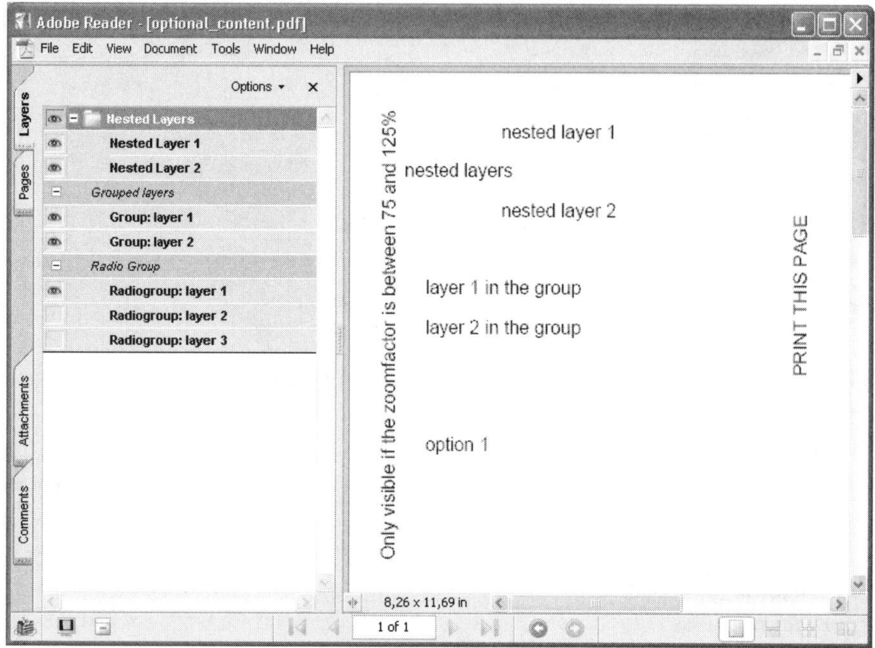


**Figure 12.11 Different groups of optional content**

First, you have a nested structure of layers. If you click the eye next to Nested Layer 1, the text *nested layer 1* disappears from the document. If you click the parent folder Nested Layers, everything that is added to this layer and to its children (Nested Layer 1 and Nested Layer 2) becomes invisible. The following code snippet shows how this is done:

```
/* chapter12/OptionalContentExample.java */
PdfLayer nested = new PdfLayer("Nested Layers", writer);
PdfLayer nested_1 = new PdfLayer("Nested Layer 1", writer);
PdfLayer nested_2 = new PdfLayer("Nested Layer 2", writer);
nested.addChild(nested_1);
nested.addChild(nested_2);
cb.beginLayer(nested);
ColumnText.showTextAligned(cb,Element.ALIGN_LEFT,
  new Phrase("nested layers"), 50, 775, 0);
cb.endLayer();
cb.beginLayer(nested_1);
ColumnText.showTextAligned(cb, Element.ALIGN_LEFT,
  new Phrase("nested layer 1"), 100, 800, 0);
cb.endLayer();
```

**Create parent layer**
**Create two children**
**Add children to parent**
**Add content to parent**
**Add content to first child**

```
cb.beginLayer(nested_2);
ColumnText.showTextAligned(cb, Element.ALIGN_LEFT,
  new Phrase("nested layer 2"), 100, 750, 0);
cb.endLayer();
```

**Add content to second child**

The nested structure is defined by using the `addChild()` method. It's not necessary to nest the `beginLayer` and `endLayer` sequences; it isn't forbidden, either. You'll use this functionality to add interactive layers to the map of Foobar; you'll add optional information locating information booths, hotels, parking space, and so on, and you'll group all the layers under different titles. If the top level of such a group doesn't have to be clickable, you can create the parent structure like this:

```
/* chapter12/OptionalContentExample.java */
PdfLayer group = PdfLayer.createTitle("Grouped layers", writer);
PdfLayer layer1 = new PdfLayer("Group: layer 1", writer);
PdfLayer layer2 = new PdfLayer("Group: layer 2", writer);
group.addChild(layer1);
group.addChild(layer2);
```

The parent of this group can't be used as a parameter for the `beginLayer()` method. The `PdfLayer` object returned by `createTitle` is a structural element; it's not an optional content layer.

Still thinking about your map of Foobar, imagine a structural element titled Streets / Rues / Straten as a parent of the layers with the street names in English, French, and Dutch. You don't want to see the names of the streets in different languages at the same time, and you don't want the street names to overlap. You should define these layers as elements of a radio group:

```
/* chapter12/OptionalContentExample.java */
PdfLayer radiogroup = PdfLayer.createTitle("Radio Group", writer);
PdfLayer radio1 = new PdfLayer("Radiogroup: layer 1", writer);
radio1.setOn(true);
PdfLayer radio2 = new PdfLayer("Radiogroup: layer 2", writer);
radio2.setOn(false);
PdfLayer radio3 = new PdfLayer("Radiogroup: layer 3", writer);
radio3.setOn(false);
radiogroup.addChild(radio1);
radiogroup.addChild(radio2);
radiogroup.addChild(radio3);
ArrayList options = new ArrayList();
options.add(radio1);
options.add(radio2);
options.add(radio3);
writer.addOCGRadioGroup(options);
```

**Create structure for parent**

**Create children**

**Add children to parent**

**Add children to ArrayList**

**Add radio group to PdfWriter**

If you open the PDF shown in figure 12.11 in Adobe Reader, clicking another option in the radio group makes "option 1" disappear. Depending on the layer you chose, "option 2" or "option 3" becomes visible.

> **NOTE** The method `setOn()` isn't limited to radio groups. You can use it to set the initial status of the `PdfLayer`. The default value is *on* (true), so the line `radio1.setOn(true)` is superfluous.

The PDF shown in the screenshot also contains two sequences of optional content we haven't discussed yet: a line mentioning the zoom factor and another one asking you to print the page. These layers are visible or invisible depending on the usage of the PDF file. This demands extra explanation.

### 12.3.3 Using a PdfLayer

Looking at the Layers tab in figure 12.11, you may assume that there are only eight layers (and two title structures) in this PDF file. In reality, two extra layers are added:

```
/* chapter12/OptionalContentExample.java */
PdfLayer not_printed = new PdfLayer("not printed", writer);
not_printed.setOnPanel(false);
not_printed.setPrint("Print", false);
cb.beginLayer(not_printed);
ColumnText.showTextAligned(cb, Element.ALIGN_CENTER,
  new Phrase("PRINT THIS PAGE"), 300, 700, 90);
cb.endLayer();
PdfLayer zoom = new PdfLayer("Zoom 0.75-1.25", writer);
zoom.setOnPanel(false);
zoom.setZoom(0.75f, 1.25f);
cb.beginLayer(zoom);
ColumnText.showTextAligned(cb, Element.ALIGN_LEFT,
  new Phrase("Only visible if the zoomfactor is between 75 and 125%"),
  30, 530, 90);
cb.endLayer();
```

The optional content groups "not printed" and "Zoom 0.75-1.25" don't appear in the Layers tab, because you set the `onPanel` value to false. We're especially interested in the methods `setPrint()` and `setZoom()`. These methods change the *usage dictionary* of the optional content.

Table 12.1 lists the methods in `PdfLayer` that change this dictionary.

**Table 12.1 Overview of `PdfLayer` methods that change the usage dictionary**

| Method | Parameters | Description |
|---|---|---|
| `setCreatorType()` | `creator, subtype` | Stores application-specific data associated with this content group. `Creator` is a text string specifying the application that created the group. `Subtype` is a name defining the type of content controlled by the group (for instance, Artwork or Technical). |
| `setExport()` | `export` | By passing a `boolean`, you can indicate the recommended state for content in this group when the document is saved by a viewer application to a format that doesn't support optional content (an earlier version of PDF or a raster image format). |
| `setLanguage()` | `language, preferred` | Specifies the language of the content controlled by this optional content group. The `language` string specifies a language and possibly a locale (for example "fr-CA" represents Canadian French). If you've specified a language, the layer that matches the system language is on, unless you set the preferred status of a language layer to true. |
| `setPrint()` | `subtype, printstate` | Specifies the state if the content in this group is to be printed. Possible values for `subtype` include "Print", "Trapped", "PrinterMarks", and "Watermark". The value for `printstate` can be true or false. |
| `setView()` | `view` | By passing a `boolean`, you can indicate that the group should be set to that state when the document is opened in a viewer application. |
| `setZoom()` | `min, max` | Specifies a range of magnifications at which the content in this optional content group is best viewed. `Min` is the minimum recommended magnification factor; `max` the maximum recommended magnification. Using a negative value for `min` sets the default to 0; for `max`, a negative value corresponds with the largest possible magnification supported by the viewer. |

This example declares that the sentence "PRINT THIS PAGE" shouldn't be printed. You see this sentence on the screen, but the text isn't visible if you print the page on paper. This can be handy if you have online forms that must be printed and filled in manually. If you're printing on paper with a preprinted header, you can show the header on screen, but you don't want to print it over the existing header on the preprinted sheet.

The sentence "Only visible if the zoom factor is between 75 and 125%" explains exactly what happens if you zoom in or zoom out: The text will disappear if the zoom factor is below 75 percent or reaches 125 percent. You'll use this in your enhanced map of Foobar: You'll show gridlines when the zoom factor is between 20 percent and 100 percent.

Another criterion that can be used to decide whether a layer should be visible is the state of a series of other layers that are grouped in an optional content membership.

### 12.3.4 Optional content membership

In the previous examples, you always added content to a single optional content group. This content is visible if the status of the group is *on* and invisible when it's *off*. You can think of more complex visibility possibilities, with content not belonging directly to a specific layer but depending on the state of different layers. An example will explain; see figure 12.12.

The word *dog* belongs to layer 1, the word *tiger* to layer 2, and the word *lion* to layer 3. The word *cat* belongs to a `PdfLayerMembership`. It's visible if either layer 2 or layer 3 is on, or both. If you make the words *tiger* and *lion* invisible, the word *cat* disappears.

This example defines another `PdfLayerMembership` that appears only if layer 2 and layer 3 both are turned off. See figure 12.13: The word *cat* has disappeared, but the words *no cat* are now visible. The words *no cat* belong to the second membership layer that is visible only if the *tiger* and *lion* layers are made invisible.

**Figure 12.12 Optional content membership policies**

**Figure 12.13 Optional content membership policies**

The following code snippet explains how to achieve this:

```
/* chapter12/LayerMembershipExample.java */
PdfLayer dog = new PdfLayer("layer 1", writer);
PdfLayer tiger = new PdfLayer("layer 2", writer);
PdfLayer lion = new PdfLayer("layer 3", writer);
PdfLayerMembership cat = new PdfLayerMembership(writer);
cat.addMember(tiger);
cat.addMember(lion);
PdfLayerMembership no_cat = new PdfLayerMembership(writer);
no_cat.addMember(tiger);
no_cat.addMember(lion);
no_cat.setVisibilityPolicy(PdfLayerMembership.ALLOFF);
cb.beginLayer(dog);
ColumnText.showTextAligned(cb, Element.ALIGN_LEFT,
  new Phrase("dog"), 50, 775, 0);
cb.endLayer();
cb.beginLayer(tiger);
ColumnText.showTextAligned(cb, Element.ALIGN_LEFT,
  new Phrase("tiger"), 50, 750, 0);
cb.endLayer();
cb.beginLayer(lion);
ColumnText.showTextAligned(cb, Element.ALIGN_LEFT,
  new Phrase("lion"), 50, 725, 0);
cb.endLayer();
cb.beginLayer(cat);
ColumnText.showTextAligned(cb, Element.ALIGN_LEFT,
  new Phrase("cat"), 50, 700, 0);
cb.endLayer();
cb.beginLayer(no_cat);
ColumnText.showTextAligned(cb, Element.ALIGN_LEFT,
  new Phrase("no cat"), 50, 700, 0);
cb.endLayer();
```

**Create two layers** (lines 2–4)

**Create first PdfLayer-Membership** (lines 5–7)

**Create second PdfLayer-Membership** (lines 8–11)

**Content linked to first membership**

**Content linked to second membership**

This example uses two out of four possible visibility policies:

- `ALLON`—Visible only if all the entries are on
- `ANYON`—Visible if any of the entries is on (this is the default)
- `ANYOFF`—Visible if any of the entries is off
- `ALLOFF`—Visible if the state of all the entries is off

This feature can be used, for instance, to inform end users that they can open the Layers panel to switch on optional layers. As soon as the end user has found this panel and has turned on at least one of the layers, you no longer need to show the message.

In the next example, you'll see other ways to change the state of an optional content layer.

### 12.3.5 Changing the state of a layer with an action

Do you remember how you wrote code to jump to an external location in chapter 4? You used `setAction()` methods of class `Chunk` to add an action. You can also create an action to turn the visibility of a layer on or off and add this action to a `Chunk`.

Figure 12.14 shows a series of questions and answers. Each answer is added to a different layer that can be turned on or off using the Layers panel to the left. Additionally, a phrase has been added. This phrase contains three `Chunks` that have been made interactive by adding actions: ON, OFF, and Toggle. Mind

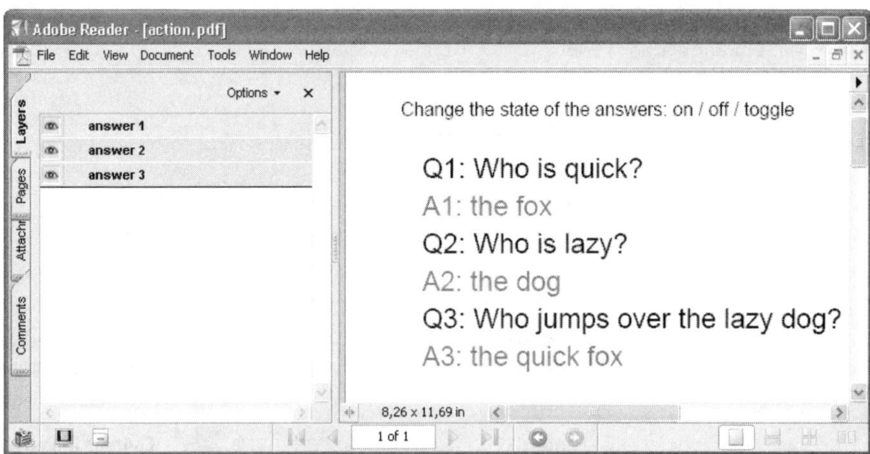


**Figure 12.14 Changing the visibility of an optional content group using actions**

the use of uppercase letters; that's how the states are defined in table 8.59 of the PDF Reference.

When you open the PDF shown in screenshot 12.14, the answers are invisible. You can click the word *on* or *toggle* to make the answers appear. If you have a quiz with lots of questions, it may be easier to have a clickable area next to each question that lets the end user show each specific answer. This approach is more user-friendly than making users find the correct layer in the panel to the left of the document. Here's the code:

```
/* chapter12/OptionalContentActionExample.java */
PdfLayer a1 = new PdfLayer("answer 1", writer);
PdfLayer a2 = new PdfLayer("answer 2", writer);
PdfLayer a3 = new PdfLayer("answer 3", writer);
a1.setOn(false);
a2.setOn(false);
a3.setOn(false);
ArrayList stateOn = new ArrayList();
stateOn.add("ON");
stateOn.add(a1);
stateOn.add(a2);
stateOn.add(a3);
PdfAction actionOn = PdfAction.setOCGstate(stateOn, true);
ArrayList stateOff = new ArrayList();
stateOff.add("OFF");
stateOff.add(a1);
stateOff.add(a2);
stateOff.add(a3);
PdfAction actionOff = PdfAction.setOCGstate(stateOff, true);
ArrayList stateToggle = new ArrayList();
stateToggle.add("Toggle");
stateToggle.add(a1);
stateToggle.add(a2);
stateToggle.add(a3);
PdfAction actionToggle = PdfAction.setOCGstate(stateToggle, true);
Phrase p = new Phrase("Change the state of the answers:");
Chunk on = new Chunk(" on ").setAction(actionOn);
p.add(on);
Chunk off = new Chunk("/ off ").setAction(actionOff);
p.add(off);
Chunk toggle = new Chunk("/ toggle").setAction(actionToggle);
p.add(toggle);
document.add(p);
```

**Create ArrayList for ON state**

**Create action object**

**Create action Chunk**

The static method `setOCGstate()` returns a `PdfAction` object. As you can see, the first parameter is an `ArrayList`. The first element in this list defines the action: The layers that are added can be turned on, turned off, or toggled. The second parameter makes sense only if you've defined radio groups. If it's false, the fact that a layer belongs to a radio group is ignored. If it's true, turning on a layer that belongs to a radio group turns off the other layers in the radio group.

Before you use all this interesting PDF functionality to enhance the map of Foobar, you should be aware of some iText-specific methods.

### 12.3.6 Optional content in XObjects and annotations

Three types of iText objects are often drawn in an optional content layer: `Images`, `PdfTemplate` objects, and annotations. For your convenience, these objects have a method `setLayer()` that can be used to define the optional content layer to which these objects belong.

The PDF shown in figure 12.15 has an `Image` (the iText logo), a `PdfTemplate` (the iText eye), and a widget annotation (a form field with text).

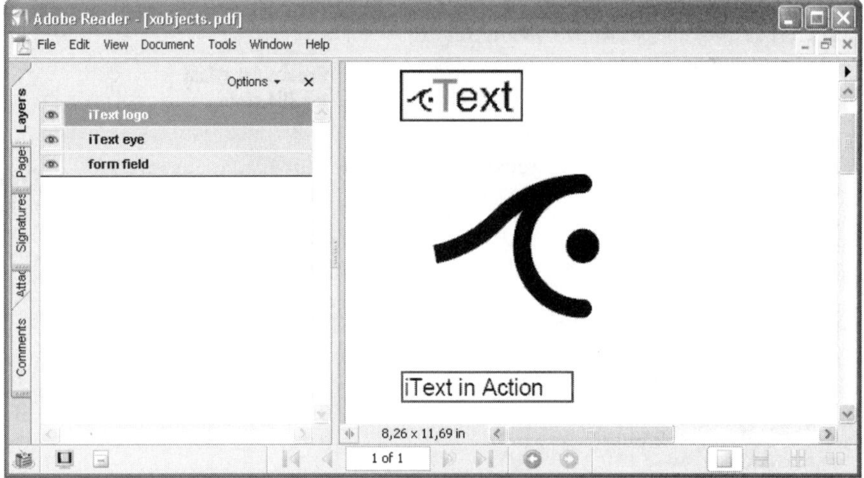


**Figure 12.15 Optional content in XObjects and annotations**

Note that we'll discuss annotations and form fields in chapter 15. But you won't have any difficulties understanding the following code sample:

```
/* chapter12/OptionalXObjectExample.java */
PdfLayer logo = new PdfLayer("iText logo", writer);
PdfLayer eye = new PdfLayer("iText eye", writer);
PdfLayer field = new PdfLayer("form field", writer);
Image image =
  Image.getInstance("../../chapter10/resources/iTextLogo.gif");
image.setAbsolutePosition(36, 780);
```

```
image.setLayer(logo);
document.add(image);

PdfTemplate template = cb.createTemplate(150, 150);
template.setLineWidth(12f);
template.arc(40f - (float) Math.sqrt(12800),
  110f + (float) Math.sqrt(12800),
  200f - (float) Math.sqrt(12800),
  -50f + (float) Math.sqrt(12800), 281.25f, 33.75f);
template.arc(40f, 110f, 200f, -50f, 90f, 45f);
template.stroke();
template.setLineCap(PdfContentByte.LINE_JOIN_ROUND);
template.arc(80f, 30f, 160f, 110f, 90f, 180f);
template.arc(115f, 65f, 125f, 75f, 0f, 360f);
template.stroke();
template.setLayer(eye);
cb.addTemplate(template, 36, 630);

TextField ff = new TextField(writer,
  new Rectangle(36, 600, 150, 620), "field1");
ff.setBorderColor(Color.blue);
ff.setBorderStyle(PdfBorderDictionary.STYLE_SOLID);
ff.setBorderWidth(TextField.BORDER_WIDTH_THIN);
ff.setText("iText in Action");
PdfFormField form = ff.getTextField();
form.setLayer(field);
writer.addAnnotation(form);
```

With these three types of objects, you no longer have to work with the methods `beginLayer()` and `endLayer()`. This will save you many lines of code when you want to enhance the map of Foobar using different layers.

## 12.4 Enhancing the map of Foobar

Previous chapters discussed the nature of the data needed to draw the map of the fictitious city of Foobar (section 10.5.1), as well as the names of the streets (section 11.6). You're now going to reuse the SVG files foobarcity.svg and streets.-svg, and you'll make extra SVG files with the names of the streets in French (rues.svg) and Dutch (straten.svg). You'll add the names of the streets in different layers, so that the end-user can choose the language he or she prefers.

Figure 12.16 shows the Dutch version of figure 11.15, with a few extra features. In the Layers panel to the left, you can now change the street names to another language by clicking one of the children of the radio group Streets / Rues / Straten.

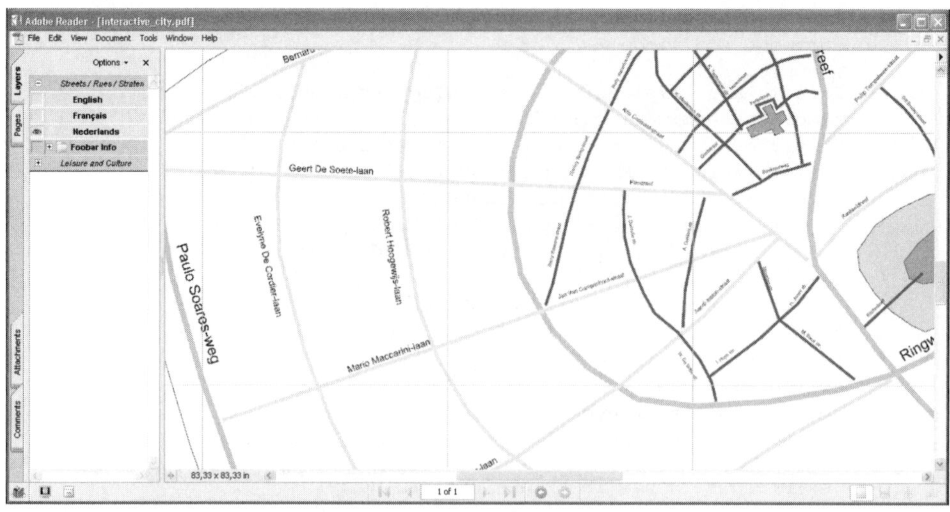


**Figure 12.16 The map of Foobar with Dutch street names**

### 12.4.1 Defining the layers for the map and the street names

In section 12.3.2, you saw that it's easy to create a radio group for the street names. Now you'll add extra layers, one with a raster image of the city of Foobar, and one with grid lines:

```
/* chapter12/FoobarCityBatik.java */
PdfLayer imageLayer = new PdfLayer("Map of Foobar", writer);
imageLayer.setZoom(-1, 0.2f);
imageLayer.setOnPanel(false);
PdfLayer vectorLayer = new PdfLayer("Vector", writer);
vectorLayer.setZoom(0.2f, -1);
vectorLayer.setOnPanel(false);
PdfLayer gridLayer = new PdfLayer("Grid", writer);
gridLayer.setZoom(0.2f, 1);
gridLayer.setOnPanel(false);
PdfLayer streetlayer =
  PdfLayer.createTitle("Streets / Rues / Straten", writer);
PdfLayer streetlayer_en = new PdfLayer("English", writer);
streetlayer_en.setOn(true);
streetlayer_en.setLanguage("en", true);
PdfLayer streetlayer_fr = new PdfLayer("Français", writer);
streetlayer_fr.setOn(false);
streetlayer_fr.setLanguage("fr", false);
PdfLayer streetlayer_nl = new PdfLayer("Nederlands", writer);
streetlayer_nl.setOn(false);
streetlayer_nl.setLanguage("nl", false);
```

**Show Image if zoom < 20%**

**Show map if zoom 20%**

**Show grid if 20% < zoom < 100%**

**Create parent for street layers**

**Create children**

```
streetlayer.addChild(streetlayer_en);
streetlayer.addChild(streetlayer_fr);
streetlayer.addChild(streetlayer_nl);
ArrayList radio = new ArrayList();
radio.add(streetlayer_en);
radio.add(streetlayer_fr);
radio.add(streetlayer_nl);
writer.addOCGRadioGroup(radio);
```

**Add children to parent**

**Declare radio group**

When you open the resulting PDF, the zoom factor will probably be lower than 20 percent. That's because you're creating a large page size, and you've changed the viewer preferences:

```
/* chapter12/FoobarCityBatik.java */
writer.setViewerPreferences(
  PdfWriter.PageModeUseOC | PdfWriter.FitWindow);
```

In chapter 13, you'll see that this makes sure the document fits the window and that the Layers panel is opened when the end user opens the file.

When the zoom factor is less than 20 percent, the image layer shows a JPEG version of the map (see figure 12.17). When you zoom in, the raster image disappears

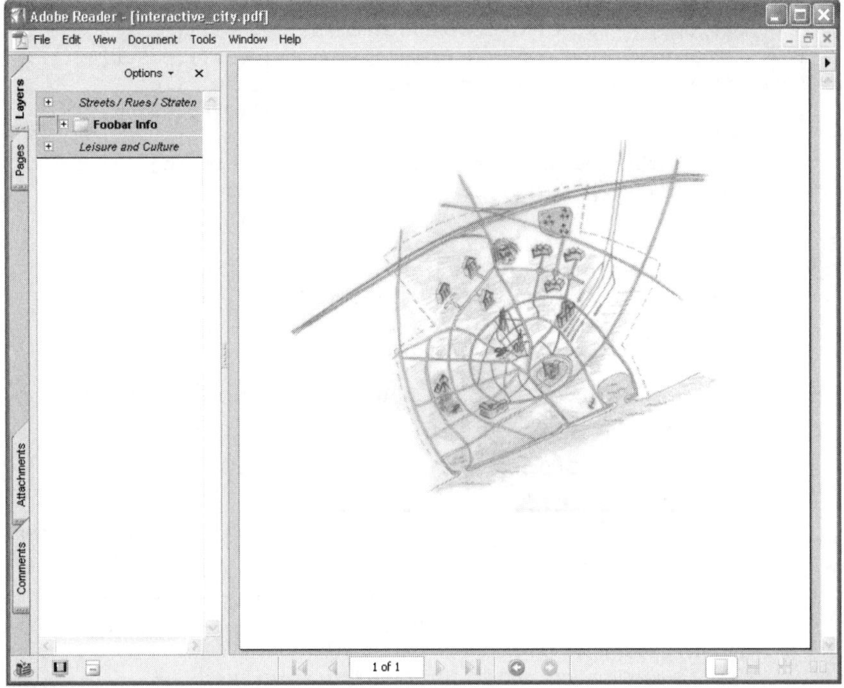


**Figure 12.17 The map of Foobar as a raster image**

as soon as you reach a zoom factor greater than or equal to 20 percent. That's the zoom factor that makes the vector data (map and grid lines) visible. Zoom in to a factor higher than 100 percent, and the grid lines disappear.

The previous snippet of code declares the structure of the optional content layers in your document. Now comes the tricky part: using Apache Batik to parse the SVG file and iText to visualize the data in the layers you just defined.

### 12.4.2 Combining iText and Apache Batik

You can find the Batik SVG Toolkit at xml.apache.org. Batik is described as "a Java-technology-based toolkit for applications or applets that want to use images in the Scalable Vector Graphics (SVG) format for various purposes, such as viewing, generation or manipulation." That sounds good: You want to use Batik in your application to view the SVG in the form of a PDF file.

First, you need Batik-specific source code to create Batik objects such as `SVGDocument`, `GVTBuilder` and `BridgeContext`:

```
/* chapter12/FoobarCityBatik.java */
String parser = XMLResourceDescriptor.getXMLParserClassName();
SAXSVGDocumentFactory factory = new SAXSVGDocumentFactory(parser);
SVGDocument city = factory.createSVGDocument(new File(
  "../../chapter10/resources/foobarcity.svg").toURL().toString());
SVGDocument streets = factory.createSVGDocument(new File(
  "../../chapter11/resources/streets.svg").toURL().toString());
SVGDocument rues = factory.createSVGDocument(new File(
  "../../chapter12/resources/rues.svg").toURL().toString());
SVGDocument straten = factory.createSVGDocument(new File(
  "../../chapter12/resources/straten.svg").toURL().toString());
UserAgent userAgent = new UserAgentAdapter();
DocumentLoader loader = new DocumentLoader(userAgent);
BridgeContext ctx = new BridgeContext(userAgent, loader);
GVTBuilder builder = new GVTBuilder();
ctx.setDynamicState(BridgeContext.DYNAMIC);
```

I won't go into the details of the Batik code; this is a book about iText, not about Batik. I'll just show you how to use the objects `builder`, `ctx`, `city`, `streets`, `rues`, and `straten` in your iText code:

```
/* chapter12/FoobarCityBatik.java */
PdfContentByte cb = writer.getDirectContent();          <-- Grab direct content
Graphics2D g2d;                                         | Create
PdfTemplate map = cb.createTemplate(6000, 6000);        | PdfTemplate/
g2d = map.createGraphics(6000, 6000,                    | Graphics2D
  new DefaultFontMapper());                             |
GraphicsNode mapGraphics = builder.build(ctx, city);      | Create/paint Batik
mapGraphics.paint(g2d);                                   | GraphicsNode
g2d.dispose();                                            |
```

```
cb.beginLayer(vectorLayer);
cb.addTemplate(map, 0, 0);
cb.endLayer();
PdfTemplate streets_en = cb.createTemplate(6000, 6000);
g2d = streets_en.createGraphics(6000, 6000,
  new DefaultFontMapper());
GraphicsNode streetGraphicsEn = builder.build(ctx, streets);
streetGraphicsEn.paint(g2d);
g2d.dispose();
streets_en.setLayer(streetlayer_en);
cb.addTemplate(streets_en, 0, 0);
```

**Add template in 3 lines**
**Create PdfTemplate/Graphics2D**
**Create/paint Batik GraphicsNode**
**Add template in 2 lines**

Note that it's possible to add the template inside a `beginLayer()/endLayer()` sequence using three lines of code, or you can use the method discussed in section 12.3.6.

After you've added these layers, you also add the raster image as described in section 12.3.5 and the grid as described in section 12.1.1:

```
/* chapter12/FoobarCityBatik.java */
Image image = Image.getInstance("../resources/map.jpg");
image.scalePercent(240);
image.setAbsolutePosition(450, 1400);
image.setLayer(imageLayer);
cb.addImage(image);
cb.saveState();
cb.beginLayer(gridLayer);
cb.setGrayStroke(0.7f);
cb.setLineWidth(2);
for (int i = 0; i < 8; i++) {
  cb.moveTo(1250, 1500 + i * 500);
  cb.lineTo(4750, 1500 + i * 500);
}
for (int i = 0; i < 8; i++) {
  cb.moveTo(1250 + i * 500, 1500);
  cb.lineTo(1250 + i * 500, 5000);
}
cb.stroke();
cb.endLayer();
cb.restoreState();
```

**Construct image**
**Transform image**
**Set layer**
**Add image to document**
**Initialize grid layer**
**Construct vertical lines**
**Construct horizontal lines**
**Stroke lines**

You already have a neat map with interesting interactive features, but now you want to add extra information.

### 12.4.3 Adding tourist information to the map

Figure 12.18 shows icons added to the map; I used glyphs from the Webdings TrueType font for the different information categories. The symbol ⓘ (somewhere near the corner of Kurt Meuleman and Patrick Debois Streets) marks the

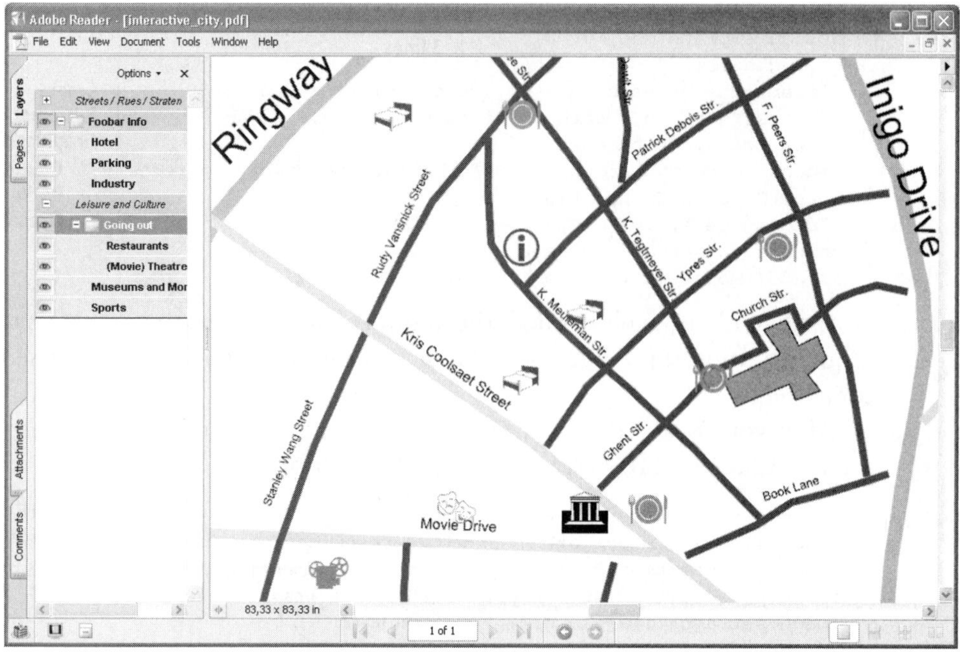


**Figure 12.18 The map of Foobar with extra information**

location of an office where you can get tourist information about the city of Foobar. The 🏛 symbol (between Kris Coolsaet Street and Movie Drive) means you'll find a monument at that location. If you click the eye next to Monuments and Musea in the Layers panel, the icon disappears.

Generating the structure of the layers is straightforward. These are some code snippets:

```
/* chapter12/FoobarCityBatik.java */
PdfLayer cityInfoLayer = new PdfLayer("Foobar Info", writer);
cityInfoLayer.setOn(false);
PdfLayer hotelLayer = new PdfLayer("Hotel", writer);
hotelLayer.setOn(false);
cityInfoLayer.addChild(hotelLayer);
PdfLayer parkingLayer = new PdfLayer("Parking", writer);
parkingLayer.setOn(false);
cityInfoLayer.addChild(parkingLayer);
(...)
PdfLayer cultureLayer =
  PdfLayer.createTitle("Leisure and Culture", writer);
PdfLayer goingoutLayer = new PdfLayer("Going out", writer);
goingoutLayer.setOn(false);
```

```
cultureLayer.addChild(goingoutLayer);
PdfLayer restoLayer = new PdfLayer("Restaurants", writer);
restoLayer.setOn(false);
goingoutLayer.addChild(restoLayer);
PdfLayer theatreLayer = new PdfLayer("(Movie) Theatres", writer);
theatreLayer.setOn(false);
goingoutLayer.addChild(theatreLayer);
PdfLayer monumentLayer =
  new PdfLayer("Museums and Monuments", writer);
monumentLayer.setOn(false);
cultureLayer.addChild(monumentLayer);
(...)
```

You've grouped and nested different layers; now you have to add content to these layers (otherwise they won't show up in the Layers panel). This is a shortened version of the code:

```
/* chapter12/FoobarCityBatik.java */
BaseFont font = BaseFont.createFont("c:/windows/fonts/webdings.ttf",
  BaseFont.WINANSI, BaseFont.EMBEDDED);
cb.saveState();
cb.beginText();
cb.setRGBColorFill(0x00, 0x00, 0xFF);
cb.setFontAndSize(font, 36);
cb.beginLayer(cityInfoLayer);
cb.showTextAligned(PdfContentByte.ALIGN_CENTER,
  String.valueOf((char)0x69), 2700, 3100, 0);
cb.beginLayer(hotelLayer);
cb.showTextAligned(PdfContentByte.ALIGN_CENTER,
  String.valueOf((char)0xe3), 2000, 1900, 0);
cb.endLayer(); // hotelLayer
cb.endLayer(); // cityInfoLayer
cb.beginLayer(goingoutLayer);
cb.beginLayer(restoLayer);
cb.setRGBColorFill(0xFF, 0x14, 0x93);
cb.showTextAligned(PdfContentByte.ALIGN_CENTER,
  String.valueOf((char)0xe4), 2650, 3500, 0);
cb.endLayer(); // restoLayer
cb.beginLayer(theatreLayer);
cb.setRGBColorFill(0xDC, 0x14, 0x3C);
cb.showTextAligned(PdfContentByte.ALIGN_CENTER,
  String.valueOf((char)0xae), 2850, 3300, 0);
cb.endLayer(); // theatreLayer
cb.endLayer(); // goingoutLayer
cb.beginLayer(monumentLayer);
cb.setRGBColorFill(0x00, 0x00, 0x00);
cb.showTextAligned(PdfContentByte.ALIGN_CENTER,
  String.valueOf((char)0x47), 3250, 2750, 0);
cb.endLayer(); // monumentLayer
cb.endText();
cb.restoreState();
```

In this example, the `beginLayer()/endLayer()` sequences are nested. Compare this code sample with the code in section 12.3.2: It's a little different, but the end result is the same.

With this example, we have finished one of Laura's most challenging assignments. It demonstrates a rather atypical use of PDF, but that doesn't mean it's less interesting.

## 12.5 Summary

After reading the last three chapters, you can make a decision when confronted with a project that involves text and graphics. If you don't like to work with PDF's graphics state operators and operands, you can consider chapters 10 and 11 to be purely informational and decide to work with the methods described in the first part of this chapter: the standard Java API and Sun's tutorial on 2D graphics. This choice is especially interesting if you need to work with a `Graphics2D` object in your application, or if you work with Swing components that are able to print themselves to a `Graphics2D` object.

Personally, I prefer working with the methods described in chapters 10 and 11, but that's because I generally write server-side applications. These applications don't have a GUI, and they don't have the benefits offered by `Graphics2D`. It's also the best choice for .NET programmers using iTextSharp or iText.NET. In .NET, there aren't any Swing components and there isn't a `Graphics2D` object.

The second part of this chapter ended this part of the book's discussion of PDF's graphics state by explaining the concept of optional content. The Foobar examples combined everything you've learned in this chapter. You even used a feature that hasn't been explained yet: setting viewer preferences so that the Layers panel is shown and the document fits the Adobe Reader window. That's a good topic to start with in the next chapter.

# *Part 4*

# *Interactive PDF*

Whereas part 3 discusses how to create a document's content, this part deals with meta content. How do you add bookmarks to a file, or headers, or footers, or a watermark? How do you add comments or a file attachment, or create and fill a form? And above all, how do you create a PDF file in a web application?

# 13 Browsing a PDF document

**_This chapter covers_**

- Setting viewer preferences
- Adding Bookmarks
- Introducing a first series of actions

If you've compiled and executed the small code samples that illustrated the past 12 chapters, you should have created more than 200 PDF files by now. Most of these examples involved step 4 in the creation process of a PDF document using iText: adding the content to a PDF document.

Now it's time to discuss another kind of content: the structural and/or interactive elements of a document. People reading an electronic soft copy of a document not only expect it to have the same characteristics as the paper hard copy; they also value interactive functionality. Studies and surveys indicate that readers find a table of contents or an outline the most important element of an eBook. Hyperlinks and illustrations are also considered important. Next in importance are page numbers and headings.

We'll deal with these and other features in the next three chapters. We'll discuss page numbers, headers, and watermarks in chapter 14, and annotations and form fields in chapter 15. In this chapter, we'll start by looking at the way a document is presented to the reader by changing the viewer preferences of Adobe Reader. You'll create thumbnails and page labels as well as the outline tree of a PDF. You'll finish with a first series of actions that can be added to a PDF document.

By the end of this chapter, you'll be able to make a new version of the course catalog with some bookmarks, thumbnail images and page labels.

## 13.1 Changing viewer preferences

If you open a document in Adobe Reader, and no viewer preferences are specified inside the document, the Reader shows the document using default settings for the zoom factor, the visibility of toolbars, and so on. The panes or panels to the left (if available) are closed by default.

For the map of Foobar, you made sure the Layers panel is open. You also don't want the end user to see an empty corner of the map or a detail of a specific street upon opening the document. Instead, you want people to see the complete city when they open the document for the first time.

To achieve this, you've defined the viewer preferences of the document like this:

```
/* chapter12/FoobarCityBatik.java */
writer.setViewerPreferences(
  PdfWriter.PageModeUseOC | PdfWriter.FitWindow);
```

If you're reading this book along with the PDF specifications, you can consult tables 3.25 and 8.1 of the PDF Reference. Not all the viewer preferences listed in these tables are supported in iText (yet), but I think we have the most important ones. The following three sections discuss the page layout, the page mode, and the viewing options.

### 13.1.1 Setting the page layout

With the following values, you can specify the page layout to be used when a document is opened:

- `PdfWriter.PageLayoutSinglePage`—Display one page at a time (this is the default).
- `PdfWriter.PageLayoutOneColumn`—Display the pages in one column.
- `PdfWriter.PageLayoutTwoColumnLeft`—Display the pages in two columns, with the odd-numbered pages on the left.
- `PdfWriter.PageLayoutTwoColumnRight`—Display the pages in two columns, with the odd-numbered pages on the right.
- `PdfWriter.PageLayoutTwoPageLeft`—Display the pages two at a time, with odd-numbered pages on the left.
- `PdfWriter.PageLayoutTwoPageRight`—Display the pages two at a time, with odd-numbered pages on the right.

At first sight, the difference between `SinglePage` and `OneColumn`, or `TwoPage` and `TwoColumn`, may not be clear. The best way to understand the difference is to open the files in Adobe Reader and scroll from one page to another. In figure 13.1, you see a document that was opened with page layout `TwoColumnLeft`. I scrolled down so that the three pages are partially visible.

If you choose View > Page Layout from the menu bar, the option Continuous—Facing is selected. Change this option to Facing, and see at what happens: Now only two pages at a time appear. The flow of the pages is no longer continuous.

Note that `TwoPageLeft` and `TwoPageRight` were introduced in PDF-1.5, so don't forget to change the PDF version as in the following code snippet:

```
/* chapter13/VPPageLayout.java */
PdfWriter writer6 = PdfWriter.getInstance(document, new
  FileOutputStream("two_page_right.pdf"));
writer6.setPdfVersion(PdfWriter.VERSION_1_5);
writer6.setViewerPreferences(PdfWriter.PageLayoutTwoPageRight);
```

With page layout preferences, you define how the pages are organized in the document window. With page mode preferences, you can define how the document opens in Adobe Reader.

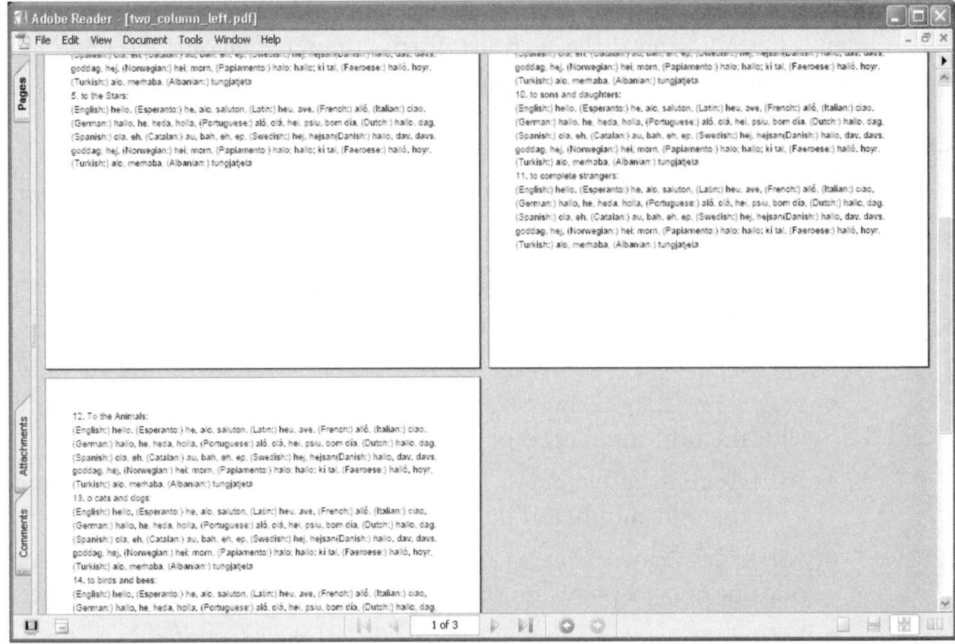

**Figure 13.1 Page layout example using `TwoColumnLeft`**

### 13.1.2 Choosing the page mode

The following list of the page mode preferences gives you an idea of the different panels available in Adobe Reader:

- `PdfWriter.PageModeUseNone`—None of the tabs on the left are selected (this is the default).
- `PdfWriter.PageModeUseOutlines`—The document outline (the bookmarks; see figure 2.3) is visible.
- `PdfWriter.PageModeUseThumbs`—Thumbnail images corresponding with the pages are visible.
- `PdfWriter.PageModeFullScreen`—Full-screen mode. No menu bar, window controls, or any other windows are visible.
- `PdfWriter.PageModeUseOC`—The optional content group panel is visible (since PDF-1.5).
- `PdfWriter.PageModeUseAttachments`—The attachments panel is visible (since PDF-1.6).

Typically, these page modes are set to stress the fact that the document has bookmarks, optional content, and so on.

With page layout and page mode, you're supposed to choose one option from each list. It doesn't make sense to choose two different page layout or page mode values (for instance, `PdfWriter.PageLayoutSinglePage | PdfWriter.PageLayoutTwoColumnLeft`), but you can always combine a page mode with a page layout option:

```
/* chapter13/VPPageModeAndLayout.java */
PdfWriter writer1 = PdfWriter.getInstance(document,
  new FileOutputStream("page_mode_and_layout.pdf"));
writer1.setViewerPreferences(PdfWriter.PageModeUseOutlines |
  PdfWriter.PageLayoutTwoColumnRight);
```

If you choose full-screen mode, you can add another option related to the panel to the left. This preference specifies how to display the document on exiting full-screen mode:

- `PdfWriter.NonFullScreenPageModeUseNone`—None of the tabs at the left are selected (this is the default).
- `PdfWriter.NonFullScreenPageModeUseOutlines`—The document outline is visible.
- `PdfWriter.NonFullScreenPageModeUseThumbs`—Thumbnail images corresponding with the pages are visible.
- `PdfWriter.NonFullScreenPageModeUseOC`—The optional content group panel is visible (since PDF 1.5).

The following code snippet opens the document in full-screen mode with a separate window showing the outlines:

```
/* chapter13/VPPageModeAndLayout.java */
PdfWriter writer2 = PdfWriter.getInstance(document,
  new FileOutputStream("full_screen.pdf"));
writer2.setViewerPreferences(PdfWriter.PageModeFullScreen |
  PdfWriter.NonFullScreenPageModeUseOutlines);
```

Note that you can exit full-screen mode using the Escape key.

A final set of viewer preferences that can be set in iText are related to the viewer options.

### 13.1.3 Viewer options

In the View menu of Adobe Reader, you can select toolbar items that must be shown or hidden. You can control the initial state of some of these options by setting the viewer preference:

- PdfWriter.HideToolbar—Hides the toolbar when the document is opened
- PdfWriter.HideMenubar—Hides the menu bar when the document is opened
- PdfWriter.HideWindowUI—Hides user-interface elements in the document's window (such as scroll bars and navigation controls), leaving only the document's contents displayed
- PdfWriter.FitWindow—Resizes the document's window to fit the size of the first displayed page
- PdfWriter.CenterWindow—Positions the document's window in the center of the screen
- PdfWriter.DisplayDocTitle—Displays the title that was added to the metadata in the top bar (otherwise, the filename is displayed)

The following code snippet combines some of the values discussed so far. Try the example, change some of the preferences, and open the resulting PDF documents to see what happens. For instance, the file generated by writer3 doesn't show the filename in the title bar; instead, it displays "Hello World in different languages," which is the title passed as PDF metadata. This may seem like a detail, but in my experience, it's these little details that make the difference for your customers:

```
/* chapter13/VPExamples.java */
PdfWriter writer1 = PdfWriter.getInstance(document,
  new FileOutputStream("hide_menu_center_window.pdf"));
writer1.setViewerPreferences(
  PdfWriter.HideMenubar | PdfWriter.CenterWindow);
PdfWriter writer2 = PdfWriter.getInstance(document,
  new FileOutputStream("no_ui_fit_window.pdf"));
writer2.setViewerPreferences(
  PdfWriter.HideWindowUI | PdfWriter.FitWindow);
PdfWriter writer3 = PdfWriter.getInstance(document,
  new FileOutputStream("display_title_two_page_left.pdf"));
writer3.setPdfVersion(PdfWriter.VERSION_1_5);
writer3.setViewerPreferences(
  PdfWriter.DisplayDocTitle | PdfWriter.PageLayoutTwoPageLeft);
document.addTitle("Hello World in different languages");
PdfWriter writer4 = PdfWriter.getInstance(document,
  new FileOutputStream("no_toolbar_use_thumbs.pdf"));
writer4.setViewerPreferences(
  PdfWriter.HideToolbar | PdfWriter.PageModeUseThumbs);
```

With the following preference values, you can determine the predominant order of the pages (this preference also has an effect on the way pages are shown when displayed side by side):

- PdfWriter.DirectionL2R—Left to right (the default)

- PdfWriter.DirectionR2L—Right to left, including vertical writing systems, such as Chinese, Japanese, and Korean

Finally, iText also supports the preference that turns off the FitToPage setting:

- PdfWriter.PrintScalingNone—Indicates that the print dialog should reflect no page scaling

This final preference is important if you want to print a PDF file on paper that is preprinted. If the viewer scales the pages to fit the paper size, you can't be sure the content printed by Adobe Reader will match with the preprinted content. For instance, you have to be careful not to print over a preprinted header and footer.

## 13.2 Visualizing thumbnails

In the previous example, you created a PDF document with the page mode set to PdfWriter.PageModeUseThumbs. Figure 13.2 shows what the resulting PDF looks like.

The Pages panel shows a thumbnail of every page automatically. This is pure Adobe Reader magic: Reader generates the thumbnail images. Note that iText can't convert PDF pages into images.

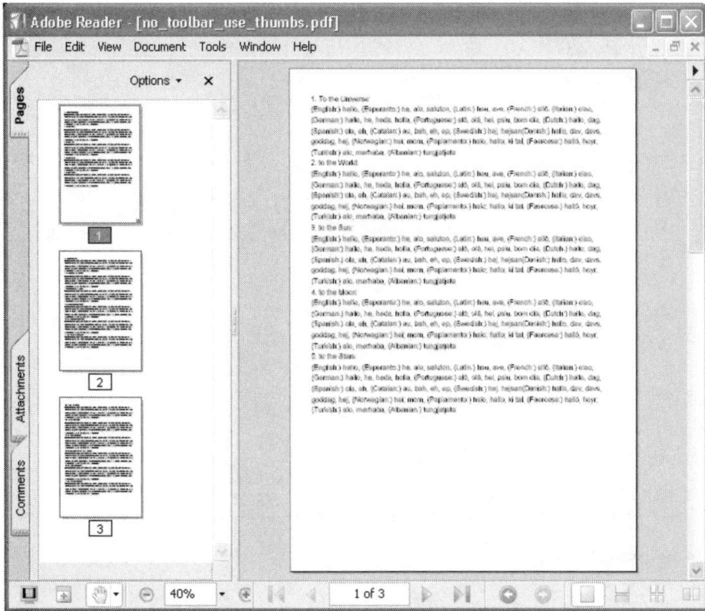


**Figure 13.2 Using thumbnails**

In the following sections, you'll learn how to change the label of these thumbnails and how to replace the thumbnail with another image.

### 13.2.1 Changing the page labels

In figure 13.3, I've opened the Pages panel in a separate window by dragging and dropping the tab. If you compare the Pages panel with the document panel, you immediately understand that it can be used as a means to browse through the document. A (red) rectangle in the Pages panel indicates the area of the document that is shown in the document window.

If you compare figure 13.2 with figure 13.3, you should notice another peculiarity. In figure 13.2, you can see the default page labels attributed automatically by Adobe Reader. In figure 13.3, I've changed the default way pages are numbered: The first page is now page i, the second is page ii, the third is page iii, and the fourth is iv. The fifth page, however, is labeled page 1; and starting with the eighth page, the numbers look like this: A-8, A-9, and so on.

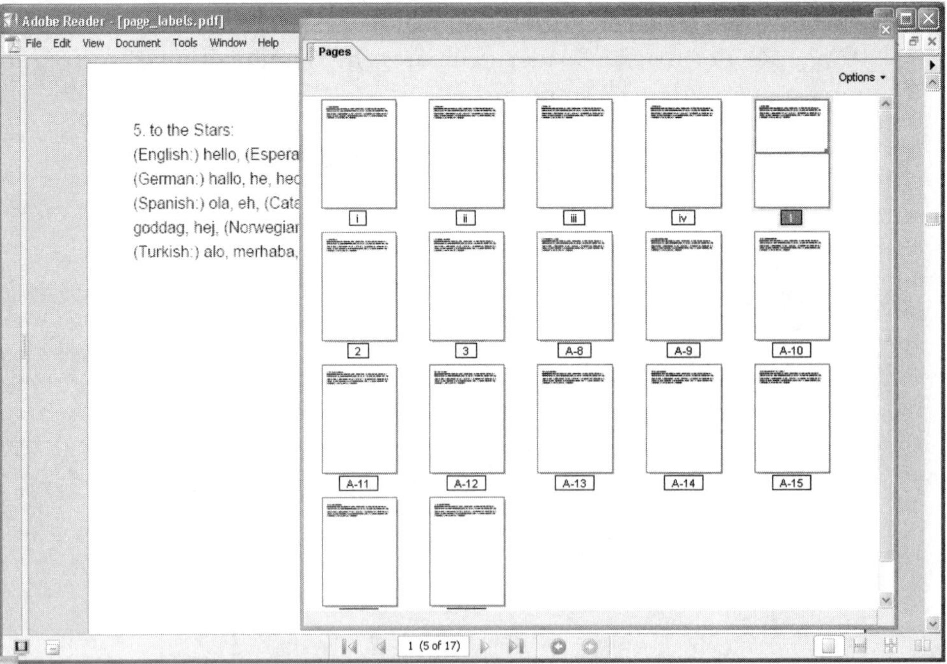


**Figure 13.3 Changing page labels**

The following code snippet changes the page labels:

```
/* chapter13/PageLabels.java */
PdfPageLabels pageLabels = new PdfPageLabels();
pageLabels.addPageLabel(1, PdfPageLabels.LOWERCASE_ROMAN_NUMERALS);
pageLabels.addPageLabel(5, PdfPageLabels.DECIMAL_ARABIC_NUMERALS);
pageLabels.addPageLabel(8, PdfPageLabels.DECIMAL_ARABIC_NUMERALS,
  "A-", 8);
writer.setPageLabels(pageLabels);
```

Take a close look at the bottom bar in the screenshots of this section. In figure 13.2, you read *page 1 of 3*. In figure 13.3, the numbering is different: *1 (5 of 17)*. The page information in figure 13.4 reads *fox dog 1 (2 of 10)*. This demands some extra explanation from the PDF Reference:

> Each page in a PDF-document is identified by an integer *page index* that expresses the page's relative position within the document. In addition, a document may optionally define page labels to identify each page visually on the screen or in print.

This example uses two of the six possible numbering types for the page labels:

- `PdfPageLabels.DECIMAL_ARABIC_NUMERALS`—Decimal Arabic numerals
- `PdfPageLabels.UPPERCASE_ROMAN_NUMERALS`—Uppercase Roman numerals
- `PdfPageLabels.LOWERCASE_ROMAN_NUMERALS`—Lowercase Roman numerals
- `PdfPageLabels.UPPERCASE_LETTERS`—Uppercase letters; A to Z for the first 26 pages, AA to ZZ for the next 26, and so on
- `PdfPageLabels.LOWERCASE_LETTERS`—Lowercase letters; a to z for the first 26 pages, aa to zz for the next 26, and so on
- `PdfPageLabels.EMPTY`—No page numbers

There are different `addPageLabel()` methods in class `PdfPageLabels`. They all take a page number as the first parameter and a numbering style as the second parameter. A method with three parameters can be used to add a `String` that serves as prefix. This method can also be used in combination with the `EMPTY` numbering style if you want to create text-only page labels.

Note that changing the numbering style resets the page number to 1. The method with four parameters lets you define the first logical page number. For instance, when I started labeling pages with "A-," I defined that the first page labeled that way should be page 8.

**TOOLBOX** `com.lowagie.tools.plugins.PhotoAlbum` *(Convert2Pdf)* If you have a directory containing images or photographs that you want to share with other people, you can use one of the plug-ins in the toolbox to create a PDF that can serve as photo album. Figure 13.4 shows an example. The Pages panel with the thumbnails is used as an overview of all the photos in the album. To show one of the photographs in the document window, click one of the thumbnails in the Pages panel.

Figure 13.4 shows an example that uses `PageLabels.EMPTY`. The PhotoAlbum plug-in uses the name of the image (minus the extension) as a page label.

**Figure 13.4 Using the PhotoAlbum plug-in**

If you have a document with a lot of text, the end user won't always be helped by the Pages panel. All the thumbnails will look more or less the same—unless you replace the thumbnail with an image that catches the eye!

### 13.2.2 *Changing the thumbnail image*

It's possible to replace the thumbnails generated by Adobe Reader with an `Image` object. In figure 13.5, the second page is selected, but the thumbnail definitely doesn't correspond with the content in the document window.

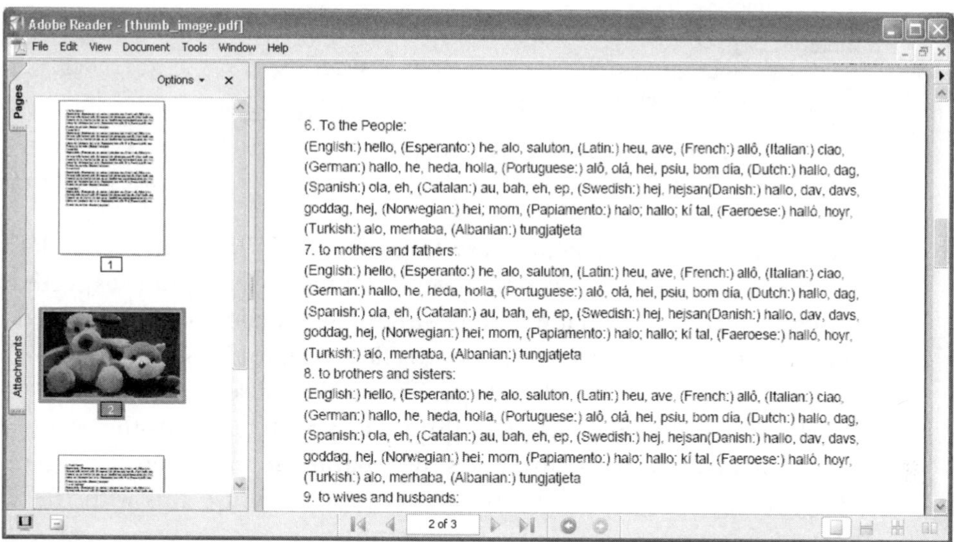


**Figure 13.5 Replacing a thumbnail with an `Image`**

With the method `setThumbnail()`, you can change the thumbnail of the current page.

```
/* chapter13/ThumbImage.java */
document.add(new Paragraph("5. to the Stars:"));
document.add(hello);
document.newPage();
writer.setThumbnail(
  Image.getInstance("../../chapter05/resources/foxdog.jpg"));
document.add(new Paragraph("6. To the People:"));
document.add(hello);
```

**Add content of page 1**

**Go to page 2**

**Set thumbnail image**

**Add content of page 2**

Page thumbnails and labels can help the end users of your document browse through the content.

In the next section, you'll add functionality that turns pages automatically.

## 13.3 Adding page transitions

By adding a transition and a value for the duration, a document can be displayed as a presentation (similar to a PowerPoint presentation). Let's rewrite the example that results in the PDF shown in figure 13.4:

```
/* chapter13/SlideShow.java */
writer.setPdfVersion(PdfWriter.VERSION_1_5);
writer.setViewerPreferences(PdfWriter.PageModeFullScreen);
```

**Set PDF version to 1.5**

**Set viewer preferences**

```
(...)
Image img2 =
  Image.getInstance("../../chapter13/resources/fox dog 2.gif");
img2.setAbsolutePosition(0, 0);
writer.setDuration(3);                    <-- Set duration (3 sec)
writer.setTransition(new PdfTransition(PdfTransition.DGLITTER, 2));  <-- Add transition (2 sec)
document.add(img2);
document.newPage();
```

The method `setDuration()` is easy to understand: The parameter defines how long the page is shown. If no duration is defined, user input is expected to go to the next page. This is what happens with the first page if you open the document generated in this example; you have to click to go to the second page. The other pages open automatically after a specific number of seconds.

The example demonstrates different possibilities of the `PdfTransition` class. The main constructor takes two parameters: a transition type and a value for the duration of the transition (don't confuse this with the value for the page duration).

There are different groups of transition types:

- `Dissolve`—The old page gradually dissolves to reveal a new one.
- `Glitter`—Similar to resolve, except that the effect sweeps across the page in a wide band moving from one side to another: diagonally (`DGLITTER`), from top to bottom (`TBGLITTER`), or from left to right (`LRGLITTER`).
- `Box`—A rectangular box sweeps inward from the edges (`INBOX`) or outward from the center (`OUTBOX`).
- `Split`—The lines sweep across the screen horizontally or vertically, inward or outward, depending on the value that was passed: `SPLITHIN`, `SPLITHOUT`, `SPLITVIN`, or `SPLITTVOUT`.
- `Blinds`—Multiple lines, evenly spaced across the screen, sweep in the same direction to reveal the new page horizontally (`BLINDH`) or vertically (`BLINDV`).
- `Wipe`—A single line sweeps across the screen from one edge to the other: from top to bottom (`TBWIPE`), from bottom to top (`BTWIPE`), from right to left (`RLWIPE`), or from left to right (`LRWIPE`).

If you don't specify a type, `BLINDH` is used. The default duration of a transition is 1 second. This is a nice feature, but it's a little off topic—you were looking for a means to browse the document. What about a good table of contents, with outlines shown in the bookmarks panel?

## 13.4 Adding bookmarks

Before you can construct an outline tree, you need to learn how to use three iText classes:

- A `PdfDestination` object allows you to define a position on a page (X, Y, zoom factor).
- A `PdfAction` object defines an action—for instance, an action to open a URL in a web browser (see section 4.2.3), an optional content state action (see section 12.3.6), and so on.
- A `PdfOutline` object is created using a `PdfDestination` and/or a `PdfAction`.

By the end of this section, you should be able to create an outline tree that is more feature-rich than the table of contents you created in chapter 4 using the objects `Chapter` and `Section`.

### 13.4.1 Creating destinations

With the class `PdfDestination`, you can create *explicit destinations* on a page, as opposed to the *named destinations* you created in chapter 4 (for instance, when you used `setName()` with an `Anchor` object, or `setLocalDestination()` with a `Chunk` object).

Table 8.2 in the PDF Reference explains the destination syntax. Let's go over the options by listing the constructors in the iText class.

#### *public PdfDestination(int type)*

You can use this constructor with two explicit destination types:

- `PdfDestination.FIT`—If you use this destination, the current page is displayed with its contents magnified just enough to fit the document window, both horizontally and vertically.
- `PdfDestination.FITB`—This option is almost identical to the previous one, but the page is displayed with its contents magnified just enough to fit the bounding box of the contents (without the margins).

Note that a page's bounding box is the smallest rectangle enclosing all of its contents.

***public PdfDestination(int type, float parameter)***

This constructor can be used with four explicit destination types:

- `PdfDestination.FITH`—The zoom factor is changed so that the page fits within the document window horizontally (the entire width of the document is visible). The parameter specifies the vertical coordinate of the top edge of the page.
- `PdfDestination.FITBH`—This option is almost identical to the previous one, but the width of the bounding box of the page is visible, not necessarily the entire width of the page.
- `PdfDestination.FITV`—The contents of the page are magnified just enough to fit the entire height of the page within the document window. The parameter is the horizontal coordinate of the left edge of the page.
- `PdfDestination.FITBV`—This option is almost identical to the previous one, but the contents are magnified just enough to fit the height of the bounding box.

***public PdfDestination(int type, float left, float top, float zoom)***

This constructor can be used for one explicit destination type:

- `PdfDestination.XYZ`—The parameter `left` defines an X coordinate, `top` defines a Y coordinate, and `zoom` defines a zoom factor.

You can also use this constructor to change the zoom factor of the current page without changing the X and/or Y position by passing negative values or zero for `left` and/or `top`.

***public PdfDestination(int type, float left, float bottom, float right, float top)***

This constructor can be used for one explicit destination type:

- `PdfDestination.FITR`—The parameters of this constructor define a rectangle. The page is displayed with its contents magnified just enough to fit this rectangle.

If the required zoom factors for the horizontal and the vertical magnification are different, the smaller of the two is used. Let's use some of these constructors to create an outline tree in a one-page example.

### 13.4.2 Constructing an outline tree

You can create an outline tree using the PdfOutline object. An outline object is constructed by defining the following:

- A parent for the outline item
- A destination or an action
- A title for the item: a String or a Paragraph (note that the style of the Paragraph isn't taken into account)
- Optionally, a boolean to indicate if the outline has to be open (the default) or closed

When you start building the tree, you don't have a parent object yet. You can get the root of the outline tree from the direct content with the method PdfContentByte.getRootOutline().

```
/* chapter13/ExplicitDestinations.java */
PdfDestination d1 = new PdfDestination(
  PdfDestination.XYZ, 300, 800, 0);                          ❶
PdfDestination d2 = new PdfDestination(
  PdfDestination.FITH, 500);                                 ❷
PdfDestination d3 = new PdfDestination(
  PdfDestination.FITR, 200, 300, 400, 500);                  ❸
PdfDestination d4 = new PdfDestination(
  PdfDestination.FITBV, 100);                                ❹
PdfDestination d5 = new PdfDestination(
  PdfDestination.FIT);                                       ❺
PdfOutline root = cb.getRootOutline();                       ❻
PdfOutline out1 = new PdfOutline(root, d1, "root", true);    ❼
PdfOutline out2 = new PdfOutline(out1, d2, "sub 1", false);  ❽
PdfOutline out3 = new PdfOutline(out1, d3, "sub 2");
new PdfOutline(out2, d4, "sub 2.1");
new PdfOutline(out2, d5, "sub 2.2");                         ❾
```

The root bookmark targets the upper-right corner ❶, the sub 1 bookmark makes the width fit the window ❷, sub 2 shows a specific rectangle ❸, and sub 2.1 makes the height fit the window ❹. Sub 2.2 makes the complete page visible ❺. To build this outline tree, you get the root object ❻. Then, you add an opened root outline ❼, a closed child ❽, and an opened child with opened children ❾.

If you try this example, you'll see that plus signs are drawn on the page. By clicking the destinations in the outline tree, you zoom in to (or zoom out from) these signs.

In addition to explicit destinations, you can also add actions to the outline tree.

### 13.4.3 Adding actions to an outline tree

You've already encountered `PdfActions` in previous chapters. You created an action to open the URL of a Wikipedia page in chapter 4; and in chapter 12, you changed the state of some optional content layers. In both examples, you used a `Chunk` and the method `setAction()`.

In the next example, you'll trigger these actions from the outline tree. In figure 13.6, you can see that it's also possible to change the style and the color of the items in the outline tree.

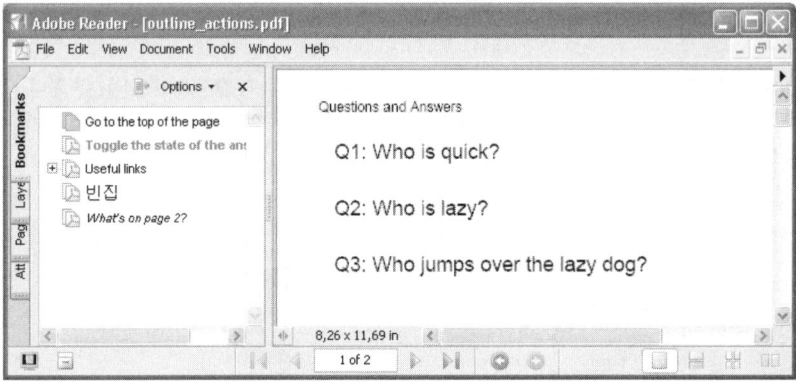


**Figure 13.6 An outline tree with different actions**

Reading the source code, you get an idea of a first series of actions supported in iText.

```
/* chapter13/OutlineActions.java */
document.add(                                                           ❶
  new Chunk("Questions and Answers").setLocalDestination("Title"));
PdfLayer answers = new PdfLayer("answers", writer);
(...)
PdfOutline root = cb.getRootOutline();        ❷
PdfOutline top = new PdfOutline(root,                ❸
  PdfAction.gotoLocalPage("Title", false),
  "Go to the top of the page");
ArrayList stateToggle = new ArrayList();                                ❹
stateToggle.add("Toggle");
stateToggle.add(answers);
PdfAction actionToggle = PdfAction.setOCGstate(stateToggle, true);
PdfOutline toggle = new PdfOutline(root, actionToggle,              ❺
  "Toggle the state of the answers");
toggle.setColor(new Color(0x00, 0x80, 0x80));
toggle.setStyle(Font.BOLD);
```

```
PdfOutline links =
  new PdfOutline(root, new PdfAction(), "Useful links");     ❻
links.setOpen(false);
new PdfOutline(links,
  new PdfAction("http://www.lowagie.com/iText"),              ❼
  "Bruno's iText site");
(...)
PdfAction chained =
  PdfAction.javaScript("app.alert('Bin-jip at IMDB');\r", writer);   ❽
chained.next(new PdfAction("http://www.imdb.com/title/tt0423866/"));  ❾
PdfOutline other = new PdfOutline(root, chained, "\ube48\uc9d1");    ❿
document.newPage();
document.add(new Paragraph("This was quite an easy quiz."));
PdfAction dest = PdfAction.gotoLocalPage(2,
  new PdfDestination(PdfDestination.FITB), writer);           ⓫
PdfOutline what = new PdfOutline(root, dest, "What's on page 2?");
what.setStyle(Font.ITALIC);                                   ⓬
```

This code first adds a named destination ❶ to the document. You get the root of the outline tree ❷ and add a local `GoTo` action ❸. Next, you create a toggle action ❹. When you use a `Paragraph` object for the title of the outline, the style and the color of the font in the paragraph aren't taken into account. If you want outline items with a color or style that is different from the default, you need to use the methods `setColor()` and `setStyle()` ❺.

Next, you add a structural outline item ❻, a URL action ❼, and a JavaScript action ❽. You now chain two actions ❾. Unicode is allowed in the outline titles ❿. Finally, you construct a local `GoTo` ⓫ and change the style to italic ⓬.

In chapter 2, you learned how to retrieve the bookmarks of an existing PDF file in the form of an XML file using the class `SimpleBookmark`. We didn't go into the details, but now that you've seen different types of bookmarks, let's take a closer look at the tags and attributes in such an XML file. (Note that not all types of bookmark entries are supported in this XML file.)

### 13.4.4 Retrieving bookmarks from an existing PDF file

In the two previous examples, the following code snippet was added to extract the bookmarks from a PDF file and to produce an XML file containing the entries of the outline tree:

```
/* chapter13/OutlineActions.java */
PdfReader reader = new PdfReader("outline_actions.pdf");
List list = SimpleBookmark.getBookmark(reader);
SimpleBookmark.exportToXML(list,
  new FileOutputStream("outline_actions1.xml"), "ISO8859-1", true);
```

If explicit destinations are used to create the outlines, you can expect an XML file similar to the one that was extracted from the PDF file generated in section 13.4.2:

```
<?xml version="1.0" encoding="ISO8859-1"?>
<Bookmark>
  <Title Action="GoTo" Page="1 XYZ 300 800 0" >root
    <Title Action="GoTo" Open="false" Page="1 FitH 500" >sub 1
      <Title Action="GoTo" Page="1 FitBV 100" >sub 2.1</Title>
      <Title Action="GoTo" Page="1 Fit" >sub 2.2</Title>
    </Title>
    <Title Action="GoTo" Page="1 FitR 200 300 400 500" >
      sub 2</Title>
  </Title>
</Bookmark>
```

Observe that the syntax of the `Page` attribute corresponds with the syntax discussed in section 13.3.1. You also see that, when using explicit destinations, a `GoTo` action is used implicitly. The possible values for the `Action` attribute are as follows:

- `GoTo`—This action can be used in combination with the attribute `Page` or `Named`.
- `GoToR`—This action opens a remote file defined in the attribute `File`. The destination inside this remote file can be defined in an attribute `Page`, `Named`, or `NamedN`. There's also the optional attribute `NewWindow`.
- `URI`—The action opens a URL defined by the attribute `URI`.
- `Launch`—The action launches an application defined in `the_file_to_open_or_execute`.

You recognize these values in the XML retrieved from the PDF file generated in section 13.4.3. There are also tags defining the color and the style:

```
<?xml version="1.0" encoding="ISO8859-1"?>
<Bookmark>
  <Title Action="GoTo" Named="Title" >
    Go to the top of the page</Title>
  <Title Color="0 0.50196 0.50196" Style="bold" >
    Toggle the state of the answers</Title>
  <Title Open="false" >Useful links
    <Title Action="URI" URI="http://www.lowagie.com/iText" >
      Bruno&apos;s iText site</Title>
    <Title Action="URI" URI="http://itextpdf.sourceforge.net/" >
      Paulo&apos;s iText site</Title>
    <Title Action="URI"
      URI="http://sourceforge.net/projects/itext/" >
```

```
        iText @ SourceForge</Title>
    </Title>
    <Title >&#48712;&#51665;</Title>
    <Title Action="GoTo" Style="italic" Page="2 FitB" >
      What&apos;s on page 2?</Title>
  </Bookmark>
```

Note that actions such as a JavaScript action or the action to toggle the answers aren't reflected in the XML. They aren't supported by the `SimpleBookmark` class.

### 13.4.5 Manipulating bookmarks in existing PDF files

One way to update/add bookmarks to an existing PDF document is to update/create an XML file. You can import the new XML file object with `SimpleBookmark.importFromXML()` and use the resulting `java.util.List` as a parameter for the method `PdfStamper.setOutlines()`.

You don't need to write any iText code; you can use the toolbox plug-ins to retrieve/update the outline tree.

**TOOLBOX** *`com.lowagie.tools.plugins.Bookmarks2XML` (Bookmarks)* Extracts the outline tree of an existing PDF document in the form of an XML file.

*`com.lowagie.tools.plugins.XML2Bookmarks` (Bookmarks)* Adds the bookmarks listed in an XML file to an existing PDF document.

If you manipulate a single document with bookmarks using `PdfStamper`, the bookmarks are preserved. Even if you insert pages, you don't need to worry about the page references: They're adjusted automatically. You can even add an extra outline item. The following example inserts a title page. You can add an extra bookmark entry that points to the (new) first page like this:

```
/* chapter13/HelloWorldManipulateBookmarks.java */
List list = SimpleBookmark.getBookmark(reader);      ❶
HashMap map = new HashMap();                 ❷
map.put("Title", "Title Page");
ArrayList kids = new ArrayList();    ❸
HashMap kid1 = new HashMap();                ❹
kid1.put("Title", "top");
kid1.put("Action", "GoTo");
kid1.put("Page", "1 FitH 806");
kids.add(kid1);
HashMap kid2 = new HashMap();               ❺
kid2.put("Title", "bottom");
kid2.put("Action", "GoTo");
kid2.put("Page", "1 FitH 36");
kids.add(kid2);
```

```
map.put("Kids", kids);   ❻
list.add(0, map);   ❼
stamper.setOutlines(list);
```

You get the `List` object with the existing bookmarks ❶. You add nested bookmarks: You create a parent entry ❷ and a list that contains the child entries ❸ (one that points to the top of the first page ❹ and another that points to the bottom ❺). You add the kids to the parent ❻ and the parent to the original bookmarks list so that it's the first item ❼ (index = 0).

The syntax used to construct this nested outline entry is similar to the syntax used in the XML files you saw in the previous subsection. The current code sample corresponds with this XML snippet:

```
<Title >Title Page
  <Title Action="GoTo" Page="1 FitH 806" >top</Title>
  <Title Action="GoTo" Page="1 FitH 36" >bottom</Title>
</Title>
```

The previous example works fine if you're using `PdfStamper` to manipulate a single document. If you're using `PdfCopy`, don't forget to set the outlines. You must concatenate the bookmarks, particularly if you're concatenating different PDF documents that have bookmarks.

The next example shows how it's done:

```
/* chapter13/HelloWorldCopyBookmarks.java */
ArrayList bookmarks = new ArrayList();
PdfReader reader = new PdfReader("HelloWorld1.pdf");
Document document =
  new Document(reader.getPageSizeWithRotation(1));
PdfCopy copy =
  new PdfCopy(document,
    new FileOutputStream("HelloWorldCopyBookmarks.pdf"));
document.open();
copy.addPage(copy.getImportedPage(reader, 1));
bookmarks.addAll(SimpleBookmark.getBookmark(reader));
reader = new PdfReader("HelloWorld2.pdf");
copy.addPage(copy.getImportedPage(reader, 1));
List tmp = SimpleBookmark.getBookmark(reader);
SimpleBookmark.shiftPageNumbers(tmp, 1, null);
bookmarks.addAll(tmp);
reader = new PdfReader("HelloWorld3.pdf");
copy.addPage(copy.getImportedPage(reader, 1));
tmp = SimpleBookmark.getBookmark(reader);
SimpleBookmark.shiftPageNumbers(tmp, 2, null);
bookmarks.addAll(tmp);
copy.setOutlines(bookmarks);
document.close();
```

In this case, the page numbers aren't updated automatically. Once you've shifted the page numbers so that they begin at the new starting position of the concatenated document, it's sufficient to use the standard methods of the `List` interface to manipulate the bookmarks.

This example isn't representative, because it takes only the first page of each document. You can automate the concatenation process in a loop. If you need some inspiration on how to achieve this, look at the source code of the Concat plug-in.

**TOOLBOX** `com.lowagie.tools.plugins.Concat` *(Manipulate)* This plug-in uses `PdfCopy` to concatenate two PDF files. It also takes bookmarks into account, but it can experience problems when the files you want to concatenate have AcroForms.

You've been adding different actions to the outline entries, but you haven't had a good overview of the types of actions yet. Let's look at the first series of actions available in PDF.

## 13.5 Introducing actions

There are two ways to create an action. In the previous chapter, you saw that you can use static methods that return a `PdfAction` instance when you want to change the state of one or more layers:

```
PdfAction.setOCGstate(ArrayList state, boolean preserveRB)
```

In chapter 4, you used one of the constructors of `PdfAction` to open a URL:

```
PdfAction(String url)
```

When you clicked the `Chunk` to which this action was added, the URL opened in a web browser.

In chapter 15, you'll see how actions that are added to a `Chunk` are in reality actions attached to an *annotation*. But first things first: Let's look at a series of constructors and static methods that are available in the `PdfAction` object. In chapter 15, we'll present form-specific actions—for instance, actions that submit an AcroForm to a web server.

### 13.5.1 Actions to go to an internal destination

The following static methods create actions that can be used to jump to another location in the current document:

```
gotoLocalPage(int page, PdfDestination dest, PdfWriter writer)
gotoLocalPage(String dest, boolean isName)
```

The first method can be used to create an *explicit destination* and the second to create a *named destination*. There are two kinds of named destinations; you make the distinction with the parameter `isName`. The `boolean` value true means you want to go to a destination defined using a PDF name; false indicates a destination defined with a PDF string. (We'll discuss the difference between a PDF name and a PDF string in chapter 18.) In iText, named destinations are generally defined using a string.

PDF viewers also support a list of *named actions* that can be created with `PdfAction(int named)`. You can use one of the following values for the parameter of this constructor:

- `PdfAction.FIRSTPAGE`—Jumps to the first page
- `PdfAction.PREVPAGE`—Jumps to the previous page
- `PdfAction.NEXTPAGE`—Jumps to the next page
- `PdfAction.LASTPAGE`—Jumps to the last page
- `PdfAction.PRINTDIALOG`—Opens a dialog box for printing

In a real-world example, you can add a header or footer to every page with a table that contains clickable areas that let you jump to the first, previous, next, or last page of the document:

```
/* chapter13/NamedActions.java */
PdfPTable table = new PdfPTable(4);
table.getDefaultCell().setHorizontalAlignment(Element.ALIGN_CENTER);
table.addCell(new Phrase(new Chunk("First Page")
  .setAction(new PdfAction(PdfAction.FIRSTPAGE))));
table.addCell(new Phrase(new Chunk("Prev Page")
  .setAction(new PdfAction(PdfAction.PREVPAGE))));
table.addCell(new Phrase(new Chunk("Next Page")
  .setAction(new PdfAction(PdfAction.NEXTPAGE))));
table.addCell(new Phrase(new Chunk("Last Page")
  .setAction(new PdfAction(PdfAction.LASTPAGE))));
```

Keep this example in mind; in the next chapter, you'll learn how to add this table to every page of your document automatically.

Just as you retrieved bookmarks in section 13.4.3, you can also retrieve the named destinations inside an existing PDF file. Two of the previous examples included the following code snippet:

```
/* chapter13/GotoActions.java */
PdfReader reader = new PdfReader("remote.pdf");
HashMap map =
  SimpleNamedDestination.getNamedDestination(reader, false);
```

```
SimpleNamedDestination.exportToXML(map,
  new FileOutputStream("remote.xml"), "ISO8859-1", true);
```

The boolean passed with the static getNamedDestination() method allows you to distinguish between named destinations that were added as a PDF string (false) or as a PDF name (true). The XML file generated with this code snippet looks like this:

```
<?xml version="1.0" encoding="ISO8859-1"?>
<Destination>
  <Name Page="2 XYZ 178.07 800 0">test</Name>
</Destination>
```

This XML file can be useful if you want to create an HTML index for the document similar to the one you made in chapter 2, or if you want to retrieve the named destinations that can be referred to by an external GoTo.

### 13.5.2 Actions to go to an external destination

Actions to jump to an external location (not necessarily a PDF document) are created using one of the following constructors:

- To an external URL—PdfAction(URL url) and PdfAction(String url)
- To a named destination in a remote PDF file—PdfAction(String filename, String name)
- To a specific page in a remote PDF file—PdfAction(String filename, int page)

You can also create an action to go to a remote file using a static method:

```
gotoRemotePage(String filename, String dest,
  boolean isName, boolean newWindow)
```

Note that you can pass an extra boolean parameter newWindow with this method. See figure 13.7 to understand what happens.

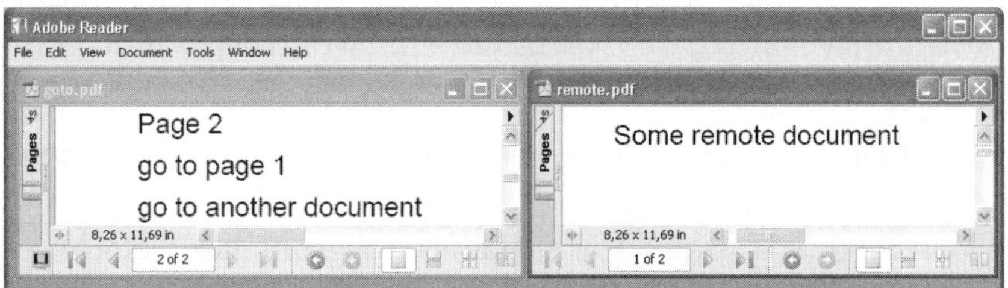


**Figure 13.7 Local and external destinations in a PDF document**

To make this screenshot, I opened the file goto.pdf; then, I clicked the sentence *go to another document*. If I had set `newWindow` to false, the window with the document goto.pdf would have been replaced with the file remote.pdf. For this example, I chose an action that opened a new window inside Acrobat Reader. If you're used to working with Firefox as your web browser, this is similar to what happens if you open a page in another tab, as opposed to what happens when you open a page in a new browser window.

As you can see in figure 13.7, goto.pdf also has an internal link to go to page 1. The following code sample demonstrates some of the actions just discussed:

```
/* chapter13/GotoActions.java */
PdfAction action = PdfAction.gotoLocalPage(2,
  new PdfDestination(PdfDestination.XYZ, -1, 10000, 0), writer);
writer.setOpenAction(action);   <-- Add action to writer
document.add(new Paragraph("Page 1"));
document.newPage();
document.add(new Paragraph("Page 2"));
document.add(new Chunk("go to page 1").setAction(
  PdfAction.gotoLocalPage(1,
  new PdfDestination(PdfDestination.FITH, 500), writer)));
document.add(Chunk.NEWLINE);
document.add(new Chunk("go to another document").setAction(
  PdfAction.gotoRemotePage("remote.pdf",
  "test", false, true)));
remote.add(new Paragraph("Some remote document"));
remote.newPage();
Paragraph p = new Paragraph("This paragraph contains a ");
p.add(new Chunk("local destination").setLocalDestination("test"));
remote.add(p);
```

**GoTo action (explicit destination)**

**GoTo action (internal destination)**

**GoTo action (external destination)**

**Create internal named destination**

Note that when you open the file goto.pdf, the viewer initially shows the second page of the document. That's because you use `setOpenAction()`, triggering an action based on a user-driven event.

### 13.5.3 Triggering actions from events

The method `setOpenAction()` is specific; it's triggered when a user opens the PDF file. With the method `setAdditionalAction()`, you can couple an action to the following events:

- `PdfWriter.DOCUMENT_CLOSE`—The action is triggered just before closing the document.
- `PdfWriter.WILL_SAVE`—The action is triggered just before saving the document.

- PdfWriter.DID_SAVE—The action is triggered just after saving the document.
- PdfWriter.WILL_PRINT—The action is triggered just before printing (part of) the document.
- PdfWriter.DID_PRINT—The action is triggered just after printing.

There's also the method setPageAction() to define what should happen for the following:

- PdfWriter.PAGE_OPEN—The action is triggered when you enter a certain page.
- PdfWriter.PAGE_CLOSE—The action is triggered when you leave a certain page.

Not all PDF consumers support these events. For instance, the events triggered when saving the document are meant for tools like Acrobat that can save forms filled in by an end user; the action can contain a script that checks whether all the fields are valid. Saving a filled-in form isn't possible with the free Adobe Reader; you can only perform a Save As, and this doesn't trigger the event.

The next code sample was tested with Adobe Reader 7.0. It opens an alert before printing the document, thanks you for reading the document just before closing the document, and warns you before entering and after leaving page 3:

```
/* chapter13/EventTriggeredActions.java */
PdfAction copyrightNotice = PdfAction.javaScript("app.alert(
    'Warning: this document is protected by copyright.');\r",
  writer);
writer.setAdditionalAction(PdfWriter.WILL_PRINT,
  copyrightNotice);
writer.setAdditionalAction(
  PdfWriter.DOCUMENT_CLOSE, PdfAction.javaScript(
  "app.alert('Thank you for reading this document.');\r",
  writer));
document.newPage();
writer.setPageAction(PdfWriter.PAGE_OPEN,
  PdfAction.javaScript
  "app.alert('You have reached page 3');\r", writer));
writer.setPageAction(PdfWriter.PAGE_CLOSE,
  PdfAction.javaScript(
  "app.alert('You have left page 3');\r", writer));
```

**Create JavaScript action**

**Action before printing**

**Action before closing**

**Action when page 3 opens**

**Action on leaving page 3**

You've been using simple JavaScript actions in this example. Let's see how you can add JavaScript to a PDF document using iText.

### 13.5.4 Adding JavaScript to a PDF document

JavaScript is discussed only briefly in the PDF Reference. You're referred to Netscape Communication's *Client-Side JavaScript Reference*, Adobe's *Acrobat JavaScript Scripting Reference*, and *Acrobat JavaScript Scripting Guide*. The JavaScript used in PDF files is almost the same JavaScript you can use in your HTML pages, but extra PDF-specific objects make it more powerful.

You can create a JavaScript action in iText by using one of the following static methods:

```
javaScript(String code, PdfWriter writer, boolean unicode)
javaScript(String code, PdfWriter writer)
```

In chapter 15, you'll use additional actions in combination with a PDF form. You'll use JavaScript to test whether the value entered by an end user is a date, and you'll do some math with a simple calculator application written in PDF and JavaScript.

To achieve this, you'll write custom JavaScript functions and add them as *document-level JavaScript* to the `PdfWriter` object. Let's try a simple example:

```
/* chapter13/DocumentLevelJavaScript.java */
writer.addJavaScript(
  "function saySomething(s) {app.alert('JS says: ' + s)}", false);
writer.setAdditionalAction(PdfWriter.DOCUMENT_CLOSE,
  PdfAction.javaScript(
  "saySomething('Thank you for reading this document.');\r",
  writer));
```

Instead of calling the `alert()` method directly, you now call a custom method that adds "JS says:" to your message. In chapter 15, you'll make extensive use of this functionality.

Note that you also used the method `next(PdfAction na)` in a previous example to chain two actions:

```
/* chapter13/OutlineActions.java */
PdfAction chained =
  PdfAction.javaScript("app.alert('Bin-jip at IMDB');\r", writer);
chained.next(new PdfAction("http://www.imdb.com/title/tt0423866/"));
```

Both actions are executed in a sequence. In this example, the JavaScript alert informs the end user that a URL will be opened. Opening a URL is, in most cases, harmless. The next action we'll discuss can be more dangerous.

### 13.5.5 Launching an application

I don't recommend it, but it's possible to launch an application from a PDF file. The PDF specification supports launching applications from Windows, Mac, and

UNIX, but passing platform-specific parameters was only defined for Windows at the time the PDF Reference 1.6 was published.

For the moment, iText only supports launch actions for Windows through these methods:

- `PdfAction(String application, String parameters, String operation, String defaultDir)`
- `createLaunch(String application, String parameters, String operation, String defaultDir)`

Note that the `application` parameter can be used to pass an application or a document. The other parameters can be `null`:

- The `parameters` are passed to the application.
- The possible `operation` values include "open" and "print."
- `defaultDir` is the default directory in standard DOS syntax.

The following code snippet creates a clickable `Chunk` to launch Windows Notepad. It opens the file <*your_dir*>/examples/chapter13/resources/test.txt:

```
/* chapter13/LaunchAction.java */
Paragraph p = new Paragraph(
  new Chunk("Click to open test.txt in Notepad.")
  .setAction(new PdfAction("c:/windows/notepad.exe",
  "test.txt", "open", "../resources/")));
```

Adobe Reader gives you a warning before starting the application, and it's important to be careful: You click a huge number of buttons every day. When you see an OK button, you click it almost automatically. To protect yourself from doing so, you'll learn how to remove launch actions from an existing PDF document in chapter 18.

We'll continue discussing actions in chapter 15. Now it's time to return to one of Laura's first assignments: creating the course catalog. With the functionality you've learned in this chapter, you can enhance the course catalog and add bookmarks, page labels, and thumbnails.

## 13.6 Enhancing the course catalog

In chapter 7, you made a course catalog based on a series of XML files and JPEG images. You parsed these XML files to create an object stack that was added to a `MultiColumnText` object. This example adapts that code slightly so that the object stack is added to a `Document` object (without using columns). You also add some code that lets you ask the XML handler for the title of the course that was parsed. You'll use this course title as an entry for the outlines in your bookmarks pane.

By adding outlines, you get a course catalog that is much easier to browse; see figure 13.8.

You now have all the titles of the courses in the left panel, which makes it easy for students to find the course descriptions they need, but you can even make it easier. JPEG images of the handbook are available for almost every course, and you can use these images as thumbnails as shown in figure 13.9.

As you can see, you don't have an image for course number 8021 (I don't think there's a book titled *JDO in Action* yet).

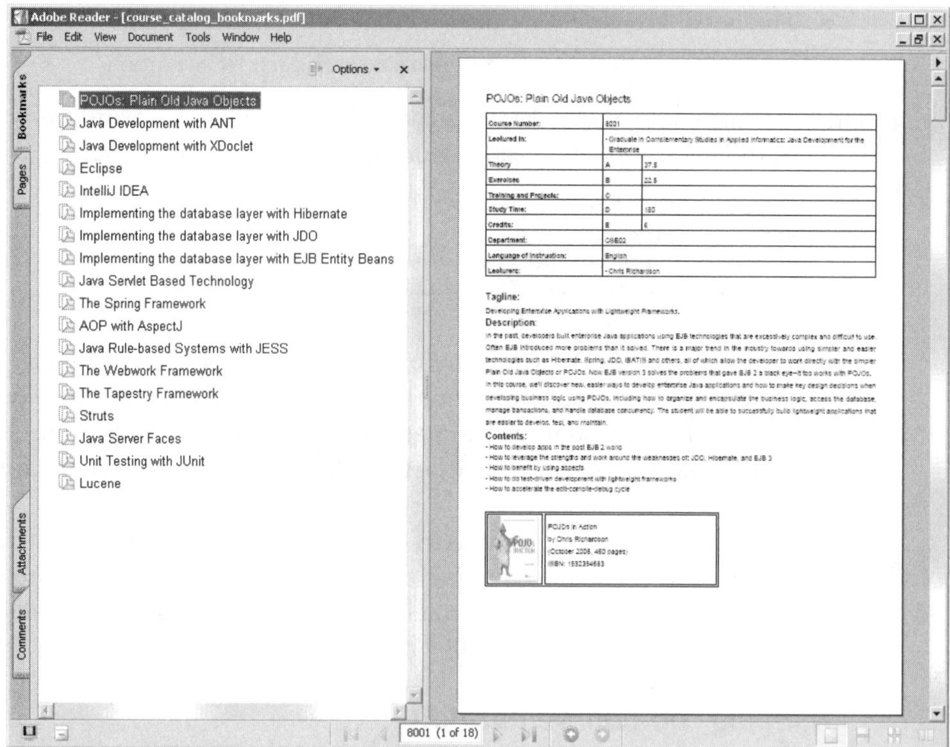


Figure 13.8 A course catalog with bookmarks

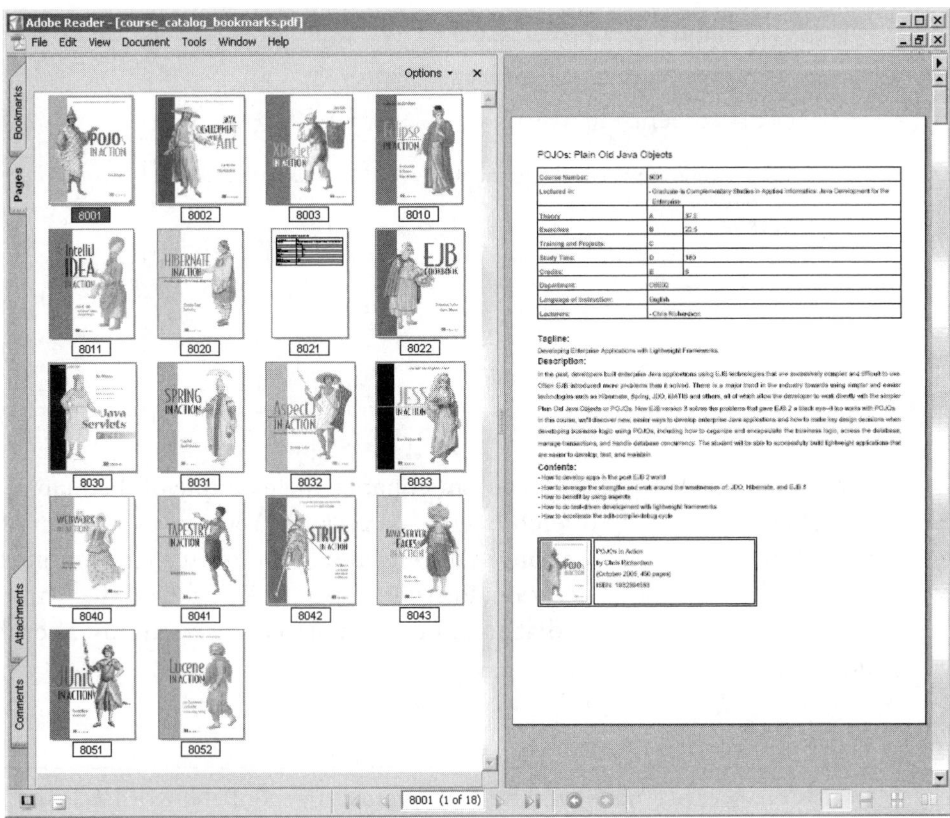


**Figure 13.9 A course catalog with thumbnails and page labels**

The following code snippet combines methods discussed in this chapter:

```
/* chapter13/CourseCatalogBookmarked.java */
Document document = new Document();
OutputStream outPDF = new FileOutputStream(
  "course_catalogue_bookmarks.pdf");
PdfWriter writer = PdfWriter.getInstance(document, outPDF);
writer.setViewerPreferences(PdfWriter.PageLayoutSinglePage
  | PdfWriter.PageModeUseOutlines);
document.open();
PdfOutline outline = writer.getRootOutline();
String[] courses = { "8001", "8002", "8003", "8010", "8011",
  "8020", "8021", "8022", "8030", "8031", "8032", "8033",
  "8040", "8041", "8042", "8043", "8051", "8052" };
CourseCatalogueBookmarked cc;
PdfPageLabels labels = new PdfPageLabels();
for (int i = 0; i < courses.length; i++) {
```

```
    cc = new CourseCatalogueBookmarked(courses[i]);
    cc.flushToDocument(document);
    int pagenumber = writer.getPageNumber();
    new PdfOutline(outline,
      new PdfDestination(PdfDestination.FIT), cc.getTitle());
    try {
      labels.addPageLabel(pagenumber, PdfPageLabels.EMPTY,
        courses[i]);
      writer.setThumbnail(Image.getInstance(
        "../../chapter07/resources/" + courses[i] + ".jpg"));
    } catch (FileNotFoundException fnfe) {
      // left empty on purpose
    }
    document.newPage();
  }
  writer.setPageLabels(labels);
  document.close();
```

If you need further practice, you can enhance the example of the map of Foobar using the functionality offered by `PdfDestination`. You can make a list of all the important sightseeing locations in the city and add this list to the outline tree. By clicking the name of the location, focus on a specific location on the map. You can even chain URL actions so that an informational web site opens just after the location is shown on the map.

## 13.7 Summary

In this chapter, we have explored different aspects of the word *browsing*. You've seen how you can define viewer preferences in a PDF document. We have discussed the contents of the Pages panel (thumbnails and page labels) and the Bookmarks panel (outlines).

You discovered that an outline tree can be more than just a table of contents, and we discussed some events triggered by an end user. In the next chapter, we'll deal with events that are triggered on the server side. When creating a document, iText keeps track of certain events: for instance, when a document is opened or closed; when a new page is started or ends; or when a paragraph, chapter, or section is added. This functionality will allow you to enhance the course catalog with extra features such as page numbers and watermarks.

# 14 Automating PDF creation

**This chapter covers**

- The theory of pages
- Page events in practice
- XML ideas for iText

In the previous chapter, we talked about events triggered in Adobe Reader by the end user. This chapter discusses events of a completely different nature: events that occur on the server side while composing a document—when a document is opened (step 3 in the PDF production process) or closed (step 5), when a new page is started or ended (step 4), and so on. These events aren't triggered by an end user or a developer, but by iText.

This functionality opens some interesting perspectives. When you add building blocks to a document, you don't care about pages. You trust that iText will send the content to the output stream each time a page is full and that a new page will be opened automatically. But you could use more control over the process if you want to add content to every page in your document—for instance, a recurring watermark. You can get this control by implementing the `PdfPageEvent` interface. This allows you to add custom functionality that is executed upon certain events. Note that you used this interface in chapter 4, when you added custom behavior to `Chunks` with the method `onGenericTag()`.

In this chapter, we'll discuss the other methods in the interface; but before we talk about page events, you should learn more about pages in general. You've used the concept of a page in all the previous examples, but there's more to a page than meets the eye.

## 14.1 Creating a page

I don't know why, but one of the frequently asked questions on the iText mailing list is how to start a new page in iText. That's easy to answer: You've used `document.newPage()` in many examples. But there is one catch: Sometimes it seems as though triggering `newPage()` doesn't have any effect.

In this section, you'll discover that this isn't a bug: It's a feature. We'll also talk about page boundaries: how to define them and how to use them. Finally, you'll lean how to reorder pages after you've created a document.

### 14.1.1 Adding empty pages

Automatic processes create undesirable empty pages in some situations. For instance, when you create a PDF based on data coming from a database, an XML file, or another source, the `newPage()` method can be called multiple times even if no data was added on the current page.

In most cases, you don't want this result; that's why iText was designed to ignore `newPage()` invocations if the current page is empty. Of course, sometimes you want to insert an empty page *on purpose*. If that is the case, you tell the writer, as in the following code sample:

```
/* chapter14/EmptyPages.java */
writer.setPageEmpty(ignore_empty);
document.newPage();
writer.setPageEmpty(ignore_empty);
document.newPage();
document.add(new Paragraph("Hello World"));
document.newPage();
writer.setPageEmpty(ignore_empty);
document.newPage();
```

If the parameter `ignore_empty` is true (the default), a document with only one page is created because three out of four `newPage()` statements in this code sample are ignored. When setting the parameter to false, a document with four pages is created: first, two empty pages, then a page saying Hello World, and then an extra empty page.

Another way to force empty pages to be inserted is to add extra content that is *outside* the page. Content that is outside the rectangle you defined when you created the document won't be visible to the end user. That brings us to the next topic: defining page boundaries.

### 14.1.2 Defining page boundaries

Until now, you have defined the size of a page using the helper class `PageSize` or by constructing an instance of the `Rectangle` object. Internally, this rectangle is called the *media box*. This page size is supposed to be equal to the size of the final document when printed on paper. In short, you've been creating PDF documents with pages that are ready for consumption.

You can also create PDF documents that are part of a prepress process with pages that have an intermediate format; in this case, the media box is larger than the finished page. The intermediate format may include additional production-related content that falls outside the boundaries of the final page.

Inside the media box, different areas can be defined: the *crop box*, the *bleed box*, the *trim box* and the *art box*. This is demonstrated in the following code snippet. Figure 14.1 shows a PDF file in which these page boundaries are defined.

Let's first look at the code used to define the different areas and then compare the code snippet with the screenshot:

```
/* chapter14/PageBoundaries.java */
Document document = new Document(new Rectangle(432, 792));      <-1 Media box: 6x11 in
PdfWriter writer = PdfWriter.getInstance(document,
  new FileOutputStream("page_boundaries.pdf"));
```

```
writer.setCropBoxSize(new Rectangle(5, 5, 427, 787));
writer.setBoxSize("bleed",
  new Rectangle(30, 30, 402, 762));
writer.setBoxSize("trim",
  new Rectangle(36, 36, 396, 756));
writer.setBoxSize("art",
  new Rectangle(72, 72, 360, 684));
```

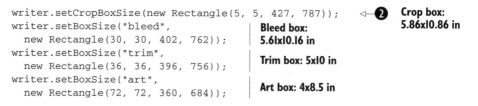

❷ **Crop box: 5.86x10.86 in**

**Bleed box: 5.61x10.16 in**

**Trim box: 5x10 in**

**Art box: 4x8.5 in**

In line ❶ you see that the media box should be 6.00 x 11.00 in. But if you look at the Document Properties window, you see that the document was clipped to 5.86 x 10.86 in. This is the size defined in line ❷ with the method `setCropBoxSize()`.

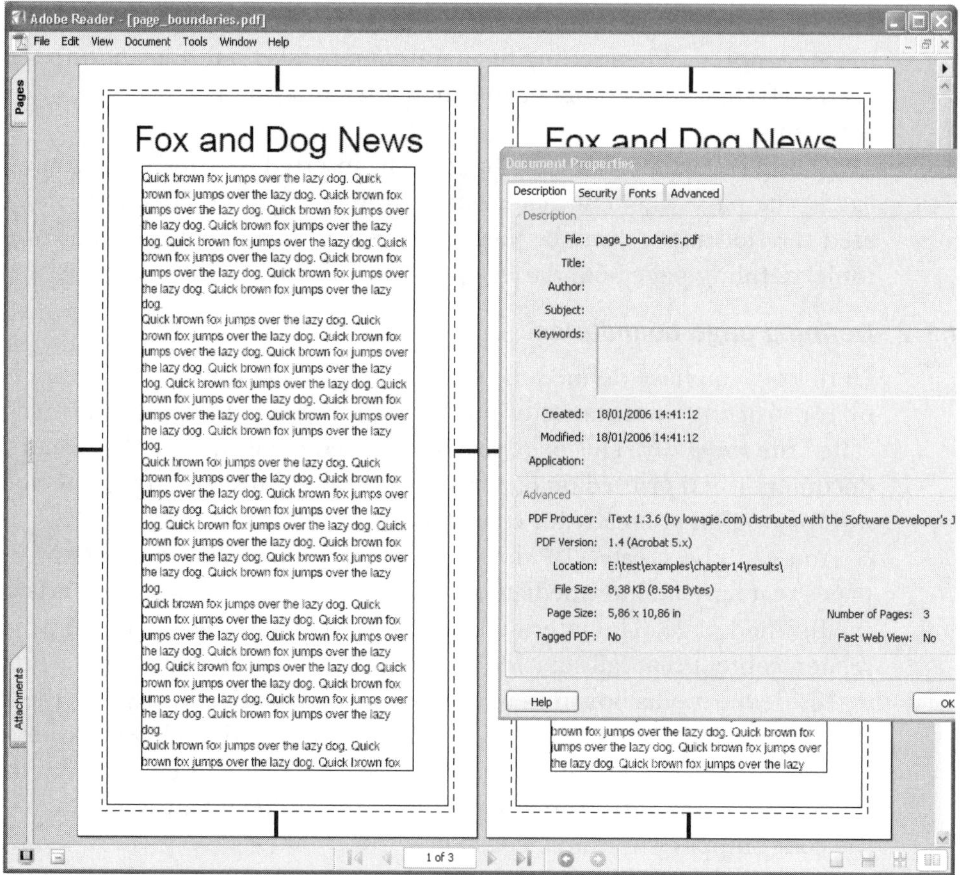


**Figure 14.1 Page boundaries**

The dashed line corresponds with the bleed box. The full line just inside the bleed box is the trim box, and the rectangle around the text is the art box. What do all these terms signify? Let's consult the PDF Reference:

- *The Media Box*—defines the boundaries of the physical medium on which the page is to be printed. It may include any extended area surrounding the finished page for bleed, printing marks, or other such purposes. It may also include areas close to the edges of the medium that cannot be marked because of physical limitations of the output device. Content falling outside this boundary can safely be discarded without affecting the meaning of the PDF file.
- *The Crop Box*—defines the region to which the contents of the page are to be clipped (cropped) when displayed or printed. Unlike the other boxes, the crop box has no defined meaning in terms of physical page geometry or intended use; it merely imposes clipping on the page contents. The default value is the page's media box.
- *The Bleed Box*—defines the region to which the contents of the page should be clipped when output in a production environment. This may include any extra bleed area needed to accommodate the physical limitations of cutting, folding, and trimming equipment. The actual printed page may include printing marks that fall outside the bleed box. The default value is the page's crop box.
- *The Trim Box*—defines the intended dimensions of the finished page after trimming. It may be smaller than the media box to allow for production-related content, such as printing instructions, cut marks, or color bars. The default value is the page's crop box.
- *The Art Box*—defines the extent of the page's meaningful content (including potential white space) as intended by the page's creator. The default value is the page's crop box.

These values are important primarily for the PDF consumer. Setting the page boundaries doesn't have any effect on the way iText creates the document. Setting the art box doesn't replace setting the page margins.

We add the text inside the art box using the `ColumnText` object:

```
/* chapter14/PageBoundaries.java */
while (ColumnText.hasMoreText(status)) {
  ct.setSimpleColumn(72, 72, 360, 684);
  status = ct.go();
  document.newPage();
}
```

We can also ask the writer to return its current page boundaries. The next code snippet uses these boundaries to add lines and a title; the rectangles, the extra marks, and the title are added in an `onEndPage` event:

```
public void onEndPage(PdfWriter writer, Document document) {
  PdfContentByte cb = writer.getDirectContent();
  cb.saveState();
  Rectangle pageSize = writer.getPageSize();        // Media box
  Rectangle trim = writer.getBoxSize("trim");       // Trim box
  Rectangle art = writer.getBoxSize("art");         // Art box
  Rectangle bleed = writer.getBoxSize("bleed");     // Bleed box
  cb.rectangle(
    trim.left(), trim.bottom(), trim.width(), trim.height());
  cb.rectangle(
    art.left(), art.bottom(), art.width(), art.height());
  cb.stroke();
  // Draw rectangles with solid lines
  cb.setLineWidth(3);
  cb.moveTo(pageSize.width() / 2, bleed.bottom());
  cb.lineTo(pageSize.width() / 2, 0);
  cb.moveTo(pageSize.width() / 2, bleed.top());
  cb.lineTo(pageSize.width() / 2, pageSize.height());
  cb.moveTo(0, pageSize.height() / 2);
  cb.lineTo(bleed.left(), pageSize.height() / 2);
  cb.moveTo(pageSize.width(), pageSize.height() / 2);
  cb.lineTo(bleed.right(), pageSize.height() / 2);
  cb.stroke();
  // Add printer marks
  cb.setLineWidth(1);
  cb.setLineDash(6, 0);
  cb.rectangle(bleed.left(), bleed.bottom(),
    bleed.width(), bleed.height());
  cb.stroke();
  // Draw rectangle with dashed lines
  cb.restoreState();
  float x = trim.left() + trim.width() / 2;
  float y = art.top() + 16;
  cb.beginText();
  cb.setFontAndSize(bf, 36);
  cb.showTextAligned(Element.ALIGN_CENTER, "Fox and Dog News", x, y, 0);
  cb.endText();
  // Add title inside trim box
}
```

This is a good example of how you'll use page events. You always add the actual content with `document.add()` or `ColumnText.go()`. The other content that is visible to the end user (page numbers, watermarks, headers, footers) or invisible (cut marks, color bars, and processing instructions) is added using page events.

But we were talking about pages. Let's find out how you can reorder pages, before we move on to an in-depth discussion of page events.

### 14.1.3 Reordering pages

The pages in a PDF file are organized in a *page tree*. Section 3.6.2 of the PDF Reference says that the page tree defines the ordering of pages in the document. The tree structure allows PDF consumer applications, using only limited memory, to quickly open a document containing thousands of pages. You'll learn more about this page tree in chapter 18 when we look under the hood of iText.

For now, it's sufficient to understand that iText constructs a page tree with different branches. If you want to be able to reorder the pages after you're done creating the document, you need to tell the writer to use the linear mode:

```
/* chapter14/ReorderPages.java */
writer.setLinearPageMode();
```

When you apply this line to the code, the page tree has no branches; every page is a leaf added directly to the root of the page tree. This allows you to change the order of the pages just before closing the document.

Let's return to the example with the index events from chapter 4 (section 4.6.3). In that example, you added regular content to a document. Once you finished adding content, you began writing an index on a new page. Suppose you want to change the order of the pages so that the index precedes the content. You must know the page number of the last page to which you have added real content:

```
/* chapter14/ReorderPages.java */
int beforeIndex = writer.getPageNumber()
```

You also need the total number of pages just after you have added the index:

```
/* chapter14/ReorderPages.java */
int totalPages = writer.getPageNumber();
int[] reorder = new int[totalPages];        <-- Create array of int
for (int i = 0; i < totalPages; i++) {
  reorder[i] = i + beforeIndex + 1;
  if (reorder[i] > totalPages)
    reorder[i] -= totalPages;                   Map new page to old one
  System.err.println("page " + reorder[i]
    + " changes to page " + (i + 1));
}
document.newPage();        <-- Finalize last page
writer.reorderPages(reorder);     <-- Reorder pages
```

If you open the document, you see that the index that was on page 6 when you executed the example in chapter 4 is now on page 1. Try clicking the page numbers in the index: They still point to the correct page, even after you change the order of the pages. Calling `newPage()` before reordering the pages is important! This method is responsible for initializing a new page, but it also does some finalization operations on the previous page. If you forget this line, you'll get an exception saying *Page reordering requires an array with the same size as the number of pages*. As explained in section 14.1.1, `newPage()` won't add an extra blank page.

This example in chapter 4 demonstrated the use of the `onGenericTag()` event. Let's see more examples of how page events can solve common problems.

## 14.2 Common page event functionality

In this section, we'll answer a series of frequently asked questions. Some of them are easy to answer—for instance, how to add a header or footer. Others can be answered in different ways depending on the desired result—for instance, how to add page numbers that say *This is page X of Y*.

The solutions presented in this section all use one or more of the following page event methods.

### 14.2.1 Overview of the PdfPageEvent methods

The `PdfPageEvent` interface defines 11 methods that are called by internal iText classes responsible for composing the PDF syntax. These methods are as follows:

- `onStartPage()`—Triggered when a new page is started. Don't add content in this event, not even a header or footer. Use this event for initializing variables or setting parameters that are page specific, such as the `transition` or `duration` parameters.
- `onEndPage()`—Triggered just before starting a new page. This is the best place to add a header, a footer, a watermark, and so on.
- `onOpenDocument()`—Triggered when a document is opened, just before `onStartPage()` is called for the first time. This is a good place to initialize variables that will be needed for all the pages of the document.
- `onCloseDocument()`—Triggered just before the document is closed. This is the ideal place to release resources (if necessary) and to fill in the total number of pages in a *page X of Y* footer.
- `onParagraph()`—In chapter 7, "Constructing columns," you used `getVerticalPosition()` to retrieve the current Y coordinate. With the `onParagraph()` method, you get this value automatically every time a new `Paragraph` is started.
- `onParagraphEnd()`—Differs from `onParagraph()` in that the Y position where the paragraph ends is provided, instead of the starting position.

- `onChapter()`—Similar to `onParagraph()`, but also gives you the title of the `Chapter` object (in the form of a `Paragraph`).
- `onChapterEnd()`—Similar to `onParagraphEnd()`, but for the `Chapter` object.
- `onSection()`—Similar to `onChapter()`, but for the `Section` object.
- `onSectionEnd()`—Similar to `onChapterEnd()`, but for the `Section` object.
- `onGenericTag()`—See section 4.6, "Generic Chunk functionality."

An extra helper class, `PdfPageEventHelper`, implements these methods. The body of all the methods in this helper class is empty. If you want to create a custom page event class, you can extend this helper class and override only those methods you need. That's what you'll do in the following sections.

### 14.2.2 Adding a header and a footer

Do you remember the example with the named actions in the previous chapter? I asked you to keep it in mind. You'll use the table with the links to the first, previous, next, and last page as a footer (see figure 14.2).

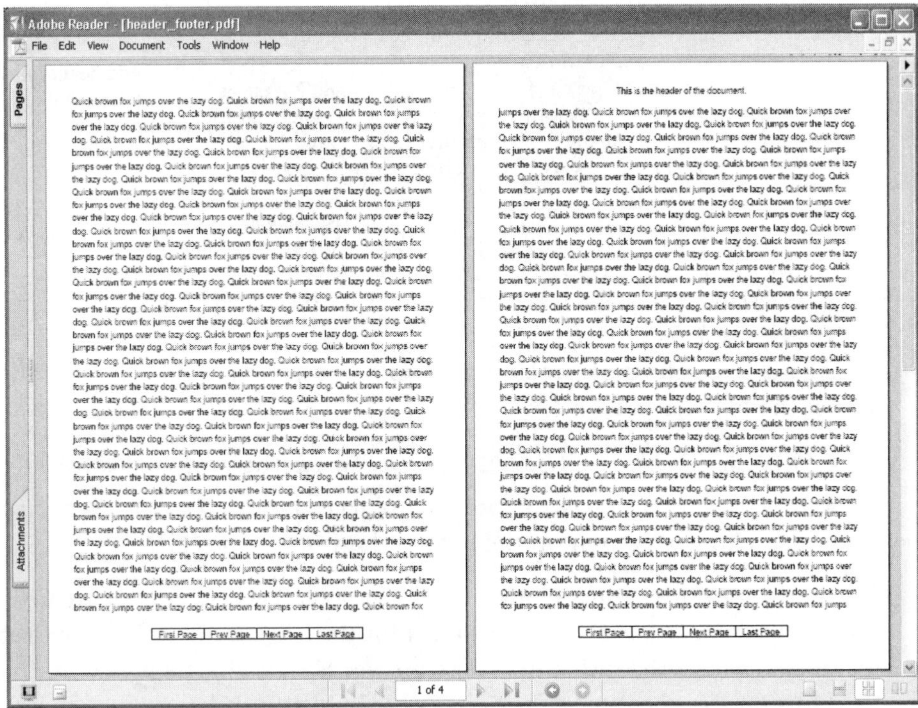


**Figure 14.2 Adding a header and a footer**

In the screenshot, you can see that a header has been added; it starts on the second page. To achieve this, you override the `onEndPage()` method:

```
/* chapter14/HeaderFooterExample.java */
protected Phrase header;
protected PdfPTable footer;

public HeaderFooterExample() {
  header = new Phrase("This is the header of the document.");
  footer = new PdfPTable(4);
  footer.setTotalWidth(300);
  footer.getDefaultCell()
    .setHorizontalAlignment(Element.ALIGN_CENTER);
  footer.addCell(new Phrase(new Chunk("First Page")
    .setAction(new PdfAction(PdfAction.FIRSTPAGE))));
  footer.addCell(new Phrase(new Chunk("Prev Page")
    .setAction(new PdfAction(PdfAction.PREVPAGE))));
  footer.addCell(new Phrase(new Chunk("Next Page")
    .setAction(new PdfAction(PdfAction.NEXTPAGE))));
  footer.addCell(new Phrase(new Chunk("Last Page")
    .setAction(new PdfAction(PdfAction.LASTPAGE))));
}
public void onEndPage(PdfWriter writer, Document document) {
  PdfContentByte cb = writer.getDirectContent();
  if (document.getPageNumber() > 1) {
    ColumnText.showTextAligned(cb,
      Element.ALIGN_CENTER, header,
      (document.right() - document.left()) / 2
      + document.leftMargin(), document.top() + 10, 0);
  }

  footer.writeSelectedRows(0, -1,
    (document.right() - document.left() - 300) /2
    + document.leftMargin(), document.bottom() - 10, cb);
}
```

Initialize header phrase

Initialize footer Table

Grab direct content

Add header if page number I

Add Phrase at absolute position

Ask Document for margins

Add table at absolute position

This code needs further explaining. Two parameters are passed to all the methods of the `PdfPageEvent` interface:

- *A* `PdfWriter` *object*—The `PdfWriter` to which the event was added
- *A* `Document` *object*—A `PdfDocument` object; *not* the `Document` instance you're using to add content in the form of high-level objects

You add the header phrase only if `document.getPageNumber()` is greater than 1. Normally, if you ask the `Document` object for the page number, it always returns 0. Why? And what's the difference? The answer is simple: The `Document` object created in step 1 is unaware of the writer object. It doesn't know if you're producing PDF, HTML, or RTF. However, as soon as you instantiate a `PdfWriter` (step 2) an instance of PdfDocument is created. This subclass of the Document class is passed as a parameter to the event.

Do *not* add content to this object; use this object for read-only purposes—for example, to get the margins of the current page. If you want the current page number, you can invoke getPageNumber() either on the PdfDocument object or on the PdfWriter passed to the event. The next code snippet demonstrates how the event was created and added to the writer:

```
/* chapter14/HeaderFooterExample.java */
Document document = new Document();
try {
  PdfWriter writer = PdfWriter.getInstance(document,
    new FileOutputStream("header_footer.pdf"));
  writer.setViewerPreferences(PdfWriter.PageLayoutTwoColumnLeft);
  writer.setPageEvent(new HeaderFooterExample());
  document.setMargins(36, 36, 54, 72);
  document.open();
  for (int k = 1; k <= 300; ++k) {
    document.add(
      new Phrase("Quick brown fox jumps over the lazy dog. "));
  }
} catch (Exception e) {
  System.err.println(e.getMessage());
}
document.close();
```

In the previous example, you initialized the header Phrase and the footer PdfPTable in the constructor of the PdfPageEvents implementation. Another option is to initialize these member variables in the onStartDocument() event, as is done in the following example.

### 14.2.3 Adding page X of Y

It's easy to change the code of the previous example so that the header or footer shows the page number: Just create a new phrase in the onEndPage() event, and use the getPageNumber() method to retrieve the current page number. Let's see how to construct a header or footer that tells the end user this is *Page X of Y.* The value for X is known; but how do you retrieve the value for Y? At the moment this information is written, there's no way of knowing the total number of pages.

There are two ways to deal with this situation:

- Create the document in memory without the *Page X of Y* information, and then create a PdfReader object and use PdfStamper to stamp a header or footer on each page. This is the most accurate method—the information is added exactly on the location you expect.

- Add the information *Page X of* in a page event, and add the same (empty) `PdfTemplate` over and over at the estimated location of the Y value of each page. In the `onCloseDocument()` event, write the actual value of Y to this single `PdfTemplate` that was added to each page.

To try the first solution, you can combine an example from chapter 2 with one of the text state methods described in chapter 11. In this chapter, you're interested in the solution that uses page events. Figure 14.3 shows a document to which text is added with `Paragraph` and `Phrase` objects. The current page number and the total number of pages are added in a footer.

This example overrides three page event methods: You perform some initializations in the `onStartDocument()` event, add a footer—including a `PdfTemplate`—

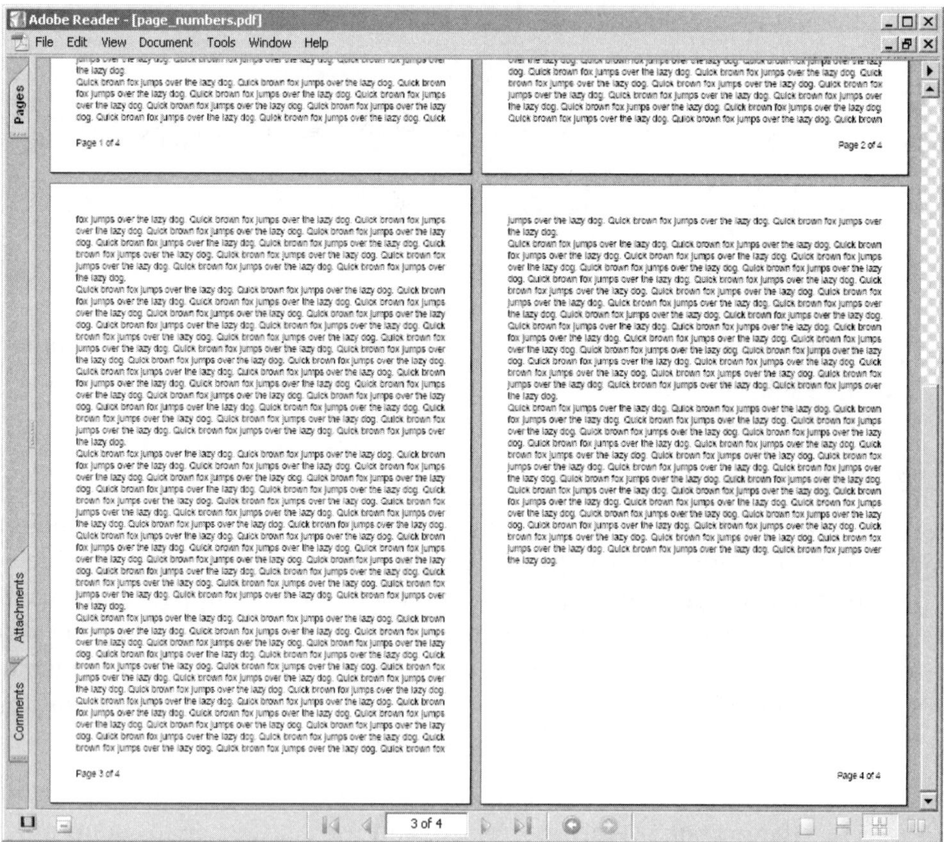


**Figure 14.3** ***Page X of Y* example**

in the `onEndPage()` event, and add the total number of pages to the `PdfTemplate` in the `onCloseDocument()` event:

```
/* chapter14/PageXofY.java */
protected PdfTemplate total;          | Event's member
protected BaseFont helv;              | variables

public void onOpenDocument(PdfWriter writer, Document document) {
  total = writer.getDirectContent().createTemplate(100, 100);    | Initialize
  total.setBoundingBox(new Rectangle(-20, -20, 100, 100));       | template
  try {
    helv = BaseFont.createFont(BaseFont.HELVETICA,       | Initialize
      BaseFont.WINANSI, BaseFont.NOT_EMBEDDED);           | base font
  } catch (Exception e) {
    throw new ExceptionConverter(e);
  }
}
public void onEndPage(PdfWriter writer, Document document) {
  PdfContentByte cb = writer.getDirectContent();
  cb.saveState();
  String text = "Page " + writer.getPageNumber() + " of ";
  float textBase = document.bottom() - 20;
  float textSize = helv.getWidthPoint(text, 12);
  cb.beginText();
  cb.setFontAndSize(helv, 12);
  if ((writer.getPageNumber() % 2) == 1) {
    cb.setTextMatrix(document.left(), textBase);      Add "Page X of"
    cb.showText(text);                                   on odd pages
    cb.endText();
    cb.addTemplate(total, document.left() + textSize, textBase);
  }
  else {
    float adjust = helv.getWidthPoint("0", 12);       Add "Page X of"
    cb.setTextMatrix(                                   on even pages
      document.right() - textSize - adjust, textBase);
    cb.showText(text);
    cb.endText();
    cb.addTemplate(total, document.right() - adjust, textBase);
  }
  cb.restoreState();
}

public void onCloseDocument(PdfWriter writer, Document document) {
  total.beginText();
  total.setFontAndSize(helv, 12);                                 Add Y
  total.setTextMatrix(0, 0);                                      value
  total.showText(String.valueOf(writer.getPageNumber() - 1));
  total.endText();
}
```

As you can see in figure 14.3, this is a good solution for the *Page X of Y* problem, but you have to keep a few things in mind.

You've created a `PdfTemplate` that is 100 by 100 user units big. That's more than large enough to add a number. You've also set the *bounding box* of the template. The bounding box is the rectangle that encloses the visible content of the form XObject. In chapter 10, you clipped images by adding them to a `PdfTemplate`. In that example, the bounding box was equal to the size of the `PdfTemplate`. In this example, you make sure the bounding box is slightly larger than the size of the `PdfTemplate` because part of the glyphs of the digits in the page number may be drawn outside the defined area—for instance, because the descender of a character added to the `PdfTemplate` goes beyond the baseline.

This solution is OK for the odd pages, where you add the footer to the left. For the even pages, you may have a problem. You don't know the value of Y in advance, so you also don't know how many digits Y has. The code introduces a parameter `adjust` that corresponds with the width of the glyph representing zero. You use this parameter to align the *Page X of Y* string. Of course, this alignment won't always be correct, especially if you expect fewer than 10 pages and end up with 10 pages or more. If you create the PDF in memory first and then use `PdfStamper` to add the footers, the positioning of the string *Page X of Y* can be done in a more accurate way.

In the next section, you'll adapt the previous example and add watermarks to each page.

### 14.2.4 Adding watermarks

Figure 14.4 resembles figure 14.3; the content is identical. The difference is that watermarks have been added.

Compare the methods `onOpenDocument()` and `onEndPage()` in the following code sample with the previous one. This example also overrides the `onStartPage()` method:

```
/* chapter14/WatermarkExample.java */
protected PdfTemplate total;
protected BaseFont helv;
protected PdfGState gstate;
protected Color color;
protected Image image;
public void onOpenDocument(PdfWriter writer, Document document) {
  total = writer.getDirectContent().createTemplate(100, 100);
  total.setBoundingBox(new Rectangle(-20, -20, 100, 100));
```

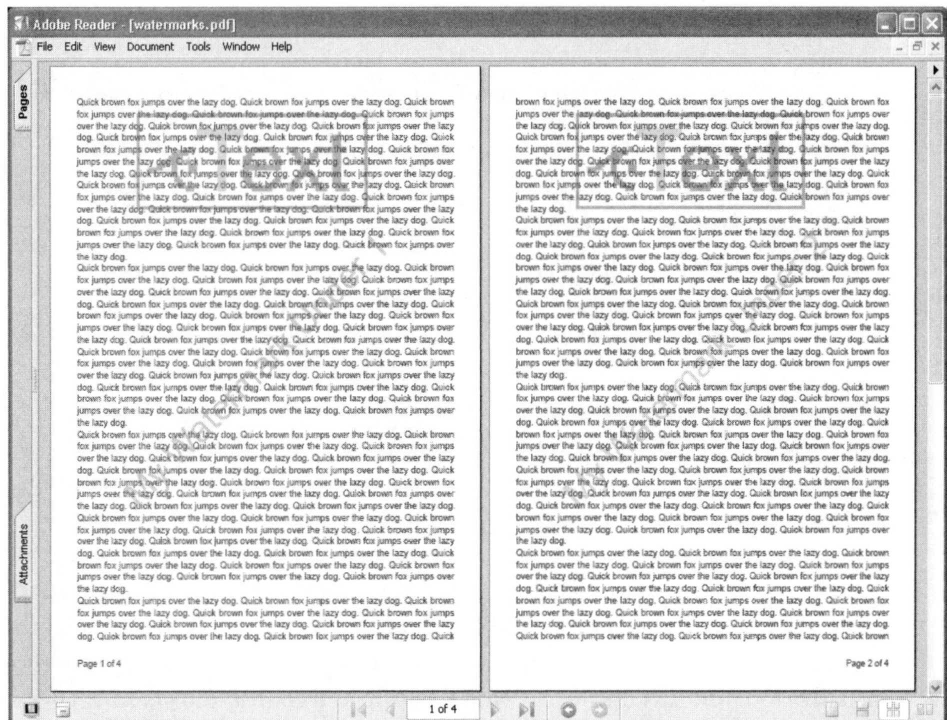


**Figure 14.4 Watermarks added with page events**

```
    try {
      helv = BaseFont.createFont(BaseFont.HELVETICA,
        BaseFont.WINANSI, BaseFont.NOT_EMBEDDED);
      image =
        Image.getInstance("../../chapter10/resources/iTextLogo.gif");
    } catch (Exception e) {
      throw new ExceptionConverter(e);
    }
    gstate = new PdfGState();
    gstate.setFillOpacity(0.3f);
    gstate.setStrokeOpacity(0.3f);
  }

  public void onStartPage(PdfWriter writer, Document document) {
    if (writer.getPageNumber() % 2 == 1) {
      color = Color.blue;
    } else {
      color = Color.red;
    }
  }
```

```
public void onEndPage(PdfWriter writer, Document document) {
  (...)
  try {
    PdfContentByte contentunder = writer.getDirectContentUnder();
    contentunder.saveState();
    contentunder.setGState(gstate);
    contentunder.addImage(image,
      image.width() * 4, 0, 0, image.height() * 4, 120, 650);
    contentunder.setColorFill(color);
    contentunder.beginText();
    contentunder.setFontAndSize(helv, 48);
    contentunder.showTextAligned(Element.ALIGN_CENTER,
      "My Watermark Under " + writer.getPageNumber(),
      document.getPageSize().width() / 2,
      document.getPageSize().height() / 2, 45);
    contentunder.endText();
    contentunder.restoreState();
  } catch (DocumentException e) {
    e.printStackTrace();
  }
}
```

Until now, you've always used `onEndPage()` to add content. It's a common misunderstanding that you should add headers and watermarks in `onStartPage()` and footers in `onEndPage()`. You can add content in the `onStartPage()` method, but I usually don't do this because it caused undesirable side-effects in earlier versions of iText. I advise you to use the `onStartPage()` method only to initialize page-specific parameters—for instance, the color of the text used for the watermark.

**NOTE** If you're adding watermarks or headers/footers with images, be sure you create the `Image` object only once—for instance, in the event's constructor or in the `onOpenDocument()` method. If you create the `Image` object in `onStartPage()` or `onEndPage()`, it will cost you not only in performance, but also in file size. You risk adding the same byte sequence (the image) to the PDF over and over again.

In the next example, you'll adapt the SlideShow example you made in the previous chapter so that the transition and duration are set in the `onStartPage()` event.

### 14.2.5 Creating an automatic slide show

In section 13.3, you learned how to add page transitions and durations. You had to define these values for every page. However, you can automate this process and set these values in a page event:

```
/* chapter14/SlideShow.java */
protected PdfTransition transition;
protected int duration;

public SlideShow(PdfTransition transition, int duration) {
  this.transition = transition;
  this.duration = duration;
}
public void setTransition(PdfTransition transition) {
  this.transition = transition;
}
public void setDuration(int duration) {
  this.duration = duration;
}
public void onStartPage(PdfWriter writer, Document document) {
  writer.setTransition(transition);
  writer.setDuration(duration);
}
```

By defining the transition and the duration as member variables, you can change their values while you're generating the document.

```
/* chapter14/SlideShow.java */
SlideShow slideshow =
  new SlideShow(new PdfTransition(PdfTransition.OUTBOX), 1);
writer.setPageEvent(slideshow);
document.open();
Image img0 =
  Image.getInstance("../../chapter13/resources/fox dog 0.gif");
img0.setAbsolutePosition(0, 0);
document.add(img0);
document.newPage();
(...)
Image img4 =
  Image.getInstance("../../chapter13/resources/fox dog 4.gif");
img4.setAbsolutePosition(0, 0);
document.add(img4);
slideshow.setTransition(new PdfTransition(PdfTransition.INBOX, 1));
  document.newPage();
(...)
Image img6 =
  Image.getInstance("../../chapter13/resources/fox dog 6.gif");
img6.setAbsolutePosition(0, 0);
writer.setTransition(new PdfTransition(PdfTransition.DISSOLVE, 1));
document.add(img6);
slideshow.setDuration(2);
document.newPage();
```

This example also demonstrates how you can change the behavior of the event while you're adding content.

This can be useful, for instance, if you want to change header text that is added in a page event dynamically while adding the actual content. In section 14.3.2, you'll parse a play by Shakespeare and display the act in the header. This means you'll change the member variable with the header text every time a new act is started, just the way you changed the duration and the transition in the previous example.

You've used `onOpenDocument()`, `onStartPage()`, `onEndPage()`, and `onCloseDocument()`. In chapter 4, you saw examples of `onGenericTag()`. The only methods in the `PdfPageEvent` interface you haven't dealt with yet are those involving `Paragraph`, `Chapter`, and `Section` objects.

### 14.2.6 Automatically creating bookmarks

Do you remember the Latin text used in chapter 7? One of the first examples in that chapter used a text file with an extract of Caesar's reports on the Gallic War; each line was wrapped in a paragraph. With the use of the `onParagraph()` event, you can create an outline entry for every paragraph that is added to the document (see figure 14.5).

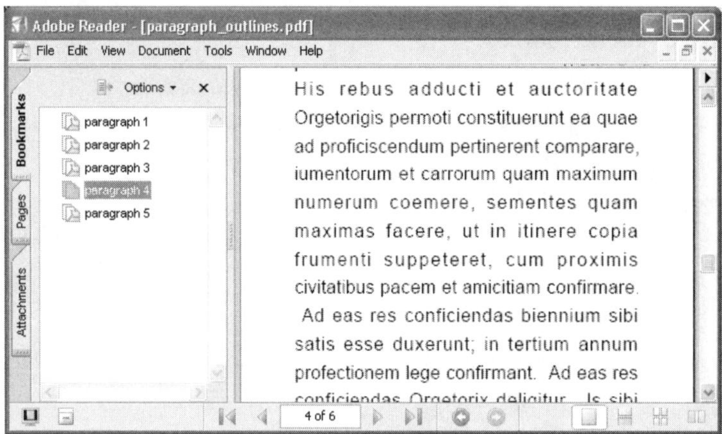


**Figure 14.5 Automatic bookmarks**

The code to read the text from the file and add it to the document is copied almost literally from the example in chapter 7. The most important difference is that you now add a page event to the document. You implement one method in this event using the functionality discussed in the previous chapter:

```
/* chapter14/ParagraphOutlines.java */
private int n = 0;
public void onParagraph(
```

```
    PdfWriter writer, Document document, float position) {
    n++;
    PdfContentByte cb = writer.getDirectContent();
    PdfDestination destination =
      new PdfDestination(PdfDestination.FITH, position);
    PdfOutline outline =
      new PdfOutline(cb.getRootOutline(),
        destination, "paragraph " + n);
}
```

Although this example is rather theoretical, the next one answers a frequently asked question: How can you create a table of contents along with the outlines in the bookmark panel?

### 14.2.7 Automatically creating a table of contents

Figure 14.6 shows an example that was used in chapter 3, but with a table of contents (TOC) added as the first page.

This example creates three files:

- chapter_events.pdf is almost identical to the file generated in chapter 3.
- toc.pdf is created using an event.
- toc_chapters.pdf is the concatenation of toc.pdf and chapter_events.pdf.

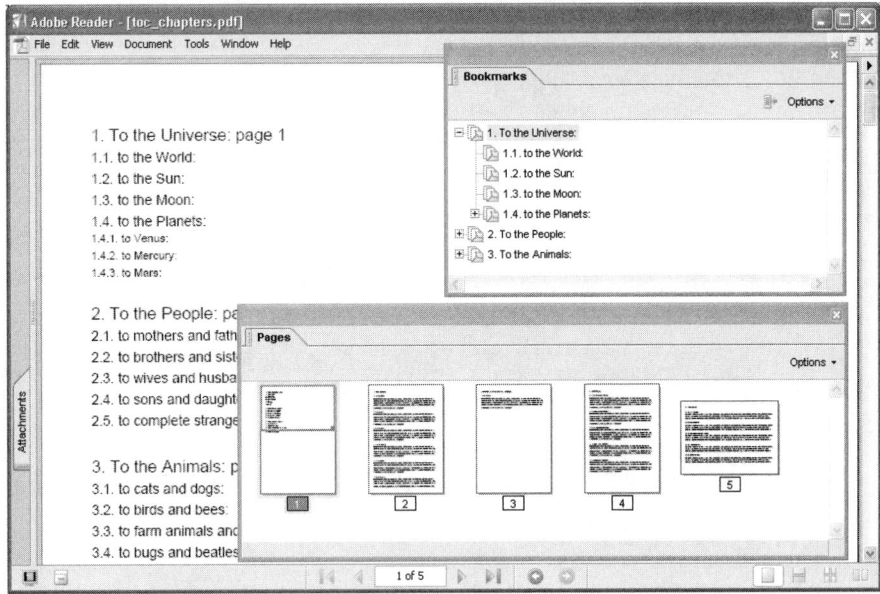


**Figure 14.6 Automatic table of contents**

You already know how to create the first file; the following code snippet creates the second file:

```
/* chapter14/ChapterEvents.java */
protected Document toc;

public ChapterEvents() {
  toc = new Document();
  try {
    PdfWriter.getInstance(toc, new FileOutputStream("toc.pdf"));
    toc.open();
  }
  catch(Exception e) {
    throw new ExceptionConverter(e);
  }
}

public void onChapter(PdfWriter writer, Document document,
  float position, Paragraph title) {
  try {
    toc.add(new Paragraph(title.content() + " page "
      + document.getPageNumber()));                    Add chapter title
  } catch (DocumentException e) {
    e.printStackTrace();
  }
}
public void onChapterEnd(PdfWriter writer, Document document,
  float position) {
  try {
    toc.add(Chunk.NEWLINE);    <-- Add newline
  } catch (DocumentException e) {
    e.printStackTrace();
  }
}
public void onSection(PdfWriter writer, Document document,
  float position, int depth, Paragraph title) {
  try {
    switch(depth) {
    case 2:
      toc.add(new Paragraph(title.content(),
        new Font(Font.HELVETICA, 10)));          Add section title
      break;
    default:
      toc.add(new Paragraph(title.content(),
        new Font(Font.HELVETICA, 8)));           Add section title
    }
  } catch (DocumentException e) {
    e.printStackTrace();
  }
}
```

```
public void onCloseDocument(PdfWriter writer, Document document) {
  toc.close();
}
```

When the file chapter_events.pdf with the content is closed, so is the file toc.pdf with the TOC entries. You can now concatenate both files. You can choose to add the TOC before or after the content. In this case, you start with the TOC:

```
/* chapter14/ChapterEvents.java */
String[] arguments =
  {"toc.pdf", "chapter_events.pdf", "toc_chapters.pdf"};
Concat.main(arguments);
```

You now have one file, toc_chapters.pdf, which starts with the TOC and continues with the document. We'll continue with more page event examples in the next section, but we'll gradually shift the scope to XML. You won't write your own handler class as you did in the Foobar examples, but you'll reuse some of the handlers shipped with iText.

## 14.3 Alternative XML solutions

All the Foobar examples you've created have been based on an XML file parsed using a SAX parser. In the real world, you'll get the data from a database. For instance, when you want to create a document with a table similar to the study program example, you won't use XML; you'll create a `PdfPTable` based on a `ResultSet` returned by a database query.

But some situations will benefit from a hybrid solution involving parsing XML in combination with database queries—for instance, if you have a letter in XML with tags that need to be replaced depending on the addressee. That's the first example in this section; in the other examples, you'll be introduced to alternatives that can be used to parse XML and/or (X)HTML.

### 14.3.1 Writing a letter on company stationery

At Ghent University, we regularly have to write letters to the students (all 27,000!). These letters have the University header and footer, but the content differs depending on specific student-related parameters (undergraduate/graduate, fulltime/halftime student, and so on). Each paragraph in the letter can take a different amount of lines. This means it's difficult to define a template with fixed fields, as we'll do in the next two chapters, when we discuss PDF forms.

I've worked on several small projects that generate letters like this. Sometimes they're generated as a separate PDF file per student that can be sent by e-mail; in

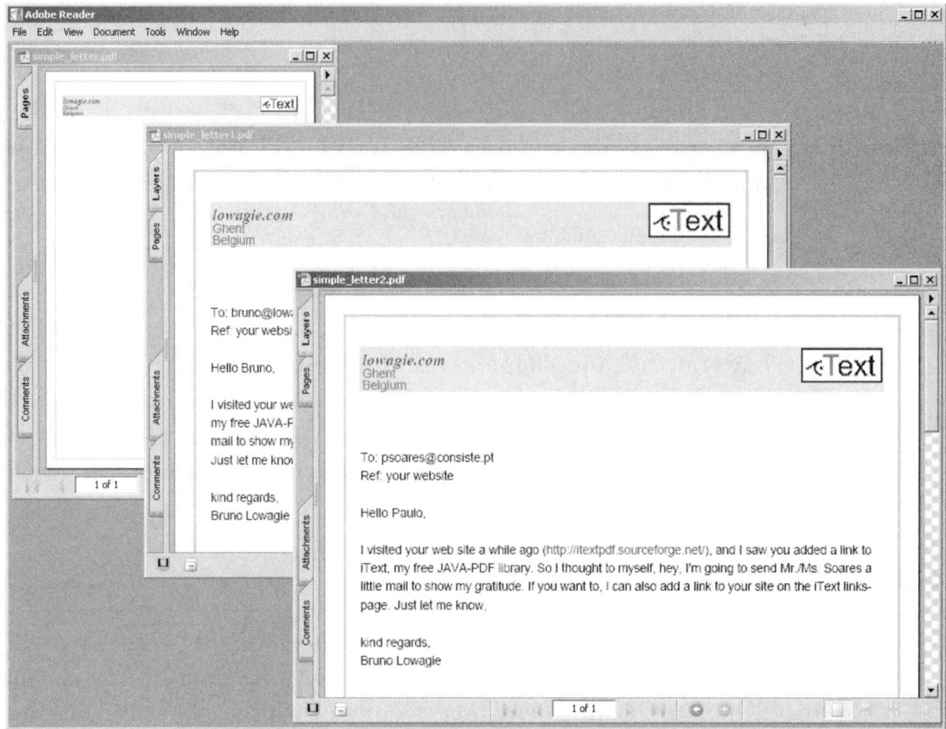


**Figure 14.7 Superimposing PDFs**

other cases, a PDF with 27,000 pages is delivered to the printing office where every letter is printed, enveloped, and sent by snail mail.

The next two examples show how it's done. You start with an existing PDF file that is used as a standard template for letters sent by your company. This is the document to the left in figure 14.7. (Note that this is a fictional example: lowagie.com isn't a company, it's my personal web site.)

Suppose I searched Google using the keyword *link:http://www.lowagie.com/iText* (meaning I want to see sites that link to my URL). Now I want to send a personalized letter to all the webmasters of the sites that link to iText (see listing 14.1).

**Listing 14.1 XML version of a thank-you letter**

```
<letter left="36" right="36" top="144" bottom="36">
To: <mail /><newline />
Ref: your website<newline />
<newline />
```

```
Hello <givenname />,<newline />
<newline />
I visited your web site a while ago (<website />), and
➥ I saw you added a link to iText, my free JAVA-PDF library.
➥ So I thought to myself, hey, I'm going to send Mr./Ms. <name />
➥ a little mail to show my gratitude.
➥ If you want to, I can also add a link to your site on the iText
➥ links-page. Just let me know,<newline />
<newline />
kind regards,<newline />
Bruno Lowagie
</letter>
```

In this XML file, some tags are left empty: givenname, name, mail, and website. These tags correspond with the fields in my database. Now I want to create a separate PDF file for every webmaster in my database. I'll use the company template as a basis and add the content from the XML merged with the data from my database.

### Writing the page events

Let's start with the stuff you know: the page event that adds the existing PDF file as a template.

```
/* chapter14/SimpleLetter.java */
protected PdfImportedPage paper;
protected PdfLayer not_printed;

public void onOpenDocument(PdfWriter writer, Document document) {
  try {
    PdfReader reader = new PdfReader("simple_letter.pdf");
    paper = writer.getImportedPage(reader, 1);
    not_printed = new PdfLayer("template", writer);
    not_printed.setOnPanel(false);
    not_printed.setPrint("Print", false);
  } catch (IOException e) {
    e.printStackTrace();
  }
}

public void onStartPage(PdfWriter writer,
  Document document) {
  PdfContentByte cb = writer.getDirectContent();
  cb.beginLayer(not_printed);
  cb.addTemplate(paper, 0, 0);
  cb.endLayer();
}
```

**Read template page once**

**Template won't be printed**

I added the standard paper page to a layer that won't be printed. This may be absurd if you plan to send these letters by e-mail, but it's a good idea if you want to print them on special company paper with a preprinted header and footer.

Now let's look at the code that parses the XML and adds the content to the page.

### *Writing the code that parses the XML*

The simplest way to parse the XML is by creating a `com.lowagie.text.xml.XmlParser` object with the document to which the content has to be added, the path to the XML file, and a *tag map*:

```
/* chapter14/SimpleLetter.java */
document = new Document(PageSize.A4);
writer = PdfWriter.getInstance(document,
  new FileOutputStream("simple_letter2.pdf"));
writer.setPdfVersion(PdfWriter.VERSION_1_5);
writer.setViewerPreferences(PdfWriter.PrintScalingNone);     <-- Set printer preference to no scaling
writer.setPageEvent(new SimpleLetter());                      <-- Set page event
XmlParser.parse(document, "../resources/simple_letter.xml",
  getTagMap("Bruno", "Lowagie",
    "bruno@lowagie.com", "http://www.lowagie.com/"));         Parse XML
```

I set the viewer preferences to avoid scaling. If you want to print the content on paper on which the company header is preprinted and that looks exactly like the template you used, you don't want the content to be scaled.

Also note that I didn't close the document; this is done by the parser object. But the most intriguing part of this code snippet is that `getTagMap()` method:

```
/* chapter14/SimpleLetter.java */
public static HashMap getTagMap(
  String givenname, String name, String mail, String site) {
  HashMap tagmap = new HashMap();
  XmlPeer peer =                                        Map root tag to
    new XmlPeer(ElementTags.ITEXT, "letter");           ElemtentTags.ITEXT
  tagmap.put(peer.getAlias(), peer);
  peer = new XmlPeer(ElementTags.CHUNK, "givenname");
  peer.setContent(givenname);
  tagmap.put(peer.getAlias(), peer);
  peer = new XmlPeer(ElementTags.CHUNK, "name");              Map other
  peer.setContent(name);                                      parameters
  tagmap.put(peer.getAlias(), peer);                          to Chunk
  peer = new XmlPeer(ElementTags.CHUNK, "mail");
  peer.setContent(mail);
  tagmap.put(peer.getAlias(), peer);
  peer = new XmlPeer(ElementTags.ANCHOR, "website");
  peer.setContent(site);                                      Map parameter site
  peer.addValue(ElementTags.REFERENCE, site);                 to Anchor
  peer.addValue(ElementTags.COLOR, "#0000FF");
```

```
    tagmap.put(peer.getAlias(), peer);
    return tagmap;
  }
```

How does this work? Most of the text objects described in chapter 4 have a constructor that takes a `Properties` object as a parameter. You can create such an element using a set of key-value pairs (the keys are constants in the `ElementTags` class).

By creating an `XmlPeer` object, you can map a custom tag (for instance, `<site>`) to a tag known by iText; such as `<anchor>` (see the `ElementTags` class for more information):

- With the method `setContent()`, you can add content to this text object.
- With the method `addValue()`, you can add the value of an attribute.
- With the method `addAlias()`, you can map an attribute in your XML to an iText attribute.

The general idea of this functionality was to have an iText Document Type Definition (DTD) that defined all the possible iText objects. In this DTD, every tag would correspond with a specific iText class and every attribute with a member variable. Unfortunately, this work was never finished.

**FAQ** *Where can I find the DTD for the iText XML?* The current DTD on the iText site is obsolete. This functionality is old, and it was never completed. It was written to serve a specific purpose, and once the XML parsing functionality was sufficient for the project I was working on, further development in this area was stopped. It's one of the things that has been on my TODO list for ages.

The biggest disadvantage of this functionality is that it uses a proprietary (and no longer existing) schema. Other libraries have been inspired by this approach and offer a more consistent DTD. The Useful Java Application Components project (UJAC) offers such a solution (with iText as PDF engine).

### *Batch-processing the XML*

The previous example makes two separate files. If you want to send these letters by snail mail, you can open every individual file and print it. This isn't practical if many letters are to be sent (remember the real-world situation at Ghent University). You could use iText to concatenate the separate files, but that approach wouldn't be efficient. If your template PDF is 1KB, and you need to produce 100 letters and add 0.1KB of data on each page, the end result will be at least 100 x (0.1 + 1) = 110 KB. We want the template to be added only once, so that the end

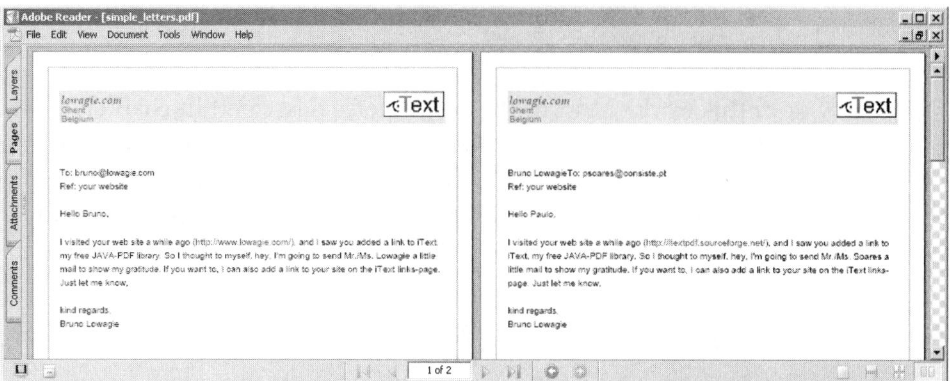

**Figure 14.8 Using an existing PDF as template**

result is more in the range of (100 x 0.1) + 1 = 11 KB (note that there's always some overhead).

The next example explains how to process all the files in one pass. The end result is a file containing all the letters in a single PDF, as shown in figure 14.8. The background of each page is a form XObject (see section 10.4.2) that is added in the `onEndPage()` method (and reused over and over).

In the `SAXiTextHandler` class, `document.open()` is triggered when the root tag is opened, and `document.close()` is triggered when a closing tag is encountered. There must be a way to avoid this. You're going to parse the same XML multiple times, once for each record in the database. It's impossible to reopen a document after it's been closed. The program will stop after processing the first record.

You can solve this problem by subclassing the `SAXiTextHandler` (the class used internally by `XmlParser`). You override the `startElement()` and `endElement()` methods. Note that the `SAXiTextHandler` class is similar to the handler classes used in the Foobar examples:

```
/* chapter14/SimpleLetters.java */
Document document = new Document(PageSize.A4, 36, 36, 144, 36);
PdfWriter writer = PdfWriter.getInstance(document,
  new FileOutputStream("simple_letters.pdf"));
writer.setPageEvent(new SimpleLetter());
document.open();
SAXParser parser = SAXParserFactory.newInstance().newSAXParser();
SimpleLetters handler = new SimpleLetters(document);
handler.setTagMap(SimpleLetter.getTagMap("Bruno", "Lowagie",
  "bruno@lowagie.com", "http://www.lowagie.com/"));
parser.parse("../resources/simple_letter.xml", handler);
document.newPage();
```

```
handler = new SimpleLetters(document);
handler.setTagMap(SimpleLetter.getTagMap(...));
parser.parse("../resources/simple_letter.xml", handler);
document.close();
```

This code snippet reuses the page events from the previous example. You take control over the SAX handler so that it no longer opens or closes the document. In step 4 you parse the XML file with a different tag map as many times as needed. (In the real world, you loop over a `ResultSet`.)

In the next example, we'll elaborate on subclassing the SAX handler.

### 14.3.2 Parsing a play

The XML version of the work of William Shakespeare was placed in the public domain by Moby Lexical Tools in 1992. Figure 14.9 shows a (famous) part of the play *Romeo and Juliet*.

I made minor changes to this XML file so that it can be parsed into a PDF document by iText. Figure 14.10 shows part of the first scene in the first act.

Instead of creating a `HashMap` object, I wrote a tag map XML file that makes the mappings. Listing 14.2 shows the most important tags (I didn't copy the complete file).

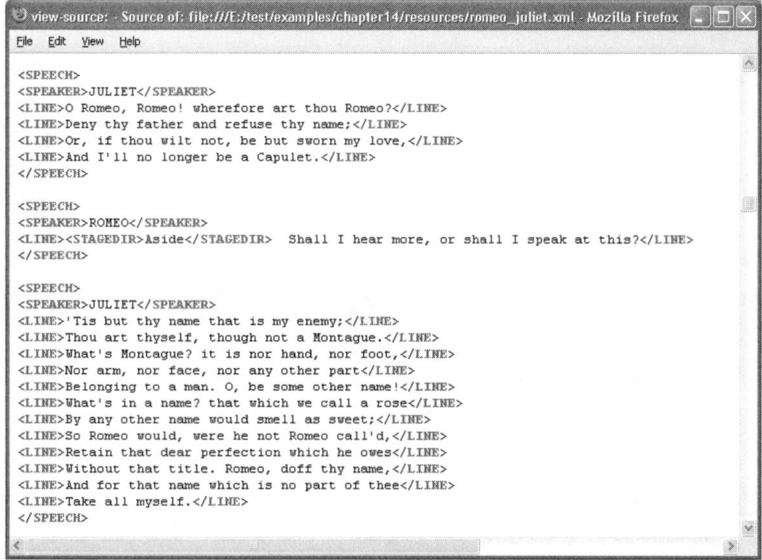


```
<SPEECH>
<SPEAKER>JULIET</SPEAKER>
<LINE>O Romeo, Romeo! wherefore art thou Romeo?</LINE>
<LINE>Deny thy father and refuse thy name;</LINE>
<LINE>Or, if thou wilt not, be but sworn my love,</LINE>
<LINE>And I'll no longer be a Capulet.</LINE>
</SPEECH>

<SPEECH>
<SPEAKER>ROMEO</SPEAKER>
<LINE><STAGEDIR>Aside</STAGEDIR>  Shall I hear more, or shall I speak at this?</LINE>
</SPEECH>

<SPEECH>
<SPEAKER>JULIET</SPEAKER>
<LINE>'Tis but thy name that is my enemy;</LINE>
<LINE>Thou art thyself, though not a Montague.</LINE>
<LINE>What's Montague? it is nor hand, nor foot,</LINE>
<LINE>Nor arm, nor face, nor any other part</LINE>
<LINE>Belonging to a man. O, be some other name!</LINE>
<LINE>What's in a name? that which we call a rose</LINE>
<LINE>By any other name would smell as sweet;</LINE>
<LINE>So Romeo would, were he not Romeo call'd,</LINE>
<LINE>Retain that dear perfection which he owes</LINE>
<LINE>Without that title. Romeo, doff thy name,</LINE>
<LINE>And for that name which is no part of thee</LINE>
<LINE>Take all myself.</LINE>
</SPEECH>
```

**Figure 14.9 XML with the play *Romeo and Juliet***

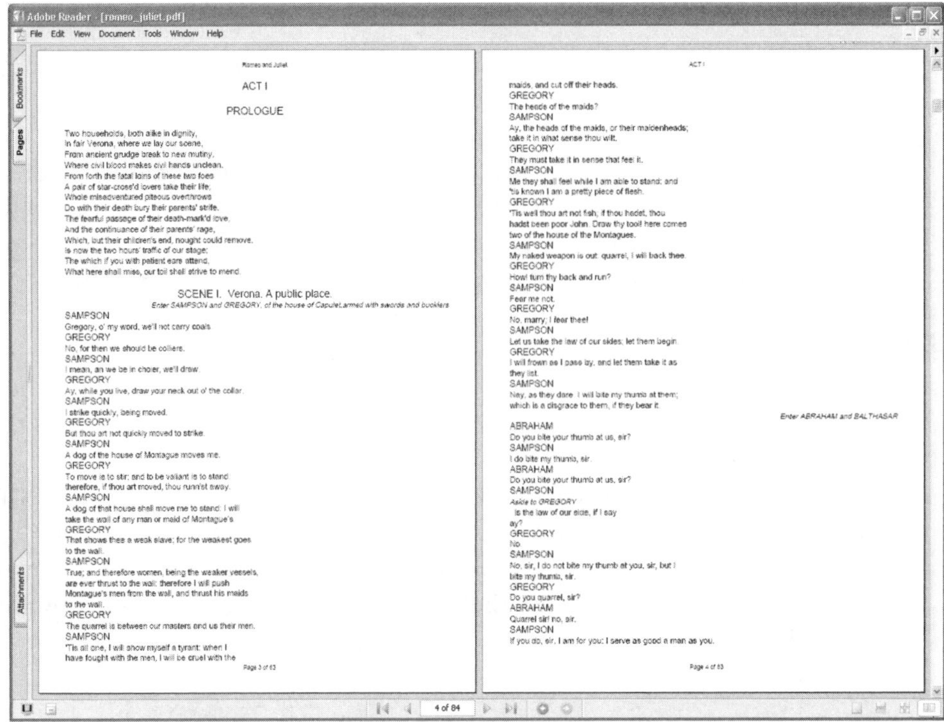

**Figure 14.10 The play *Romeo and Juliet* in PDF**

Compare the tags in the tag map with figures 14.9 and 14.10. The `ACT` tag corresponds with an iText `Chapter`, the `SCENE` tag with a `Section`. No extra chapter or section numbers are added (`numberdepth` = 0). `SPEECH` blocks are left aligned; the stage directions (`STAGEDIR`) are right aligned and italic, and so on.

**Listing 14.2 Tag mappings in tagmap.xml**

```
<tagmap>
  <tag name="itext" alias="PLAY" />
  <tag name="newpage" alias="NEWPAGE" />
  <tag name="newline" alias="NEWLINE" />
  <tag name="title" alias="TITLE">
    <attribute name="size" value="14" />
    <attribute name="align" value="Center" />
  </tag>
  <tag name="chapter" alias="ACT">
    <attribute name="numberdepth" value="0" />
  </tag>
```

```
    <tag name="section" alias="SCENE">
      <attribute name="numberdepth" value="0" />
    </tag>
    <tag name="paragraph" alias="SPEECH">
      <attribute name="leading" value="14" />
      <attribute name="align" value="Left" />
    </tag>
    <tag name="paragraph" alias="LINE">
      <attribute name="leading" value="15" />
      <attribute name="size" value="11" />
      <attribute name="align" value="Left" />
    </tag>
    <tag name="paragraph" alias="STAGEDIR">
      <attribute name="leading" value="14" />
      <attribute name="size" value="10" />
      <attribute name="style" value="italic" />
      <attribute name="align" value="Right" />
    </tag>
  </tagmap>
```

In figure 14.10, page numbers are added, as well as a header with the title of the play for the odd page numbers and the current act for the even page numbers. The PDF document starts with an unnumbered page. It lists all the characters in the play and the number of SPEECH blocks per actor (see figure 14.11).

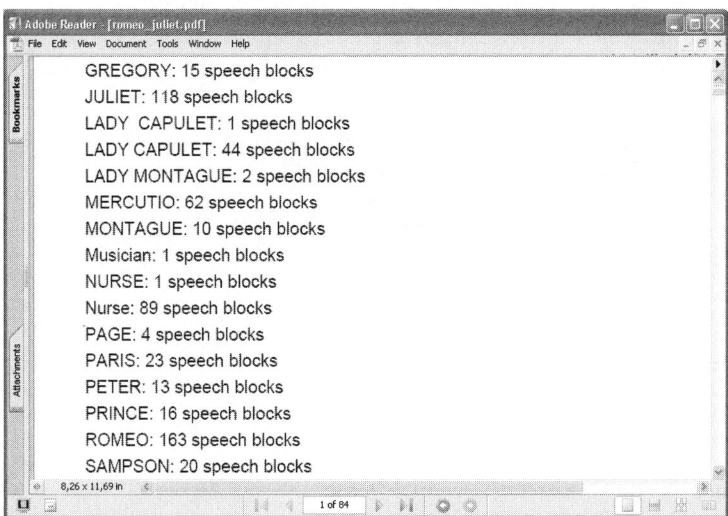


**Figure 14.11 Counting the speech blocks of every actor**

The page numbers, the variable header, and the list with speakers are generated automatically using page events, as is demonstrated in the following code snippet (`MyPageEvents` is an inner class of class `RomeoJuliet`).

```
/* chapter14/RomeoJuliet.java */
MyPageEvents extends PdfPageEventHelper
  TreeSet speakers = new TreeSet();
  PdfContentByte cb;
  PdfTemplate template;
  BaseFont bf = null;
  String act = "";

  public void onGenericTag(PdfWriter writer, Document document,
    Rectangle rect, String text) {
    speakers.add(new Speaker(text));
  }

  public void onOpenDocument(PdfWriter writer, Document document) {
    try {
      bf = BaseFont.createFont(BaseFont.HELVETICA, BaseFont.CP1252,
        BaseFont.NOT_EMBEDDED);
      cb = writer.getDirectContent();
      template = cb.createTemplate(50, 50);
      writer.setLinearPageMode();
    } catch (Exception e) { }
  }

  public void onChapter(PdfWriter writer, Document document,
    float paragraphPosition, Paragraph title) {
    act = title.content();
  }

  public void onEndPage(PdfWriter writer, Document document) {
    int pageN = writer.getPageNumber();
    String text = "Page " + pageN + " of ";
    float len = bf.getWidthPoint(text, 8);
    cb.beginText();
    cb.setFontAndSize(bf, 8);
    cb.setTextMatrix(280, 30);
    cb.showText(text);
    cb.endText();
    cb.addTemplate(template, 280 + len, 30);
    cb.beginText();
    cb.setFontAndSize(bf, 8);
    cb.setTextMatrix(280, 820);
    if (pageN % 2 == 1) {
      cb.showText("Romeo and Juliet");
    } else {
      cb.showText(act);
    }
```

```
      cb.endText();
    }
  }
```

Just as in the previous example, `SAXmyHandler` is subclassed so that the document isn't closed when the final closing tag is encountered. When a `SPEAKER` closing tag is encountered, you add a new line:

```
/* chapter14/RomeoJuliet.java */
public void endElement(String uri, String lname, String name) {
  if (myTags.containsKey(name)) {
    XmlPeer peer = (XmlPeer) myTags.get(name);
    if (isDocumentRoot(peer.getTag())) {
      return;
    }
    handleEndingTags(peer.getTag());
    if ("SPEAKER".equals(name)) {
      try {
        TextElementArray previous =
        (TextElementArray) stack.pop();
        previous.add(new Paragraph(16));
        stack.push(previous);
      }
      catch (EmptyStackException ese) {
      }
    }
  } else {
    handleEndingTags(name);
  }
}
```

**Ignore closing tag PLAY**

**Add extra newline after SPEAKER**

In the previous example, you didn't want the document to close because you needed to parse the same XML file over and over again. Here you don't parse the XML more than once, but you add the speech-block count (figure 14.11) and move it to the start of the document:

```
/* chapter14/RomeoJuliet.java */
RomeoJuliet rj = new RomeoJuliet();
Document document = new Document(PageSize.A4, 80, 50, 30, 65);
try {
  PdfWriter writer = PdfWriter.getInstance(document,
    new FileOutputStream("romeo_juliet.pdf"));
  MyPageEvents events = rj.new MyPageEvents();
  writer.setPageEvent(events);
  SAXParser parser =
    SAXParserFactory.newInstance().newSAXParser();
  RomeoJulietMap tagmap =
    rj.new RomeoJulietMap("../resources/tagmap.xml");
  parser.parse("../resources/romeo_juliet.xml",
    rj.new MyHandler(document, tagmap));
```

**Create page events**

**Create SAXParser and TagMap**

```
    int end_play = writer.getPageNumber();
    events.template.beginText();
    events.template.setFontAndSize(events.bf, 8);
    events.template.showText(String.valueOf(end_play));
    events.template.endText();
    document.newPage();
    writer.setPageEvent(null);
    Speaker speaker;
    for (Iterator i =
      events.speakers.iterator(); i.hasNext();) {
      speaker = (Speaker) i.next();
      document.add(new Paragraph(speaker.getName() + ": "
        + speaker.getOccurrance() + " speech blocks"));
    }
    int end_doc = writer.getPageNumber();
    int[] reorder = new int[end_doc];
    for (int i = 0; i < reorder.length; i++) {
      reorder[i] = i + end_play + 1;
      if (reorder[i] > end_doc)
        reorder[i] -= end_doc;
    }
    document.newPage();
    writer.reorderPages(reorder);
  } catch (Exception e) {
    e.printStackTrace();
  }
  document.close();
```

**Update Y in Page X of Y**

**Trigger newPage/ disable page events**

**Add speech-blocks count**

**Reorder pages**

The functionality demonstrated in this example serves its purpose in some projects, but for the moment nobody is working on this part of the iText library. This is a pity, because there's a lot of room for improvement. For instance, we could improve the XHTML parsers that are shipped with iText.

### 14.3.3 Parsing (X)HTML

One of the frequently asked questions on the iText mailing list is, "Does iText provide HTML2PDF functionality?" The official answer is no; you're advised to use HtmlDoc or ICEbrowser.

This answer may come as a surprise, because you've parsed the Foobar flyer and the iText class `com.lowagie.text.html.HtmlParser` uses the functionality described in the previous section. In this `html` package, a tag map contains a subset of the available HTML tags. Figure 14.12 shows an example of an XHTML file in a browser and a PDF generated based on this XHTML.

What's wrong with this example? Well, maybe this specific example is more or less OK, but you risk being disappointed when you start parsing your own HTML pages.

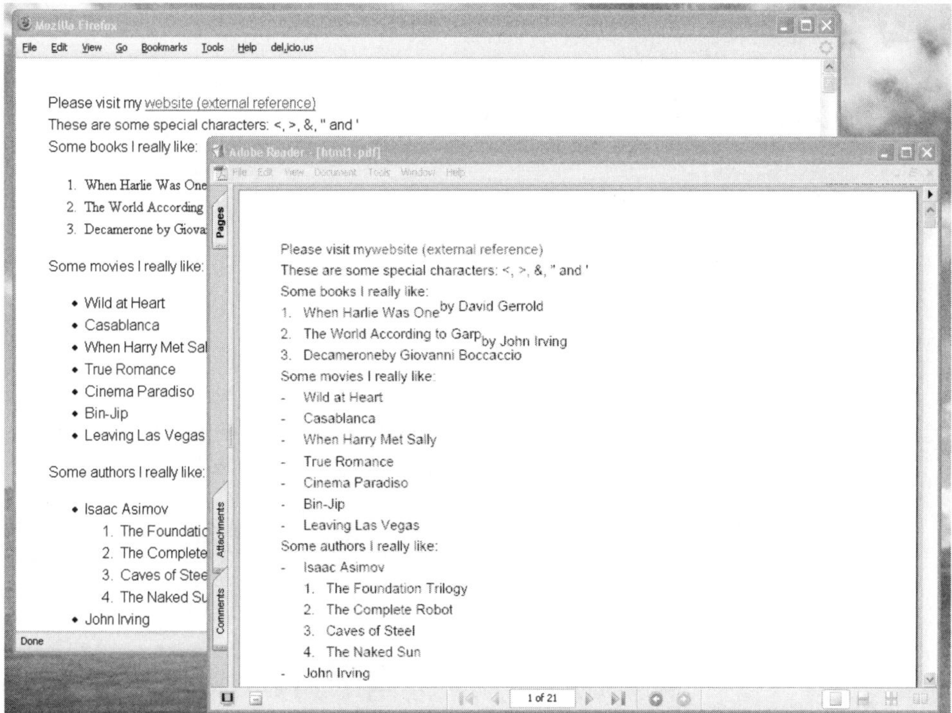


**Figure 14.12 Parsing HTML**

First, there's the nature of HTML. It wasn't designed to define the exact design of a document, and it's impossible to store the layout of a page using HTML tags. You can use CSS, but if you open the same HTML/CSS page in Internet Explorer, Netscape, Firefox, Mozilla, Opera, and so on, there will always be differences in the way the different browsers render the content of the file. It's not a good idea to use HTML as original format for your documents.

Second, parsing HTML isn't the core business of iText. When I develop something new, I try not to reinvent the wheel. If another product already offers some functionality, it wouldn't be smart to invest time writing my own implementation (unless I can do it better or add value). I already mentioned ICEbrowser; this tool parses HTML to a `Graphics2D` object and uses the `PdfGraphics2D` object in iText to generate PDF. That's a completely different approach.

This being said, the code used to generate the HTML in figure 14.12 looks like this:

```
/* chapter14/HtmlParseExample.java */
Document document = new Document();
try {
  PdfWriter.getInstance(document, new FileOutputStream("html1.pdf"));
  HtmlParser.parse(document, "../resources/example.html");
}
catch(Exception e) {
  e.printStackTrace();
}
```

In spite of all the warnings, there is even an alternative way to parse HTML using iText.

### 14.3.4 Using HtmlWorker to parse HTML snippets

Compare figure 14.12 with figure 14.13. At first sight, the end result is worse: Style seems to be lost when you use the alternative approach discussed in this section.

The code to generate the PDF in figure 14.13 takes a few more lines:

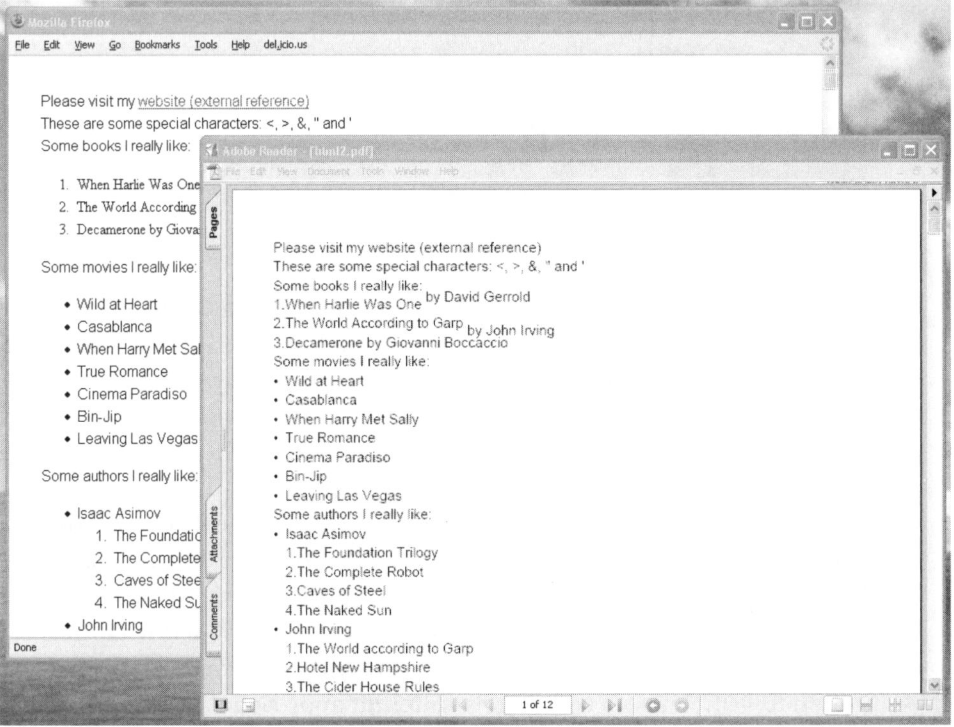


**Figure 14.13 Parsing HTML**

```
/* chapter14/ParsingHtml.java */
Document document = new Document();
StyleSheet st = new StyleSheet();                  | Define custom
st.loadTagStyle("body", "leading", "16,0");        | styles
try {
  PdfWriter.getInstance(
    document, new FileOutputStream("html2.pdf"));
  document.open();
  ArrayList p = HTMLWorker.parseToList(                    | Parse HTML into list
    new FileReader("../resources/example.html"), st);      | of iText objects
  for (int k = 0; k < p.size(); ++k)         | Add objects to
    document.add((Element)p.get(k));         | document
}
catch(Exception e) {
  e.printStackTrace();
}
document.close();
```

If you give this example a closer look, you'll discover this functionality has interesting advantages:

- You can define your own styles per tag/class.
- You can parse HTML snippets.

You typically won't use `HtmlWorker` to parse complete HTML files with an `<html>`, `<head>`, and `<body>` tag, but rather to parse small snippets of HTML.

I don't say it's good design, but I know some projects that store `Strings` with HTML tags in a database. For instance, if you have a database of product names, you can store *i*Text like this—`<i>i</i>Text`—because the *i* in *i*Text was originally printed in italic. There are also examples of situations where people are allowed to enter markup when they fill in a form. For instance, if you're keeping a blog, you can use a subset of HTML tags.

`HtmlWorker` can deal with a limited set of HTML tags. Suppose you have an HTML snippet that looks like this:

```
<ol>
  <li>When Harlie Was One <span class="sf">(by David Gerrold)</span></li>
  <li>The World According to Garp <span>(by John Irving)</span></li>
  <li>Decamerone <span class="classic">(by Giovanni Boccaccio)</span></li>
</ol>
```

Figure 14.14 shows this HTML snippet rendered in a browser window. In the Adobe Reader window, you see a PDF to which the HTML snippet was added three times, each time using another style.

The HTML snippet uses the tags `ol`, `li`, and `span` and the attribute `class`. The first time you add the snippet to the PDF document, you only define the leading

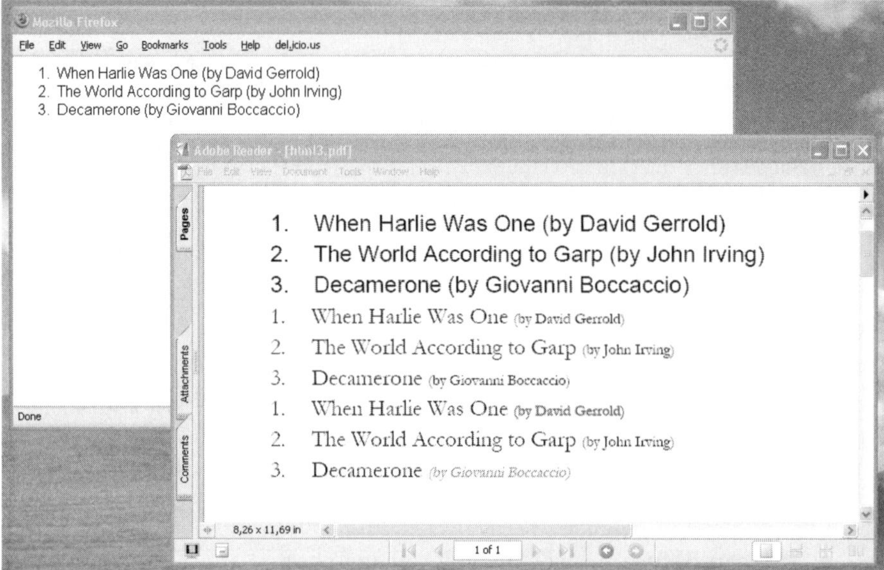


**Figure 14.14 Parsing HTML snippets**

of the tag that encloses all the other content: `ol`. The second time, you change the font of the `li` tags and the font size of the `span` tags. Finally, you change the color and style of tags that are marked using the `class` attribute: science fiction books are rendered in blue/bold; classics are rendered in red/italic. Here's the code:

```
/* chapter14/ParsingHtmlSnippets.java */
StyleSheet styles = new StyleSheet();
styles.loadTagStyle("ol", "leading", "16,0");
PdfWriter.getInstance(document, new FileOutputStream("html3.pdf"));
document.open();
ArrayList objects;
objects = HTMLWorker.parseToList(
  new FileReader("../resources/list.html"), styles);
for (int k = 0; k < objects.size(); ++k)
  document.add((Element)objects.get(k));
FontFactory.register("c:\\windows\\fonts\\gara.ttf");
styles.loadTagStyle("li", "face", "garamond");
styles.loadTagStyle("span", "size", "8px");
objects = HTMLWorker.parseToList(
  new FileReader("../resources/list.html"), styles);
for (int k = 0; k < objects.size(); ++k)
  document.add((Element)objects.get(k));
styles.loadStyle("sf", "color", "blue");
styles.loadStyle("sf", "b", "");
```

```
styles.loadStyle("classic", "color", "red");
styles.loadStyle("classic", "i", "");
objects = HTMLWorker.parseToList(
  new FileReader("../resources/list.html"), styles);
for (int k = 0; k < objects.size(); ++k)
  document.add((Element)objects.get(k));
```

If you need to know more about this functionality, please consult the online docs.

In the meantime, we've drifted away from the main topic of this chapter: page events. Let's finish with an example that will help Laura enhance the course catalog.

## 14.4 Enhancing the course catalog (part 2)

To add a header, footer, and watermark to the course catalog, you can reuse the code from section 13.6. The main difference is that you add page events to create a PDF that looks like figure 14.15.

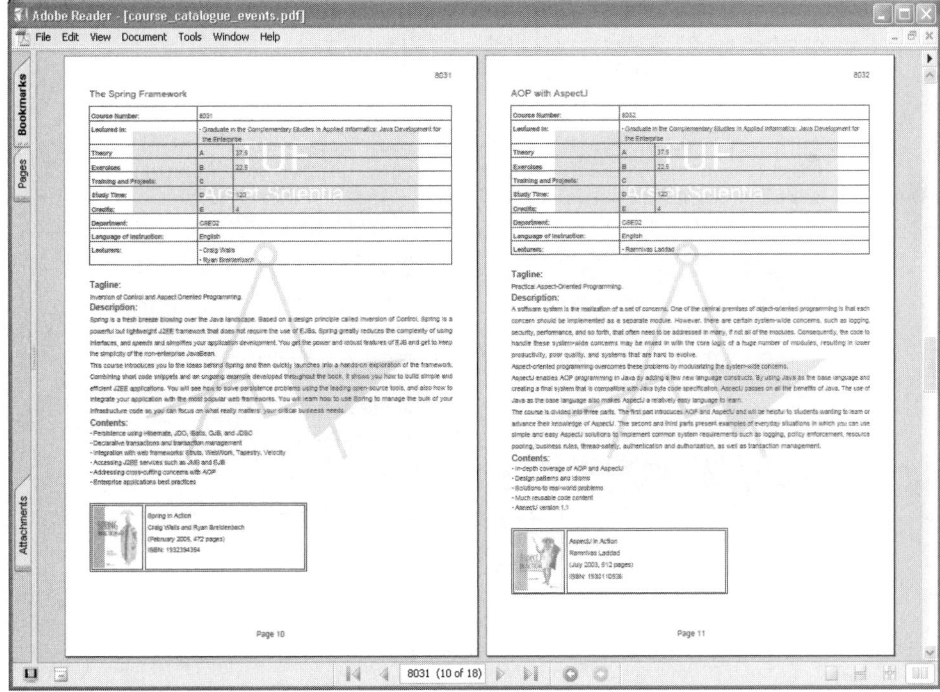

**Figure 14.15 Course catalog with watermarks, headers, and page numbers**

After reading this chapter, you shouldn't have any trouble writing the code for the custom page events:

```
/* chapter14/CourseCatalogEvents.java */
protected String header = "";
protected BaseFont helv;
protected Image image;
protected PdfGState gstate;

public void setHeader(String header) {
  this.header = header;
}

public void onOpenDocument(PdfWriter writer, Document document) {
  try {
    helv = BaseFont.createFont(BaseFont.HELVETICA,
      BaseFont.WINANSI, BaseFont.NOT_EMBEDDED);
    image = Image.getInstance(
      "../../chapter05/resources/shield_tuf.gif");
  } catch (Exception e) {
    throw new ExceptionConverter(e);
  }
  gstate = new PdfGState();
  gstate.setFillOpacity(0.1f);
  gstate.setStrokeOpacity(0.3f);
}

public void onEndPage(PdfWriter writer, Document document) {
  PdfContentByte directcontent = writer.getDirectContent();
  directcontent.saveState();
  String text = "Page " + writer.getPageNumber();
  float textBase = document.bottom() - 20;
  float textSize = helv.getWidthPoint(text, 12);
  directcontent.beginText();
  directcontent.setFontAndSize(helv, 11);
  directcontent.showTextAligned(Element.ALIGN_RIGHT,
    header, document.right(), 810, 0);
  directcontent.showTextAligned(Element.ALIGN_CENTER,
    text, (document.right() + document.left()) / 2, 28, 0);
  directcontent.endText();
  directcontent.restoreState();
  PdfContentByte contentunder = writer.getDirectContentUnder();
  contentunder.saveState();
  contentunder.setGState(gstate);
  try {
    contentunder.addImage(image,
      image.width(), 0, 0, image.height(), 100, 200);
  } catch (DocumentException e) {
    e.printStackTrace();
  }
  contentunder.restoreState();
}
```

This concludes Laura's course catalog assignment. In chapter 17, you'll reuse the file you just generated to create a personalized course catalog on demand.

## 14.5 Summary

Page events offer a solution for some page-specific problems like adding watermarks, page numbers, headers, footers, transitions, and durations. Note that none of the page events uses `document.add()`.

In the examples, you used page events to gather meta-information based on content: You created outlines and a table of contents. While explaining page events, we took a tangent showing you that it's possible to parse XML and even HTML. The most important conclusion is that iText may not be the ideal product to parse complete HTML files, but `HTMLWorker` is a useful class to parse snippets of HTML.

As explained in the chapter introduction, page events are triggered on the server side during the document-creation process. In the next chapter, we'll return to the client side. We'll discuss annotations, and you'll learn that the fields in a form use a special type of annotations called *widget annotations*.

# 15 Creating annotations and fields

**This chapter covers**

- Annotations: overview of the most common types
- Fields: buttons, text fields, choice fields
- Forms: a second series of actions

In chapter 2, you learned how to fill in form fields using `PdfStamper`. We didn't go into the details of form filling, nor did we discuss how a PDF containing an *interactive form* (an AcroForm) can be created using iText objects. Most fields in such a form use *widget annotations* to represent their appearance and to manage user interactions.

That's why we'll begin this chapter by explaining how to add annotations to a PDF document. In the second part of this chapter, you'll use widget annotations to create three types of form fields: button, text, and choice fields. You'll learn about a fourth type, signature fields, in the next chapter.

By adding form fields to a document, you implicitly create a PDF with an AcroForm. In chapter 2, you saw examples of how to use the fields of an AcroForm as placeholders to add new data. We'll look more closely at this functionality in chapter 16. In this chapter, you'll use these forms to retrieve information from an end user.

## 15.1 Introducing annotations

*Annotation* is a generic name for all kinds of interactive content added to a PDF document, including textual notes, multimedia content such as movies and sounds, file attachments, and so on. Not all types of annotations available in PDF are supported in iText, but you'll learn that there's a way to work around this problem. Let's start with the most elementary types of annotations.

### 15.1.1 Simple annotations

In the first example, some squares are drawn at absolute locations. They indicate the clickable areas defined in a series of annotations. The file simple_annotations2.pdf, shown in figure 15.1, displays such a square. A small MPEG movie plays inside this square when you open the corresponding file in Adobe Reader.

The second PDF document shown in figure 15.1 displays a text annotation that was added without specifying coordinates. It's positioned at the current Y coordinate in a sequence of paragraphs. The `Paragraphs` and `Annotation` were added with `document.add()`.

Both files demonstrate all the annotation types supported in the class `com.lowagie.text.Annotation`. These annotations are also supported in `com.lowagie.text.pdf.PdfAnnotation`. The classes have only two differences:

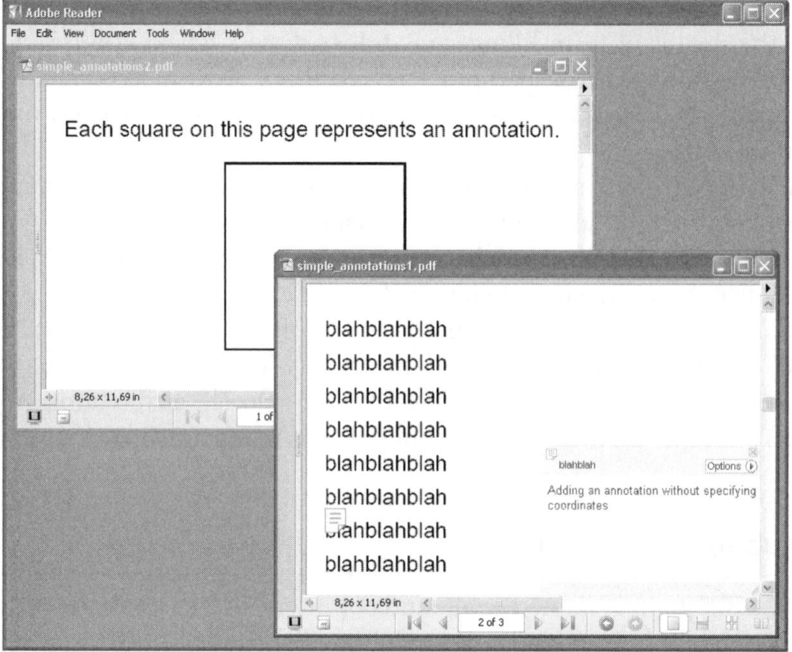


**Figure 15.1 Simple annotations**

- An `Annotation` object is added to the `Document` object, whereas a `PdfAnnotation` is added to the `PdfWriter` instance.
- `PdfAnnotation` supports more annotation types and possibilities. If a specific annotation type isn't available in iText, `PdfAnnotation` offers you the flexibility to compose your own annotation dictionary.

Let's review the annotation types supported in the simple class.

### Text annotations

A *text annotation* represents a sticky note attached to a point in the PDF document. When closed, the annotation appears as an icon. Figure 15.2 shows the types of icons that are available.

When you move the mouse pointer over the icon, the title and the content of the text annotation are visible as a tool tip. When you double-click on the icon, or if *open* is defined as the default display value, a post-it like message appears (see figure 15.1). Figure 15.2 also shows the Comments panel. If you open this panel, you get a per-page overview of all the annotations.

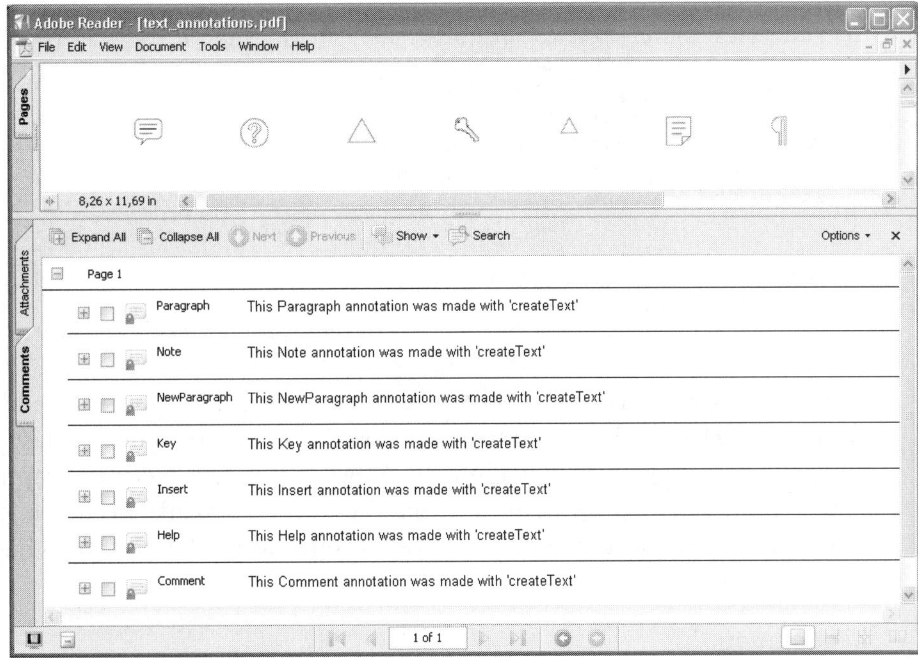


**Figure 15.2 Text annotations**

With class `Annotation`, you can only create a text annotation with a Note icon that is closed by default:

```
/* chapter15/SimpleAnnotations.java */
Annotation a1 = new Annotation("authors",
  "Maybe it's because I wanted to be an author ...",
  250f, 700f, 350f, 800f);
```

The PDF in figure 15.2 was made using the `PdfAnnotation` class.

```
/* chapter15/TextAnnotations.java */
writer.addAnnotation(
  PdfAnnotation.createText(writer,
    new Rectangle(50, 780, 70, 800),
    "Comment", "...", false, "Comment"));
writer.addAnnotation(
  PdfAnnotation.createText(writer,
    new Rectangle(100, 780, 120, 800),
    "Help", "...", true, "Help"));
writer.addAnnotation(
  PdfAnnotation.createText(writer, new Rectangle(50, 700, 70, 720),
    "Insert", "...", false, "Insert"));
```

```
writer.addAnnotation(
  PdfAnnotation.createText(writer,
    new Rectangle(100, 700, 120, 720),
    "Key", "...", true, "Key"));
writer.addAnnotation(
  PdfAnnotation.createText(writer, new Rectangle(50, 620, 70, 640),
    "NewParagraph", "...", false, "NewParagraph"));
writer.addAnnotation(
  PdfAnnotation.createText(writer,
    new Rectangle(100, 620, 120, 640),
    "Note", "...", true, "Note"));
writer.addAnnotation(
  PdfAnnotation.createText(writer, new Rectangle(50, 540, 70, 560),
    "Paragraph", "...", false, "Paragraph"));
```

The `boolean` value passed with the `createText()` method specifies whether the text annotation should be open (true) or closed (false) by default. The last parameter specifies the type of icon: Comment, Help, Insert, Key, NewParagraph, Note, or Paragraph. See figure 15.2 to see what these icons look like in Adobe Reader.

Another type of annotation you've already encountered in previous chapters is the link annotation.

### Link annotations

A *link annotation* represents either a hypertext link to a destination elsewhere in the document (see, for instance, section 13.4.1, "Creating destinations") or an action to be performed (for example, section 13.5, "Introducing actions"). You created such annotations in chapter 4 when you added a link or an action to a `Chunk`. Behind the scenes, an annotation was created:

```
/* chapter15/SimpleAnnotations.java */
Annotation a2 = new Annotation(250f, 550f, 350f, 650f,       URI action
  new URL("http://www.lowagie.com/iText/"));                  (java.net.URL)
Annotation a3 = new Annotation(250f, 400f, 350f, 500f,       URI action (String)
  "http://www.lowagie.com/iText");
Annotation a4 = new Annotation(250f, 250f, 350f, 350f,       Named action
  PdfAction.LASTPAGE);
...
Annotation a6 = new Annotation(100f, 550f, 200f, 650f,       Remote GoTo action
  "simple_annotations1.pdf", "mark");                         (named destination)
Annotation a7 = new Annotation(100f, 400f, 200f, 500f,       Remote GoTo action
  "simple_annotations1.pdf", 2);                              (specific page)
Annotation a8 = new Annotation(100f, 250f, 200f, 350f,       Launch action
  "C://windows/notepad.exe", null, null, null);
```

Again, the `PdfAnnotation` class offers more possibilities to create link annotations. You can create an annotation using any action or destination, named or explicit (see chapter 14):

```
/* chapter15/Annotations.java */
writer.addAnnotation(
  PdfAnnotation.createLink(writer,
  new Rectangle(200f, 700f, 300f, 800f),
  PdfAnnotation.HIGHLIGHT_INVERT,
  PdfAction.javaScript("app.alert('Hello');\r", writer)));
writer.addAnnotation(
  PdfAnnotation.createLink(writer,
  new Rectangle(200f, 550f, 300f, 650f),
  PdfAnnotation.HIGHLIGHT_OUTLINE,
  "top"));
writer.addAnnotation(
  PdfAnnotation.createLink(writer,
  new Rectangle(200f, 400f, 300f, 500f),
  PdfAnnotation.HIGHLIGHT_PUSH, 1,
  new PdfDestination(PdfDestination.FIT)));
```

**Annotation that triggers action**

**Annotation that goes to named destination**

**Annotation linking to explicit destination**

This functionality is used by iText when you define an `Anchor` with a reference to an external or internal document. Actions are used to jump to an external document; destinations to jump to another location in the current document.

With `PdfAnnotation`, you can also define the highlighting mode:

- `PdfAnnotation.HIGHLIGHT_NONE`—No highlighting (the default)
- `PdfAnnotation.HIGHLIGHT_INVERT`—Inverts the content of the annotation square when clicked
- `PdfAnnotation.HIGHLIGHT_OUTLINE`—Inverts the annotation's border when clicked
- `PdfAnnotation.HIGHLIGHT_PUSH`—Displays the annotation as if it was being pushed below the surface of the page

There's also a `PdfAnnotation.HIGHLIGHT_TOGGLE`, but this option can be used only in widget annotations; it has the same meaning as `HIGHLIGHT_PUSH` (which is preferred).

A final annotation type is supported by the `Annotation` class; you can use it to add a movie to your document.

### *Movie annotations*

If you want to add an animated picture to a PDF file, you need a media clip. For PDF versions 1.4 or earlier, only MOV, MPG, and AVI are supported; versions 1.5 and later support ASF, ASX, AVI, IVF, MLV, MP2, MPA, MPE, MPEG, MPG, MPV2, SPL, SWF, WM, WMP, WMV, WMX, and WVX.

I used the images of the animated GIF from chapter 5 to create an MPEG file:

```
/* chapter15/SimpleAnnotations.java */
Annotation a5 = new Annotation(100f, 700f, 200f, 800f,
  "../resources/foxdog.mpg", "video/mpeg", true);
```

The last parameter in the constructor specifies that the video should be played immediately when the resulting PDF document is opened. Note that you may get a Manage Trust for Multimedia Content alert. You can choose to play the video just once, or you can add it to a list of trusted multimedia content.

The MPEG isn't embedded into the PDF document in this example. The next example embeds the movie:

```
/* chapter15/Annotations.java */
PdfFileSpecification fs =
  PdfFileSpecification.fileEmbedded(writer,
  "../resources/foxdog.mpg", "foxdog.mpg", null);
writer.addAnnotation(PdfAnnotation.createScreen(writer,
  new Rectangle(200f, 700f, 300f, 800f), "Fox and Dog", fs,
  "video/mpeg", true));
```

If you don't want to embed the file, you can replace the `PdfFileSpecification` method `fileEmbedded()` with the method `url()` to refer to a URL, or `file-External()` to refer to a file on the file system.

This concludes the list of annotations supported in class `Annotation`. Let's continue our overview with more annotations that are supported in class `PdfAnnotation`.

## 15.1.2 Other types of annotations

If you look at Table 8.16 in Adobe's PDF Reference Manual, you'll immediately see that new types of annotations have been added with every new PDF version. Not all of these types are supported directly in iText, but that doesn't mean you can't use iText to create such annotations.

In the following code sample, a text annotation is created by adding different key-value pairs to a `PdfAnnotation` object:

```
/* chapter15/Annotations.java */
PdfAnnotation annotation =
  new PdfAnnotation(writer,
  new Rectangle(100, 750, 150, 800));
annotation.put(PdfName.SUBTYPE, PdfName.TEXT);
annotation.put(PdfName.OPEN,
  PdfBoolean.PDFTRUE);
annotation.put(PdfName.T, new PdfString("custom"));
annotation.put(PdfName.CONTENTS,
  new PdfString("This is a custom built text annotation."));
writer.addAnnotation(annotation);
```

**Create undefined annotation**

**Define as TEXT annotation**

**Annotation should be open by default**

**Add title and contents**

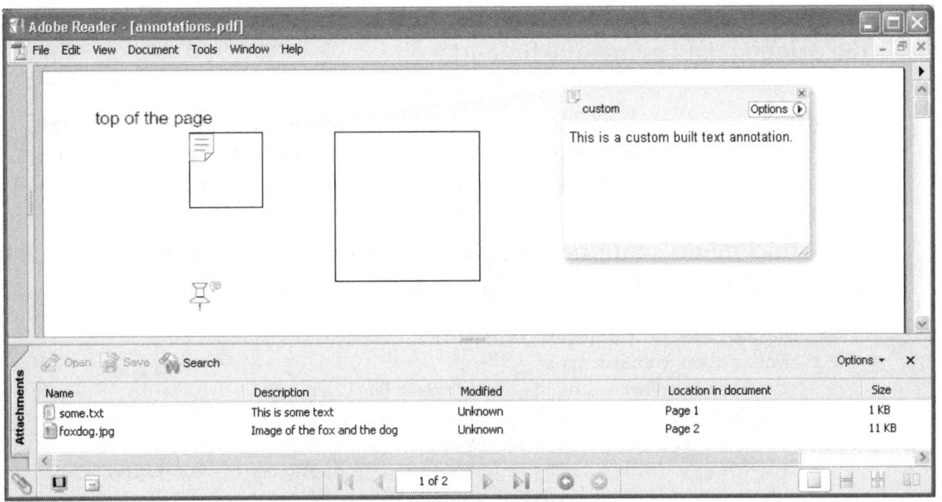


**Figure 15.3 Annotations added using the `PdfAnnotation` class**

Consult the PDF Reference to look up which keys you can add and what values are valid for each key. As you can see, you also need iText objects such as `PdfBoolean`, `PdfString`, and so on. These objects correspond with the PDF objects as they are defined in the PDF Reference. In reality, a `PdfAnnotation` is a special type of `PdfDictionary`. You can find an overview of these basic PDF objects in chapter 18.

Figure 15.3 shows a PDF to which the custom text annotation has been added.

Just below the custom text annotation is a pin; it symbolizes a file attachment. In the attachments pane, you see that two attachments are added to the file: one on each page.

### *File attachments*

The following code sample shows how to add a file called some.txt containing "some text" to a PDF file. You also add a description that is used in the attachments pane:

```
/* chapter15/Annotations.java */
writer.addAnnotation(
  PdfAnnotation.createFileAttachment(writer,
  new Rectangle(100f, 650f, 150f, 700f), "This is some text",
  "some text".getBytes(), null, "some.txt"));
```

The file some.txt is embedded into the PDF document. This functionality is often used when creating reports based on a source in XML, CSV, or another format that can be parsed. If you create a table in PDF, all structure is lost. You can't extract the data that was used to create the document from the PDF file, unless you add the original data as an attachment!

**TOOLBOX** `com.lowagie.tools.plugins.ExtractAttachment` *(Various)* You can use iText to extract all the attachments added to a PDF document. Note that this plug-in doesn't remove the attachments.

The attachments pane in figure 15.3 also lists a second attachment. This time, you pass a path to the file instead of an array of bytes:

```
/* chapter15/Annotations.java */
PdfAnnotation attachment =
  PdfAnnotation.createFileAttachment(writer,
  new Rectangle(400f, 250f, 500f, 350f),
  "Image of the fox and the dog",
  null, "../../chapter05/resources/foxdog.jpg", "foxdog.jpg");
attachment.put(PdfName.NAME, new PdfString("Paperclip"));
writer.addAnnotation(attachment);
```

Another difference in the previous code snippet is that you add "Paperclip" as a name. Other possible values are "PushPin" (the default), "Graph," and "Tag." The paperclip is visible in figure 15.4, along with more annotation types.

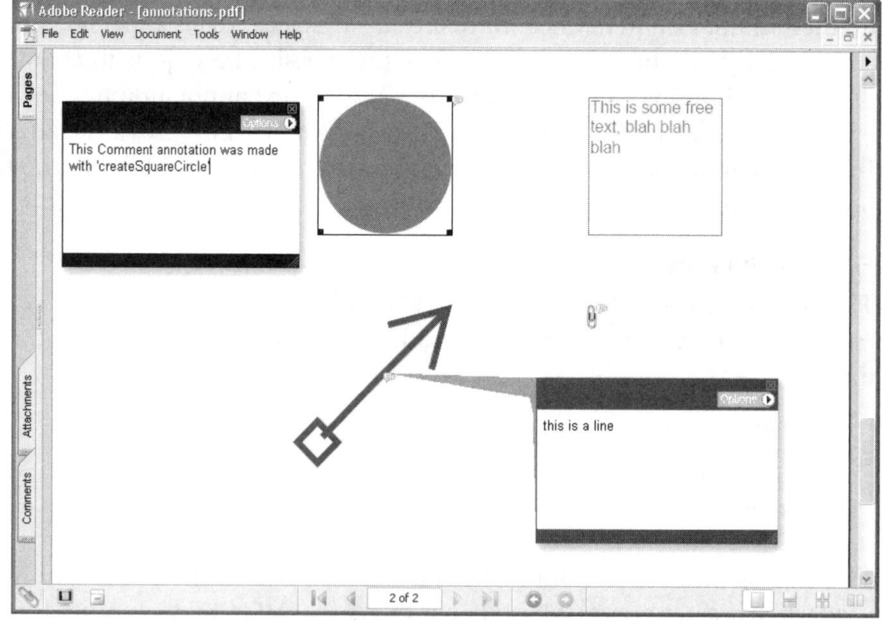


**Figure 15.4 Annotations added using class `PdfAnnotation`**

Let's finish this first series of annotation types with the other annotation types that are visible in the screenshot.

### Free text annotations

A *free text annotation* differs from the text annotations discussed so far:

- There is no open or closed state—the text is always visible.
- You can add rich text strings or a text stream (PDF-1.5).
- You can display the annotation as a callout (PDF-1.6).

This is how the free text annotation in the screenshot was created:

```
/* chapter15/Annotations.java */
PdfContentByte pcb = new PdfContentByte(writer);
pcb.setColorFill(new Color(0xFF, 0x00, 0x00));
writer.addAnnotation(
  PdfAnnotation.createFreeText(writer,
    new Rectangle(200f, 700f, 300f, 800f),
    "This is some free text, blah blah blah", pcb));
```

Note that iText only offers a convenience method for the simplest free text annotations. If you need more complex functionality, consult the PDF Reference. Basically, you can create any type of free text annotation. In the next code snippet, you'll use the `PdfDictionary` method `put()` to create a circle and a line annotation dictionary with extra entries.

### Line, square, and circle annotations

A *line annotation* displays a single straight line. If you want to use the annotation as an arrow, you can define different types of line endings. To use the annotation as a dimension line, you can add leader lines.

Square and circle annotations display (in spite of their name) a rectangle or an ellipse on the page; iText also supports stamp, ink, pop-up, and other annotations, but I won't discuss all those types in this book. The PDF Reference also defines polygon and polyline annotations, and so on, but these types don't have convenience methods in iText.

Let's look at the code that generates the circle and line annotations in figure 15.4:

```
/* chapter15/Annotations.java */
PdfAnnotation shape1 = PdfAnnotation.createSquareCircle(writer,
  new Rectangle(200f, 400f, 300f, 500f),
  "This Comment annotation was made with 'createSquareCircle'",
  false);
```

**Create circle annotation**

```
float[] red = { 1, 0, 0 };                                    Define and set
shape1.put(new PdfName("IC"), new PdfArray(red));             interior color
writer.addAnnotation(shape1);
PdfAnnotation shape2 = PdfAnnotation.createLine(writer,           Create line
  new Rectangle(200f, 250f, 300f, 350f), "this is a line",        annotation
  200, 250, 300, 350);
shape2.put(PdfName.C, new PdfArray(red));      <-- Set color of line
PdfArray lineEndingStyles = new PdfArray();
lineEndingStyles.add(new PdfName("Diamond"));                 Define and set
lineEndingStyles.add(new PdfName("OpenArrow"));               line endings
shape2.put(new PdfName("LE"), lineEndingStyles);
shape2.put(PdfName.BS, new PdfBorderDictionary(5,             Define and set
  PdfBorderDictionary.STYLE_SOLID));                          border style
writer.addAnnotation(shape2);
```

As you can see, iText is a flexible library: By using the lowest level objects summed up in chapter 18, you can create any object defined in the PDF Reference. In section 15.2, we'll focus on widget annotations that can be used as fields in an AcroForm; but let's finish this section with examples of annotations that are added to an image or a chunk.

### 15.1.3 Adding annotations to a chunk or image

The previous examples define the absolute position of the clickable area using the coordinates of the lower-left and upper-right corners of a rectangle. You can use table, cell, or page events to position them, but there are also two high-level objects to which annotations can be added in order to make them clickable.

You already have experience with Chunks and annotations:

```
/* chapter15/AnnotatedChunks.java */
PdfAnnotation text = PdfAnnotation.createText(
  writer, new Rectangle(200f, 250f, 300f, 350f),
  "Fox", "The fox is quick", true, "Comment");
PdfAnnotation attachment = PdfAnnotation.createFileAttachment(
  writer, new Rectangle(100f, 650f, 150f, 700f),
  "Image of the fox and the dog",
  getBytesFromFile(new File("../../chapter05/resources/foxdog.jpg")),
  null, "foxdog.jpg");
PdfAnnotation javascript =
  new PdfAnnotation(writer, 200f, 550f, 300f, 650f,
  PdfAction.javaScript("app.alert('Wake up dog!');\r", writer));
Chunk fox = new Chunk("quick brown fox").setAnnotation(text);
Chunk jumps = new Chunk(" jumps over ").setAnnotation(attachment);
Chunk dog = new Chunk("the lazy dog").setAnnotation(javascript);
document.add(fox);  document.add(jumps);  document.add(dog);
```

Now you're going to create clickable `Images`:

```
/* chapter15/AnnotatedImages.java */
Image gif =
  Image.getInstance("../../chapter10/resources/iTextLogo.gif");
gif.setAnnotation(
  new Annotation(0, 0, 0, 0, http://www.lowagie.com/iText"));
gif.setAbsolutePosition(30f, 750f);
document.add(gif);
Image jpeg =
  Image.getInstance("../../chapter05/resources/foxdog.jpg");
jpeg.setAnnotation(new Annotation("picture",
  "quick brown fox jumps over the lazy dog", 0, 0, 0, 0));
jpeg.setAbsolutePosition(120f, 550f);
document.add(jpeg);
```

When the first image (the iText logo) is clicked, the iText home page opens. A file attachment containing the JPEG is added to the image displayed in the document.

If you delve into the PDF Reference, you'll discover that you can set annotation flags to make an annotation invisible, hidden, printable, and so on. You can also define the appearance of an annotation; this is especially important for widget annotations. This brings us to the subject of form fields.

## 15.2 Creating an AcroForm

Widget annotations are used to represent the fields in interactive forms called *AcroForms*. The PDF Reference says that "a PDF document may contain any number of fields appearing on any combination of pages, all of which make up a single, global interactive form spanning the entire document." Note that if you compare a form in PDF with forms in an HTML document, you'll discover some similarities but also huge differences. A PDF document can have only one form! Each field in a PDF document is defined by a *field dictionary*. Fields can be organized hierarchically, and the children of a field can contain widget annotations.

The PDF Reference states that "as a convenience, when a field has only a single associated widget annotation, the contents of the field dictionary and the annotation dictionary may be merged into a single dictionary containing entries that pertain to both a field and an annotation." It's not necessary to understand all this theoretical stuff immediately. We'll look at examples, and you'll learn what is meant in these definitions by creating your first AcroForms.

AcroForms support four types of fields:

- `Btn`—Button fields
- `Tx`—Text Fields
- `Ch`—Choice Fields
- `Sig`—Signature fields

Let's see how to create the first three types of widget annotations (we'll save signature fields for later).

### 15.2.1 Button fields

Let's start with the PDF Reference definition:

> A button field represents an interactive control on the screen that the user can manipulate with the mouse. There are three types of button fields:
>
> - A pushbutton is a purely interactive control that responds immediately to user input without retaining a permanent value.
> - A check box toggles between two states, on and off.
> - Radio button fields contain a set of related buttons that can each be on or off. Typically, at most one radio button in a set may be on at any given time, and selecting any one of the buttons automatically deselect all the others.

Figure 15.5 shows examples of each type of button field.

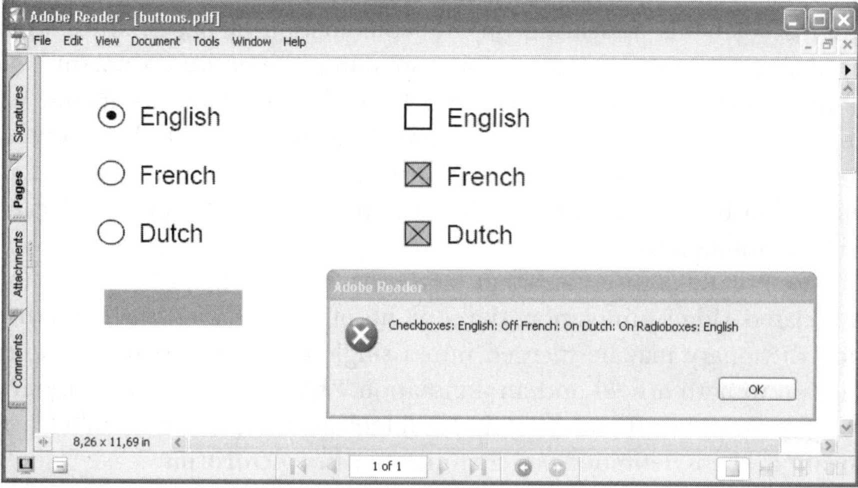


**Figure 15.5 A PDF file with different button fields**

You recognize a set of radio buttons, a set of check boxes, and a grey rectangle that is a pushbutton. When it's clicked, a JavaScript method is invoked that shows the state of the radio buttons and check boxes in an alert message. When you add a button, radio button, or check box in HTML, every browser knows how to visualize these button fields. This isn't the case when you add a button to a PDF file. You have to define the appearance of each form field.

### *Adding a pushbutton*

The appearance of a (widget) annotation is created with the class `PdfAppearance`. This is a subclass of `PdfTemplate` (see section 10.4.2), so it shouldn't have many secrets for you. Next, you define three appearances for the widget annotation that displays the pushbutton field:

```
/* chapter15/Buttons.java */
PdfAppearance normal = cb.createAppearance(100, 50);
normal.setColorFill(Color.GRAY);
normal.rectangle(5, 5, 90, 40);  normal.fill();
PdfAppearance rollover = cb.createAppearance(100, 50);
rollover.setColorFill(Color.RED);
rollover.rectangle(5, 5, 90, 40);  rollover.fill();
PdfAppearance down = cb.createAppearance(100, 50);
down.setColorFill(Color.BLUE);
down.rectangle(5, 5, 90, 40);  down.fill();
```

**Normal (gray rectangle)**

**Rollover (red rectangle)**

**Down (blue rectangle)**

You don't add any hierarchy to this pushbutton. The single pushbutton field corresponds with a single widget annotation. In other words, you don't have to use two separate dictionaries, one defining the field and another defining the widget annotation. Both dictionaries can be merged into one, as explained in the PDF Reference.

This merger is done implicitly in iText: The class `PdfFormField` extends `PdfAnnotation`. The next code snippet adds dictionary entries that are specific for form fields as well as entries that are specific for annotations:

```
/* chapter15/Buttons.java */
PdfFormField pushbutton = PdfFormField.createPushButton(writer);
pushbutton.setFieldName("PushAction");
pushbutton.setAppearance(
  PdfAnnotation.APPEARANCE_NORMAL, normal);
pushbutton.setAppearance(
  PdfAnnotation.APPEARANCE_ROLLOVER, rollover);
pushbutton.setAppearance(
  PdfAnnotation.APPEARANCE_DOWN, down);
pushbutton.setWidget(new Rectangle(40, 650, 150, 680),
  PdfAnnotation.HIGHLIGHT_PUSH);
```

**Create form field dictionary**

**Set field name (field dictionary)**

**Set appearances (annotation dictionary)**

**Set other annotation dictionary entries**

```
pushbutton.setAction(
  PdfAction.javaScript("this.showButtonState()", writer));
writer.addAnnotation(pushbutton);
```

**Add action to annotation dictionary**

This code sample defines different appearance streams for the annotation. This applies for other annotation types, too. You can define three appearance streams:

- `APPEARANCE_NORMAL`—The annotation's normal appearance
- `APPEARANCE_ROLLOVER`—The appearance when you move the mouse pointer over the annotation
- `APPEARANCE_DOWN`—The appearance of the annotation when you click the mouse button

Except for certain link annotations and the movie annotation, you can also set an action that must be performed when the annotation is clicked. In the buttons example, you call a JavaScript method that shows the state of the radio buttons and check boxes.

### *Adding radio buttons*

A radio button field is a set of related buttons. Typically, a radio button field corresponds with a set of widget annotations. If you want to add a radio button field, you must create a field dictionary and add separate widget annotation dictionaries. Such a widget annotation has different appearance streams depending on the appearance state:

```
/* chapter15/Buttons.java */
PdfAppearance[] radiobuttonStates = new PdfAppearance[2];
radiobuttonStates[0] = cb.createAppearance(20, 20);
radiobuttonStates[0].circle(10, 10, 9);
radiobuttonStates[0].stroke();
radiobuttonStates[1] = cb.createAppearance(20, 20);
radiobuttonStates[1].circle(10, 10, 9);
radiobuttonStates[1].stroke();
radiobuttonStates[1].circle(10, 10, 3);
radiobuttonStates[1].fillStroke();
```

**Off (single circle)**

**On (two concentric circles)**

For these radio buttons, you only define the normal appearance. (You could define a rollover and down appearance as well.) You need two appearance streams for the normal appearance, because a radio button can have an On state and an Off state.

Let's create the radio button field with field name `language` and English as the default value (stored as a `PdfName`) and then loop over the languages array:

```
/* chapter15/Buttons.java */
String[] languages = { "English", "French", "Dutch" };
PdfFormField language =
  PdfFormField.createRadioButton(writer, true);
language.setFieldName("language");
language.setValueAsName(languages[0]);
for (int i = 0; i < languages.length; i++) {
  rect = new Rectangle(40, 806 - i * 40, 60, 788 - i * 40);
  addRadioButton(writer, rect,
    language, languages[i], radiobuttonStates, i == 0);
}
```

The method you used in the loop looks like this:

```
/* chapter15/Buttons.java */
private static void addRadioButton(PdfWriter writer,
  Rectangle rect, PdfFormField radio, String name,
  PdfAppearance[] onOff, boolean on) {
  PdfFormField field = PdfFormField.createEmpty(writer);      <- Create empty PdfFormField object
  field.setWidget(rect, PdfAnnotation.HIGHLIGHT_INVERT);      <- Define widget annotation
  if (on)
    field.setAppearanceState(name);                           | Set default
  else                                                        | appearance
    field.setAppearanceState("Off");                          | state
  field.setAppearance(
    PdfAnnotation.APPEARANCE_NORMAL, "Off", onOff[0]);        | Give On state
  field.setAppearance(                                        | custom name
    PdfAnnotation.APPEARANCE_NORMAL, name, onOff[1]);
  radio.addKid(field);      <- Add widget to parent
}
```

The three radio buttons shown in figure 15.5 are three widget annotations defined in three different dictionaries. They're associated with one radio button field dictionary.

The end user can select only one option in a radio button field. When the Java-Script code snippet `this.getField('language').value` is used, one of the custom names for the On state is returned: English, French, or Dutch. Check boxes are also a type of button field, but they differ from radio buttons: You can choose more than one option.

### *Adding check boxes*

Again, you must define the different states of the button:

```
/* chapter15/Buttons.java */
PdfAppearance[] checkboxStates = new PdfAppearance[2];
checkboxStates[0] = cb.createAppearance(20, 20);       |
checkboxStates[0].rectangle(1, 1, 18, 18);             | Off (rectangle)
checkboxStates[0].stroke();                            |
```

```
checkboxStates[1] = cb.createAppearance(20, 20);
checkboxStates[1].setRGBColorFill(255, 128, 128);
checkboxStates[1].rectangle(1, 1, 18, 18);
checkboxStates[1].fillStroke();
checkboxStates[1].moveTo(1, 1);                    On (rectangle with X)
checkboxStates[1].lineTo(19, 19);
checkboxStates[1].moveTo(1, 19);
checkboxStates[1].lineTo(19, 1);
checkboxStates[1].stroke();
```

You can give these buttons any appearance you want. You could reuse the appearance of the radio button, but that might confuse the end user, who is used to a radio button being circular and a check box being rectangular:

```
/* chapter15/Buttons.java */
private static void createCheckbox(PdfWriter writer, Rectangle rect,
  String name, PdfAppearance[] onOff) {
  PdfFormField field = PdfFormField.createCheckBox(writer);   <-1
  field.setWidget(rect, PdfAnnotation.HIGHLIGHT_INVERT);   <-2
  field.setFieldName(name);   <-3
  field.setValueAsName("Off");   <-4
  field.setAppearanceState("Off");   <-5
  field.setAppearance(
    PdfAnnotation.APPEARANCE_NORMAL, "Off", onOff[0]);
  field.setAppearance(                                        6
    PdfAnnotation.APPEARANCE_NORMAL, "On", onOff[1]);
  writer.addAnnotation(field);
}
```

This code sample creates the form field ❶ and defines the widget annotation ❷. You set the field name ❸, the field value ❹, and the default appearance state ❺. Then, you add the normal appearances ❻.

In the buttons example, you use `PdfFormField` to create pushbuttons, radio buttons, and check boxes. You create `PdfAppearance` objects using the methods discussed in chapters 10 and 11. But there's an alternative way that you may find easier to use.

Let's rewrite the example using convenience classes.

### Convenience classes for button fields

Figure 15.6 shows a PDF file that contains button fields similar to those in figure 15.5; but these buttons were created using the convenience classes `PushButtonField` and `RadioCheckField`.

These classes offer a more user-friendly way to create button fields. Glyphs from the ZapfDingbats font are used to visualize the On state. The pushbutton contains an icon (the iText eye) and some text.

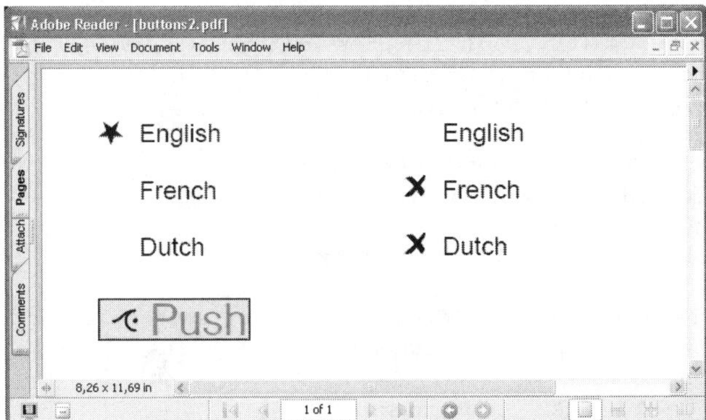


**Figure 15.6**
**A PDF document with buttons**

The code to create the pushbutton is as follows:

```
/* chapter15/Buttons2.java */
PushbuttonField push = new PushbuttonField(writer,
  new Rectangle(40, 650, 150, 680), "pushAction");       ❶
push.setBackgroundColor(Color.YELLOW);
push.setBorderColor(Color.BLACK);                         ❷
push.setText("Push");
push.setTextColor(Color.RED);
push.setTemplate(template);
push.setScaleIcon(PushbuttonField.SCALE_ICON_ALWAYS);
push.setLayout(PushbuttonField.LAYOUT_ICON_LEFT_LABEL_RIGHT);   ❸
PdfFormField pushbutton = push.getField();   ❹
pushbutton.setAction(
  PdfAction.javaScript("this.showButtonState()", writer));   ❺
writer.addAnnotation(pushbutton);
```

You first create the `PushbuttonField` ❶. Next, you set the background and border colors ❷, and define the text, the icon, and their positions ❸. You get the form field object ❹, and finally add an action ❺.

You no longer have to draw the button yourself. You define a background and border color. You add text and define the text color. You can add a `PdfTemplate` (or an `Image`) that acts as an icon. In other words, you get numerous methods to set the border width, the font and font size, and so on, that let you create a pushbutton in a more intuitive way. When you're done defining the attributes of your `PushbuttonField`, you can get a `PdfFormField` object. If necessary, you can add other dictionary entries, such as a JavaScript action.

For the other two button types, you use another convenience class to rewrite the `addRadioButton()` and `createCheckbox()` methods:

```
/* chapter15/Buttons2.java */
private static void addRadioButton(PdfWriter writer, Rectangle rect,
  PdfFormField radio, String name, boolean on)
  throws IOException, DocumentException {
  RadioCheckField check =                                      ❶
    new RadioCheckField(writer, rect, null, name);
  check.setCheckType(RadioCheckField.TYPE_STAR);          ❷
  check.setChecked(on);    ❸
  radio.addKid(check.getRadioField());    ❹
}
private static void createCheckbox(PdfWriter writer, Rectangle rect,
  String name) throws IOException, DocumentException {
  RadioCheckField check =                                      ❺
    new RadioCheckField(writer, rect, name, "On");
  check.setCheckType(RadioCheckField.TYPE_CROSS);    ❻
  writer.addAnnotation(check.getCheckField());    ❼
}
```

This code sample first creates a `RadioCheckField` ❶ whose On appearance is a star ❷. You set the default state ❸, and add the radio button as a `PdfFormField` ❹. You can also create a `RadioCheckField` ❺ whose appearance is an X ❻. Finally you add the check box as a `PdfFormField` ❼.

Using the code of the two button examples, you can ask end users for their mother tongue (only one answer possible) and for their knowledge of other languages (preferably more than one). You could define an action that submits this information to a site and add it to the pushbutton, but that will have to wait for the next section.

Let's continue with the next type of form field: text fields.

### 15.2.2 Creating text fields

The definition given by the PDF Reference is easy to understand:

> A text field is a box or space in which the user can enter text from the keyboard. The text may be restricted to a single line or may be permitted to span multiple lines.

Figure 15.7 shows examples of such text boxes.

Again there are two ways to create the `PdfFormField`: a difficult way that gives you more control over what happens, and an easier way that uses the convenience class `TextField`.

By studying the code that creates a text field without the convenience class, you get some insight into the way text fields are organized in a PDF file:

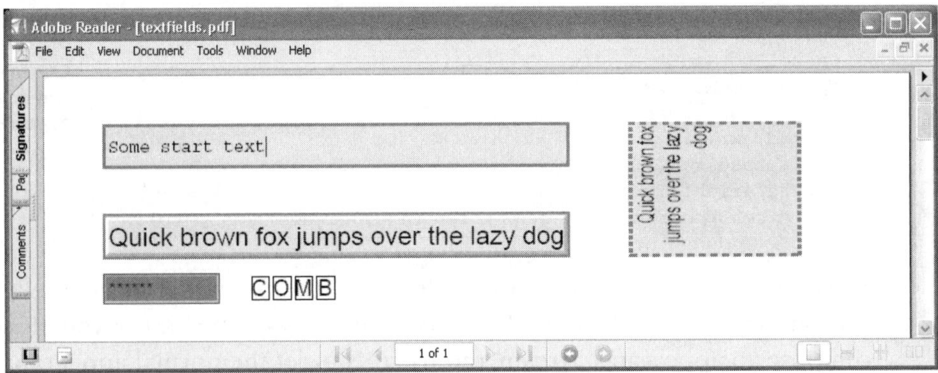


**Figure 15.7 Different types of text fields**

```
/* chapter15/TextFields.java */
BaseFont helv = BaseFont.createFont(
  BaseFont.COURIER, BaseFont.WINANSI, BaseFont.NOT_EMBEDDED);
String text = "Some start text";
PdfFormField field =
  PdfFormField.createTextField(writer, false, false, 0);
field.setWidget(new Rectangle(40, 780, 360, 810),
  PdfAnnotation.HIGHLIGHT_INVERT);
field.setFlags(PdfAnnotation.FLAGS_PRINT);
field.setFieldName("some_text");
field.setValueAsString(text);
field.setDefaultValueAsString(text);
field.setMKBorderColor(Color.RED);
field.setMKBackgroundColor(Color.YELLOW);
field.setBorderStyle(
  new PdfBorderDictionary(2,
  PdfBorderDictionary.STYLE_SOLID));
field.setPage();
PdfAppearance tp = cb.createAppearance(320, 30);
PdfAppearance da = (PdfAppearance)tp.getDuplicate();
da.setFontAndSize(helv, 12);
field.setDefaultAppearanceString(da);
tp.saveState();
tp.setColorStroke(Color.RED);
tp.setLineWidth(2);
tp.setColorFill(Color.YELLOW);
tp.rectangle(1, 1, 318, 28);
tp.fillStroke();
tp.restoreState();
tp.beginVariableText();
tp.saveState();
tp.rectangle(2, 2, 318, 28);
```

Annotations: **Create field/widget dictionary** · **Make annotation printable** · **Set field dictionary entries** · **Set widget-specific appearance attributes** · **Set border style** · **Create normal and default appearance**

```
tp.clip();
tp.newPath();
tp.beginText();
tp.setFontAndSize(helv, 12);
tp.setTextMatrix(4, 11);
tp.showText(text);
tp.endText();
tp.restoreState();
tp.endVariableText();
field.setAppearance(PdfAnnotation.APPEARANCE_NORMAL, tp);
writer.addAnnotation(field);
```

**Create normal and default appearance**

As you can see, it's a lot of work to define all the parts that make a text field. It isn't sufficient to set the default text (with `setValueAsString()`); you also have to compose an appearance stream and use this to set the normal appearance of the annotation and the default appearance of the field. It pays off to use the `TextField` convenience class.

The following code snippet creates a similar text field using fewer lines of code. I even added some extra options—the border style is beveled, the text is centered, and you indicate that the field is required:

```
/* chapter15/TextFields.java */
TextField tf1 =
  new TextField(writer, new Rectangle(40, 720, 360, 750), "fox");
tf1.setBackgroundColor(Color.YELLOW);
tf1.setBorderColor(Color.RED);
tf1.setBorderWidth(2);
tf1.setBorderStyle(PdfBorderDictionary.STYLE_BEVELED);
tf1.setText("Quick brown fox jumps over the lazy dog");
tf1.setAlignment(Element.ALIGN_CENTER);
tf1.setOptions(TextField.REQUIRED);
writer.addAnnotation(tf1.getTextField());
```

When you use the `TextField` class, a lot of work is done for you. By default, an annotation isn't printed. If you leave out the line that sets the `FLAGS_PRINT` option in the first code sample, the text field isn't printed. Unless you change the visibility (with the method `setVisibility()`), the `FLAGS_PRINT` option is set by default in a `TextField`.

`TextField` also creates an appearance stream based on the text and the styles you define. Note that this appearance is an approximation of the way Adobe Reader renders the content of a text field. As soon as you click the text field and enter another `String`, you see differences in the offset of the text, depending on the version of Adobe Reader you're using.

The next code snippet creates a multiline text field rotated 90 degrees:

```
/* chapter15/TextFields.java */
TextField tf2 =
  new TextField(writer, new Rectangle(400, 720, 520, 810), "dog");
tf2.setBackgroundColor(Color.YELLOW);
tf2.setBorderColor(Color.RED);
tf2.setBorderWidth(2);
tf2.setBorderStyle(PdfBorderDictionary.STYLE_DASHED);
tf2.setText("Quick brown fox jumps over the lazy dog");
tf2.setAlignment(Element.ALIGN_RIGHT);
tf2.setOptions(TextField.MULTILINE | TextField.REQUIRED);
tf2.setRotation(90);
writer.addAnnotation(tf2.getTextField());
```

By changing the options, you can create different types of text fields. The following code creates a password field:

```
/* chapter15/TextFields.java */
TextField tf3 =
  new TextField(writer, new Rectangle(40, 690, 120, 710), "secret");
tf3.setBackgroundColor(Color.RED);
tf3.setBorderColor(Color.BLUE);
tf3.setBorderWidth(1);
tf3.setBorderStyle(PdfBorderDictionary.STYLE_INSET);
tf3.setText("secret");
tf3.setOptions(TextField.PASSWORD);
writer.addAnnotation(tf3.getTextField());
```

Some forms display their text fields as a set of boxes, one per character that has to be entered. Sometimes a scanned paper document is used as background for the AcroForm, and the boxes are already present. You must make sure every character that is entered by the end user fits into the preprinted boxes. You can do this by setting the `TextField.COMB` option:

```
/* chapter15/TextFields.java */
TextField tf4 =
  new TextField(writer, new Rectangle(140, 690, 200, 710), "comb");
tf4.setMaxCharacterLength(4);
tf4.setOptions(TextField.COMB);
tf4.setText("COMB");
writer.addAnnotation(tf4.getTextField());
```

You can find other methods (`setFont()`, `setFontSize()`, and so on) and other options (`READ_ONLY`, `FILE_SELECTION`, and so on) in the Javadoc information and the PDF Reference. The `TextField` class can also be used as a convenience class to create the two types of choice fields that are described in the PDF Reference.

### 15.2.3 Creating choice fields

The PDF Reference says the following:

> A choice field contains several text items, one or more of which may be selected as the field value. The items may be presented to the user in either of two forms:
>
> - A scrollable list box
> - A combo box consisting of a drop down-list optionally accompanied by an editable text box in which the user can type a value other than the predefined choices.

Figure 15.8 demonstrates the different types of choice fields; the first two were created with class `PdfFormField` only; the last two were created with the convenience class `TextField`.

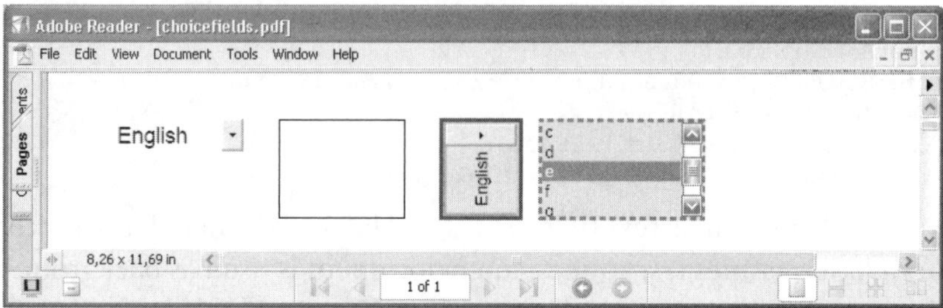


**Figure 15.8 Different types of choice fields**

The first two examples let the end user choose one out of four languages. Unfortunately, you see the options in the list (the empty rectangle in the screenshot) only after you click the rectangle. Let's look at the code and find out why:

```
/* chapter15/ChoiceFields.java */
String options[] = {"English", "French", "Dutch", "German"};
PdfFormField combo =
  PdfFormField.createCombo(writer, true, options, 0);
combo.setWidget(new Rectangle(40, 780, 120, 800),
  PdfAnnotation.HIGHLIGHT_INVERT);
combo.setFieldName("languageCombo");
combo.setValueAsString("English");
writer.addAnnotation(combo);
PdfFormField field = PdfFormField.createList(writer, options, 0);
PdfAppearance app = cb.createAppearance(80, 60);
app.rectangle(1, 1, 78, 58);
app.stroke();
```

```
field.setAppearance(PdfAnnotation.APPEARANCE_NORMAL, app);
field.setWidget(new Rectangle(140, 740, 220, 800),
  PdfAnnotation.HIGHLIGHT_OUTLINE);
field.setFieldName("languageList");
field.setValueAsString("English");
writer.addAnnotation(field);
```

You pass the array with the different options to the `createCombo()` and `createList()` methods and, as a result, get a `PdfFormField` as in the previous examples. You don't do much work to create the appearance streams, and that shows when you open the PDF document. Or rather, it doesn't show. Instead of the second choice field in the screenshot, you see a black rectangle. If you did more work on your appearance stream, you could avoid this result. But that would mean lots of extra work.

Fortunately, you can also use the `TextField` class, as in the following code snippets. Note that you change the visibility of the combo box; if you print the page shown in figure 15.8, only the fourth choice field is visible:

```
/* chapter15/ChoiceFields.java */
TextField tf1 = new TextField(
  writer, new Rectangle(240, 740, 290, 800), "comboLanguage");
tf1.setBackgroundColor(Color.YELLOW);
tf1.setBorderColor(Color.BLUE);
tf1.setBorderWidth(2);
tf1.setFontSize(10);
tf1.setBorderStyle(PdfBorderDictionary.STYLE_INSET);
tf1.setVisibility(TextField.VISIBLE_BUT_DOES_NOT_PRINT);
tf1.setChoices(new String[]{"English", "French"});
tf1.setChoiceExports(new String[]{"EN", "FR"});
tf1.setRotation(90);
writer.addAnnotation(tf1.getComboField());
TextField tf2 = new TextField(
  writer, new Rectangle(300, 740, 400, 800), "listLanguage");
tf2.setBackgroundColor(Color.YELLOW);
tf2.setBorderColor(Color.RED);
tf2.setBorderWidth(2);
tf2.setBorderStyle(PdfBorderDictionary.STYLE_DASHED);
tf2.setFontSize(10);
tf2.setChoices(
  new String[]{"a", "b", "c", "d", "e", "f", "g", "h"});
tf2.setChoiceSelection(4);
writer.addAnnotation(tf2.getListField());
```

Note that you define the default selection of the list box: You select the element with index 4 (the fifth element in the list). You also make a distinction between the choices shown in the combo box and the export value of each of these options; this value will be sent to the server once you add a submit button.

As I mentioned in section 1.2.2, an AcroForm can be submitted in different ways. Let's find out how to create a PDF with an AcroForm that can be submitted to a server.

## 15.3 Submitting a form

In the previous section, you created forms with all kinds of fields; but you couldn't submit the data entered in these fields, because you didn't add a button with a submit action.

**FAQ** *Can an end user save a (partially) filled in AcroForm?* If end users view the form in the free Adobe Reader, they can print the form, but there's no way to save it (unless the PDF was rights-enabled using Acrobat Professional). Users can only save a blank copy of the form. They need the full Acrobat or other third-party software (for instance, JPedal) to save the data entered in the form.

Figure 15.9 shows a form with text fields and buttons, opened in a browser.

If you look closely at the extra bar that appears when the form opens, you see the confirmation of what I told you about saving and printing the form. I also selected two check boxes on the right side of the toolbar: fields than can be filled in get a blue background; fields that are required get a thick red border.

Before we talk about the buttons labeled POST, FDF, XFDF, RESET, HIDE, and SHOW, let's look at how the form was created—specifically, at the names given to the fields.

### 15.3.1 Choosing field names

In the previous examples, you created fields that had no (or almost no) hierarchy. The *partial name* of the field was equal to the *fully qualified name*. The fully qualified field name is constructed from the partial field names of the field and all of its ancestors. The names are separated by a period.

In figure 15.9, you have a table with fields of information about a sender and similar fields about a receiver. Instead of defining a flat structure with fields named sender_name, sender_address, receiver_name, receiver_address, and so on, you create two parent fields: sender and receiver. You use the same partial field names for name, address, postal_code and email.

The fully qualified names of those fields are sender.name, sender.address, receiver.name, receiver.address, and so on. This hierarchy will prove to be useful

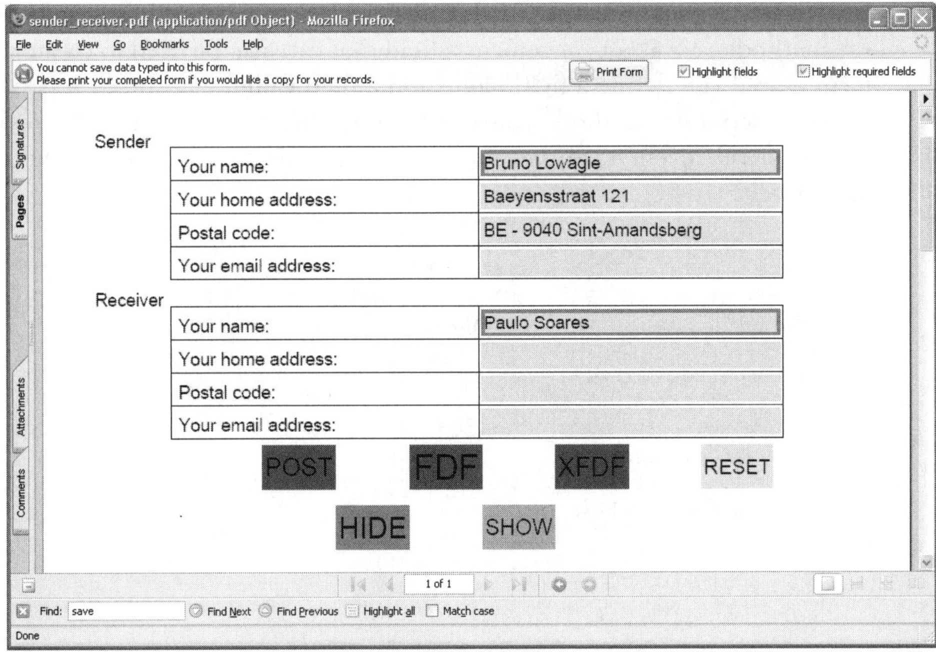


**Figure 15.9 A form with submit buttons in a browser**

later. Note that you can have two different (representations of) fields with the same fully qualified name, provided that they have the same parent, have no children of their own, and differ only in properties that specify their visual appearance. The PDF Reference says, "Fields with the same fully qualified name must have the same field type, value and default value."

Just as you created an empty form field for the radio button field, you create a field that acts as the parent of the data fields containing the information about the sender and the receiver:

```
/* chapter15/SenderReceiver.java */
document.add(new Paragraph("Sender"));
PdfFormField sender = PdfFormField.createEmpty(writer);
sender.setFieldName("sender");
document.add(createTable(writer, sender));
writer.addAnnotation(sender);
document.add(new Paragraph("Receiver"));
PdfFormField receiver = PdfFormField.createEmpty(writer);
receiver.setFieldName("receiver");
document.add(createTable(writer, receiver));
writer.addAnnotation(receiver);
```

This example uses an empty field; you can use any other field instead. Note that the method `createEmpty()` returns a field that can also be used to create a hidden form field if you define a field name and a field value.

In a separate method, you create the table that contains the text fields. You let a cell event take care of creating the fields and adding them to the parent field:

```
/* chapter15/SenderReceiver.java */
private static PdfPTable createTable(
  PdfWriter writer, PdfFormField parent) {
  PdfPTable table = new PdfPTable(2);
  PdfPCell cell;
  table.getDefaultCell().setPadding(5f);
  table.addCell("Your name:");
  cell = new PdfPCell();
  cell.setCellEvent(
    new SenderReceiver(writer, parent, "name", true));
  table.addCell(cell);
  ...
  table.addCell("Your email address:");
  cell = new PdfPCell();
  cell.setCellEvent(
    new SenderReceiver(writer, parent, "email", false));
  table.addCell(cell);
  return table;
}
public void cellLayout(
  PdfPCell cell, Rectangle rect, PdfContentByte[] cb) {
  TextField tf = new TextField(writer,
    new Rectangle(rect.left(2), rect.bottom(2),
                  rect.right(2), rect.top(2)),
    partialFieldName);
  if (required) tf.setOptions(TextField.REQUIRED);
  tf.setFontSize(12);
  try {
    parent.addKid(tf.getTextField());
  } catch (Exception e) {
    throw new ExceptionConverter(e);
  }
}
```

You have now created text fields that correspond with the borders of the cell in the second column (minus a padding of two points).

Note that you pass a `boolean` as a last parameter to construct the cell event. You set this parameter to true for the name fields, and as a result, the flag `FF_REQUIRED` is set. That explains why these fields get a red rectangle in figure 15.9; using the `setFieldFlags()` method in `PdfFormField` would have the same result. Other options include FF_READ_ONLY, which makes the field read-only, and FF_NO_EXPORT, meaning end users can fill out the field but its value isn't exported when they click the submit button. Submitting a form is a form action; let's find out how to add such an action.

### 15.3.2 Adding actions to the pushbuttons

Figure 15.9 shows two rows of buttons. The most important are the three first buttons in the first row. You create them by adding a submit action to a pushbutton:

```
/* chapter15/SenderReceiver.java */
PushbuttonField button1 = new PushbuttonField(writer,
  new Rectangle(150, 560, 200, 590), "submitPOST");
button1.setBackgroundColor(Color.BLUE);
button1.setText("POST");
button1.setOptions(PushbuttonField.VISIBLE_BUT_DOES_NOT_PRINT);
PdfFormField submit1 = button1.getField();
submit1.setAction(
  PdfAction.createSubmitForm("http://your.domain.com/", null,
  PdfAction.SUBMIT_HTML_FORMAT | PdfAction.SUBMIT_COORDINATES));
writer.addAnnotation(submit1);
```

You create a button using the convenience class PushbuttonField. You want this button to be visible on the screen, but not if somebody prints the form (for instance, to fill it in manually).

The key method in this code snippet is PdfAction.createSubmitForm(). By adding this action to the pushbutton form field, you create a button that submits the form to the URL passed as the first parameter. The second parameter is null because you want to submit all the fields (except those flagged with the FF_NO_EXPORT flag). If you want to specify by name the fields that must be exported, you should pass an array with these names instead. The third parameter defines the submit method; extra options can be defined.

Basically, you can submit an AcroForm four ways: as an HTML query string, as a Forms Data Format (FDF) form, as an XFDF form, and as PDF if you're using the full Acrobat. The buttons labeled POST, FDF, and XFDF in figure 15.9 demonstrate the three first possibilities that are available in Adobe Reader. Before we discuss the extra options that were added, let's look at a small JSP file that writes the InputStream of the request to the OutputStream of the response. That way, you'll see what happens:

```
<%@ page import="java.io.*" %><%
  BufferedReader reader = new BufferedReader(
    new InputStreamReader(request.getInputStream()));
```

```
    BufferedWriter writer = new BufferedWriter(
      new OutputStreamWriter(response.getOutputStream()));
    response.setContentType("text/plain");
    String line;
    while ((line = reader.readLine()) != null) {
      writer.write(line);
      writer.write("\n");
    }
    reader.close();
    writer.close();
  %>
```

This code shows what is sent to the server in plain text if you submit the form from a web browser. If you submit it from Adobe Reader, you get an error because Adobe Reader doesn't accept plain text. You can adapt the example to return content of type "`application/pdf`," "`application/vnd.fdf`," or "`application/vnd.adobe.xfdf`." But for now, let's look at what happens when you click the POST button on the form.

### Submitting as HTML

Because you define the submit action as a `SUBMIT_HTML_FORMAT`, the data in your form is submitted to the server as an HTML POST. You can retrieve the parameters from the request object; the JSP file shows you this query string:

```
receiver.address=&receiver.email=&receiver.name=Paulo+Soares
➥ &receiver.postal_code=&sender.address=Baeyensstraat+121
➥ &sender.email=&sender.name=Bruno+Lowagie&sender.postal_code=9040
➥ &submitPOST.x=31&submitPOST.y=12
```

The first eight fields are the fields in the form. The option `SUBMIT_COORDINATES` was added to the or-sequence defining the submit action, so you also get two extra fields: `submitPOST.x` and `submitPOST.y`. The submit button is 50 x 30 user units. When I clicked the button, the mouse was pointing at the pixel x=31 and y=12 inside this button. This isn't important information in this example, but it can be useful if you want a pushbutton that acts as a clickable map.

Note that you can change this in an HTML GET action by adding the option `SUBMIT_HTML_GET` to the or-sequence. Don't do this if your form contains text fields that have the `FILE_SELECTION` flag set. If a form has a file-select control, the submission uses the MIME content type multipart/form-data.

### Submitting as FDF

The default submit option is "submit as FDF." That's why the action of the second button is created with 0 as a parameter for the options:

```
/* chapter15/SenderReceiver.java */
submit2.setAction(PdfAction.createSubmitForm("...", null, 0));
```

The output of the JSP page now looks quite different. Note that I added extra indentation to make the file readable:

```
%FDF-1.2
%âãÏÓ
1 0 obj
<</FDF
  <</Fields
    [<</T(receiver)/Kids
      [<</T(address)>>
        <</T(email)>>
        <</T(name)/V(Paulo Soares)>>
        <</T(postal_code)>>]
    >>
    <</T(sender)/Kids
      [<</T(address)/V(Baeyensstraat 121)>>
       <</T(email)>>
       <</T(name)/V(Bruno Lowagie)>>
       <</T(postal_code)/V(9040)>>]
    >>
    <</T(submitFDF)>>]
  /ID[<02309484A35CD6A7A648BB1431F7DCE1>
    <9B6324F7920A629294C0F1EB4611783C>]
  /F(http://blowagie.users.mcs2.netarray.com/sender_receiver.pdf)>>
>>
endobj
trailer
<</Root 1 0 R>>
%%EOF
```

This looks almost like a small PDF file. After reading chapter 18, you'll be able to distinguish a trailer, an object with nested dictionaries, and so on. This is a file in FDF. With `com.lowagie.text.pdf.FdfReader`, you can parse this file to retrieve the field names and corresponding values.

Instead of creating the submit button with value 0 (submit as FDF), you can use the options `SUBMIT_EXCL_F_KEY` and `SUBMIT_EMBED_FORM`. The first option excludes the F key (with the URI of the original form), and the second option embeds the original form as a content stream in the F entry of the FDF file. iText also provides the options `SUBMIT_CANONICAL_FORMAT`, `SUBMIT_INCLUDE_APPEND_SAVES`, `SUBMIT_INCLUDE_ANNOTATIONS`, and `SUBMIT_EXCL_NON_USER_ANNOTS`, as defined in the PDF Reference.

If you download or store this file on your file system, you can open it in Adobe Reader. Adobe Reader searches for the original form specified in the F entry (if available) and shows this form filled with the data in the FDF file. This is a compact way to save the form data. In the next chapter, you'll learn how to create an FDF file using iText and how to merge an FDF file with a PDF file that has a corresponding AcroForm.

Since PDF-1.4, an XML version of FDF has been introduced: XFDF.

### *Submitting as XFDF*

XFDF is less compact than FDF (I repeat: I added white space to the output to make it readable), but it has the advantage that you don't need a class like `FdfReader` to understand what's inside. You can use any XML parser:

```
<?xml version="1.0" encoding="UTF-8"?>
<xfdf xmlns="http://ns.adobe.com/xfdf/" xml:space="preserve">
<fields>
  <field name="receiver">
    <field name="address"/>
    <field name="email"/>
    <field name="name"><value>Paulo Soares</value></field>
    <field name="postal_code"/>
  </field>
  <field name="sender">
    <field name="address"><value>Baeyensstraat 121</value></field>
    <field name="email"/>
    <field name="name"><value>Bruno Lowagie</value></field>
    <field name="postal_code"><value>9040</value></field>
  </field>
  <field name="submitXFDF"/>
</fields>
<ids original="02309484A35CD6A7A648BB1431F7DCE1"
  modified="9B6324F7920A629294C0F1EB4611783C"/>
  <f href="http://blowagie.users.mcs2.netarray.com/sender_receiver.pdf"/>
</xfdf>
```

Looking at the FDF and at the XFDF file, you now understand the benefits of adding some hierarchy to your field names. The information on the sender is kept nicely between a `field` tag with attribute `name="receiver"`. The same goes for the sender. This makes it easier to parse the file (or to transform it with an XSLT).

The action added to the XFDF button is constructed like this:

```
/* chapter15/SenderReceiver.java */
PdfAction.createSubmitForm("...", null, PdfAction.SUBMIT_XFDF);
```

Note that you have fewer options with XFDF: It won't work with file-selection fields, and you can't combine it with the options listed in the previous subsection on FDF (except for `SUBMIT_CANONICAL_FORMAT`).

Beginning with PDF-1.4, you can also submit the document as PDF.

### Submitting as PDF

On the server side, you receive a copy of the PDF file with the fields filled in. If the option `SUBMIT_PDF` is set, all other options are ignored except `SUBMIT_HTML_GET`. This can be important to know if you accept the PDF in the `doGet()` or `doPost()` method of your servlet.

### Reset, hide, and show fields

We've dealt with three of the six buttons shown in figure 15.9. If you click the HIDE button, these buttons disappear, leaving RESET, HIDE, and SHOW (see figure 15.10). Note that I also deselected the check boxes in the form toolbar. This way, the form looks exactly as intended, without the blue background and the red border.

The three remaining buttons are created similarly to the POST, FDF, and XFDF buttons. The main difference lies in the line that sets the action.

The code sample that creates these buttons doesn't need much explanation: Reset does more or less the same as the reset button in an HTML form, but you can pass an array of names to reset only part of the fields. With the flag, you specify whether the fields in the array should be included (0) or excluded (1). The

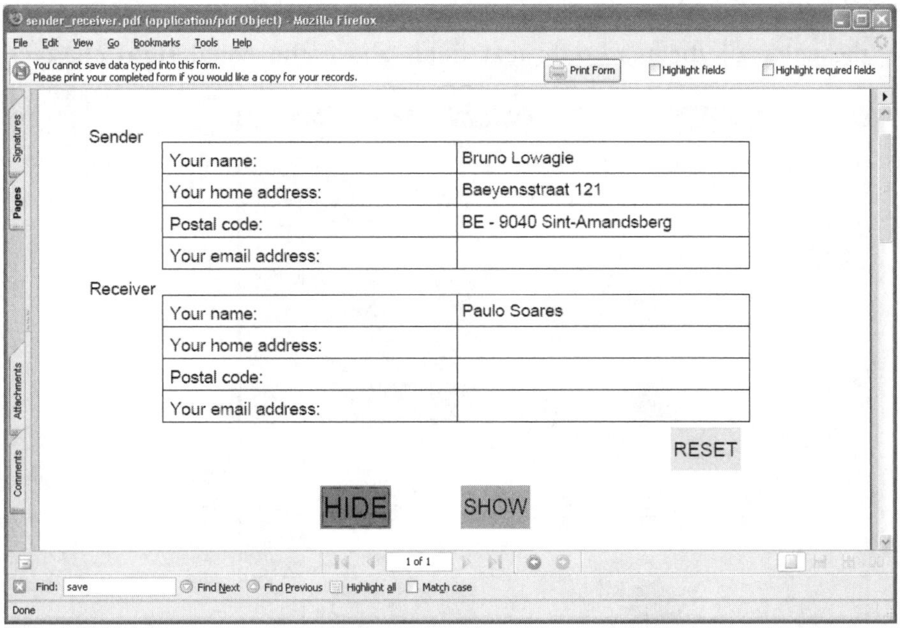

**Figure 15.10 A form with (hidden) submit buttons**

HIDE and SHOW buttons can be used to hide (true) or show (false) the objects listed in the buttons array. The `createHide()` action isn't limited to pushbuttons; you can use it to hide or show other fields as well:

```
/* chapter15/SenderReceiver.java */
reset.setAction(PdfAction.createResetForm(null, 0));
String[] buttons = { "submitPOST", "submitFDF", "submitXFDF" };
hide.setAction(PdfAction.createHide(buttons, true));
show.setAction(PdfAction.createHide(buttons, false));
```

If you know a little JavaScript, you can add all kinds of other actions—for instance, to validate a field or to change its value.

### 15.3.3 Adding actions

In section 13.5.4 you triggered actions from events such as "will print," "page open," and "document close." You can now add another series of events triggered by annotations and fields. A first series can be triggered by annotations in general.

The calculator shown in figure 15.11 is a good example of how to use JavaScript in a PDF file. The figure shows a series of pushbuttons labelled with digits from 0 to 9, four operators, and the equal sign, as well as C and CE to clear the screen.

When you enter the active area of the widget annotation of a pushbutton, the value of the read-only text field (above the equal sign) changes. In the

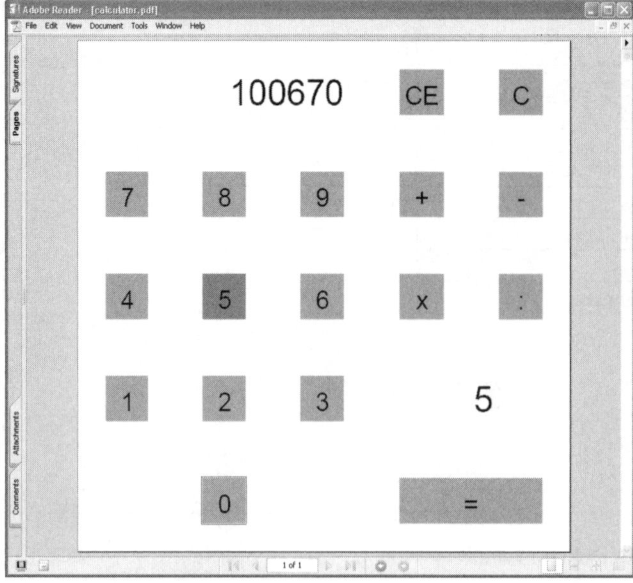


**Figure 15.11**
**A simple calculator in PDF**

screenshot, the mouse pointer has just entered the button labelled with the digit 5. When you exit the active area of a button, the read-only text field is blanked out. When you click a button, a mouse down event and a mouse up event occur. You listen to the mouse up events to change the value of the other read-only text field (the one showing the number 100670 in the screenshot).

Depending on the button that is clicked, you call another JavaScript method:

```
/* chapter15/Calculator.java */
private static void addPushButton(
  PdfWriter writer, Rectangle rect, String btn, String script) {
  float w = rect.width();
  float h = rect.height();
  PdfFormField pushbutton = PdfFormField.createPushButton(writer);
  pushbutton.setFieldName("btn_" + btn);
  pushbutton.setAdditionalActions(PdfName.U,
    PdfAction.javaScript(script, writer));                    Mouse up event
  pushbutton.setAdditionalActions(PdfName.E,
    PdfAction.javaScript("this.showMove('" + btn + "');", writer));  Mouse enters
  pushbutton.setAdditionalActions(PdfName.X,
    PdfAction.javaScript("this.showMove(' ');", writer));      Mouse exits
  PdfContentByte cb = writer.getDirectContent();
  pushbutton.setAppearance(PdfAnnotation.APPEARANCE_NORMAL,
    createAppearance(cb, btn, Color.GRAY, w, h));
  pushbutton.setAppearance(PdfAnnotation.APPEARANCE_ROLLOVER,
    createAppearance(cb, btn, Color.RED, w, h));
  pushbutton.setAppearance(PdfAnnotation.APPEARANCE_DOWN,
    createAppearance(cb, btn, Color.BLUE, w, h));
  pushbutton.setWidget(rect, PdfAnnotation.HIGHLIGHT_PUSH);
  writer.addAnnotation(pushbutton);
}
```

Other possible values for actions for annotations can be found in table 8.40 in the PDF Reference. In the next example, you'll use `Fo` (get FOcus) and `Bl` (lost focus or BLur) for the upper text field in figure 15.12.

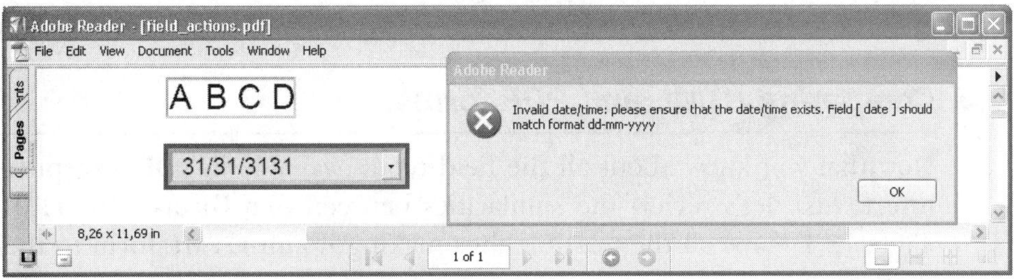


**Figure 15.12 A keystroke event that validates a date**

The upper text field is called comb, and the code to create it is more or less the same as the code to create the comb field in figure 15.7. The only difference is that you add actions:

```
/* chapter15/FieldActions.java */
PdfFormField field = textfield.getTextField();
field.setAdditionalActions(new PdfName("Fo"),
  PdfAction.javaScript("app.alert('COMB got the focus');",
  writer));
field.setAdditionalActions(new PdfName("Bl"),
  PdfAction.javaScript("app.alert('COMB lost the focus');",
  writer));
field.setAdditionalActions(new PdfName("K"),
  PdfAction.javaScript "event.change =
  event.change.toUpperCase();", writer));
```

**Get focus annotation event**

**Lost focus annotation event**

**Keystroke field event**

The `K` (Keypress) event in the code snippet is a field-specific event (meaning it won't work for annotations). These events are listed in table 8.42 of the PDF Reference. The `change` property of the JavaScript object `event` contains the value of the key that was just stroked. In this case, you change the character to uppercase. With this simple line of code, you can force the input text to be in uppercase only.

The alert box shown in the screenshot is triggered by the other field: an editable combo box with dates. I deliberately entered an invalid date, causing an alert box to open:

```
/* chapter15/FieldActions.java */
field = date.getComboField();
field.setAdditionalActions(PdfName.K, PdfAction.javaScript(
  "AFDate_KeystrokeEx( 'dd-mm-yyyy' )", writer));
```

You don't have to write the method that validates the date. Adobe Reader comes with precanned functions that let you validate and format dates, times, currencies, and so on. Unfortunately, this is beyond the scope of this book.

We started section 15.2 by saying you would find similarities as well as differences if you compared AcroForms with HTML forms. Let's make the comparison.

## 15.4 Comparing HTML and PDF forms

Now that you know about all the field types available in PDF (except for signature fields), let's review the similarities between AcroForms and HTML forms. Table 15.1 maps all the possible tags making up an HTML form to their counterparts in PDF.

**Table 15.1 Comparing HTML form elements with PDF fields**

| HTML form element | PDF field |
|---|---|
| `input type="Hidden"` | A `PdfFormField` with a name and a value, but without a widget annotation (you can also use a hidden text box) |
| `input type="Text"` | A single-line text field |
| `input type="Password"` | A text field with the option `PASSWORD` on |
| `input type="File"` | A text field with the option `FILE_SELECTION` on (be careful how you submit a form with a file selection field) |
| `input type="ReadOnly"` | A text field with the option `READ_ONLY` on |
| `textarea` | A multiple-line text field |
| `select` | A choice field (a list or a combo box); in HTML, you define the number of lines that must be shown in a select box |
| `input type="checkbox"` | A button of type check box |
| `input type="radio"` | A button of type radio button; note that you add different widget annotations to one form field in PDF |
| `input type="submit"` | A pushbutton to which a submit action is added |
| `input type="reset"` | A pushbutton to which a reset action is added |
| `input type="image"` | A pushbutton to which a special submit action is added (with the option `SUBMIT_COORDINATES`) |
| `input type="button"` | A pushbutton (with or without an action) |

HTML forms as well as PDF forms can be used in a transaction between an end user and the form provider, but the approach between the two types of interactive forms is quite different. If your form is short—for instance, a two-box login form—you should prefer HTML over PDF.

If your form gets really complex, you can opt to split an HTML form over different pages and store the partial results on the server side. You can also provide a good PDF form (one or more pages) and let the user fill in the complete form before submitting it to the server. If you have control over the working environment of the end users, you can provide a viewer that will save a partially filled-in form locally on the client side. While creating the PDF form, make good use of the field hierarchy so you have structured field names.

A PDF form is typically preferred when you want to keep the layout of an existing paper form: Some people fill in the form online, whereas other people print it and fill it in manually. HTML forms don't look nice when printed out.

In general, you won't use iText to create your form. Creating a good form requires specific skills. You'll probably ask somebody who knows how to work with Acrobat to create it. They can add all the fields we've summed up here, and you'll use chapter 16 to fill in the form programmatically.

If you have a form that previously existed on paper only, you can scan it and add fields. After reading this chapter, you probably doubt that iText is the right tool for this. You could take a ruler and measure all the locations of every field on the paper form so you can use iText to add widgets on the right places, but you're right: That's not the ideal way of achieving the result you want.

Let's put what you've learned in this chapter into perspective and find out if there is a better way.

## 15.5 Summary

This chapter is important because you need to know about forms in order to understand the next chapter about reading and filling an AcroForm in an existing PDF document. You can use iText to create such a PDF document, but it requires intensive programming. In most cases, it's a better idea to use a form that was created with another program, such as Acrobat. Make sure the PDF is created with the right type of form. For the time being, there is only limited support for forms created with Adobe Designer (XFA forms).

If you insist on creating AcroForms using iText, you can do so. You can build your own GUI application to create a document with a form and use iText as the engine that builds your PDF and AcroForm. If you don't want to reinvent the wheel, use a product that already uses iText. With JPedal, you can view a PDF file and combine this viewer with iText to add all the necessary widgets. There's a tutorial on how to achieve this on jpedal.org. JPedal can also be used to save form data. A cool forms feature in this product is that the forms objects are converted into Java Swing gadgets; you can add your own listeners and build your own form server functionality. But that's beyond the scope of this book—this is *iText in Action*, not *JPedal in Action*.

You haven't helped Laura in this chapter. You know she needs forms that allow the future students at Foobar to fill in a learning agreement; but that will have to wait until chapter 17, where you'll combine the functionality learned in this and the next chapter to create, manage, and fill two types of forms.

# 16 Filling and signing AcroForms

**This chapter covers**

- Reading and updating form fields
- Working with (X)FDF
- Signing a PDF document
- Verifying a signed PDF

In chapter 15, you created a PDF file with an AcroForm using iText. At the end of the chapter, you read that it isn't important to use iText to do this. The main purpose of the previous chapter was to get familiar with the types of form fields.

In this chapter, you'll use this newly acquired knowledge to retrieve data from an existing form and from an (X)FDF file. You're also going to fill in form fields programmatically, and you'll flatten the forms you've filled out. You already had an introduction to these techniques in chapter 2, but now we'll take a closer look.

There's also an important field type we haven't dealt with yet: the signature field. The third section of this chapter explains how to add a signature field with a digital signature.

## 16.1 Filling in the fields of an AcroForm

The PDF file shown in figure 16.1 contains an AcroForm. Just by looking at it, you see that it contains text fields, a list (listing programming languages), a combo box (that allows you to select your mother tongue) and buttons. By clicking the buttons, you discover that the Preferred Language options are a set of radio buttons and the Knowledge Of options are check boxes.

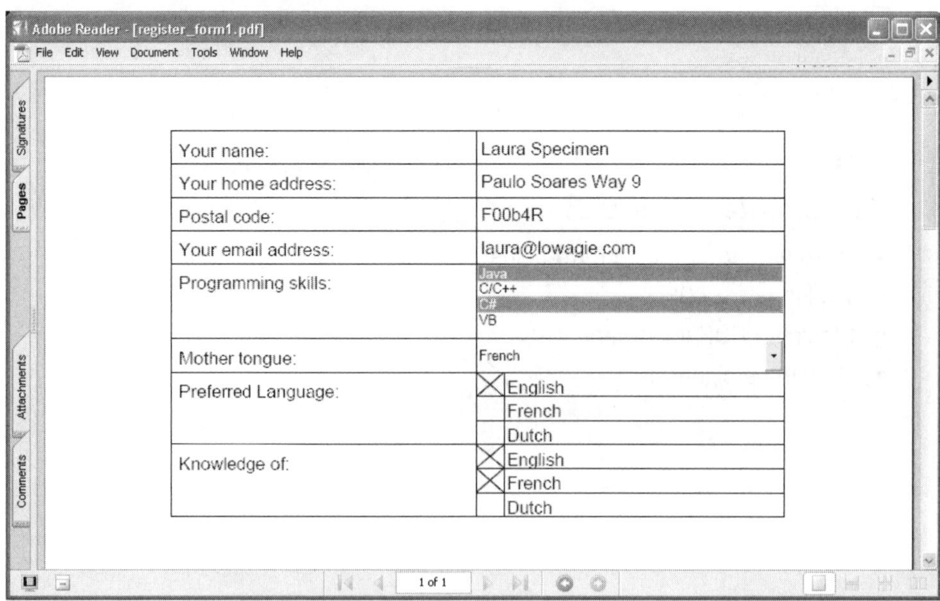


**Figure 16.1 An existing AcroForm**

I created the form myself using iText, so I know the names of all the fields, but let's pretend the PDF was given to you by a third party. The first thing you need to do is retrieve the names and types of all the fields.

### 16.1.1 *Retrieving information about the fields (part 1)*

Here's the code for this example:

```
/* chapter15/RegisterForm1.java */
PdfReader reader = new PdfReader("register_form1.pdf");
AcroFields form = reader.getAcroFields();   <-❶
HashMap fields = form.getFields();   <-❷
String key;
for (Iterator i = fields.keySet().iterator(); i.hasNext(); ) {   <-❸
  key = (String) i.next();
  System.out.print(key + ": ");
  switch(form.getFieldType(key)) {   <-❹
    case AcroFields.FIELD_TYPE_CHECKBOX:
      System.out.println("Checkbox");
      break;
    case AcroFields.FIELD_TYPE_COMBO:
      System.out.println("Combobox");
      break;
    case AcroFields.FIELD_TYPE_LIST:
      System.out.println("List");
      break;
    case AcroFields.FIELD_TYPE_NONE:
      System.out.println("None");
      break;
    case AcroFields.FIELD_TYPE_PUSHBUTTON:
      System.out.println("Pushbutton");
      break;
    case AcroFields.FIELD_TYPE_RADIOBUTTON:
      System.out.println("Radiobutton");
      break;
    case AcroFields.FIELD_TYPE_SIGNATURE:
      System.out.println("Signature");
      break;
    case AcroFields.FIELD_TYPE_TEXT:
      System.out.println("Text");
      break;
    default:
      System.out.println("?");
  }
}
```

The code retrieves an `AcroFields` object from a `PdfReader` instance ❶. In chapter 2, you used an `AcroFields` object retrieved from a `PdfStamper` object to change the value of one or more fields, but now you'll first inspect the properties of every field.

You get the fields as a `HashMap` ❷ and you loop over every key in the map ❸ to find out the type of each field ❹.

If you run this example, the following output is written to `System.out`:

```
person.knowledge.French: Checkbox
person.language: Combobox
person.email: Text
person.preferred: Radiobutton
person.name: Text
person.programming: List
person.postal_code: Text
person.address: Text
person.knowledge.English: Checkbox
person.knowledge.Dutch: Checkbox
```

You can now use this information to set the value of the text fields as demonstrated in the example in chapter 2. If you want to set the value of the button and choice fields, you need extra information:

```
/* chapter15/RegisterForm1.java */
System.out.println("Possible values for person.programming:");
String[] options = form.getListOptionExport("person.programming");
String[] values = form.getListOptionDisplay("person.programming");   ❶
for (int i = 0; i < options.length; i++)
  System.out.println(options[i] + ": " + values[i]);
System.out.println("Possible values for person.language:");
options = form.getListOptionExport("person.language");
values = form.getListOptionDisplay("person.language");   ❷
for (int i = 0; i < options.length; i++)
  System.out.println(options[i] + ": " + values[i]);
System.out.println("Possible values for person.preferred:");
String[] states = form.getAppearanceStates("person.preferred");   ❸
for (int i = 0; i < states.length; i++)
  System.out.println(states[i]);
System.out.println("Possible values for person.knowledge.English:");
states = form.getAppearanceStates("person.knowledge.English");   ❹
for (int i = 0; i < states.length; i++)
  System.out.println(states[i]);
```

This code sample retrieves the options available in the Programming Skills list ❶, the Mother Tongue combo box ❷, and the Preferred Language radio button field ❸. You also retrieve the possible values of the English button (one of the Knowledge Of check boxes) ❹.

This code snippet also writes information to `System.out`:

```
Possible values for person.programming:
  JAVA: Java
  C: C/C++
```

```
    CS: C#
    VB: VB
  Possible values for person.language:
    EN: English
    FR: French
    NL: Dutch
  Possible values for person.preferred:
    NL
    Off
    EN
    FR
  Possible values for person.knowledge.English:
    Off
    On
```

This output tells you that you can choose between EN, FR, or NL to fill in the field person.language and that you should use the value On if you want to select the field person.knowledge.English.

### 16.1.2 Filling fields

The form in figure 16.1 was filled in manually. Now let's fill in the form using iText. The next code snippet should look familiar: It looks almost exactly like the HelloWorldForm example in chapter 2. The main difference is that you also fill out check-box, radio-button, list, and combo-box fields:

```
/* chapter16/FillAcroForm1.java */
reader = new PdfReader("register_form1.pdf");
stamper = new PdfStamper(reader,
  new FileOutputStream("registered1_1.pdf"));
AcroFields form = stamper.getAcroFields();
form.setField("person.name", "Laura Specimen");
form.setField("person.address", "Paulo Soares Way 1");
form.setField("person.postal_code", "F00b4R", "FOOBAR");
form.setField("person.email", "laura@lowagie.com");
form.setField("person.programming", "JAVA");
form.setField("person.language", "FR");
form.setField("person.preferred", "EN");
form.setField("person.knowledge.English", "On");
form.setField("person.knowledge.French", "On");
form.setField("person.knowledge.Dutch", "Off");
stamper.close();
```

If you look at the line that sets the postal code, you notice something odd: Apart from the fact that Foobar City has a strange postal code, you use three parameters in the `setField()` method.

- The first parameter defines the field you want to change.
- The second parameter defines the value of the field.
- The optional third parameter sets the display value.

If you open the resulting PDF file, you won't see F00b4R, but FOOBAR. Only when you click the field or submit the form do you see that the actual value isn't FOOBAR, but F00b4R.

Note that, although the list box allows multiple selects, selecting more than one value programmatically isn't supported (yet).

In chapter 2, you learned that you can rename a field with the method `renameField()`. The next code snippet demonstrates how to change the entries in a choice field (a list or combo box). In this example, you're limited if you want to set the value of the mother tongue: You can only choose between English, French, and Dutch. If you want to fill the form with data for the co-developer of iText, Paulo Soares, you should be able to add Portuguese to the combo box. No problem—you can redefine the entries in a choice field with the method `setListOption()`:

```
/* chapter16/FillAcroForm1.java */
String[] combo_options = { "EN", "FR", "NL", "PT" };
String[] combo_values =
  { "English", "French", "Dutch", "Portuguese" };
form.setListOption("person.language", combo_options, combo_values);
form.setField("person.language", "PT");
```

Note that you haven't flattened the forms in this first series of examples. When the form is opened, the end user can change the values that were filled in programmatically. This can be useful if the form is part of a document workflow and you want to serve the end user a form with some fields that are prefilled—for instance, based on information that's already in your database.

Maybe you want the end user to change some of the fields, but not all of them. Some fields should be made read-only. There are different ways to do this. You could use partial form flattening, like this:

```
/* chapter16/FillAcroForm1.java */
reader = new PdfReader("registered1_2.pdf");
stamper = new PdfStamper(
  reader, new FileOutputStream("registered1_3.pdf"));
stamper.setFormFlattening(true);
stamper.partialFormFlattening("person.name");
stamper.close();
```

There's one major disadvantage if you use this approach. The following code snippet no longer works:

```
/* chapter16/FillAcroForm1.java */
reader = new PdfReader("registered1_3.pdf");
form = reader.getAcroFields();
System.out.println(form.getField("person.name"));
```

The method `getField()` returns null because the field person.name is no longer there. There's only a `String` painted on a canvas.

A better solution is to change the flags of the field containing the name so that the field is read-only:

```
/* chapter16/FillAcroForm1.java */
reader = new PdfReader("registered1_2.pdf");
stamper = new PdfStamper(
  reader, new FileOutputStream("registered1_4.pdf"));
form = stamper.getAcroFields();
form.setFieldProperty("person.name",
  "setfflags", PdfFormField.FF_READ_ONLY, null);
form.setFieldProperty("person.programming",
  "clrfflags", PdfFormField.FF_MULTISELECT, null);
form.setFieldProperty(
  "person.language", "bgcolor", Color.RED, null);
stamper.close();
```

When you compare both PDF files, you won't see much difference between the field that no longer exists in registered1_3.pdf and the read-only field in registered1_4.pdf. Neither can be changed by the end user, but when you use `form.getField("person.name")` on registered1_4.pdf, the name that was entered originally in the read-only field is returned correctly.

The previous code sample uses two variations of the `setFieldProperty()` method. The first can be used to change the annotation and/or the field flags. Valid values for the second parameter are as follows:

- "flags," "setflags," or "clrflags"—Replaces, adds, or removes the flags of the widget annotation, respectively. The possible values for these flags can be found in the class `PdfAnnotation`.
- "fflags," "setfflags," or "clrfflags"—Replaces, adds, or removes the field flags, respectively. The possible values can be found in the class `PdfFormField` (the constants starting with `FF_`).

The second variation of the `setFieldProperty()` method can be used to change one of the following properties:

- "textfont"—Changes the text font. The third parameter for this entry should be of type `BaseFont`.
- "textcolor"—Changes the color of the text. The value for this entry is of type `java.awt.Color`.
- "textsize"—Sets the text size. You can pass a `Float` as the third parameter.
- "bgcolor"—Sets the background color. The value for this entry is a `java.awt.Color`. If it's null, the background is removed.
- "bordercolor"—Sets the border color. The value for this entry is a `java.awt.Color`. If it's null, the border is removed.

The previous code sample didn't specify the fourth parameter of these two methods; you just passed null. The method expects an array of `int` values. If a field is represented by more than one widget, you can sum up the indexes of the widgets of which you want to change the property. Passing null means you want to process all the widgets.

In section16.1.1, you retrieved the name, type, and possible values of each field in the AcroForm. Now let's look at how you can retrieve information about the widgets.

### 16.1.3 Retrieving information from a field (part 2)

The `AcroFields` class has an inner class called `Item` that contains different `ArrayList` objects. The next code snippet lists the contents of two of these member variables:

```
/* chapter16/FillAcroForm1.java */
AcroFields.Item item = form.getFieldItem("person.preferred");    ❶
PdfDictionary dict;
PdfName name;
System.out.println("pages: " + item.page);    ❷
for (Iterator i = item.merged.iterator(); i.hasNext(); ) {
  dict = (PdfDictionary)i.next();
  for (Iterator it = dict.getKeys().iterator(); it.hasNext(); ) {    ❸
    name = (PdfName)it.next();
    System.out.println(name.toString() + ": " + dict.get(name));
  }
  System.out.println("------------------------------------");
}
```

You take the `AcroFields.Item` object for the radio button field person.preferred ❶. The "page" list contains these values: [1, 1, 1] ❷. This field is represented by three widget annotations that all appear on page 1. The lists "values," "widgets," and "merged" contain a PDF dictionary for each widget. The dictionaries in "values" contain field-specific entries. Those in "widgets" contain annotation-specific entries. These dictionaries are merged in the "merged" list ❸. To understand the meaning of each entry, you'll need to study the PDF Reference (section 8.4.1, "Annotation dictionaries"; and section 8.6.2, "Field Dictionaries").

Although it's interesting to know that you can retrieve this valuable information, you don't have to go through all this trouble for the most important data: the page number and the coordinates. Call the method `getFieldPositions()`, and it gives you an array containing the page number(s) and the coordinates of every widget. The number of values in the array is always a multiple of five:

```
/* chapter16/FillAcroForm1.java */
float[] positions = form.getFieldPositions("person.preferred");
for (int i = 0; i < positions.length; ) {
  System.out.print("Page: " + positions[i++]);       <-- Page number
  System.out.print(" [ " + positions[i++]);         <-- Lower-left X
  System.out.print(", " + positions[i++]);         <-- Lower-left Y
  System.out.print(", " + positions[i++]);         <-- Upper-right X
  System.out.print(", " + positions[i++]);         <-- Upper-right Y
  System.out.println(" ]");
}
```

In the case of the person.preferred radio button field, the following values are returned:

```
Page: 1.0 [ 297.5, 630.0, 316.52, 646.0 ]
Page: 1.0 [ 297.5, 614.0, 316.52, 630.0 ]
Page: 1.0 [ 297.5, 598.0, 316.52, 614.0 ]
```

This information will be useful if you're using the fields as placeholders. You can retrieve the location of fields that mark an area, remove the fields, and add extra data using `PdfStamper.getOverContent()` or `PdfStamper.getUnderContent()`.

Fields can be removed using one of these methods:

- `removeFieldsFromPage(int page)`—Removes all the fields from a page
- `removeField(String name, int page)`—Removes the fields with name `name` from page `page`
- `removeField(String name)`—Removes a field from a document

You saw examples that performed this flattening process automatically in chapter 2; now you'll add more complexity.

### 16.1.4 Flattening a PDF file

The next example uses a form that's a little different from the one in the previous examples (see figure 16.2). It contains the same four text fields but adds a button on the left side.

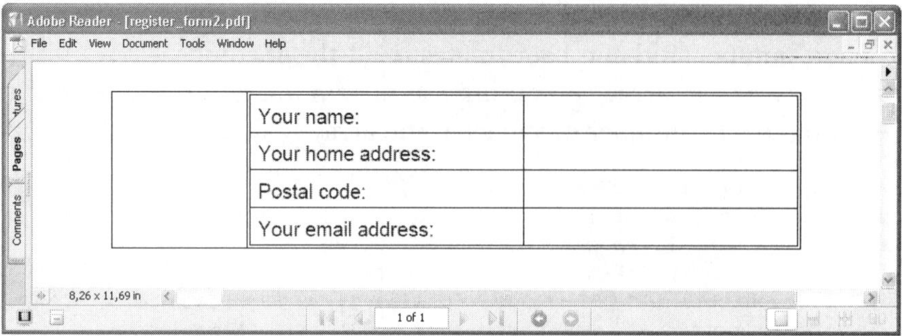


**Figure 16.2 A simple form that will be filled and flattened**

You won't use the button for any action or user input; it's there as a placeholder. Figure 16.3 shows the same form, but now Laura's personal data is filled in and her photograph appears at the location indicated by the button field. (Don't you think Laura is a beauty? As a matter of fact, she looks just like my wife.)

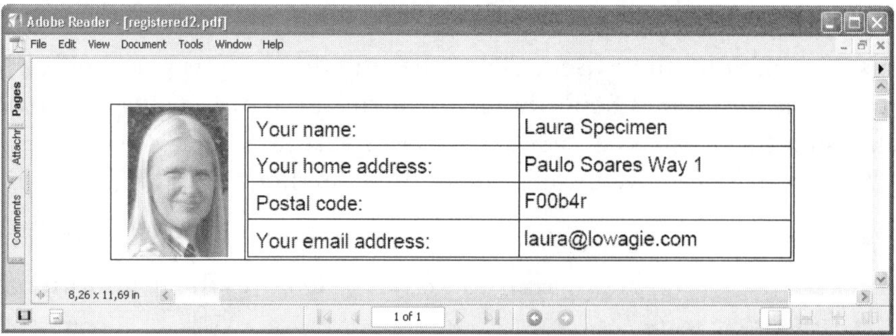


**Figure 16.3 The form after it's been filled in and flattened**

Let's look at a code sample to see how it's done:

```
/* chapter16/FillAcroForm2.java */
reader = new PdfReader("register_form2.pdf");
stamper = new PdfStamper(
  reader, new FileOutputStream("registered2.pdf"));
```

```
AcroFields form = stamper.getAcroFields();
form.setField("person.name", "Laura Specimen");
form.setField("person.address", "Paulo Soares Way 1");
form.setField("person.postal_code", "F00b4r");
form.setField("person.email", "laura@lowagie.com");
float[] photograph =
  form.getFieldPositions("person.photograph");
Rectangle rect = new Rectangle(
  photograph[1], photograph[2], photograph[3], photograph[4]);
Image laura = Image.getInstance("../resources/Laura.jpg");
laura.scaleToFit(rect.width(), rect.height());
laura.setAbsolutePosition(
  photograph[1] + (rect.width() - laura.scaledWidth()) / 2,
  photograph[2] + (rect.height() - laura.scaledHeight()) / 2);
PdfContentByte cb = stamper.getOverContent((int)photograph[0]);
cb.addImage(laura);
stamper.setFormFlattening(true);
stamper.close();
```

**Fill in text fields**

**Get placeholder data**

**Get/scale photo**

**Position photo**

**Add photo**

**Set flattening to true**

As you see, you don't need any new functionality to create this PDF, but you should know a few extra things if you want to optimize the process.

### 16.1.5 *Optimizing the flattening process*

In chapter 14, you learned how to combine XML and page events to generate a large number of letters in a batch. This is a good solution when you need continuous text, but often you can use standard forms with only a limited set of fields at fixed coordinates. In this case, it's better to use a PDF file with an AcroForm.

If you want one big resulting file containing all the letters, you can choose between two options. The most economic way to create your large PDF file is to do the following:

1. Retrieve the field positions from the AcroForm in the original PDF file.
2. Create a flattened version of the original PDF document.
3. Create a page event that reads the flattened form in `onOpenDocument()` and adds it in `onEndPage()`.
4. Loop over all the records in your database, and add the fields at the corresponding positions.

The other solution is to create separate files for each record and to concatenate them afterward. Note that your final PDF file will be larger. When you use page events, the form is added only once; if you concatenate separate files that all contain the original form, you have a lot of redundancy. It can pay to choose the first option. But it's up to you to choose the solution that offers the best answer for your requirements. If it's important for you to generate separate files (for instance, because you intend to send them by e-mail), you can optimize the flattening process. Look at the following code snippet:

```
/* chapter16/FillAcroForm2.java */
HashMap fieldCache = new HashMap();
for (int i = 0; i < db.length; i++) {
  reader = new PdfReader("register_form2.pdf");
  stamper = new PdfStamper(reader,
    new FileOutputStream("registered_" + (i + 1) + ".pdf"));
  form = stamper.getAcroFields();
  form.setFieldCache(fieldCache);
  form.setExtraMargin(12, -3);
  form.setField("person.name", db[i][0]);
  form.setField("person.address", db[i][1]);
  form.setField("person.postal_code", db[i][2]);
  form.setField("person.email", db[i][3]);
  stamper.setFormFlattening(true);
  stamper.close();
}
```

This example uses two new methods:

- `setFieldCache()`—Sets a cache for field appearances. Parsing the existing PDF to create a new `TextField` is expensive in terms of time. For those tasks that repeatedly fill the same PDF with different field values, using `setFieldCache()` offers a dramatic speed advantage. There's one downside: If you have choice fields, you sometimes get odd results, because you can't reuse the appearance of a list or a combo box.
- `setExtraMargin()`—Sets extra margins in text fields to better mimic the Acrobat layout. I already mentioned that the appearance of a field created by iText doesn't always correspond exactly with the appearance when the field is rendered in Adobe Acrobat or Reader. Depending on the version of Acrobat used to create the form, you can have small unwanted offsets. You can correct these offsets by specifying extra margins that are applied to every field in the form.

I've slightly exaggerated the extra margins so you can see a clear difference if you compare figure 16.4 with figure 16.3. The content of the fields in figure 16.4 is shifted 12 points to the right and 3 points to the top (or rather, –3 points to the bottom).

Another common problem when filling fields is that you have to fill in forms in batches with data that fits the field for 99 percent of the records.

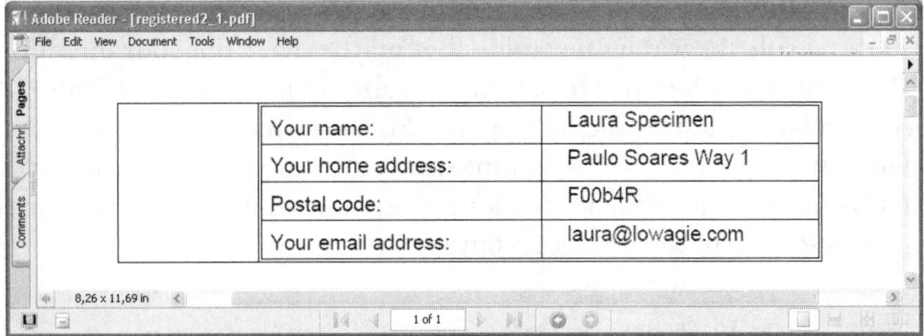


**Figure 16.4 This form was filled in using a small offset**

Unfortunately, there are always a few records with strings that don't fit into the rectangle defined in your form; this problem is demonstrated in the upper PDF file in figure 16.5.

In the upper PDF file, the content of the field is truncated. Because the form is flattened, an end user can't scroll to the right to see what's missing. There are different ways to solve this problem. You can set the options of the field so that the multiline flag is on. This way, the content can be split over several lines. Unfortunately, this won't help if the height of the field isn't sufficient to display multiple lines.

Another solution is to retrieve the coordinates of the field as you did before, with the photograph placeholder. You can then adapt the font size so that the

**Figure 16.5 A form with data that doesn't fit into a field**

content fits the rectangle, or you can add the string to the direct content so that it extends outside the widget rectangle (but maybe that's not your intention).

The simplest solution is to set the font size to 0. According to the PDF Reference, Acrobat auto-sizes the text in an AcroForm's text field to best fill the area. When flattening a text field with font size 0, iText does the same thing. The bottom PDF file in figure 16.5 has two long field values that are drawn using different font sizes so they fit the widget rectangle:

```
/* chapter16/FillAcroForm2.java */
reader = new PdfReader("register_form2.pdf");
stamper = new PdfStamper(
  reader, new FileOutputStream("registered2_Y.pdf"));
form = stamper.getAcroFields();
form.setFieldProperty(
  "person.name", "textsize", new Float(0), null);
form.setField(
  "person.name", "Somebody with a very, very long name.");
form.setFieldProperty(
  "person.address", "textsize", new Float(0), null);
form.setField(
  "person.address", "and a very, very long address too");
stamper.setFormFlattening(true);
stamper.close();
```

Using the `setField()` method is one way to fill in form data. In the previous chapter, you learned about the Forms Data Format (FDF). Let's find out if you can merge a PDF file with an FDF or XFDF file.

## 16.2 Working with FDF and XFDF files

In chapter 15, you used FDF and XFDF as an interesting way to receive (and store) data submitted to a server. You saw that such a file can be opened in Adobe Reader to show the PDF referred to in the (X)FDF file with all the fields filled in. In this chapter, you'll use an (X)FDF file to merge (and flatten) the data with the original PDF file.

Let's create sample FDF files first.

### 16.2.1 Reading and writing FDF files

For this series of examples, you'll work with a form that is a reduced version of the form shown in figure 16.2. It has the same text fields, but not the button. You'll construct an `FdfWriter` object and add the values for four fields; you'll also add the file that contains an AcroForm with these fields:

```
/* chapter16/FillAcroForm3.java */
FdfWriter fdf = new FdfWriter();
fdf.setFieldAsString("person.name", "Bruno Lowagie");
fdf.setFieldAsString(
  "person.address", "Baeyensstraat 121, Sint-Amandsberg");
fdf.setFieldAsString("person.postal_code", "BE-9040");
fdf.setFieldAsString("person.email", "bruno@lowagie.com");
fdf.setFile("register_form3.pdf");
fdf.writeTo(new FileOutputStream("register_form3.fdf"));
```

The result is an FDF file that looks like this:

```
%FDF-1.2
%âãÏÓ
1 0 obj
<</FDF
  <</F(register_form3.pdf)
    /Fields[
      <</T(person)
        /Kids[
        <</T(address)/V(Baeyensstraat 121, Sint-Amandsberg)>>
        <</T(postal_code)/V(BE-9040)>>
        <</T(email)/V(bruno@lowagie.com)>>
        <</T(name)/V(Bruno Lowagie)>>]
      >>]
   >>
>>
endobj
trailer
<</Root 1 0 R>>
%%EOF
```

Note that I added indentation to make the FDF readable. You can now use this FDF file to fill in the form fields:

```
/* chapter16/FillAcroForm3.java */
PdfReader pdfreader = new PdfReader("register_form3.pdf");
PdfStamper stamp =
  new PdfStamper(
    pdfreader, new FileOutputStream("registered3.pdf"));
FdfReader fdfreader = new FdfReader("register_form3.fdf");
AcroFields form = stamp.getAcroFields();
form.setFields(fdfreader);
stamp.close();
```

Normally you won't perform these two steps after each other.

You can use `FdfWriter` to create FDF files for direct use. If you open the FDF generated in the first code sample in Adobe Reader, it looks exactly the same as the PDF produced in the second sample.

Or, you may have a repository of FDF files that was gathered, for instance, by storing all the FDF files submitted to your web server. Now you want to merge all these FDF files with the original PDF file programmatically and maybe flatten them and concatenate all the files into one large file.

You may also receive an FDF file submitted to the server and use `FdfReader` to retrieve the values of the fields. The next example explains the last option. First, you generate an FDF file based on one of the previously generated PDF files containing an AcroForm (the PDF in figure 16.1):

```
/* chapter16/FillAcroForm3.java */
reader = new PdfReader("registered1_1.pdf");
form = reader.getAcroFields();
FdfWriter fdf = new FdfWriter();
form.exportAsFdf(fdf);
fdf.setFile("register_form1.pdf");
fdf.writeTo(new FileOutputStream("registered1.fdf"));
```

This code sample exports an `AcroFields` object from an existing PDF file to an FDF file. The check boxes in the original PDF file are translated to FDF like this:

```
<</T(knowledge)
  /Kids[
    <</T(English)/V/On>>
    <</T(French)/V/On>>
    <</T(Dutch)/V/Off>>
  ]
>>
```

The values in text fields such as person.name are between angle brackets; they're stored as PDF strings. The values of the check boxes are stored in a different way: for instance, /On or /Off. These are PDF names. To create an FDF containing this snippet, you have to use the method `FdfWriter.setFieldAsName()` instead of `setFieldAsString()`.

Now that you have this more complex FDF file, you can read it with `FdfReader`:

```
/* chapter16/FillAcroForm3.java */
fdfreader = new FdfReader("registered1.fdf");
System.err.println(fdfreader.getFileSpec());
HashMap fields = fdfreader.getFields();
String key;
for (Iterator i = fields.keySet().iterator(); i.hasNext(); ) {
  key = (String) i.next();
  System.err.println(key + ": " + fdfreader.getFieldValue(key));
}
```

This is typically what you'll do if you want to interpret the data sent as FDF to a server instead of just storing the FDF file. The output of the code sample looks like this:

```
register_form1.pdf
person.knowledge.French: On
person.language: FR
person.preferred: EN
person.email: laura@lowagie.com
person.name: Laura Specimen
person.postal_code: F00b4R
person.knowledge.English: On
person.programming: JAVA
person.address: Paulo Soares Way 1
person.knowledge.Dutch: Off
```

In chapter 18, we'll return to this functionality and demonstrate how to retrieve the actual PDF object such as a PDF name or a PDF dictionary.

In the previous chapter, you also learned about XFDF; iText can read these files.

### 16.2.2 Reading XFDF files

For the moment, there's no XFDF writer in iText. The structure of an XFDF file is simple. I made an example manually:

```
<?xml version="1.0" encoding="UTF-8"?>
<xfdf xmlns="http://ns.adobe.com/xfdf/" xml:space="preserve">
<fields>
  <field name="person">
    <field name="name"><value>Bruno Lowagie</value></field>
    <field name="address">
      <value>Baeyensstraat 121, Sint-Amandsberg</value>
    </field>
    <field name="postal_code"><value>BE-9040</value></field>
    <field name="email"><value>bruno@lowagie.com</value></field>
  </field>
</fields>
<f href="../results/register_form3.pdf"/>
</xfdf>
```

The code to read the fields in this XFDF and to merge the XFDF with an AcroForm in an existing PDF is similar to the code in the previous section on FDF. Add an *X* here and there, and you're done:

```
/* chapter16/FillAcroForm3.java */
XfdfReader xfdfreader =
  new XfdfReader("../resources/formfields.xfdf");
System.err.println(xfdfreader.getFileSpec());
```

```
fields = xfdfreader.getFields();
for (Iterator i = fields.keySet().iterator(); i.hasNext(); ) {
  key = (String) i.next();
  System.err.println(key + ": " + xfdfreader.getFieldValue(key));
}
reader = new PdfReader(xfdfreader.getFileSpec());
stamper = new PdfStamper(
  reader, new FileOutputStream("registered3X.pdf"));
form = stamper.getAcroFields();
form.setFields(xfdfreader);
stamper.close();
```

Note that the hints given in section 16.1.5 are also valid when you fill (multiple) forms using an FDF or an XFDF form as the data source: You can flatten the form, set an extra margin, and set a cache for the appearances using the same methods as described earlier.

At the end of chapter 15, we compared PDF forms with forms in HTML. Now that you've seen how to fill in a PDF form, we can add one major advantage offered by PDF forms: An AcroForm is an ideal way to define a template that can be used in an automated batch process.

But there's more: The AcroForm technology also allows you to add a digital signature to a file.

## 16.3 Signing a PDF file

In the previous chapter, we talked about annotations and form fields in an AcroForm. We discussed three types of form fields: buttons, text fields, and choice fields. We mentioned that an AcroForm can also contain a fourth type of form field: signature fields. Let's start with a simple example that adds an empty signature field to a PDF.

### 16.3.1 Adding a signature field to a PDF file

Figure 16.6 shows a PDF file with a personal message from Laura, your friend at Foobar. The PDF has a signature field, but as you can read in the Signatures pane, the signature field isn't signed (yet).

Creating such a PDF is easy; you only need to add these two lines:

```
/* chapter16/UnsignedSignatureField.java */
PdfAcroForm acroForm = writer.getAcroForm();
acroForm.addSignature("foobarsig", 73, 705, 149, 759);
```

Of course, when Laura sends me a personal message, I want to be sure it's sent by Laura and not by anyone else. Anyone can create a PDF document with an empty

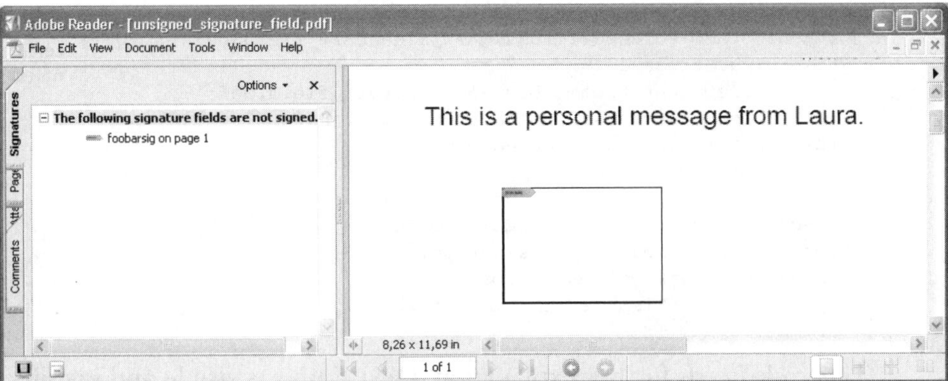


**Figure 16.6 A PDF with an unsigned signature field**

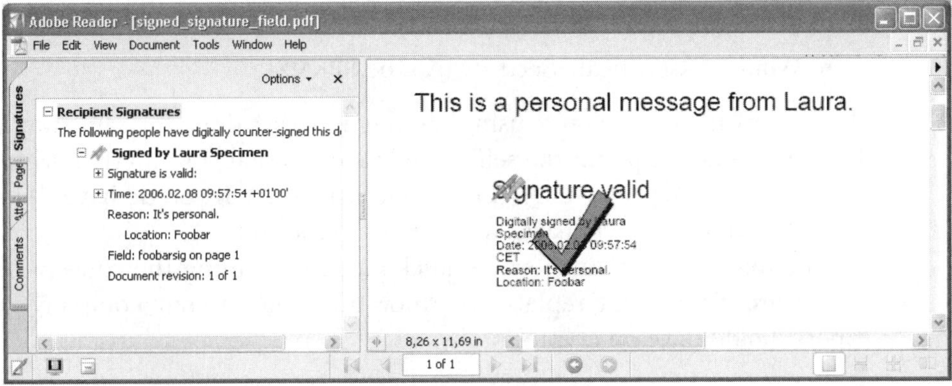


**Figure 16.7 A PDF with a signed signature field**

signature field. You need a signature field with a real digital signature, as shown in figure 16.7.

To create this PDF file, you use `PdfReader` to read the document with the signature field, and you add the signature like this:

```
/* chapter16/SignedSignatureField.java */
KeyStore ks = KeyStore.getInstance(KeyStore.getDefaultType());
ks.load(
  new FileInputStream("../resources/.keystore"),
  f00b4r".toCharArray());
PrivateKey key =
  (PrivateKey) ks.getKey("foobar", "r4b00f".toCharArray());
```

**A java.security.KeyStore object**

**A java.security.PrivateKey object**

```
Certificate[] chain = ks.getCertificateChain("foobar");
reader = new PdfReader("unsigned_signature_field.pdf");
FileOutputStream os =
  new FileOutputStream("signed_signature_field.pdf");
PdfStamper stamper = PdfStamper.createSignature(reader, os, '\0');
PdfSignatureAppearance appearance
  = stamper.getSignatureAppearance();
appearance.setCrypto(key, chain, null,
  PdfSignatureAppearance.SELF_SIGNED);
appearance.setReason("It's personal.");
appearance.setLocation("Foobar");
appearance.setVisibleSignature("foobarsig");
stamper.close();
```

**A java.security.cert.Certificate object**

This code needs further explanation. iText supports visible and invisible signing using the following modes:

- Self signed (Adobe.PPKLite)
- VeriSign plug-in (VeriSign.PPKVS)
- Windows Certificate Security (Adobe.PPKMS)

No matter what mode you're using, signing is always done the same way in iText. The next section explains the self-signed mode so that you can try it without having to acquire a key from a Certificate Authority (CA). If you do have a key signed by a CA, you'll have to make small changes to the code.

The following sections form a quick guide explaining the concept of digital signatures. They don't replace the know-how you or your company's security expert should have on cryptography.

### 16.3.2 Using public and private keys

Do you remember the exchange students at the University of Foobar? Most of these students are enrolled in a program at a university in their own country (the sending institution). They take some courses at the university in Foobar (the receiving institution). After taking exams for these courses, the students want to go home with a document listing the grades they've obtained for each course. This document can act as a transcript of records so that the sending institution can take the grades into account when calculating an end result for the complete program.

Because TUF is a *technological* university, it can't afford to use the old-fashioned paper solution with stamps and hand-written signatures. The university has a reputation to defend, and it wants to use an electronic document. Of course, you don't want the students to be able to change their grades before the document reaches its destination. That's why you'll add a digital signature.

This signature contains a digest of the data inside the document. You encrypt the digest using your *private key*. This key is part of a pair; you also have a *public key*. As the names indicate, you should keep the private key private, whereas the public key should be open to the public.

Both keys are related, but they can't be derived from each other. Due to the nature of this key pair, the digest you encrypt with your private key can only be decrypted using your public key. This is a public key (aka *asymmetric* key) cryptography system, where one key is for encoding and the other for decoding.

Somewhere between the receiving institution (receiving the student, but sending the document) and the sending institution (receiving the transcript of records), malicious students could try to change their grades. Unfortunately for them, when the digest is decrypted using the public key of the institution that issued the document, the digest won't correspond with the altered content, and the fraud will be exposed.

But maybe students are smarter than you think. They don't have your private key, so they can't create a valid signature. However, they can create a new private and public key and pretend this is an official key pair. That way, students can try to fool their university.

To solve this problem, you call in a third party that is beyond suspicion: a *Certificate Authority*. The CA checks whether the public key of the University of Foobar really originated from the University of Foobar and wasn't made up by a student. The CA generates a *certificate* by signing the public key of the University of Foobar with its own private key. Whoever receives a message that can be decrypted with this certificate knows for sure that the University of Foobar was the sender.

That's a short version of the theory. The main question is: How can you generate a private/public key pair and obtain a certificate?

### 16.3.3 Generating keys and certificates

Many tools allow you to create a private/public key pair, but because you're developing in Java, you'll use the keytool that comes with the JDK:

```
$ keytool -genkey -alias foobar -keyalg RSA -keystore .keystore
Enter keystore password:  f00b4r
What is your first and last name?
  [Unknown]:  Laura Specimen
What is the name of your organizational unit?
  [Unknown]:  FCSE
What is the name of your organization?
  [Unknown]:  TUF
What is the name of your City or Locality?
  [Unknown]:  Foobar
```

```
What is the name of your State or Province?
  [Unknown]:
What is the two-letter country code for this unit?
  [Unknown]:  BE
Is CN=Laura Specimen, OU=FCSE, O=TUF, L=Foobar,
  ST=Unknown, C=BE correct?
  [no]:  yes

Enter key password for <foobar>
        (RETURN if same as keystore password):  r4b00f
```

The resulting file .keystore contains your private key, so keep it private. If you're going to sign your document using self-signed mode, you can generate a certificate that can be used to decrypt messages encrypted with your private key like this:

```
keytool -export -alias foobar -file foobar.cer -keystore .keystore
Enter keystore password:  f00b4r
Certificate stored in file <foobar.cer>
```

The resulting file foobar.cer can now be used to validate a PDF file that was signed using the private key in the .keystore file. I repeat my warning: Everyone can generate such a key pair. Answer the questions asked by `keytool` with Laura's data, and if you can persuade the people at the receiving end that it's not a bogus certificate—you can pretend to be her.

To avoid this problem, Laura should generate a Certificate Signing Request (CSR) that can be sent to a CA. It's done like this.

```
keytool -certreq -keystore .keystore -alias foobar -file foobar.csr
Enter keystore password:  f00b4r
Enter key password for <foobar>r4b00f
```

A file foobar.csr is generated. You send this file to your CA, and you receive a Privacy Enhanced Mail (PEM) file. This file contains your public key signed by the CA using the CA's private key. This public key can be decrypted with the CA's public key, which comes in the form of a Distinguished Encoding Rules (DER) file.

Import these files into your keystore, and you'll be able to export a PFX file that can be used to sign your documents.

**NOTE** The Acrobat VeriSign plug-in only works with VeriSign certified keys. To sign documents with VeriSign, you need a key that is certified by VeriSign. You can acquire a 60-day trial key or buy a permanent key at verisign.com.

The Microsoft Windows Certificate works with any trusted certificate. In addition to the VeriSign certificate, you can also use a free Thawte certificate, available at Thawte.com.

Normally, you don't have to deal with this stuff as a Java developer. You should get all the needed files from your company's security expert. In the next sections, you'll learn how to use these files to add a digital signature to a PDF document.

## 16.3.4 Signing a document

Let's start with a document that doesn't have any fields—just a personal message from Laura (see figure 16.8). You want to add a signature to this document, just as you did in section 16.3.1, but now you'll do it step by step.

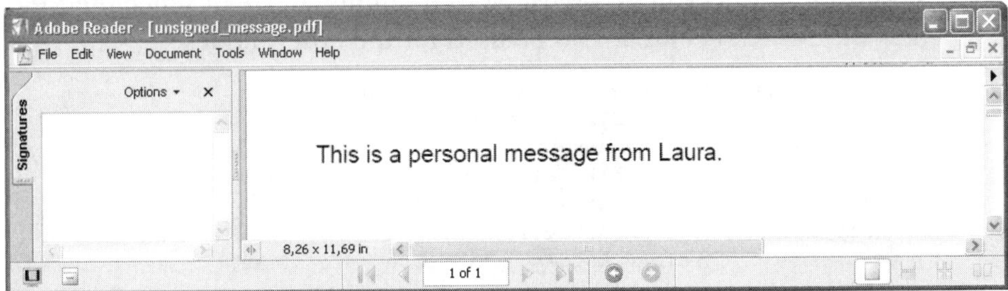


**Figure 16.8 A plain message with no fields**

### KeyStore, PrivateKey and Certificate[]

First you'll need to create a `Keystore` object. The Javadocs from Sun say the following:

> This class represents an in-memory collection of keys and certificates. It manages two types of entries:
>
> - *Key Entry*—this type of keystore entry holds very sensitive cryptographic key information, which is stored in a protected format to prevent unauthorized access. Typically, a key stored in this type of entry is a secret key, or a private key accompanied by the certificate chain for the corresponding public key.
> - *Trusted Certificate Entry*—this type of entry contains a single public key certificate belonging to another party. It's called a trusted certificate because the keystore owner trusts that the public key in the certificate indeed belongs to the identity identified by the subject (owner) of the certificate.
>
> Each entry in a keystore is identified by an "alias" string. In the case of private keys and their associated certificate chains, these strings distinguish among the different ways in which the entity may authenticate itself.

In the previous section, you generated a keystore called .keystore with password f00b4r, containing an alias "foobar" corresponding with a private key with password r4b00f. Let's load this keystore in the application and see if you can get access to the key entry and the trusted certificate entry:

```
/* chapter16/SignedPdf.java */
KeyStore ks = KeyStore.getInstance(KeyStore.getDefaultType());
ks.load(new FileInputStream("../resources/.keystore"),
  "f00b4r".toCharArray());
PrivateKey key = (PrivateKey) ks.getKey("foobar",
  "r4b00f".toCharArray());
Certificate[] chain = ks.getCertificateChain("foobar");
```

This code snippet can be used if you're signing a PDF in self-signed mode. The next one, which is similar, can be used for the other modes:

```
KeyStore ks = KeyStore.getInstance("pkcs12");
ks.load(new FileInputStream("my_private_key.pfx"),
  "my_password".toCharArray());
String alias = (String)ks.aliases().nextElement();
PrivateKey key = (PrivateKey)ks.getKey(alias,
  "my_password".toCharArray());
Certificate[] chain = ks.getCertificateChain(alias);
```

The file my_private_key.pfx is the PFX file mentioned in the previous section—you need a CA to generate this file.

### *Creating the signature*

Now that you have a `PrivateKey` object and a `Certificate` array, you can sign the file:

```
/* chapter16/SignedPdf.java */
reader = new PdfReader("unsigned_message.pdf");
FileOutputStream os = new FileOutputStream("signed_message.pdf");
PdfStamper stamper = PdfStamper.createSignature(reader, os, '\0');    ❶
PdfSignatureAppearance appearance =                       ❷
  stamper.getSignatureAppearance();
appearance.setCrypto(key, chain, null,                    ❸
  PdfSignatureAppearance.SELF_SIGNED);
appearance.setReason("It's personal.");                   ❹
appearance.setLocation("Foobar");
appearance.setVisibleSignature(                           ❺
  new Rectangle(30, 750, 500, 565), 1, null);
stamper.close();
```

The code to get the `PdfStamper` object ❶ is different from what you did before when you wanted to add plain content to an existing PDF file. To understand why, you need some background information about digital signatures in PDF.

The PDF Reference says:

> Signatures are created by computing a *digest* of the data (or part of the data) in a document, and storing the digest in the document. To verify the signature, the digest is recomputed and compared with the one stored in the document. Differences in the digest values indicate that modifications have been made since the document was signed.

In iText, you create a signature using one of the `createSignature()` methods. The binary null that is used in line ❶ means you don't want to change the PDF version of the original PDF; you can replace it with one of the `VERSION_X_Y` constants in `PdfWriter` if necessary.

Next, you create a `PdfSignatureAppearance` object ❷ and set the crypto information ❸: The first three parameters are the `PrivateKey`, the `Certificate` array, and (optionally) a Certificate Revocation List (`java.security.cert.CRL`). The fourth parameter defines the mode. Possible values are as follows:

- PdfSignatureAppearance.SELF_SIGNED—Adobe.PPKLite
- PdfSignatureAppearance.WINCER_SIGNED—Adobe.PPKMS
- PdfSignatureAppearance.VERISIGN_SIGNED—VeriSign.PPKVS

There are five different layers in a signature's appearance. These layers are XObjects that can be drawn on top of each other:

- n0—Background layer.
- n1—Validity layer, used for the unknown and valid state; contains, for instance, a yellow question mark.
- n2—Signature appearance, containing information about the signature. This can be text or an XObject that represents the handwritten signature.
- n3—Validity layer, containing a graphic that represents the validity of the signature when the signature is invalid.
- n4—Text layer, for a text presentation of the state of the signature.

In iText, you can retrieve these layers as a `PdfTemplate` object using the method `getLayer()`. The example only uses the methods `setReason()` and `setLocation()` ❹. These methods define the text that is added in the n2 layer. Consult the Javadocs if you need to know more about the other methods available in `PdfSignatureAppearance`.

With the method `setVisibleSignature()`, you define the location of the signature on a certain page ❺. The name of the signature is generated automatically because you pass a null value.

### *Validating the PDF in Adobe Reader*

To get a better understanding of what all these layers mean, let's look at some images. Figure 16.9 shows a PDF signed in self-signed mode.

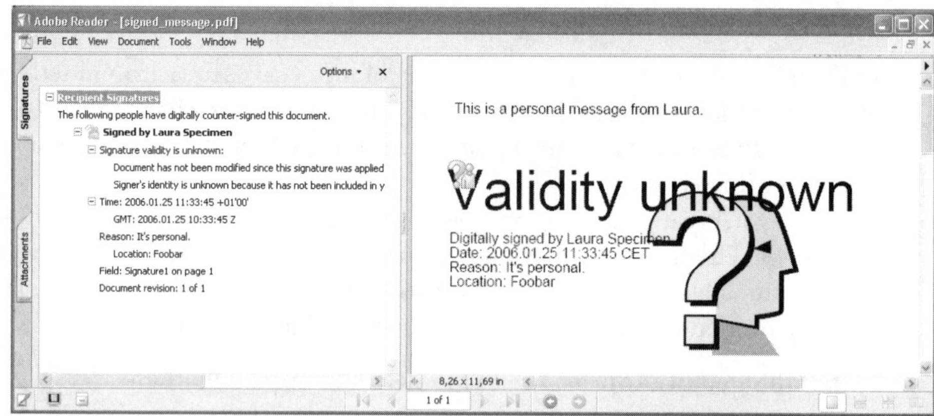


**Figure 16.9 A signed PDF document with an unknown state**

The validity is unknown because Laura's certificate hasn't been added to your list of trusted identities; you didn't use a key from a CA to sign the document. If you click the signature, you get a dialog box that offers you different possibilities for trusting Laura. For instance, you can send her an e-mail asking her to send you her certificate. Once her certificate is added to the trusted identities, you can validate the signature. Figure 16.10 shows the result of these actions.

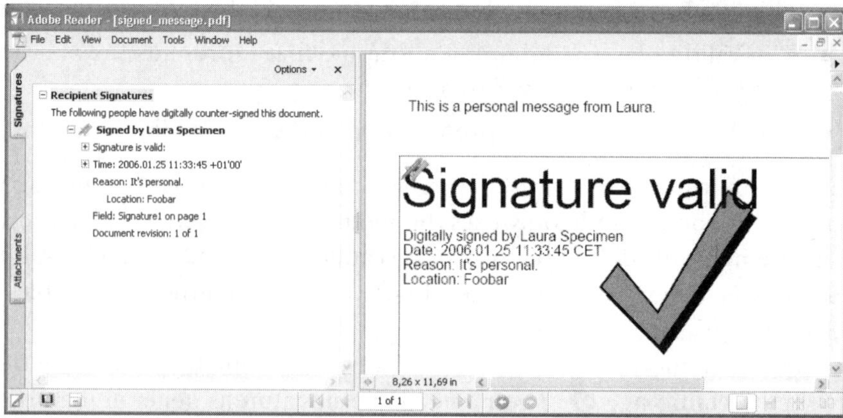


**Figure 16.10 A signed PDF document with a valid signature**

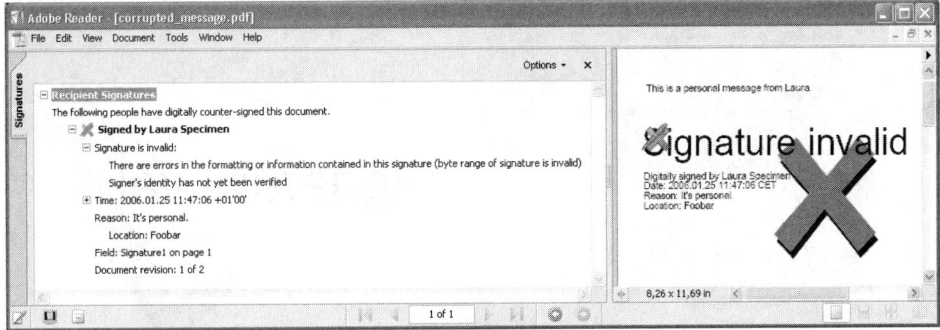


**Figure 16.11 A signed PDF document with an invalid signature**

Suppose you tamper with the signed document; for instance, you use `PdfCopy` to create a new PDF document that looks exactly like the original. When you open this new PDF file, you'll immediately notice that something happened to it (see figure 16.11).

You added visible digital signatures in the previous examples. If you omit the `setVisibleSignature()` method in line ❹, an invisible signature is added, as demonstrated in figure 16.12.

The examples in this book generate *ordinary* or *recipient* signatures. If you want to add a *certifying* or *author* signature, you need to add one more line to the code:

```
PdfSignatureAppearance.setCertified(true);
```

One of the main differences is that with recipient signatures, you can revise the document and add more than one recipient digital signature. The changes are reflected in the document revision number. On the other hand, you can add *only one* author signature to a document with iText.

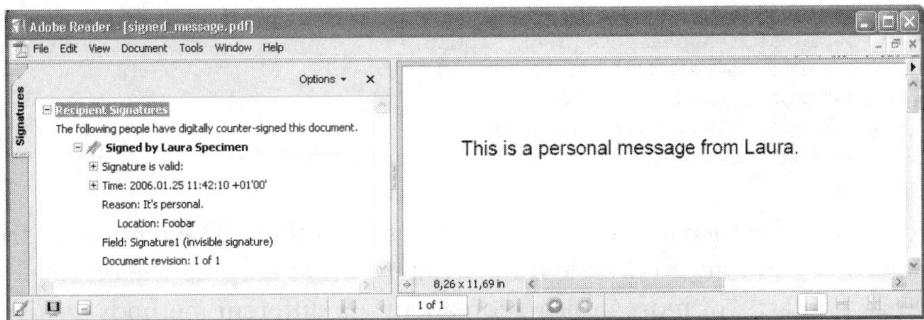


**Figure 16.12 A signed PDF document with a valid invisible signature**

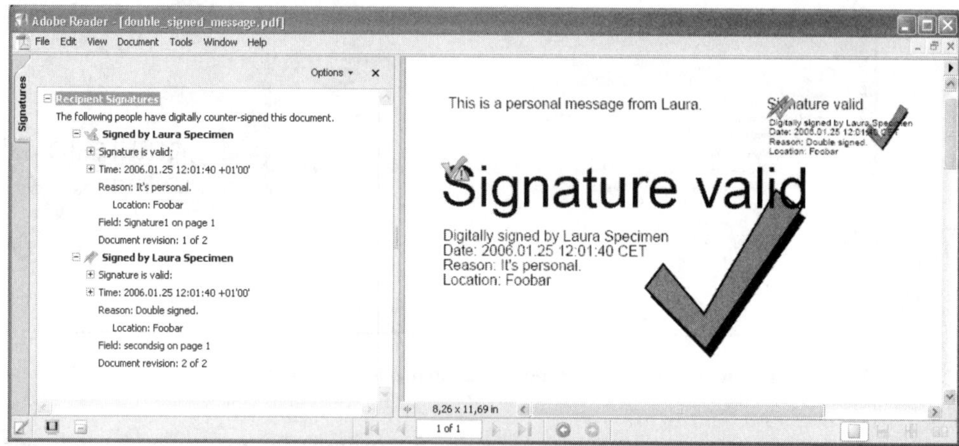

**Figure 16.13 A signed PDF document with a two valid signatures**

Figure 16.13 shows a PDF file based on the document shown in figures 16.10, to which an extra signature has been added. In the Signatures panel, you see that one signature belongs to revision 1 and the other to revision 2. A yellow triangle with an exclamation point appears next to the checkmark of the original signature; this triangle warns you that the signature doesn't cover the latest revision of the document. Here's the code:

```
/* chapter16/SignedPdf.java */
reader = new PdfReader("signed_message.pdf");          <-- Read signed PDF
FileOutputStream os =
  new FileOutputStream("double_signed_message.pdf");
PdfStamper stamper =                                          | Create second
  PdfStamper.createSignature(reader, os, '\0', null, true);   | signature
PdfSignatureAppearance appearance =
  stamper.getSignatureAppearance();
appearance.setCrypto(key, chain, null,
  PdfSignatureAppearance.SELF_SIGNED);
appearance.setReason("Double signed.");
appearance.setLocation("Foobar");
appearance.setVisibleSignature(
  new Rectangle(300, 750, 500, 800), 1, "secondsig");
stamper.close();
```

Note the difference in the `createSignature()` method. The parameter true indicates that you want to update the document while keeping the original (signed) revision intact. For more information about the different methods to create a signature, consult the Javadoc information.

In the previous examples, you've learned the basics of signing a PDF document; iText has taken care of creating the hash and the signature. It's also possible to sign a document using an external hash and/or an external signature. More examples are provided on the iText site.

### Using a smart card for signing

Until now, you've assumed that the keystore or the PFX file was read from a safe place on your system. If you want to sign a document using a smart card, you must consult the card's API for a method that extracts the certificate from the card.

**FAQ** *How do I extract a private key that is on my smart card?* If you could extract a private key from a smart card, there would be a serious security problem. Your private key is secret, and the smart card should be designed to keep this secret safe. You don't want an external application to use your private key; instead, you send a hash to the card, and the card returns a signature or a PKCS#7 message. PKCS refers to a group of Public Key Cryptography Standards. PKCS#7 defines the Cryptographic Message Syntax Standard.

If you're working with a smart card, you can't create a `PrivateKey` object. You have to send the hash to your smart card reader, and the card returns a signature or a PKCS#7. Appendix D provides an example of how to sign a PDF using an electronic identity card. You'll have to adapt this example according to the type of smart card you're using.

In figures 16.10 and 16.12, the signed PDF file is validated in Adobe Reader. But if you receive hundreds of PDF files, you'd have to hire somebody to open every PDF file in Adobe Reader to check if the signatures were valid. A better solution is to check the validity programmatically.

## 16.4 Verifying a PDF file

If you return to figure 16.9, you see a file whose status is unknown. When opening a PDF document with signatures added in WINCER or VERISIGN mode, you only have to click the signature to verify it. You don't need the certificate of the person who sent you the mail, just the CA's *root certificate*. Normally, this certificate is already present in Adobe Reader, and you must select the setting Trust All Root Certificates.

When verifying the signatures in a PDF file programmatically, the CA's root certificate should be present in a cacerts file installed along with your Java Runtime Environment (JRE). This cacerts file is a keystore that can be loaded using this single code line:

```
KeyStore ks = PdfPKCS7.loadCacertsKeyStore();
```

The next code sample shows how you can get the names of all the signature fields in the AcroForm of a PDF file. You loop over these signatures and inspect them:

```
/* chapter16/SignedPdf.java */
reader = new PdfReader("double_signed_message.pdf");
AcroFields af = reader.getAcroFields();
ArrayList names = af.getSignatureNames();
String name;
for (Iterator it = names.iterator(); it.hasNext();) {
  name = (String) it.next();
  System.out.println("Signature name: " + name);                 <-- Show signature name
  System.out.println("Signature covers whole document: "         | Entire document
    + af.signatureCoversWholeDocument(name));                    | covered?
  System.out.println("Document revision: "              | Signature belongs to
    + af.getRevision(name)                              | which revision?
    + " of " + af.getTotalRevisions());                 |
  FileOutputStream os = new FileOutputStream("revision_"
    + af.getRevision(name) + ".pdf");
  byte bb[] = new byte[8192];
  InputStream ip = af.extractRevision(name);
  int n = 0;                                                     Restore revision
  while ((n = ip.read(bb)) > 0)
    os.write(bb, 0, n);
  os.close();
  ip.close();
  PdfPKCS7 pk = af.verifySignature(name);
  Calendar cal = pk.getSignDate();
  Certificate pkc[] = pk.getCertificates();                      Document
  System.out.println("Subject: "                                 modified?
    + PdfPKCS7.getSubjectFields(pk.getSigningCertificate()));
  System.out.println("Document modified: " + !pk.verify());
  Object fails[] =
    PdfPKCS7.verifyCertificates(pkc, ks, null, cal);
  if (fails == null)                                             Verify
    System.out.println(                                          document
    "Certificates verified against the KeyStore");               against
  Else                                                           keystore
    System.out.println("Certificate failed: " + fails[1]);
}
```

If you look closely at this code sample, you see that it does more than just verify the signatures. It checks whether the signature covers the whole document. You extract revision information and restore the original revision. This example uses the double-signed document. You restore the original revision; this results in a file that is identical to the original signed_message.pdf.

Of course, the verification against the cacerts keystore fails unless you've imported Laura's certificate into cacerts. If you choose not to do this, you must create a `KeyStore` in memory and use a `CertificateFactory` to load the foobar.cer file created in section 16.3.3:

```
/* chapter16/SignedPdf.java */
CertificateFactory cf = CertificateFactory.getInstance("X509");
Collection col = cf.generateCertificates(
  new FileInputStream("../resources/foobar.cer"));
KeyStore ks = KeyStore.getInstance(KeyStore.getDefaultType());
ks.load(null, null);
for (Iterator it = col.iterator(); it.hasNext();) {
  X509Certificate cert = (X509Certificate) it.next();
  System.err.println(cert.getIssuerDN().getName());
  ks.setCertificateEntry(
    cert.getSerialNumber().toString(Character.MAX_RADIX), cert);
}
```

If you loop over the signatures using this `KeyStore`, the signatures prove to be valid. There are two signature fields in the file double_signed_message.pdf, so the following is written to `System.out`:

```
Signature name: Signature1
Signature covers whole document: false
Document revision: 1 of 2
Subject:
  {O=[TUF], CN=[Laura Specimen], OU=[FCSE], C=[BE],
   L=[Foobar], ST=[Unknown]}
Document modified: false
Certificates verified against the KeyStore
Signature name: secondsig
Signature covers whole document: true
Document revision: 2 of 2
Subject:
  {O=[TUF], CN=[Laura Specimen], OU=[FCSE], C=[BE],
   L=[Foobar], ST=[Unknown]}
Document modified: false
Certificates verified against the KeyStore
```

The first signature is named Signature1, and it doesn't cover the whole document. That's correct: The double-signature example adds an extra signature on top of a file that already had a signature. In other words, Signature1 belongs to revision 1 of 2 of the document. The signature belongs to Laura Specimen, and the content covered by the signature wasn't changed. Note that this doesn't mean the complete document wasn't changed!

The second signature is named secondsig, and it does cover the complete document. It also belongs to Laura, and the contents weren't changed. And that's that. You now know how to add a digital signature to a PDF file and how to verify signatures in an existing PDF file.

## 16.5 Summary

This chapter was the logical continuation of chapter 15. In the previous chapter, we discussed annotations with the goal of learning more about the way the fields of an AcroForm appear in a PDF file. We didn't go into the details of form creation, but you've learned enough to know what to do when confronted with a PDF file containing an AcroForm.

You've learned how to use such a PDF document as a template. You've added data in many ways: using the `setField()` method of an `AcroFields` object, using an (X)FDF file, and even using the absolute coordinates retrieved from the fields' widget annotations. That turned out to be quite easy.

The final part of this chapter dealt with a special type of field: signature fields. We discussed the basic mechanisms of signing that should get you started.

In the past 16 chapters, we've covered a lot of functionality in literally hundreds of small standalone examples. It's high time that we looked at web applications and how to adapt these examples so that you can create a PDF document on the fly and serve it to a web browser.

# 17

# *iText in web applications*

***This chapter covers***

- How to use iText in a web application
- How to avoid the most common pitfalls
- How to use PDF in a web application

One of the main requirements of the project that led to the development of iText was that my colleagues and I at Ghent University had to be able to serve PDF documents on the fly using Java servlets. This book has included an abundance of standalone examples. You didn't need to install an application server to compile and execute them.

In this chapter, you'll integrate some of these code samples into a web application. You'll create a personalized version of the course catalog, and you'll retrieve data from a Forms Data Format (FDF) file submitted using a static PDF document with an AcroForm. But first, let me list some common pitfalls that can stand in the way of creating PDF documents on the fly.

## 17.1 Writing PDF to the ServletOutputStream: pitfalls

Fifteen chapters ago, you made a simple "Hello World" example. In the example, you created a PDF file in five steps (see also listing 2.1):

1. Create a document.
2. Create a `PdfWriter` using `Document` and `OutputStream`.
3. Open the document.
4. Add content to the document.
5. Close the document.

When we discussed step 2 (see section 2.1.2), I told you that you can write the PDF file to any `java.io.OutputStream`, including a `javax.servlet.ServletOutputStream`, returned by the `getOutputStream()` method of a `(Http)ServletResponse` object.

Let's do the test! The following code sample extends the `HttpServlet` class and overrides the `doGet()` method:

```
/* chapter17/HelloWorldServlet.java */
public void doGet(HttpServletRequest request,
  HttpServletResponse response)
  throws IOException, ServletException {
  String presentationtype =                          | Get presentationtype
    request.getParameter("presentationtype");        | parameter
  Document document = new Document();   <-- Step 1
  try {
    if ("pdf".equals(presentationtype)) {                                | Step 2
      response.setContentType("application/pdf");                      | for PDF
      PdfWriter.getInstance(document, response.getOutputStream());      | file
    }
```

```
      else if ("html".equals(presentationtype)) {
        response.setContentType("text/html");
        HtmlWriter.getInstance(document,
        response.getOutputStream());
      }
      else if ("rtf".equals(presentationtype)) {
        response.setContentType("text/rtf");
        RtfWriter2.getInstance(document,
        response.getOutputStream());
      }
      else {
        response.sendRedirect(
          "http://itextdocs.lowagie.com/tutorial/");
        return;
      }
      document.open();
      document.add(new Paragraph("Hello World"));
      document.add(new Paragraph(new Date().toString()));
    }
    catch(DocumentException de) {
      de.printStackTrace();
      System.err.println("document: " + de.getMessage());
    }
    document.close();
  }
```

Step 2 for HTML file

Step 2 for RTF file

On error, send redirect

Step 3

Step 4

Step 5

Figure 17.1 shows two browser windows:

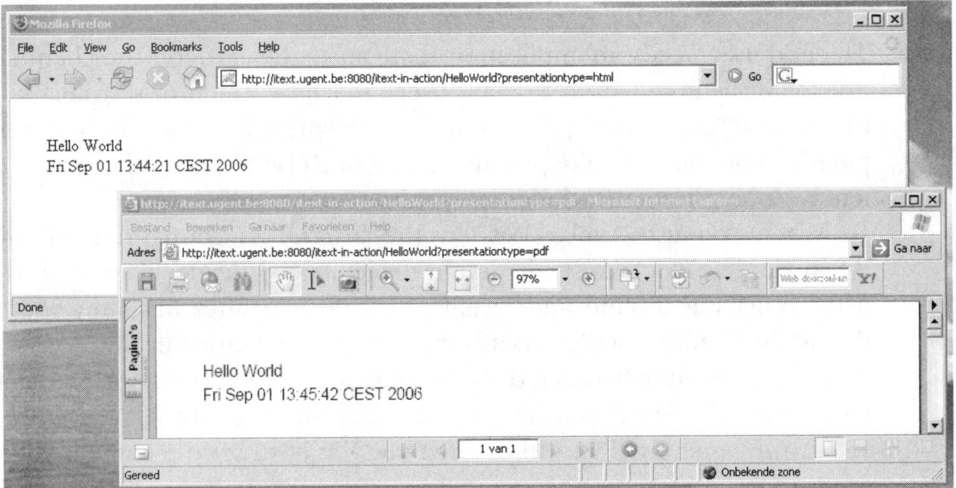


**Figure 17.1 iText in action in a web application**

- A FireFox window showing an HTML page produced by this servlet
- A Microsoft Internet Explorer (IE) window showing a PDF page produced by the same servlet, but with another value for the `presentationtype` parameter

It works like a charm! At least, it works like a charm for me; it may or may not work for you or your customers. In spite of Murphy's Law, this functionality almost always works in the demo version; but once you go into production you'll probably get reports from users saying they see only gibberish, or white pages, or annoying error pages.

Trust me; I have experience with this stuff. In most cases, these problems aren't a result of bad PDF or bad iText code. They're caused by one or more known browser issues, or by a wrong browser configuration at the client side.

The following section helps you work around the most common client-side problems.

### 17.1.1 Solving problems related to content type-related problems

The previous example could produce PDF, HTML, and RTF. This book focuses on PDF. The content type of a PDF file is "application/pdf." On the server side, you need to add this content type to the content header. This can be done with the method `setContentType()`:

```
/* chapter17/HelloWorldServlet.java */
response.setContentType("application/pdf");
```

The end user needs an application that can render PDF on the client side. If a PDF viewer is installed on the end user's machine, the browser must know that files of type "application/pdf" should be interpreted by the PDF viewer or a PDF plug-in. Note that if you're producing FDF or XFDF files, you should use the content type "application/vnd.fdf" or "application/vnd.adobe.xfdf."

When you use Adobe Reader, the browser is configured automatically. When you install a browser, it should detect Adobe Reader if present. If you do it the other way around and install Adobe Reader after installing the browser, the Adobe Reader installer installs the web plug-in automatically.

If the association between the content type and the PDF viewer isn't made correctly, the end user will probably see gibberish starting with *%PDF-1.4 %âãÏÓ* and so on (the same problem will occur if you forget to set the content type on the server side).

Some browsers ignore the content type defined in the header. IE is known to look at the file extension, rather than the content type. PDFs ending with .pdf are rendered fine in IE (providing the plug-in was installed correctly). But as soon as you serve a PDF from a servlet, you may get complaints from your end users. Adding a dummy parameter ending in .pdf (for instance, http://myserver.com/servlet/MyServlet?dummy=dummy.pdf) is one way to deal with this problem, but it's not the most elegant.

You could use the `Content-Disposition` header like this:

```
response.setHeader("Content-Disposition",
  " inline; filename=my.pdf");
```

Or, if you want the PDF to be saved, rather than to be viewed in the browser, you can force the browser to open a Save As dialog box like this:

```
response.setHeader("Content-Disposition",
  " attachment; filename=\"my.pdf\"");
```

Note that not every version of every browser deals with this header correctly.

If you're familiar with servlets, you know another way to solve the filename problem: You can define a servlet-mapping in your web.xml file that maps URLs ending in *.pdf to a facade servlet that handles all your PDF documents. The following XML snippet is an example hosted on itext.ugent.be, the support site for this book hosted by Ghent University:

```
<servlet-mapping>
  <servlet-name>OutSimplePdf</servlet-name>
  <url-pattern>/simple.pdf</url-pattern>
</servlet-mapping>
```

The next section looks at a code snippet of the servlet `OutSimplePdf`. This servlet also works around another known problem: the blank-page phenomenon.

### 17.1.2 Troubleshooting the blank-page problem

It's been a while since this question turned up on the iText mailing list (especially since I wrote a tutorial chapter about it), but in the past we got many questions about the blank-page problem. This problem can have different causes: server-related and/or browser-related; never iText-related.

Let's start with some rules of thumb:

- Always begin writing code that runs as a standalone example. If the example doesn't work in its standalone version, it won't work in a web application either, but at least you can rule out all problems related to the server or the browser.
- Start with simple code based on the examples in this book. If it works, gradually add complexity until something goes wrong. Don't post complete

servlet examples on the mailing list. We only look at standalone examples that can reproduce the problem. If you do post a servlet-related problem, don't forget to mention what application server you're using, and always post the exception that was thrown.

- Always test your application on different machines, using different browsers, even if there isn't any problem. Some web applications won't ever show problems when tested on one type of browser, but they will fail when using another browser.
- Before posting a question to the mailing list, add an extra `PdfWriter` instance to your application so that two PDF files are generated simultaneously (see the examples in section 2.1.2). One PDF file should be sent to the client side through the `HttpResponse` object; another should be saved to a file on the server side (remember the note in section 7.2.1: be careful when using columns).

When you've followed all these rules, you should be able to determine the nature of the problem—more specifically, is it a server-side problem or a client-side problem?

### *Server-related problems*

If you've followed the final rule of thumb, start by opening the file generated on the server side. If it isn't a valid PDF file, there are three possibilities:

- An iText class is missing. Check whether you added the iText.jar file to the `CLASSPATH`. Check whether you have more than one version in your `CLASSPATH` (different versions can lead to conflicts). Check whether the jar is compiled with the correct compiler: If the jar is compiled with JDK 1.4 and your server runs on a 1.3 JRE, you'll get exceptions saying some classes aren't found, even if they're in the iText.jar.
- There's a resource missing. Normally, the exception should give you a fair idea about what's wrong. The most common problem is that font files aren't found because the path you used can't be reached by the application server, or because the application server runs as a user that doesn't have the permission to read the file.
- On a UNIX-based server, you need to install an X server. In section 2.1.4, a FAQ callout tells you how to solve X-related problems that typically occur when you're using `Graphics2D` or the `Color` class.

If the file generated on the server side is OK, look at the file generated on the client side. If it doesn't open correctly in Adobe Reader, try opening it in a plain text editor, but make sure it's a text editor that preserves binary characters.

If you see lots of question marks in the page streams, the problem is server-related; your server probably flattens all bytes with a value higher than 127. The pages are shown in Adobe Reader because the page structure is OK but the content of the pages is corrupted—hence the blank pages. Consult your web (or application) server manual to find out how to solve this problem.

If you see HTML, change the extension from .pdf to .html and look at it in a browser; you'll probably see an error page in HTML generated by your server. Exceptions happen; deal with them. If necessary, send an error page to the client, but don't forget to set the content type to "text/html"; otherwise, Adobe Reader will open with an error message saying the file doesn't begin with %PDF. If you check the page for HTML, don't forget to look at the end of the file. Once, people spent days searching for a bug I was able to fix in a minute just by looking at the PDF file in a text editor: They had sent the PDF to the browser, followed by a stream of plain HTML. Adobe Reader said the file was damaged and couldn't be repaired.

If the file generated on the client side is OK or if none of the problems mentioned so far match your situation, chances are the problem is browser-related. Don't despair! Just because a problem is browser-related doesn't mean it's impossible to solve by changing settings on the server side.

#### *Browser-related problems*

When no content length is specified in the header of your dynamically generated file, the browser reads blocks of bytes sent by the web server. Firefox, Mozilla, and Netscape detect when the stream is finished and use the correct size of the dynamically generated file. Some versions of IE are known to have problems truncating the stream to the right size: The real size of the PDF file is smaller than the size assumed by IE. The surplus of bytes can contain gibberish, and this leads to problems.

The only way you can work around this issue is to specify the content length in the response header. Setting this header has to be done *before* any content is sent. Unfortunately, you only know the length of the file *after* you've created it. This means you can't send the PDF to the `ServletOutputStream` obtained with `response.getOutputStream()` right away. Instead, you must create the PDF on your file system or in memory first, so that you can retrieve the length, add the length to the response header, and then send the PDF. That's a pity, because if you're generating large PDF files, you risk a timeout in the browser-server communication. We'll deal with this problem in section 17.1.5. First, let's find out how to create a PDF file in memory:

```
/* chapter17/OutSimplePdf.java */
Document document = new Document();
ByteArrayOutputStream baos = new ByteArrayOutputStream();
PdfWriter.getInstance(document, baos);
document.open();
document.add(new Paragraph(msg));
document.close();
```

You've now generated a PDF in memory using a `ByteArrayOutputStream`. Next, you retrieve the size of the byte array and then send the bytes to the servlet's output stream:

```
/* chapter17/OutSimplePdf.java */
response.setContentType("application/pdf");   <-1
response.setContentLength(baos.size());   <-2
ServletOutputStream out = response.getOutputStream();   <-3
baos.writeTo(out);   <-4
out.flush();   <-5
```

This code sample sets the content type ❶, sets the content length ❷, gets the `ServletOutputStream` ❸, writes the PDF to the `OutputStream` ❹, and then flushes the stream ❺.

Remember that you can also set the content disposition header. Mailing-list subscribers have shared their experiences with the community and told us that it's also safe to set the following response header values:

```
/* chapter17/OutSimplePdf.java */
response.setHeader("Expires", "0");
response.setHeader("Cache-Control",
  "must-revalidate, post-check=0, pre-check=0");
response.setHeader("Pragma", "public");
```

Note that response headers have to be set before the content is sent to the output stream. You can't prevent the PDF file from being cached on the client side. The PDF viewer needs to read the file from the file system. This isn't an iText-specific issue: It's true for all PDF files served on the Web. In the file permissions overview listed in section 3.3.3, you saw that it's impossible to disable the Save As button. Even if you could, doing so would be of no use: The PDF file is always cached.

Figure 17.2 shows a simple form with a text area. Depending on the parameter passed to the JSP, the submit method of the form is `GET` or `POST`. You can enter any text you want and then click the submit button; a PDF file containing your message is generated (see figure 17.3).

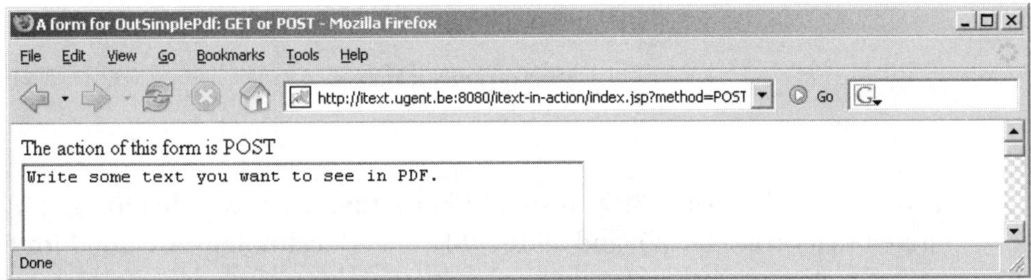


**Figure 17.2 A simple JSP file with a text area in an HTML form**

The PDF in the screenshot was generated with the servlet we just discussed: `OutSimplePdf`. You can test it by using one of these URLs:

- http://itext.ugent.be:8080/itext-in-action/index.jsp?method=GET
- http://itext.ugent.be:8080/itext-in-action/index.jsp?method=POST

The code of the JSP that generates the form in HTML is simple:

```
<html>
  <head>
      <title>A form for OutSimplePdf: GET or POST</title>
  </head>
  <body>
<%
    String method = request.getParameter("method");
    if (method == null) method = "GET";
%>
    The action of this form is <%= method %>
    <form action="simple.pdf" method="<%= method%>">
      <textarea name="msg" cols="50" rows="20">
```

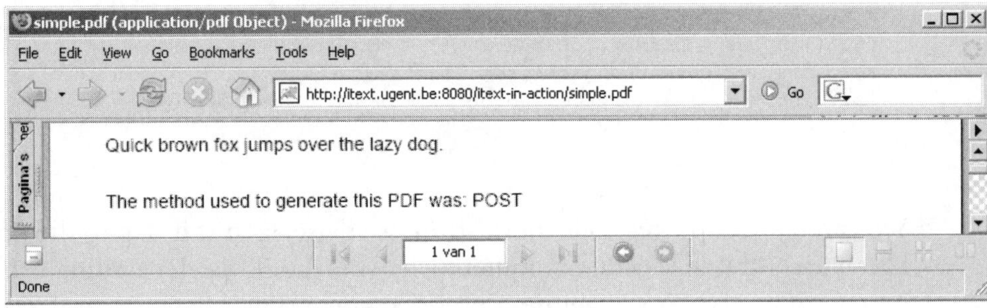


**Figure 17.3 The resulting PDF after posting a message**

```
        Write some text you want to see in PDF.
        </textarea><br />
        Click to see PDF: <input type="Submit" value="GeneratePDF">
      </form>
    </body>
  </html>
```

If you're familiar with JSP, you should know that it's a bad idea to use JSP to generate binary content. JSP and all the JSP-related technology are good for building HTML web sites. A JSP file can be also used as a forwarder to a servlet, but it isn't recommended to generate a PDF file from a JSP page.

In the next section, you'll find out why.

### 17.1.3 Problems with PDF generated from JSP

I can't repeat it enough: It's a bad idea to use JSP to generate binary content. I don't say it isn't possible to integrate iText in a JSP page. Surf to http://itext.ugent.be:8080/itext-in-action/helloworld.jsp: The link works for me and gives me a PDF file saying "Hello World," but it won't necessarily work for you.

First I'll give you the code that works for me, and then I'll tell you what can go wrong if you try to adapt the sample and deploy the JSP on your system:

```
<%@
page import="java.io.*,com.lowagie.text.*,com.lowagie.text.pdf.*"
%><%
response.setContentType( "application/pdf" );
Document document = new Document();
ByteArrayOutputStream buffer = new ByteArrayOutputStream();
PdfWriter.getInstance( document, buffer );
document.open();
document.add(new Paragraph("Hello World"));
document.close();
DataOutput output =
  new DataOutputStream( response.getOutputStream() );
byte[] bytes = buffer.toByteArray();
response.setContentLength(bytes.length);
for( int i = 0; i < bytes.length; i++ ) {
  output.writeByte( bytes[i] );
}
%>
```

You can try to copy this code, but I strongly advise against it. Up to the present, I haven't heard one sensible argument why you should prefer writing a JSP page instead of a servlet to generate a PDF document, but I know several arguments against doing so:

- Some servers assume that JSP output isn't binary, so you get the question-mark problem mentioned earlier. PDF files written to the file system of the server open without problems. When served to a client, the PDF opens, but you only see blank pages.
- JSP pages are compiled to servlets internally. Granted, to serve HTML, it's easier to write a JSP page (or code using a similar technology) than to write a servlet; but I know from experience that it's the other way round for PDF. Most of the workarounds listed in this section are hard to implement in a JSP file. Integrating iText in a servlet is less error prone than integrating iText in a JSP page.
- If you copy the JSP example and start working from there, you'll probably add indentation, newlines, spaces, carriage returns, and so on. If you're used to writing JSPs, it should be second nature to do this. Although this is good for most of the code you're writing, it's forbidden if you want to generate binary content!

The third reason is the most common problem. Adding formatting characters such as newlines and spaces has no impact on HTML pages, but now you're generating PDF. These characters are invisible to the human eye, but they're compiled into the servlet and they can cause problems:

- You can get the exception *`getOutputStream()` has already been called for this response*. This happens because the JSP has newlines or spaces that cause the output writer to be opened before you call `response.getOutputStream()`.
- Your PDF risks being corrupt. You can't add characters at arbitrary places in a binary file, but that's exactly what the servlet does with your newlines and spaces. The cross-reference of the PDF file generated with the JSP won't point to the correct byte positions.

We can't help you with these kinds of problems. Our answer will always be to use servlets instead of JSP. I can only repeat: It's a bad idea to use JSPs to generate binary data.

But writing JSP isn't always a bad idea; as a matter of fact, you can solve the next problem with a simple JSP file.

### 17.1.4 Avoiding multiple hits per PDF

In web analytics, a *hit* is when an end user requests a page from your web server and this page is sent to the user's browser directly. When you enter the URL http://itext.ugent.be:8080/itext-in-action/simple.pdf in the location bar of your browser, one PDF file opens in your browser window using a PDF viewer plug-in, and you probably assume that one hit is registered in the logs on the server side.

This is true if you're using Firefox, Mozilla, or Netscape, but again there's a problem with IE. IE hits the server multiple times with the same request for every dynamically generated binary file. You can't predict how many hits one single request will generate; it could be two or three hits, or occasionally just one. This behavior can be a real pain, for instance if you're updating a database or keeping statistics for every PDF that is served. Setting the cache parameters like this

```
response.setHeader(
  "Cache-Control", "must-revalidate, post-check=0, pre-check=0");
```

can help, but there's no guarantee it will work for all browsers. The only foolproof solution I know of is using the `embed` tag in an HTML file:

```
<html>
<body leftMargin="0" topMargin="0" scroll="no">
  <embed src="http://myserver/pdfCreationServlet"
    width="100%" height="100%"
    type="application/pdf" fullscreen="yes" />
</body>
</html>
```

Because this problem is IE specific, you can use JSP to check the user agent before sending the PDF file:

```
<%
  String user = request.getHeader("User-Agent");
  if(user.indexOf("MSIE") != -1 && user.indexOf("Windows") != -1) {
    out.print(
      "<body leftMargin=\"0\" topMargin=\"0\" scroll=\"no\">");
    out.print("<EMBED src=\"simple.pdf?msg="
      + user
      + "\" width=\"100%\" height=\"100%\"  fullscreen=\"yes\" "
      + "type=\"application/pdf\">");
  }
  else{
    response.sendRedirect("simple.pdf?msg=" + user);
  }
%>
```

Granted, this also triggers two hits, one for the JSP file and one for the servlet generating the PDF, but that isn't the issue. The problem is that with IE, you can never predict how many times the server will execute the servlet code; using this small JSP sample, you're sure the code will execute only once per request.

### 17.1.5 *Workaround for the timeout problem*

As I mentioned before, it's a pity you have to buffer the PDF in a `ByteArrayOutputStream` just because some browsers need to know the length of the generated PDF file in advance. At Ghent University, we had to generate reports with grades for several thousand students in one document.

This document could become large, but that wasn't our main problem. Our Achilles heel was database access. The database system that was used initially was old, and database access was slow, especially when the server load was high. People sometimes failed to retrieve the PDF because the browser-server connection timed out.

If I had been able to serve little bits of PDF at a time to the client side (for instance, by writing binary code directly to the `ServletOutputStream` each time a page was finished), this timeout wouldn't have occurred, but I had to support IE clients too.

Eventually, I solved the problem by serving HTML feedback as long as the PDF wasn't finished. The HTML showed the total number of students and the number of students added to the PDF so far. I also made a progress bar by stretching a pixel in an image with a width of 0 to 100:

```
<img src="pixel.gif"
  height="10" width="<%= myPdf.getPercentage() %>">
```

This HTML page was refreshed every 3 seconds until the PDF was finished.

The example that follows simplifies this solution. The PDF is generated in a Java `Thread`. Figure 17.4 shows a text message that says what percentage of the PDF is finished and after how many seconds the page will be refreshed.

The PDF is being created in the background; when this process is finished, you see a simple PDF form with a button to get the PDF (see figure 17.5).

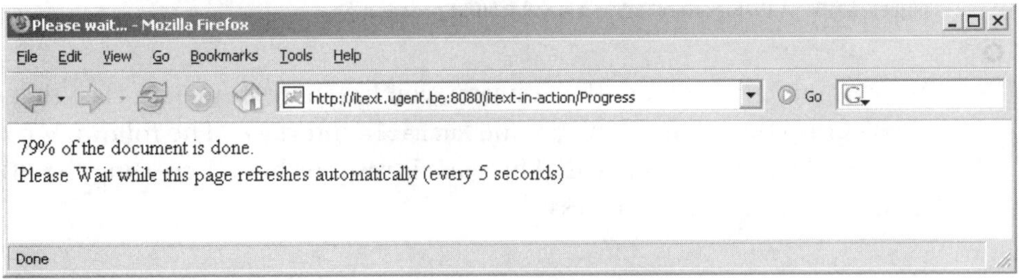


**Figure 17.4 A message while waiting for a PDF file to be created**

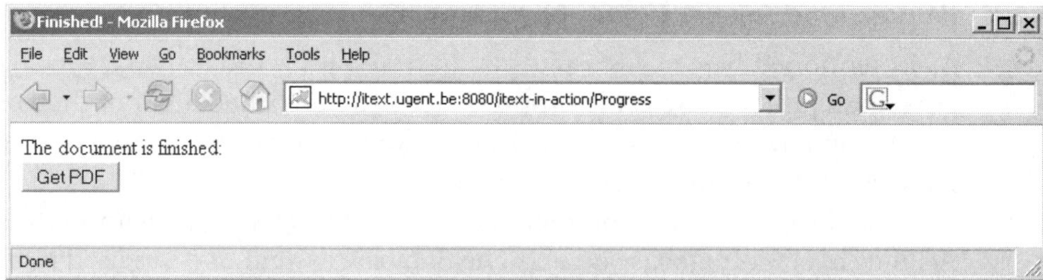


**Figure 17.5 A message that the PDF has been created successfully**

The PDF is attached to the personal session of the current user. If this user clicks the button, the PDF is fetched from this session object. The resulting PDF is shown in figure 17.6.

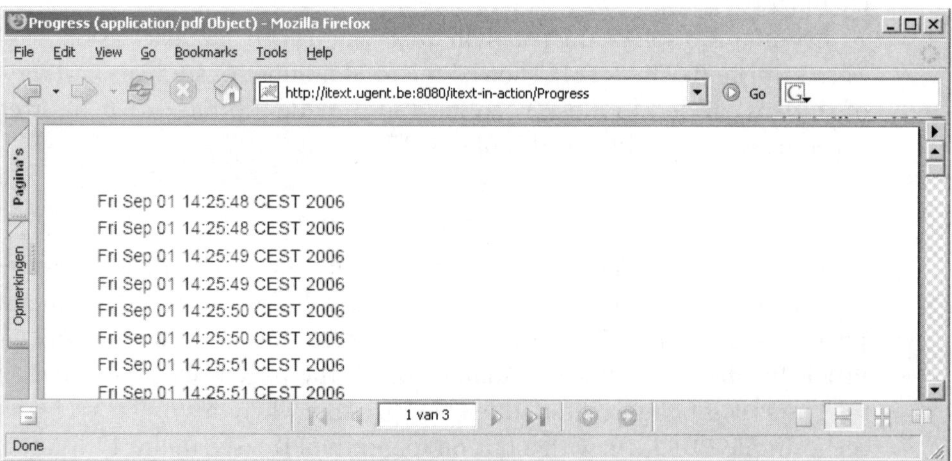


**Figure 17.6 A PDF generated in a background process**

If you want to implement this solution, you first have to make a class that extends class `Thread` or that implements the `Runnable` interface. The following code sample uses the inner class `MyPdf`. This class is responsible for creating the PDF document in a background process:

```
/* chapter17/ProgressServlet.java */
public class MyPdf implements Runnable {

  ByteArrayOutputStream baos = new ByteArrayOutputStream();   <-1
  int p = 0;   <-2
```

```
    public void run() {
      Document doc = new Document();
      try {
        PdfWriter.getInstance(doc, baos);
        doc.open();
        while (p < 99) {                                   <-3
          doc.add(new Paragraph(new Date().toString()));
          Thread.sleep(500);                               <-4
          p++;                                             <-5
        }
      } catch (DocumentException e) {
        p = -1;                                            <-6
        e.printStackTrace();
      } catch (InterruptedException e) {
        p = -1;                                            <-6
        e.printStackTrace();
      }
      doc.close();
      p = 100;                                             <-7
    }

    public ByteArrayOutputStream getPdf() throws DocumentException {   <-8
      if (p < 100) {
        throw new DocumentException(                       9
          "The document isn't finished yet!");
      }
      return baos;
    }

    public int getPercentage() {
      return p;
    }
  }
```

This code first constructs the `ByteArrayOutputStream` ❶. You keep track of the percentage that is finished ❷ and continue if the percentage is less than 99 ❸. `Thread.sleep(500)` deliberately slows down the process ❹; otherwise, you'd probably get the PDF file immediately, and you wouldn't see the mechanism in action. If all goes well, the percentage is increased ❺; on error, the percentage is invalidated ❻. When finished, the percentage is set to 100 ❼, and you can get the PDF `ByteArrayOutputStream` ❽. The code throws an exception if the process isn't finished ❾.

In this example, the `doGet()` method serves the HTML. It returns useful information as long as the PDF isn't finished using extra helper methods:

```
/* chapter17/ProgressServlet.java */
public void doGet(
  HttpServletRequest request, HttpServletResponse response)
  throws IOException, ServletException {
```

```
    HttpSession session = request.getSession(true);      <-- Get user's session
    Object o = session.getAttribute("myPdf");             <-- Retrieve MyPdf object
    MyPdf pdf;
    if (o == null) {
      pdf = new MyPdf();
      session.setAttribute("myPdf", pdf);                 Create one, if none
      Thread t = new Thread(pdf);
      t.start();
    }
    else {
      pdf = (MyPdf)o;      <-- Get it, if there is one
    }
    response.setContentType("text/html");     <-- Content type HTML!
    switch (pdf.getPercentage()) {           <-- Choose message to return
      case -1:
        isError(response.getOutputStream());
        return;
      case 100:
        isFinished(response.getOutputStream());
        return;
      default:
        isBusy(pdf, response.getOutputStream());
        return;
    }
  }

  private void isBusy(MyPdf pdf, ServletOutputStream stream)
    throws IOException {
    stream.print("<html>\n\t<head>\n\t\t"
      + "<title>Please wait...</title>\n\t\t"
      + "<meta http-equiv=\"Refresh\" content=\"5\">"              Create
      + "\n\t</head>\n\t<body>");                                   server-busy
    stream.print(String.valueOf(pdf.getPercentage()));              message
    stream.print("% of the document is done.<br>\n"
      + "Please Wait while this page refreshes automatically "
      + "(every 5 seconds)\n\t</body>\n</html>");
  }

  private void isFinished(ServletOutputStream stream)
     throws IOException {
    stream.print("<html>\n\t<head>\n\t\t<title>Finished!</title>"
      + "\n\t</head>\n\t<body>");                                    Create
    stream.print("The document is finished:<form method=\"POST\">"    finished
      + "<input type=\"Submit\" value=\"Get PDF\">"                   message
      + "</form>\n\t</body>\n</html>");
  }

  private void isError(ServletOutputStream stream)
    throws IOException {
    stream.print("<html>\n\t<head>\n\t\t<title>Error</title>"
      + "\n\t</head>\n\t<body>");                                    Create error
    stream.print("An error occured.\n\t</body>\n</html>");            message
  }
```

This is what happens: The first time you hit the server, a new `MyPdf` is added to your personal user session and a `Thread` generating the PDF is started. As long as the PDF isn't generated completely (that is, as long as percentage < 100), a Please Wait message is sent to the browser showing the percentage done. Once the PDF is finished, the end user gets a form with a button to fetch the PDF from the `doPost()` method:

```
/* chapter17/ProgressServlet.java */
public void doPost (
  HttpServletRequest request, HttpServletResponse response)
  throws IOException, ServletException {
  HttpSession session = request.getSession(false);
  try {
    MyPdf pdf = (MyPdf) session.getAttribute("myPdf");
    session.removeAttribute("myPdf");
    ByteArrayOutputStream baos = pdf.getPdf();
    response.setHeader("Expires", "0");
    response.setHeader("Cache-Control",
      "must-revalidate, post-check=0, pre-check=0");
    response.setHeader("Pragma", "public");
    response.setContentType("application/pdf");
    response.setContentLength(baos.size());
    ServletOutputStream out = response.getOutputStream();
    baos.writeTo(out);
    out.flush();
  }
  catch(Exception e) {
    isError(response.getOutputStream());
  }
}
```

This is a simplified example of a solution I've been using for more than seven years. It's not only a technical solution, it also works on a psychological level. People tend to be impatient. They don't like to wait for that Internet page to come, not knowing if the connection got lost, if they should hit the reload button, if the server went down… Give them feedback, and time seems to go a lot faster!

With all these troubleshooting suggestions in mind, you should be able to adapt the standalone examples from this book and rewrite them as servlets in a web application. This isn't limited to the PDF-creation examples.

In the next section, you'll put the theory into practice and make some Foobar web applications.

## 17.2 Putting the theory into practice

In your first Foobar web application, you'll reuse the course catalog and write a servlet that retrieves its outlines. You'll use the bookmarks to create an HTML form so that students can select a set of courses and create a personalized course catalog containing only the pages that are of interest to them.

### 17.2.1 A personalized course catalog

Suppose you have a large catalog. In order to save bandwidth, you don't want to serve the complete catalog to every individual customer: You want to provide a means so that the customer can select parts of the catalog.

If you apply this example to the course catalog you created in section 14.4, you can make an HTML form based on the bookmarks added to the file (see also section 13.6). A simple HTML file with such a form is shown in figure 17.7.

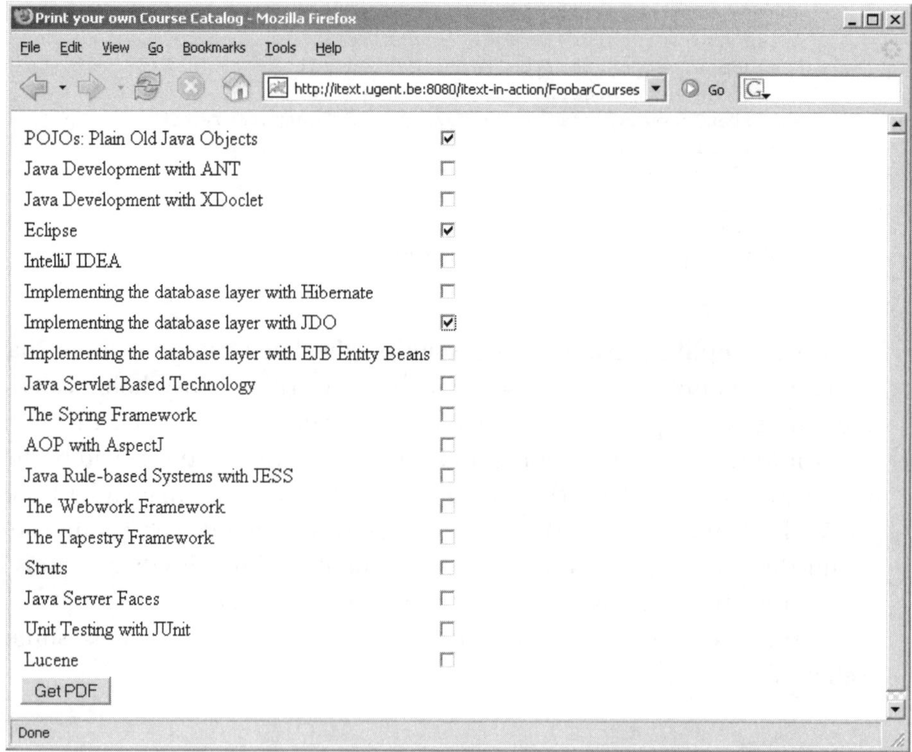


**Figure 17.7 A list of courses extracted from the bookmarks of the course catalog**

This HTML page is generated in the `doGet()` method of a servlet:

```
/* chapter17/FoobarCourses.java */
PdfReader reader = new PdfReader(resource);
List list = SimpleBookmark.getBookmark(reader);
Map bookmark;
stream.print("<html>\n\t<head>\n\t\t<title>Print your
➥ own Course Catalog</title>\n\t</head>\n\t<body>");
stream.print(msg);
stream.print("<form method=\"POST\"><table>");
int p = 0;
for (Iterator i = list.iterator(); i.hasNext(); ) {
  bookmark = (Map) i.next();
  stream.print("<tr><td>");
  stream.print((String)bookmark.get("Title"));
  stream.print(
    "</td><td><input type=\"Checkbox\" name=\"page\" value=\""
    + (++p));
  stream.print("\"></td>");
}
stream.print(
  "</table><input type=\"Submit\" value=\"Get PDF\"></form>
  ➥ \n\t</body>\n</html>");
```

The code is straightforward and assumes that every bookmark entry corresponds with one page. When you click the button, the servlet's `POST` action is triggered. Three courses are selected in figure 17.7. The result is shown in figure 17.8: a PDF document with only three pages—the pages with the description of the selected courses.

The servlet's `doPost()` method contains code from chapter 2:

```
/* chapter13/FoobarCourses.java */
String[] pages = request.getParameterValues("page");      <-- Get parameters
StringBuffer selection = new StringBuffer();                  entered by student
if (pages.length == 0) {
  response.setContentType("text/html");
  makeHtml(response.getOutputStream(),                     Select at least
  "You must at least choose one!");                        one course
  return;
}
selection.append(pages[0]);
for (int i = 1; i < pages.length; i++) {
  selection.append(",");                                    Compose select
  selection.append(pages[i]);                               string
}
PdfReader reader = new PdfReader(resource);
reader.selectPages(selection.toString());                   Repeat code
int p = reader.getNumberOfPages();                          from chapter 2
Document document = new Document();
```

```
ByteArrayOutputStream baos = new ByteArrayOutputStream();
PdfCopy copy = new PdfCopy(document, baos);
document.open();
for (int i = 0; i < p; ) {
  i++;
  copy.addPage(copy.getImportedPage(reader, i));
}
copy.setViewerPreferences(PdfWriter.PageModeUseThumbs);
document.close();
response.setHeader("Expires", "0");
response.setHeader(
  "Cache-Control", "must-revalidate, post-check=0, pre-check=0");
response.setHeader("Pragma", "public");
response.setContentType("application/pdf");
response.setContentLength(baos.size());
ServletOutputStream out = response.getOutputStream();
baos.writeTo(out);
out.flush();
```

**Repeat code from chapter 2**

**Send PDF to browser**

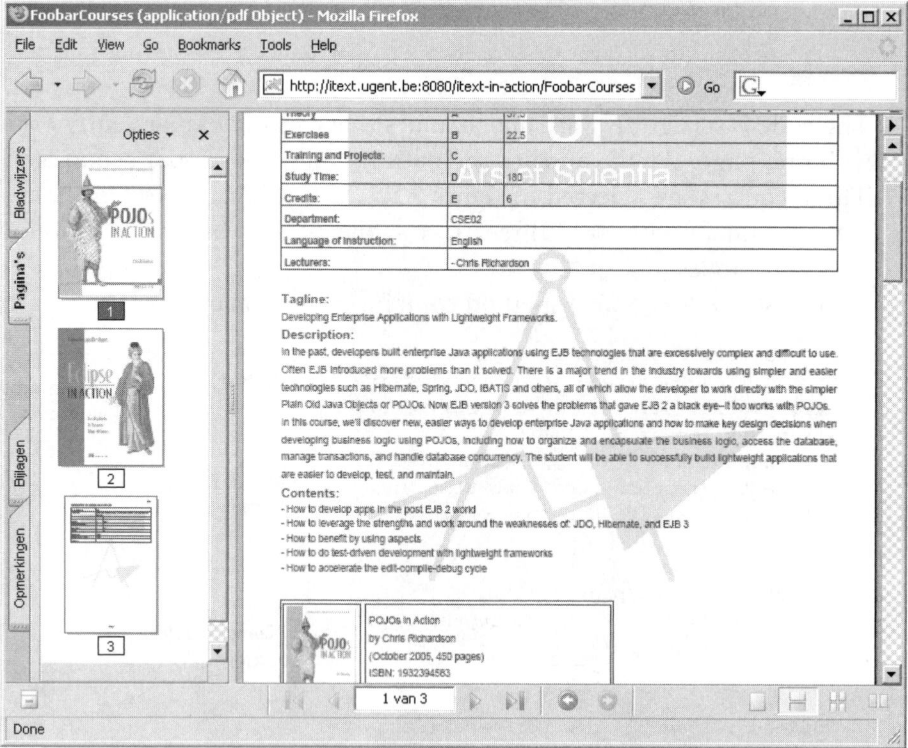


Figure 17.8 A PDF file with a selection of pages

A useful exercise would be to adapt the example so that it uses `PdfCopy` instead of `PdfStamper`. Or you could take any other standalone example from this book and integrate it into a servlet.

Now that students can create their own personalized course catalog, you want to give them the means to subscribe. For the following example, I was inspired by the European Credit Transfer System (ECTS). This is a system that allows students who are enrolled in one university to take courses from another educational institution, provided there's a learning agreement. In the next section, you'll create a learning agreement form in a standalone example. You'll put this form online and write a JSP file that accepts an FDF file and retrieves the fields that were filled in by the student.

### 17.2.2 Creating a learning agreement form

Note that the form you'll create in the next example isn't the official ECTS document. I removed some of the fields that have to be filled in by the institutions, and I added an extra field that lets you add a letter of recommendation. See figure 17.9.

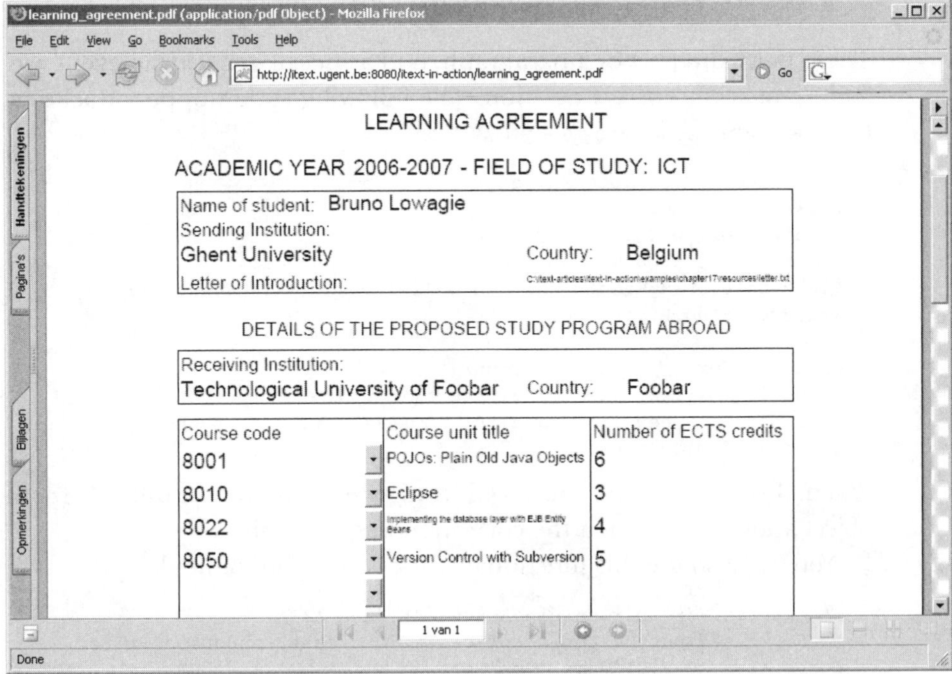


**Figure 17.9 An example of a learning agreement form**

In chapter 15, I told you that creating such a form is typically done in the full Acrobat application, but I used iText to create it because I want to illustrate interesting functionality that wasn't discussed in the chapters on forms:

- Using a special event class to add fields
- Using JavaScript to fill in fields automatically
- Using a text field with the option `FILE_SELECTION`

Once we've dealt with these extra features, you'll see what happens if you submit the filled-in form to the server.

### *Using FieldPositioningEvents*

Figure 17.9 includes a line saying

```
ACADEMIC YEAR 2006-2007 - FIELD OF STUDY: ICT
```

There are two text fields in this line:

- *academic_year*—Contains *2006-2007*
- *field_of_study*—Contains the letters *ICT*

These fields are part of a paragraph, and a special generic tag event was used to add them at the correct position. The following code snippet attaches a generic tag with name `academic_year` to a `Chunk`:

```
/* chapter17/FoobarLearningAgreement.java */
PdfWriter writer =
  PdfWriter.getInstance(document,
    new FileOutputStream("learning_agreement.pdf"));
FieldPositioningEvents fpe = new FieldPositioningEvents();
writer.setPageEvent(fpe);
...
Chunk academic_year = new Chunk("                    ");
academic_year.setGenericTag("academic_year");
Paragraph p = new Paragraph(30, "ACADEMIC YEAR ", font);
p.add(academic_year);
```

When iText renders the `Chunk` with the generic tag, the `FieldPositioningEvents` object adds a text field at the corresponding position.

You can also use this functionality for other types of fields:

```
/* chapter17/FoobarLearningAgreement.java */
PdfFormField pushbutton = PdfFormField.createPushButton(writer);
pushbutton.setFieldName("PushMe");
pushbutton.setWidget(
  new Rectangle(0, 0), PdfAnnotation.HIGHLIGHT_PUSH);
```

```
pushbutton.setAction(PdfAction.createSubmitForm(
  "learning_agreement.jsp", null, 0));
fpe.addField("pushMe", pushbutton);;
...
Chunk submit = new Chunk("    Click to submit     ");
submit.setGenericTag("pushMe");
p = new Paragraph(submit);
p.setAlignment(Element.ALIGN_CENTER);
document.add(p);
```

But in this case you first have to register the field to the event. If you scroll to the bottom of the page, you see a pushbutton field with the text *Click to submit*.

Note that if you hadn't registered a field named pushMe, a text field would be added. Now the pushbutton with the name PushMe and the URL learning_agreement.jsp is added because the name of the generic tag corresponds with the name of a field that was registered to the field-positioning object.

This field-positioning class also implements the `PdfPCellEvent` interface. This is even more interesting because you can use it to create a field that fits exactly inside a table cell. This means you don't have to write your own `cellLayout()` method. The following code snippet adds a text field named student_name; the widget rectangle corresponds exactly with the border of the cell:

```
/* chapter17/FoobarLearningAgreement.java */
cell.setCellEvent(
  new FieldPositioningEvents(writer, "student_name"));
```

The code to add the table where the student can fill in the courses that are part of the learning agreement adds a bit more complexity:

```
/* chapter17/FoobarLearningAgreement.java */
table = new PdfPTable(3);
table.setTableEvent(new FoobarLearningAgreement());
table.getDefaultCell().setBorder(PdfPCell.RIGHT);
table.addCell("Course code");
table.addCell("Course unit title");
table.getDefaultCell().setBorder(PdfPCell.NO_BORDER);
table.addCell("Number of ECTS credits");
PdfFormField[] lines = new PdfFormField[16];
FieldPositioningEvents kid;
TextField combo;
PdfFormField comboField;
for (i = 0; i < 16; i++) {
  lines[i] = PdfFormField.createEmpty(writer);
  lines[i].setFieldName("course_" + i);
  cell = new PdfPCell();
  cell.setFixedHeight(22);
  cell.setBorder(PdfPCell.RIGHT);
```

**Create 16 parent fields**

```
    combo = new TextField(writer, new Rectangle(0, 0), "code");
    combo.setChoices(new String[]{});
    comboField = combo.getComboField();
    comboField.setAdditionalActions(PdfName.K,
      PdfAction.javaScript("updateCourse(event);", writer));
    kid = new FieldPositioningEvents(lines[i], comboField);
    kid.setPadding(0.5f);
    cell.setCellEvent(kid);
    table.addCell(cell);
    cell = new PdfPCell();
    cell.setFixedHeight(22);
    cell.setBorder(PdfPCell.RIGHT);
    kid = new FieldPositioningEvents(writer, lines[i], "name");
    kid.setPadding(0.5f);
    cell.setCellEvent(kid);
    table.addCell(cell);
    cell = new PdfPCell();
    cell.setFixedHeight(22);
    cell.setBorder(PdfPCell.NO_BORDER);
    kid = new FieldPositioningEvents(writer, lines[i], "credits");
    kid.setPadding(0.5f);
    cell.setCellEvent(kid);
    table.addCell(cell);
  }
  document.add(table);
  for (i = 0; i < 16; i++) {
    writer.addAnnotation(lines[i]);
  }
```

**Create combo box as child**

**Create field-positioning event**

**Padding for field position**

**Add event to cell**

**Add child named name**

**Add child named credits**

The previous code snippet creates 16 parent fields: course_0 to course_15. Three children are added to each of these fields in the `for` loop:

- "code" is a combo box without any options. If an option is changed, a JavaScript method is called. The field is added with a field-positioning event that is created with the parent field and a child field. When the event is triggered, the child is added to the parent.
- "name" is added to the parent in an event. The event creates the text field.
- "credits" is added to the parent in an event. The event creates the text field.

The fact that you add a combo box without options is odd. If you look at figure 17.9, you see that at least the combo boxes course_0.code to course_3.code contain different course numbers. These values aren't added when you create the combo box, but are added by JavaScript code that is executed when the document is opened.

### *Using JavaScript to manipulate fields*

In this example, I've added a big chunk of JavaScript code. The first part of this code sample reads the data for the course fields from the CSV file courses.csv. Arrays are created with all the course codes, names, and credits. The `items` object contains a comma-separated list with all the possible codes, starting with an empty string.

You loop over the 16 fields in the form. You set the items for all the combo boxes, change some properties of the name fields, and set default values:

```
/* chapter17/FoobarLearningAgreement.java */
StringBuffer js = new StringBuffer(
  "var code = new Array();\nvar name = new Array();\n"
  + "var credits = new Array();\n");
StringBuffer items = new StringBuffer("''");
BufferedReader reader =
  new BufferedReader(new FileReader("../resources/courses.csv"));
String line;
float pos;
int i = 0;
while ((line = reader.readLine()) != null) {
  StringTokenizer js_courses = new StringTokenizer(line, ";");
  line = js_courses.nextToken();
  items.append(", '").append(line).append("'");
  js.append("code[").append(i).append("] = '");
  js.append(line).append("';\n");
  js.append("name[").append(i).append("] = '");
  js.append(js_courses.nextToken()).append("';\n");
  js.append("credits[").append(i).append("] = '");
  js.append(js_courses.nextToken()).append("';\n");
  i++;
}
reader.close();
js.append("for (i = 0; i < 16; i++) {\n");
js.append("  f = this.getField('course_' + i + '.code');\n");
js.append("  f.setItems([").append(items.toString());
js.append("]);\n");
js.append("  f = this.getField('course_' + i + '.name');\n");
js.append("  f.textSize = 0;\n");
js.append("  f.multiline = true;\n");
js.append("};\n");
js.append("this.getField('academic_year').value = '2006-2007';");
js.append("this.getField('field_of_study').value = 'ICT';");
js.append("this.getField('student_name').setFocus();");
js.append("function updateCourse(event) {\n");
js.append("  target = event.target.name;\n");
js.append("  parent = target.substring(0, target.length - 5);\n");
js.append("  for (c = 0; c < code.length; c++) {\n");
js.append("    if (event.value == code[c]) {\n");
js.append(
  "      this.getField(parent + '.name').value = name[c];");
```

```
js.append(
  "        this.getField(parent + '.credits').value = credits[c];");
js.append("    }\n");
js.append("  }\n");
js.append("  this.getField(parent + '.name').setFocus();");
js.append("}\n");
writer.addJavaScript(js.toString());
```

The previous code snippet includes the JavaScript function `updateCourse()`. It's triggered when the value of the combo box is changed. It automatically fills in the name of the course and the number of credits.

In other words, when students select a course code, they don't have to fill in the course title and number of credits; this is done automatically in the JavaScript function `updateCourse()`. As an exercise, you could add an extra row to the table with a field that calculates the total number of credits.

One more special feature shown in figure 17.9 needs further explanation. Next to the words *Letter of Introduction* is the path to a local file on my machine. Isn't this odd? What happens if you send this form to a server? Isn't the information about a file useless when you send it to a remote computer? It would be if the field containing the path wasn't a text field with the file-selection flag on.

### *Using file selection fields*

If you enroll as an exchange student in a foreign university, you need a letter written by your promoter at your own university. By adding a file-selection field to the learning agreement, students can attach a digital copy of this letter to their learning agreement.

If you set the option `FILE_SELECTION` for a text field, the text that is entered should be the pathname of a file whose contents are to be submitted as the value of the field. Because it's not user-friendly to have the end user type in this path manually, I added a bit of extra JavaScript as an additional action triggered by a mouse-up event:

```
/* chapter17/FoobarLearningAgreement.java */
TextField letter =
  new TextField(writer, new Rectangle(0, 0), "letter");
letter.setOptions(TextField.FILE_SELECTION);
PdfFormField introduction = letter.getTextField();
introduction.setAdditionalActions(PdfName.U,
   PdfAction.javaScript(
     "this.getField('letter').browseForFileToSubmit();"
     + "this.getField('receiving_institution').setFocus();",
     writer));
cell.setCellEvent(new FieldPositioningEvents(writer, introduction));
table.addCell(cell);
```

Now, when the student clicks the text field, a file-selection dialog box opens. The Acrobat JavaScript Scripting Guide says that "the path entered through the dialog is automatically assigned as the value of the text field."

It's also important to read what the PDF Reference has to say about file selection fields:

- For fields submitted in HTML Form Format, the submission uses the MIME content type multipart/form-data.
- For Forms Format Data Format (FDF) submission, the value of the V entry in the FDF field dictionary is a file specification identifying the selected file.
- XML format is not supported for file-select controls; therefore, no value is submitted in this case.

This is a chapter on using iText in web applications, so you'll submit the form as an FDF file and learn how to retrieve the string values of the fields in a JSP file.

### 17.2.3 Reading an FDF file in a JSP page

When a student submits the learning agreement form, you could save the complete FDF file on the server side for later use. Another option would be to save the data in a database. But you mustn't forget that the University of Foobar is a fictional institution, so you're just going to read the FDF file and display the data that was entered, as in figure 17.10.

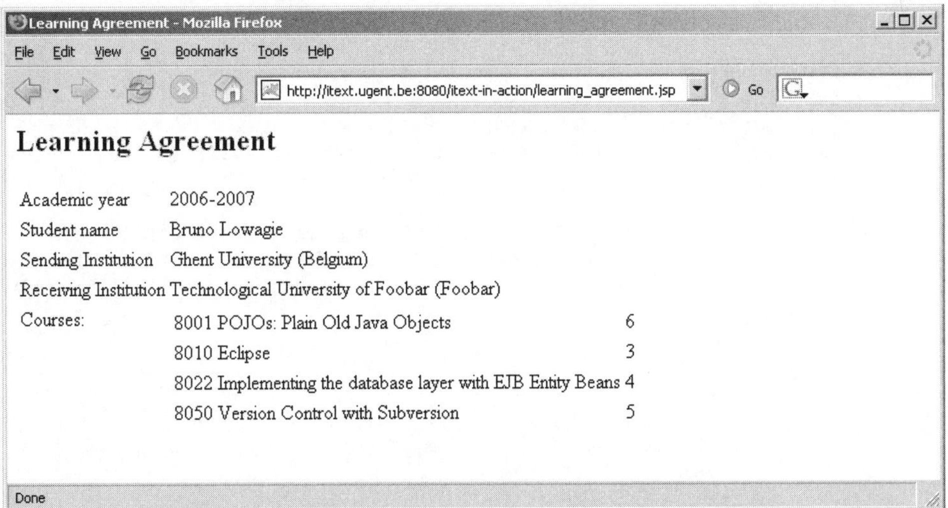


**Figure 17.10 The JSP file showing part of the data entered in the PDF form**

Let's look at the JSP code that produces this HTML file:

```
<%@ page import="java.io.*,java.util.HashMap,com.lowagie.text.pdf.*" %>
<% FdfReader reader = new FdfReader(request.getInputStream()); %>
<html>
  <head><title>Learning Agreement</title></head>
  <body>
    <h2>Learning Agreement</h2>
    <table>
      <tr>
        <td>Academic year</td>
        <td><%= reader.getFieldValue("academic_year") %></td>
      </tr>
      <tr>
        <td>Student name</td>
        <td><%= reader.getFieldValue("student_name") %></td>
      </tr>
      <tr>
        <td>Sending Institution</td>
        <td><%= reader.getFieldValue("sending_institution") %>
        (<%= reader.getFieldValue("sending_country") %>)</td>
      </tr>
      <tr>
        <td>Receiving Institution</td>
        <td><%= reader.getFieldValue("receiving_institution") %>
        (<%= reader.getFieldValue("receiving_country") %>)</td>
      </tr>
      <tr>
        <td valign="Top">Courses:</td>
        <td>
          <table>
<%
String parent;
for (int i = 0; i < 16; i++) {
  parent = "course_" + i + ".";
  if (reader.getFieldValue(parent + "code") != null) {
%>
          <tr>
           <td><%= reader.getFieldValue(parent + "code") %></td>
           <td><%= reader.getFieldValue(parent + "name") %></td>
           <td><%= reader.getFieldValue(parent + "credits") %></td>
          </tr>
<%
  }
}
%>
          </table>
        </td>
      </tr>
    </table>
  </body>
```

```
</html>
<%
  reader.close();
%>
```

Only one thing is missing in this code: It doesn't extract the letter of introduction. If you use `reader.getFieldValue("letter")`, a null value is returned. This doesn't mean the value of the field is missing in the FDF file. If you store the FDF file and inspect it, you see that a field with `/T` equal to "letter" actually has a value `/V`. But the value isn't a PDF string or a PDF name object: It's either a PDF dictionary with the file specification or an indirect reference to such a dictionary.

If you want to extract the file that was submitted using the learning agreement form, you need to look under the hood. By coincidence, this is the title of the next chapter, so let's deal with this problem then.

## 17.3 Summary

In previous chapters, you learned almost all about iText and its capacity to create and/or manipulate PDF files. Although this was interesting, one serious obstacle remained: What if you want to use your iText know-how in a web application?

It shouldn't be difficult to copy and paste the code of the book examples into a servlet and to change `new FileOutputStream("myPdf.pdf")` into `response.getOutputStream()`, but experience has taught me otherwise. This chapter has included lots of tips and tricks to avoid most of the common pitfalls.

In the second part of this chapter, you wrote more Foobar examples: one that creates a personalized course catalog on the fly, and another that creates a form that can be used to submit data in the Forms Data Format. With these examples, you've completed almost all of Laura's assignments. There is one problem left: How do you extract a file from an FDF file? To answer this question, you need to know more about PDF objects and about the way iText implements the PDF specification.

In other words, you have to look under the hood.

# 18 Under the hood

**This chapter covers**

- Under the hood of PDF: the syntax
- Under the hood of iText: design decisions
- How to access and change PDF syntax using iText

Writing a book on iText is like writing a never-ending story. Every new iText release brings new functionality. Every time Adobe publishes a new PDF specification, there's room for new features. By the time this book is published, I'll probably have to write more chapters describing new classes and new methods. That's a good sign; it proves the library is very much alive.

This book has given you a comprehensive overview of the functionality that is present in iText 1.4. The Foobar examples demonstrate pseudo real-life applications, illustrating the classes and methods dealt with in the different chapters. The most important functionality has been discussed in depth, but I've also tried to pay attention to some of the more specialized features. When it wasn't possible to go into detail, I've referred you to other sources (the Javadocs, the PDF Reference, online information, and so forth).

In this final chapter, I'll give you a glimpse of what's under the hood of iText.

## 18.1 Inside iText and PDF

On different occasions, I've talked about the strengths of iText:

- In chapter 2, I talked about the architecture of the library—how it combines ease of use with speed.
- In chapter 6, I discussed the most important building blocks: the table classes.
- In chapter 12, I explained how you can use iText in your Swing applications using `PdfGraphics2D`.
- In chapter 16, you learned how to use forms as a template.
- In chapter 17, you saw that iText is an ideal library if you want to create PDF documents for the Web.

In the future, you'll probably see new functionality appear. Support for XML Forms Architecture (XFA) has just been added; maybe better PDF/A support is next. This is just one of the many opportunities that lie ahead for the developers of iText.

### 18.1.1 Factors of success

Different factors make iText a successful library. First, consider the many working hours Paulo Soares has spent writing new functionality for iText. I'm the initial developer of iText, but Paulo is the developer who turned iText the library into iText the product, a piece of highly commercial Free/Open Source Software. Note that I don't see any contradiction in the previous sentence: You can use iText for free, and that makes it a commercially interesting product for you. iText is integrated into many other commercial products and applications (Eclipse/BIRT, JasperReports, ICEbrowser, and so on).

Although Paulo has become iText's main developer, I took up the task of writing the documentation. I think this is a second factor for success that is often underestimated by developers: A good product deserves good documentation. That's what iText users keep telling me, and I won't contradict them.

But there's a third factor. It's rather technical and low-level, but this book wouldn't be complete without it. One of the basic strengths of iText is that it's highly extensible. Once you know how iText works internally, it's relatively easy to implement new functionality that is introduced in the PDF Reference. In this chapter, I'll give you a concise overview of what makes iText work internally, technically, at the lowest level. I'll talk about the file structure of a PDF document and about the PDF objects that compose a PDF document.

### 18.1.2 The file structure of a PDF document

In chapter 2, you wrote a simple PDF file saying "Hello World" to the `System.out`. We had a short discussion about the content stream of a page, based on listing 2.2. This was a small fragment of a PDF file. If you take a closer look at the complete file, you can distinguish four parts:

- *The header*—Discussed in section 2.1.3. It specifies the PDF version and contains a comment section that ensures that the file's content is treated as binary content.
- *The body*—Contains the PDF objects that make up the document: pages, outlines, annotations, and so on. We'll discuss the *basic types* of PDF objects in the next section.
- *The cross-reference table*—Contains information that allows random access to the *indirect objects* in the body.
- *The trailer*—Gives the location of the cross-reference table and of certain special objects in the body of the file.

A PDF consumer such as Adobe Reader starts reading the file at the end. Listing 2.2 was only a small snippet of the uncompressed "Hello World" example. Listing 18.1 shows the complete file. Note that I changed the indentation to make the file more readable. Don't do this with a real PDF file; you'll soon learn that doing so corrupts the file.

**Listing 18.1 A complete PDF file**

```
%PDF-1.1
%âãÏÓ
2 0 obj <</Length 55>>stream
q
BT
36 806 Td
0 -18 Td
/F1 12 Tf
(Hello World)Tj
ET
Q
endstream
endobj
4 0 obj
<< /Type/Page /Contents 2 0 R /Parent 3 0 R /Resources <<
    /ProcSet [/PDF /Text /ImageB /ImageC /ImageI]
    /Font<</F1 1 0 R>>
  >> /MediaBox[0 0 595 842]
>>
endobj
1 0 obj
<< /Type/Font /BaseFont/Helvetica /Subtype/Type1
   /Encoding/WinAnsiEncoding
>>
endobj
3 0 obj
<< /Count 1 /Type/Pages /Kids[4 0 R] >>
endobj
5 0 obj
<< /Type/Catalog /Pages 3 0 R >>
endobj
6 0 obj
<<
  /CreationDate(D:20060210143110+01'00')
  /Producer(iText 1.4 \(by lowagie.com\))
  /ModDate(D:20060210143110+01'00')
>>
endobj
xref
0 7
0000000000 65535 f
0000000273 00000 n
0000000015 00000 n
0000000360 00000 n
0000000117 00000 n
0000000410 00000 n
0000000454 00000 n
```

File header

File body

Cross-reference table

```
trailer
<<
  /ID
    [<64003e8594bfd3db6dd3d28867eac68b>
     <d24e67314073f6c8ef1700036dd6f22e>]
  /Root 5 0 R
  /Size 7
  /Info 6 0 R
>>
startxref
635
%%EOF
```

**File trailer**

Now, let's pretend you're a PDF consumer: Let's start reading this file at the end.

### *The file trailer*

The last line of each PDF file (including the one shown in listing 18.1) should contain the end-of-file marker `%EOF`. The two preceding lines contain the keyword `startxref` and the byte offset of the cross-reference table—that is, the position of the word `xref` counted from the start of the file.

The trailer begins with the keyword `trailer`, followed by the *trailer dictionary*. In the "Hello World" example, the first entry of this dictionary is a *file identifier*. The `/Size` entry shows the total number of entries in the file's cross-reference table. There are two references to special dictionaries in the body: The `/Root` entry refers to the *catalog dictionary* and the `/Info` entry to the *information dictionary*. We discussed this dictionary in section 2.1.3; it contains PDF-specific metadata.

Other possible entries in the trailer dictionary are the `/Encrypt` key, which is required if the document is encrypted, and the `/Prev` key, which is present only if the file has more than one cross-reference section. If you want to see an example of a PDF file with two cross-reference tables, run the following code:

```
/* chapter18/HelloWorld.java */
PdfReader reader = new PdfReader("HelloWorld.pdf");
PdfStamper stamper = new PdfStamper(reader,
  new FileOutputStream("updated.pdf"), '\0', true);
PdfContentByte cb = stamper.getOverContent(1);
cb.beginText();
cb.setFontAndSize(BaseFont.createFont(
  BaseFont.HELVETICA, BaseFont.WINANSI, BaseFont.EMBEDDED), 12);
cb.showTextAligned(Element.ALIGN_LEFT, "Hello People", 36, 770, 0);
cb.endText();
stamper.close();
```

At first sight, this looks like a typical `PdfStamper` example from chapter 2. The only difference is that you use extra parameters to create the stamper object. The binary null (`'\0'`) ensures that the PDF version of the original PDF file won't be changed. The `boolean` value indicates whether the original file should be appended (true) or updated (false). This example tells iText to preserve the original file; the extra content is added at the end of the file after the original end-of-file marker.

When you open the file created with this code snippet in a text editor, you see that the first part of the file is an exact copy of listing 18.1. Instead of replacing the original objects, an extra part is added (see listing 18.2).

**Listing 18.2 The part that is appended to listing 18.1 by `PdfStamper`**

```
...     <- Paste listing 18.1 here
7 0 obj
<</Type/Font/BaseFont/Helvetica/Subtype/Type1
  /Encoding/WinAnsiEncoding>>
endobj
8 0 obj <</Length 2>>stream
q
endstream
endobj
9 0 obj <</Length 59>>stream
Q
q
BT
/Xi0 12 Tf
1 0 0 1 36 770 Tm
(Hello People)Tj
ET
Q
endstream
endobj
4 0 obj<< Type/Page /Contents[8 0 R 2 0 R 9 0 R]
  /Parent 3 0 R /Resources <<
    /ProcSet [/PDF/Text/ImageB/ImageC/ImageI]
    /Font<</F1 1 0 R/Xi0 7 0 R>>
  >> /MediaBox[0 0 595 842]
>>
endobj
6 0 obj<<
  /CreationDate(D:20060210153542+01'00')
  /Producer(iText 1.4 \(by lowagie.com\)
  /ModDate(D:20060210153542+01'00')>>
endobj
xref
0 1
```

Appended body

Appended cross-reference table

```
0000000000 65535 f
4 1
0000001162 00000 n
6 4
0000001341 00000 n
0000000921 00000 n
0000001008 00000 n
0000001056 00000 n
trailer
<</Prev 635/Root 5 0 R/Size 10/Info 6 0 R>>
startxref
1522
%%EOF
```

**Appended cross-reference table**

**Appended trailer**

The structure of the original file is kept intact, but an extra body part, cross-reference table, and trailer are appended. The value of the `/Prev` entry points at the original `startxref`.

**NOTE** There's usually no reason why you'd need to be able to restore the original file. That's why `PdfStamper` sets the append mode to false by default. You're obliged to use the append mode only when your original document contains a digital signature (see section 16.3.4). If you use `PdfStamper` to update the original revision of the document, the signature is made invalid (see figure 16.11).

Looking at the file body in both listings, you see that the objects aren't ordered by number. In listing 18.1, the object order is 2, 4, 1, 3, 5, 6. In listing 18.2, the order is 7, 8, 9, 4, 6. To a PDF consumer, the object order doesn't make any difference. What matters is the cross-reference table.

### *The cross-reference table*

The cross-reference table stores the information to locate every indirect object in the body. For reasons of performance, a PDF consumer doesn't read the entire file. Imagine a document with 10,000+ pages. If you ask to see the last page, the consumer doesn't have to know what's inside the 9,999 previous pages. It can use the cross-reference table to find the requested page in no time.

The cross-reference table contains two types of lines:

- *Lines with two numbers*—For instance, `0 7` means the next line is about object 0 in a series of 7 consecutive objects. In listing 18.2, `6 4` means the next 4 lines represent objects 6, 7, 8, and 9.

- *Lines with exactly 20 bytes*—A 10-digit number represents the byte offset; a 5-digit number is used for the generation number of the object. If these numbers are followed by the keyword `n`, the object is in use. Otherwise, the keyword `f` is present, meaning the object is free. These three parts are separated by a space character and end with a 2-byte end-of-line sequence.

The first entry in the table is always free and has a generation number of 65,535. Except for this 0 object, all objects in the cross-reference table initially have generation number 0. You won't see objects with another generation number when using iText.

The objects referred to in the cross-reference table are called *indirect*. They can be referred to by other objects using their *label*: the object number and its generation number. If you look at the trailer dictionary, you see that the catalog dictionary is referred to with the indirect reference `5 0 R`. An indirect reference doesn't always point to a dictionary; there are other types of objects.

### 18.1.3 Basic PDF objects

All PDF objects in iText are derived from the abstract class `PdfObject`. The `PdfIndirectObject` and `PdfIndirectReference` classes are special; they can only be created internally by iText.

All the other objects can be boiled down to one of the eight types listed in Table 18.1; see also appendix A.9. This table shows the mapping between the eight basic PDF objects (see the PDF Reference sections 3.2.1–3.2.8) and the corresponding subclass of `PdfObject` in iText.

**Table 18.1 Overview of the basic PDF objects**

| PDF object | iText object | Description |
|---|---|---|
| Boolean | `PdfBoolean` | This type is similar to the `boolean` type in programming languages and can be true or false. |
| Numeric object | `PdfNumber` | There are two types of numeric objects: integer and real. You've used them frequently to define coordinates, font sizes, and so on. |
| String | `PdfString` | String objects can be written two ways:<br>(1) As a sequence of literal characters enclosed in parentheses ( ).<br>(2) As hexadecimal data enclosed in angle brackets < >. |
| Name | `PdfName` | A name object is an atomic symbol uniquely defined by a sequence of characters. You've been using names as keys for dictionaries, to define a destination on a PDF page, and so on. |

*continued on next page*

**Table 18.1 Overview of the basic PDF objects** *(continued)*

| PDF object | iText object | Description |
|---|---|---|
| Array | `PdfArray` | An array is a one-dimensional collection of objects, arranged sequentially: for instance, the coordinates of a rectangle: `[ llx lly urx ury ]`. |
| Dictionary | `PdfDictionary` | A dictionary is an associative table containing pairs of objects, known as dictionary entries. We'll discuss them in more detail later. |
| Stream | `PdfStream` | Like a string object, a stream is a sequence of bytes. The main difference is that a PDF consumer reads a string entirely, whereas a stream can be read incrementally. Strings are generally used for small parts of data and streams for large amounts of data. |
| Null object | `PdfNull` | This type is similar to the null object in programming languages. Setting the value of a dictionary entry to null is equivalent to omitting the entry. |

You used these objects frequently in the previous chapters:

- `PdfAction`, `PdfOutline`, and `PdfLayer` are only a few of the many subclasses of the `PdfDictionary` object.
- `PdfDate` extends `PdfString` because a date is a special type of string.
- `PdfRectangle` is a special type of `PdfArray` because it's an array of four values: `[llx,lly,urx,ury]`.

When new PDF objects are introduced in the PDF Reference, a new subclass of one of these basic objects can be created in iText. In section 15.1.2, you saw that a `PdfAnnotation` is a special type of dictionary. You learned that if you want to use a specific annotation type that is in the PDF Reference but not yet supported in iText, you can create your own annotation using the methods inherited from the `PdfDictionary` object. This makes iText a highly extensible library.

The basic types of PDF objects are useful when you create a new PDF file, but in the next sections you'll see why they're also important when reading an existing PDF.

### 18.1.4 Climbing up the object tree

By reading the trailer and retrieving the position of every object in the body from the cross-reference table, you can climb up the object tree and see what's inside the PDF.

In chapter 2, you used the method `PdfReader.getInfo()` to get a `HashMap` with keys and values. This was a convenience method. In the next example, you'll learn how to get the information dictionary as a `PdfDictionary` object. You use the `PdfLister` class to list the contents of the different objects. This class displays PDF objects in a more or less human-readable way:

```
/* chapter18/ClimbTheTree.java */
PrintStream list = new PrintStream(new FileOutputStream("objects.txt"));
PdfLister lister = new PdfLister(new PrintStream(list));
PdfDictionary trailer = reader.getTrailer();          | Get and list trailer
lister.listDict(trailer);                             |
PdfIndirectReference info =                                 | Get indirect reference
  (PdfIndirectReference)trailer.get(PdfName.INFO);          | to information
lister.listAnyObject(info);                      Show information dictionary
lister.listAnyObject(reader.getPdfObject(info.getNumber()));  <-
```

This sample retrieves the indirect reference of the information dictionary with the method `get(PdfName.INFO)`. An object of type `PRIndirectReference` is returned. This is a subclass of `PdfIndirectReference` that is used by `PdfReader`.

The `PdfLister` prints its value as `28 0 R`. You use the reader to get the object with number 28:

```
<<
/CreationDate (D:20060215100658+01'00')
/Producer (iText 1.4 (by lowagie.com))
/ModDate (D:20060215100658+01'00')
>>
```

This is an alternative (more technical) way to get the metadata from a PDF file. Observe that `PdfLister` unescapes all PDF strings to make them human-readable.

Note that iText uses the inner classes `PdfWriter.PdfTrailer`, `PdfDocument.PdfInfo`, and `PdfDocument.PdfCatalog` in the creation process of a PDF file. When iText is reading a PDF, these objects are returned as plain `PdfDictionary` objects.

### *The catalog dictionary*

You can retrieve the catalog dictionary in a similar way using the method `get(PdfName.ROOT)`, or you can use the `getCatalog()` method:

```
/* chapter18/ClimbTheTree.java */
PdfDictionary root = reader.getCatalog();
lister.listDict(root);
```

The catalog dictionary can contain references to the viewer preferences, page labels, the AcroForm, XMP metadata, and so on. You can retrieve all these extra entries with iText, but none of them are present in this example. When you look at the output of the lister, you see only three entries: the dictionary's type, a reference to the outline tree, and a reference to the pages tree:

```
<<
/Type /Catalog
/Outlines 9 0 R
/Pages 4 0 R
>>
```

In the following code snippets, we'll examine the outline and the pages dictionary. Consult the PDF Reference if you want to know more about the syntax used for other entries.

### Retrieving the bookmarks

The *outline tree* is a dictionary that keeps a count of the bookmarks. It also refers to the first and last objects in the bookmark list. You can retrieve the outline dictionary through `/Outlines` in the catalog dictionary. Its value is an indirect reference (`9 0 R`):

```
/* chapter18/ClimbTheTree.java */
PdfDictionary outlines = (PdfDictionary)reader.getPdfObject(
  ((PdfIndirectReference)root.get(PdfName.OUTLINES)).getNumber());
lister.listDict(outlines);
PdfObject first = reader.getPdfObject(
  ((PdfIndirectReference)outlines.get(PdfName.FIRST)).getNumber());
lister.listAnyObject(first);
```

The outline tree looks like this:

```
<<
/Count 17
/Type /Outlines
/Last 21 0 R
/First 10 0 R
>>
```

This example lists only the first element:

```
<<
/Count 4
/Parent 9 0 R
/Dest [
1 0 R
/FitH
806
]
/Last 14 0 R
/Title (1. To the Universe:)
/First 11 0 R
/Next 15 0 R
>>
```

The title of this bookmark is "1. To the Universe." The destination is the page described in object 1 (`1 0 R`). Keep this number in mind! The zoom factor is set to fit horizontally at the Y position 806.

The parent of this outline entry is the object with number 9; that's the number that was referred to from the catalog dictionary. This first outline entry has four children; the dictionary contains a reference to the first and the last children. You can also fetch the next outline entry.

You now have all the information needed to reconstruct the complete list of bookmarks. In section 13.4.4, you used class `SimpleBookmark` to do this. It's obvious why this class was called "simple": It hides the complexity of outline dictionaries by offering `HashMap` objects or an XML file. It also goes over the *pages dictionary* to retrieve the logical page number of the page referred to in the `/Dest` entry. Looping over the pages dictionary is what you'll do manually in the next code snippet.

#### The pages/page dictionary

The *page tree* is also defined in a dictionary. You get it the same way you retrieved the outline tree:

```
/* chapter18/ClimbTheTree.java */
PdfDictionary pages = (PdfDictionary)reader.getPdfObject(
  ((PdfIndirectReference)root.get(PdfName.PAGES)).getNumber());
lister.listDict(pages);
PdfArray kids = (PdfArray)pages.get(PdfName.KIDS);
PdfIndirectReference kid_ref;
PdfDictionary kid = null;
for (Iterator i = kids.getArrayList().iterator(); i.hasNext(); ) {
  kid_ref = (PdfIndirectReference)i.next();
  kid = (PdfDictionary)reader.getPdfObject(kid_ref.getNumber());
  lister.listDict(kid);
}
```

The *pages tree* contains the page count and the references to all the children:

```
<<
/Count 3
/Type /Pages
/Kids [
1 0 R
5 0 R
7 0 R
]
>>
```

The elements in the child array can refer to another *pages dictionary*; this is the case when the pages tree has branches (see also section 14.1.3). Or they can refer to a *page dictionary*; this is the case in this example—each element in the child array refers to a *single* page. You recognize the reference to the first page (`1 0 R`). It's the first element in the array, so now you know that the `/Dest` entry of your first outline refers to the first page.

In this example, the page dictionary for page 3 looks like this:

```
<<
/Type /Page
/Contents 8 0 R
/Parent 4 0 R
/Resources <<
  /ProcSet [ /PDF /Text /ImageB /ImageC /ImageI ]
  /Font <</F1 2 0 R>>
>>
/MediaBox [0 0 595 842]
/Rotate 90
>>
```

You recognize the page size and the rotation; this is a page in landscape. The most important entry in the resources dictionary is the reference to the font. The contents of the page are stored in a stream object with object number 8.

In the next section, you'll extract and edit the text inside this stream.

## 18.2 Extracting and editing text

Now comes the hard part: How do you retrieve the content? A stream object is a combination of a dictionary object followed by 0 or more bytes bracketed by the keywords `stream` and `endstream`.

### 18.2.1 Reading a page's content stream

The value of the `/Contents` entry can refer to different content streams, listed in a PDF array. This is typically the case if you use `PdfStamper`; iText doesn't change the content stream but adds an extra content stream before (under) and/or after (above) the existing content stream.

I must stress that this is a simple example. The `/Contents` entry is an indirect reference to a single stream object. Let's fetch the content stream of page 3. The object returned is of type `PRStream`. This is a special subclass of `PdfStream` that is used by `PdfReader`.

You can get the first part of the stream (the stream dictionary) by listing this object as a dictionary; remember that `PdfStream` is derived from `PdfDictionary`. The actual bytes of the stream can be retrieved with `PdfReader.getStreamBytes-Raw()` or `PdfReader.getStreamBytes()`. If your PDF document was generated using iText, the first method gives you the compressed content stream; the latter gives you the uncompressed stream:

```
/* chapter18/ClimbTheTree.java */
PdfIndirectReference content_ref =
  (PdfIndirectReference) kid.get(PdfName.CONTENTS);
PRStream content =                                           Get PdfStream
  (PRStream)reader.getPdfObject(content_ref.getNumber());    object
lister.listDict(content);                              <-- Show stream dictionary
byte[] contentstream = PdfReader.getStreamBytes(content);    Retrieve/show
list.println(new String(contentstream));                     stream
PRTokeniser tokenizer = new PRTokeniser(contentstream);     Loop over
while (tokenizer.nextToken()) {                              content stream
  if (tokenizer.getTokenType() == PRTokeniser.TK_STRING) {   Show all PDF
    list.println(tokenizer.getStringValue());                Strings
  }
}
```

The stream dictionary of page 3 contains two entries: `<< /Filter /FlateDecode /Length 460 >>`.

As you can see, the stream was compressed (filter `/Flatedecode`) to 460 bytes. The actual uncompressed stream looks like this:

```
0 1 -1 0 595 0 cm
q
BT
36 559 Td
0 -18 Td
/F1 12 Tf
(3. )Tj
(To the Animals:)Tj
0 -18 Td
0 -18 Td
(3.1. )Tj
(to cats and dogs:)Tj
0 -18 Td
(\(English:\) hello, \(Esperanto:\) he, alo, saluton,
➥ \(Latin:\) heu, ave, \(French:\) allô, \(Italian:\) ciao,
➥ \(German:\) hallo, he, heda, holla, \(Portuguese:\) alô,)Tj
0 -18 Td
...
ET
Q
```

With `PRTokeniser` (mind the British *s*, instead of the American *z*), you can split a PDF content stream into its most elementary parts. For this example, we're only interested in PDF strings. You filter them out, and the contents of the PDF file are written to `PrintStream`:

```
3.
To the Animals:
3.1.
to cats and dogs:
(English:) hello, (Esperanto:) he, alo, saluton, (Latin:) heu, ave,
(French:) allô, (Italian:) ciao, (German:) hallo, he, heda, holla,
(Portuguese:) alô, olá, hei, psiu, bom día, (Dutch:) hallo, dag,
(Spanish:) ola, eh, (Catalan:) au, bah, eh, ep,
(Swedish:) hej, hejsan (Danish:) hallo, dav, davs, goddag, hej,
(Norwegian:) hei; morn, (Papiamento:) halo; hallo; kí tal,
(Faeroese:) halló, hoyr, (Turkish:) alo, merhaba, (Albanian:) tungjatjeta
...
```

What you have here is a poor man's text extractor. It works well for this example, but it won't work with most PDF files that can be found in the wild. Many aspects should be taken into account if you want to use iText as a text-extraction library.

### 18.2.2 Why iText doesn't do text extraction

In the previous example, all the text was in one contiguous block. In reality, the different letters of the text can be drawn in any random order. Consider the two following examples. Both result in a file that looks like figure 18.1.

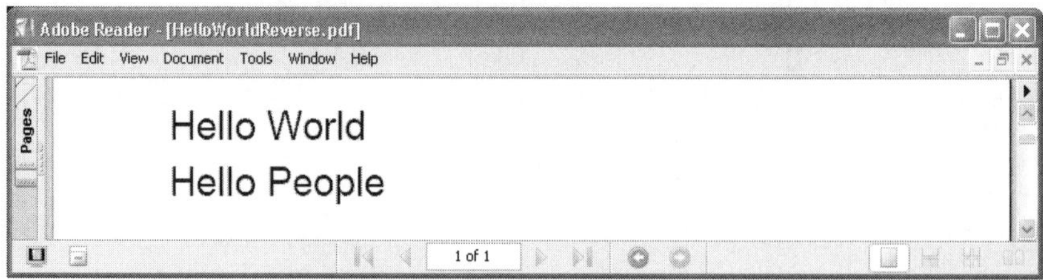


**Figure 18.1 A simple "Hello World" document**

The first example uses the code you know from chapter 4:

```
/* chapter18/HelloWorldStream.java */
PdfWriter.getInstance(document, new FileOutputStream(filename));
document.open();
document.add(new Paragraph("Hello World"));
document.add(new Paragraph("Hello People"));
```

This example gives you a PDF page that can easily be parsed using `PRTokeniser`. It returns two lines: "Hello World" and "Hello People." But PDF documents aren't always created that way. For reasons that are far beyond the scope of this book, the order in which the strings appear in the content stream can be totally different. Let's look at the second example:

```
/* chapter18/HelloWorldReverse.java */
PdfWriter writer = PdfWriter.getInstance(document,
  new FileOutputStream("HelloWorldReverse.pdf"));
document.open();
PdfContentByte cb = writer.getDirectContent();
BaseFont bf = BaseFont.createFont(
  BaseFont.HELVETICA, BaseFont.CP1252, BaseFont.NOT_EMBEDDED);
cb.beginText();
cb.setFontAndSize(bf, 12);
cb.moveText(88.66f, 367);
cb.showText("ld");
cb.moveText(-22f, 0);
cb.showText("Wor");
cb.moveText(-15.33f, 0);
cb.showText("llo");
cb.moveText(-15.33f, 0);
cb.showText("He");
cb.endText();
PdfTemplate tmp = cb.createTemplate(250, 25);
tmp.beginText();
tmp.setFontAndSize(bf, 12);
tmp.moveText(0, 7);
tmp.showText("Hello People");
tmp.endText();
cb.addTemplate(tmp, 36, 743);
```

Now, when you pass the content stream to `PRTokeniser`, four strings are returned, in this order: "ld," "Wor," "llo," and "He." The string "Hello People" is added in a `PdfTemplate`, meaning it's in the PDF file as a separate form XObject. You have to run the `PRTokeniser` on the content of this XObject too if you want the complete content.

Even if all the characters are in the right order, there may be kerning information between letters, adjusting the space between the letters so they look better (for instance, between the *ll*s of the word *Hello*). That's one aspect that should be considered and that makes it difficult to extract text from a content stream.

Another aspect is the encoding. It's possible for a PDF to have a font containing characters marked *a*, *b*, *c*, and so on, but for the shapes drawn in the PDF file for each character not to correspond with the glyphs *a*, *b*, and *c* (remember the Shavian example in chapter 8). An application can create a different encoding for each specific PDF document—for instance, in an attempt to obfuscate. More likely, the PDF-generating software does this deliberately, such as when a large font is used but all the text can be shown using only 256 different glyphs. In this case, the software picks character names at random according to the glyphs that are used.

Another possibility is that the text in the content stream consists of raw glyph indexes: the *n*th character of this font. You then have to write code that goes through the character mapping and is able to find the right letter.

Note that you'll also encounter PDF files that were created from scanned images. The content stream of each of the pages in such a document contains a reference to an `Image` XObject. You won't find a PDF string in the stream. In chapter 12, you created PDF documents with glyphs drawn by a `Graphics2D` object; again, you won't find any PDF strings. In these cases, Optical Character Recognition (OCR) is your only recourse.

If you refine the code sample, you can take some of the hurdles I just explained and extract the text from PDFs, but certainly not from every PDF file imaginable. Moreover, it's not our intention to reinvent the wheel. If you want to extract data from an existing PDF file, other tools offer this functionality—for instance, PDFBox (see pdfbox.org).

Other tools claim they can be used to edit a traditional PDF document.

### *18.2.3 Why you shouldn't use PDF as a format for editing*

A recurring remark about `PdfWriter`, `PdfCopy`, and `PdfStamper`, is that the API isn't intuitive. Why can't you just take reader objects, select pages, and then concatenate all of them using a writer? Or even better: Why can't you take the content stream of a page, look up some words, and replace them or insert extra content at that specific position?

In chapter 2, I stressed the fact that iText can be used for manipulating a PDF file, *not* for editing a PDF document. Let's find out the difference using an example that adds an extra string to the content stream. This example comes with a firm warning: do not try this at home!

```
/* chapter18/HelloWorldStream.java */
StringBuffer buf = new StringBuffer();
int pos = contentStream.indexOf("Hello World") + 11;
buf.append(contentStream.substring(0, pos));
buf.append(", Hello Sun, Hello Moon, Hello Stars, Hello Universe");
buf.append(contentStream.substring(pos));
String hackedContentStream = buf.toString();
Document document = new Document(PageSize.A6);
PdfWriter writer
  = PdfWriter.getInstance(document, new
   FileOutputStream("HelloWorldStreamHacked.pdf"));
document.open();
PdfContentByte cb = writer.getDirectContent();
cb.setLiteral(hackedContentStream);
document.close();
```

**Alter existing content stream**

**Add new content stream literally**

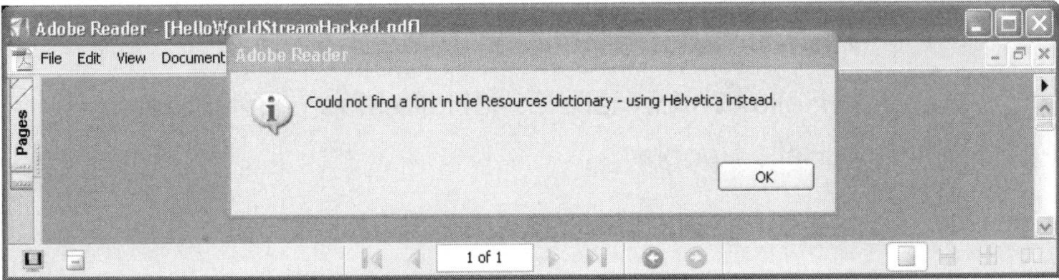


**Figure 18.2 Copying a page the wrong way**

This example demonstrates what goes wrong if you take the content stream of one page and copy it to a new PDF file. When you open the resulting file, you get at least the error shown in figure 18.2.

When you copy the content stream, you also copy references to objects that aren't in the stream. In this case, you copy a reference to a font (`/F1`), but there is no font with this name in the new PDF file.

It gets even worse if you try to copy a page that has XObjects or annotations; you have to make sure you copy all the objects the page needs. Note that iText does all this work behind the scenes—for instance, when you ask the `PdfCopy` for a `PdfImportedPage` object.

The previous code sample is a dirty hack. For argument's sake, let's hack the hack and see what happens if you use `PdfStamper` to change the content stream:

```
/* chapter18/HelloWorldStreamHack.java */
PdfReader reader = new PdfReader("HelloWorldStream.pdf");
byte[] streamBytes = reader.getPageContent(1);      <— Get content stream
StringBuffer buf = new StringBuffer();
int pos = contentStream.indexOf("Hello World") + 11;     Change content
buf.append(contentStream.substring(0, pos));                 stream
buf.append(", Hello Sun, Hello Moon, Hello Stars, Hello Universe");
buf.append(contentStream.substring(pos));
String hackedContentStream = buf.toString();
PdfStamper stamper = new PdfStamper(reader,
  new FileOutputStream("HelloWorldStreamHack.pdf"));      Set page content
reader.setPageContent(1, hackedContentStream.getBytes()); <— with PdfStamper
stamper.close();
```

I used a shortcut to get the content stream: `PdfReader.getPageContent()`. I used the corresponding setter method to replace the stream: `PdfReader.setPageContent()`. In between, I made some changes to the content. You already used these methods in section 3.3.2 to decompress a PDF file.

**Figure 18.3 A PDF document that was altered by using a hack**

After you execute this code sample, the new PDF file has the original text "Hello World" and "Hello People," but you expect the first line to be extended with ", Hello Sun, Hello Moon, Hello Stars, Hello Universe." Look at figure 18.3 to see if you succeed.

This time, no alert was triggered, the PDF syntax is correct, and the file is valid; but the document doesn't look the way you expect. The words *Hello Universe* are in the file, in the content stream of the page, but they aren't visible because they're drawn outside the page boundaries.

This is normal; PDF isn't Word, RTF, or HTML. Word, RTF, and HTML documents are interpreted by an application that defines the layout. If you change a sentence in an HTML file and it doesn't fit on one line, the text wraps, causing the layout to change.

This isn't possible in traditional PDF; the PDF syntax defines the layout. I listed the advantages of this approach (speed, reliability, and so on) in part 1, but you should consider traditional PDF to be a read-only format. This code sample does something you never should do: It changes the content of a traditional PDF file more or less manually. It's a serious misconception to think you can open a PDF file in Notepad, change some text, save the file, and expect it to be OK. This example shows that you may be able to preserve the binary streams. You may succeed in updating the cross-reference stream. But you can't expect the layout to be OK if you add text or replace one word with another.

The conclusion of this section is that you shouldn't use iText to extract or edit text. At the same time, it also aims to give you a better understanding of the Portable Document Format. There are tools that claim you can edit traditional PDF documents, and some of them work—but make sure you're aware of the limits inherent in the nature of PDF. If you need a tool to edit a traditional PDF file, you should probably reconsider your design.

This being said, you can use everything you've learned in this chapter to manipulate a PDF file. In section 18.4, you'll use the iText toolbox to make a tree view of a PDF file and to remove launch actions. You'll also write code to change the URL of a form and to retrieve a file from an FDF file. But first, let's say a word about rendering PDF.

## 18.3 Rendering PDF

We started the previous section with an example that uses the class `PRTokeniser`. This class returns tokens of different types: PDF strings, PDF names, start and end sequences of PDF arrays and PDF dictionaries, and so on. If you ever plan to write a PDF viewer, you'll have to write code that interprets all this information, translating the PDF syntax into drawing operations.

This is beyond the scope of iText. A simple search on the Internet will tell you a plethora of other tools (free as well as propriety software) can be used to view a PDF. It wasn't the intention of the iText developers to reinvent the wheel.

In general, these tools can also be used to print a PDF file.

### 18.3.1 How to print a PDF file programmatically

If you post the question "How can I print a PDF file programmatically?" on the mailing list, you can expect two kinds of answers.

- *An easy answer*—iText doesn't render PDF. The question is off-topic.
- *A difficult answer*—In some cases, you can use a workaround; in other cases, you need another tool.

Why is the second answer difficult? Java (cl)aims to be platform independent; but printing is a platform-dependent process. A printer is a device in the context of an operation system. You need a printer driver to convert the data to be printed in a form that is specific for your printer.

#### Sending PDF to the printer

If your printer understands PDF, you can send the PDF stream generated by iText to the printer directly. In a code snippet submitted to the mailing list by I. Canellos, a method `generatePdf()` creates a PDF document that is written to the output stream passed as a parameter. This output stream is a `PipedOutputStream` connected to the input stream that feeds the printer:

```
PipedInputStream pdf_in = new PipedInputStream();
PipedOutputStream pdf_out = new PipedOutputStream();
DocFlavor myFlavor = DocFlavor.INPUT_STREAM.AUTOSENSE;
pdf_in.connect(pdf_out);
Doc d = new SimpleDoc(pdf_in, myFlavor, new HashDocAttributeSet());
```

```
generatePdf(pdf_out);
PrintService[] ps =
  PrintServiceLookup.lookupPrintServices(myFlavor, null);
PrintService service =
  ServiceUI.printDialog(null, 100, 100, ps, ps[0],  myFlavor, null);
DocPrintJob dpj = service.createPrintJob();
dpj.print(d, pas);
```

You can try this solution, but it works only if you send the stream to a printer that can take PDF natively. In most cases, printer drivers expect PostScript (PS) or Printer Command Language (PCL), not PDF. You need a program that can translate PDF to PS or PCL.

Another solution that was posted on the mailing list involves the Line Printer Remote (LPR) protocol. This is a set of programs that provides printer spooling and network print-server functionality for UNIX-like systems. There is an LPR client plug-in in the iText toolbox, and you'll find an LPR class in the package `com.lowagie.tools`. Of course, this won't work on all systems.

You can also print a PDF file using a PDF viewer.

### *Using a viewer application to print a PDF*

If you've installed Adobe Reader on a Windows machine, you can open the PDF viewer from the command line using the `acrord32` command. Appendix C discusses the `/A` option that lets you open a document and specify viewer preferences. In the following code snippet, the `/p` option prints the file and the `/h` option suppresses the printer dialog:

```
String osName = System.getProperty("os.name" );
//FOR WINDOWS 95 AND 98 USE COMMAND.COM
if(osName.equals("Windows 95") || osName.equals("Windows 98")){
    Runtime.getRuntime().exec(
      "command.com /C start acrord32 /p /h" + claim.pdf);
}
//FOR WINDOWS NT/XP/2000 USE CMD.EXE
else {
    Runtime.getRuntime().exec(
      "cmd.exe start /C acrord32 /p /h" + claim.pdf);
}
```

This code snippet is integrated and slightly adapted for Mac users in the `Executable` class in the package `com.lowagie.tools`. Note that the `/A` option is documented by Adobe, but the `/p` and `/h` options are undocumented and probably unsupported by Adobe. It's also known that the Reader process keeps running after the file is printed.

Maybe it's a better idea to use Adobe Reader by addressing it with a tool like pdfp (hosted on noliturbari.com); I quote: "pdfp is a command-line batch printer that uses Adobe Reader or Acrobat via the DDE interface to print multiple PDFs to the default or (optionally) specified printer."

In the past, Adobe developed a JavaBean that could be used to view and print a PDF file, but the development of this bean was discontinued before it was fully functional.

If you're looking for an active Free/Open Source library that lets you print PDF files, you're better off with PDFBox or JPedal. Note that JPedal is a Java PDF library with GPL and proprietary versions. The GPLed software is a subset of the complete library. Other proprietary libraries and products include IceSoft's ICEPDF and Crionics' jPDF Printer. These are just products that come to mind; the list is far from complete.

A good free alternative is offered by GhostScript. GhostScript is a set of C programs that can interpret PS as well as PDF. It can convert PS to PDF and vice versa. If you don't mind writing C code, you can address GhostScript to print a PDF file programmatically.

One of the major downsides all these solutions have in common is that you need to run a program on a client machine. You don't know what printer drivers are installed on the client side. You don't know if the end user has Adobe Reader. You don't know if you can execute a program on their machine.

But people keep asking: "How can you print a PDF document on the client side of a web application?"

### 18.3.2 Printing a PDF file in a web application

If you're sure the end user is viewing the file using Internet Explorer, you can try to find an ActiveX component that can print PDF. Note that using such a component raises security as well as licensing issues. It may be safer to ask the end user to install the Adobe Reader plug-in.

In section 13.5.4, you learned how to add document-level JavaScript. You can add the following snippet of document-level JavaScript to every PDF created by your web application:

```
/* chapter18/SilentPrinting.java */
writer.addJavaScript("this.print(false);", false);
document.add(new Paragraph("Testing Silent Printing with iText"));
```

This code causes the PDF to be printed on the end user's default printer as soon as the user opens it. According to the Acrobat JavaScript Scripting Reference, the first parameter of the `print()` method is a `boolean`. If false, it suppresses the print dialog box: The document can be printed without any extra user interaction.

That's one of the reasons some people disable the JavaScript interpreter in their PDF viewer. People generally don't like it when their printer starts spitting out pages unexpectedly. In other words, this isn't exactly a good solution.

**FAQ** *Is it possible to allow printing, but not saving?* From time to time, people ask if it's possible to set the permissions of a PDF file so that the file can be printed on the client machine, but not viewed or saved. This is impossible for many reasons. You can't expect a PDF document to be rendered on a client machine without sending information about how to render it. In section 3.3.3, I explained that disabling the save button is useless. Another common question is whether you can set a permission so that a PDF can be printed only once. If you need that kind of protection for your document, you need a Digital Rights Management solution. To summarize, when people ask me if it's possible to print a file programmatically, I prefer giving the simple answer: This is beyond the scope of iText.

We've spent two sections telling you what iText can't do:

- You shouldn't extract text from a PDF using iText.
- You shouldn't use iText to edit a PDF file.
- You can't use iText to view a PDF file.
- You can't use iText to convert PDF to an image (or generate thumbnails).
- You can't use iText to print a PDF file.

In the next section, we'll return to the low-level functionality discussed in the first section of this chapter. You can achieve interesting document manipulations using low-level iText functionality.

## 18.4 Manipulating PDF files

In the first section, you climbed the object tree, but I didn't provide an image showing this tree structure. That was on purpose; I can give you something much better than an image. Open the iText toolbox, and you'll find a plug-in called TreeViewPDF that allows you to browse the object tree. Carsten Hammer is still working on this tool, but already it is beyond price for a developer manipulating low-level PDF objects.

### 18.4.1 Toolbox tools

Look at figure 18.4. You immediately recognize the file you read in the Climb-TheTree example in section 18.1.3. I opened the page tree and the outline tree nodes. The Pagesnode shows an array with three elements. The node of this last page is open, showing the entries in the page dictionary of the third page. The Content entry is selected; you can inspect the content stream in the lower pane of the plug-in.

This plug-in is useful if you want to learn more about the structure of a PDF file. Other plug-ins allow you to change the value of specific PDF objects.

For instance, there's a plug-in that lets you replace all the launch actions in a PDF file with harmless JavaScript alerts. (Remember that launch actions can launch an application on the end user's operating system.)

The original code for this plug-in was written to remove all these potentially dangerous actions from PDF files submitted to a repository by the visitors of a

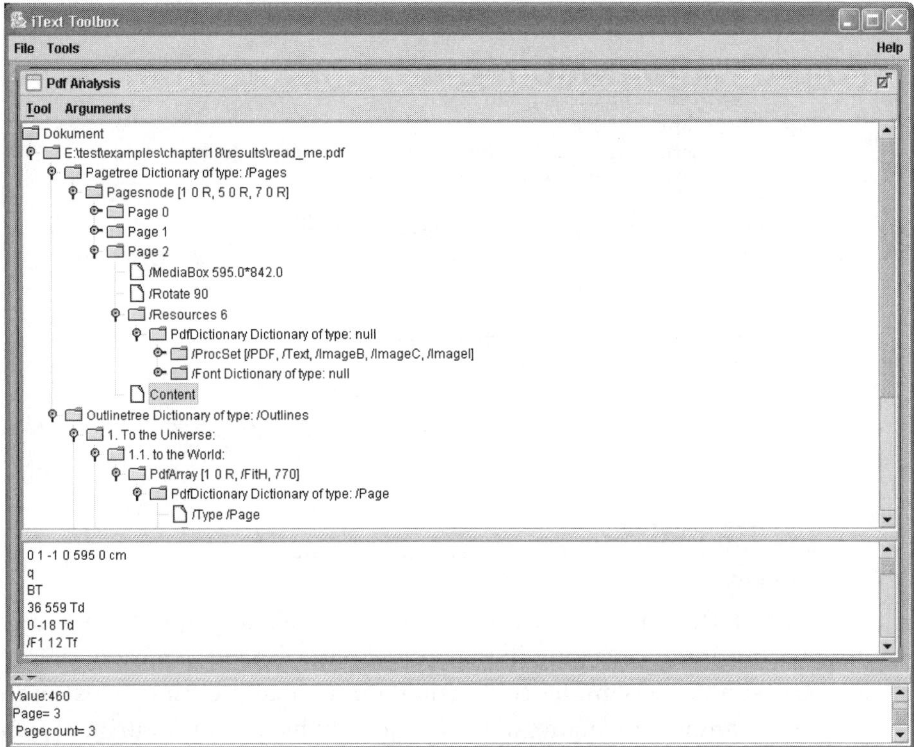


**Figure 18.4 Tree view of a PDF file**

company web site. Granted, the end user gets a warning when such an action is triggered, but you know how easy it is to click an OK button without reading the warnings listed in the dialog box. It's better to be safe than sorry. Here's the code:

```
PdfReader reader = new PdfReader(src.getAbsolutePath());
PdfObject o;
PdfDictionary d;
PdfDictionary l;
PdfName n;
for (int i = 1; i < reader.getXrefSize(); i++) {
  o = reader.getPdfObject(i);
  if (o instanceof PdfDictionary) {
    d = (PdfDictionary)o;
    o = d.get(PdfName.A);
    if (o == null) continue;
    if (o instanceof PdfDictionary) {
      l = (PdfDictionary)o;
    }
    else {
      PRIndirectReference r =(PRIndirectReference)o;
      l = (PdfDictionary)reader.getPdfObject(r.getNumber());
    }
    n = (PdfName)l.get(PdfName.S);
    if (PdfName.LAUNCH.equals(n)) {
      if (l.get(PdfName.F) != null) {
        System.out.println("Removed: " + l.get(PdfName.F));
        l.remove(PdfName.F);
      }
      if (l.get(PdfName.WIN) != null) {
       System.out.println("Removed: " + l.get(PdfName.WIN));
       l.remove(PdfName.WIN);
      }
      l.put(PdfName.S, PdfName.JAVASCRIPT);
      l.put(PdfName.JS, new PdfString(
        "app.alert(
           'Launch Application Action removed by iText');\r"));
    }
  }
}
PdfStamper stamper =
  new PdfStamper(reader, new FileOutputStream(dest));
stamper.close();
```

If you check the (growing) list of tools in the toolbox, you'll find plenty of other plug-ins (for instance, a plug-in that extracts attachments). Most of these plug-ins were based on code samples contributed on the mailing list by iText users.

More examples are always welcome, but you have to take into account that not all code samples can be turned into plug-ins. In the next section, you'll write code to complete the Foobar example you started in the previous chapter.

## 18.4.2 The learning agreement (revisited)

In section 17.2.2, you made an online form that foreign students can use to fill in a learning agreement. Clicking a pushbutton field submits the form to the server as an FDF form. Suppose other universities ask Laura if they can use this form, too. It wouldn't make sense to let them use a form that submits the data to the Technological University of Foobar. They should be able to change the URL to which the form is submitted.

### Changing the submit URL

This question arises on the mailing list now and then. Let's read the learning_agreement.pdf file you created in the previous chapter with `PdfReader` and get the reference of the `PushMe` button. A `PdfDictionary` object is returned (you created this button as a `PdfFormField`, which is a subclass of `PdfDictionary`).

Now it's up to you to get the action and change the URL:

```
/* chapter18/ChangeURL.java */
PdfReader reader =
  new PdfReader("../resources/learning_agreement.pdf");
PdfStamper stamper = new PdfStamper(reader, new
   FileOutputStream("learningagreement.pdf"));
AcroFields form = stamper.getAcroFields();
HashMap fields = form.getFields();
AcroFields.Item field = (AcroFields.Item)fields.get("PushMe");
PRIndirectReference ref =
  (PRIndirectReference)field.widget_refs.iterator().next();
PdfDictionary object =
  (PdfDictionary)reader.getPdfObject(ref.getNumber());
PdfDictionary action = (PdfDictionary)object.get(PdfName.A);
PdfDictionary file = (PdfDictionary)action.get(PdfName.F);
file.put(PdfName.F, new PdfString("[...]/agreementform.jsp"));
stamper.close();
```

To understand this example, you need to know that the name of a field action is `A`, and that the URL is a PDF string in the `F` entry of an `F` dictionary; that's the kind of information you'll find in the PDF Reference. With the PDF Reference next to you and iText as a low-level PDF tool, you can implement almost any feature you need.

Figure 18.5 shows the form with the altered URL.

To see the difference from the form created in the previous chapter, click the submit button; another URL is used.

The JSP file to which you submit the data is similar to the JSP file you used before, but now it's able to extract the file letter.txt that was uploaded to the server.

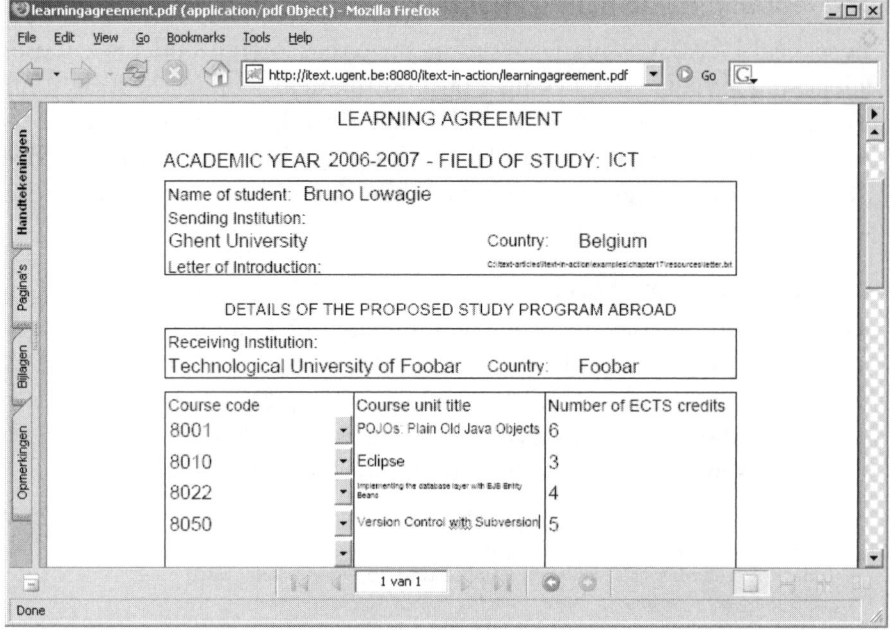


**Figure 18.5 A learning agreement form**

### *Extracting a file from an FDF*

When you click the submit button, you see the data that's been entered, including the contents of the plain-text file that was submitted (see figure 18.6).

The following code sample is simple; it assumes you're sending a file that is plain text. You should adapt it if, for instance, you want the students to upload a photograph:

```
<%
HashMap fields = reader.getFields();
PdfDictionary field = (PdfDictionary)fields.get("letter");
if (field != null) {
  PdfIndirectReference ir =
    (PRIndirectReference)field.get(PdfName.V);
  PdfDictionary filespec =
    (PdfDictionary)reader.getPdfObject(ir.getNumber());
  PdfDictionary ef = (PdfDictionary)filespec.get(PdfName.EF);
  ir = (PRIndirectReference) ef.get(PdfName.F);
  PRStream stream = (PRStream)reader.getPdfObject(ir.getNumber());
  String letter = new String(reader.getStreamBytes(stream));
%>
</tr>
```

```
<tr><td valign="Top">Letter of Introduction</td>
<td><pre>
<%= letter %>
</pre></td></tr>
<% } %>
```

Parsing an FDF file is done the same way as parsing a PDF file. You can adapt the JSP code to extract the bytes of a file that is attached to a PDF file, or you can use the plug-in I mentioned earlier.

**TOOLBOX** `com.lowagie.tools.plugins.ExtractAttachments` *(Various)* You can use this toolbox plug-in to extract file attachments. As an exercise, you can extract the attachments from the file annotations.pdf (see figure 15.3). The result is a JPG showing a fox and a dog, and a simple text file.

The plug-in has a public static method `unpackFile()`. Given a `PdfReader` instance and a `PdfDictionary` with the file specification, you can use this method to extract

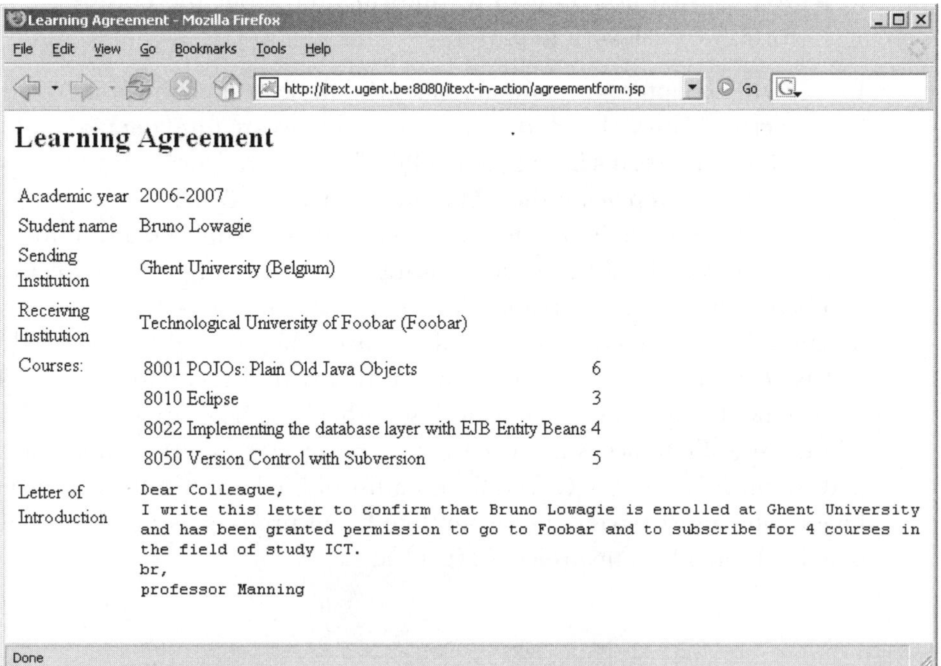


**Figure 18.6 A JSP file showing the contents of an FDF submitted to the server**

an attached file to an output path of your choice without having to open the toolbox manually.

Once you have a good understanding of PDF, you'll be able to solve lots of similar problems by writing your own iText code. Of course, it's not easy to master the Portable Document Format. The PDF Reference is about 1,200 pages long, so take your time—it's not a book you can read overnight. This chapter was meant to give you a head start.

## 18.5 Summary

Looking under the hood of PDF and iText, you should recognize a lot of the functionality discussed in previous chapters:

- We focused on the "Hello World" examples from the introduction.
- You saw how the content you added using the basic building blocks of part 2 translates into the PDF syntax discussed in part 3.
- You learned how PDF stores information about the outlines, pages, and forms we dealt with in part 4.

In a way, this chapter is a summary of this book, seen from the point of view of the PDF specialist. You've learned that some problems are fundamental and inherent to PDF; for instance, it's hard to edit a PDF file. But you've also seen that problems can be solved by replacing the right entries in a PDF dictionary.

Of course, we didn't go into much detail. If you want to know more about the PDF syntax, you should consider reading the PDF Reference. I repeat that it's a good companion for this book, and vice versa. This book helps you picture the functionality explained in the PDF Reference. I hope it's also convinced you that PDF is an interesting document format with a rich history and a bright future.

Finally, I hope you enjoy working with iText. The appendices that follow address specific topics, such as barcodes, how to sign a PDF using a smart card, and so on. In appendix G, you'll find a list of books and URLs you may want to investigate, and I started an incomplete list of projects using iText. I hope that one day I can add your project to this list.

# A Class diagrams

This appendix has been added for your convenience. It contains class diagrams that explain the relationships between several of the most important iText classes. It's important to realize that these diagrams don't provide the complete model; many attributes and methods have been omitted in order to make the diagrams presentable.

Most classes are represented in a rectangle containing three parts:

- The name of the class or interface. Sometimes the names of the superclass or the interfaces that were implemented are added in the upper-right corner.
- A (partial!) list of attributes.
- A (partial!) list of methods.

Every attribute or method name is preceded by a sign:

- A plus-sign (+) means the attribute or method is public.
- A minus-sign (-) means the attribute or method is private.
- A number or cardinality-sign (#) means the attribute or method is protected.
- A tilde (~) means the attribute or method is package protected.

A subclass is connected to its superclass by a solid line with a triangle shape on the superclass end. The relationship between a class and the interface that is implemented is represented by a dotted line with a triangle shape on the interface end.

Dependencies are illustrated using a solid line with an open arrow. The graphical representation of an aggregation is a solid line with a clear diamond shape at the end.

# A.1 PDF/RTF/HTML creation classes

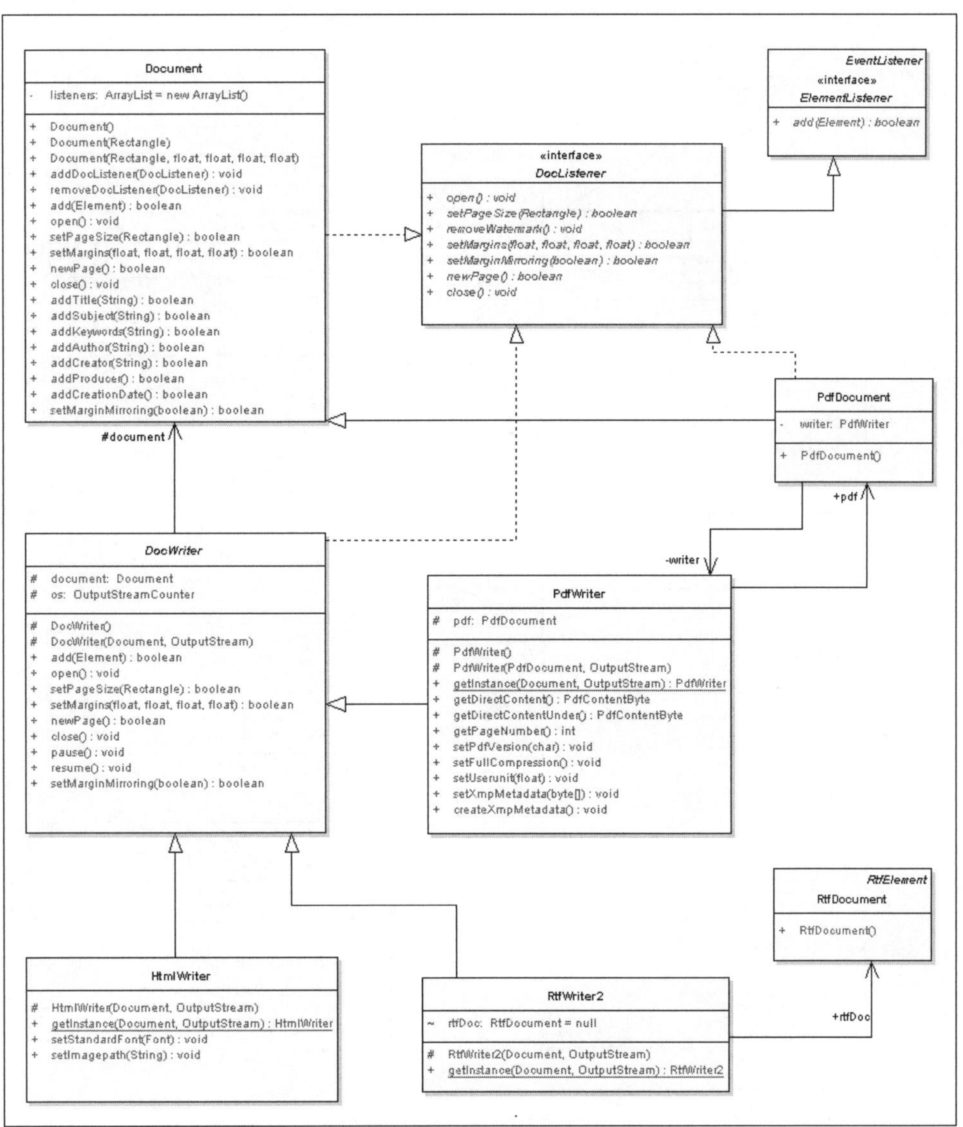


**Figure A.1 Overview of the classes discussed in section 2.1**

## A.2 PDF manipulation classes

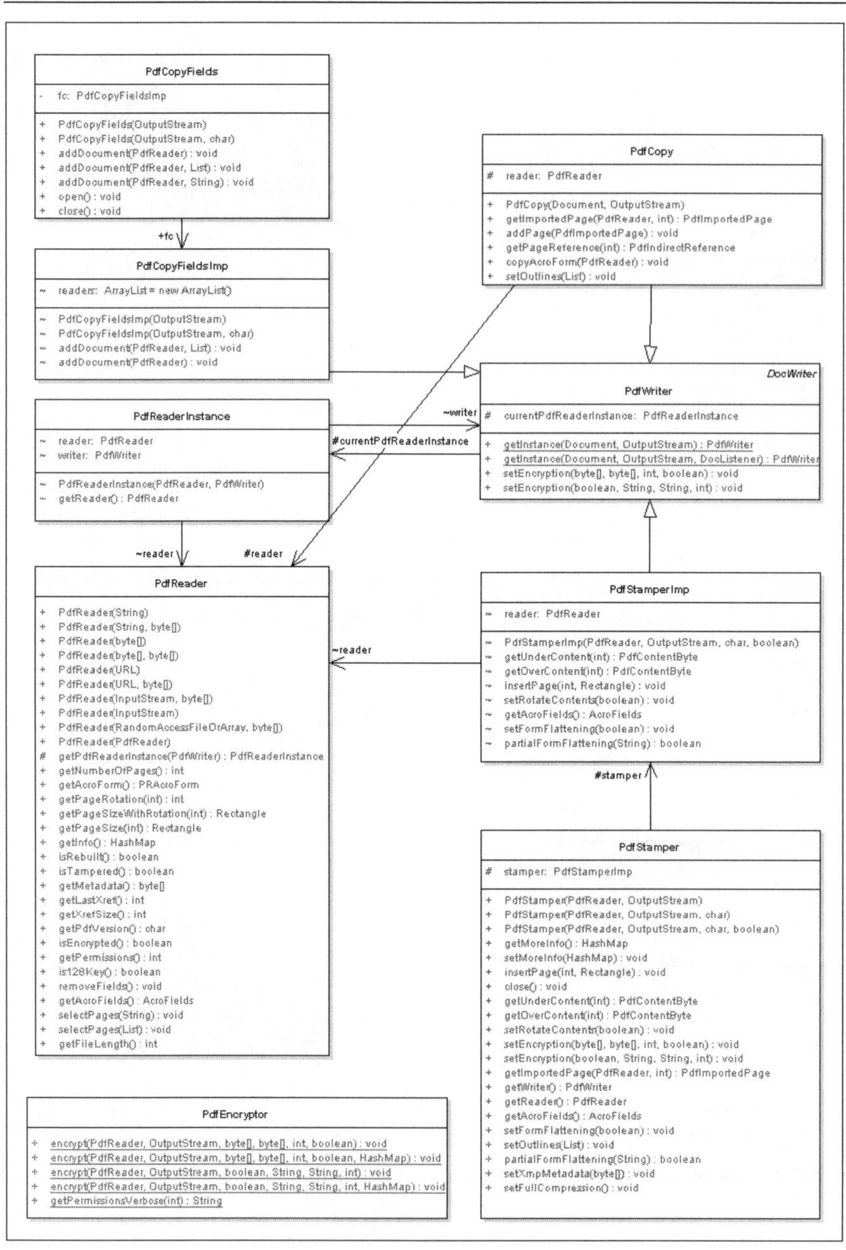


**Figure A.2 Overview of the classes discussed in section 2.2**

## A.3 Text element classes

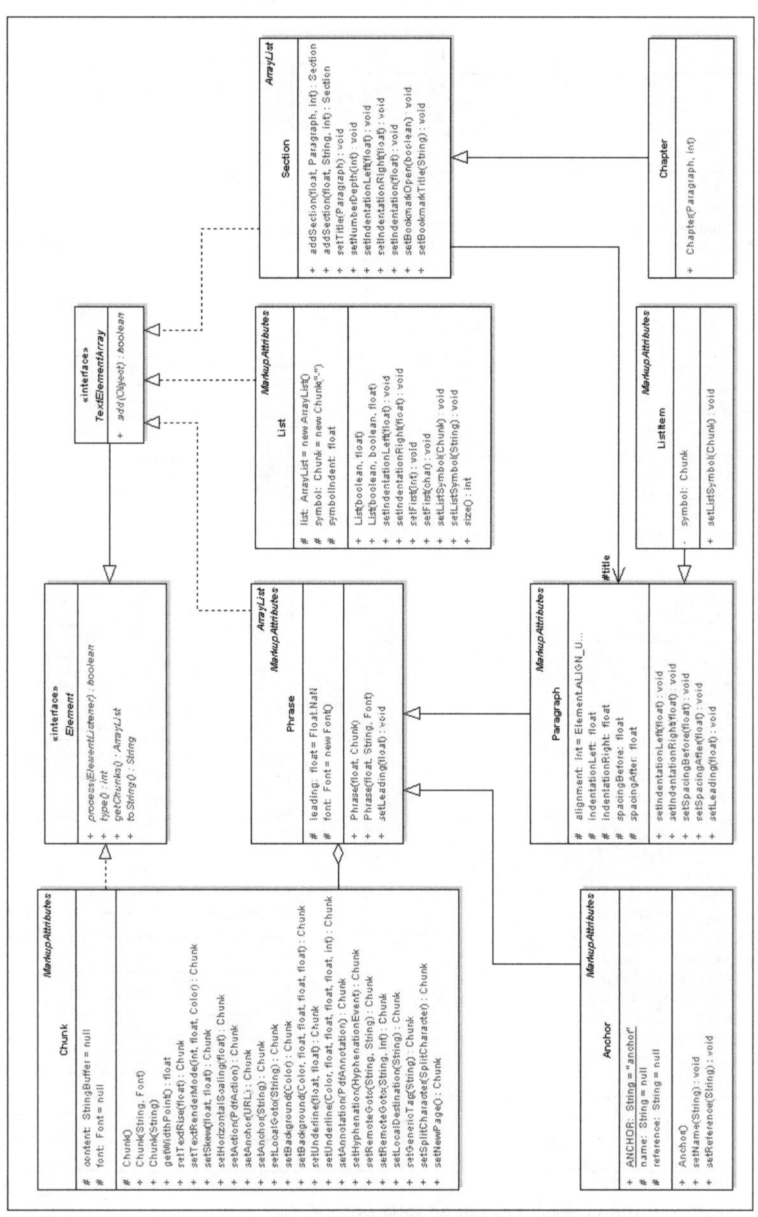


**Figure A.3 Overview of the classes discussed in chapter 4**

## A.4 Image classes

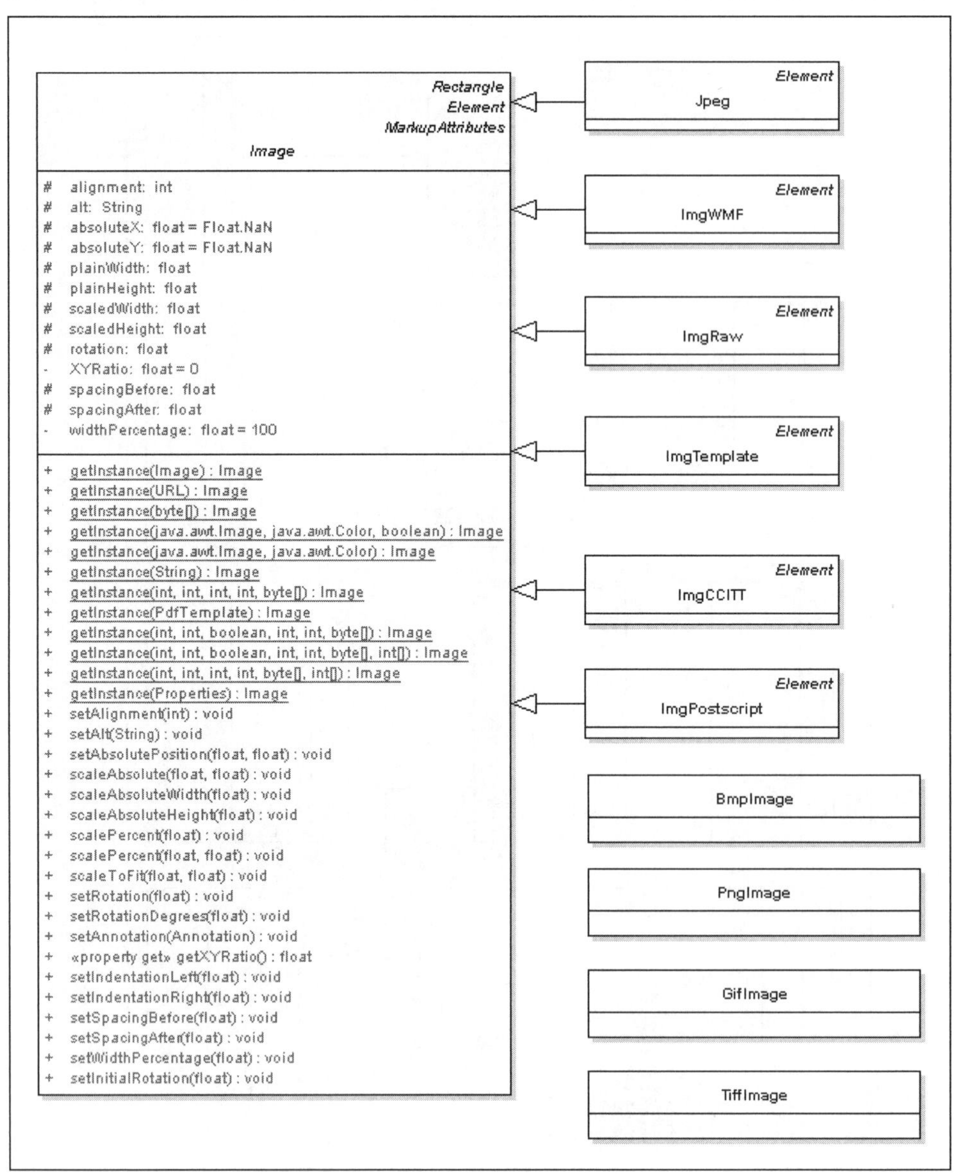


**Figure A.4 Overview of the classes discussed in chapter 5**

## A.5 Barcode classes

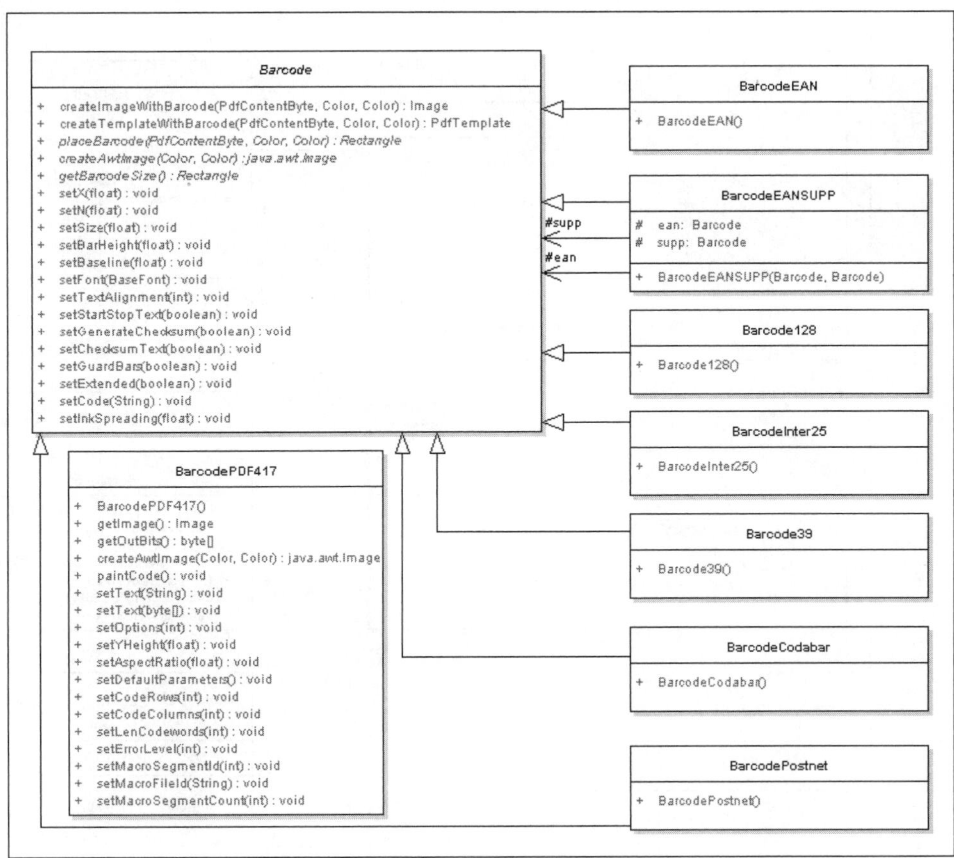


**Figure A.5 Overview of the `barcode` classes discussed in chapter 5 and appendix B**

## A.6 Table classes

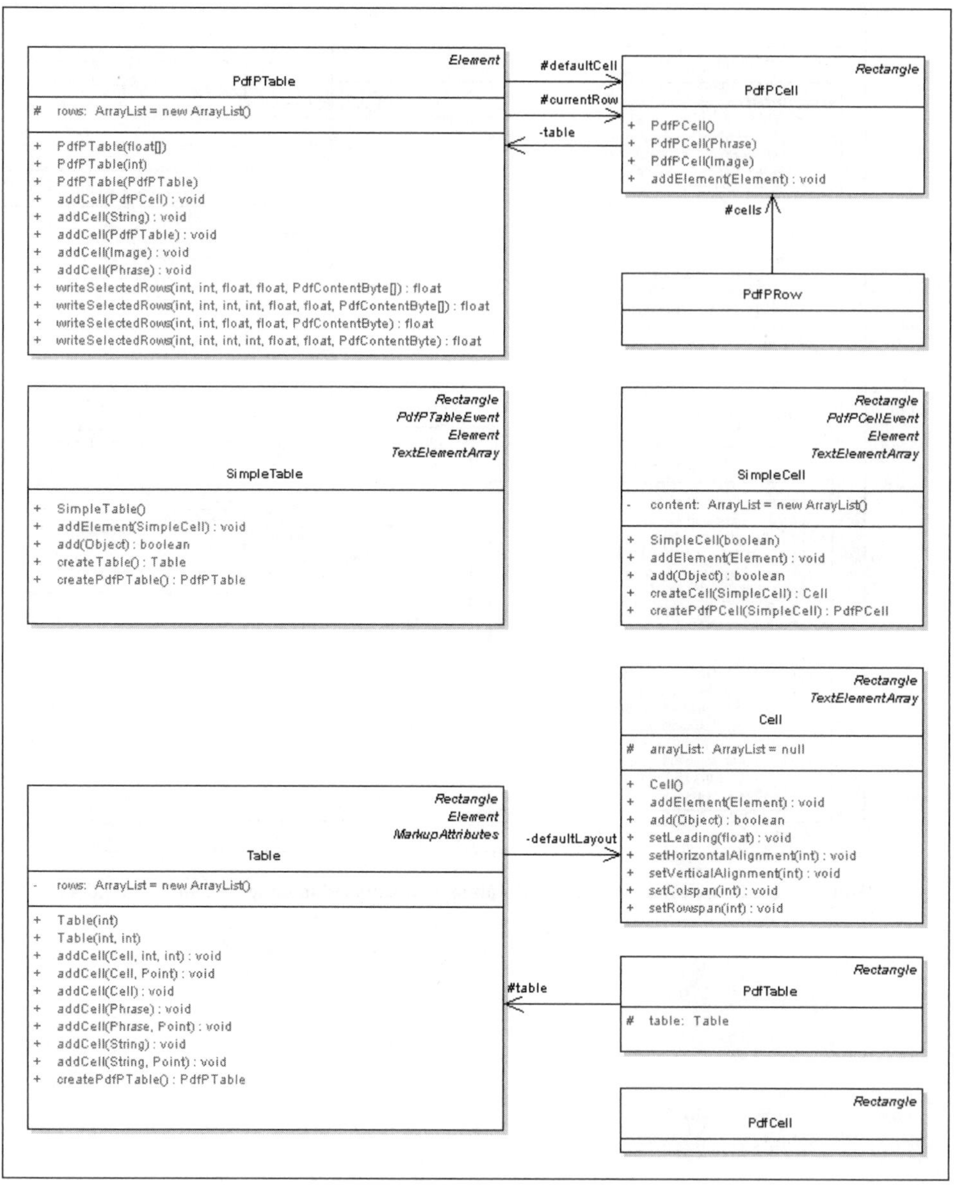


**Figure A.6 Overview of the classes discussed in chapter 6**

## A.7 Font classes

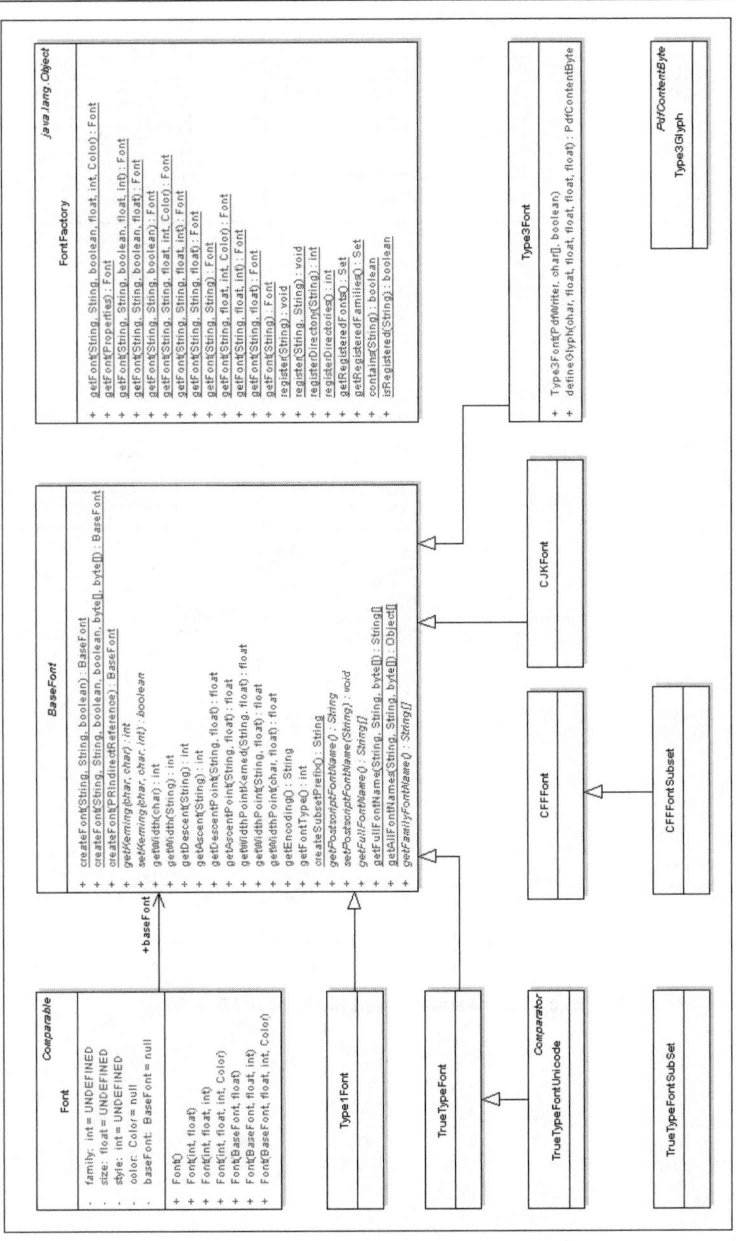


**Figure A.7 Overview of the classes discussed in chapter 8**

## A.8 Color classes

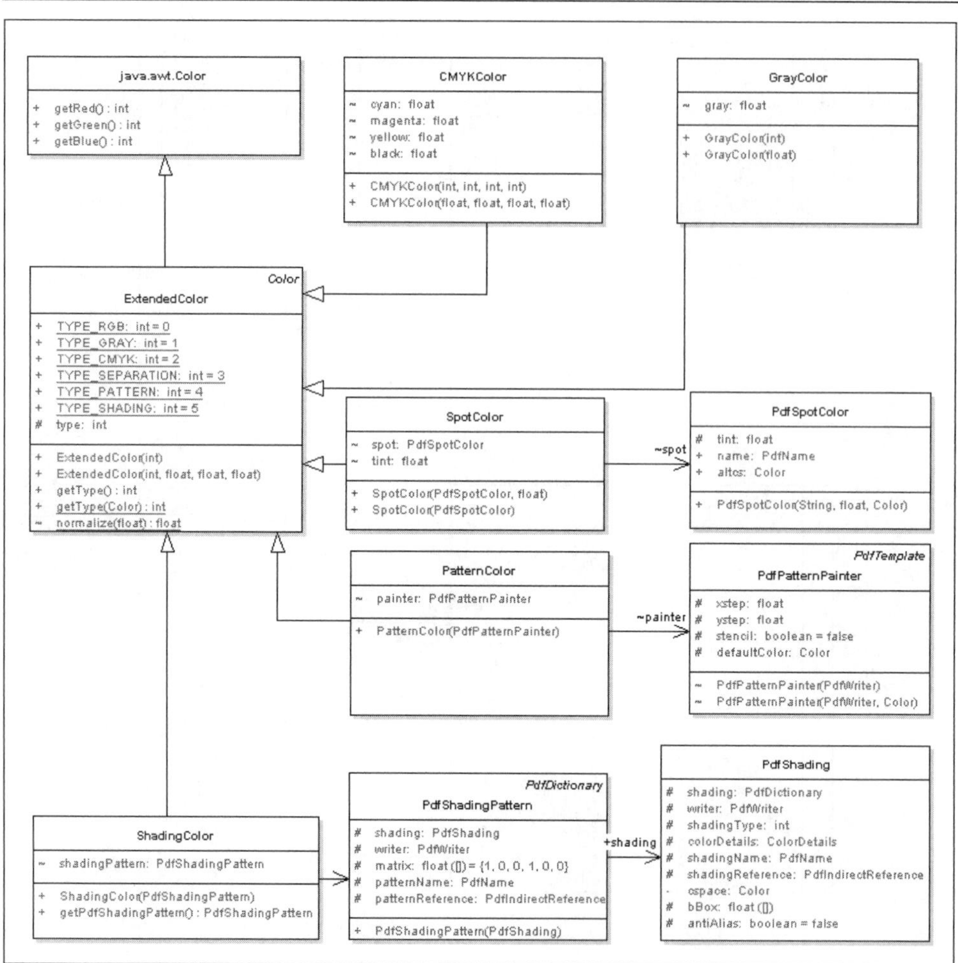


**Figure A.8 Overview of the `Color` classes discussed in chapter 10**

## A.9 PdfObject classes

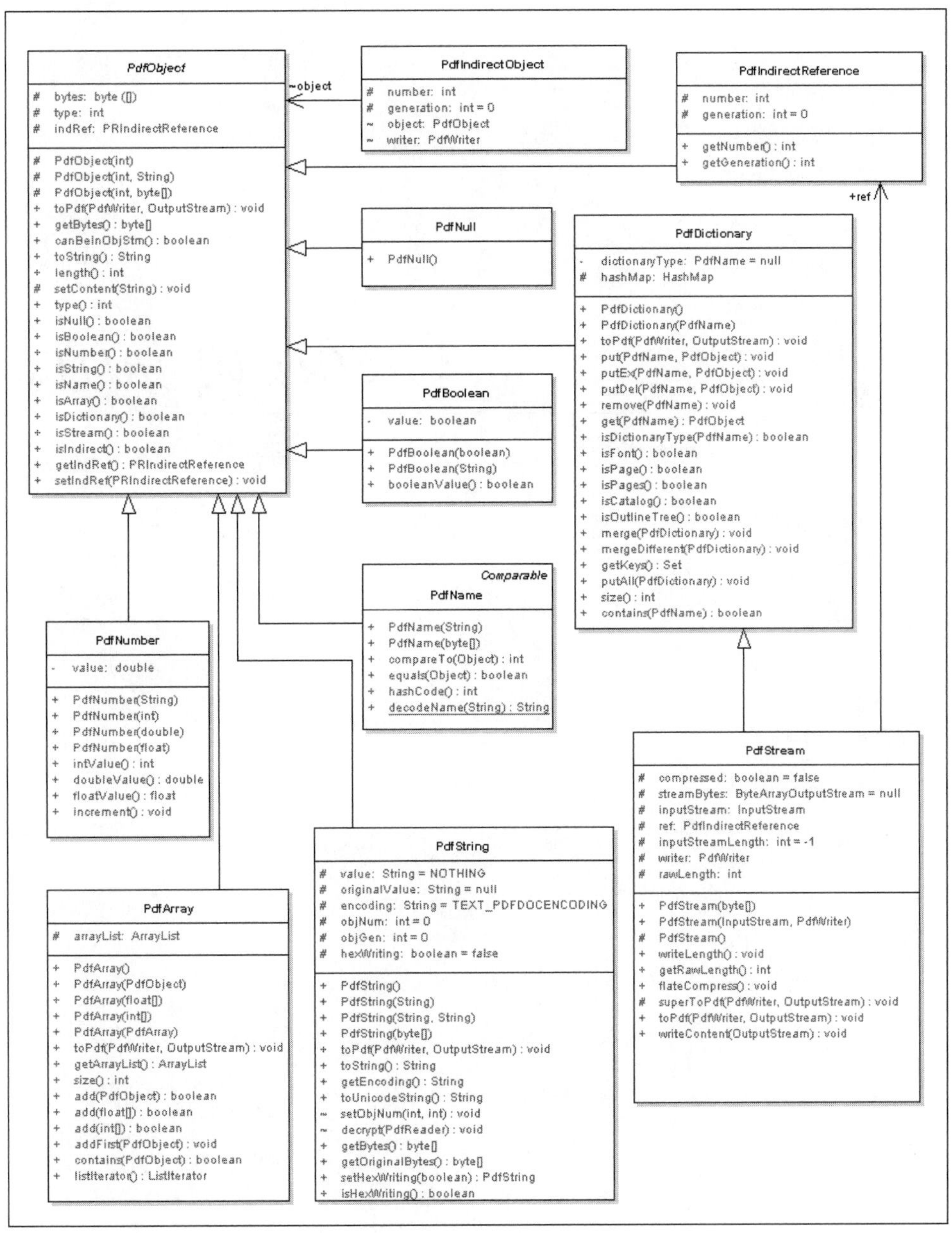


**Figure A.9 Overview of the classes discussed in chapter 18**

# B Creating barcodes

We briefly discussed the abstract class `com.lowagie.text.pdf.Barcode` in chapter 5, and appendix A section A.5 gave you an overview of the `Barcode` subclasses. These classes provide a user-friendly way to create an `Image` instance that represents a barcode.

This could be a `com.lowagie.text.Image` or a `java.awt.Image` class. There's also a method to place the barcode on a `PdfContentByte` object and to create a `PdfTemplate` containing the barcode.

In this appendix, which is a specific extension of chapter 5, we'll look at an example of every barcode type supported in iText.

## B.1 Barcodes to identify products

If you live in America or Canada and you go to your retail store, you're probably familiar with Universal Product Code (UPC) barcodes. These codes aren't really as universal as the name suggests. Most of the rest of the world uses European Article Number (EAN) barcodes; Japan uses JAN (which is just another name for EAN). These standards are different and similar at the same time. They're different in the sense that EAN and UPC codes represent a different number of digits; but similar in the way the barcode to represent this code is generated.

To ensure consistent terminology around the world, the Global Trade Item Number (GTIN) was introduced. GTIN is a new term, not a new standard. It's an all-numeric system that uniquely identifies trade items (products and services) that are sold, delivered, warehoused, and billed throughout retail and commercial distribution channels. It embraces EAN/UCC-8, EAN/UCC-12 (UPC), EAN-UCC-13, and EAN/UCC-14. The acronym UCC stands for the Uniform Code Council. The numbers indicate the number of digits represented by the barcode: 8, 12, 13, or 14.

**NOTE** When you want to store GTIN barcode values in a database, it's advised that you store a 14-digit number for reasons of uniformity and forward compatibility. Even if you're using EAN-13, EAN-8, or UPC barcodes that don't have 14 digits, you should use right justifying and zero padding at the left.

iText supports all these types of barcodes, albeit under different names. We'll look at the different types by summing up the iText classes used to produce GTIN-compliant barcodes

### *com.lowagie.text.pdf.BarcodeEAN*

Although this classname refers to EAN, the class can be used to produce a range of barcodes: EAN-13, UPC-A, EAN-8, UPC-E, supplemental 5, and supplemental 2. The default type is EAN-13 (see figure B.1).

**Figure B.1 EAN-13 barcodes**

These barcodes were generated like this:

```
/* chapter05/Barcodes.java */
PdfContentByte cb = writer.getDirectContent();          <-- Grab direct content
BarcodeEAN codeEAN = new BarcodeEAN();
codeEAN.setCode("4512345678906");      <-- Set code (including check digit)
Paragraph p = new Paragraph("default: ");
p.add(new Chunk(
  codeEAN.createImageWithBarcode(cb, null, null), 0, -5));   <-- Create Image object
codeEAN.setGuardBars(false);       <-- No guard bars
p.add(" without guard bars: ");
p.add(new Chunk(
  codeEAN.createImageWithBarcode(cb, null, null), 0, -5));
codeEAN.setBaseline(-1f);     <-- Move text above bars
codeEAN.setGuardBars(true);      <-- This line is ignored!
p.add(" text above: ");
p.add(new Chunk(
  codeEAN.createImageWithBarcode(cb, null, null), 0, -5));
p.setLeading(codeEAN.getBarcodeSize().height());
document.add(p);
```

In the Barcodes.java example, you create barcodes as an iText `Image` instance. The method that creates this instance needs a `PdfContentByte` object obtained from the writer to which the image object will be added. The other two parameters (which are null in this example) represent the colors of the barcode and the text under or above the bars. In some of the examples that follow, you'll change this value. EAN and UPC barcodes have a check digit, but you have to calculate this checksum yourself before setting the code.

**Figure B.2 UPC-A barcode of the PDF Reference**

UPC-A is similar to EAN-13, but it has only 12 digits; see figure B.2.

The code is almost identical to the previous snippet. The only difference is that you set the type:

```
/* chapter05/Barcodes.java */
BarcodeEAN codeEAN = new BarcodeEAN();
codeEAN.setCodeType(Barcode.UPCA);
codeEAN.setCode("785342304749");
document.add(codeEAN.createImageWithBarcode(cb, null, null));
```

Some retail items are small, and it's difficult to put a full-sized EAN-13 or UPC-A barcode on the package. If this is the case, an EAN-8 or UPC-E barcode can be used (see figure B.3).

As you can see, these barcodes don't take a lot of space; moreover, I reduced the height of the bars:



**Figure B.3 EAN-8 and UPC-E barcodes**

```
/* chapter05/Barcodes.java */
BarcodeEAN codeEAN = new BarcodeEAN();
codeEAN.setCodeType(Barcode.EAN8);
codeEAN.setBarHeight(codeEAN.getSize() * 1.5f);
codeEAN.setCode("34569870");
document.add(codeEAN.createImageWithBarcode(cb, null, null));
codeEAN.setCodeType(Barcode.UPCE);
codeEAN.setCode("03456781");
document.add(codeEAN.createImageWithBarcode(cb, null, null));
```

`BarcodeEAN` can also generate supplemental-5 and supplemental-2 barcodes. These are the codes you'll use as second argument in the constructor of the following class.

### *com.lowagie.text.pdf.BarcodeEANSUPP*

EAN-13, UPC-A, EAN-8, and UPC-E allow for a supplemental two- or five-digit number to be appended to the main barcode. This was designed for use on publications and periodicals. For instance, the supplemental two-digit number can indicate a month from January (01) to December (12).

If you add a supplemental five-digit barcode to an EAN-13 barcode representing an International Standard Book Number (ISBN), you get a *Bookland* code. The 13 digits of the ISBN barcode are composed of five parts in the following order:

- Start number: 978 or 979
- Country or language code
- Publisher number code
- Item number code
- Checksum character

The additional five-digit barcode contains a currency and recommended retail price. Figure B.2 is the UPC-A code of the PDF Reference (fifth edition), which could be used in retail stores. Figure B.4 shows the Bookland code of the PDF Reference. Both barcodes can be found on the back of the book.

ISBN 0-321-30474-8

9 780321 304742 55499

**Figure B.4 Bookland code of the PDF Reference**

Do you recognize the ISBN number in the barcode number? The supplemental code tells you that the recommended retail price is $54.99 (in most stores, the PDF Reference isn't that expensive). I also made the text blue for a change:

```
/* chapter05/Barcodes.java */
BarcodeEAN codeEAN = new BarcodeEAN();
codeEAN.setCodeType(Barcode.EAN13);
codeEAN.setCode("9780321304742");
BarcodeEAN codeSUPP = new BarcodeEAN();
codeSUPP.setCodeType(Barcode.SUPP5);
codeSUPP.setCode("55499");
codeSUPP.setBaseline(-2);
BarcodeEANSUPP eanSupp =
  new BarcodeEANSUPP(codeEAN, codeSUPP);
document.add(eanSupp.createImageWithBarcode(cb, null, Color.blue));
```

**Create EAN-13 code**

**Create SUPP5 code**

**Combine both in BarcodeEANSUPP code**

If you inspect this code and try it on your computer, you'll see that some of the properties of the barcode are changed. I won't discuss all these properties right now, but a table with all the properties per barcode type appears in section B.3 (table B.3).

Let's continue with another GTIN barcode.

### *com.lowagie.text.pdf.Barcode128*

Code 128 provides much more detail than the single-product EAN barcodes. It's used to describe properties such as the number of products included, weight, dates, and so on.

Different specifications dictate how the Code 128 symbology is to be printed. With iText, you can set the code type to `Barcode.CODE128`, which is the original, plain Code 128, to `Barcode.CODE128_RAW`, where the code attribute has the codes from 0 to 105 followed by \uffff and the human-readable text, or to `Barcode.CODE128_UCC`, with support for UCC/EAN-128 and *application identifiers* (see table B.1).

Plain Code 128 can encode all 128 ASCII characters and 4 special function codes (see table B.2). It's capable of encoding two characters in the space of one character width—this is called *double density*. It's an interesting barcode to put a maximum amount of information on a minimum amount of space.

This all sounds complex, so let's look at some examples to get the idea. The upper barcode in figure B.5 is a plain barcode (the default; `Barcode.CODE128`); the lower returns 0123456789 when scanned, and the human-readable text says *My Raw Barcode (0-9)*. It was created by setting the type to `Barcode.CODE128_RAW`.

**Figure B.5 Code 128 (plain and raw)**

A concatenation of the machine-readable code, the \uffff character, and the human-readable text is entered as parameter of the `setCode()` method:

```
/* chapter05/Barcodes.java */
document.add(new Paragraph("Barcode 128"));
Barcode128 code128 = new Barcode128();
code128.setCode("0123456789 hello");
document.add(code128.createImageWithBarcode(cb, null, null));
code128.setCode("0123456789\uffffMy Raw Barcode (0 - 9)");
code128.setCodeType(Barcode.CODE128_RAW);
document.add(code128.createImageWithBarcode(cb, null, null));
```

The `Barcode128` class contains a `Hashtable` with a series of Application Identifiers (AIs). An AI is a prefix that is used to identify the meaning and the format of the data that follows it. AIs have been defined for many types of information: dates, quantity, measurements, locations, and so on. Table B.1 shows some of the most common examples (there are too many to list in this book).

**Table B.1 Nonrestrictive list of Application Identifiers**

| AI | Description |
|---|---|
| (00) | Serial Shipping Container Code; identification of a logistic unit. Used to support tracking and reception operations. |
| (01) | Identification of a trade item; 14-digit GTIN. |
| (02) | Indicates that the data field includes the GTIN of the contained trade items. The logistic unit isn't a trade item in itself. |
| (10) | Identifies a batch or lot number. The data field following the AI is always a batch number not exceeding 20 alphanumeric characters. |
| (11) | Production date in the form YYMMDD. |
| (13) | Packaging date. |
| (15) | Minimum durability date (Quality). |

*continued on next page*

**Table B.1 Nonrestrictive list of Application Identifiers** *(continued)*

| AI | Description |
|---|---|
| (17) | Maximum durability date (Security). |
| (90) | Information mutually agreed on between trading partners. |
| (402) | Shipment Identification Number (Bill of Lading); a globally unique number that identifies a logical grouping of physical units for the purpose of a transport shipment. |
| (420) | Ship-to (deliver-to) postal code. This can facilitate shipment sorting, consolidation, and general automated package handling; maximum of 20 alphanumeric characters. |
| (421) | Postal code of the addressee (international format). |
| (3100) to (3109) | Net weight in kilograms. The last digit in the AI is a decimal-point indicator. |

I also mentioned that Code 128 allows the use of four function codes. Table B.2 explains what these codes are for.

**Table B.2 Special function codes in Code 128**

| Function code in iText | Description |
|---|---|
| `Barcode128.FNC1` | Reserved for EAN applications |
| `Barcode128.FNC2` | Used to instruct the barcode reader to concatenate the current message with the next one |
| `Barcode128.FNC3` | Code to instruct the barcode reader to perform a reset |
| `Barcode128.FNC4` | For future use or closed system applications |

Figure B.6 shows a shipping code, with a Shipment Identification Number, information mutually agreed on between the trading partners, and the postal code of the addressee.

24132399420058289370000005042235 6

**Figure B.6 Shipment barcode**

This is also a plain Code 128, but it uses AI terminology. Because the blocks with type 402 and 90 can have a variable length, FNC1 is used as a demarcation character. This example also uses methods to change the way the barcode looks:

```
/* chapter05/Barcodes.java */
String code402 = "24132399420058289";
```

Shipment Identification Code

```
String code90 = "3700000050";        ⇐ Information agreed on between partners
String code421 = "422356";      ⇐ Postal code of addressee
StringBuffer data = new StringBuffer(code402);
data.append(Barcode128.FNC1);
data.append(code90);                              Concatenate content
data.append(Barcode128.FNC1);
data.append(code421);
Barcode128 shipBarCode = new Barcode128();
shipBarCode.setX(0.75f);
shipBarCode.setN(1.5f);
shipBarCode.setSize(10f);                               Change defaults
shipBarCode.setTextAlignment(Element.ALIGN_CENTER);
shipBarCode.setBaseline(10f);
shipBarCode.setBarHeight(50f);
shipBarCode.setCode(data.toString());
document.add(shipBarCode.createImageWithBarcode(cb,
Color.black, Color.blue));
```

The next examples demonstrate the UCC/EAN-128 barcode. It uses the same code set as Code 128, but without the function codes FNC2, FNC3, and FNC4. Only FNC1 is used, to enable barcode scanners and processing software to autodiscriminate between UCC/EAN-128 and other barcode symbologies. FNC1 follows the start character of the bar. The AIs are added to the code (see figure B.7).

**Figure B.7 UCC/EAN-128 barcodes**

If you only work with content fields that have a fixed length, you can omit the brackets that indicate the AI, as is done for the lower barcode in figure B.7. But it's always safer to use brackets, as in the upper barcode:

```
/* chapter05/Barcodes.java */
Barcode128 uccEan128 = new Barcode128();
uccEan128.setCodeType(Barcode.CODE128_UCC);
uccEan128.setCode("(01)00000090311314(10)ABC123(15)060916");
document.add(
  uccEan128.createImageWithBarcode(cb, Color.blue, Color.black));
uccEan128.setCode("0191234567890121310100035510ABC123");
document.add(uccEan128.createImageWithBarcode(cb,
Color.blue, Color.red));
```

Remember that I talked about GTIN and how iText supports, for instance, EAN/UCC-14, but under other names? One way to represent an EAN/UCC-14 code is by using Code 128 with AI 01 (see figure B.8).

**Figure B.8 Code 128 with AI 01 as an EAN/UCC-14 barcode**

This is how the figure was generated:

```
/* chapter05/Barcodes.java */
Barcode128 uccEan128 = new Barcode128();
uccEan128.setCodeType(Barcode.CODE128_UCC);
uccEan128.setCode("(01)28880123456788");
document.add(
  uccEan128.createImageWithBarcode(cb, Color.blue, Color.black));
```

Whereas single products get an EAN code, and mass-packaged products get a Code 128, a carton of products often gets an Interleaved 2 of 5 barcode.

### *com.lowagie.text.pdf.BarcodeInter25*

This is a numerical barcode that encodes pairs of digits; the first digit is encoded in the bars, and the second digit is encoded in the spaces interleaved with them. As you see in figure B.9 and the corresponding code sample, I used non-numeric characters that are printed in the text, but these characters don't generate bars; iText ignores them.

**Figure B.9 Interleaved 2 of 5 barcodes**

Here's the code:

```
/* chapter05/Barcodes.java */
BarcodeInter25 code25 = new BarcodeInter25();
code25.setGenerateChecksum(true);
code25.setCode("41-1200076041-001");
document.add(code25.createImageWithBarcode(cb, null, null));
code25.setCode("411200076041001");
document.add(code25.createImageWithBarcode(cb, null, null));
code25.setCode("0611012345678");
code25.setChecksumText(true);
document.add(code25.createImageWithBarcode(cb, null, null));
```

The checksum in an Interleaved 2 of 5 barcode is optional, but you can let iText add it with the method `setGenerateChecksum()`. The generated checksum isn't shown in the human-readable text by default; if you want to see it appear in the text, you have to use the method `setChecksumText()`.

If you construct an Interleaved 2 of 5 barcode with 13 digits + checksum and add guard bars, you get an ITF14 barcode. This type of code is also a valid GTIN barcode with 14 digits. I repeat: GTIN isn't a new standard. It's a new term for a series of existing barcodes.

You've seen all possible flavors of GTIN and EAN.UCC barcodes that are used for identifying products, but barcodes can be used for many other purposes.

## B.2 Barcodes for postal services and other industries

POSTNET, PLANET, Code39, and Codabar are other barcode types supported by iText. Let's see in what context these barcodes are used.

### com.lowagie.text.pdf.BarcodePostnet

The United States Postal Service (USPS) uses a combination of the POSTal Numeric Encoding Technique (POSTNET) sorting code and the PostaL Alpha Numeric Encoding Technique (PLANET) code to direct and identify mail.

Currently, three forms of POSTNET codes are in use: a 5-digit ZIP code, a 9-digit ZIP+4, and an 11-digit delivery point code. The delivery point added to the ZIP+4 code usually consists of the last two digits of the address or PO box. The PLANET Code is an 11-digit code assigned by the USPS.

Both types are encoded in a sequence of half- and full-height bars. They start and end with a full-height bar. The encoded address information followed by a check digit is between these two *frame* bars. You don't have to worry about this check digit. It's added by iText automatically. See figure B.10.

ZIP

ZIP+4

ZIP+4 and dp

Barcode Planet

**Figure B.10 Barcodes for the United States Postal Service**

If you compare the POSTNET code with the PLANET code in the figure, you see that the PLANET code symbology is the inverse of the POSTNET symbology:

```
/* chapter05/Barcodes.java */
BarcodePostnet codePost = new BarcodePostnet();
codePost.setCode("01234");
document.add(codePost.createImageWithBarcode(cb, null, null));
codePost.setCode("012345678");
document.add(codePost.createImageWithBarcode(cb, null, null));
codePost.setCode("01234567890");
document.add(codePost.createImageWithBarcode(cb, null, null));
BarcodePostnet codePlanet = new BarcodePostnet();
```

**POSTNET code for ZIP code**

**POSTNET code for ZIP+4 code**

**POSTNET code with delivery point**

```
codePlanet.setCode("01234567890");
codePlanet.setCodeType(Barcode.PLANET);
document.add(codePlanet.createImageWithBarcode(cb, null, null));
```

**PLANET code**

The next barcode we'll discuss is widely used in the pharmaceutical industry. It's also the standard code for the US Department of Defense.

### *com.lowagie.text.pdf.Barcode39*

The 3 of 9 code (Code39) can encode numbers, uppercase letters (A–Z), and symbols (- . ' '$ / + % *). Figure B.11 shows two variations: barcode 3 of 9 and barcode 3 of 9 extended.

Barcode 3 of 9

Barcode 3 of 9 extended

**Figure B.11 Code39 barcodes**

A Code39 barcode has the following structure:

- An asterisk as start character
- Any number of (valid) characters
- A checksum digit (optional; Code39 doesn't require a check digit)
- An asterisk as stop character

The asterisks before and after the content are added by iText automatically. Note that the asterisk may only be used as a start and stop character; you can't use it in the content of the barcode. By default, iText doesn't add a checksum digit. Again, you can use the methods `setGenerateChecksum()` and `setChecksumText()` as you did with the Interleaved 2 of 5 barcode.

I didn't add a checksum in the examples:

```
/* chapter05/Barcodes.java */
Barcode39 code39 = new Barcode39();
code39.setCode("ITEXT IN ACTION");
document.add(code39.createImageWithBarcode(cb, null, null));
```

Extended Code39 can encode all 128 ASCII characters. This is achieved by shifting the characters using the $, /, %, and + symbols. For instance, `$P` equals 0, `$Q` equals 1, `$R` equals 2, and so on:

```
/* chapter05/Barcodes.java */
Barcode39 code39ext = new Barcode39();
code39ext.setCode("iText in Action");
code39ext.setStartStopText(false);
code39ext.setExtended(true);
document.add(code39ext.createImageWithBarcode(cb, null, null));
```

Remember that if your barcode reader doesn't support full ASCII Code39, you'll get shifted characters as if they were plain Code39 characters.

Finally, there's the Codabar barcode.

#### *com.lowagie.text.pdf.Codabar*

Codabar is used to store numerical data only, but the letters A, B, C, and D are used as start and stop characters (start and stop characters have to match: A123A is OK; A123B isn't). The Codabar barcode is used in blood banks, the shipping industry, libraries, and other industries.

**Figure B.12 Codabar example**

Figure B.12 shows a simple example.

The code to produce this barcode is straightforward:

```
/* chapter05/Barcodes.java */
BarcodeCodabar codabar = new BarcodeCodabar();
codabar.setCode("A123A");
codabar.setStartStopText(true);
document.add(codabar.createImageWithBarcode(cb, null, null));
```

Now that you've been introduced to all the types of (one-dimensional) barcodes, let's see how you can change some of their properties.

## B.3 Barcode properties

The previous examples used `createImageWithBarcode(PdfContentByte, Color, Color)`. Instead of creating an iText `Image` instance, you can add the barcode directly to a `PdfContentByte` object with `placeBarcode(PdfContentByte, Color, Color)` or create a `PdfTemplate` with `createTemplateWithBarcode(PdfContentByte, Color, Color)`.

In these methods, the `Color` parameters define the color of the barcode and the text. If both parameters are null, the current fill color is used. If only the text color is null, the bar color is used for the text.

You can also create a `java.awt.Image` of the barcode (without text) using the method `createAwtImage(Color, Color)`. In this method, the second color parameter defines the background color of the barcode.

Throughout the examples, we've played with other properties. Now it's time for an overview per barcode type.

### *Overview of barcode properties*

The property x (adjustable with `setX()`) holds the minimum width of a bar. Except for the POSTNET code, this value is set to 0.8 by default. You can set the amount of ink spreading with `setInkSpreading()`. This value is subtracted from the width of each bar. The actual value depends on the ink and the printing medium; it's 0 by default. The property n holds the multiplier for wide bars for some types, the distance between two barcodes in EANSUPP, and the distance between the bars in the USPS barcodes.

The property `font` defines the font of the text (if any). If you want to produce a barcode without text, you have to set the barcode font to null with `setFont()`. You can change the size of the font with `setSize()`, and with `setBaseline()` you can change the distance between text and barcode. Negative values put the text above the bar.

Changing the bar height can be done with `setBarHeight()`. For USPS codes, you can also change the height of the short bar with `setSize()`. USPS codes don't have text.

Finally, there are methods to generate a checksum and to make the calculated value visible in the human-readable text (or not). You can also set the start/stop sequence visible for those barcodes that use these sequences.

If you don't use any of the methods to change the properties, a default is used. Table B.3 shows the default values for each of the properties per class that extends the abstract `Barcode` class.

**Table B.3 Default properties of the different barcode classes**

| Code: | EAN | EANSUPP | 128 | Inter25 | 39 | Codabar | POSTNET |
|---|---|---|---|---|---|---|---|
| **Type** | EAN13 | - | CODE128 | - | - | CODABAR | POSTNET |
| **x** | 0.8f | | | | | | 0.02f * 72f; |
| **n** | - | 8 | - | 2 | | | 72f / 22f |
| **Font** | `BaseFont.createFont(BaseFont.HELVETICA, BaseFont.WINANSI, BaseFont.NOT_EMBEDDED)` | | | | | | - |
| **Size** | 8 | | | | | | 0.05f * 72f |

*continued on next page*

**Table B.3 Default properties of the different barcode classes** *(continued)*

| Code: | EAN | EANSUPP | 128 | Inter25 | 39 | Codabar | POSTNET |
|---|---|---|---|---|---|---|---|
| **Baseline** | Size | | | | | | - |
| **Bar height** | Size * 3 | | | | | | 0.125f * 72f |
| **Text alignment** | - | - | Element.ALIGN_CENTER | | | | - |
| **Guardbars** | True | - | - | - | - | - | - |
| **Generate checksum** | User | User | - | False | False | False | - |
| **Text checksum** | - | - | - | False | False | False | - |
| **start/stop text** | - | - | - | - | True | False | - |

The class diagram in section B.5 shows that one barcode class doesn't extend the class `com.lowagie.text.pdf.Barcode`: the class that produces a PDF417 barcode.

## B.4 Two-dimensional barcodes

The title of this subsection is somewhat a *contradictio in terminis*; two-dimensional barcodes are no longer codes with bars. That's why they're sometimes referred to as *matrix codes*, which is a more accurate term. The important difference from plain barcodes is that they don't consist of bars and spaces, but are made using dots, squares, and even hexagons organized in a matrix. They're read in two dimensions, and they can represent a lot more data than one-dimensional barcodes.

For the moment, iText only supports PDF417.

### com.lowagie.text.pdf.BarcodePDF417

The *PDF* acronym of this matrix code doesn't refer to the Portable Document Format; it stands for Portable Data File. A PDF417 barcode can store up to 2,170 characters, and the symbology is capable of encoding the entire ASCII set (255 characters).

The text you add to the barcode is converted to bytes using the encoding cp437. `BarcodePDF417` isn't a subclass of `Barcode`, but it has `getImage()` and `createAwtImage()` methods. There is no method to get a `PdfTemplate`, because

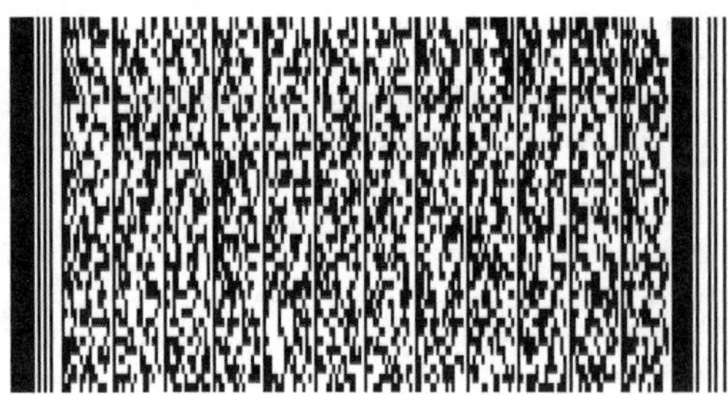

**Figure B.13 PDF417 matrix code**

the matrix code is constructed in a completely different way. A CCITT G4 image is constructed internally; if needed, you can get the raw image bits with `getOutBits()`; you can get the dimensions with `getBitColumns()` and `getCodeRows()`.

Figure B.13 was generated with the default options: `yHeight` of 3 (this is the height of the Y pixel relative to X) and an aspect ratio of 0.5 (the proportion of rows versus columns).

The code is as follows:

```
/* chapter05/Barcodes.java */
BarcodePDF417 pdf417 = new BarcodePDF417();
String text = "It was the best of times... (...)";
pdf417.setText(text);
Image img = pdf417.getImage();
img.scalePercent(50, 50 * pdf417.getYHeight());
document.add(img);
```

Use the methods `setCodeColumns()`, `setCodeRows()`, `setAspectRatio()`, and/or `setYHeight()` to define the number of columns, the number of rows, the aspect ratio, and the `yHeight` value; iText can change these values to keep the barcode valid, based on the options you set with the method `setOptions()`. The options are listed in table B.4.

**Table B.4 PDF417 option values**

| Option value | Description |
|---|---|
| `PDF417_USE_ASPECT_RATIO` | The autosize is based on `aspectRatio` and `yHeight` (this is the default). |
| `PDF417_FIXED_RECTANGLE` | The size of the barcode is at least `codeColumns*codeRows`. |
| `PDF417_FIXED_COLUMNS` | The size is at least `codeColumns`, with a variable number of `codeRows`. |

*continued on next page*

**Table B.4 PDF417 option values** *(continued)*

| Option value | Description |
|---|---|
| `PDF417_FIXED_ROWS` | The size is at least `codeRows`, with a variable number of `codeColumns`. |
| `PDF417_USE_ERROR_LEVEL` | The error level correction is set by the user. It can be 0 to 8; if this option isn't set, the error level correction is set automatically according to ISO 15438 recommendations. |
| `PDF417_USE_RAW_CODEWORDS` | No text interpretation is done, and the content of codewords is used directly. |
| `PDF417_INVERT_BITMAP` | This inverts the output bits of the raw bitmap that is normally bit one for black. It affects only the raw bitmap. |
| `PDF417_USE_MACRO` | You can split the PDF417 barcode into several segments to represent even more data. This is called Macro PDF417. You need the methods `setMacroSegmentId()`, `setMacroSegmentCount()`, and `setMacroFileId()` to create these segments. |

Other examples of matrix codes are Data Matrix, MaxiCode, and Semacode, but these aren't supported in iText (yet).

New types of barcodes are added to iText from time to time. For more information, please consult the web site or the mailing list.

# C Open parameters

In chapter 13, we discussed viewer preferences. By adding these preferences to the document, you define the initial state of the document when it's opened by an end user. In chapter 18, you used Adobe Reader from the command line with the `/p` option to print a PDF document.

This appendix discusses the parameters that can be passed to Adobe Reader along with the `/A` option. The same syntax can be used in the URL of a (static or dynamic) PDF file served on a web site.

The following line called from a DOS box opens the PDF Reference on page 573:

```
AcroRd32.exe /A "page=573" d:/pdf/PDFReference16.pdf
```

The following URL opens the PDF Reference hosted at adobe.com on page 573 with zoom factor 100 percent:

```
http://partners.adobe.com/public/developer/en/pdf/
➥ PDFReference16.pdf#page=573&zoom=100
```

Table 13.1 lists the most important parameters that can be passed with the `/A` option with command line, or using a # sign after the URL in the location bar of a browser.

**Table C.1 Syntax of the open parameters**

| Parameter and value | Description |
|---|---|
| `nameddest=name` | Specifies a named destination in the PDF. |
| `page=pagenum` | Jumps to a specific page. *Pagenum* indicates the actual page, not the label you may have given to the page. |
| `zoom=scale`<br>`zoom=scale,left,top` | Sets the zoom and scroll factors. A scale value of 100 gives 100 percent zoom.<br>Left and top are in a coordinate system where 0,0 is the top left of the visible page, regardless of document rotation. |
| `view=fit`<br>`view=fit,parameter` | The value for fit can be Fit, FitH, FitV, FitB, FitBH, or FitBV. The parameter has the same meaning as described in section 13.3.1. Note that this isn't supported from the command line. |
| `viewrect=left,top,width,height` | Opens the file so that the rectangle specified with the parameters is visible. Note that this isn't supported from the command line. |
| `pagemode=mode` | The mode can be none, bookmarks, or thumbs. |

*continued on next page*

**Table C.1 Syntax of the open parameters** *(continued)*

| Parameter and value | Description |
|---|---|
| `scrollbar=1\|0` | Enables/disables the scrollbars. |
| `toolbar=1\|0` | Shows/hides the toolbar. |
| `statusbar=1\|0` | Shows/hides the status bar. |
| `navpanes=1\|0` | Shows/hides the navigation panes and tabs. |
| `search=wordlist` | Opens the Search UI and searches for the words specified in the wordlist. The words must be enclosed in quotes and separated by spaces; for instance: #search="iText PDF". |

You should recognize most of the terminology from chapter 13. The functionality described in this appendix isn't iText specific, but it can be useful when you're building a web application involving PDF documents—particularly when you want to refer to different locations in one and the same document (without any built-in viewer preferences).

Note that you used this functionality in chapter 2 when you used the toolbox plug-in `HtmlBookmarks` to create an HTML index based on the outline tree of a PDF document.

# D

# *Signing a PDF with a smart card*

In chapter 16, you learned how to add a digital signature to a PDF document using a (self-signed) certificate and a private key that is present somewhere on the file system. I also mentioned that this certificate and key are sometimes stored on a smart card.

Figure D.1 shows an example of such a smart card. It's a copy of my identity card.

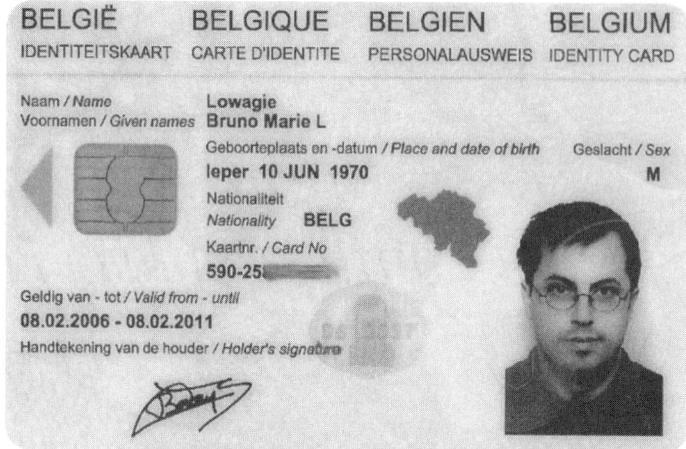


**Figure D.1 A smart card containing my personal information**

Belgium is one of the first countries in the world to issue an electronic identity card (eID) as official proof of identity for its citizens. This identity card looks like a regular bankcard, with basic identity information in visual format, such as personal details and a photograph. It also contains a chip with the same information printed legibly on the card, the address of the card holder, and the identity and signature keys and certificates.

The next example (written by Philippe Frankinet) uses this special card to add a digital signature to a PDF document. This example requires middleware that is specific for the type of smart card and smart card reader you're using. It's impossible to write a universal example that will work for every device and every type of card. The example is provided for your interest only; you'll have to adapt it according to the requirements of your project:

```
Certificate[] certs = new Certificate[1];
BelpicCard scd = new BelpicCard("");
certs[0] = scd.getNonRepudiationCertificate();
PdfReader reader = new PdfReader("unsigned.pdf");
```

```
FileOutputStream fout = new FileOutputStream("signed.pdf");
PdfStamper stamper = PdfStamper.createSignature(reader, fout, '\0');
PdfSignatureAppearance sap = stamper.getSignatureAppearance();
sap.setCrypto(
  null, certs, null, PdfSignatureAppearance.SELF_SIGNED);      <-❷
sap.setReason("How to use iText a Belgian eID");
sap.setLocation("Belgium");
sap.setVisibleSignature(new Rectangle(100, 100, 200, 200), 1, null);
sap.setExternalDigest(new byte[128], new byte[20], "RSA");     <-❸
sap.preClose();
PdfPKCS7 sig = sap.getSigStandard().getSigner();    <-❹
byte[] content = streamToByteArray(sap.getRangeStream());                  ❺
byte[] hash = MessageDigest.getInstance("SHA-1").digest(content);
byte[] signatureBytes = scd.generateNonRepudiationSignature(hash);     <-❻
sig.setExternalDigest(signatureBytes, null, "RSA");
PdfDictionary dic = new PdfDictionary();
dic.put(PdfName.CONTENTS,                                              ❼
  new PdfString(sig.getEncodedPKCS1()).setHexWriting(true));
sap.close(dic);
```

This example is quite different from the examples you've seen elsewhere. In chapter 16, you learned how to retrieve the certificate and the private key from a keystore. Now you have to fetch the certificate from the smart card ❶. After you create a reader and a stamper object, you create a signature appearance.

You don't pass the private key with the method `setCrypto()` ❷. The private key is on the smart card, and there would be a serious security problem if you could read this private key. You have to sign the hash externally on the smart card reader ❸. To achieve this, you create a `PdfPKCS7` instance ❹. `PdfPKCS7` is a class that does all the processing related to signing. You create a hash of the document's contents ❺ and use middleware to sign it ❻. The signature appearance is stored as a PDF dictionary; `sap.close()` adds the `CONTENTS` entry to the signature ❼.

This example uses the GoDot library. This library was written by Danny De Cock, and it can only be used with the Belgian eID. The object `be.godot.sc.-engine.BelpicCard` retrieves the certificate ❶ and signs the hash ❻. You'll have to replace these lines with code that addresses software that is specific for your type of smart card and smart card reader.

If you need to know more about external hashes and/or external signatures, consult the online how-to examples written by Paulo Soares: http://itextpdf.-sourceforge.net/howtosign.html.

If you want to know more about the Belgian eID, read my presentation notes for GovCamp Brussels: http://itext.ugent.be/articles/eid-pdf/.

# E
# *Dealing with exceptions*

The examples in this book are for demonstration purposes only. They're conceived so that you can easily run them on your own computer, and I have tried to keep them as short as possible. Most of the time, the iText-related code is inside a `try-catch` sequence. In most cases, I print the stack trace to the `System.out` when something goes wrong. That's OK for simple standalone applications; but in your own business applications, you should do something more intelligent in the `catch` clauses. Let's look at what can go wrong when you're producing a PDF document.

## E.1 iText-specific exception classes

There are four important exception classes in iText, but you'll probably never encounter two of them. `PdfException` and `BadPdfFormatException` in the package `com.lowagie.text.pdf` are for internal use only. We'll only discuss the most common exceptions.

### E.1.1 com.lowagie.text.BadElementException

A `BadElementException` is thrown when you try to create a basic building block using parameters that are valid for Java but that are wrong for iText. Here are some examples:

- You try to create a `Table` with zero or fewer columns. This doesn't make sense, so an exception is thrown. In newer versions of iText, exceptions like this are gradually being replaced by a `java.lang.IllegalArgumentException`—for instance, when you create a barcode object using data that doesn't conform to the type of barcode you chose.
- You want to add one basic building block to another with `addElement()`, but iText doesn't allow nesting of those elements. In this case, you risk a `BadElementException`. Because some of the text elements are derived from `java.util.ArrayList` overriding the `add()` methods, which are methods that obviously don't know any iText-specific exceptions, you may get a `java.lang.ClassCastException` instead.

`BadElementException` is a subclass of `DocumentException`.

### E.1.2 com.lowagie.text.DocumentException

`DocumentException` is the most general exception in iText. If you try to add content *before* opening the `Document`, a `DocumentException` is thrown with the message: *The document isn't open yet; you can only add meta information*. When you try adding metadata *after* opening the `Document` object, the result is the following error message: *The document is open; you can only add Elements with content.* The same happens for the other functionality that needs to be done before opening the `Document`; for instance, encryption can only be added before opening the document. After the `Document` is closed, a `DocumentException` can be thrown, saying *The document is closed. You can't add any Elements.*

`DocumentExceptions` are also thrown while you're manipulating a PDF document—for instance, *The original document was reused. Read it again from file* or *Append mode requires a document without errors even if recovery was possible.*

## E.2 Standard Java exceptions

As you're writing and reading to and from output and input streams, the most important Java exceptions you'll have to deal with are those in the package `java.io`.

### E.2.1 java.io.IOException

An `IOException` may be thrown *by* iText, but hardly ever *because of* iText. In most cases, you have to look for the reason in your file system or J2EE environment. Do you have access to the file you're reading? Do you have sufficient permissions to write in the directory of the file you're creating?

If you're experimenting with the examples, you may experience the same problem I encounter almost daily while writing and testing the examples: the `OutputStream` to a HelloWorld.pdf file can't be created because the file is already open in Adobe Reader (the file is in use, locked by the operating system).

The most obvious `IOException` occurs when you're trying to use a resource that can't be found. Especially when using relative paths, you must make sure you start from the correct directory. This can be confusing when you're working with a servlet container. You'll have to check the documentation of your application server to know how to change the JVM's working directory.

Another `IOException` you may encounter when closing the `Document` says *The document has no pages.* Suppose you're adding rows from a database to a `Document` in a loop, iterating over a `ResultSet`. If the `ResultSet` retrieved from the database is empty, and you aren't adding any other objects to the `Document`, the file is closed and doesn't contain any pages. When a user opens the file, Adobe Reader gives an error. Rather than send a bad PDF to the end user, iText prefers to throw an exception.

### E.2.2 java.lang.RuntimeException

A `RuntimeException` can be thrown because of bad parameters passed by the system or the end user, but iText also needs to throw `RuntimeExceptions` that are caused by programming errors. One of the things Java programmers have to get used to when writing complex iText code is that iText often shifts error checking from compile time to runtime, not by choice, but out of necessity.

For instance, in chapter 10, you saved and restored the state. If you try to restore the state without having saved it first, you get a `RuntimeException`. The compiler isn't able to check whether you use `restoreState()` *after* `saveState()` and not *before*. Moreover, if an unbalanced save/restore happens at runtime, there is no obvious way to cure this problem in a `catch` clause. Whatever you do, you can get odd side effects in the resulting PDF. Again: You don't want to send corrupt PDF files to the end user.

These are some `RuntimeExceptions` and their possible causes:

- `NullPointerException`—This occurs, for instance, when you forget to set a variable that is necessary to continue. In the text block of HelloWorldAbsolute.java (see chapter 2), you might forget to set the font and size before adding the text. In that case, you'd get an exception with this message: *Font and size must be set before writing any text.*
- `UnsupportedOperationException`—When a class extends a superclass or implements an interface, it isn't always possible to override or implement all the methods. For instance, a table cell is a `Rectangle`, but before it's rendered to a specific format—PDF, HTML, RTF—it doesn't make sense to ask for the dimensions of the table cell. Even after it's added to the `Document`, the value isn't available, as you could be rendering the cell in different formats at the same time.

What you have here are programming bugs; you shouldn't work around them or, even worse, ignore them by using an empty `catch` clause. You should fix the bugs. That's why iText often uses the `ExceptionConverter` class.

### E.2.3 Converting checked exceptions

I don't want to debate whether checked exceptions are a blessing or a mistake. There are other places for such discussions. I know, I plead guilty, I swallow all exceptions in the short examples that come with this book, but in your applications you should replace the comment section and handle the exceptions—even if this means converting a checked exception into an unchecked exception with this class: `com.lowagie.text.ExceptionConverter`.

The iText developers found this class on a mailing list a long time ago. It was probably posted by Heinz Kabutz. In his article "Does Java need checked Exceptions?" Bruce Eckel, author of the famous book *Thinking in Java*, renamed `ExceptionConverter` to `ExceptionAdapter`. This class is used in iText to change a checked exception into an unchecked one (`ExceptionConverter` extends `RuntimeException`) when unrecoverable damage is done to the PDF file while generating it. You don't want to send a corrupt PDF to end user without having the slightest clue that something went wrong. In my experience, it's always better to throw a `RuntimeException` giving end users no PDF than to give them a bad PDF.

## E.3 Virtual machine errors

I bet you don't like the sound of the dreaded word *error*. I must confess, I had to take a break before I could finish this appendix and tell you about two errors that pop up now and then on the mailing list.

### E.3.1 java.lang.OutOfMemoryError

In section 2.1.5, I told you that iText tries to free as much memory as possible, as soon as possible. It's important not to store too much content in one big object. For instance, iText can't flush the contents of a table object before you add it to the `Document`. If you create a table that spans 1,000 pages, all the content of this table object remains in memory. You should cut the table into small portions and add them little by little, so that iText can flush the content gradually.

Unfortunately, there are internal iText objects that can't be flushed to the `OutputStream` until the end, when the `Document` is closed: the reference table, the page tree, and so on. If you're generating documents that have a huge number of pages containing lots of special objects that have to be kept in memory, you may need to throw extra memory at them. You can do this by starting the JVM with the `-Xmx` option—for instance, `-Xmx128m` or `-Xmx256m`. Otherwise, the default maximum memory will probably be only 64 MB, which may not be enough for your document.

### E.3.2 Class or method not found error

These are some weird errors. Many people have lost a lot of time because they don't know where to look for the class or method that is supposed to be missing. They open the iText.jar they just installed, and see the presence of a class or a method; but when they try to use it, the JVM tells them it can't find the class or method.

The most obvious reason for these errors is that the class or method is indeed missing; but there are other possibilities you should take into account. You can get this kind of error when you use a jar that is compiled with another version of the JDK than your JVM. In that case, you should build the jar yourself, using your own JDK.

Another possibility is that you have two different versions of iText in your `CLASSPATH`. You can have only one active iText version in your `CLASSPATH`. This is especially tricky when you're upgrading or when you're using other products that have an iText.jar in their distribution in the same environment.

# F

# *Pdf/X, Pdf/A, and tagged PDF*

This book focuses on traditional PDF and PDF documents with AcroForms. Those are the most important and most widespread types of PDF. In chapter 3, we also talked about specific subsets of the PDF specification that are defined in an ISO standard. I told you that iText supports two versions of the PDF/X standard, and that different aspects of the PDF/A specification are under development. The *X* stands for eXchange; PDF/X is used in the prepress sector. The *A* stands for Archiving; PDF/A has been advanced as the standard format for long-term preservation of documents.

Let's find out more about creating PDF/X- and PDF/A-compliant documents with iText.

## F.1 PDF/X

If you want to make sure the file you're generating conforms to one of the PDF/X specifications supported by iText, you have to add an extra line between the second and third step in the PDF-creation process: `PdfWriter.setPDFXConformance(pdfxversion)`.

The value of the parameter must be one of the following constants:

- `PdfWriter.PDFXNONE`—The default. No conformance tests are done.
- `PdfWriter.PDFX1A2001`—The files are PDF/X-1a:2001 compliant.
- `PdfWriter.PDFX32002`—The files are PDF/X-3:2002 compliant.

Once the PDF/X version is set, iText throws a `PdfXConformanceException` as soon as you try to do something that isn't in accordance with the ISO standard. The message that comes with this exception (which extends `java.lang.RuntimeException`) explains what went wrong.

The following example adapts the initial "Hello World" example (listing 2.1):

```
/* chapterF/HelloWorldPdfX.java */
writer.setPDFXConformance(PdfWriter.PDFX1A2001);     <-❶
document.open();
Font font = FontFactory.getFont("c:/windows/fonts/arial.ttf",
  BaseFont.CP1252, BaseFont.EMBEDDED, Font.UNDEFINED,          ❷
  Font.UNDEFINED, new CMYKColor(255, 255, 0, 0));   <-❸
document.add(new Paragraph("Hello World", font));
```

This code conforms to PDF/X-1a:2001 ❶. This means you have to embed the font into the PDF file ❷. If you want to use color, you need to define it with the class `CMYKColor` ❸.

If you want to see the exception in action, you can change the CMYK color to `new Color(0x00, 0x00, 0xFF)`; the `java.awt.Color` object is translated to an RGB color, and this isn't allowed in PDF/X-1a:2001.

Or, you can try to replace `BaseFont.EMBEDDED` with `BaseFont.NOT_EMBEDDED`. This also throws a `PdfXConformanceException` because all fonts must be embedded according to the PDF/X standard. The size of the resulting HelloWorld-PdfX.pdf file is a lot bigger than your original HelloWorld.pdf because the glyph descriptions of all the characters in your "Hello World" string are embedded.

Other functionality that breaks PDF/X conformance includes encryption, layers, image masks, transparency, and blend modes. The same goes more or less for PDF/A.

## F.2 PDF/A

Just like PDF/X, the PDF/A specification lists a number of things that are inappropriate in a PDF file that is intended for long-term preservation. PDF/A conformity is similar to PDF/X-3 (fonts need to be embedded, audio and video is forbidden, and so on), but for the moment iText doesn't have a method `setPdfAConformance()`.

As mentioned in chapter 3, PDF/A isn't only about restrictions. Self-documentation is also important in a PDF/A file. In a PDF/A file, you should always find an XMP metadata stream. The *eXtensible Metadata Platform* (XMP) is a standard format for the creation, processing, and interchange of metadata. XMP isn't limited to the PDF or PDF/A format. TIFF, JPEG, PNG, SVG, and so on can also contain XMP data, but that is beyond the scope of this book.

In chapter 2, you added PDF-specific metadata to the information dictionary. This is fine for Adobe Reader, but applications that aren't PDF-aware can't read this meta-information. By adding the metadata as an unencrypted XML content stream following the XMP schema, you can work around this problem. The XML/XMP inside the PDF document can be detected and parsed by any application that is able to read a file. Note that this type of metadata isn't reflected in the Document Properties tab of Adobe Reader. In Acrobat 7, you can find the XMP metadata by choosing File > Document Properties > Additional Metadata.

An XMP metadata stream can be added to any component for which it's relevant to have metadata. For instance, you can add an XMP stream to the PDF page dictionary of every page in your document. PDF/A needs an XMP stream in the document catalog.

### F.2.1 Creating an XMP metadata stream

In iText XMP streams are added to the document catalog:

```
/* chapterF/HelloWorldXmpMetadata.java */
ByteArrayOutputStream os = new ByteArrayOutputStream();
XmpWriter xmp = new XmpWriter(os);    <-❶
XmpSchema dc = new DublinCoreSchema(XmpSchema.FULL);
XmpArray subject = new XmpArray(XmpArray.UNORDERED);
subject.add("Hello World");
subject.add("XMP");                                              ❷
subject.add("Metadata");
dc.setProperty(DublinCoreSchema.SUBJECT, subject.toString());
xmp.addRdfDescription(dc);
PdfSchema pdf = new PdfSchema(XmpSchema.SHORTHAND);
pdf.setProperty(PdfSchema.KEYWORDS, "Hello World, XMP, Metadata");  ❸
pdf.setProperty(PdfSchema.VERSION, "1.4");
xmp.addRdfDescription(pdf);
xmp.close();
writer.setXmpMetadata(os.toByteArray());    <-❹
```

You can use `XmpWriter` ❶ to create the XMP stream and `setXmpMetadata()` ❹ to add the bytes of this stream to the root object. As you can see in the source code, you add different XMP schemas to the `XmpWriter` object: `DublinCoreSchema` ❷ and `PdfSchema` ❸. All the possible XMP schemas are described in the XMP specification. Only the most common schemas are implemented in iText, but you can extend the abstract class `XmpSchema` if you need support for the other ones.

The PDF/A specification contains a table titled *crosswalk between document information dictionary and XMP properties*. This table is implemented in iText so that you can add XMP metadata without having to worry about the XMP specifications, Dublin Core, and other schemas. You can use the methods discussed in section 2.1.3 and invoke `createXmpMetadata()` to generate the XMP stream automatically:

```
/* chapterF/HelloWorldXmpMetadata2.java */
document.addTitle("Hello World example");
document.addSubject("This example shows how to add metadata");
document.addKeywords("Metadata, iText, step 3");
document.addCreator("My program using iText");
document.addAuthor("Bruno Lowagie");
writer.createXmpMetadata();
document.open();
```

If you open the resulting PDF in a plain text editor, you'll see an XML section that looks like this:

```
<?xpacket begin='ï»¿' id='W5M0MpCehiHzreSzNTczkc9d' ?>
<x:xmpmeta xmlns:x='adobe:ns:meta/'>
<rdf:RDF xmlns:rdf='http://www.w3.org/1999/02/22-rdf-syntax-ns#'>
<rdf:Description rdf:about=''
```

```
    xmlns:dc='http://purl.org/dc/elements/1.1'>
    <dc:format>application/pdf</dc:format>
    <dc:subject>This example shows how to add metadata</dc:subject>
    <dc:title>Hello World example</dc:title>
    <dc:creator>
      <rdf:Seq><rdf:li>Bruno Lowagie</rdf:li></rdf:Seq>
    </dc:creator>
  </rdf:Description>
  <rdf:Description rdf:about=''
    xmlns:dc='http://ns.adobe.com/pdf/1.3/'
    pdf:Producer='iText1.3.3 by lowagie.com'
    pdf:Keywords='Metadata, iText, step 3' />
  <rdf:Description rdf:about=''
    xmlns:dc='http://ns.adobe.com/xap/1.0'>
    <xmp:CreateDate>2005-09-01T11:42:49.000Z</xmp:CreateDate>
    <xmp:CreatorTool>My program using iText</xmp:CreatorTool>
    <xml:ModifyDate>2005-09-01T11:42:49.000Z</xml:ModifyDate>
  </rdf:Description>
  </rdf:RDF>
  </x:xmpmeta>
  (padding recommended by the XMP Specification)
  <?xpacket ends='w' ?>
```

Applications that don't understand PDF syntax but are able to extract and read XMP can now retrieve the metadata from the PDF you created.

### F.2.2 Existing PDF files and XMP metadata

The XMP metadata stream from the document catalog of an existing PDF file can be extracted with the method `getMetadata()`:

```
/* chapterF/HelloWorldReadMetadata.java */
if (reader.getMetadata() == null) {
  System.out.println("No XML Metadata.");
}
else {
  System.out.println("XML Metadata: " +
    new String(reader.getMetadata()));
}
```

Suppose you have a repository of existing PDF documents with PDF-specific metadata but without an XMP metadata stream. You can retrieve the information `Map` and use this `Map` as a parameter for `XmpWriter`. Use `PdfStamper.setXmpMetadata()` to add this stream to the existing document:

```
/* chapterF/HelloWorldAddMetadata.java */
ByteArrayOutputStream baos = new ByteArrayOutputStream();
XmpWriter xmp = new XmpWriter(baos, info);
xmp.close();
stamper.setXmpMetadata(baos.toByteArray());
stamper.close();
```

This XMP functionality was added to iText only recently. If `setPdfAConformance()` were to be added to iText, you'd be able to produce a Level B-conforming PDF/A file. Level B mainly ensures that the visual appearance of a file is preserved over the long term.

Level A conformance demands richer internal information, which is necessary for the preservation of the document's logical structure and content text stream in natural reading order. Additionally, Level A conformance facilitates the accessibility of conforming files for physically impaired users.

That's what tagged PDF is about.

## F.3 Tagged PDF

Do you remember the different types of PDF discussed in chapter 3? We talked about the fact that traditional PDF doesn't know about the structure of text: As far as traditional PDF is concerned, text is just shapes painted on a canvas. PDF/A Level B conformance ensures that you'll always be able to render such a document correctly.

In PDF version 1.4, a new type of PDF was introduced: tagged PDF. When reading a tagged PDF file, applications can recognize text structure types such as paragraphs, headings, tables, and so on. That's what you need for PDF/A Level A conformance.

### F.3.1 Standard structure types

The purpose of tagged PDF is not only to prescribe how the PDF should be read, but also to allow a tagged PDF consumer application to distinguish what part is real content in a specific context and what part of the content can be disregarded.

For instance, a text-to-speech engine probably shouldn't read running heads or page numbers out loud. Specific types of elements of page content can be disregarded or replaced with alternate text (for instance, an image can be replaced by a description of the image).

Standard structure types are defined, divided into these four categories:

- *Grouping elements*—Group other elements into sequences and hierarchies, but have no direct effect on layout. For instance, Document, Part, Sect (section), Div, TOC, and so on.
- *Block-level structure elements (BLSEs)*—Describe the overall layout of content on the page: paragraph-like elements (P, H, H1-H6), list elements (L, LI, Lbl, LBody), and the table element (Table).

- *Inline-level structure elements (ILSEs)*—Describe the layout of content within a BLSE: Span, Quote, Note, Reference, and so on.
- *Illustration elements*—Compact sequences of content that are considered to be unitary objects with respect to page layout: Figure, Formula, and Form.

The content of such a structure is enclosed in a marked-content sequence.

### F.3.2 Marked content

Marked-content operators were introduced in PDF-1.2. They identify a portion of a PDF content stream as a marked-content element of interest to a particular application (for instance, a tagged PDF consumer).

With iText, you can define a `PdfStructureElement` and add marked content to the direct content with the methods `beginMarkedContentSequence()` and `endMarkedContentSequence()`. The following example shows how you can generate a tagged PDF file, writing text to the direct content:

```
/* chapterF/MarkedContent.java */
Document document = new Document();
PdfWriter writer = PdfWriter.getInstance(document,
  new FileOutputStream("marked_content.pdf"));
writer.setTagged();
document.open();
PdfStructureTreeRoot root = writer.getStructureTreeRoot();
PdfStructureElement eTop =
  new PdfStructureElement(root, new PdfName("Everything"));
root.mapRole(new PdfName("Everything"), new PdfName("Sect"));
PdfStructureElement e1 = new PdfStructureElement(eTop, PdfName.P);
PdfStructureElement e2 = new PdfStructureElement(eTop, PdfName.P);
PdfStructureElement e3 = new PdfStructureElement(eTop, PdfName.P);
PdfContentByte cb = writer.getDirectContent();
BaseFont bf = BaseFont.createFont(BaseFont.HELVETICA,
  BaseFont.WINANSI, false);
cb.setLeading(16);
cb.setFontAndSize(bf, 12);
cb.beginMarkedContentSequence(e1);
cb.beginText();
cb.setTextMatrix(50, 804);
for (int k = 0; k < text1.length; ++k) {
  cb.newlineShowText(text1[k]);
}
cb.endText();
cb.endMarkedContentSequence();
cb.beginText();
cb.setTextMatrix(50, 700);
for (int k = 0; k < 2; ++k) {
  cb.beginMarkedContentSequence(e2);
```

```
    cb.newlineShowText(text2[k]);
    cb.endMarkedContentSequence();
  }
  cb.endText();
  cb.beginMarkedContentSequence(e3);
  cb.beginText();
  cb.setTextMatrix(50, 400);
  cb.showText("It was the ");
  PdfDictionary dic = new PdfDictionary();
  dic.put(new PdfName("ActualText"), new PdfString("best"));
  cb.beginMarkedContentSequence(new PdfName("Span"), dic, true);
  cb.showText("worst");
  cb.endMarkedContentSequence();
  cb.showText(" of times.");
  cb.endText();
  cb.endMarkedContentSequence();
```

If you look at the Advanced section in the Document Properties > Description tab of the resulting PDF, you'll see the file is of type tagged PDF. If you decompress the file, you'll see sequences like this:

```
/P <</MCID 4>> BDC
BT
1 0 0 1 50 400 Tm
(It was the )Tj
/Span <</ActualText(best)>> BDC
(worst)Tj
EMC
( of times.)Tj
ET
EMC
```

The P means this is a paragraph; MCID 4 is the Marked Content ID. The marked content operators are BDC and EMC. A nested marked content sequence is tagged as type Span.

In the resulting PDF, the word *worst* is shown on the screen; but if you try to copy/paste this small paragraph, the actual text *best* is copied. You can also test this by trying the Adobe Reader 7.0 feature View > Read Out Loud. On screen, you see *this is the worst of times*, but Adobe Reader reads *this is the best of times*.

## F.4 To be continued

This PDF/A and tagged PDF functionality is new in iText, so I can't tell you much more about it for now. For more information, consult the iText history file and look for the words *PDF/A* and *tagged PDF*. Code contributions are always welcome.

# G Resources

## PDF in general

Adobe Systems Inc. http://www.adobe.com/.

———. *PDF Reference Version 1.6*. 5th ed. Adobe Press, 2004.

———. "What is PDF?" http://www.adobe.com/products/acrobat/adobepdf.html.

Steward, Sid. *PDF Hacks*. O'Reilly Media, Inc., 2004.

Warnock, John. "The Camelot Paper." 1991.

## Publications by Adobe Systems Incorporated

Acrobat 7.0 PDF Open Parameters. 2005.

Acrobat JavaScript Scripting Reference. 2005.

Acrobat JavaScript Scripting Guide. 2005.

Adobe Type 1 Font Format. Reading, MA: Addison-Wesley, 1990.

Font technical notes. http://partners.adobe.com/public/developer/font/index.html.

———.Technical Note #5004: Adobe Font Metrics File Format Specification v4.1. 1998.

———.Technical Note #5015: Type 1 Font Format Supplement. 1994.

———.Technical Note #5176: The Compact Font Format Specification v1.0. 2003.

OpenType User Guide for Adobe Fonts. 2005.

*PostScript Language Reference*. 3rd ed. Reading, MA: Addison-Wesley, 1999.

XMP Specification. http://www.adobe.com/products/xmp/pdfs/xmpspec.pdf.

## Font-related bibliography and sites

American Mathematical Society. http://www.ams.org/. Links to Type 1 fonts: http://www.ams.org/tex/type1-fonts.html.

David McCreedy's Gallery of Unicode Fonts. http://www.travelphrases.info/fonts.html.

Devroye, Luc. http://jeff.cs.mcgill.ca/~luc/. (Contains many font-related links.)

Fondu (a set of programs to interconvert between Mac font formats and PFB, TTF, OTF, and BDF files on UNIX). http://fondu.sourceforge.net/.

Languagegeek.com. http://www.languagegeek.com/font/fontdownload.html. (The free aboriginal serif for the word *peace* in Cherokee was found here.)

Microsoft Typography. http://www.microsoft.com/typography/. Including the OpenType Specification: http://www.microsoft.com/typography/otspec/.

OpenType Q&A. http://store.adobe.com/type/opentype/qna.html.

Repository of TrueType fonts. http://chanae.walon.org/pub/ttf/.

Say PEACE in all languages! http://www.columbia.edu/~fdc/pace/. This page inspired the SayPeace examples. See also: http://www.columbia.edu/~fdc/ (home page of Frank da Cruz).

Shavian alphabet. http://www.omniglot.com/writing/shavian.htm.

Shavian OpenType fonts. http://www.30below.com/~ethanl/fonts.html.

Unicode Consortium. http://www.unicode.org/. "Where's my character" page: http://www.unicode.org/standard/where/.

———. The Unicode Standard 4.0. Reading, MA: Addison Wesley, 2003.

Utopia font. ftp://ctan.tug.org/tex-archive/fonts/utopia/.

## *iText-related links*

iText at Ghent University: http://itext.ugent.be/.

iText home page. http://www.lowagie.com/iText/.

iText documentation. http://itextdocs.lowagie.com/.

iText at SourceForge. http://sourceforge.net/projects/itext/.

Lesser GNU Public License. http://www.gnu.org/copyleft/lesser.html.

Mozilla Public License. http://www.mozilla.org/MPL/.

Soares, Paulo. iText site. http://itextpdf.sourceforge.net/.

## *Links to PDF tools mentioned in the book*

Adobe Acrobat family. http://www.adobe.com/products/acrobat/main.html.

Apache FOP. http://xmlgraphics.apache.org/fop/.

C# port (iTextSharp). http://itextsharp.sourceforge.net/.

Cold Fusion. http://www.adobe.com/products/coldfusion/.

Crionics. http://www.crionics.com/.

Eclipse/BIRT. http://www.eclipse.org/birt/.

Folio. http://defoe.sourceforge.net/folio/.

ICESoft. http://www.icesoft.com/.

J# port (iText.NET). http://www.ujihara.jp/iTextdotNET/.

JasperReports. http://jasperreports.sourceforge.net/.

JFreeChart. http://www.jfree.org/jfreechart/. (See also the JFreeChart Developer Guide.)

JPedal. http://www.jpedal.org/.

PDFBox. http://www.pdfbox.org/.

Pdfp and other interesting tools. http://www.noliturbare.com/ChicksTools.html.

PdfTk. http://www.accesspdf.com/pdftk/.

## *Limited list of other projects and products using iText*

Datavision OS reporting tool. http://datavision.sourceforge.net/.

Display Tag Library. http://displaytag.sourceforge.net/.

DocMan document manager. http://docman.sourceforge.net/.

Google Calendar. http://www.google.com/calendar/.

iReport visual report builder for JasperReports. http://ireport.sourceforge.net/.

NASA Panoply NETCDF Viewer. http://www.giss.nasa.gov/tools/panoply/thanks.html.

PDFDoclet: Javadoc API to PDF. http://pdfdoclet.sourceforge.net/.

Topaz (electronic signatures). http://www.topazsystems.com/software/download/java/index.htm.

UJAC Useful Java Application Components. http://ujac.sourceforge.net/

Your project?

# index



*The names of all the code examples in the book have been set in **bold font** for easier identification.*

## C

## D

## E



## F

## G

## I



## J

## R



## S

## T

## U



## V



## W

## *MORE JAVA TITLES FROM MANNING*

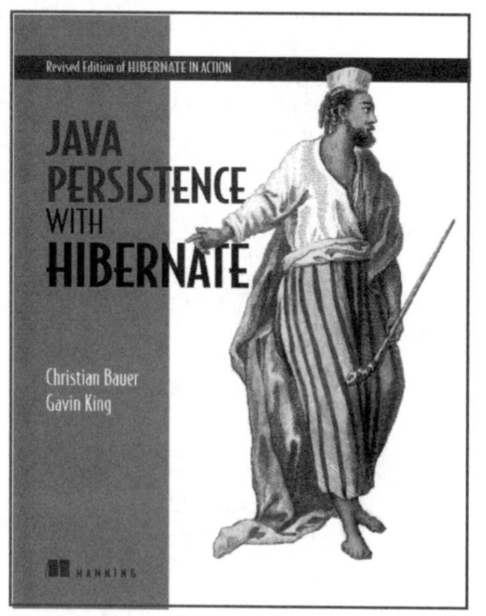


*Java Persistence with Hibernate:*
*Revised Edition of* Hibernate in Action

by Christian Bauer and Gavin King
ISBN: 1-932394-88-5
Foreword by Linda DeMichiel
880 pages
$49.99
November 2006

*Groovy in Action*

by Dierk Koenig with Andrew Glover,
Paul King, Buillaume Laforge,
and Jon Skeet
Foreword by James Gosling
ISBN: 1-932394-84-2
420 pages
$44.99
December 2006

*For ordering information on these and other Manning titles,*
*please visit www.manning.com*

## MORE JAVA TITLES FROM MANNING

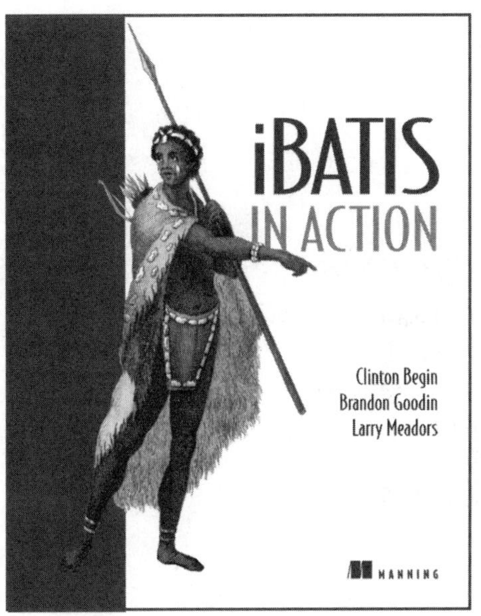


*iBATIS in Action*

by Clinton Begin, Brandon Goodin, and Larry Meadors
ISBN: 1-932394-82-6
350 pages
$44.99
December 2006

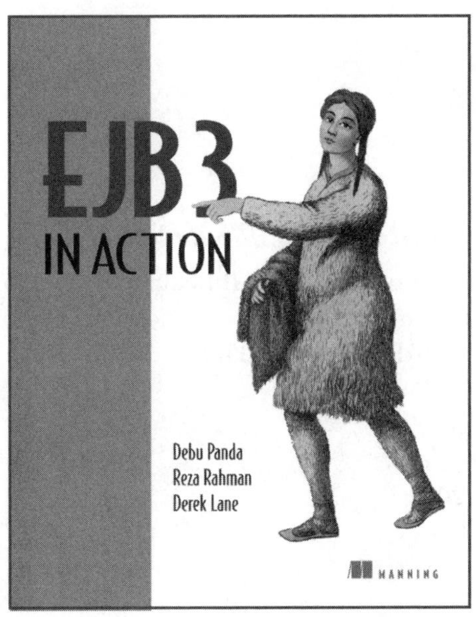


*EJB3 in Action*

by Debu Panda, Reza Rahman, and Derek Lane
ISBN: 1-932394-93-1
500 pages
$44.99
February 2007

*For ordering information on these and other Manning titles, please visit www.manning.com*

## MORE JAVA TITLES FROM MANNING

*Ajax in Practice*
by David Crane, Jord Sonneveld,
and Bear Bibeault
ISBN: 1-932394-99-0
450 pages
$44.99
February 2007

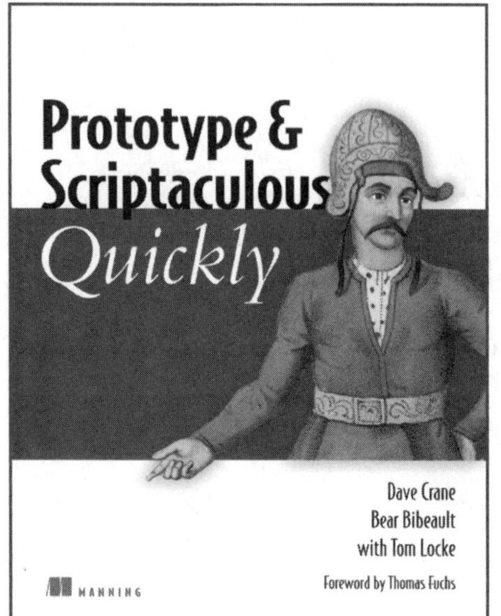


*Prototype and Scriptaculous Quickly*
by David Crane and Bear Bibeault
with Tom Locke
Foreword by Thomas Fuchs
ISBN: 1-933988-03-7
350 pages
$44.99
March 2007

*For ordering information on these and other Manning titles, please visit www.manning.com*